Intellectual Interactions in the Islamic World

The Institute of Ismaili Studies
Shiʿi Heritage Series, 6

Previously published titles:
1. Daftary, Farhad. *A History of Shiʿi Islam* (2013).
2. Daftary, Farhad, and Gurdofarid Miskinzoda, eds. *The Study of Shiʿi Islam: History, Theology and Law* (2014).
3. Mir-Kasimov, Orkhan. *Words of Power: Hurufi Teachings Between Shiʿism and Sufism in Medieval Islam* (2015).
4. Asatryan, Mushegh. *Controversies in Formative Shiʿi Islam: The Ghulat Muslims and their Beliefs* (2017).
5. De Cillis, Maria. *Salvation and Destiny in Islam: The Shiʿi Ismaili Perspective of Ḥamīd al-Dīn al-Kirmānī* (2018).

Intellectual Interactions in the Islamic World

The Ismaili Thread

Edited by
Orkhan Mir-Kasimov

I.B.TAURIS
in association with
THE INSTITUTE OF ISMAILI STUDIES
LONDON, 2020

I.B. TAURIS
Bloomsbury Publishing Plc
50 Bedford Square, London, WC1B 3DP, UK
1385 Broadway, New York, NY 10018, USA

In association with
The Institute of Ismaili Studies
Aga Khan Centre, 10 Handyside Street, London N1C 4DN
www.iis.ac.uk

First published in Great Britain 2020

Front cover image: Iskandar (in the likeness of Sultan Husain Baiqara) with the seven sages, from the Khamsa of Nizami; British Library MS Or 6810, fol. 214r. Opaque watercolour. Herat, AH900/1494–5CE. (© The British Library Board)

Back cover image: Steel plaque from a shrine, inscribed with the shahāda, with the added phrase *'Ali wali Allah*. Iran, 11th/17th century. (Courtesy of the Aga Khan Museum, Toronto, AKM617)

A catalogue record for this book is available from the British Library.

A catalog record for this book is available from the Library of Congress

ISBN HB: 978-1-83860-485-1
PB: 978-1-83860-488-2
eISBN: 978-1-83860-487-5
ePDF: 978-1-83860-486-8

Series: Shiʿi Heritage Series

Typeset by RefineCatch Limited, Bungay, Suffolk
Printed and bound in Great Britain

The Institute of Ismaili Studies

The Institute of Ismaili Studies was established in 1977 with the object of promoting scholarship and learning on Islam, in the historical as well as contemporary contexts, and a better understanding of its relationship with other societies and faiths.

The Institute's programmes encourage a perspective which is not confined to the theological and religious heritage of Islam, but seeks to explore the relationship of religious ideas to broader dimensions of society and culture. The programmes thus encourage an interdisciplinary approach to the materials of Islamic history and thought. Particular attention is also given to issues of modernity that arise as Muslims seek to relate their heritage to the contemporary situation.

Within the Islamic tradition, the Institute's programmes promote research on those areas which have, to date, received relatively little attention from scholars. These include the intellectual and literary expressions of Shiʿism in general, and Ismailism in particular.

In the context of Islamic societies, the Institute's programmes are informed by the full range and diversity of cultures in which Islam is practised today, from the Middle East, South and Central Asia, and Africa to the industrialized societies of the West, thus taking into consideration the variety of contexts which shape the ideals, beliefs and practices of the faith.

These objectives are realised through concrete programmes and activities organized and implemented by various departments of the Institute. The Institute also collaborates periodically, on a programme-specific basis, with other institutions of learning in the United Kingdom and abroad.

The Institute's academic publications fall into a number of inter-related categories:

1. Occasional papers or essays addressing broad themes of the relationship between religion and society, with special reference to Islam.
2. Monographs exploring specific aspects of Islamic faith and culture, or the contributions of individual Muslim thinkers or writers.
3. Editions or translations of significant primary or secondary texts.
4. Translations of poetic or literary texts which illustrate the rich heritage of spiritual, devotional and symbolic expressions in Muslim history.
5. Works on Ismaili history and thought, and the relationship of the Ismailis to other traditions, communities and schools of thought in Islam.
6. Proceedings of conferences and seminars sponsored by the Institute.
7. Bibliographical works and catalogues which document manuscripts, printed texts and other source materials.

This book falls into category six listed above.

In facilitating these and other publications, the Institute's sole aim is to encourage original research and analysis of relevant issues. While every effort is made to ensure that the publications are of a high academic standard, there is naturally bound to be a diversity of views, ideas and interpretations. As such, the opinions expressed in these publications must be understood as belonging to their authors alone.

Shiʿi Heritage Series

Shiʿi Muslims, with their rich intellectual and cultural heritage, have contributed significantly to the fecundity and diversity of the Islamic traditions throughout the centuries, enabling Islam to evolve and flourish both as a major religion and also as a civilisation. In spite of this, Shiʿi Islam has received little scholarly attention in the West, in medieval as well as modern times. It is only in recent decades that academic interest has focused increasingly on Shiʿi Islam within the wider study of Islam.

The principal objective of the *Shiʿi Heritage Series*, launched by the Institute of Ismaili Studies, is to enhance general knowledge of Shiʿi Islam and promote a better understanding of its history, doctrines and practices in their historical and contemporary manifestations. Addressing all Shiʿi communities, the series also aims to engage in discussions on theoretical and methodological issues, while inspiring further research in the field.

Works published in this series will include monographs, collective volumes, editions and translations of primary texts, and bibliographical projects, bringing together some of the most significant themes in the study of Shiʿi Islam through an interdisciplinary approach, and making them accessible to a wide readership.

Table of Contents

PART SIX: THE INTERACTION AND CIRCULATION OF KNOWLEDGE ACROSS RELIGIOUS AND GEOGRAPHICAL BOUNDARIES

Note on Transliteration, Dates and Abbreviations

The system of transliteration used in this book for the Arabic and Persian scripts is that adopted in the third edition of the *Encyclopaedia of Islam*, with certain variations (for instance چ is transliterated as 'ch'). The lunar years of the Islamic calendar are generally followed throughout the text and notes by the corresponding Gregorian solar years (for example, 11/632). The years of the Islamic era, initiated by the emigration (*hijra*) of the Prophet Muhammad from Mecca to Medina in July 622, commonly abbreviated in the Latin form AH (=*Anno Hegirae*), have been converted to the corresponding dates of the Christian era, abbreviated as AD (=*Anno Domini*), on the basis of the conversion tables given in Greville S. P. Freeman-Grenville, *The Muslim and Christian Calendars* (London, 1963). In Iran (called Persia in the West until 1936), a solar Islamic calendar was officially adopted in the 1920s. The Islamic dates of the sources published in modern Iran are, therefore, solar (Persian, Shamsi), coinciding with the corresponding Christian years starting on 21 March. For the transliteration of Indian languages/scripts, see the preliminary notes in individual chapters.

Introduction[*]

Orkhan Mir-Kasimov

Like any other Islamic group, in the course of history, the Ismailis were in permanent interaction with many of the other groups and movements that make up the complex fabric of Islamic civilisation. However, even if information concerning exchanges and mutual influences between various domains of Ismaili thought and other doctrinal trends in Islam is to be found in the secondary material, it is often dispersed and scattered through those studies which are more general in nature.[1] There are only a few monographs which focus on specific

---

* In this Introduction, I use some material from the report on the conference 'Intellectual Interactions in the Islamic World: The Ismaili Thread' which took place at the Institute of Ismaili Studies, London, 19–21 October 2016. The report was published in *Shiʿi Studies Review*, 1 (2017), pp. 261–264. Most of the chapters in this volume developed from the papers presented at that conference.

[1] For example, the seminal works on Ismaili history and thought, such as M.G.S. Hodgson's *The Order of Assassins: The Struggle of the Early Nizârî Ismâʿîlîs Against the Islamic World* (The Hague, 1955), Farhad Daftary's *The Ismāʿīlīs: their History and Doctrines* (Cambridge, 1990), Michael Brett's *The Rise of the Fatimids: The World of the Mediterranean and the Middle East in the Tenth Century C.E.* (Leiden, 2002), or the numerous works of Daniel De Smet, Maribel Fierro, Heinz Halm, Wilferd Madelung, Paul Walker, and others, contain substantial information about historical and doctrinal relationships between various Ismaili groups and other, Shiʿi as well as non-Shiʿi, branches of Islam, but this information does not constitute the central point of these works and is presented as part of a much broader discourse. Similarly, some works on other groups as, for example, Ahmet Yaşar Ocak's works on Anatolian mysticism, contain interesting indications of possible or actual Ismaili influence, which invite reflection and may stimulate further research. The only collection of articles known to me which comes close to the idea of the present volume is perhaps *Ismāʿīlī Contributions to Islamic Culture* edited by S.H. Nasr (Tehran, 1977). However, even if some

instances of interaction between the Ismailis and non-Ismaili doctrines in Islam.[2] The goal of the present volume is to bring this topic to the fore through a collection of articles reflecting the most recent scholarship in the relevant fields.

The fundamental idea that informs the approach of this volume is that Islamic civilisation is not and has never been a monolith. In fact, it consists of various groups and movements which, throughout the centuries, have enjoyed complex relationships with each other. These relationships have various aspects – social, political, commercial, spiritual, intellectual, artistic and so on – and every aspect gives us a specific point of view regarding the place of any given group within the whole. For example, a study on the spiritual and intellectual doctrines of a Sufi order will provide a picture quite different from, though complementary to, the study of its social and political connections.

Starting from this basic understanding, this volume focuses on one group – namely, the Ismailis – and on one aspect – namely, the intellectual aspect – of their relationships with other groups and movements of the Islamic world. Thus it is as if, in the complex texture of Islamic civilisation, we were following one thread in the pattern – the Ismaili one – observing how it has been interwoven with other threads throughout history.

A substantial part of our knowledge of the relationships between the Ismailis and other Islamic groups is based on the historical literature. An approach to the issue of interactions from the point of view of intellectual history can complement this historical dimension and give us a more balanced understanding of the place occupied by the Ismaili branch of Shiʿi Islam within the broader Islamic context.

Addressing the issue of intellectual interactions between the Ismaili and non-Ismaili groups and branches of Islam from a holistic and

---

continuity can be traced from *Ismāʿīlī Contributions* to this volume, the scope and perspective of each are substantially different. While the former was concerned with the 'role of Ismāʿīlism in Islamic history' as well as with Ismaili influence on 'various intellectual and artistic aspects of Islamic civilization and culture', this work focuses on the exchanges that took place between the Ismailis and other Islamic groups and remains confined mainly to the intellectual sphere, however broadly defined.

[2] A recent example is Michael Ebstein's *Mysticism and Philosophy in al-Andalus: Ibn Masarra, Ibn al-ʿArabī and the Ismāʿīlī Tradition* (Leiden and Boston, 2014).

interdisciplinary perspective, this volume also seeks to provide a panoramic overview of this area of study and to reflect the diversity of various groups and spheres of interaction. In this regard, I would like to mention the famous Sufi tale of the elephant in the darkened room, which resurfaced several times at the conference where most of the papers included in this volume were presented. Each of the scholars participating in this project largely specialises in one area of Islamic studies. Like the people in the darkened room, each scholar can therefore only feel one part of the elephant, like a leg, an ear or the trunk, that is, contribute to the study of one of the aspects and spheres of intellectual interactions. Only by bringing together our perceptions forged in different disciplines and areas of specialisation can we attempt to present a global picture of an issue of such complexity, that is to say, a constituent part as it appears through the prism of its interactions with other parts within the complex body of Islamic civilisation.

However, this diversity comes at a price. First, this volume is not, and could not possibly be, fully comprehensive, that is, it does not cover all possible spheres of intellectual interaction nor all possible groups that participated in these interactions in the course of history. Second, because of the obvious limitations of space, several spheres of interaction are represented by only one or two papers; and conversely, some papers can be related not to one, but to two or more spheres of interaction, for example, to Sufism and to the issue of religious authority; or to mysticism and philosophy. This has made it difficult to divide the volume into thematic parts, and it should be remembered that these divisions are mostly conventional and generally porous. Several chapters in this volume can be seen as the starting point for establishing thematic sections or even producing individual volumes in possible future developments of this project. In this sense, this publication should be considered as a first attempt at mapping an area the details of which will be hopefully developed in future studies.

The contributions to this volume include papers on incipient Ismailism as well as its main branches such as the Fatimids, the Nizārīs, the Ṭayyibīs, and Pamiri and Indian Ismailism, and their interactions with various other Shiʿi and non-Shiʿi groups in areas such as philosophy, law, mysticism, hermeneutics and interreligious dialogue. While the Fatimids and the Nizārī Ismailis have attracted significant scholarly interest, other branches of the Ismailis are still relatively little studied, and the papers in this volume will hopefully contribute to expanding our knowledge of their doctrines and traditions.

The volume is divided into six parts, with chapters in every part being organised according to thematic and chronological criteria:

Part One, 'In the Eyes of Others: Mutual Reflections in Polemical and Doctrinal Literature' investigates how the Ismaili vision of other Islamic groups and, conversely, how the other's vision of the Ismailis is reflected in polemical and doctrinal literature of Ismaili, Twelver and Sunni authors. Polemic is one form of intellectual interaction. It can be based on a deep knowledge of the opponent's thought, but it can also create a distorted image of the other, especially in the context of rivalry and competition when the polemic is an expression of ideological and political hostility. Farhad Daftary's chapter analyses the political reasons that lie behind the medieval Sunni anti-Ismaili polemical works. The purpose of many of these works was to provide an ideological and religious basis for the Abbasid struggle against the rival Fatimid and later Nizārī Ismaili conception of the religious and political authority which disputed the Abbasid claim to the legitimate leadership of the Islamic world. Largely unconcerned with the actual content of Ismaili doctrines, these polemical works are responsible for the creation of the 'black legend' depicting Ismailis in an extremely negative and distorted way. The modern progress in Ismaili studies, based on authentic Ismaili sources, has gradually overcome the influences of the 'black legend' and has reached a more balanced understanding of the Ismaili intellectual heritage and its contributions to Islamic thought and culture. For their part, the Ismailis also engaged into ideologically motivated polemics against other Muslim groups, in which they discussed the doctrinal standpoints of these groups and compared them with the corresponding points of the Ismaili doctrine aiming to demonstrate the superiority of the latter. Paul Walker in his paper analyses the early Ismaili polemical literature including the works of such authors as Abū ʿAbd Allāh al-Shīʿī (d. 298/911), Abū Tammām (fl. fourth/tenth century), Abū Ḥātim al-Rāzī (d. ca. 322/934), al-Qāḍī al-Nuʿmān (d. 363/974), Abū Yaʿqūb al-Sijistānī (d. after 361/971) and Ḥamīd al-Dīn al-Kirmānī (d. after 411/1020). Roy Vilozny's paper examines the Twelver and Zaydī views of the Ismailis as they appear in Ibn

Bābawayh al-Shaykh al-Ṣadūq's (d. 381/991) *Kamāl al-dīn wa-tamām al-niʿma,* mainly in the context of Twelver anti-Zaydī polemics. Although fragmentary, this early refutation of the Ismailis, which significantly does not mention the Fatimids, invites reflection on its historical context. Toby Mayer's paper is a study of *Maṣāriʿ al-muṣāriʿ*, Naṣīr al-Dīn al-Ṭūsī's (d. 672/1274) critical response to Muḥammad al-Shahrastānī's (d. 548/1153) critique of Ibn Sīnā's (d. 428/1037) thought. Although *Maṣāriʿ* is a polemical work, it does not constitute a direct form of polemic between Ismailis and non-Ismailis. However, both al-Ṭūsī and al-Shahrastānī were prominent scholars closely associated with the Ismaili tradition, and therefore this work contains rich material for reflection on the interactions between the Ismaili thought and Avicennan tradition of Islamic philosophy, as well as insights into al-Ṭūsī's complex intellectual and spiritual journey.

Part Two, 'Authority and Law', explores intellectual interactions in the sphere of religious and political authority. Religious law has always been one of the main pillars of religious and political power in Islam, and its relationship with the authority of the divinely-inspired imam is one of the most fascinating issues marking the development of Shiʿi, especially Twelver and Ismaili, legal thought. Agostino Cilardo's chapter in this part directly addresses this issue by comparing the status of the jurist in Fatimid and Sunni sources. Maribel Fierro's paper explores the influence and conceptualisation of certain Fatimid rituals in the broader context of the Maghrib and Umayyad al-Andalus and the way these rituals are linked to religious and political authority. Michael Ebstein studies Ibn al-ʿArabī's (d. 638/1240) concept of the divine Command (*amr*) including its cosmic, historical and socio-political aspects, and compares it with the theory of *amr* developed in the works of Ismaili thinkers that would have had a significant influence on the perception of this concept in Andalusian and Maghribi intellectual milieux.

Part Three, 'The Ikhwān al-Ṣafāʾ, Theosophical and Philosophical Trends' brings together papers discussing various intellectual trends and their possible or factual connections with the Ismailis. Carmela Baffioni investigates the contents of a curious and perhaps oldest, version of the Epistle 50 of the *Rasāʾil Ikhwān al-Ṣafāʾ*. Her study suggests the existence of two parallel manuscript traditions of the *Rasāʾil,* one of which establishes a connection with proto-Ismaili and Ismaili philosophical doctrines. Daryoush Mohammad Poor analyses the development of the Nizārī Ismaili doctrines in connection with contemporary Iranian intellectual circles, including the work of such figures as Sanāʾī Ghaznawī (d. 525/1131), ʿAyn al-Quḍāt Hamadānī (d. 526/1131) and Muḥammad al-Shahrastānī, arguing that the Nizārī Ismailis were closely connected to these circles and that the articulation of Ismaili doctrines was deeply influenced by the ideas circulating amongst them. Janis Esots examines the parallels between the works of Ismaili thinkers and those of one of the most prominent figures of the Safavid Shiʿi intellectual tradition, Mullā Ṣadrā Shīrāzī (d. 1050/1640). These parallels could either be the result of Mullā Ṣadrā's unacknowledged familiarity with the works of leading Ismaili thinkers or of the existence of a common source used by Ismaili authors as well as by Mullā Ṣadrā. The former option falls directly into the scope of the intellectual interactions between the Ismaili and non-Ismaili groups, while the latter is relevant to the related question of the assimilation of the intellectual heritage of Antiquity by the Ismailis and other trends in Islam.

Part Four, 'Mystical Trends', explores intellectual interactions in the area of Islamic esotericism which is not Sufi in nature, including early Shiʿi esotericism and eclectic mystical and messianic movements. Scrutinising the structure of the *Kitāb al-Kashf*, one of the earliest texts in the literary tradition of the Ismailis, Mushegh Asatryan finds traces of Ismaili polemics against the Shiʿi groups known as 'exaggerators' (*ghulāt*) or, to use the author's expression, the 'Ghulat-Nuṣayrī' tradition. The text analysed in this paper provides evidence to show that already at that early stage there was a tendency to formulate a distinct Ismaili interpretation of the doctrines common to many of the early Shiʿi groups. Daniel De Smet's paper examines another case of a distinctively Ismaili assimilation and interpretation of the early Shiʿi cosmological and anthropological material that was developed in works by Ṭayyibī authors, who also rejected the interpretation of this material adopted by the *ghulāt* groups. The paper shows how the early Shiʿi esoteric traditions were incorporated into Ṭayyibī esoteric doctrines and discusses the channels of transmission by which these traditions reached the Ṭayyibīs. Also related to the transmission of the early Shiʿi esoteric doctrines, Orkhan Mir-Kasimov's paper compares the doctrinal texts pertaining to the Nizārī Ismaili theory of Resurrection (*qiyāma*) and the works of Faḍl Allāh Astarābādī (d. 796/1394), an eighth/fourteenth century mystical and messianic thinker and the founder of the influential movement known as Ḥurūfism. Consistent doctrinal parallelisms, analysed against the background of other textual and historical evidence, provide some material for reflection on the possible influence of the Ismaili theory of *qiyāma,* strongly focused on the messianic age, on the mystical and messianic movements which played an important ideological and socio-political role in shaping of the eastern Islamic world in the period following the Mongol invasions.

Still within the area of mysticism, Part Five, 'Ismaili-Sufi Relationships in Badakhshan', is focused on the interactions between the Ismaili and the Sufi ethos in the specific, and largely under-studied, cultural context of Badakhshan. Nourmamadcho Nourmamadchoev examines the close interconnection of the Ismaili, Sufi and Twelver Shiʿi elements in the important and complex text related to the Ismaili ritual practice of the region, the *Chirāgh-nāma.* Abdulmamad Iloliev's paper deals with the amalgamation of Sufi and Ismaili ideas in the concept of *wilāya* as expounded by Mubārak-i Wakhānī (d. 1903), a mystical thinker and poet from Badakhshan, in his *Risāla-yi chihil dunyā.*

Part Six, 'The Interaction and Circulation of Knowledge across Religious and Geographical Boundaries' addresses the issues of religious and cultural cross-pollination involving Ismaili intellectual traditions. This part opens with Delia Cortese's paper on the material means for the transmission of knowledge in medieval societies, namely on the circulation of books across geographical, confessional and religious boundaries in the Fatimid cultural context. The paper highlights a specific aspect of intellectual interactions, namely the personal contacts based on the exchange of books between scholars belonging to various confessional and intellectual trends. Wafi Momin's paper addresses the dialectics of balance between Islamic and Hindu elements in the Satpanth tradition, associated with an offshoot of the Indian Nizārī Ismaili tradition. Instead of perceiving the terms Islamic and Hindu as referring to clear-cut and unvarying categories that came to form an equally invariable Satpanth synthesis, the author proposes a more nuanced approach which regards the cross-pollination of Islamic and Indian cultural and religious symbols as a living process responsive to historical changes and socio-political transformations. Analysing the *Ginān* literature produced in the Satpanth tradition, Wafi Momin identifies various layers of interaction between Muslim and Hindu ideas and forms of mythology. Shafique Virani studies how the Zoroastrian festival of the vernal equinox, Nawrūz, generally incorporated into various Islamic cultural contexts, was integrated into an Ismaili interpretational framework in three distinct cultural and linguistic environments, namely the Arabic of the Islamic heartlands, the Persian of Iranian and Central Asian traditions, and the various South Asian languages of the Indo-Pakistan subcontinent. Mauro Zonta explores the issue of the Ismaili influence on medieval Jewish thought, focusing on the interactions between Ismailism and the ideas of Yemeni Jewish philosophers.

As mentioned above, it is hoped that this volume will constitute a contribution to our understanding of the infinite richness and diversity, as well as the interconnection of the intellectual traditions, of Islam and will further our knowledge of various Ismaili traditions and doctrines across a broad historical and geographical span in the context of their interactions with other groups and trends in the Islamic world.

I want to take this opportunity to express my sincere gratitude to all the participants for their collaboration and for their valuable contributions without which this publication would have been impossible. Neither the conference nor the edited volume could be brought to completion without the help of many colleagues at the Institute of Ismaili Studies. While it is impossible to mention all those whose help was instrumental at different stages of this project, I would like to thank Farhad Daftary for supporting this initiative from the start, Gurdofarid Miskinzoda and Maria De Cillis for accepting this volume for publication in the *Shiʿi Heritage Series*, the anonymous peer reviewers for their detailed feedback and insightful suggestions, Tara Woolnough for her assistance through the publishing process and Isabel Miller for her patient, thoughtful and rigorous reading and editing of the text.

The preparation of this volume was marked by a note of deep sadness as two contributors, Professors Agostino Cilardo and Mauro

Zonta, passed away during the summer and autumn of 2017. They were no longer with us to check the proofs of their papers. With the help of their colleagues, we have done our best to prepare their chapters for publication. My special thanks go to Professor Carmela Baffioni, who immediately offered her help, and to Professors Ronald C. Kiener, Giancarlo Lacerenza and Tzvi Langermann who read the texts and provided many useful comments and suggestions. Needless to say, I alone am to blame for any possible errors and shortcomings in the final versions. May these texts be a modest homage to the memory of our much missed colleagues.

PART ONE

IN THE EYES OF OTHERS: MUTUAL REFLECTIONS IN POLEMICAL AND DOCTRINAL LITERATURE

1

Sunni Perceptions of the Ismailis: Medieval Perspectives

Farhad Daftary
(The Institute of Ismaili Studies)

Imam Jaʿfar al-Ṣādiq succeeded in consolidating Imāmī Shiʿism, one of the major early Shiʿi communities, on a quiescent basis. It was also in the time of this ʿAlid imam that the central Shiʿi doctrine of the imamate was articulated.[1] The doctrine was based on the belief in the permanent need of mankind for a divinely guided, sinless and infallible (*maʿṣūm*) imam who, after the Prophet Muhammad, would act as the authoritative teacher and guide of men in all their spiritual affairs. This imam was entitled to temporal leadership as much as to religious authority, but his mandate did not depend on his actual rule. The doctrine further taught that the Prophet himself had designated his cousin and son-in-law (married to his daughter, Fāṭima), ʿAlī b. Abī Ṭālib, as his legatee or *waṣī* and successor, under divine command. After ʿAlī, the imamate was to be transmitted by an explicit designation or *naṣṣ* amongst the descendants of ʿAlī and Fāṭima, and after al-Ḥusayn b.

[1] The basic conception of the Imāmī Shiʿi doctrine of the imamate, as expressed in numerous *ḥadīth*s reported mainly from Imam Jaʿfar al-Ṣādiq, is preserved in the earliest corpus of Imāmī *ḥadīths*, compiled by Abū Jaʿfar Muḥammad al-Kulaynī's *al-Uṣūl min al-kāfī*, ed. ʿAlī A. al-Ghaffārī (3rd ed., Tehran, 1388/1968), vol. 1, pp. 168–548, and retained by the Ismailis in the foremost legal compendium of Fatimid times, compiled by al-Qāḍī Abū Ḥanīfa al-Nuʿmān b. Muḥammad, *Daʿāʾim al-Islām*, ed. Asaf A. A. Fyzee (Cairo, 1951–1961), vol. 1, pp. 14–98; English trans., *The Pillars of Islam*, tr. A. A. A. Fyzee, completely revised by I. K. Poonawala (New Delhi, 2002–2004), vol. 1, pp. 18–122.

ʿAlī, it would continue in the Ḥusaynid ʿAlid line until the end of time. This Ḥusaynid ʿAlid imam, the sole legitimate spiritual authority at any given time, is also in possession of a special knowledge or *ʿilm*, and has perfect understanding of the exoteric (*ẓāhir*) and esoteric (*bāṭin*) meanings of the Qurʾan and the message of Islam. This doctrine, retained by the later Ismailis, posed a serious challenge to the legitimacy of the Abbasid caliphs as the spiritual spokespersons of all Muslims. Indeed, the doctrine of the imamate provided the basic theological framework by means of which the Ismaili imams would confront the Sunni establishment.

On the death of Imam Jaʿfar al-Ṣādiq in 148/765, the Imāmī Shiʿis split into several groups. One group, maintaining the established Imāmī tradition of quiescence, eventually evolved into the Ithnāʿasharī or Twelver branch of Shiʿism. There were other Kūfan-based Imāmī splinter groups that now recognised Ismāʿīl, the eponym of the Ismāʿīliyya, or his son Muḥammad b. Ismāʿīl, as their new imam. These earliest Ismailis adopted a politically active policy against the established Sunni order under the Abbasids. In fact, a line of imams, who did not initially claim the Ismaili imamate openly, now began to organise a dynamic, revolutionary Ismaili movement against the Abbasids. Referring to their movement as *al-daʿwa al-hādiya*, or the 'rightly guiding mission', the religio-political message of this anti-Abbasid movement was disseminated by a network of *dāʿīs*, summoners or missionaries.

It was soon after the middle of the third/fourth century that Ismaili *dāʿīs* began to appear in southern Iraq, Persia, Yemen, Sind, and, later, in Central Asia and North Africa.[2] The early Ismaili *daʿwa* met with particular success in Ifrīqiya, where the *dāʿī* Abū ʿAbd Allāh al-Shīʿī was active among the Kutāma Berbers of the Lesser Kabylia mountains (in present-day eastern Algeria) from 280/893. He converted the bulk of the Kutāma Berbers and transformed them into a disciplined army. By 290/903, Abū ʿAbd Allāh had commenced his conquest of Ifrīqiya, covering today's Tunisia and eastern Algeria. Since 184/800 the Aghlabids, who were Sunni, had ruled over this part of the Maghrib

[2] See F. Daftary, *A Short History of the Ismailis* (Edinburgh, 1998), pp. 36–45.

and Sicily as vassals of the Abbasids. But by 296/909, the Aghlabids had actually been overthrown. Meanwhile, ʿAbd Allāh al-Mahdī, the central leader of the *daʿwa* who succeeded to the leadership in 286/899 and claimed the imamate openly, had embarked on a fateful journey from the secret headquarters of the *daʿwa* at Salamiyya, in Syria, that eventually took him to Ifrīqiya. There, on 20 Rabīʿ II 297/4 January 910, al-Mahdī was proclaimed as caliph.[3] This marked the foundation of the Fatimid caliphate. The new Ismaili Shiʿi dynasty came to be known as Fatimid, derived from the Prophet's daughter Fāṭima, to whom al-Mahdī and his successors traced their ʿAlid ancestry.

The foundation of the Fatimid caliphate marked the crowning success of the early Ismailis. The religio-political *daʿwa* of the Ismailis had finally led to the establishment of a state or *dawla* headed by the Ismaili imam. This represented not only a great success for the Ismailis, but for all Shiʿi Muslims as well. Since the days of ʿAlī b. Abī Ṭālib, this was the first time that an ʿAlid imam from the Prophet's family, or the *ahl al-bayt*, had succeeded to the leadership of an important Muslim state. Fatimid victory, thus, heralded the fulfilment of a long-awaited Shiʿi ideal, frustrated and delayed for more than two centuries by numerous defeats and setbacks.

The Ismaili imam had always claimed to possess sole legitimate religious authority as the divinely appointed and infallible spiritual guide of all Muslims. By acquiring political power, and then transforming the Fatimid *dawla* into a vast flourishing empire, the Ismaili imam now effectively presented his Shiʿi challenge to Abbasid hegemony and Sunni interpretations of Islam. Henceforth, the Ismaili Fatimid caliph-imam could readily act as the spiritual spokesman of Shiʿi Islam in general, much in the same way that the Abbasid caliph was the mouthpiece of Sunni Islam. In line with their universal claims, the Fatimid caliph-imams did not abandon their *daʿwa* activities on assuming power. Aiming to extend their authority and rule over the

[3] Al-Qāḍī al-Nuʿmān b. Muḥammad, *Iftitāḥ al-daʿwa*, ed. W. al-Qāḍī (Beirut, 1970), pp. 249–258; ed. F. Dachraoui (Tunis, 1975), pp. 293–306; English trans., *Founding the Fatimid State: The Rise of an Early Islamic Empire*, tr. H. Haji (London, 2006), pp. 205–213.

entire Muslim society and beyond, they retained a network of *dāʿīs*, operating on their behalf as religio-political agents both inside and outside Fatimid dominions.

In the immediate aftermath of the foundation of the Fatimid caliphate, the Sunni establishment launched what amounted to an official anti-Ismaili propaganda campaign. The overall aim of this systematic and prolonged campaign, fully endorsed and supported by the Abbasid caliphs, was to discredit the entire Ismaili movement from its origins onward so that the Ismailis could be readily condemned as *malāḥida*, heretics or deviators from the true religious path. Muslim heresiographers, theologians, jurists and historians participated variously in this anti-Ismaili campaign. In particular, Sunni polemicists fabricated the necessary evidence that would lend support to the condemnation of the Ismailis on specific doctrinal grounds. They concocted detailed accounts of the supposed sinister objectives, immoral teachings and libertine practices of the Ismailis, while refuting the ʿAlid genealogy of the Ismaili Fatimid caliph-imams. Some polemicists also fabricated travesties in which they attributed a variety of abhorrent beliefs and practices to the Ismailis. And these forgeries circulated widely as genuine Ismaili treatises and, eventually, they were used as genuine Ismaili source materials by subsequent generations of Muslim authors writing about the Ismailis.

By spreading these defamations and fictitious accounts, the polemicists and other anti-Ismaili authors gradually created, in the course of the fourth/tenth century, coinciding with the first century of Fatimid rule, a 'black legend'.[4] Accordingly, Ismailism was mischievously depicted as the arch-heresy (*ilḥād*) of Islam, carefully designed by a certain ʿAbd Allāh b. Maymūn al-Qaddāḥ, or some other non-ʿAlid impostor, or possibly even a Jewish magician disguised as a Muslim, aiming at destroying Islam from within. By the end of the fourth/tenth century, this fiction with its elaborate details and stages of initiation culminating in atheism, had been accepted as an accurate and reliable description of Ismaili beliefs and practices, leading to further anti-Ismaili polemics and heresiographical accusations as well as

[4] W. Ivanow produced a number of pioneering studies on this 'black legend'; see especially his *The Alleged Founder of Ismailism* (Bombay, 1946).

intensifying the animosity of other Muslim communities towards the Ismailis. The defamatory components of this anti-Ismaili 'black legend' continued to fire the imagination of countless generations of Sunni writers throughout the medieval times.

Many of the essential components of this 'black legend', relating especially to the origins and early history of Ismailism, may be traced to a certain Sunni jurist and polemicist called Abū ʿAbd Allāh Muḥammad b. ʿAlī b. Rizām al-Ṭāʾī al-Kūfī, better known as Ibn Rizām. He lived in Baghdad during the first half of the fourth/tenth century. Around 340/951, Ibn Rizām wrote a major treatise in refutation of the Ismailis, also referred to as Bāṭinīs (Esotericists) by their detractors. Ibn Rizām's anti-Ismaili tract, called possibly *Kitāb Radd ʿalāʾl-Ismāʿīliyya*, or *al-Naqḍ ʿalāʾl-Bāṭiniyya*, does not seem to have survived, but it is quoted by Ibn al-Nadīm in his famous catalogue of Arabic books, *al-Fihrist*,[5] completed in 377/987. More importantly, Ibn Rizām's tract was used extensively a few decades later by another polemicist, the Sharīf Abu'l-Ḥusayn Muḥammad b. ʿAlī, an ʿAlid from Damascus better known as Akhū Muḥsin. An early ʿAlid genealogist, Akhū Muḥsin wrote his own anti-Ismaili tract, consisting of historical and doctrinal parts, around 372/982. This work, too, has not survived. However, long fragments from Akhū Muḥsin's account have been preserved by several later sources, notably the Egyptian historians al-Nuwayrī (d. 733/1333), Ibn al-Dawādārī (d. after 736/1335), and al-Maqrīzī (d. 845/1442), who was the first authority to have identified Ibn Rizām as the principal source of Akhū Muḥsin while condemning both sources as unreliable.[6] It is interesting to note that the

[5] Ibn al-Nadīm, *Kitāb al-Fihrist*, ed. G. Flügel (Leipzig, 1871–1872), vol. 1, pp. 186–187; ed. M. R. Tajaddud (2nd ed., Tehran, 1973), pp. 238–239.

[6] Shihāb al-Dīn Aḥmad b. ʿAbd al-Wahhāb al-Nuwayrī, *Nihāyat al-arab fī funūn al-adab*, vol. 25, ed. M. J. ʿA. al-Ḥīnī (Cairo, 1984), pp. 187–317; Abū Bakr ʿAbd Allāh b. al-Dawādārī, *Kanz al-durar wa-jāmiʿ al-ghurar*, vol. 6, ed. Ṣ. al-Munajjid (Cairo, 1961), pp. 6–21, 44–156; Taqī al-Dīn Aḥmad b. ʿAlī al-Maqrīzī, *Ittiʿāẓ al-ḥunafāʾ bi-akhbār al-aʾimma al-Fāṭimiyyīn al-khulafāʾ*, vol. 1, ed. J. al-Shayyāl (Cairo, 1967), pp. 22–29, 151–202; ed. Ayman F. Sayyid (Damascus, 2010), vol. 1, pp. 20–27, 173–231; English trans., *Towards a Shiʿi Mediterranean Empire: Fatimid Egypt and the Founding of Cairo*, tr. Shainool Jiwa (London, 2009), pp. 122–180.

unreliability of Ibn Rizām had already been pointed out by his contemporary, the Iraqi chronicler al-Masʿūdī, in his last work completed by 345/956, a few years after Ibn Rizām had produced his tract.[7]

It was in Akhū Muḥsin's polemical treatise that a certain *Kitāb al-Siyāsa* ('Book of Methodology'), one of the most popular early travesties attributed to Ismailis themselves, came to be mentioned for the first time. Used by several generations of polemicists and heresiographers as a major source of information on the secret doctrines and practices of the Ismailis, this anonymous text contained all the ideas needed to condemn the Ismailis as heretics on account of their alleged libertinism (*ibāḥa*) and atheism. Akhū Muḥsin claims to have read this book and quotes passages from it on the procedures for winning new converts that were supposedly followed by Ismaili *dāʿīs*, and for instructing the novices through some seven stages of initiation (*balāgh*) leading ultimately to atheism and unbelief.[8] The same book, or perhaps another forgery entitled *Kitāb al-Balāgh* ('Book of Initiation'), was seen shortly afterwards by Ibn al-Nadīm.[9] Needless to add that the Ismaili tradition knows of these fictitious accounts only through the polemics of its enemies.

The anti-Ismaili polemical writings provided a major source of information for Sunni heresiographers, who produced another important category of sources against the Ismailis. One of the most widely circulating of these heresiographies was the one written, in the 420s/1030s, by ʿAbd al-Qāhir b. Ṭāhir al-Baghdādī (d. 429/1037). He also had access to the anti-Ismaili works of Ibn Rizām and Akhū Muḥsin and claims to have used the *Kitāb al-Siyāsa* as well. In fact, al-Baghdādī claims that this book was sent by ʿAbd Allāh al-Mahdī, the founder of the Fatimid dynasty, to Abū Ṭāhir al-Jannābī

[7] Abu'l-Ḥasan ʿAlī b. al-Ḥusayn al-Masʿūdī, *Kitāb al-Tanbīh wa'l-ishrāf*, ed. M. J. de Goeje (Leiden, 1894), p. 396.

[8] The Arabic text of this forged account, together with its English translation, was partially reconstructed by S. M. Stern, on the basis of fragments preserved by al-Nuwayrī and other sources; see S. M. Stern, 'The "Book of the Highest Initiation" and other Anti-Ismāʿīlī Travesties', in his *Studies in Early Ismāʿīlism* (Jerusalem and Leiden, 1983), pp. 56–83.

[9] Ibn al-Nadīm, *al-Fihrist*, ed. Flügel, p. 189; ed. Tajaddud, p. 240.

(d. 332/944), the leader of the Qarmaṭī state of Bahrayn. By this allegation al-Baghdādī not only attempted to accord authenticity to this forgery, but also made the Qarmaṭīs subservient to the Fatimids in order to defame all Ismailis for the atrocities committed by Abū Ṭāhir and the Qarmaṭīs. A similar stance was adopted by many other Sunni writers. Modern scholarship has shown that the dissident Qarmaṭīs of Bahrayn, who awaited the return of the seventh Ismaili imam (Muḥammad b. Ismāʿīl) as their Mahdi, did not recognise Abū ʿAbd Allāh al-Mahdī and his successors on the Fatimid throne as their imams.[10]

At any rate, al-Baghdādī devoted a long chapter in his heresiography to the refutation of the Ismailis, referred to as the Bāṭinīs.[11] He opens the chapter by stating that the damage caused by the Bāṭiniyya to Muslim groups is greater than those caused by the Jews, Christians and Magians (Majūs); he then quotes long extracts from the *Kitāb al-Siyāsa*, describing the seven degrees of initiation into Ismailism, giving each stage a name, and leading finally to the state of unbelief (*al-khalʿ wa'l-salkh*).[12] He also refutes the ʿAlid descent of the Fatimids. The polemical and heresiographical traditions, in turn, influenced Muslim historians, theologians and jurists, while systematically turning other Muslim communities against the Ismailis.

The Sunni authors were not generally interested in collecting accurate information on the internal divisions of Shiʿi Islam as they treated all Shiʿi interpretations of Islam as 'heterodoxies' and, indeed, deviations from the true path. On the other hand, the Imāmī (Twelver) Shiʿi heresiographers, such as al-Nawbakhtī (d. after 300/912) and al-Qummī (d. 301/913–14), were better informed on the internal divisions of Shiʿism and, despite intending to defend the legitimacy of their own line of imams and the Imāmī community, did not maliciously misrepresent the Ismailis. In fact, these earliest Imāmī

---

10 See W. Madelung, 'The Fatimids and Qarmaṭīs of Baḥrayn', in F. Daftary (ed.), *Mediaeval Ismaʿili History and Thought* (Cambridge, 1996), pp. 21–73.

11 Abū Manṣūr ʿAbd al-Qāhir b. Ṭāhir al-Baghdādī, *al-Farq bayn al-firaq*, ed. M. Badr (Cairo, 1328/1910), pp. 265–299; English trans., *Moslem Schisms and Sects*, Part II, tr. A. S. Halkin (Tel-Aviv, 1935), pp. 107–157.

12 Al-Baghdādī, *al-Farq*, pp. 278 ff.; trans., pp. 131 ff.

heresiographers remain our main sources of information on the opening phase of Ismailism.[13] Under the circumstances, the Sunni writers, who were more interested in refuting than understanding, would not have availed themselves of authentic Ismaili sources, even if such sources were more readily available to them.

Meanwhile, the Fatimid Ismaili *daʿwa* had continued to spread successfully in many lands. The *daʿwa* was greatly expanded under the sixth Fatimid caliph-imam, al-Ḥākim bi-Amr Allāh (386–411/996–1021). The *daʿwa* now became particularly active outside the Fatimid state, in the eastern regions of the Muslim world, especially in Iraq and Persia where the inhabitants were familiar with different Shiʿi traditions. Indeed, Ismailism achieved its greatest and most enduring success outside Fatimid dominions where, ironically, the Ismailis were often persecuted. On the other hand, the Ismailis continued to represent a minority within the boundaries of the Fatimid state, both in Ifrīqiya and Egypt, where Shiʿism had never developed any deep roots.

A large number of Ismaili *dāʿī*s were assigned to Iraq, Persia and, later, to Central Asia, where they targeted various social strata. In Iraq, the seat of the Abbasid caliphate, the *dāʿī*s seem to have concentrated their efforts on local rulers and Arab tribal chiefs, with whose support they aimed to bring about the downfall of the Abbasids.[14] Foremost amongst the *dāʿī*s operating in Iraq and Persia during the reign of al-Ḥākim, was Ḥamīd al-Dīn al-Kirmānī (d. after 411/1020), an eminent philosopher and one of the most learned Ismaili theologians of the Fatimid period.[15] He was particularly active in Baṣra and Baghdad,

---

[13] See al-Ḥasan b. Mūsā al-Nawbakhtī, *Kitāb al-Firaq al-Shīʿa*, ed. H. Ritter (Istanbul, 1931), pp. 37–41, 57–60; Saʿd b. ʿAbd Allāh al-Qummī, *Kitāb al-Maqālāt wa'l-firaq*, ed. M. J. Mashkūr (Tehran, 1963), pp. 50–55, 63–64, 80–83.

[14] See Paul E. Walker, 'The Ismaili *Daʿwa* in the Reign of the Fatimid Caliph al-Ḥākim', *Journal of the American Research Center in Egypt*, 30 (1993), pp. 161–182; reprinted in his *Fatimid History and Ismaili Doctrine* (Aldershot, 2008), article III; and his *Caliph of Cairo: Al-Hakim bi-Amr Allah, 996–1021* (Cairo and New York, 2009), pp. 119–133.

[15] See Paul E. Walker, *Ḥamīd al-Dīn al-Kirmānī: Ismaili Thought in the Age of al-Ḥākim* (London, 1999); Ismail K. Poonawala, *Biobibliography of Ismāʿīlī Literature* (Malibu, CA, 1977), pp. 94–102; F. Daftary, 'Ḥamid-al-Din Kermāni', *EIR*, vol. 11, pp. 639–641.

the very seat of the Abbasid caliphate. In 401/1010–11, Qirwāsh b. al-Muqallad (391–442/1001–1050), the ʿUqaylid ruler of Mawṣil, Kūfa, and other towns, whose family adhered to Shiʿism, acknowledged the suzerainty of the Fatimids and had the *khuṭba* read in the name of al-Ḥākim. In the same year, ʿAlī al-Asadī, chief of the Banū Asad, declared his loyalty to al-Ḥākim in Ḥilla and other districts in Iraq under his control.

Alarmed by the success of the Ismaili *daʿwa* within Abbasid territories, and indeed at the very doorstep of Baghdad, the Abbasid caliph al-Qādir (381–422/991–1031) now decided to take more severe measures against the Ismailis. In 402/1011, he launched his own personal anti-Fatimid propaganda campaign. He assembled a number of Sunni and Shiʿi scholars at his court in Baghdad, and commanded them to declare in a written statement that al-Ḥākim and his predecessors were impostors with no genuine Fatimid ʿAlid ancestry.[16] This so-called Baghdad manifesto, which was also influenced by aspects of the earlier anti-Ismaili 'black legend', was read in mosques throughout the Abbasid lands, to the deep annoyance of al-Ḥākim. In addition, al-Qādir commissioned several theologians, including the Muʿtazilī ʿAlī b. Saʿīd al-Iṣṭakhrī (d. 404/1013–14), to write treatises in refutation of the Fatimids and their doctrines. Be that as it may, the Ismaili *daʿwa* continued unabated in the eastern regions, calling forth further hostile reactions from the Sunni establishment. Several decades later, in 444/1052, the Abbasid caliph al-Qāʾim (422–467/1031–1075) sponsored yet another anti-Fatimid manifesto in Baghdad.[17]

By the end of the fifth/eleventh century, the widespread literary campaign against the Ismailis had been astonishingly successful

---

[16] The text and the list of the signatories of this Baghdad manifesto, with slight variations, may be found in Ibn al-Jawzī, *al-Muntaẓam*, ed. F. Krenkow (Hyderabad, 1357–1362/1938–1943), vol. 7, p. 255; Ibn Khaldūn, *The Muqaddimah*, tr. F. Rosenthal (2nd ed., Princeton, 1967), vol. 1, pp. 45–46; al-Maqrīzī, *Ittiʿāẓ*, ed. al-Shayyal, vol. 1, pp. 43–44; ed. Sayyid, vol. 1, pp. 42–43; Ibn Taghrībirdī, *al-Nujūm al-zāhira fī mulūk Miṣr wa'l-Qāhira* (Cairo, 1348–1392/1929–1972), vol. 4, pp. 229–231.

[17] See, for instance, Ibn Muyassar, *Akhbār Miṣr*, ed. Ayman F. Sayyid (Cairo, 1981), p. 13; Ibn Taghrībirdī, *al-Nujūm*, vol. 5, p. 53; see also H. Laoust, 'Les agitations religieuses à Baghdad aux IVe et Ve siècles de l'hégire', in Donald S. Richards (ed.), *Islamic Civilisation, 950–1150* (Oxford, 1973), pp. 175 ff.

throughout the central Islamic lands. The revolt of the Persian Ismailis, initially led by the *dāʿī* Ḥasan-i Ṣabbāḥ (d. 518/1124), against the Sunni Saljūq Turks, the new overlords of the Abbasids, called forth another prolonged and vigorous Sunni reaction against the Ismailis in general and the Nizārī Ismailis in particular. It may be recalled that the succession to the eighth Fatimid caliph-imam, al-Mustanṣir (427–487/1036–1094), was disputed between his original heir-designate son, Nizār (d. 488/1095), and his younger son al-Mustaʿlī, who was actually installed to the Fatimid caliphate by the powerful vizier al-Afḍal. Ḥasan-i Ṣabbāḥ upheld Nizār's cause and severed his ties with Cairo.

This succession dispute led to the major Nizārī-Mustaʿlian schism in the Ismaili *daʿwa* and community. Al-Mustaʿlī and his successors in the Fatimid dynasty were also acknowledged as imams by the Mustaʿlian Ismailis concentrated in Egypt, Syria and Yemen. On the other hand, the Ismailis of the Saljūq dominions, who were already engaged in revolutionary activities against the Saljūqs, gave their allegiance to the newly founded Nizārī Ismaili *daʿwa*. Mustaʿlian Ismailism, which survived only in its later Ṭayyibī form, soon found a permanent stronghold in the highlands of Yemen, far from the Abbasid centres of power. But the Nizārīs now posed a serious political challenge to the established Sunni order under the Abbasids and their Saljūq overlords. Consequently, it was the politically active Nizārī Ismailis who received the wrath of the Sunni establishment.

The new literary campaign, accompanied by incessant military attacks on the Nizārī Ismaili strongholds in Persia, was spearheaded by Niẓām al-Mulk, the Saljūq vizier and virtual master of Saljūq dominions for more than two decades, with the full endorsement of the Abbasid caliph and the Saljūq sultan. Niẓām al-Mulk, who was an outspoken enemy of the Ismailis and evidently had access to the earlier anti-Ismaili works of Ibn Rizām and Akhū Muḥsin, devoted a long chapter in his *Siyāsat-nāma* ('The Book of Government') to the condemnation of the Ismailis who, according to him, aimed 'to abolish Islam, to mislead mankind and cast them into perdition.'[18] This work,

[18] Niẓām al-Mulk, *Siyar al-mulūk (Siyāsat-nāma)*, ed. H. Darke (2nd ed., Tehran, 1347 Sh./1968), p. 311; English trans., *The Book of Government or Rules for Kings*, tr. H. Darke (2nd ed., London, 1978), p. 231.

giving counsel to the Saljūq sultan Malik Shāh (465–485/1073–1092), was completed in 484/1091, but eleven chapters (including chapter 46 on the Ismailis) were added in the following year, shortly before the vizier was assassinated in 485/1092. These additional chapters focus on the dangers which threatened the Saljūq state, notably those posed by certain Iranian movements as well as the Ismailis. The attack on the Ismailis was a response to their growing influence in Persia. Indeed, in just two years after establishing himself in the fortress of Alamūt in 483/1090, Ḥasan-i Ṣabbāḥ had carved out a territorial state for the Persian Ismailis in the very midst of the Saljūq sultanate; he was also enjoying popular support from Persians of different social classes who despised the alien rule of the Saljūq Turks.

However, the earliest polemical treatise against the Persian Ismailis of the Alamūt period was written by Abū Ḥāmid Muḥammad al-Ghazālī (d. 505/1111), the most renowned contemporary Sunni theologian and jurist. He was, in fact, commissioned by the Abbasid caliph al-Mustaẓhir (487–512/1094–1118) to write a major work in refutation of the Bāṭinīs – another designation meaning Esotericists coined for the Ismailis by their detractors who accused them of dispensing with the *ẓāhir*, or the commandments and prohibitions of the *sharīʿa*, because they claimed to have found access to the *bāṭin*, or the inner meaning of the Islamic message as interpreted by the Ismaili imam. In this widely circulating book, commonly known as *al-Mustaẓhirī* and completed shortly before al-Ghazālī left his teaching post at the Niẓāmiyya Madrasa in Baghdad in 488/1095, the author elaborates his own version of the Ismaili system of graded initiation leading to the ultimate stage of atheism (*al-khalʿ wa'l-salkh*).[19] He uses specific designations in reference to each of the seven stages, similarly to al-Baghdādī's list.

---

19 Abū Ḥāmid Muḥammad al-Ghazālī, *Faḍā'iḥ al-Bāṭiniyya wa-faḍā'il al-Mustaẓhiriyya*, ed. ʿA. Badawī (Cairo, 1964), especially pp. 21–36; English trans., in Richard J. McCarthy, *Freedom and Fulfillment. An Annotated Translation of Al-Ghazālī's al-Munqidh min al-Ḍalāl and other Relevant Works of al-Ghazālī* (Boston, 1980), pp. 185–195. See also F. Mitha, *Al-Ghazālī and the Ismailis: A Debate on Reason and Authority in Medieval Islam* (London, 2001).

Al-Ghazālī aims his polemics particularly against the doctrine of *taʿlīm*, or authoritative teaching by the Ismaili imam, as articulated in a vigorous form by Ḥasan-i Ṣabbāḥ. The doctrine of *taʿlīm* posed a serious intellectual challenge to the Sunni establishment as it also refuted afresh the legitimacy of the Abbasid caliph as the spiritual spokesman of the Muslims. This doctrine, essentially a reformulation of the old Shiʿi doctrine of the imamate, served as the basis of all the subsequent doctrinal positions of the early Nizārī Ismailis. Subsequently, al-Ghazālī wrote several shorter works in refutation of the Ismailis,[20] and his defamations were adopted by other Sunni writers who, like Niẓām al-Mulk, were for the most part also familiar with the earlier 'black legend'. It is interesting to note that the Nizārī Ismailis themselves never responded to al-Ghazālī's polemics, but a detailed refutation of his *al-Mustaẓhirī* was much later written in Yemen by the fifth chief *dāʿī* of the Ṭayyibī Mustaʿlian Ismailis, ʿAlī b. Muḥammad b. al-Walīd (d. 612/1215).[21] The Mustaʿlians of Yemen had their own local conflicts with their Zaydī Shiʿi neighbours and, later, with the Sunni Ottomans who occupied Yemen in 945/1538. Be that as it may, a variety of Sunni authors, including especially Saljūq chroniclers, participated actively in the renewed propaganda against the Nizārī Ismailis, while Saljūq armies persistently failed to dislodge the Nizārīs from their mountain fortresses. In fact, by the final years of Ḥasan-i Ṣabbāḥ's life Nizārī-Saljūq relations had entered a new phase of 'stalemate'.[22]

After decades of conflict with the Sunni world, followed by stalemate and isolation, many Nizārī Ismailis had become weary of their situation. Under the circumstances, the sixth lord of Alamūt, Jalāl

---

[20] See for instance, al-Ghazālī's *al-Qisṭās al-mustaqīm*, ed. V. Chelhot (Beirut, 1959), especially pp. 40–102; English trans., in McCarthy, *Freedom and Fullfilment*, pp. 287–332.

[21] ʿAlī Ibn al-Walīd, *Dāmigh al-bāṭil wa-ḥatf al-munāḍil*, ed. M. Ghālib (Beirut, 1982), 2 vols. See also H. Corbin, 'The Ismāʿīlī Response to the Polemic of Ghazālī', in S. H. Nasr (ed.), *Ismāʿīlī Contributions to Islamic Culture* (Tehran, 1977), pp. 67–98.

[22] See Carole Hillenbrand, 'The Power Struggle Between the Saljuqs and the Ismaʿilis of Alamūt, 487–518/1094–1124: The Saljuq Perspective', in Daftary (ed.), *Mediaeval Ismaʿili History and Thought*, pp. 205–220; F. Daftary, 'Ismaili-Seljuq Relations: Conflict and Stalemate', in E. Herzig and S. Stewart (ed.), *The Age of the Seljuqs: The Idea of Iran, VI* (London, 2015), pp. 41–57.

al-Dīn Ḥasan (607–618/1210–1221), attempted a daring rapprochement with the Sunni world. He ordered his followers to adopt the *sharīʿa* in its Sunni form and invited Sunni jurists to instruct his people. The outside world, and especially the Abbasid caliph al-Nāṣir, accepted Jalāl al-Dīn Ḥasan's reform; and, in 608/1211 the caliph issued a decree to that effect. The Ismaili imam was now recognised as an *amīr* amongst the *amīr*s, and his rights over the territories of the Nizārī Ismaili state were officially acknowledged by the Abbasid caliph and other Muslim rulers. All the Nizārīs obeyed the new instruction without any dissent, as Ḥasan was the infallible imam who guided his community and contextualised the interpretation of the *sharīʿa* as he deemed appropriate. The Nizārīs evidently regarded their imam's declarations as reflecting the strict imposition of *taqiyya*, which could take any form of accommodation to the outside world as deemed necessary by the imam of the time. The Nizārī Ismaili imam's new policy had obvious political advantages for the Nizārī community, which had survived very precariously under highly adverse circumstances. By his bold decision the imam had now ensured territorial security for the Nizārīs as well as peace and safety for his community. Under Ḥasan's son and successor, ʿAlāʾ al-Dīn Muḥammad (618–653/1221–1255), the penultimate lord of Alamūt, the Sunni *sharīʿa* was gradually relaxed.

The ameliorated situation of the Nizārīs proved short-lived, however. With the appearance of the all-conquering Mongol hordes in southwestern Asia, the fate of the Nizārī Ismaili state was sealed. Ironically, the destruction of the Shiʿi Ismaili state and the Sunni Abbasid caliphate were the twin objectives of the Mongols, which were achieved with some difficulty and much bloodshed. The surrender of Alamūt in 654/1256 signalled the fall of the Ismaili state, followed a couple of years later by the demise of the Abbasid caliphate. In subsequent centuries, the Nizārī Ismailis, devoid of any political prominence, survived as religious minorities in many lands, often dissimulating under the guise of Sunnism to escape persecution by various local dynasties. Strangely, the creed of their perennial adversaries now served the Nizārīs as a protective shield against intermittent persecution.

The Ismailis continued to be misrepresented throughout the centuries until the modern progress in Ismaili studies, based on the recovery and study of a large number of genuine Ismaili texts – manuscript sources preserved in many collections in Yemen, Syria, Persia, Afghanistan, Central Asia and South Asia. These manuscripts, which were not available to earlier generations of non-Ismaili Muslim writers, revealed the richness and diversity of the Ismaili literary and intellectual traditions.[23] As a result of the modern scholarship in the field, initiated in the 1930s, we have increasingly come to have a much better understanding of the true nature of Ismaili history and the contributions of this historically misunderstood Shiʿi community to Islamic thought and culture. The scholarly study of the Ismailis, which by the closing decades of the twentieth century had already greatly deconstructed many of the seminal anti-Ismaili legends of medieval times, promises to dissipate the remaining misrepresentations of the Ismailis rooted either in hostility or the imaginative ignorance of earlier generations.

[23] In addition to Professor Poonawala's already-cited *Biobibliography of Ismāʿīlī Literature*, see W. Ivanow, *Ismaili Literature: A Bibliographical Survey* (Tehran, 1963), and F. Daftary, *Ismaili Literature: A Bibliography of Sources and Studies* (London, 2004).

2

Ismaili Polemics Against Opponents in the Early Fatimid Period

Paul E. Walker
(University of Chicago)

The standard dictionary definition of a polemic is a contentious argument that is intended to support a specific position through a contrary position. It is mostly seen in arguments about controversial topics, particular those concerned with religion and religious doctrine. The practice of such argumentation is called polemics and it commonly contains aggressive attack on or refutation of the opinions or principles of another and involves the art or practice of disputation or controversy.

Ismaili writings from the Fatimid period abound in refutations of their opponents. Some are quite explicit, naming specific individuals for repudiation, frequently in substantial detail. A number of this type appear as separate treatises, each devoted to a single person. We have a list of such works by al-Qāḍī al-Nuʿmān (d. 363/974): against Ibn Surayj (d. 306/918), al-Shāfiʿī (204/820), Ibn Qutayba (d. 276/889), Mālik (d. 179/796), and Abū Ḥanīfa (d. 150/767). Another example is al-Kirmānī's (d. after 411/1020–21) polemic against Abū Bakr al-Rāzī (d. ca. 313/925 or 323/935), his *al-Aqwāl al-dhahabiyya*. Yet others do not single out a named opponent but rather a school or sect. It is quite common to find, for example, a refutation of those who pretend to philosophy. Al-Kirmānī wrote separate chapters of his *Tanbīh al-hādī* against them, as well as the Twelvers, the Zaydīs and the Nusayrī *ghulāt*. Both al-Nuʿmān and al-Kirmānī devoted separate sections to the refutation of those who uphold *taqlīd*, or *qiyās*, or advocate the use of *naẓar*, *istiḥsān*, *istidlāl*, and *ijmāʿ*, or *ijtihād* and personal *ra'y*. In addition there is a whole range of materials wherein, rather than individuals or groups, a category or item of doctrine is refuted generically. Much of this effort by the *daʿwa* to censure its enemies and detractors has become better known especially recently with attention to the works of al-Nuʿmān, particularly his *Ikhtilāf uṣūl al-madhāhib*. Important new material, however, is to be found in the unpublished work of al-Kirmānī, his *Tanbīh al-hādī wa'l-mustahdī* just mentioned. And there is much more in the work of a variety of authors from just prior to and the first century and a half subsequent to the founding of the Fatimid state.

The Ismaili *daʿwa* operated in the first instance as appeal, aiming to attract the loyalty of those who accepted membership either to an unnamed supreme leader, the imamate, before the declaration of the caliphate, or to the reigning imam-caliph once the empire had come into existence. The *daʿwa* is thus a summons whose basic function is to bring followers into the fold. But a key step in this process often involved a concerted effort to break down and render null and void any pre-existing religious affiliation that might be held by the target individual. The process is typically described as 'breaking' and a specialist assigned to do it is the 'One who breaks' (*mukāsir*), although most ranking agents of the *daʿwa* are thought to have performed a similar operation.

The exact technique employed likely varied and depended heavily on the capacity of the potential novice. However the action itself is often mentioned in connection with the administration of the oath of allegiance and fidelity which was a fairly routine rite of admission to the *daʿwa*. An early treatise by Abu'l-ʿAbbās, brother of Abū ʿAbd Allāh al-Shīʿī (both d. 298/911), comments: 'in the inner meaning of the law, the one for whom the *dāʿī* breaks the external on which the novice previously relied because he did not know the [true] interpretation or its meanings, he is in the position of someone captured from the land of ignorance, being moved to the land of knowledge.' The *dāʿī*s are 'those who break the people of outward meaning [from earlier beliefs] and then place the oath of covenant on the necks of those of the believers who respond to the appeal of truth.'[1] From a century

[1] Wilferd Madelung and Paul E. Walker (ed.), *Two Works from the Earliest Fatimid Daʿwa in North Africa: Sermons by Abū ʿAbdallāh al-Shīʿī and a Letter by His Brother Abu'l-ʿAbbās on Fiscal Obligations to the Imam* (forthcoming).

later we find the following confirmation in a manual that outlines the proper conduct of the *dāʿī*. Once the agent of the *daʿwa* ascertains that the novice's 'objective is God and true religion, he is first to break him down and extirpate those notions he previously upheld, so that his prior beliefs have then become so thoroughly destroyed he no longer has an argument in their favour. . . . Shower him with arguments . . . until he has been broken down and wants to take the oath.'[2]

Thus polemic was built into the programme of the *daʿwa* even at its most basic level. Every agent who hoped to further the Ismaili cause, to convert new members and expand the appeal, needed the tools required to countermand and nullify the arguments put forth by opponents of various kinds. In short they required not only firm knowledge of doctrine, but how to defend it and deflect contentions that ran counter to it. At the most sophisticated levels of argument, it obviously helped to have at hand the kind of works mentioned earlier, some themselves impressive masterpieces of polemical reasoning, but all in service to the *daʿwa*.

Of course not all propagation of the appeal began with obvious polemical argumentation. A particularly subtle technique is represented in a record of Abū ʿAbd Allāh's preaching in the period before the proclamation of the state.[3] His general method involved casting doubt without direct confrontation. He would suggest that the misdeeds and errors committed by the communities of earlier prophets, mostly as described or hinted at in Qurʾanic passages, had almost exact parallels in the actions of Islamic counterparts. The pharaohs of the Muslim community were repeating the evils perpetrated by the pharaohs at the time of the Israelites. What befell the earlier groups when they went astray are now matched by those who deny the family of the Prophet and fail to follow their lead. In fact argument of this type easily expands. The mistakes of the present mirror actions in the

---

2 Aḥmad b. Ibrāhīm al-Naysāburī, *al-Risāla al-mūjaza al-kāfiya fī ādāb al-duʿāt*, ed. Verena Klemm, trans. by Paul E. Walker as *A Code of Conduct: A Treatise on the Etiquette of the Fatimid Ismaili Mission* (London and New York, 2011), pp. 60–61.

3 See Wilferd Madelung and Paul E. Walker (ed.), *Two Works from the Earliest Fatimid Daʿwa in North Africa: Sermons by Abū ʿAbdallāh al-Shīʿī and a Letter by His Brother Abu'l-ʿAbbās on Fiscal Obligations to the Imam* (forthcoming).

past. As several versions of a well-known *ḥadīth* insist: 'The Apostle of God said: "This community will not abandon the practice of previous generations so much as this thumb leads the one that follows it."' Ḥudhayfa b. al-Yamān[4] said: 'There was nothing with the Israelites but that its like will be with you.' 'The messenger of God warned his community against disunion and mutual difference and he informed them that they will perpetrate what the nations that came before them perpetrated. And so he said: "Surely you will follow the practice of the Israelites in a completely identical manner, exactly alike."' 'You shall keep to the path of those who came before you in a completely identical manner and to take after them exactly, whether inch by inch, cubit by cubit or yard by yard, to the point that, were they to enter the burrow of a lizard, you would enter it as well.'

From this basic hard to challenge claim, which in and of itself has no direct link to a doctrinal position, he could move progressively on to more and more overt cases of sin, corruption and degradation specifically within the Islamic community following the death of the Prophet when it refused to acknowledge the succession of ʿAlī b. Abī Ṭālib (d. 40/661). Finally it would become clear that accepting the appeal of agents acting on behalf of the true guardian of God's religion, the about to appear Mahdi, was the sole avenue to salvation.

Yet another polemical technique, one that might seem quite unorthodox – assuming that there exists anything like an orthodox method in polemical writing – can be found in the 'Chapter on Satan' by an obscure Eastern *dāʿī* known to us only as Abū Tammām (fl. fourth/tenth century).[5] In it all the erring sects of Islam are condemned as a whole and as individual movements, each being established by a satan leading his followers away from the true religion.

The text that contains the heresiographical 'Chapter on Satan' comes from a fourth/tenth century Ismaili work called *Kitāb al-Shajara*. Even

---

[4] Ḥudhayfa b. al-Yamān was one of the Prophet's Companions.

[5] Wilferd Madelung and Paul E. Walker, *An Ismaili Heresiography: The "Bāb al-Shayṭān" from Abū Tammām's* Kitāb al-Shajara. Critical edition of the Arabic text (with) an English translation and introduction (Leiden, 1998).

in the tradition of the *daʿwa* of his own or parallel Ismaili groups who preserve what is left of his book, its author is known only by the *kunya*, Abū Tammām. Nevertheless, from internal evidence, it is clear that he either lived and wrote in Khurāsān, or came from there or both. He was also a disciple of the famous *dāʿī* and philosopher, Muḥammad al-Nasafī, who was executed by Samanid authorities in 332/943, and who is mentioned frequently with special reverence in various places in the *Shajara*.

The 'Chapter on Satan' is actually one part of a fairly large work and the general structure of the whole treatise is not necessarily polemical. At the outset, the author expresses his intention to explain in this work the following classes of beings: angels (*al-malāʾika*), jinn, satans (*al-shayāṭīn*), devils (*al-abālisa*), and humans (*al-ins*), as they exist both in potentia and in actuality. He says that he will do so in response to a request from a colleague who has become perplexed on this issue. The satans in potentia are those, he says, who adhere to the exterior and who are far from the truth, that is, who stay away from it. These satans have supporters of only one sort, the devils, because those who adhere to exterior realities consider matters from one aspect exclusively and that is from its exterior and not its interior, its shell and not its kernel.

The author continues by also relating the well-known *ḥadīth* of the Prophet, in which he said:

> The tribe of Israel broke up after Moses into seventy-one sects that are in hell except for one that is in paradise; the community of Jesus broke up after him into seventy-two sects that are in hell except for one that is in paradise; and my community will break up into seventy-three sects that will be in hell except for one among them that will be in paradise.

For Abū Tammām,

> there is no doubt that, for each one of these sects, a chief or a leader summons the people to his particular opinion and belief. These are the satans that the messenger of God mentioned. What fits exactly the words of the messenger of God is the fact that the proponents of external meaning have divided into seventy-two sects, while the partisans of inner meanings remain in the same state they were when the messenger of God departed from this

> world. There has not occurred among them any breaking apart or mutual opposition or irresolution as has occurred among the proponents of external meanings who curse and repudiate each other. In our view this fact establishes the correctness of the doctrines of the proponents of inner meaning and the corruption of the various dogmas held by the proponents of external meaning who curse each other because God has said: 'Had it not been from other than God, surely they would have found in it much disagreement.' From this we learn that, if the doctrines of the proponents of external meaning were actually taken from God, they would not now be in disaccord. I will here spell out these divisions and sects one by one and explain briefly and concisely the beliefs of each of them.

The divisions and sects in his list, each of which was founded or led by a satan, are the Muʿtazila, the Khawārij, the Ḥadīthiyya, the Qadariyya, the Anthropomorphists, the Murji'a, the Zaydiyya, the Kaysāniyya, the ʿAbbāsiyya, the Ghāliya, and the Imāmiyya, along with the various sub-branches of each. In total they are seventy-two; all destined for hellfire. The seventy-third Islamic group, the 'one among them that will be in paradise', are of course the Ismaili Shiʿa.

Any heresiography is by its very nature polemical; it seeks to identify, expose and condemn the groups its author considers heretics. This Ismaili example is, however, relatively unique. Nearly all those from the classical period of Islam that we possess are Sunni, or composed from the Sunni viewpoint. Abū Tammām's 'Chapter on Satan' is the only one that expresses the Shiʿa perspective. But it also strongly denounces a whole series of Shiʿi groups, among them the Zaydiyya and the Imamiyya. Most striking, however, is its censure of several favoured imams of Sunni legal and theological schools, among them Mālik b. Anas, al-Shāfiʿī, Aḥmad b. Ḥanbal (d. 241/855), Abū Ḥanīfa, and ʿAlī b. Ismāʿīl al-Ashʿarī (d. 324/935–36).

The following examples will illustrate Abū Tammām's methods and provide some idea of how thorough – with what detail – he both describes and refutes these heretical tendencies.

> *Azāriqa*
>
> The first [of the Khawārij] is the Azāriqa related to Nāfi' b. al-Azraq. This Nāfi' was the first to create dissension among the Khawārij. It was he who instigated the dissociation from those

who remained at home and the testing of those who attempted to join his army. The Azāriqa do not dissociate from those of the early generation among the Khawārij who came before them and who associated with the quietists and failed to declare them unbelievers. They say instead that this matter has become clear to us but it was hidden from them. The Azāriqa uphold strict determinism in the manner that was taught by Jahm. They maintain further that whoever remains in the territory of unbelief is an unbeliever and nothing avails him but to emigrate away from there. They also sanction the torment of children [in the hereafter].[6]

Shāfiʿiyya

The second sect [of the Ḥadīthiyya] is the Shāfiʿiyya, the followers of Muḥammad b. Idrīs al-Shāfiʿī. They maintain that the most excellent of people after the messenger of God, was Abū Bakr, then ʿUmar, then ʿUthmān, and then ʿAlī, and that these caliphs are the four who were rightly guided. They say further that the messenger of God died and did not appoint a successor and that the community appointed for themselves Abū Bakr as leader. According to them he was more deserving of the imamate than anyone else, and the messenger of God had said, 'My community will not agree on an error.' They affirm reasoning by analogy and personal endeavour although they do not accept the establishment of a ruling on the basis of discretion. They hold that ʿAlī b. Abī Ṭālib was right in all of his wars but that Ṭalḥa, al-Zubayr, Muʿāwiya, ʿA'isha, and ʿAmr b. al-ʿĀṣ argued for fighting him and exerted personal judgment to that end. All of them are in paradise just as God said, 'And We shall remove from their hearts any lurking sense of injury as brothers facing each other on raised couches.' They say that beasts will be resurrected and thereafter become dry dust by the order of God and that the unbeliever will want to be in their state when he cries out, 'O would that I were become dry dust.' As for the children and the insane, they will, by the mercy of God, be entered into paradise. Al-Shāfiʿī had numerous differences with Abū Ḥanīfa and other legal experts in the Islamic community on matters of legal rulings

6 *An Ismaili Heresiography*, trans., p. 35.

and the law. Handling the penis negates the ablution according to him.[7]

Jahmiyya

The first sect [of the Qadariyya] is the Jahmiyya related to Jahm b. Ṣafwān. They say that faith is cognisance and conviction in the heart rather than confession and excluding the rest of the acts of obedience. If a man were to live a hundred years and acknowledge God and recognise Him in the heart but never confess to this with his tongue, he is nonetheless a believer. They maintained as well that God's knowledge is originated. God knew from eternity that a thing will come into being but did not know it as existing. When a thing has come into existence, it may be said God knows it as having come into existence. That God's knowledge is other than He is proven because of the temporal origination of knowledge. Examples are the humans, the heavens, the Torah, the Furqān [Qur'an], the Gospels, the earth, and other kinds of created things. Jahm argued that he would not say that God knew eternally because, if he were to say that, it would require that there have been another eternally with Him. He agreed that he would not say He was eternally either knowing or ignorant because knowing is an act of His. When He performs the act of knowing, He has knowledge. If He performs the act of ignorance, He is in fact ignorant. Thus Jahm would say that all ignorance in this world, as well as knowledge, is an act of God. They hold that the will of God [encompasses] all the actions of humans, as for example those of obedience and disobedience, in the same way as they maintained is the case with knowledge. They say that the Qur'an was created, and that God will not be seen by anyone in the afterlife. God is the Creator of things, their Innovator, and the Maker of created things. None of His creation can possibly act or bring something into being and all the acts that we witness that are ascribed to the animals are actually due to God's acting through them, as is the case for the sun, the moon, and dying. Therefore, when you say a man became an unbeliever or had faith or moved or disobeyed or was obedient,

[7] *An Ismaili Heresiography*, trans., pp. 45–46.

committed adultery, or stole, that is the same as your saying the sun set, the moon rose, so-and-so died, grew long, grew short, or the tree dried up. All the actions in this world are actually acts of God. God will punish the servants on the day of resurrection for what He did on their behalf, not for what they did for themselves since they have no acts of their own. It is possible that God will punish all of the people and the closest angels and will reward the hypocrites and the satans and preserve them forever in His paradise. They state: this appears to us to be unjust but it is not unjust in regard to God because He is not like us and because we are merely His chattel and slaves who are not to question His actions. The proof is that, if it were possible for humans on their own to have actions, either of movement or of rest, they could adjust the heavens and the earth. If that were possible, they would seek it, but it is impossible. They say further that motions are bodies; it is absurd for them to be non-corporeal for the reason that what is non-corporeal is God Himself and nothing is like Him. They hold that God acts unjustly, capriciously, and imposes a legal burden on His servants which they do not have the ability to fulfil but all that is not, on His part, unjust but rather for Him it is a bounty and a charity. That occurs only on the part of someone under command and prohibition whereas He, the mighty and glorious, is not subject to command and prohibition.[8]

[8] The entry on Jahm continues as follows: 'They deny the punishment of the grave, Munkar and Nakīr, and the Balance. We do not claim, they say, that God is a thing but rather that He is the Maker of things. Their proof that God, the exalted, is the Maker of things is that thingness applies only to the created and it is impossible that God have any of the characteristics of creatures. They uphold rebellion against an unjust ruler by any means available to them, by the sword or what is less than it. According to them, paradise and hell have not now been created and will not occur except at their proper time; they will be created following the day of resurrection but they will not endure after God creates them. This group believes that paradise and hell may be annihilated, and they draw support for this from the statement of God, the mighty and glorious, "He is the First and the Last. He was in the beginning when there was nothing and, likewise, He will be at the end when there will be nothing with Him".' *An Ismaili Heresiography*, trans., pp. 49–51.

Karrāmiyya

The third sect is the Karrāmiyya related to Muḥammad b. Karrām al-Sijistānī. They maintain that God is a body adjoining the throne, that He will be seen in the next life, and that the Qurʾan is uncreated. Muḥammad b. Karrām was a man given to self-mortification and asceticism. He claimed that he was a person who relied solely on God and that he had intended to go into the desert with many of those who followed him without provisions, water, or riding mounts. The ruler prevented him from doing that and threw him in prison, saying, 'This man will destroy himself and these other poor wretches as well. It is incumbent on us to stop him and to assume control over him.' The Karrāmiyya say that the prophet was never the proof [*ḥujja*] and that was because he died and God's proof will not die. They insist also that there is nothing among us that is the word of God; the Qurʾan is only a narration of the words of God and a narration is not the same as the narrated. They claim further that there is not, in the heart of any of the saints, the prophets, or the faithful, faith in God. That is because faith with God is speech rather than cognisance, assent, or the rest of the acts of obedience. The location of speech is not in the heart but rather solely on the tongue. They maintain that the hypocrites are actually believers. On the matter of the acts of humans, they hold doctrines like those of the Najjāriyya. There are, however, oddities in which they stand alone and among these is their claim that a woman is unlawful to anyone who has had sexual intercourse with her mother. Another is permitting their associates, whenever in the middle of a dispute with opponents and the opponent asks them for a *ḥadīth* from the prophet in accord with their doctrine, to invent the *ḥadīth* spontaneously for that particular occasion and to attribute it to the prophet and use it as their proof of that doctrine. Their argument for this is that their doctrines are true and the prophet would only have spoken the truth and summoned to it. Thus, when they relate of him that he said this or that in which they believe, they have been quite truthful. According to them the people will be assembled [at the Resurrection] in Jerusalem and their leader Muḥammad b. Karrām gathered from Khurāsān and its vicinity more than five thousand families and moved them to Jerusalem. Thereafter when the people gather to assemble there, having already moved to it at present, it will be easier for them on the day of resurrection in that they will be closer to the assembling point. They hold that God creates conviction in the hearts of His servants although He did not create it in the hearts of some of them. It is a gift from God which humans have no ability to acquire on their own. The capacity, they insist, precedes the act.[9]

Sabāʾiyya

The second sect [of the Ghāliyya] is the Sabāʾiyya, related to ʿAbd Allāh b. Sabaʾ. They claim that the imam after the messenger of God was ʿAlī b. Abī Ṭālib. He is the Mahdi who will fill the earth with justice as it is now full of wrongdoing and oppression. ʿAbd Allāh b. Sabaʾ once said to the person who brought to al-Madāʾin the news of the death of ʿAlī b. Abī Ṭālib, 'By God, if you brought us the brains of ʿAlī seven hundred times over, we would still know that he will not die until he returns and drives the Arabs with his rod.' As a result when this was reported to Ibn ʿAbbās, he remarked, 'If we had known that, we would not have married off his womenfolk nor parcelled out his inheritance.' They also have a number of evil doctrines other than this.[10]

Wāqifiyya

The fourth sect [of the Imāmiyya] is the Wāqifiyya. They say that the imam after the messenger of God, was ʿAlī b. Abī Ṭālib, then al-Ḥasan, then al-Ḥusayn, then ʿAlī b. al-Ḥusayn, then Muḥammad b. ʿAlī, then Jaʿfar b. Muḥammad, and then Mūsā b. Jaʿfar. Mūsā was the seventh of the imams and he did not die nor will he die until he reigns over the world, both the east of it and the west, and until he fills the earth with justice as it is now full of wrongdoing and oppression. He is the Qāʾim and the Mahdi. They are called the Wāqifiyya because they stop [*waqafū*] with Mūsā b. Jaʿfar and do not go beyond him to any others after him. Some of their opponents call them the Mamṭūra. It is said the reason for that is because once a member of their group debated Yūnus b. ʿAbd al-Raḥmān who was from the Qaṭʿiyya. Yūnus at one point said to him, 'You people are of less weight to me than rain-soaked dogs,' and this term stuck to them thereafter.[11]

---

[9] *An Ismaili Heresiography*, trans., pp. 58–59.

[10] *An Ismaili Heresiography*, trans., p. 100.

[11] *An Ismaili Heresiography*, trans., pp. 113–114.

Much of the information in this kind of heresiographical text simply repeats material gleaned from older works in the Islamic tradition of this genre, although Abū Tammām does add a few of his own personal observations and does include accounts of several sects that either do not appear elsewhere or not in as complete detail. There is, however, an interesting Ismaili parallel in the massive treatise on lexicography by Abū Ḥātim al-Rāzī (d. 322/933–34), his *Kitāb al-Zīna*, which offers a rich treasure of information about Arabic words and technical terms. One section of it provides, as the author says, 'an account of the names (*alqāb*) of the various sects in Islam'.[12] Under each he recounts details – often derogatory – that we would otherwise find in an Islamic heresiography. Ultimately it is not so obvious a polemic because, among the long list of sects, he incorporates an account of what we assume is his own, the 'Ismāʿīliyya',[13] and not all the others are clearly condemned and denounced, perhaps because they advocate doctrines not antithetical to his own.

A more overtly polemic work by Abū Ḥātim, although again not quite of the standard form, is his *Aʿlām al-nubuwwa*, which is his after-the-fact record of an encounter and debate with the famous physician, Abū Bakr al-Rāzī (Rhazes).[14] For reasons not completely obvious this al-Rāzī drew the ire of a number of Ismaili *dāʿīs* who felt called upon each to compose a substantial work whose main purpose was the condemnation of this man. A second, by al-Kirmānī, will be discussed later. Here we can take up Abū Ḥātim's diatribe against 'the heretic' and the ideas he stood for. It might be noted, however, that Abū Bakr does not really speak for himself in this work. What he had said or advocated in the meeting of the two comes to us in the words of his Ismaili opponent. Still the material in this book that supposedly reflects the views of Abū Bakr conforms to what we know about them otherwise.

The principal issue is prophecy, which is fundamental to Islam in general and Ismailism in particular but which Abū Bakr

---

[12] Abū Ḥātim al-Rāzī, *Kitāb al-Zīna fi'l-kalimāt al-islāmiyya al-ʿarabiyya*, ed. Saʿīd al-Ghānamī (Beirut, 2015), vol. 1, pp. 487–569.

[13] Ibid., pp. 527–530.

[14] Abū Hātim al-Rāzī, *Aʿlām al-nubuwwa*, ed. and trans. by Tarif Khalidi as *The Proofs of Prophecy* (Provo, UT, 2011).

apparently rejected, claiming the prophets were frauds and their so-called revelations of no value. He argued that the revealed text was essentially incoherent nonsense. Another point of contention was creation. Abū Bakr upheld a doctrine that recognised five eternal principles: God, matter, soul, time and place. The universe had come to be out of the interaction of these five. Abū Ḥātim brought up these and other issues that he explains and refutes, broadly denouncing Abū Bakr's reliance on and devotion to ancient Greek philosophy, most especially Socrates and Plato. One of his arguments is especially interesting, as it became a standard part of the Ismaili rejection of the pre-eminence of philosophy over revelation. In Abū Ḥātim's view the ancient philosophers failed to reach a consensus on crucial points. Instead they each favoured mere opinions where they should have attained certainty. What is of ultimate value in the sciences and philosophy has come from the prophets. The overall argument is clear from key chapter titles and runs as follows:

> An account of what transpired between me and the heretic; concerning his argument that the five are eternal, with no other eternal except them, and the debate about time and space; that the world is created; conflict among philosophers regarding principles; a summary of divergences among views of philosophers; which of the two groups is more deceitful?; there is no divergence among prophets regarding principles; all religious laws are true, but falsehood has been mixed with them; further views of the heretic; the prophets as originators of the sciences and the philosophers as their heirs.

In terms of the sheer number of and variety of polemics credited to a single Fatimid authority, it would be the work of al-Qāḍī al-Nuʿmān, whose voluminous output included many examples. At least six titles of those he wrote contain the Arabic phrase *al-radd ʿalā* (the refutation of), which is a standard indication of a polemic. Additional Arabic verbs that might be used for this purpose are *faḍaḥa* (to disclose or uncover someone's faults), *afḥama* (to silence with counter arguments), and *afsada* (to denigrate, thwart, devalue). But, as we have seen, polemical rejection of an opponent can come in many forms. Al-Qāḍī al-Nuʿmān's treatise, often called, using a simple title, *Kitāb al-Manāqib wa'l-mathālib*,[15] and which might be translated as 'Book of Virtues and Vices', is actually titled *Kitāb al-Manāqib li-ahl bayt rasūl Allāh al-nujabā' wa'l-mathālib li-banī Umayya al-luʿanā'*, which translates as 'Book of the Virtues of the House of God's Messenger, the most noble, and the Vices of the House of Umayya, the accursed ones'. It thus has two intentions: one to celebrate the virtues of the Prophet's own family and most especially of the imams of the Fatimid line; and the other to castigate and condemn the Umayyad house. This second aspect is decidedly polemical, although the polemic is dispersed and accompanied by its opposite, a laudatory glorification of the competing lineage.

Significantly, he begins his review of the subject with generations of both lines reaching back even prior to the Prophet himself. His first chapter recounts the virtues of ʿAbd Manāf b. Qusay and the origin of the dispute between his two sons. From there he continues in parallel lines, on one side Hāshim and the other ʿAbd Shams, and then ʿAbd al-Muṭṭalib and Umayya, and next the Prophet's father ʿAbd Allāh and Ḥarb b. Umayya. Eight chapters and eight examples of this type of parallel follow. A key passage at the end concerns the Andalusian Umayyads, most specifically ʿAbd al-Raḥmān III (r. 300–350/912–961) and his caliphate, which al-Qāḍī al-Nuʿmān regards as particularly despicable. At this point the polemical nature of the whole work concludes with a vehement attack on this rival caliphate.

About the Umayyads of Spain in general he says:

> These were all wicked rulers, of vile standing, of despicable intentions, who drank wine, passed time with musical instruments, amused themselves with young boys, caroused with fools, listened to singing girls, ate forbidden things, transgressed regulations, in the same way as their forefathers in the past.[16]

The advent of ʿAbd al-Raḥmān III then brought changes, making the situation far worse.

---

[15] Al-Qāḍī al-Nuʿmān, *al-Manāqib wa'l-mathālib*, ed. M. A. al-ʿAtiyya (Beirut, 2012).

[16] *Al-Manāqib wa'l-mathālib*, p. 400.

> He exceeded the boundaries and crossed over into what none of his forefathers had done. . . . He called himself 'Commander of the Believers', coined money, decorated *ṭirāz* with his name. . . . The vileness of his condition and meanness of his character and intentions and the shamelessness of his opinions was caused by what we have cited as the malicious states of his forefathers that had come together in him. . . . He was well known and famous . . . for sexual intercourse with his young boys, group after group. . . . That went along with his openly drinking wine, listening to singing girls, playing *ṭanbūr*s and *ʿūd*s. The keepers of pleasure houses visited him from remote lands and he settled them with him accordingly, in close proximity, and he gave them abundant gifts and favours. . . . He had his subjects believe a [vile] behaviour good, thereby permitting them these same transgressions. . . . So they amused themselves with young boys, openly practicing pederasty in public. Daughters were shared among them as they accustomed her [to it] young and proceeded with the same when older. Among them fornication was evident and they flaunted openly sedition and wealth. They did commerce in wine in their markets, safe with him from this manifesting of crime that was due to their own moral depravity.[17]

Of al-Qāḍī al-Nuʿmān's treatises that employ the more formal indication of a polemic, most are now lost.[18] One was devoted to the Khawārij, six others to specific named individuals: Aḥmad b. Surayj, a famous Shāfiʿī scholar of the third/ninth century (d. 306/918), Mālik b. Anas (or someone of his school), Abū Ḥanīfa, someone called al-ʿAtakī (or al-Ghatakī, al-ʿItakī, according to Poonawala, or either al-ʿUtbī or al-ʿUtaqī),[19] Ibn Qutayba (*Risālat dhāt al-bayān fi'l-radd ʿalā Ibn Qutayba*), which still exists,[20] and finally al-Shāfiʿī himself in a work

---

[17] *Al-Manāqib wa'l-mathālib*, pp. 400–401.

[18] For a complete list of titles see Ismail Poonawala, *Biobibliography of Ismāʿīlī Literature* (Malibu, CA, 1977), pp. 48–68 (section on 'Polemics and Refutations', pp. 62–65).

[19] Al-Qāḍī al-Nuʿmān, *Ikhtilāf uṣūl al-madhāhib*, ed. and trans. Devin J. Stewart as *Disagreements of the Jurists* (New York, 2015), p. xiii.

[20] Al-Qāḍī al-Nuʿmān, *Risālat dhāt al-bayān fi'l-radd ʿalā Ibn Qutayba*, critical edition by Avraham Hakim as *The Epistle of the Eloquent Clarification Concerning the Refutation of Ibn Qutayba by al-Qāḍī al-Nuʿmān b. Muḥammad (d. 363/974)* (Leiden, 2012).

called *al-Risāla al-miṣriyya fi'l-radd ʿalā al-Shāfiʿī*, which may have been aimed at an Egyptian audience in preparation for the Fatimid invasion of 367/969. All of these appear to have concerned law and legal theory. Yet one more is important here. That is his *Ikhtilāf uṣūl al-madhāhib* ('Disagreements of the Jurists'),[21] which according to the author's grandson and fully authorised transmitter of it,[22] has the complete title 'The Islamic Legal Schools' Conflicting Principles of Interpretation and Refutation of Those Who Contradict the True Doctrine Therein', with the phrase *al-radd ʿalā man khālafa al-ḥaqq fīhā* and its stipulation added, thereby making its polemical intent more obvious.

The main issue in this work from the Ismaili side was the authority of the Fatimid imams, all of them, but particularly al-Muʿizz for whom al-Nuʿmān composed this work. On the opposing side were those legal scholars and would-be experts who claimed that they could determine the law and rulings of the religion by methods other than appeal to these same imams and thus derive legal judgment from sources that lack authority. For al-Qāḍī al-Nuʿmān the only valid means to ascertain true doctrine in the absence of an explicit ruling is to follow the practice of Muhammad and that of the guiding imams, the people of his house. Arbitrary submission to authorities (*taqlīd*) is impermissible except in this latter situation. He rejects consensus (*ijmāʿ*), speculation (*naẓar*), analogy (*qiyāṣ*), preference (*istiḥsān*), inference (*istidlāl*), interpretation and personal judgment (*ijtihād* and *ra'y*) and any person or party that upholds one or more of these methods as a valid way to determine the law. To each he devoted a separate chapter of substantial length and detail.

At about the same time that al-Qāḍī al-Nuʿmān reached the pinnacle of Fatimid authority in service to al-Muʿizz, Abū Yaʿqūb al-Sijistānī, active in far away Khurāsān, attain a similar status as one of the most influential voices in the *daʿwa*. By then he had accepted the imamate of the Fatimids and now supported them whereas earlier he may have hesitated. Of the several treatises by him that have been

---

21 See note 19 above.

22 See the grandson's preface to the book, ibid., pp. 2–3.

preserved and were studied within the *daʿwa*, most contain either whole sections or individual chapter that constitute a polemic of one kind or another. Al-Sijistānī took pains to refute a long list of doctrines that he found faulty, ranging from key points of metaphysics – items of contention in Neoplatonic thought, for example – to issues in Islamic religious principles. He, for example, adamantly rejects bodily resurrection. But there are many more we might cite. For a work that has as its principal aim a type of polemic, it is essential to mention his *al-Iftikhār* ('The Boast').[23] Apparently when he composed this treatise, which appears to come fairly late in his career, perhaps just before he was martyred, he was not particularly concerned to shield his views from the opposition. Quite the contrary. In it he states most of his claim as a challenge: We, he says, are the Proponents of Truth, you are not. He then castigates all those who fail to acknowledge the true imams and the doctrines they promote, which, for him, constitute true Islam.

His enemies and opponents are both specific individuals and broader categories. He denounces 'ignorance like that of the literalists (al-Ḥashwiyya)', 'conceit like that of the theologians (al-Mutakallimīn)', and 'presumption like that of the Philosophers (al-Falāṣifa)'. Yet he will also run through a list of Umayyad and Abbasid caliphs each noted for evil and depravity. In fact his chapter on the imamate is especially interesting for this reason. His purpose is to establish the absolute right of the Fatimid imams to rule as the only true and proper authorities in the Islamic community. As the Ismailis regard ʿAlī b. Abī Ṭālib as the Legatee (al-Waṣī) and the foundation of the imamate, he begins with Ḥasan whose confrontation with Muʿāwiya in no way denied him the imamate, the treaty they made notwithstanding. Next is the 'Accursed son of the Accursed' Yazīd. Those who uphold his caliphate have the blood of Ḥusayn on their hands. Yazīd did many bad and un-Islamic things and he is ultimately, according to al-Sijistānī, the 'Accursed Tree' (*al-shajara al-malʿūna*) mentioned in Qurʾan 17:60. It is common in Ismaili writings to insist that the Umayyads are the 'accursed tree', which is also the Tree of Zaqqūm, and to castigate the whole lineage accordingly. But al-Sijistānī would rather, at least in

---

23 Abū Yaʿqūb al-Sijistānī, *Kitāb al-Iftikhār*, ed. I. Poonawala (Beirut, 2002).

this instance, make the reference specific to Yazīd. He and not the rest was the Accursed Tree.[24]

As he continues his polemic, to each successive valid imam of the Fatimid line he opposes either the Umayyad or Abbasid usurper. ʿAbd al-Mālik b. Marwān was famous for drinking wine and for destroying the Kaʿba, both signs of his unfitness for the caliphate. Al-Sijistānī's general method is to ask pointedly: Where do you stand with respect to. . . and then name the enemy, for example, al-Walīd b. Yazīd who he calls the Zindīq (which can be translated as heretic). The Abbasid caliph al-Manṣūr is mentioned simply as al-Dawānīqī; al-Amīn is Ibn Zubayda. The latter was a shameless reprobate, inattentive and careless, devoting himself to poets and their praise of wine. Al-Ma'mūn was guilty of yet another sin. He spent the treasury of the Muslims on translations of the works of Greek atheist and materialist philosophers.[25] One more example here is his reference to the caliph al-Muqtadir as 'your *muqtadir*', as if to say dismissively, 'the one you believe holds power'.

The next major figure in the Ismaili arsenal of polemicists would be Ḥamīd al-Dīn al-Kirmānī, whose numerous writings span a period that appears to correspond fairly exactly with the reign of al-Ḥākim (386–441/996–1021). In his case we have eighteen titles that survive and an almost equal number that are lost. Many are relatively small having probably been issued as single pamphlets, but some are substantial. As we ought to expect, polemics or polemical intent prompted him to compose several. Like his predecessor in the *daʿwa*, Abū Ḥātim, he was eager to refute Abū Bakr al-Rāzī. The latter's *al-Ṭibb al-rūḥānī* ('Spiritual Medicine') he decided needed an answer, a denunciation, for its pretence to know something about the medicine of the soul. He called his treatise *al-Aqwāl al-dhahabiyya* ('The Golden Sayings').[26] In al-Kirmānī's view the admitted pre-eminence of Abū Bakr in the medicine of physical ailments and their treatment in no way qualified him to administer to the illnesses of the soul. As he put it: in the former field he is a vigorous stallion who gallops at will, but in the latter he is

[24] *Al-Iftikhār*, pp. 171–172.

[25] *Al-Iftikhār*, p. 175.

[26] Ḥamīd al-Dīn al-Kirmānī, *al-Aqwāl al-dhahabiyya*, ed. Ṣalāḥ al-Ṣāwī (Tehran, 1977).

a dried up and withered limb devoid of benefit. The maladies of the soul can be cured only by the medicine of prophetic religion as dispensed by the living imam and his *daʿwa*.

After his attack on Abū Bakr, al-Kirmānī turned his attention to al-Jāḥiẓ whose *Kitāb al-ʿUthmāniyya* was universally rejected by the Shiʿis for its refusal to recognise the superiority of ʿAlī over ʿUthmān, or even Abū Bakr and ʿUmar. It was also pro-Abbasid. Al-Kirmānī's answer was the *Maʿāṣim al-hudā wa'l-iṣāba fī tafḍīl ʿAlī ʿalā al-ṣaḥāba*[27] ('The Protecting Links to Guidance and the Validation of the Superiority of ʿAlī Over the Companions'). The first part, his specific reply to al-Jāḥiẓ, is lost but the second survives. Curiously when it comes to Abū Bakr's virtues, al-Kirmānī admits that he can only recount the good that he had once done before the Prophet's death. Al-Ḥākim had issued clear orders in the year 401 that the Companions are henceforth to be mentioned only in connection to these earlier acts, not to those committed in the subsequent period.

Of his pamphlets,[28] one is a refutation of the Zaydī imam and another of the proto-Druze figure Ḥasan al-Farghānī, who was known as al-Akhram. As the second of these was composed in the middle of 408/1017–18 in Cairo, it is quite specific as to date, occasion and its opponent, and what it claims about al-Akhram and his associates is key evidence concerning the formation of what later became the Druze. Al-Kirmānī adamantly denies that the imamate will end with al-Ḥākim, that he is the messiah, or is actually God incarnate as upheld by these people.

Among his more substantial works, two, his *al-Maṣābīḥ fī ithbāt al-imāma*[29] ('Lights to Illuminate the Proof of the Imamate'), and *Tanbīh al-hādī wa'l-mustahdī*[30] ('The Exhortation to the Guiders and the Guided')

---

[27] Ḥamīd al-Dīn al-Kirmānī, *Maʿāṣim al-hudā wa'l-iṣāba fī tafḍīl ʿAlī ʿalā al-ṣaḥāba*, MS 724, Institute of Ismaili Studies.

[28] Eleven of his short pieces, including these two, were gathered together in the Ismaili manuscript tradition and were published in modern times as *Majmūʿat rasāʾil al-Kirmānī*, ed. M. Ghālib (Beirut, 1987).

[29] Ḥamīd al-Dīn al-Kirmānī, *al-Maṣābīḥ fī ithbāt al-imāma*, tr. as *Master of the Age: An Islamic Treatise on the Necessity of the Imamate*, with a critical edition, full translation, introduction and notes by Paul E. Walker (London, 2007).

[30] Ḥamīd al-Dīn al-Kirmānī, *Kitāb al-Hādī wa'l-mustahdī*, MS 723, Institute of Ismaili Studies, MS 57, Fyzee Collection, Bombay University Library.

would normally not be categorised as polemic even though they each contain interesting sections with clear polemical intent. The major purpose of the first is to validate the imamate of al-Ḥākim in as explicit a manner as possible, thereby not merely to prove the obligation of the Muslim community to admit that the imamate is an essential institution of Islamic governance, but to recognise specifically the Fatimid imam-caliph who held it at the time of writing. Thus the reign of al-Ḥākim is a critical factor. And, in that sense, this is a political work with a clear agenda to establish the right of the Fatimid dynasty to universal allegiance against all other claimants, Abbasids, Umayyads, Zaydīs and the rest.

Designation is crucial. The community cannot validly elect an imam; its choice determines nothing in that regard and, if expressed, has no meaning. ʿAlī b. Abī Ṭālib was designated by the Prophet, a point al-Kirmānī attempts to prove, before he next traces the line of imams from him to Jaʿfar al-Ṣādiq and to the latter's son Ismāʿīl. From there it must, he says, continue in Ismāʿīl's progeny. Ultimately, it reaches the Fatimid caliphs and specifically al-Ḥākim, the sixth of them. Al-Kirmānī provides a list of what an imam does and what virtues he displays. Moreover, he names all those in his time who claim the imamate but who either are not qualified for it or fail to perform the actions it requires or fulfil the duties required of them as true imams. His roster of false imams has special interest. They are Aḥmad b. Isḥāq (al-Qādir), the Abbasid caliph in Baghdad, al-Hārūnī (al-Muʾayyad biʾllāh), the Zaydī imam in Hawsam in Gilan, ʿUmar al-Nazwānī, the Ibadī imam in ʿUmān, the Umayyad ruler in Spain and the Maghrib, and the leaders of the Qarmatian remnant in al-Aḥsāʾ. His references cite quite specific individuals of a fairly limited time and set of places (about 404/1013). He also mentions the expected imam of the Twelver Shiʿis.

Here in what follows we can see, in tabular form, what specific failings invalidate the claims of all these men.[31]

> Aḥmad b. Isḥāq, who resides in Baghdad[32]: he is not a lineal descendant of al-Ḥusayn; he is not pure in soul due to his consumption of forbidden things (*suḥt*) and his setting the price of

---

[31] *Master of the Age*, trans., pp. 119–121.

[32] The Abbasid caliph al-Qādir, who ruled from 381/991 to 422/1031.

wine that is sold for him on his estates in Baghdad and its hinterland and for the ignorance deeply rooted in him due to the lack of knowledge; the existence in him by his own admission of things connected to the imamate that he does not know and his utilisation of resources in ways not religiously commendable; being devoid of the knowledge associated with the religious declaration of God's absolute oneness and his reliance on the leaders of the Postponers (al-Murji'a), such as Abū Bakr al-Bāqillānī, and others; contempt for the regulations of God, not commanding the good and forbidding the bad in his own household and entourage, let alone for any other Muslims; being devoid of the designation of the person who occupies the place of the apostle and instead having been put in office by the August Amir Bahā' al-Dawla, may God's mercy be upon him.[33]

Al-Ḥārūnī al-Ḥasanī, who resides in Hawsam[34]: he is not a lineal descendant of al-Ḥusayn; he is not pure in body because of leprosy that has taken hold of him, nor in the soul because of his ignorance of God's true oneness; the existence in him of his judging all matters out of ignorance and his responding to questions asked of him with what is he has not learned from his own school's doctrine or that of any other; being devoid of the knowledge associated with the declaration of God's oneness and his reliance on the statements of the Ḥashwiyya[35] and others like them; the existence in him of contempt for the regulations of God, the lands of the Muslims being devoid of an appeal (*daʿwa*) of his to God; lacking the nobility conferred by designation and appointment, he being like the others who have not inherited the imamate.

---

[33] Bahā' al-Dawla was the Buyid supreme ruler (*amīr*) in Iraq and then southern Persia as well from 379/989 to his death in Jumādā II 403/December 1012. In 381/991 he had deposed the Abbasid caliph al-Ṭā'iʿ and replaced him with the same man's cousin, Aḥmad b. Isḥāq, who took the throne name al-Qādir bi'llāh.

[34] This person is Abu'l-Ḥasan al-Mu'ayyad bi'llāh Aḥmad b. al-Ḥusayn b. Hārūn, the Zaydī imam in the Caspian region until his death in 411/1020. Al-Kirmānī dedicated the treatise mentioned earlier, *al-Risāla al-kāfiya fi'l-radd ʿalā al-Hārūnī al-Ḥusaynī (or al-Ḥasanī) al-Zaydī* ('The Effective Treatise in Refutation of al-Hārūnī al-Ḥusaynī the Zaydī') against this man who had written his own denunciation of al-Ḥākim and the Ismailis.

[35] The term *ḥashwiyya* often refers to the extreme literalist doctrine of the Proponents of Ḥadīth or to those who mindlessly relate *ḥadīths*, even contradictory ones, without attempting to determine if they are valid and reasonable.

> ʿUmar al-Nazwānī,[36] who resides in Jabāl ʿUmān: he is not a lineal descendant of al-Ḥusayn; he is not pure of body on account of leprosy that has taken hold of him and settled in most of his limbs, nor in soul due to ignorance; there exists in him by his own admission what he does not know; being devoid of religious knowledge; the existence in him of contempt for the regulations of God, not commanding the good and prohibiting the bad; lack of designation and appointment.
>
> The Umayyad, who resides in al-Andalus: he is not a lineal descendant of al-Ḥusayn; he is not pure due to his being from the Tree of Zaqqūm which is the Umayyad clan; there exists in him by his own admission what is not his business; being devoid of knowledge; there exists in him contempt for the regulations of God in his promoting among his subjects behaviour not that of the prophet; lacking the designation and appointment.
>
> Those who call themselves the Lords, who reside in al-Aḥsāʾ[37]: they are not lineal descendants of al-Ḥusayn; they are not pure because of drinking wine; there exists among them the expenditure of their funds for purposes not religiously commendable; there exists among them contempt for the regulations of God in their permitting forbidden acts; they are devoid of religious knowledge; they lack the designation and appointment.

Earlier in the same work he had reviewed in a similar fashion all those Companions of the Prophet who either claimed superiority over ʿAlī or were possibly so considered. In this instance he does list Abū Bakr's faults (again in tabular form) in addition to a couple of his merits.[38]

> Abū Bakr: he did not have revelation from God; he was not chaste because of his having drunk wine in the period of Jāḥiliyya and his commission of mortal sins; he was not designated by God or by His apostle; he was not pure nor purified, he had worshipped idols and had prostrated himself to them and not God; he was

[36] This man who is here said to be the Ibāḍī imam at the time is otherwise unknown.

[37] He refers to the Qarmatians in Bahrayn who are, according to what al-Kirmānī says about them, at this time completely excluded from the Ismaili fold. For their relations with the Fatimids in the period just prior to this, see Daftary, *The Ismāʿīlīs*, p. 194.

[38] *Master of the Age*, trans., pp. 97–98.

> not brave or recognised for strength and bravery; he was pious not covetous; he was generous, spending freely; he was not selected by God nor by His apostle, and he was not dear to either of them nor among those described as such; he was not among those characterised by ascetic restraint; he was not just in the exercise of authority and did not show mercy to the daughter of God's apostle when he seized her property unlawfully; he came early to Islam; he did not have knowledge of the Book of God nor is one mentioned for that; he was not knowledgeable about what is permitted and what is forbidden and is not cited for that; he was not someone who knew the interpretation; he did not understand how to make judgments and deferred the argument in such matters to ʿAlī; and he was not close to God nor to His apostle.

Yet one final example in this survey is the second text mentioned above, *Tanbīh al-hādī wa'l-mustahdī*. Al-Kirmānī wrote it, as he says, because he observed that the Muslims (*ahl al-qibla*) had broken up into factions in conformity to each group's individual viewpoint. In doing so they had abandoned true religion. He now sets about rectifying this situation by first outlining acceptable doctrine, namely that of the Ismaili *daʿwa*, on matters such as the imamate, the *sharīʿa*, faith, purity, prayer, alms-giving, fasting, pilgrimage, *jihād*, obedience to the imam, the oath and covenant, knowledge of interpretation (*ta'wīl*) and others, each in its own chapter. That section is not polemical. But after this basic exhortation to awaken the desire for proper adherence to the teachings of the imams, he moves on to criticise those who fail to obey. Significantly the first chapter of this part warns against the corruptions of those who pretend to philosophy (*al-mutafalsafūn*). Next come the false beliefs of the Muʿtazila and those who uphold inference and speculation (*ahl al-istidlāl wa'l-naẓar*) and their ignominies, followed by the Ashʿarīs with an explanation of their errors. From here he adopts a course much like that found in al-Qāḍī al-Nuʿmān's *Ikhtilāf*, with chapters refuting the doctrines of those who uphold *qiyās*, then *ra'y* and *ijtihād*, next *istiḥsān*, the people who accept *taqlīd* (*ahl al-taqlīd*) and then *ijmāʿ*.

The following chapter admonishes against the warped doctrine of those 'who refer to themselves as the Qaṭʿiyya Imāmiyya Ithnā ʿashariyya'. After that he takes on the Zaydiyya whose corrupt beliefs put them in opposition to the Book of God and the law of

Muhammad. And one more in this polemical section denounces the delusion of the Ghulāt, specifically the Nuṣayriyya and Isḥāqiyya and those who agree with their doctrines and infidelities.

At this point we might conclude this exploration of early Ismaili polemics by raising an issue that is peculiar to its *daʿwa*. Given the well-known reticence – some would say notorious reluctance – on their part to disclose publicly much of their esoteric doctrine, what portion of the polemical material in the surviving works actually entered an open debate in which both sides participated actively? Or was all this conceived and elaborated solely from a safe distance? The one direct piece of evidence for an exchange in a public setting is Abū Ḥātim's confrontation with Abū Bakr, which supposedly occurred in a formal session of disputation, or at least an initial debate between them appears to have taken place during such an occasion.

Membership of the Ismaili *daʿwa* came from the very beginning with a strict requirement that imposed on the novice an oath of allegiance in which he or she swore never to reveal the secret teachings about to be received. *Dāʿīs* obviously maintained a cautiously circumspect demeanour both to protect themselves and their doctrines from hostile scrutiny but also to observe this rule of imposed secrecy. Without authorisation a *dāʿī* could not speak about the *daʿwa* to others. They were simply not to discuss delicate doctrinal matters in the presence of outsiders. And yet it is clear from the material presented above that the agents of the *daʿwa* engaged in rather heated argument denouncing opponents and in defending the Ismaili understanding of Islam. Many of them were highly educated and knew in full detail the issues of contention among the various parties and the history of the sectarian divisions that had arisen in the community. Ultimately, however, the answer may lie in the nature of polemic which, in general, involves the exposure and denunciation of an opponent's views without necessarily confessing to the most problematic of the doctrines one held oneself. The Ismailis could actively promote vigorous refutation, even denunciation, of various opponents and enemies by attacking them for what they deemed false doctrines, manifest sins and glaring errors, while still, even so, hiding, and thus preserving, their own esoteric traditions which, had they become better known, might have more seriously threatened or weakened their position.

3

On the Limited Representation of the Ismailis in al-Ṣadūq's (d. 381/991) *Kamāl al-dīn*[*]

Roy Vilozny
(University of Haifa)

It is generally agreed that *Kamāl al-dīn wa-tamām al-niʿma* by Ibn Bābawayh, known as al-Shaykh al-Ṣadūq (d. 381/991), is of the most important milestones in the process of institutionalising the notion of the Twelfth imam's occultation and eschatological return as one of the Imāmiyya's fundamental articles of faith. Al-Ṣadūq's motivation in compiling this work several decades following the onset of the greater occultation (329/941) was derived – if we take his introduction to the work at face value – from the realisation of the degree of perplexity (*ḥayra*) among his fellow Imāmīs.[1] Partly since this state of perplexity resulted – or at least had the potential of resulting – in the adoption of non-Imāmī views by members of the Imāmī community, al-Ṣadūq devotes considerable theological effort to attempting to refute what he

* I am grateful to Etan Kohlberg for his attentive reading of an earlier version of this paper and for his insightful comments.

[1] See *Kamāl al-dīn wa-tamām al-niʿma*, ed. Ḥusayn al-Aʿlamī (Beirut, 2004), pp. 14–15. See also M. A. Amir-Moezzi, 'A Contribution on the Typology of Encounters with the Hidden Imam', in his *The Spirituality of Shiʿi Islam* (New York and London, 2011), p. 445, where he argues that 'al-Ṣadūq may be considered as the main architect of the rendering canonical of material pertaining to the hidden Imam, his occultation and eschatological return'. See in addition R. Vilozny, 'What Makes a Religion Perfect: al-Ṣadūq's (d. 381/991) *Kamāl al-dīn* Revisited', in M. A. Amir-Moezzi, M. De Cillis, O. Mir-Kasimov and D. De Smet (ed.), *Esotérisme shi'ite, ses racines et ses prolongements* (Turnhout, 2016), pp. 476–480, where al-Ṣadūq's reasons for writing the work are discussed at length.

considers to be erroneous groups. This sort of endeavour, one should bear in mind, was not unusual at the time and ought to be seen in the broader context of the ongoing debate in the fourth/tenth century between religious thinkers of a variety of sects and the respective production of rich heresiographical literature.[2]

Among the groups refuted by al-Ṣadūq, one finds mainly various forms of Shiʿism, both those that could be regarded as a concrete threat to the Imāmiyya during his life as well as others that were no longer in existence. It appears that for al-Ṣadūq, refuting the latter was no less important than refuting the former. This attitude may have resulted from a variety of reasons and it is enough to mention here al-Ṣadūq's overall tendency to address the problem of the imamate in general and the Twelfth imam's occultation in particular from a historical perspective, along a chronological axis that stretches from the creation of the first man until the time of the composition of *Kamāl al-dīn*.[3] In other words, for him – and in this respect he was not exceptional among Islamic thinkers – making sense of the present depended largely on the way one perceived both the past and the relationship between past and present to which the ascription of continuity and consecutiveness was indispensable.

---

[2] In this context, the first volume of J. van Ess' recent contribution, *Der Eine und das Andere: Beobachtungen an islamischen häresiographischen Texten* (Göttingen, 2010), is worthy of mention, in particular Part 2, section B, which deals with the fourth/tenth century. Although *Kamāl al-dīn* is not a typical heresiographical treatise, the numerous parts in it that concern various sects, including the Ismāʿīliyya, certainly fit within the boundaries of this literary genre and reflect the intellectual climate at the time of its composition.

[3] See *Kamāl al-dīn*, pp. 16–17, where al-Ṣadūq introduces his *al-khalīfa qabla al-khalīqa* theory, according to which a ruler, a *khalīfa*, was put on earth before the creation of mankind. He bases this view mainly on his understanding of Q 2:30 – a verse which al-Ṣadūq, interestingly and despite its diverse interpretations by early Qurʾan commentators, refers to as a *muḥkam*, i.e. conveying a clear message – in which God informs the angels about His intention to create a *khalīfa*. On the difficulties that this verse and particularly the term *khalīfa* – which for al-Ṣadūq clearly represents the imam's prototype – raise see G. S. Reynolds, *The Qurʾān and its Biblical Context* (New York, 2010), pp. 40–43.

The historical manifestations of Shiʿism that al-Ṣadūq refutes include the Kaysāniyya who followed Muḥammad b. al-Ḥanafiyya,[4] the Nāwūsiyya who believed in the mahdiship of Jaʿfar al-Ṣādiq,[5] the *wāqifa* who halted the lineage of the imamate with Mūsā al-Kāẓim and another *wāqifa* group that halted it with al-Ḥasan al-ʿAskarī.[6] Remarkably, al-Ṣadūq's refutation of these sects revolves around what he regards as their false identification of the person in whom they halted the line of the imamate, whose death they denied and to whom they ascribed an eschatological return. Al-Ṣadūq's means of proving the falsity of such claims is centred on providing what he considers as undeniable proofs (mainly traditions on the authority of the imams) for the death of this or that alleged hidden imam.[7] The notions of *waqf*, *ghayba* and *rajʿa* are thus depicted in this context as legitimate ideas that circulated in the Islamic community as early as the Prophet's death and the debated issue was not their content but rather their object of ascription.

As contemporary ideological rivals, two movements take centre stage: the Muʿtazila[8] and the Zaydiyya.[9] This is not surprising, given that al-Ṣadūq wrote *Kamāl al-dīn* towards the end of his career in Rayy, which by that time had become a centre of Imāmī Shiʿism with a strong inclination towards Muʿtazilī theology and Zaydism.[10] With regard to the Zaydiyya, al-Ṣadūq offers the reader an explanation for their centrality in *Kamāl al-dīn*, stating that this is 'the most challenging (or difficult) sect for us [that is, the Imāmiyya]' (*wa-hiya ashaddu al-firaq ʿalaynā*).[11] Indeed, in accordance with this statement, al-Ṣadūq devotes significantly more room to discussing the Zaydiyya and refuting their arguments against the Imāmiyya than he does to any other

---

4 See W. Madelung, 'Kaysāniyya', *EI*2.

5 See 'Nāwūsiyya', *EI*2.

6 On the term *al-wāqifa* see H. Halm, 'al-Wāḳifa', *EI*2.

7 See *Kamāl al-dīn*, pp. 42–53.

8 Ibid., pp. 67–70.

9 Ibid., pp. 98–128.

10 See W. Madelung, 'Imamism and Muʿtazilite Theology', in T. Fahd (ed.), *Le Shīʿisme Imāmite* (Paris, 1970), pp. 17–21.

11 See *Kamāl al-dīn*, p. 128.

group. These arguments are manifold and include attacks on both the general Imāmī conception of the imamate as well as concrete cases of adherence to the wrong imams.

Although the Muʿtazila pose no less challenging difficulties, the impression is that the debate with them is milder. Al-Ṣadūq's remark regarding the Zaydiyya could also be regarded as corresponding to the gradual incorporation, and perhaps despite his initial objection, of Muʿtazilī theology into Imāmī thought in his time. Furthermore, al-Ṣadūq's relatively restrained criticism of the Muʿtazila in *Kamāl al-dīn* may be related to the fact that he wrote it in Rayy under the restrictions of the Muʿtazilī Būyid vizier, al-Ṣāḥib b. ʿAbbād (d. 385/995).[12] This also goes hand in hand with the obvious fact that, unlike Zaydism, Muʿtazilism did not necessarily entail sectarian affiliation.

In addition to al-Ṣadūq's direct confrontation with these contemporary ideological movements, he cites various anonymous Imāmī scholars including, surprisingly, *mutakallimūn*.[13] A well-known example are the relatively long passages that al-Ṣadūq quotes from Ibn Qiba al-Rāzī's (d. before 319/931) apologetic debate with hypothetical or concrete spokesmen for the Muʿtazilīs and Zaydīs. In the second part of his *Crisis and Consolidation* (which is referred to further below), Hossein Modarressi published the Arabic text of Ibn Qiba's debates with the Muʿtazila and the Zaydiyya along with an English translation.[14]

Whether through quotations by Imāmī scholars such as Ibn Qiba al-Rāzī, or through al-Ṣadūq's own comments about a variety of past and present Islamic sects, one gets the impression that *Kamāl al-dīn* was written in the light of an intense awareness of heresiographical

12 See W. Madelung, 'Imamism and Muʿtazilite Theology', pp. 17–21.

13 See *Kamāl al-dīn*, p. 70, where the text reads *wa-qāla ghayruhu min mutakallimī mashāyikh al-imāmiyya*.

14 See H. Modarressi, *Crisis and Consolidation in the Formative Period of Shīʿite Islam: Abū Jaʿfar ibn Qiba al-Rāzī and His Contribution to Imāmite Shīʿite Thought* (Princeton, 1993), where, in addition to the original extracts from *Kamāl al-dīn* and their translation, Modarressi presents a brief overview of the main Muʿtazilī (p. 133) and Zaydī (p. 169) arguments against the Imāmiyya that al-Ṣadūq cites.

polemic. Seen in this light, the lack of a significant, explicit discussion of the Ismāʿīliyya is remarkable. This lack is even more puzzling when one bears in mind that the composition of *Kamāl al-dīn* must have taken place during the last decades of the fourth/tenth century, that is, when various forms of Ismailism flourished in both the Western and Eastern parts of the Islamic world: from the Fatimid capital in Cairo (est. 359/970) and the impressive spread of missionaries (*dāʿīs*), including some prolific authors, around the eastern provinces, to the Qarmaṭī communities in Baḥrayn, Persia and Khurāsān. Several battles over territory in Syria and Palestine took place between the Fatimids and the Qarmaṭīs of Baḥrayn – who at one point (in Damascus and al-Ramla, 360/971) were even aided by Būyid troops. In the 370s/980s, following the death of ʿAḍud al-Dawla (d. 372/983), several armed clashes between the Qarmaṭīs of Baḥrayn and the Būyids occurred in Iraq at Kūfa and Baṣra.[15]

In what follows, the scant information in *Kamāl al-dīn* regarding the Ismailis will be presented and analysed in an attempt to reconstruct al-Ṣadūq's perception of this alternative manifestation of Shiʿism. Interestingly, all references to the Ismāʿīliyya are evoked by Zaydī rivals who try to refute the Ḥusaynid lineage of the Imāmī imams as well as the notion of the Twelfth imam's occultation. The strategy behind the Zaydī emphasis on matters of dispute between the Ismāʿīliyya and the Imāmiyya must have derived from their conviction that this would be useful in their refutation of the Imāmiyya. It is due to this attitude that the reader indirectly gets a rare glimpse of al-Ṣadūq's position on the Ismailis. This comes to the fore at varying degrees of explicitness in al-Ṣadūq's treatment of the following three Zaydī arguments:

(a) The first Zaydī argument of relevance is that if the number of imams had been twelve, Imam Jaʿfar al-Ṣādiq would have known it and would not have designated his son Ismāʿīl, who died in his father's lifetime. The famous *badāʾ* tradition – *mā badā li-llāh fī shayʾ kamā badā lahu fī Ismāʿīl* – according to which Imam Jaʿfar al-Ṣādiq is said to have explained this change in the predetermined course of events

---

15 See W. Madelung, 'Ḳarmaṭī', *EI2*.

by ascribing to God the action expressed by the ambiguous verb *badā* is presented by the Zaydīs as a clear proof that this problematic designation had actually taken place. Al-Ṣadūq unequivocally rejects the claim that Jaʿfar designated Ismāʿīl and offers a different interpretation of the *badāʾ* tradition, namely, that nothing was as evident (*ẓahara* which could indeed be used as a synonym of *badā*) to God as the case of Ismāʿīl whom God caused to die before his father to make it clear that he would not be the imam after Jaʿfar al-Ṣādiq. According to him, a group that considered Ismāʿīl their imam invented the baseless story about his designation which evidently contradicts prophetic and Imāmī teachings regarding the twelve imams.[16] Al-Ṣadūq also clarifies in this context what the genuine meaning of the Imāmī theological concept of *badāʾ* is, which is of less relevance for the present discussion.[17]

To further highlight the absurdity of Ismāʿīl's alleged designation, al-Ṣadūq provides several accounts that present Ismāʿīl in a very negative light, including his father's description of him as disobedient and different from him and his ancestors i.e. the previous imams. Of utmost interest is a story by Walīd b. Ṣubayḥ, a disciple of Jaʿfar al-Ṣādiq,[18] who is said to have told Imam Jaʿfar al-Ṣādiq that he saw Ismāʿīl drinking (clearly illicit intoxicating beverages) somewhere with a group of people and at the same time saw him praying piously at the Kaʿba until its curtains turned wet from his tears. Imam al-Ṣādiq's explanation for this inconceivable story was that in order to try Ismāʿīl,

---

[16] See *Kamāl al-dīn*, p. 75, where the Arabic text reads: *wa-innamā hādhihi ḥikāya walladahā qawm qālū bi-imāmat Ismāʿīl.*

[17] Ibid, pp. 75–76 where al-Ṣadūq cites a tradition on the authority of Jaʿfar al-Ṣādiq who is said to have declared: 'dissociate yourselves from the one who claims that something may appear to God today of which He was unaware yesterday' (*man zaʿama anna Allāh yabdū lahu fī shayʾ al-yawm lam yaʿlamhu amsi fa-braʾū minhu*). Following this, al-Ṣadūq stresses that *badāʾ* for the Imāmiyya is synonymous with *ẓuhūr* and does not carry the sense of regret. The concept is of course more complex than that; see in addition 'Badā" in *EI2* (I. Goldziher and A. S. Tritton) and *EI3* (M. A. Amir-Moezzi), as well as M. M. Bar-Asher, *Scripture and Exegesis in Early Imāmī Shiism* (Leiden, 1999), pp. 210–212.

[18] See H. Modarressi, *Tradition and Survival: A Bibliographical Survey of Early Shīʿite Literature* (Oxford, 2003), vol. 1, p. 391.

Satan used to appear in his form.[19] Al-Ṣadūq concluded as a result that since it is well attested that Satan cannot take the form of a prophet or a *waṣiyy*, it is unlikely that Jaʿfar designated Ismāʿīl (*fa-kayfa yajūzu an yanuṣṣa ʿalayhi biʾl-imāma?*).[20] Al-Ṣadūq's reliance on this fantastic story to prove that Ismāʿīl was inadequate is remarkable.

Although al-Ṣadūq blames this group for falsely ascribing the imamate to Ismāʿīl, it is unclear at this point whether for him this group stands for the Ismāʿīliyya. The matter becomes clear from the following question that al-Ṣadūq ascribes to the Zaydīs: 'By what means do you [i.e. the Imāmiyya] reject the imamate of Ismāʿīl and what is your proof against the Ismāʿīliyya that believe in his imamate?'[21] Al-Ṣadūq's reply to this is comprised of three categories:

1. Traditions of the kind mentioned earlier (i.e. about the falsity of claiming that Jaʿfar designated Ismāʿīl as well as accounts that prove Ismāʿīl's moral ineligibility to become imam).
2. Traditions affirming the explicit designation (*naṣṣ*) of twelve imams, naturally to the exclusion of Ismāʿīl.
3. Traditions confirming the death of Ismāʿīl during his father's lifetime.[22]

---

19 See *Kamāl al-dīn*, p. 76; see F. Daftary, 'The Earliest Ismāʿīlīs', *Arabica*, 38 (1991), p. 219, where he suggests that traditions in this spirit, including accusations of drinking, represent later fabrications by anti-Ismaili sources. However, al-Ṣadūq's emphasis in his interpretation of the story is not on Ismāʿīl's illicit behaviour but rather on the possibility that Satan would appear in his form. On this see further below, note 22.

20 See *Kamāl al-dīn*, p. 76.

21 Ibid.

22 Ibid., pp. 76–77; in one of these traditions Imam Jaʿfar al-Ṣādiq is depicted as kissing Ismāʿīl following his death. Jaʿfar is said to have done so on Ismāʿīl's forehead, chin and neck twice prior to the body's washing and preparation for burial and once afterwards. In addition to the legal implications of the imam's behaviour in this situation, we are told by al-Ṣadūq that the fact that Jaʿfar ordered others to wash his son's body indicates that Ismāʿīl had not been designated as imam. Had that been the case, al-Ṣadūq says, he would have to be washed by an imam. Al-Ṣadūq's way of arriving at this conclusion reminds one of the logic he applied in the story about Satan that was discussed earlier: Ismāʿīl's ineligibility to be imam is attested by the attitude of others (Satan and his father) towards him. The added value in this tradition for al-Ṣadūq's purpose is of course the repetition of the kissing several times, an act that ascertains Jaʿfar's intimate contact with the deceased and leaves little room for doubt with regard to the latter's identity.

(b) The followers of Ismāʿīl are also briefly mentioned in another argument that al-Ṣadūq ascribes to the Zaydiyya in which they raise the following difficulty: if the tradition regarding the designation of twelve imams is genuine, why were there so many doubts regarding the imamate following Jaʿfar al-Ṣādiq's death? According to this Zaydī argument, at this juncture a group of the Shiʿis asserted that ʿAbd Allāh b. Jaʿfar was the imam, another said that it was Ismāʿīl and a third faction were perplexed. Some of the perplexed even tried to follow ʿAbd Allāh for a while and left him when they realised that he was not suitable. Following this experience, the latter are portrayed as being undecided whether they should follow the Murjiʾa, the Qadariyya or the Ḥarūriyya (that is, the Khawārij). At which stage Mūsā al-Kāẓim is said to have called upon these perplexed to accept his imamate. That even a prominent scholar such as Zurāra b. Aʿyan (d. ca. 148–49/766–67) is said to have died without knowing who would be the imam after al-Ṣādiq is presented in the Zaydī argument as further evidence of the soundness of their cause.[23]

The emphasis in this allegedly Zaydī argument is not on the Ismāʿīliyya but rather on the diversity of opinions and state of confusion that befell the Imāmiyya following Jaʿfar al-Ṣādiq's death. In his elaborate reply, al-Ṣadūq does not discuss each of the groups mentioned in the Zaydī argument separately but rather stresses the following points:

1. It is not argued, according to him, that all Shiʿis knew the identity of all twelve imams at the time of Jaʿfar al-Ṣādiq's death. Rather, he stresses the fact that the Apostle of God had informed the community that he would be followed by twelve imams, his heirs. Nevertheless, this tradition along with the names of the twelve imams circulated among Shiʿi savants.
2. It is likely in al-Ṣaduq's opinion that although the above-mentioned prophetic tradition (apparently in its Imāmī version which

---

[23] Ibid., p. 80 and see in addition H. Modarressi, *Tradition and Survival*, vol. 1, s.v. 234, 'Zurāra b. Aʿyan'.

included the twelve imams' names) was in circulation among Imāmī traditionists, not all members of the community were exposed to it. As to the claim regarding Zurāra, al-Ṣadūq asserts that Zurāra had in fact practiced *taqiyya* and refrained from exposing the identity of al-Ṣādiq's heir before Mūsā al-Kāẓim gave him his explicit permission,[24] thus portraying him as a pious devotee who died while practising a fundamental Shiʿi duty rather than a perplexed Imāmī.[25]

3. Al-Ṣadūq provides evidence in the form of Imāmī traditions for the designation of Mūsā al-Kāẓim.[26]

In short, what one can conclude from this *en passant* mention of the Ismāʿīliyya is that for al-Ṣadūq the Ismāʿīliyya, just like the other sects that emerged following Jaʿfar al-Ṣādiq's death, came into being as a result of there being Imāmīs who were not sufficiently acquainted with prophetic or Imāmī teachings. This is of course a milder approach than the one mentioned earlier, in which al-Ṣadūq explicitly accused the Ismāʿīliyya of fabricating a designation story. It reflects, I would suggest, al-Ṣadūq's ability, perhaps due to the circumstances he personally experienced, to appreciate the degree of perplexity into which a community could be thrown following the death of its leader, including erroneous beliefs regarding the succession. After all, his entire *Kamāl al-dīn* is intended for perplexed Imāmīs.

(c) The third discussion of the Ismāʿīliyya – by far the most elaborate in *Kamāl al-dīn* – is incorporated in al-Ṣadūq's citation of Abū Jaʿfar b. Qiba al-Rāzī's refutation (*naqḍ*) of *Kitāb al-Ishhād* by Abū Zayd al-ʿAlawī (d. 326/938) whom Modarressi reckons to be a Zaydī scholar

---

[24] See *Kamāl al-dīn*, pp. 80–82.

[25] Traditions depicting this episode are followed by others that highlight Zurāra's elevated status in the eyes of the imams, see *Kamāl al-dīn*, pp. 81–82.

[26] Evidence for the explicit designation (*naṣṣ*) of Mūsā al-Kāẓim is also incorporated in some of the traditions that address the case of Zurāra. See for example *Kamāl al-dīn*, pp. 80–81, where the eighth imam, ʿAlī al-Riḍā, is said to have declared that Zurāra knew that al-Riḍā's father was explicitly designated by his father [i.e. Imam Jaʿfar al-Ṣādiq].

of the late third/ninth century.[27] What we actually have here, between the lines of Ibn Qiba's debate with the Zaydīs, is a concise pamphlet against the Ismailis. Although, as shown by Modarressi, Ibn Qiba's *Naqḍ Kitāb al-ishhād* is referred to in Imāmī bibliographical sources such as Ibn Shahrāshūb's *Maʿālim al-ʿulamāʾ*,[28] I was unable to determine whether the text is extant independently of *Kamāl al-dīn*.[29] Since a comparison between the two texts is – at least for the moment – not feasible, the possibility that the version in *Kamāl al-dīn* was reworked by al-Ṣadūq cannot be ruled out. Whether or not the extracts in *Kamāl al-dīn* and Ibn Qiba's original work are identical, as Modarressi argues,[30] it is clear that al-Ṣadūq – notwithstanding the gap of several decades that probably separated Ibn al-Qiba's work and *Kamāl al-dīn* – regarded it as a valuable source for the refutation of those considered by him as the Imāmiyya's fiercest rivals, the Zaydiyya. It is thus only logical that al-Ṣadūq deemed Ibn Qiba's arguments against the Ismāʿīliyya, which are intertwined with the latter's response to the Zaydīs, to be no less valid.

As in the two previous cases, the author of *Kitāb al-Ishhād* also refers to the Ismailis as an example of the anarchy and lack of unity among the Imāmiyya following the death of Jaʿfar al-Ṣādiq. According to Abū Zayd al-ʿAlawī's heresiographical mapping of the circumstances at that vital historical juncture, a group called the Shumayṭiyya believed that ʿAbd Allāh b. Jaʿfar al-Ṣādiq was the imam by both

---

[27] See H. Modarressi, *Crisis and Consolidation*, p. 121 (no. 6), the date of Abū Zayd al-ʿAlawī is not given by Modarressi but rather found in several Zaydī internet sites as well as in Jamāl al-Shāmī's introduction to his 2014 edition of *Kitāb al-Ishhād* (which includes the Zaydī arguments exclusively) on the basis of *Kamāl al-dīn* (see: http://zaidiah.com/articles/2367). It is noteworthy that both Ibn Qiba and Abū Zayd al-ʿAlawī were from Rayy.

[28] See Ibn Shahrāshūb, *Maʿālim al-ʿulamāʾ*, ed. Muḥammad Ṣādiq Baḥr al-ʿUlūm (Beirut, n.d.), pp. 95–96.

[29] The work is not mentioned by C. Brockelmann in his *Geschichte der arabischen Litteratur* nor by F. Sezgin in his *Geschichte des arabischen Schrifttums*.

[30] See H. Modarressi, *Crisis and Consolidation*, p. 121, where Modarressi argues – and I do not know on which basis – that, with the exception of the opening formula and Ibn Bābawayh's introductory remarks, the version in *Kamāl al-dīn* is identical.

inheritance (*bi'l-wāritha*) and designation (*waṣiyya*).[31] Remarkably, this allegedly Zaydī depiction of the Shumayṭiyya is different from the one found in heresiographical sources such as al-Qummī, al-Nawbakhtī and al-Shahrastānī (as well as a variety of secondary sources).[32] While the account cited by al-Ṣadūq depicts the Shumayṭiyya as the followers of ʿAbd Allāh b. Jaʿfar, the other sources assert that they followed Muhammad, Jaʿfar al-Ṣādiq's younger son. Both Modarressi's Arabic text and the English translation of Ibn Qiba's debate with the Zaydīs are in line with this common definition of the Shumayṭiyya. However, all the copies of *Kamāl al-dīn* that I checked (including the one edited by ʿAlī Akbar al-Ghaffārī of which Modarressi made use in *Crisis and Consolidation*) refer to the Shumayṭiyya as those who followed ʿAbd Allāh. Unless there is an additional version of *Kamāl al-dīn* of which I am unaware, this is highly interesting, as it reflects a deviation – perhaps due to a simple mistake – from the common perception of the sectarian situation following Jaʿfar al-Ṣādiq's death. The fact that it appears as it is in *Kamāl al-dīn* may be indicative of the limited access to heresiographical sources that the three relevant authors, Abū Zayd al-ʿAlawī, Ibn Qiba and al-Ṣadūq, had. It should be pointed out that Ibn Qiba's response, which will be discussed later, does not include a refutation of the Shumayṭiyya.

---

[31] See *Kamāl al-dīn*, p. 105. It should be mentioned that prior to this argument (p. 104), the author of *Kitāb al-Ishhād* refers to the Khaṭṭābiyya but not to those of this group who transferred their allegiance to Ismāʿīl and it is thus of less relevance to the present discussion. Yet, this short reference contains a brief description of the Khaṭṭābiyya's doctrines: arresting in Jaʿfar al-Ṣādiq and claiming his *rajʿa* (that is, very similar to the Nāwūsiyya, see above). Ibn Qiba refutes them as *ghulāt* and not surprisingly asserts the death of al-Ṣādiq. See in addition F. Daftary, 'The Earliest Ismāʿīlīs', pp. 217–218, where, inter alia, Daftary remarks that information about the Khaṭṭābiyya's doctrines is very fragmentary.

[32] See H. Halm, 'Shumayṭiyya' in *EI2* and F. Daftary, 'The Earliest Ismāʿīlīs', pp. 219–220; see Saʿd b. ʿAbd Allāh al-Ashʿarī al-Qummī, *Kitāb al-Firaq wa'l-maqālāt*, ed. Muḥammad Jawād Mashkūr (Tehran, 1341 Sh./1963), vol. 1, pp. 86–87; al-Nawbakhtī, *Firaq al-Shīʿa* (Beirut, 2012), pp. 125–126; Muḥammad b. ʿAbd al-Karīm al-Shahrastānī, *al-Milal wa'l-niḥal*, ed. Aḥmad Fahmī Muḥammad (Beirut, 1992), part I, p. 168.

The heresiographical mapping which is put forward by Abū Zayd al-ʿAlawī includes a second group, called the Faṭḥiyya, who believed in the *imāma* of Ismāʿīl for the very same reasons, that is, inheritance and designation. This description requires some clarification. According to Abū Zayd al-ʿAlawī, prior to the Faṭḥiyya's adherence to Ismāʿīl, they too believed in the *imāma* of ʿAbd Allāh but since no one of those who believed in his *imāma* survived, they were named the Ismāʿīliyya.[33] In other words, once the Faṭḥiyya disappeared, the Ismāʿīliyya became the appellation of those believing in Ismāʿīl's imamate, regardless of whether they originally followed ʿAbd Allāh (that is, were ex-Faṭḥiyya) or asserted Ismāʿīl's imamate immediately following his death. Although the entire discussion is supposed to revolve around the events following al-Ṣādiq's death, it seems that al-Qummī and al-Nawbakhtī called the latter group al-Ismāʿīliyya al-Khāliṣa, that is, those who denied Ismāʿīl's death already during al-Ṣādiq's lifetime.[34] As for the dimensions of these groups, Ibn Qiba remarks elsewhere that they were insignificant. According to him, whoever is acquainted with the history of the Imāmiyya knows that those who maintained the *imāma* of ʿAbd Allāh and Ismāʿīl were only a few deviators.[35] In other words, he claims that the degree of perplexity was not such that could shake the foundations of the Imāmiyya.

To conclude his argument, the Zaydī author asserts that a sect of the Faṭḥiyya – which here clearly stands for the Ismāʿīliyya – known by the name al-Qarāmiṭa, believed in the *imāma* of Muḥammad b. Ismāʿīl b. Jaʿfar, again, due to inheritance and designation.[36] Other than their

---

[33] See *Kamāl al-dīn*, p. 105, H. Modarressi, *Crisis and Consolidation*, p. 177 (Arabic) and pp. 210–211 (English translation).

[34] See Saʿd b. ʿAbd Allāh al-Ashʿarī al-Qummī, *Kitāb al-Firaq wa'l-maqālāt*, vol. 1, pp. 79–83 and al-Nawbakhtī, *Firaq al-Shīʿa*, pp. 114–116; see F. Daftary, 'The Earliest Ismāʿīlīs', pp. 220–221.

[35] See *Kamāl al-dīn*, p. 109.

[36] Ibid., p. 105; H. Modarressi, *Crisis and Consolidation*, p. 177 (Arabic) and pp. 210–211 (English translation). In addition to these groups, the author of *Kitāb al-Ishhād* mentions those who stopped the imamate with Mūsā and expected his return (*wa-tartaqibu rajʿatahu*), but since this development happened apparently around Mūsā's death, it is of less relevance for the present discussion. For details regarding the Shumayṭiyya and Qarāmiṭa, see the corresponding entries in *EI*.

appellation, the description of this group is in line with what al-Qummī and al-Nawbakhtī call the Mubārakiyya, that is, those who at first followed Ismāʿīl and only later (following al-Ṣādiq's death) upheld Muhammad's imamate.[37] At any rate, it is noteworthy that the Ismāʿīliyya are referred to as Faṭḥiyya in both the Zaydī argument and in Ibn Qiba's response, to which we now turn.

In this response, Ibn Qiba refutes the Faṭḥiyya – which here again clearly stands for the early Ismāʿīliyya – by what he regards as an indisputable, evident proof, namely, that Ismāʿīl died before his father and that a dead person cannot succeed a living one but rather the other way around.[38] This refutation is completely along the lines of al-Ṣadūq's general methodology in the heresiographical parts of his *Kamāl al-dīn*.

The Qarāmiṭa, on the other hand, are refuted on purely ideological grounds and not only due to their erroneous belief that it was Muḥammad b. Ismāʿīl rather than Mūsā al-Kāẓim who succeeded Jaʿfar al-Ṣādiq. Ibn Qiba's main argument is that they abolished Islam as a whole by abrogating its law and introducing all sorts of sophistry. The Qarāmiṭa's own claim that Jaʿfar al-Ṣādiq or his legatee designated a person who called for the nullification of Islam and the abrogation of its law is according to Ibn Qiba a sufficient proof of the fallacy of their doctrine.[39]

It is important to draw attention to Ibn Qiba's choice of words: 'Jaʿfar b. Muḥammad [i.e. al-Ṣādiq] *or his legatee* appointed a person who called for the nullification of Islam'. This phrasing indicates a degree of ambiguity with regard to whether the Qarāmiṭa maintained the imamate/mahdiship of Muḥammad b. Ismāʿīl directly following Jaʿfar or only after Ismāʿīl. This ambiguity may reflect the various early Ismaili versions regarding the identity of the seven imams in the cycle of Islam. At any rate, it is evident that Ibn Qiba was aware of the Qarmaṭī notion that Muḥammad b. Ismāʿīl's *rajʿa* as the Mahdi would

---

37 See F. Daftary, 'The Earliest Ismāʿīlīs', pp. 220–221.

38 See *Kamāl al-dīn*, p. 105.

39 See *Kamāl al-dīn*, pp. 105–106, H. Modarressi, *Crisis and Consolidation*, pp. 177–178 (Arabic) and p. 212 (English translation).

entail the abrogation of the law which was revealed to the Prophet Muhammad. This notion was propagated in al-Nasafī's (d. 332/943) *Kitāb al-Maḥṣūl* with which Ibn Qiba may have been acquainted, but antinomian tendencies may have characterised the Qarmaṭīs earlier. It is hard to tell whether Ibn Qiba's depiction of the Qarmaṭīs as abolishing Islam refers only to their antinomian ideology or also to their violent campaigns in Iraq under the leadership of Abū Ṭāhir al-Jannābī during the 320s/930s including the conquest of Mecca in 317/930, that is, around about the time of Ibn Qiba's death.[40]

Conclusion

This fragmentary information is highly valuable. It allows us a glimpse into the way the Ismailis may have been perceived by a Zaydī scholar and two Imāmīs. All three, one should bear in mind, resided in Rayy and their life and work stretch over about one hundred years, starting from the late third/ninth century. As noted earlier, since of all three texts (*Kitāb al-Ishhād*, *Naqḍ Kitāb al-ishhād* and *Kamāl al-dīn*) only *Kamāl al-dīn* has come down to us, it is hard to determine to what degree, if at all, the scant details regarding the Ismāʿīliyya in *Naqḍ Kitāb al-ishhād* were reworked by al-Ṣadūq. To the best of my knowledge there are no other Imāmī anti-Ismaili works from the third/ninth and fourth/tenth century that have survived.[41] We have evidence that anti-Qarmaṭī works, such as *al-Radd ʿalāʾl-Qarāmiṭa* by al-Faḍl b. Shādhān al-Naysābūrī (d. 260/873–74)[42] and a work under the same title by the renowned al-Kulaynī (d. 329/941), were compiled during this time though none of them has come down to us. Interestingly, a work under the title *al-Radd ʿalāʾl-Ismāʿīliyya* is ascribed to al-Nuʿmānī (d. 360/971), who like al-Ṣadūq, dedicated an independent treatise to

---

40 See W. Madelung, 'Ḳarmaṭī', *EI2*.

41 An early Zaydī-Muʿtazilī treatise against the Ismāʿīliyya is ascribed to Abuʾl-Qāsim al-Bustī (lived around 400/1000), see S. M. Stern, *Studies in Early Ismāʿīlism* (Jerusalem and Leiden, 1983), part II, ch. 7.

42 See T. Bayhom-Daou, 'al-Faḍl b. Shādhān al-Naysābūrī', *EI3*.

the occultation of the Twelfth imam. However, since his polemical work against the Ismāʿīliyya has not survived, it is impossible to tell against what sort of Ismāʿīliyya it was written.[43] The fact that al-Nuʿmānī devotes a chapter in his *Kitāb al-Ghayba* to the repudiation of Ismāʿīl's designation may suggest that *al-Radd ʿalāʾl-Ismāʿīliyya* resembled *Kamāl al-dīn* in refuting mainly the early Ismailis and the Qarāmiṭa.

No less significant is the lack of any reference in *Kamāl al-dīn* to the Fatimid state or to its *daʿwa* in the east of the Islamic world. Stern's assessment that, at least politically, the Fatimid mission in the east failed could provide a partial explanation. According to Stern, although Rayy, al-Ṣadūq's city of residence while working on *Kamāl al-dīn*, as well as other cities in Persia, Transoxania and Khurāsān, served as a base for the Fatimid *daʿwa* in the eastern provinces as early as the third/ninth century, it never gained significant popular support there.[44] The question of whether al-Ṣadūq was aware of important Ismaili works that were produced by Ismaili *dāʿī*s from this area, such as Abū Ḥātim al-Rāzī (d. 322/933–34), al-Nasafī (d. 332/943, the author of the aforementioned *Kitāb al-Maḥṣūl*) and Abū Yaʿqūb al-Sijistānī (d. after 361/971), remains unanswered at this point. It is nevertheless likely that by the time of *Kamāl al-dīn*'s composition these works were already classified as Fatimid and were not in circulation in an area devoid of significant pro-Fatimid Ismaili communities.[45]

Finally, one could reasonably argue that once al-Ṣadūq had refuted the early Ismailis, the refutation of any later Ismaili manifestations, including the Fatimids, seemed redundant. This, however, stands in contradiction to the refutation of the Qarmaṭīs that found its expression in *Kamāl al-dīn*. It is possible that al-Ṣadūq sought to provide the

---

[43] See M. M. Bar-Asher, *Scripture and Exegesis in Early Imāmī Shiism* (Leiden, 1999), pp. 63–64.

[44] See S. M. Stern, *Studies in Early Ismāʿīlism*, part II, ch. 3. 'The Early Ismāʿīlī missionaries in North-West Persia and in Khurāsān and Transoxania', pp. 189–233.

[45] Ibid., p. 223 and see in addition P. Walker, 'Dāʿī (in Ismāʿīlī Islam)', *EI2*, where he asserts that although these three authors were initially Qarmatian, al-Sijistānī eventually acknowledged the Fatimids and edited versions of works by all three were accepted in Cairo.

perplexed believer with a remedy against various sorts of immediate, concrete threats rather than remote ones such as the Fatimid challenge.[46] Despite these seemingly sensible explanations, the impression remains that *Kamāl al-dīn* is characterised by a degree of detachment from the historical circumstances prevailing at the time of its composition.

[46] The impression from al-Ṣadūq's introduction to *Kamāl al-dīn* is that he was mostly preoccupied by the degree of perplexity in the eastern provinces (Mashhad, Nishāpur, Bukhāra), see *Kamāl al-dīn*, pp. 14–15.

4

'The Places where the Wrestler was Thrown Down' (*Maṣāriʿ al-muṣāriʿ*) and the Question of Ṭūsī's Rejection of his Prior Nizārī Identity

Toby Mayer
(The Institute of Ismaili Studies)

Introduction: 'The Lady Doth Protest too much, Methinks'

The biography of Khwāja Naṣīr al-Dīn al-Ṭūsī (d. 672/1274) reflects the extreme volatility of the times through which he lived; a period over which he ended up exercising a presiding role of sorts. It is likely that the Mongols' massive predations in the region, starting from 617/1220, formed the original circumstances in which he took refuge with the Nizārī Ismaili governor of Quhistān around 632/1235.[1] But two decades later, the special advisory relationship he would gain with the Mongol conqueror and first Ilkhanid dynast, Hülagü Khān, whose 'court sage' he has sometimes been called,[2] gave Ṭūsī rare powers to shape his whole milieu directly. Hülagü gave him the position of administering all religious endowments and even appointed him vizier.[3] One text in particular marks the volte-face that the Khwāja had had around its time of writing. The *Maṣāriʿ* appears to have been written early in his relationship with Hülagü, during the crucial period

[1] F.J. Ragep, *Naṣīr al-Dīn al-Ṭūsī's* Memoir on Astronomy *(al-Tadhkira fī ʿilm al-hayʾa)* (New York, 1993), 2 vols, vol. 1, p. 11.

[2] M. Minovi and V. Minorsky, 'Naṣīr al-Dīn Ṭūsī on Finance', *Bulletin of the School of Oriental and African Studies*, 10, 3 (1940), pp. 755–789, at p. 767.

[3] Khalīl b. Aybak al-Ṣafadī, *al-Kitāb al-Wāfī biʾl-wafayāt* (Leipzig, 1931—), 20 vols, vol. 1, p. 183.

1257–1259.[4] In these years the Mongols, having destroyed Ṭūsī's erstwhile home, the Nizārī fortress of Alamūt in the Alburz mountains, and put to death its last incumbent imam, Rukn al-Dīn Khurshāh, would go on to successfully besiege Baghdad and kill the last Abbasid caliph to reign there, al-Mustaʿṣim. The text is thus an intellectual vehicle for the re-configuration that Ṭūsī's identity had undergone.[5]

In it he responds aggressively to a critique of the thought of the supreme representative of Muslim Peripateticism Abū ʿAlī Ibn Sīnā (d. 429/1037), which had been completed over a century earlier, probably around 1141,[6] by Muḥammad b. ʿAbd al-Karīm al-Shahrastānī (d. 548/1153).[7] The deeper doctrinal premises for Shahrastānī's attempted challenge to the Avicennan system, titled 'The Wrestling Match' (*al-Muṣāraʿa*), derive from Ismailism, such that this text forms part of the cumulatively decisive evidence of Shahrastānī's clandestine adoption of the latter alongside his official identity as an Ashʿarī and Shāfiʿī. Although Khwāja Naṣīr, for his part, had also been an esteemed associate of the Nizārī branch of Ismailism, responsible for some of its most important philosophical texts, he now appeared to

---

[4] Naṣīr al-Dīn al-Ṭūsī, *Maṣāriʿ al-muṣāriʿ*, ed. W. Madelung (Tehran, 2004), editor's introduction, p. 2.

[5] It was, of course, not the only such signal. His *Risāla fi'l-imāma*, *al-Firqa al-nājiya*, the substituted dedication of the *Akhlāq-i Nāṣirī* claiming his stay with the Nizārīs was against his will, and the postscript which he added later to the *Ḥall mushkilāt al-ishārāt* may also be mentioned. In the latter, Ṭūsī again implies that he had been kept at Alamūt under duress: 'I wrote most of [*Ḥall mushkilāt al-ishārāt*] in circumstances so harsh that none worse than them is possible (*fī ḥālin ṣaʿbin lā yumkinu aṣʿabu min-hā*) etc.' Ibn Sīnā, *al-Ishārāt wa'l-tanbīhāt (maʿa sharḥ Naṣīr al-Dīn al-Ṭūsī)*, ed. Sulaymān Dunyā (Cairo, 1377/1958), vols 3–4, p. 906.

[6] Muḥammad b. ʿAbd al-Karīm al-Shahrastānī, *Kitāb al-Muṣāraʿa* (translated as 'Struggling with the Philosopher'), ed. and tr. W. Madelung and T. Mayer (London and New York, 2001), editor's introduction, pp. 12–13.

[7] Shahrastānī can be regarded as a major luminary of the Sunni intellectual scene under the Saljūq dynasty. He is best known for his universal heresiography, the *Kitāb al-Milal wa'l-niḥal* ('The Book of Religions and Sects') and for his manual of Kalām thought in the Ashaʿrī tradition, the *Nihāyat al-aqdām fī ʿilm al-kalām* ('The Furthest Steps Taken in the Discipline of Kalām'). For an outline of his life and works see Toby Mayer (tr.), *Keys to the Arcana: Shahrastānī's esoteric commentary on the Qur'an* (Oxford, 2009), translator's introduction, pp. 3–19.

turn firmly against it. In his counter to Shahrastānī's 'Wrestling Match' (evoking its name in its own title, 'The Places where the Wrestler was Thrown Down' *Maṣāriʿ al-muṣāriʿ*) Ṭūsī gave strident defences of his intellectual cynosure, Ibn Sīnā, missing no opportunity to scorn Shahrastānī's arguments as unworthy of the latter's intellectual eminence and to denounce them as reflexes of the thought of the Ismailis.[8] Ṭūsī, throughout, seems intensely concerned to dissociate himself from the Nizārī community, against the background of its virtual destruction by Hülagü's Mongols, and his own religious re-alignment with Twelver Shiʿism, to whose intellectual heritage he would now go on to contribute seminal texts, notably the *Qawāʿid al-ʿaqāʾid* and the *Tajrīd al-iʿtiqād*.

The heightened, very personal significance of the *Maṣāriʿ* in Ṭūsī's oeuvre is indicated by its heated, polemical atmosphere, contrasting sharply with the other texts in which he likewise represents Ibn Sīnā against his critics, such as Fakhr al-Dīn al-Rāzī and Qūnawī. Prophetic *ḥadīth*s counsel against speaking ill of the dead but Ṭūsī apparently had no qualms whatsoever in this case, indeed, the *Maṣāriʿ* has a pungency and bitterness as if directed against a living foe, not someone dead for over a century. The denunciation has an added dimension which must surely be noted: in Ṭūsī's own fascinating contribution to the genre of *confessiones*, *Sayr wa sulūk*, he mentions that his original introduction to the Ismaili *daʿwa* was orchestrated by his father whose education (*tarbiyat*) was through an uncle who had been Shahrastānī's own direct disciple. As if this highly intriguing personal detail were not enough, implicating Shahrastānī in Ṭūsī's own involvement in

---

8 See Wilferd Madelung, 'Aš-Šahrastānīs Streitschrift gegen Avicenna und ihre Widerlegung durch Naṣīr ad-Dīn aṭ-Ṭūsī', *Akten des VII. Kongresses für Arabistik und Islamwissenschaft* [= *Abhandlungen der Akademie der Wissenschaften in Göttingen: philologisch-historische Klasse*, ed. A. Dietrich, ser. 3, no. 98] (Göttingen, 1976), pp. 250–259. For a study of the part of the book in which Ṭūsī defends Ibn Sīnā's teaching that the world is pre-eternal against Shahrastānī's criticisms, see Toby Mayer, 'The Absurdities of Infinite Time: Shahrastānī's Critique of Ibn Sīnā and Ṭūsī's Defence', in Rotraud Hansberger, M. Afifi al-Akiti and Charles Burnett (ed.), *Medieval Arabic Thought: Essays in Honour of Fritz Zimmermann* (London and Turin, 2012), pp. 105–134.

Ismailism in his earlier career, he even refers to him here as *dāʿī al-duʿāt* Tāj al-Dīn-i Shahrastāna.[9] His use of the title *dāʿī al-duʿāt* (missionary of missionaries) is a conundrum. Although it was applied vaguely in Sunni sources, it seems to correspond with the rank of *bāb al-abwāb* (gate of gates), the *daʿwa* hierarchy's administrative head, immediately after the imam.[10] In view of the fact that Ṭūsī was addressing an eminently Nizārī Ismaili readership in *Sayr wa sulūk*,[11] there is an argument that his inclusion of the title is neither random nor empty but is a genuine protocol reflecting the specific rank which Shahrastānī had attained in the *daʿwa* at some time in the course of his life.[12] Ṭūsī himself was referred to in Nizārī contexts by the same high title, notably in the preface to the *Taṣawwurāt*. Be that as it may, the contrast with Ṭūsī's contemptuous manner of referring to Shahrastānī in the *Maṣāriʿ* could not be more extreme. In this text, in effect, he has publicly seceded – in the loudest terms – from his own deeper religio-intellectual identity, signified by the person of Shahrastānī. But 'the lady doth protest too much, methinks . . .' The intent here is to re-read the *Maṣāriʿ*, with its buried, pivotal significance in Ṭūsī's intellectual and personal development, in the light of this memorable, if clichéd, line from Shakespeare's Hamlet.

---

9 Naṣīr al-Dīn al-Ṭūsī, *Contemplation and Action: The Spiritual Autobiography of a Muslim Scholar*, ed. and tr. S. J. Badakhchani (London and New York, 1999), p. 26 (English) and p. 3 (Persian).

10 Farhad Daftary, *The Ismāʿīlīs: Their History and Doctrines* (Cambridge, 1990), p. 227.

11 He evidently presented *Sayr wa sulūk* to the aforementioned Nizārī governor of Quhistān, Naṣīr al-Dīn al-Muḥtasham, to whom he refers in the text as Muẓaffar b. Mu'ayyad. Ṭūsī, *Contemplation and Action*, p. 25 and note 10, p. 67.

12 It is to be noted that the title page of the unicum of Shahrastānī's Qur'anic commentary alludes to the author as Tāj al-Milla wa'l-Dīn Muḥammad b. ʿAbd al-Karīm al-Shahrastānī, and the honorific expression just preceding the name has been scratched out. It seems likely that the erased words were *dāʿī al-duʿāt*, the manuscript having been transcribed and preserved within the Twelver Shiʿi Banū Hamūya family. The other honorifics *al-imām al-muḥaqqiq*, which are instead neutral in connotation, have been left in place. Tāj al-Dīn Muḥammad b. ʿAbd al-Karīm Shahristānī, *Mafātīḥ al-asrār* (facsimile edition of the unique manuscript at the Library of the Islamic Consultative Assembly) (Tehran, 1989), 2 vols, vol. 1, fol. 1a.

As perhaps the greatest scholastic thinker in the Muslim Avicennan tradition, the meticulous, pedantic, style of Ṭūsī's thought clashes with that of Shahrastānī, whom he regularly blames for arguing in ways beneath those befitting philosophy. By turns he chides him for employing reasoning typical of jurisprudence,[13] of Kalām theology,[14] and even of rhetoric and poetics (*al-khaṭṭābiyyāt al-shiʿriyya*).[15] Perhaps alluding to Shahrastānī's actual, historical role at the Baghdad Niẓāmiyya college as official preacher (511–514/1117–1120) and his composition of elaborate sermons, as in the case of his Persian language *Majlis-i maktūb dar Khwārazm*, Ṭūsī insults him as 'this preacher' (*hādha'l-wāʿiẓ*)[16] and makes the aspersion against him that 'he is talking for trading and fame-seeking (*ṭalab al-jāh*) with the commonalty, as is the custom of those who give pious admonition, and he does not aim thereby at the truth'.[17] The harsh judgment in part surely arises from the more scriptural basis of Shahrastānī's approach to philosophical issues in the 'Wrestling Match', which has less to do with religious oratory than with his sincere belief that his counter-Avicennan system had a deeper scriptural or 'prophetic' authority. Ṭūsī affects not to understand the strongly scriptural impulse in Shahrastānī's ways of speaking and thinking in the 'Wrestling Match', at one point declaring: 'The exegesis of the Qur'an is too lofty to use in the context of mere intellectual wrestling with another person and one should only undertake it after purifying the soul from blameworthy traits and base distractions, including disputatiousness, "wrestling", and so on.'[18]

Ṭūsī's constant, almost hysterical, derision of Shahrastānī is not easy to square with the technicality and subtlety of his defence of Ibn Sīnā that fills the book's pages. For all its curtness, the philosophical tenor of the *Maṣāriʿ* is dense and demanding, hardly bearing out its author's claim that the arguments he is refuting are risible and imbecilic. The constant irritability and scorn thus give this reader an

13 E.g., Ṭūsī, *Maṣāriʿ*, pp. 220–221, 218.
14 E.g., Ṭūsī, *Maṣāriʿ*, p. 160.
15 E.g., Ṭūsī, *Maṣāriʿ*, p. 146.
16 E.g., Ṭūsī, *Maṣāriʿ*, p. 51.
17 Ṭūsī, *Maṣāriʿ*, p. 180.
18 Ṭūsī, *Maṣāriʿ*, pp. 113–114.

impression of Ṭūsī's discomposure – quite at odds with the one intended. Whatever their idiosyncrasy and (let it be admitted) repetitiveness in the first three chapters, Shahrastānī's criticisms of the Avicennan system challenge it at its deepest levels, such as its ontology, theory of predication, its cosmogony, and its premise that we can probe divinity itself through ratiocination. It is understandable, then, that all this seriously vexed Ṭūsī. But there is a further, vital sense in which Ṭūsī 'doth protest too much': his *own* earlier Ismaili intellectual affiliation seems to inform parts of his attack on Shahrastānī. His habit of snubbing Shahrastānī over the Ismaili origin of his teachings cannot hide the fact that aspects of his defence of Ibn Sīnā may themselves have that origin.

Although three out of five topics (all but the first and last topic) which are dealt with in the book appear to belong narrowly to theology,[19] it gradually emerges that Ibn Sīnā's basic 'systemic' premises are at stake throughout – premises which generate his theology but which in the first instance pertain to his analysis of beings in the widest sense. Shahrastānī's critique is therefore marked by an insight that the theological and non-theological aspects of philosophy are intimately, mutually implicative. Just as the non-theological aspect directly generates conclusions in theology, the theological aspect directly generates conclusions in the non-theological aspect such as, say, cosmology. The point is underlined by the fact that the final, ostensibly purely cosmological, discussion of the world's pre-eternity is, unexpectedly, largely resolved by Shahrastānī on the basis of his own theology, Ismaili in character.[20] The authors of the two texts, Shahrastānī with

[19] Five principal issues form the subject of each successive chapter in Shahrastānī's earlier book and thus dictate the structure of Ṭūsī's later reply: (1) the division of being; (2) the existence of the Necessary Being, i.e., God; (3) the unicity of the Necessary Being; (4) the knowledge of the Necessary Being; and (5) the Avicennan claim of the world's pre-eternity.

[20] He states that the divine origin must be raised above conceptual twins, of which space-time (to use this Einsteinian anachronism) is a central example. It would be as blasphemous and absurd to subject God to time as to subject God to space. Ibn Sīnā, he argues, has failed to see the analogy of time with space, thus that time must be like space in its inherent finitude. Ibn Sīnā effectively subjects the divinity to time by speaking of time as an un-incepted dimension occupied by God (as well as the world).

his Ismaili bent and Ṭūsī with his Avicennan bent, negotiate the interrelation of the non-theological and theological in wholly opposed ways. Shahrastānī is at pains in the *Muṣāraʿa* to show that Ibn Sīnā produces absurdities (principally that of divine composition) by including the godhead within the scope of his wider analytical framework.[21] Shahrastānī himself has his own, largely distinct, Ismaili analytical framework parallel to Ibn Sīnā's, but at any rate, he refuses to extend it to include the godhead. The only way that it implies conclusions for his theology is *a contrario*. Ṭūsī, for his part, in the *Maṣāriʿ* is emphatic that the theology which results for Shahrastānī is unworkable and rationally incoherent. His own, essentially reactive, project is to modify Ibn Sīnā's analytical framework to obviate the absurdities (principally that of divine composition) which Shahrastānī has alleged must ensue when the framework is extended to comprehend the godhead.

Pulling back to a height and looking at Ṭūsī's involved defence of Avicennism against Shahrastānī, three facets may be discerned, examples of which will be given: (1) the defensive interpretation of Ibn Sīnā; (2) the critique of Shahrastānī's anti-Avicennan, Ismaili system; and (3) the intimation of an alternative, pro-Avicennan, Ismaili system. In the first he interprets the terms of Ibn Sīnā's analytical framework, as just mentioned, so as to put Ibn Sīnā's thought beyond the reach of Shahrastānī's contentions; in the second facet he criticises the

---

The theological reflex to assert God's transcendence of paired concepts is, of course, typical of Ismaili thought. See T. Mayer, 'Shahrastānī's Ḥanīf Revelation: A Shīʿī Philosophico-Hemeneutical System', in F. Daftary and G. Miskinzoda (ed.), *The Study of Shiʿi Islam. History, Theology and Law* (London and New York, 2014), pp. 563–583, at pp. 580–581.

[21] Although the infliction of composition on the godhead by Ibn Sīnā is Shahrastānī's prime contention, there are other absurdities which he claims follow from his inclusion of It within structures properly confined to the matrix of realities subordinate to It, e.g., the absurdities which afflict the Avicennan bid to explain the God-world relation through the cosmogonic principle that 'only one proceeds from the One'. These last absurdities are said by Shahrastānī to arise from Ibn Sīnā's tacitly viewing God as merely the top member of the cosmological hierarchy. He is instead to be viewed as wholly outside the hierarchy, all of whose members are co-dependent on Him. Ṭūsī, *Maṣāriʿ*, p. 184. Also see T. Mayer, 'Shahrastānī's Ḥanīf Revelation', p. 577. Discussed further below in this chapter.

philosophical coherence of Shahrastānī's counter-Avicennan system; and in the third facet he criticises Shahrastānī's *interpretation* of Ismaili thought in his counter-Avicennan system, as being inaccurate, and he even hints at ways in which Ismaili teachings may after all support or coincide with Ibn Sīnā's ideas. This last aspect has momentous implications, as it suggests a deeper perspectival unity than one might expect, underlying the ostensive volte-face in the Khwāja-i Ṭūs's intellectual identity.

Defensive Interpretation of Ibn Sīnā

It is, however, in the preponderant, first of these three broad approaches in the *Maṣāriʿ* that Ṭūsī is in the role for which he is probably best known and most celebrated in the history of Muslim philosophy, that is, as Ibn Sīnā's faithful interpreter, moulding and developing the Avicennan system in the face of challenges to it with striking philosophical genius. With his mastery of Peripatetic philosophy in general and Ibn Sīnā's thought in particular, Ṭūsī is acutely skilful in knowing which concepts and positions he can adopt in a given argument. He has recourse to Aristotelian logic[22] while ridiculing Shahrastānī for his own 'logic-chopping' (*tamanṭuq*).[23] He will sometimes interpret Ibn Sīnā more loosely than Shahrastānī does, and at other times he will interpret Ibn Sīnā more strictly and literally than Shahrastānī does, according to the given dispute. For example, when Shahrastānī raises the matter of Ibn Sīnā's self-contradiction in his denying considerations (*iʿtibārāt*) in the Necessary Being and then his affirming that the Necessary Being has three considerations insofar as it is an intellect, is intellecting, and is intellected, Ṭūsī replies: 'There is a difference between our statement "it is [say] twofold in consideration" (*huwa ithnān fi'l-iʿtibār*), and our statement "it has two considerations" (*lahu iʿtibārān ithnān*). For the former entails multiplicity but the latter does not entail it – instead, it entails that [the subject in question] *possesses*

---

22 E.g., he accuses Shahrastānī of the fallacious inference of the converse (*īhām al-ʿaks*), Ṭūsī, *Maṣāriʿ*, pp. 55–56. See below in this chapter for further mention of this.

23 Ṭūsī, *Maṣāriʿ*, p. 184.

a multiplicity.'[24] I.e., multiplicity in the former case is intrinsic to the subject but in the latter case is merely extrinsic to it – the Necessary Existent, for its part, being only taken to have multiple *iʿtibārāt* in this innocuous, second sense. In his defensive arguments, it is precisely this non-complicative character of 'considerations' which leads Ṭūsī to evoke them, as confirmed by their mental or 'intelligible' (*ʿaqlī*) status. It is relevant that he derives the term *iʿtibār* (consideration) from *ʿubūr* (passing beyond), thus underlining that considerations are external to the subject to which they pertain, adding that 'what is meant by it is taking something with reference to (*bi'l-qiyās ilā*) something else'.[25]

At any rate, the Khwāja's defensive exegesis here is clearly rooted in syntactical minutiae and insists on weighing them more strictly than does Shahrastānī. On these grounds Ṭūsī can accommodate Ibn Sīnā's apparent self-contradiction in affirming and denying *iʿtibārāt* in regard to the Necessary Being. However, elsewhere he will read Ibn Sīnā contrariwise and take his meaning more loosely than does Shahrastānī. In relation to the latter's complaint that the *shaykh al-raʾīs*, in certain contexts, applies to the Necessary Being terms like species and quiddity despite ultimately believing in their inapplicability to It, Ṭūsī declares 'The door of extended meaning and figuration (*bāb al-tawassuʿ wa'l-majāz*) is not blocked in arguing'.[26] Ṭūsī again evokes figuration when he castigates Shahrastānī for not permitting Ibn Sīnā to combine acting and the transcendence of acting in the case of God's pre-eternal generation of the universe: '[Shahrastānī] does not allow [extended meaning, *tawassuʿ*] in the proposition of someone who says, "The Creator did not act, and then He acted" in the sense of the two of them being combined.'[27] Despite its casually accusatory tone, this statement, in effectively advocating that the principle of non-contradiction be suspended in understanding divine agency, is logically, highly avant-garde of Ṭūsī. Later in the discussion of this same issue we even find that, in the face of one of Shahrastānī's major points, Ṭūsī relinquishes the claim that Ibn Sīnā's argument for the

---

24 Ṭūsī, *Maṣāriʿ*, p. 127.
25 Ṭūsī, *Maṣāriʿ*, p. 130.
26 Ṭūsī, *Maṣāriʿ*, p. 89.
27 Ṭūsī, *Maṣāriʿ*, p. 179.

world's pre-eternity from divine generosity was truly intended to be 'demonstrative' (*mubarhin*) at all, rather than merely 'clarificatory' (*mubayyin*).[28] He has earlier relinquished the claim, again in the face of Shahrastānī's challenge, that Ibn Sīnā's elaborate emanative scheme had really been put forward based on apodixis (*'alā sabīl al-qaṭ'*) rather than as a tentative, heuristic model (*'alā sabīl al-tamthīl*).[29] Selectivity of another kind is displayed in the fact that the Khwāja sometimes takes his stand on nominality[30] and at other times on the strong realist element in Ibn Sīnā's philosophy, as when he opposes Shahrastānī's claim that universals have no extramental existence: 'This statement is false. For human individuals external to the mind are commonly associated in what individual donkeys and cattle are *not* associated in, nor individual stones and trees. And the thing held in common between

---

[28] Ibn Sīnā's argument in question for the world's pre-eternity states: 'It is then conceivable for you in the judgement of the intellect to admit that [God] might have created the world temporally ahead of its time. If that is conceivable but He did *not* create, He was idle from generosity!' Shahrastānī retorts: 'The imagination conceives of and the intellect postulates another world beyond the world, above and beneath, and postulates the volume of the universe as greater and less than it actually is – however, on condition that *it be essentially finite*, since the proof is established that an infinite body is impossible. Likewise, the intellect postulates a time or an existent temporally prior to the world – however on condition that it be finite, for an infinite time is impossible.' In other words, Ibn Sīnā's argument from God's generosity begs the more fundamental question of whether the world can extend back in time to infinity. Ibn Sīnā did not believe that the world could extend outwards in space to infinity, therefore he did not introduce God's generosity into that issue – as if God were lacking in generosity for not bringing about a world which is spatially infinite. In response, Ṭūsī's defence states that Ibn Sīnā had never intended the argument from divine generosity to be actually demonstrative: 'Ibn Sīnā did not say that so as to prove demonstratively (*lam yaqul dhālika Ibn Sīnā mubarhinan*), but he said it so as to clarify (*mubayyinan*) the way to conceive of the postulate of [an earlier] time, supposing that time is finite.' Ṭūsī, *Maṣāri'*, p. 182.

[29] Ṭūsī, *Maṣāri'*, p. 99.

[30] E.g., when Shahrastānī, in opposing an infinite regress of natural causes, speaks of the vicious circularity (*al-dawr*) that obtains between such things as eggs and chickens, and seeds and trees, Ṭūsī retorts with typical sarcasm: 'O you most learnèd of scholars! You are conversant with this vicious circularity, which lay people and children inquire into, but it is only a vicious circle *nominally* (*laysa bi-dawrin illā fi'l-lafẓ*).' Ṭūsī, *Maṣāri'*, p. 190.

them external to the mind is called a "universal" and is [further] qualified as the "natural" [universal].'[31]

I am drawing attention in these examples to an obviously strategic component in Ṭūsī's philosophical stances in the *Maṣāriʿ* but it would surely be facile to draw the conclusion from such examples (whose contradictoriness doubtless diminishes or dissolves when each argument is treated in its specific, detailed context) that Ṭūsī is simply arbitrary or unsystematic in his approach to Ibn Sīnā's thought in mounting his defence. Such examples rather demonstrate his highly skilful handling of Ibn Sīnā's philosophy as a pliant system – indeed, as an extendable project rather than the brittle, enclosed edifice assumed in attacks like Shahrastānī's. In reality, in this first facet of his approach in the *Maṣāriʿ* Ṭūsī can be seen to elaborate a defence which draws on a highly defined, stable set of ideas bequeathed him by Ibn Sīnā. Fundamental to the set are 'considerations' (*iʿtibārāt*), especially in view of their mental or intelligible status (*al-iʿtibārāt al-ʿaqliyya*) and also 'relations' of similar status (*al-iḍāfāt al-ʿaqliyya*), predicational ambiguity (*al-tashkīk*), and especially the ambiguity of existence (*tashkīk al-wujūd*). These philosophical tools of course have a much wider role in Ṭūsī's distinctive treatment of Ibn Sīnā's thought and are found, for example, in his commentary on the *Ishārāt*, *Ḥall mushkilāt al-ishārāt*, often in specific response to the criticisms of Ibn Sīnā's argumentation typical of Fakhr al-Dīn al-Rāzī,[32] as also in Ṭūsī's

[31] Ṭūsī, *Maṣāriʿ*, p. 68. It is intriguing that Ṭūsī also emphasises the natural universal in defence of Ibn Sīnā's argument for extramental imperceptible entities at the opening of the Metaphysics of the *Ishārāt*. There Fakhr al-Dīn al-Rāzī argued against the reality of such entities, which are in some ways the currency of Ibn Sīnā's metaphysics, that if all the perceptible adjuncts are removed from perceptibles, nothing existent is left at all, and Ṭūsī responds with the case of the natural universal – a datum which supposedly has subsistence in the extramental world despite not in itself being an object of sense perception. Ibn Sīnā, *al-Ishārāt wa'l-tanbīhāt* with Ṭūsī's commentary, ed. S. Dunyā (Cairo, 1377–1380/1957–1960) vol. 3, p. 438, lines 6–7.

[32] See e.g., T. Mayer, 'Faḫr ad-Dīn ar-Rāzī's Critique of Ibn Sīnā's Argument for the Unity of God in the *Išārāt*, and Naṣīr ad-Dīn aṭ-Ṭūsī's Defence', in David C. Reisman (ed.) with the assistance of Ahmed H. Al-Rahim, *Before and After Avicenna* (Leiden: Brill, 2003), pp. 199–218, at p. 212 ff. Also see T. Mayer, 'Avicenna against Time Beginning: The Debate between the Comentators on the *Ishārāt*', in Peter Adamson (ed.), *Classical Arabic Philosophy: Sources and Reception* (London and Turin, 2007), pp. 125–149, at pp. 140–146.

involved correspondence with Ṣadr al-Dīn al-Qūnawī, known as the *Murāsalāt*,[33] and also other works.[34]

Expectedly, then, they are also to be found operating – in varying degrees – in the text which concerns us, the *Maṣāri*ʿ. Although at first a lesser role seems given to *iʿtibāriyya* (considerationality),[35] Ṭūsī does make important use of it. One use, against Shahrastānī, of ascribing a merely 'considerational' status to this or that divine aspect or relation is that (A) considerations are non-complicative for the subject (thus preserving divine simplicity),[36] yet (B) considerations can nonetheless function as real factors in divine agency. This allows Ṭūsī to 'have it both ways': God's simplicity is ensured by their externality to Him and their mental status (Ṭūsī even calls them 'non-existential', *ʿadamiyya*); yet they can be attributed, causally, with a pivotal role. In view of (A), when Shahrastānī asserts: 'The absolutely one is that which involves no multiplicity, and the multiplicity of these aspects and considerations [= spoken of by Ibn Sīnā] negates unqualified, pure unity', Khwāja Naṣīr can respond: 'Since the multiple aspects and considerations are external to the essence of the One, they do not defile its unity', and what is more he observes: 'Although external entities [consisting of these considerations] are implied by the plurality of things other than the [divine] essence, there is no existence whatsoever of a single [consideration] within possibility.'[37] It is precisely these traits

33 G. Schubert, *Annäherungen: Der mystisch-philosophische Briefwechsel zwischen Ṣadr ud-Dīn-i Qōnawī und Naṣīr ud-Dīn-i Ṭūsī* (Wiesbaden, 1995).

34 A recent doctoral thesis has been entirely dedicated to this aspect of Ṭūsī's thought: Wahid M. Amin, *Naṣīr al-Dīn al-Ṭūsī and the Avicennan Tradition: Metaphysics and Mental Existence* (DPhil. thesis, University of Oxford, 2017). For a broader account than would be appropriate in the present chapter, this study is recommended.

35 'Consideration' is admittedly a cumbersome English rendering of *iʿtibār*, but has been adopted to bring out the highly specific ontological status of these factors as purely 'ratiocinate' entities. Ṭūsī readily employs the term *iʿtibārāt* in place of near-synonyms used by Ibn Sīnā such as *ḥaythiyyāt* and *wujūh* (aspects), precisely to stress this ratiocinate status, vital to his defence of Avicennan cosmology.

36 As was just mentioned: Ṭūsī argues that Ibn Sīnā's proposition that the Necessary '*possesses* considerations' underscores the point that no complexity is thereby implied within It.

37 Ṭūsī, *Maṣāri*ʿ, p. 82.

of 'considerations' which lead Ṭūsī to evoke them in his defensive articulation of Avicennan cosmogony. Notwithstanding their non-complicative character, they are, in view of (B), the factors through which the Necessary Being is responsible for the emanation of numerous existents. As Ṭūsī argues: 'If it is said: "These considerations are not existential entities, so how would multiplicity emanate from the One because of them?" I respond: non-existential conditions (*al-shurūṭ al-ʿadamiyya*) perhaps complete the agency of the agent, such as the non-existence of griminess on a garment for dyeing it.'[38] This example given of a non-existential condition is amusingly workaday but the gist of what Ṭūsī aims to achieve through speaking of divine causation in terms of 'considerations' is clear: he is trying to explain God's necessitation of a multiplicity of effects despite His absolute simplicity. Ṭūsī believes he can do this through the mediation of 'considerations'. The latter do not, correctly speaking, have causal status, but they are objective factors or 'conditions' (*shurūṭ*) in causality.

We next come to cases of ambiguity. In the second chapter, on the Necessary Being's existence, Shahrastānī points out an apparently blatant contradiction between, on the one hand, Ibn Sīnā's division of 'necessary being' into two (that which is necessary in itself, and that which is necessary through something else), and on the other hand, his denial that there could be two necessary beings. Ṭūsī responds: 'The subject of the first proposition is "necessary being" in a sense different from the "necessary being" which cannot apply to two essences.' Basic to Ṭūsī's reply here is the claim that the 'necessity of existence' is ambiguous: 'the necessity of existence does not apply equivalently (*bi'l-sawiyya*) to necessity by itself and necessity by another, rather [it applies] by ambiguity (*bi'l-tashkīk*).'[39] 'Necessary being' in the eminent sense applicable to the intrinsically necessary being, i.e., the divine principle, cannot be thought of as shared between numerous subjects, but 'necessary being' in the sense applicable to both the intrinsically necessary being and also extrinsically necessary, i.e., contingent,

38 Ṭūsī, *Maṣāriʿ*, p. 95.

39 Ṭūsī, *Maṣāriʿ*, p. 46.

beings necessitated by something else, *can* be thought of as shared between numerous subjects.[40]

Next, in the third chapter, on the Necessary Being's unity, Shahrastānī observes that unity is something predicated of the Necessary in Itself, the intellect, the soul, and in fact, of all other beings. He then proposes that: 'If it is [predicated] by way of univocity, allow it to be suited to be a genus, and allow every species to be differentiated by a differentia – and that is composition.' Now according to Ibn Sīnā, composition is, of course, not contradictory for entities which are contingent, but it is considered by him to be absolutely contradictory for the intrinsically necessary being with which he identifies the godhead, as it implies that being's dependence on sub-parts which precludes true necessity. Following this logic through, Shahrastānī insists that unity (*al-waḥda*) must be equivocal (i.e., *bi'l-ishtirāk al-lafẓī*), concluding: 'Let us make that evident, and mention the divisions of unity such that when we say: "He (exalted is He) is one, but not like numerically single things" the unity is unadulterated and absolute.'[41] Shahrastānī will shortly derive his own Neoplatonic, virtually mystical, approach to God's unity from this same doctrine of unity's equivocity: 'Unity is applied to Him (exalted is He) and to existents purely equivocally. He is one unlike the "ones" mentioned – one such that the two opposites, unity and multiplicity, both emanate from Him, one in the sense that He brings things that are "one" into existence. He was unique in unicity, then He made it overflow on His creation.'[42] In answer, Ṭūsī scoffs: 'This consists in the talk of preachers and orators!' He instead flatly denies that unity is predicated equivocally, tending to shun equivocity as it removes the subject from the purview of the deductive reasoning central to the entire project of Avicennan philosophy. The response, which, as we have already seen, is wholly typical of him, is instead to specify that unity is predicated on the basis of ambiguity. This maintains the applicability of reason to it, but crucially removes it

[40] We might also explain Ṭūsī's point as follows: necessity can be considered in an exclusive sense, negatively conditioned (*bi-sharṭ lā shay'*) and also in an inclusive sense, as 'general necessity', unconditioned (*lā bi-sharṭ shay'*). Amin, *Naṣīr al-Dīn al-Ṭūsī and the Avicennan Tradition*, pp. 113–114.

[41] Ṭūsī, *Maṣāriʿ*, p. 109.

[42] Ṭūsī, *Maṣāriʿ*, p. 115.

from the genus-differentia composition characteristic of the subjects of univocal predicates. Thus the Necessary can be attributed with unity in some recognisable, common sense yet remain a perfect simplex, in line with Avicennan theology.[43]

More decisive in our two authors' dispute than the question of the predicational status of the two cases just mentioned, necessity and unity, is that of existence itself (*ḥaml al-wujūd*). The second chapter of Shahrastānī's text concerns God's existence, and at its centre is a contention to which he returns repeatedly from slightly differing angles. Shahrastānī thus contends that it is implied by the Avicennan division of existence between the necessary and the contingent that existence itself is a kind of generic unity, a quasi-genus. Next, according to the classic Aristotelian understanding, whatever falls within a genus is marked out from others within the same genus by a differentia. Therefore Ibn Sīnā's divine principle is a composite of the quasi-genus, existence, and the differential factor, necessity. But a composite is in fact contingent.[44] Shahrastānī himself asserts that the proper solution, as in the case of unity, just mentioned, and all other such attributes

---

[43] Ṭūsī, *Maṣāriʿ*, p. 109. In fact there is an added twist here. He also accepts that, from a certain viewpoint, unity is also predicated of God univocally – presumably in the sense that Ṭūsī of course accepts that God is also 'one' in the basic numerical sense of oneness. But he adds: 'If unity is predicated by way of univocity, no composition necessarily follows [for the subject], since not everything fitting to be a genus, *is* a genus. Instead, it is perhaps non-essential.'

[44] He takes up the opening proposition of Ibn Sīnā's proof of God in which existence itself is dichotomised: 'In your statement [Ibn Sīnā] "we do not doubt that there is existence, and either it is necessary in itself or it is contingent in itself", you have made a counterpart for the Necessary of Existence, namely the contingent in itself. It is implied by that, that existence includes two divisions which are equal in respect of existence-status, so that it is suited to be a genus or a concomitant tantamount to a genus. And one of the divisions is distinguished by a meaning which is suited to be a differentia or tantamount to a differentia. Thus the essence of the Necessary of Existence is compounded of a genus and a differentia, or what is tantamount to them by way of concomitants. That contradicts absolute independence. For whatever is compounded from two things or from two considerations – a generality and a specificity – is deficient, in need firstly of its constituents for its reality to be realised, and in need secondly of the thing which compounds it for it to bring its quiddity about in existence.' Ṭūsī, *Maṣāriʿ*, p. 55.

apparently held in common by God and others, is to acknowledge existence's equivocity (*ishtirāk al-lafẓ*). This in effect purges existence of homogeneity, leaving it as utterly variant commensurate with the variety in the subjects of which it is predicated.[45] In his characteristically polemical response to this solution, Ṭūsī declares that 'as for the ruling that existence is amongst purely equivocal terms, it is the teaching of the dross of the Kalām theologians, such as the Ashʿarites and the adherents of Abu'l-Ḥusayn [al-Baṣrī] amongst the Muʿtazilites – and anyone untainted in their intellect would enjoin its falsity!'[46]

Although it is true that the eponym of the Ashʿarite school was indeed credited (strictly speaking, anachronistically) with this doctrine,[47] it seems that Shahrastānī was here, highly distinctively and originally, attempting to co-ordinate his extensive Kalām learning with Ismaili theological reflexes. He was aiming to articulate in terms shared with wider Muslim intellectual discourse the pointedly Ismaili elevation of the godhead *beyond* being, which had indeed been singled out by Ghazālī in *Faḍā'iḥ al-bāṭiniyya* (unwarrantedly, if understandably) as disguised atheism.[48] Shahrastānī thus used both formulations, endorsing their essential exchangeability: either we can say God is above existence, or we might in certain contexts speak of God as having existence in a uniquely transcendental, humanly incomprehensible manner, in view of existence's equivocity. At any rate, through this stance existence ceases to be treated as a quasi-generic reality common to both God and creatures, with ruinous consequences for the former's absolute simplicity.

Shahrastānī next dismisses any attempt on Ibn Sīnā's part to evade this latter consequence by asserting a tertium quid *between* univocity and equivocity, namely, the ambiguity of existence (*tashkīk al-wujūd*): 'When the man [Ibn Sīnā] had become aware of the like of this absurd

---

45 Ṭūsī, *Maṣāriʿ*, p. 56.

46 Ṭūsī, *Maṣāriʿ*, p. 88.

47 See e.g., Fakhr al-Dīn al-Rāzī, *al-Maṭālib al-ʿāliya*, ed. Aḥmad al-Saqqā (Beirut, 1407/1987), 9 vols, vol. 1, pp. 291–292.

48 'It seems that, in general, [the Ismailis] have in mind denying the Maker. For if they were to affirm that He is non-existent, it would not be accepted from them. Rather, they prevent people from calling Him existent – and this is the very same denial with a change of expression; but they are clever and call this denial deanthropomorphism.' R.J. McCarthy (tr.), *Freedom and Fulfillment* (Boston, 1980), p. 169.

implication, he invented for himself a division beyond the univocal, designating it "the ambiguous". That is not in the logic of the sages, nor will it protect him from starvation, nor is the absurd implication fended off by it!'[49] In this way, Shahrastānī flatly denies any philosophical authority for this supposed predicational tertium quid. Moreover he proposes that unless existence is frankly and unqualifiedly declared to be equivocal the problem of divine composition will remain, since an ambiguous predicate arguably has the same traits fundamentally incompatible with divine simplicity, as a univocal predicate:

> We say, granted that existence is amongst what is ambiguous, and that [the ambiguous] is [indeed] another division. Is it not the case that existence is common to them both [i.e., the necessary and the contingent] with some sort of generality, and necessity is specific to [the case of the Necessary Being] with some sort of specificity; and that by which it is general is different from that by which it is particular? Then, It involves the compounding of two aspects by way of two terms, each of which signifies something different from what the second signifies. That negates absolute unity.[50]

An initial feature of Ṭūsī's response to mention is that, of course, he pointedly rejects existence's genericity, which Shahrastānī alleges must follow from Ibn Sīnā's approach. Shahrastānī, he says, supposes that because Ibn Sīnā subdivides existence into necessary and contingent existence, existence is a kind of genus. This, however, 'involves the fallacy of the converse (*īhām al-ʿaks*), namely, that [Shahrastānī] heard that every genus, or what is tantamount to a genus, is subject to division, so he took it that whatever is subject to division is a genus or tantamount to it.'[51] Next, concerning Shahrastānī's rejection of the tertium quid, ambiguity, Ṭūsī, with a certain predictability, says 'apparent from all that [Shahrastānī] says here is that he does not understand the meaning of ambiguity at all!'[52] He continues: 'If he had understood the meaning of ambiguity he would have grasped that what is marked by

[49] Ṭūsī, *Maṣāriʿ*, p. 58.
[50] Ṭūsī, *Maṣāriʿ*, p. 63.
[51] Ṭūsī, *Maṣāriʿ*, p. 55. The fallacy of the converse: $(p \supset q) \wedge q \therefore p$.
[52] Ṭūsī, *Maṣāriʿ*, p. 63.

ambiguity is classed among accidents, so the compositeness of the divisions does not follow from its inclusion of divisions, since the compositeness of simplexes does not follow from their being associated in accidents.'[53] That is, only a factor which is *essentially* constitutive of a subject will compound it, and existence qua ambiguous is instead accidental to its subject according to Ibn Sīnā's well-known teaching.[54] Ṭūsī additionally answers Shahrastānī's claim that predicational ambiguity is randomly invented by Ibn Sīnā and lacks earlier philosophical authority, declaring that this last view simply indicates Shahrastānī's lack of learning in the philosophical tradition. At some date later than the original, apparently hurried context in which he wrote the *Maṣāriʿ*, he has conscientiously transcribed into the book at this point six passages from earlier philosophers as evidence that Ibn Sīnā has not put forward the ambiguity of existence without all philosophical precedent or authority.[55] Ṭūsī transcribes passages which demonstrate the contrary from Aristotle's Topics, Alexander of Aphrodisias's commentary at the beginning of the Categories as transmitted by Yaḥyā b. ʿAdī, Abū Bishr Mattā b. Yūnus's commentary on Porphyry's *Eisagōgē*, and three separate quotations from the works of Abū Naṣr al-Fārābī.[56]

Critique of Shahrastānī's Counter-Avicennan System

The next, second, of the three facets to exemplify is Ṭūsī's attack on the system of ideas which Shahrastānī holds up as the proper alternative to Ibn Sīnā's deficient philosophy. Although he never unfolds it in

---

53 Ibid. The reference here is, in the first place, to relative simplexes such as the separate intellects which are understood not to be compounded by their joint possession of accidental attributes.

54 To be more precise: existence is accidental to quiddity in the case of everything except the Necessary Existent.

55 Madelung suggests that the quotations were added 'soon after he settled down in Marāgha in 657/1259', Marāgha being the town where he founded the college observatory that would prove to be one of his life's greatest achievements. Ṭūsī, *Maṣāriʿ*, editor's introduction, p. 2.

56 Ṭūsī, *Maṣāriʿ*, pp. 58–62.

thorough detail, Shahrastānī refers to this esoteric philosophical system in the last section of each chapter, entitled 'the true choice' (*al-mukhtār al-ḥaqq*). While he designates the body of doctrines in question with evocative euphemisms such as 'the Ḥanīf revelation' (*al-sharʿ al-ḥanīfī*) and 'the measuring instrument of prophecy' (*miʿyār al-nubuwwa*), it is clear that it enshrines a form of Ismaili thought.[57] Ṭūsī is at pains to show that this supposed competitor of Avicennism is unworkable. A major feature of this competing approach is the attempt to raise the godhead above contraries (*mutaḍāddāt*) and also above hierarchically disposed entities (*mutarattibāt*). According to Shahrastānī, it is wrong to involve God in any such relationship, since whatever is subject to such a relation is not divine. God is instead to be viewed as the transcendental cause of the entire hierarchy, and of any two oppositional realities. The second of these two reflexes of his reasoning applies pre-eminently to existence, whose opposite is non-existence. God, he says, should be viewed as transcending both existence and non-existence, and as causing both. Implicit here is of course the familiar Ismaili elevation of God above existence itself. Moreover, it is from this premise that Shahrastānī derives his own proof of God, insofar as he takes any proof to be feasible, in the *Muṣāraʿa*: 'He is necessary in His existence in the sense that He necessitates the existence of other than Him, and annihilates.'[58] He sums up his reasoning in a form of parable:

> Contraries are litigants and variant things are legal appellants, and their Judge is not numbered amongst either of His two appellants, the two litigants before Him. Instead, 'the truth' is applied to the Judge in the sense that He manifests the truth and establishes it, not in the sense that He disputes with one of the two litigants such that He would sometimes be equal to him and at others at variance with him. So existence and nonexistence . . . are contraries – and exalted be God above contraries and rivals! 'So do not knowingly make rivals for God' (Qur'an 2:22).[59]

---

[57] As argued, e.g., by W. Madelung, 'Aspects of Ismāʿīlī Theology: The Prophetic Chain and the God Beyond Being', in S.H. Nasr (ed.), *Ismāʿīlī Contributions to Islamic Culture* (Tehran, 1977), pp. 53–65. Also see my 'Shahrastānī's Ḥanīf Revelation', pp. 573–574.

[58] Ṭūsī, *Maṣāriʿ*, p. 75.

[59] Ṭūsī, *Maṣāriʿ*, pp. 75–76.

In the critique as a whole this is a highly indicative passage, condensing a central feature of the counter-Avicennan system of ideas to which Shahrastānī subscribes. In his answer, Ṭūsī not only makes explicit that this is a reflex specific to Ismaili thought, but asserts its fundamental incoherence:

> What [Shahrastānī] describes is the doctrine of the proponents of authoritative instruction (*al-taʿlīmiyyūn*),[60] for they declare: He (exalted is He) is neither existent nor non-existent, but He is the origin of existence and non-existence, and so on for every two opposites or two ranked things. For He is exalted above both, or rather He is the judge of both of them and the bestower of both of them, and the most specific of His attributes is generosity (*al-jūd*). It is replied to them: the bestower and the seeker of bestowal are two hierarchically ranked things, and the judge between two opposites and the non-judge between them are [themselves] two opposites! In sum: that is akin to the talk of preachers and poets, and is unfitting for a [philosophical] wrestling match and debate.[61]

In this way, Ṭūsī trenchantly argues that the twofold bid, characteristic of Shahrastānī's higher theology, to think of the godhead as beyond *all* hierarchical relationships and beyond *all* paired, oppositional relationships, can never succeed, and indeed that Shahrastānī himself cannot extricate his theology from such frameworks. Moreover, according to Ṭūsī, Shahrastānī's notion of upholding the godhead's transcendence of all opposites will wreak havoc with his deepest theological tasks, such as establishing God's oneness: 'Unity and multiplicity are two opposite attributes, and likewise the one and the many which is the opposite of it. So if God is *not* to be characterised as the one which is the opposite of the many, how is one to prove the

---

60 It is notable that the term *taʿlīmiyya* was generally reserved for the Nizārī Ismailis. Farhad Daftary, 'Naṣīr al-Dīn al-Ṭūsī and the Ismāʿīlis of the Alamut Period', in N. Pourjavady and Ž. Vesel (ed.), *Naṣīr al-Dīn al-Ṭūsī, Philosophe et Savant du XIIIe Siècle* (Tehran: Presses Universitaires d'Iran; Institut Français de Recherche en Iran, 2000), pp. 59–67, at p. 65.

61 Ṭūsī, *Maṣāriʿ*, pp. 87–88.

negation of multiplicity from Him (exalted is He), in line with His uniqueness?'[62]

Likewise, Ṭūsī attacks Shahrastānī's supposition that his theology, in cleaving to the godhead's absolute ineffability, succeeds in preserving It from any kind of composition entailed by attributions, in contrast to the alleged failure of Ibn Sīnā's theology in that regard. When Shahrastānī, for instance, urges that Ibn Sīnā's famous substitute-formula for God, 'the Necessary of Existence', inevitably projects complicating distinctions into the godhead, 'unless [Ibn Sīnā] shuns these divisions and expressions altogether, so that he says [instead of "the Necessary of Existence"]: It is an indeterminate reality (*ḥaqīqa munakkara*)[63] which is ineffable [literally "lacking a word", *ʿadīmat al-ism*]', Ṭūsī retorts: 'This formulation [of Shahrastānī's] is also composed from four things: (1) "a reality", (2) "indeterminate", (3) "lacking" and (4) "word" – they being different significations. So in consequence, what he disapproved of for someone else has taken place [for him too]!'[64] According to Ṭūsī the error lies in Shahrastānī's blunter view of attribution which takes it to be objectively complicating for the subject unless declared to be equivocal. Instead, as we saw above, Ṭūsī takes it that the ambiguity (*tashkīk*) and the mental, i.e., considerational, status of a given attribute is enough to safeguard the divine subject from composition.

The relations (*iḍāfāt*) of other things to God in Ibn Sīnā's cosmology are similarly voided by Ṭūsī of their complicating impact, no longer implying, as Shahrastānī claims, objective corresponding aspects (*wujūh* or *ḥaythiyyāt*) in God. Ṭūsī, in passing, gives a compressed argument for this: '[Shahrastānī] reckons that if the thing has aspects (*ḥaythiyyāt*) in consideration of its relation (*iḍāfa*) with things different from it, then that thing is composed of a multiplicity – and this is forbidden [in the case of the Necessary Being]. Yet the point (*al-nuqṭa*) has aspects commensurate with every point *other* than it in existence, to infinity, yet its comprising an infinity of things does not follow from

[62] Ṭūsī, *Maṣāriʿ*, p. 114.

[63] The *Maṣāriʿ* here has *ḥaqīqa munakkara*, instead of the reading *ḥaqīqatun mā* found in Madelung and Mayer, *Struggling with the Philosopher* (London, 2001), p. 27 (Arabic).

[64] Ṭūsī, *Maṣāriʿ*, p. 50.

that!'[65] In this resourceful line of reasoning, Ṭūsī has implicitly evoked the Aristotelian principle that an actualised infinity is absurd. Recall that in the Aristotelian, thus also the Avicennan, teaching, space is 'continuous', i.e., potentially divisible to infinity, such that there is no atomistic final term reachable in its subdivision. If the relation of every potential point of this continuous space with some single selected point were to entail a different corresponding aspect within the selected point, then the latter would absurdly comprise an actual infinity of aspects. Instead, the relations and their corresponding aspects are simply considerational, so no such infinity is entailed in the relatum-term. The argument's force is evidently enhanced by the extreme juxtaposition of the actual infinity of aspects which would supposedly ensue, and the zero-dimensional point.

An Alternative, Pro-Avicennan, Ismaili System?

The third possible facet of Khwāja Naṣīr's approach can finally be mooted. The author's immersion in Ismaili thought is clear at some junctures in the text, such that he is not above correcting Shahrastānī for his supposed misinterpretation of Ismaili teachings. Very notable in this regard is the involved discussion[66] concerning Shahrastānī's attack on Ibn Sīnā's cosmological principle that 'only one proceeds from the One'. Some passages in Ṭūsī's answer are highly revealing. Shahrastānī at one point says:

> Since the Necessary of Existence is one in every respect, and It necessitates a single Intellect from an 'aspect', then let the Intellect also necessitate a single thing from an aspect. For it only necessitates something in consideration of its benefiting from that which necessitates *it*, not in consideration of what it has in itself, so that it follows that existence is arranged from individuals in a continuous sequence, not in unequal quantities and variant individuals. But existence is the opposite of that, so it is incoherent.[67]

---

65 Ṭūsī, *Maṣāriʿ*, pp. 71–72.

66 Madelung's edition, pp. 91–109.

67 Ṭūsī, *Maṣāriʿ*, p. 105.

Shahrastānī's reasoning is that existence is not a long, single cause-effect sequence as might be implied by Ibn Sīnā's cosmogonic formula 'only one proceeds from the One'. By contraposition, the formula is thus falsified.

The nub of Ṭūsī's answer is that the formula does not negate the emergence of multiplicity but seeks instead to *explain* it. He therefore attacks Shahrastānī's misunderstanding, or wilful misrepresentation, of this principle, from which faulty premise he draws the obviously absurd single-chain cosmos. How Shahrastānī has interpreted the principle is that the First Intellect's production of what is beneath it is purely through what comes to it from its divine cause, and '*not* through the consideration of what it has in itself' (*lā bi-ʿtibāri mā lahu bi-dhātihi*). According to Ṭūsī this is quite incorrect, so he reiterates the point already referred to, that a 'consideration', possessed by something in itself, can indeed function as a basis for the emanation of what is beneath it, and the multiplicity of emanant entities can indeed be traced to such a consideration, 'though the consideration [per se] is unsuited to be a cause, it is suited to be a condition (*sharṭ*), since a multiplicity emanates from the One on account of it.'[68] It is precisely through emanative bases in the form of different isolable 'considerations' that Ṭūsī elaborates the explanation of Ibn Sīnā's cosmogony, using a complex combinatorial calculus.[69]

How, then, is all this subsumed within the third facet, i.e., articulated by Ṭūsī against Sharastānī in terms of a pro-Avicennan interpretation of Ismailism? In the passage confronting us, Ṭūsī seeks to lend further credence to this Avicennan 'consideration-based' cosmogony by invoking the theory attributed to Pythagoras: 'In the entailment of multiplicity on account of the "considerations" lies a mighty mystery

---

[68] Ṭūsī, *Maṣāriʿ*, p. 105.

[69] It is presented in slightly different ways in different contexts. For the version in our text, see Ṭūsī, *Maṣāriʿ*, pp. 95–96. For a general discussion of this calculus see Roshdi Rashed, 'Combinatoire et métaphysique: Ibn Sīnā, al-Ṭūsī et al-Ḥalabī', in R. Rashed and J. Biard (ed.), *Les Doctrines de la Science de l'Antiquité à l'Âge Classique* (Leuven, 1999), pp. 61–86. Also see Nicholas Heer, 'Al-Rāzī and al-Ṭūsī on Ibn Sīnā's Theory of Emanation', in P. Morewedge (ed.), *Neoplatonism and Islamic Thought* (Albany, 1992), pp. 111–125.

in regard to creation which Pythagoras declared on the authority of the sages, inasmuch as he said: If "one" is established, "not-one" is entailed facing it, so a two-ness (*thanwatun*) results. [Pythagoras] stated: "This is the origin of multiplicity". Ṭūsī's allusion is clearly to the doctrine of the 'Indefinite Dyad' (*aoristos duas*), attributed to Pythagoras and taken up (with modifications) by Plato before passing to the Neoplatonists. Ṭūsī's invocation of it here is simply insofar as this ancient theory traces multiplicity, not to the One itself, but to its correlative 'consideration', a 'not-one, which faces it' (*lā-wāḥid bi-izā'ihi*). The negative, or non-existential, status of this root-factor for all subsequent multiplicity, is crucial to Ṭūsī here. He mentions in addition an analogy, as he sees it, in Zoroastrian teaching: the principle of all evils (*mabda' li'l-shurūr*) is the great angel Yazdān's shadow (*ẓill*), known as Ahriman, and whereas Yazdān has an existential nature (*ṭabī'a wujūdiyya*), the latter has a non-existential nature (*ṭabī'a 'adamiyya*).[70] The basic intent behind these comparisons is straightforward enough: to lend support to the Avicennan claim that a non-existential 'consideration' can be the source of the cosmos.

By citing these specific ancient precedents for this Avicennan idea, Ṭūsī is perhaps also surreptitiously deflating Shahrastānī's reputation as a nonpareil Muslim authority on doctrines past and present, based on his *Kitāb al-Milal*. Be that as it may, it is an intriguing challenge to find the actual historical basis for Ṭūsī's next, rather crucial, claim about the Pythagorean doctrine in question. He makes out that the Ismailis themselves suggest that their cosmology – the cosmology which Shahrastānī took himself to be promoting – derived from Pythagoras.[71] Ṭūsī comments sardonically, 'Perhaps this wrestler

---

[70] Ṭūsī, *Maṣāri'*, p. 106.

[71] This reference to a belief, apparently internal to the Ismaili tradition, that Ismaili thought is linked to Pythagoras is hard to substantiate. See Wilferd Madelung and Paul E. Walker, 'The *Kitāb al-Rusūm wa'l-izdiwāj wa'l-tartīb* Attributed to 'Abdān (d. 286/899): Edition of the Arabic Text and Translation', in Omar Alí-de-Unzaga (ed.), *Fortresses of the Intellect: Ismaili and Other Islamic Studies in Honour of Farhad Daftary* (London and New York, 2011), pp. 103–165, at pp. 108–109. The strong, explicit Pythagorean empathies in the *Rasā'il Ikhwān al-Ṣafā'* may constitute some basis for Ṭūsī's claim of Ismailism's link with Pythagoras. *Risāla* 32 is, notably,

forgot what he drew from his instructors.' His subsequent remarks thus upbraid Shahrastānī for rejecting Avicennan cosmogony on behalf of his alternative model, supposedly of Pythagorean origin, which bore an essential resemblance to it. Indeed, according to Ṭūsī, not just he but Shahrastānī's Ismaili teachers *themselves* advocated the basic, underlying agreement of this supposedly Pythagorean scheme and the so-called Aristotelian scheme which is enshrined in Ibn Sīnā's axiom 'only one proceeds from the One'.[72]

Khwāja Naṣīr here re-formulates the problem of cosmogony using the pointedly Ismaili terminology used by Shahrastānī himself. He frames the Pythagorean scheme, on the one hand, as accenting contrariety (*al-taḍādd*), with the cosmos being envisaged as emerging from a primal contrary relation between one and not-one (with hierarchy following secondarily as all the numbered entities deriving from the 'not-one'); and he frames the Aristotelian (hence Avicennan) scheme, on the other hand, as accenting hierarchy (*al-tarattub*), with the cosmos instead being envisaged as emerging from a primal hierarchical relation between the One and its singular first effect (with contrariety following secondarily as the accidental existence and non-existential quiddity of the first effect). But to repeat, according to Ṭūsī, any real conflict of the two cosmogonic scenarios, the Ismaili-Pythagorean one and the Aristotelian-Avicennan one, was denied by the Ismaili thinkers who promoted the former of these theories and who were

---

dedicated to Pythagorean doctrines. Also see Alessandro Bausani, 'Die Bewegungen der Erde in *Kitāb Ikhwān aṣ-Ṣafā*: ein vor-philolaisch-pythagoraisches System?', *Zeitschrift für Geschichte der Arabisch-Islamischen Wissenschaften*, 1 (1984), pp. 88–99. It was not unusual for non-Ismaili Muslim authors to associate Pythagoras with Ismailism, e.g., the Egyptian historian al-Maqrīzī (d. 845/1442). See, Taqī al-Dīn Aḥmad al-Maqrīzī, *al-Mawā'iẓ wa'l-i'tibār fī dhikr al-khiṭāṭ wa'l-āthār* (Cairo, 1270), vol. 1, p. 349. Al-Ghazālī, in passing, links the Ismailis, Pythagoras and the Brethren of Purity in the section on 'Ta'limism' in his *Munqidh*. R.J. McCarthy, *Freedom and Fulfillment*, p. 77.

[72] It must be noted that Aristotle (d. 322 BC) himself did not advocate emanation or procession (*proodos*), a cosmological theory which only became associated with his philosophy through the later impact of Neoplatonism, especially Plotinus (d. 270 CE). Aristotle's name here is evidently shorthand for the Greco-Arabic philosophical tradition represented pre-eminently by al-Fārābī and Ibn Sīnā.

Shahrastānī's instructors. They themselves interpreted the theories as concordant. Why then, Ṭūsī effectively asks, is Shahrastānī himself so hostile to the Avicennan scheme?[73] To summarise Ṭūsī's brief but highly noteworthy discussion in these pages: (A) he defends Ibn Sīnā's considerational cosmogony through Pythagoras's theory of a primal 'not-one' facing 'one'; (B) he points out that Shahrastānī's own Ismaili teachers equated their cosmogony with that of Pythagoras; and (C) he points out that Shahrastānī's Ismaili teachers even claimed the compatibility of their supposedly Pythagorean cosmogony and Aristotle's (in reality, Ibn Sīnā's) cosmogony. It is imperative to note that Ṭūsī has here taken up the very same Ismaili system of concepts which elsewhere in the *Maṣāriʿ* he seems to debunk, and he has corrected Shahrastānī's reading of this Ismaili system as contradicting Avicennism. Ṭūsī instead advocates its broad compatibility with Avicennism.

Let us move on to a second noteworthy passage, also evidential for the third facet of Ṭūsī's approach. Shahrastānī's opposition to the axiom 'only one proceeds from the One' is driven by the sense that, in treating the godhead as the hierarchy's top member, in an exclusive relation with the first effect, the axiom unwittingly subjects It to the cosmological hierarchy which depends on It.[74] According to Shahrastānī it is more fitting to view the entire hierarchical structure, with its agential relations from above to below, as *in toto* directly dependent on the godhead. The emanative and causal sequences internal to the hierarchy are real, but all of them constitute a global effect of the godhead, which is in a single relation to its entire effect. Shahrastānī presents this idea in various ways, such as: 'Why might not the universe be related to [the godhead] in a single manner without any difference between what emanates from It essentially, without mediation and through the first intention (*bi'l-qaṣd al-awwal*), not through the second intention (*lā bi'l-qaṣd al-thānī*), and between what emanates

[73] '[Shahrastānī's instructors] denied that Aristotle contradicted [Pythagoras], for [Aristotle] made hierarchy the origin of the emergence of multiplicity. They meant that he said: From the One emanates another one (*ṣadara ʿan al-wāḥid wāḥid ākhar*), which is other than the First in rank and power.' Ṭūsī, *Maṣāriʿ*, p. 106.

[74] As was already mentioned above, see note 21.

from It contrary to that?'[75] It is clear that in this distinctive trend in his interpretation of Ismaili cosmology, Shahrastānī retains the influence of the strong theistic determinism characteristic of his prior Ashʿarī affiliation.

In answer to this last statement Ṭūsī again remonstrates with Shahrastānī for neglecting his own fundamental Ismaili teachings in attacking Ibn Sīnā's theory of cosmogony, but from a new angle to the one just discussed, concerning the precedent of Pythagoras. Ṭūsī declares:

> [Shahrastānī] and his [Ismaili] colleagues do not allow that God's creation has any way back to Him save by one access, which is a single individual in their view, and they judge that the final return is a reversion to the origin. Why, then, did [Shahrastānī] reject someone [viz. Ibn Sīnā] who says, 'The origin consists in a single effect which is the closest of effects to Him'?[76]

Ṭūsī is here availing himself of the teaching, to which he takes Shahrastānī to have adhered, that creation must finally revert to the Creator through a unique entity, which is characteristically referred to as a single 'individual' (*shakhṣ wāḥid*) in order to underscore its ultimate religious identification with the imam. To underline this reciprocity of identity between the imam's person and the cosmological endpoint, Ṭūsī adds, 'Especially given that [Shahrastānī's] doctrine is that every individual here [on earth] has an archetype among the immaterial entities and every immaterial entity there has an individual *here* – with them calling the former the "sources" (*maṣādir*) and the latter the "loci of manifestation" (*maẓāhir*).' This is evidently an

---

[75] Ṭūsī, *Maṣāriʿ*, p. 119. Another way in which Shahrastānī articulates the same claim is through turning Ibn Sīnā's modal ontology against his cosmogony: everything other than the intrinsically necessary godhead is contingent in its existence, i.e., whether it is as senior in rank as, say, a separate intellect or as junior in rank as, say, a sublunary rock. Shahrastānī ventures, 'It is [therefore] necessary for all contingents to be related to Him in the same way, without the mediation of an intellect.' Quoted in Ṭūsī, *Maṣāriʿ*, p. 97. Also see my 'Shahrastānī's Ḥanīf Revelation', p. 577.

[76] Ṭūsī, *Maṣāriʿ*, p. 118.

allusion to the highly characteristic Ismaili notion of a socio-cosmic matrix involving a parallelism between each ranked intellect of the celestial world and each ranked individual of the missionary hierarchy, culminating in the imam at its summit, co-ordinate with the divine Command. The Khwāja-i Ṭūs is here enlisting his deep acquaintance with Nizārī Ismaili doctrines in his rebuttal.[77] His main point to Shahrastānī is that if he espouses these teachings on the final reversion of the cosmos to God via the unique 'individual', he should equally assent to the original projection of the cosmos via the same, since '[Shahrastānī's Ismaili authorities] judge that the final return (*al-maʿād*) is a reversion to the origin (*al-mabdaʾ*)'.

Khwāja Naṣīr presents all this as strictly ad hominem argumentation against Shahrastānī but the prevalence of Ismaili catchwords in this passage of the *Maṣāriʿ*, as in the one just discussed, suggests some disingenuousness in that pretext. It similarly seems to show him letting down his guard and effectively slipping back into the expert co-ordination of Nizārī and Avicennan thought which he had promoted during his years as the most esteemed of Nizārī scholars under the imamate of ʿAlāʾ al-Dīn Muḥammad III. He acknowledges an underlying harmony of the systems and takes Shahrastānī to task for believing otherwise. Continuing, Ṭūsī thus challenges, 'Why might not the universe's return to [God] and the universe's "science" be in a single manner, without them being linked within the chain of giving perfection and seeking perfection, of giving instruction and receiving instruction to a single individual who is the intermediary between creatures and their Creator?'[78] I.e., since Shahrastānī is bent on denying the universe's emanation via a single intermediary, let him, for consistency, also deny the intermediary's other functions in the cosmological return, in bringing the hierarchy of beings to perfection (*al-ikmāl*) and imparting instruction (*al-taʿlīm*), as attested in Ismaili

[77] In his Nizārī period works Ṭūsī himself employs this model and the terminology of the 'sources' (*maṣādir*) and the 'loci of manifestation' (*maẓāhir*). See e.g., S.J. Badakhchani (ed. and tr.), *Paradise of Submission: A Medieval Treatise on Ismaili Thought. A New Persian Edition and English Translation of Ṭūsī's* Rawḍa-yi taslīm (London and New York, 2005), § 516, § 517, pp. 169–170.

[78] Ṭūsī, *Maṣāriʿ*, p. 119.

teaching. The individual's function in origination is of a piece with these other roles, and Avicennan cosmogonic theory acutely defends that very originating function. Ṭūsī is angered, quite simply, by Shahrastānī's inability to recognise the deep complimentariness of Avicennan cosmology and Nizārī Ismaili teachings. The Khwāja-i Ṭūs here clearly betrays reflexes which correspond with his earlier Nizārī identity and sit very oddly with his new presentation of his identity.

If the above co-ordination with Ismaili cosmology is taken seriously, it is implied that Khwāja Naṣīr is not so much focused on the First Intellect in his defence of the formula 'only one proceeds from the One', as on the entity termed the Command (*al-amr*) which lies *beyond* the First Intellect as such, though assimilated to it (i.e., taken to be the upper aspect of it) in some Ismaili thinkers' treatments. It is obviously the Command which is alluded to in the Ismaili doctrine, just quoted from Ṭūsī, concerning the return of the universe to God and the idea that the chain of seeking perfection and instruction culminates in 'a single individual who is the intermediary between creatures and their Creator', hence who should likewise, Ṭūsī argues, be acknowledged by Shahrastānī in regard to the universe's origination. What, if any, is the evidence in the *Maṣāri*ʿ that Ṭūsī acknowledges two traits which would be critical in establishing that the entity he has in mind is indeed the Command, namely: (1) its transcendence of the First Intellect such that it is instrumental in the latter's emanation, and (2) its radical divine/non-divine duplexity?

Some reference by Ṭūsī to the second of these defining characteristics of the Command in Ismaili teaching, is encountered through an arguable misunderstanding, on his part, of the following statement from Shahrastānī: 'The general can be particularised step by step till it reaches a limit in a single thing which is a "worshipper" (*ʿabd*) . . . Just as the particular can be generalised step by step till it reaches a limit in "the universe" (*al-kull*).'[79] I have elsewhere taken the thrust of Shahrastānī's broader point here to be that Ibn Sīnā's principle that 'only one may proceed from the One', if it has any truth at all, would be adequately fulfilled by the culmination of our perspective at a level

[79] Quoted Ṭūsī, *Maṣāri*ʿ, pp. 116–117.

of total generality, from which viewpoint the universe is indeed a unitary thing which proceeds from God.[80] Ṭūsī however reads him contrariwise, such that it is the unique 'worshipper' reached via the perspective of total specificity which Shahrastānī ventures might serve as the subject of the famous cosmogonic axiom. On this basis Ṭūsī next makes the following noteworthy comment:

> [Shahrastānī's Ismaili] associates do not allow his judgement about that thing unique in its pure 'worshipper-hood'. Rather they say: it is an *intermediary* (*wāsiṭa*) between Him and His worshippers. So it is [only] a worshipper through the aspect which it has relative to the worshippers, they designating it the world of similarity; and it is not a worshipper through the aspect which it has relative to the One Worshipped, they designating it the world of dissimilarity; and it is the absolute 'One' in itself, not relative to others, they designating this modus the world of oneness.[81]

Thus Ṭūsī, again occupied here in correcting his opponent's supposedly weak grasp of Ismaili doctrine, stresses that the world's crowning individual is *not* properly characterised as 'unique in pure worshipper-hood' (*al-wāḥid bi'l-'ubūdiyyati'l-maḥḍa*). The whole point about the Command is rather that it is a true intermediary, thus duplex in identity: it is only a worshipper (*'abd*) on the creational side, i.e., from the viewpoint of comparability (which Ṭūsī gives the Ismaili designation 'the world of similarity', *kawn al-mushābaha*); it is not a worshipper on the side facing God who is the object of worship (*ma'būd*), i.e., from the viewpoint of its difference from creation (Ṭūsī giving this differentiative viewpoint the Ismaili designation 'the world of dissimilarity', *kawn al-mubāyana*); and it may even be identified with the godhead from the viewpoint of the latter's utter unity (Ṭūsī giving this highest viewpoint the Ismaili designation 'the world of oneness', *kawn al-waḥda*).[82]

---

80 T. Mayer, 'Shahrastānī's Ḥanīf Revelation', p. 576,

81 Ṭūsī, *Maṣāri'*, p. 117.

82 The triple terminology of *kawn-i mushābahat*, *kawn-i mubāyanat* and *kawn-i waḥdat* is found in Ṭūsī's Ismaili works. See e.g., Ṭūsī, *Contemplation and Action*, p. 42, and Badakhchani, *Paradise of Submission* p. 64.

To deal, then, with the question of whether the *Maṣāriʿ* involves any mention of the first of the Command's definitive traits – its transcendence of the First Intellect which, for its part, is only generated through it. In the *Maṣāriʿ*, Ṭūsī's presentation of the inverted tree of emanations, rooted in 'considerations', is very close to what he says in other texts in exploring the Avicennan model of cosmogony. The *Maṣāriʿ* version involves the same complex analysis in which twelve entities, no less, are produced on three descending levels.[83] The interpretation of Ibn Sīnā's model which Ṭūsī produced when in his earlier Nizārī habitat has been convincingly argued to bear the influence of Ismaili cosmology and, despite the ostensibly strongly anti-Ismaili context of the *Maṣāriʿ*, he evidently saw fit to retain it in the *Maṣāriʿ* as it stood. In this I draw on Professor Landolt's hypothesis that the Command, which Ṭūsī put forward in *Sayr wa sulūk* as an indispensable solution to more than one philosophical mystery and which he there presents as a compelling feature of Ismaili teachings, is also alluded to – highly implicitly – in his commentary on the *Ishārāt*. There, in defending Ibn Sīnā against Fakhr al-Dīn al-Rāzī, Ṭūsī had carefully distinguished the First Intellect as such from the truly primary and simple reality contiguous with the Necessary Being and implicated in Its agency, thus the true subject of the axiom 'only one proceeds from the One'. He declared this reality to be the 'existence' without which the quiddity of the First Intellect would not itself become existentialised at all. To quote from Landolt's discussion: 'Were it not for this primordial creative act located somewhere between the First Principle and the *quiddity* of the Prime Intellect, no quiddity at all would actually *exist*. This, I submit, amounts to the same crucial point Ṭūsī is making... in *Sayr wa Sulūk* (Nos. 25–26) regarding the necessity of the divine *Amr* as an intermediary between the First Principle and the "Universal Intellect".'[84] In his defensive *Ishārāt* commentary, Ṭūsī availed himself of

---

[83] See the discussion in Heer, 'Al-Rāzī and al-Ṭūsī on Ibn Sīnā's Theory of Emanation'.

[84] Hermann Landolt, 'Khwāja Naṣīr al-Dīn al-Ṭūsī (597/1201-672/1274), Ismāʿīlism, and *Ishrāqī* Philosophy', in N. Pourjavady and Ž. Vesel (ed.), *Naṣīr al-Dīn al-Ṭūsī: Philosophe et Savant du XIIIe Siècle* (Tehran, 2000), pp. 13–30, at p. 26.

this solution in the face of Rāzī's searching criticism of Ibn Sīnā's theory, in which he had showed that the First Intellect inescapably comprises different kinds of multiplicity, and so would strictly violate Ibn Sīnā's principle that 'only one proceeds from the One'. As Nicholas Heer puts this point: 'For al-Ṭūsī the first effect is by no means synonymous with the first intelligence. It is, in fact, only the first aspect of the first intelligence to emanate, namely, its existence. The first effect is thus a single entity, whereas the first intelligence is multiple.'[85]

In brief, it becomes apparent that Ṭūsī's discussion in the *Maṣāriʿ* rehearses precisely the same scheme:

> As for when the First Intellect emanates from [the First Principle], the considerations have been multiplied, and that is insofar as the [very] existence of the thing which emanates [i.e., the First Intellect] has [1] a consideration and is an entity other than the First [Principle]; its 'otherness' also has a quiddity, and this is [2] a consideration other than the consideration of its existence.[86]

Ṭūsī here, as in his other detailed analyses of Ibn Sīnā's cosmogony, retreats from the notion of the First Intellect as the reality immediately abutting the godhead, to make his aforementioned distinction of the First Intellect's (1) existence and (2) quiddity. He reifies its existence as 'an entity other than the First [Principle]' (*huwa mawjūdun ghayru'l-awwal*). To frame the First Intellect's existence as an existent (*mawjūd*) in its own right is perhaps contrived and paradoxical-sounding. It additionally begs the key question of whether the division into existence and quiddity is not simply an analytical (*taḥlīlī*) distinction as Ṭūsī himself might claim in other contexts. But for these very reasons it underlines the ingenuity of what Ṭūsī is effecting to do and alerts us to its abnormality: he is straining to entify something between God and the First Intellect, using the matrix of relations available to him in Avicennan cosmogony. It was, notwithstanding the more Avicennan vocabulary, a defining reflex of Ismaili cosmology to treat the existentiation of the Universal Intellect as a hypostasis in its own right, hence the earlier Ismaili nomenclature employed for the Command: *kūnī*,

---

85 Heer, 'Al-Rāzī and al-Ṭūsī on Ibn Sīnā's Theory of Emanation', p. 121.

86 Ṭūsī, *Maṣāriʿ*, p. 94.

from the Arabic existentiating imperative *kun* (Be!). The distinct Avicennan philosophical context has dictated that Ṭūsī slightly shift the basis for the hypostasis from, so to speak, the existentiating (*ījād*) to the existing (*wujūd*) of the First Intellect, but the upshot is the same. The existence of the First Intellect is taken to be a hypostasis in its own right which adjoins God insofar as it directly proceeds from Him, but from another angle is other than God. The quiddity of the First Intellect signifies the aspect of 'otherness' (*ghayriyya*) while the existence of the First Intellect is the true referent of the principle 'only one proceeds from the One'. We are, in sum, confronted in the *Maṣāriʿ* by the same refinement discernible from a decade earlier in Ṭūsī's *Ishārāt* commentary, a refinement of, arguably, direct Ismaili inspiration.

It may be observed that all the above-mentioned testaments to Ṭūsī's lingering acknowledgment of a pro-Avicennan Ismaili system in the *Maṣāriʿ*, congregate around a single, albeit vital, issue: cosmogony. So are there other issues in the book, in which the same conjunction of Avicennism and Ismailism looms in some way in Ṭūsī's discussion? One other possible example, at least, may be mentioned which could well prove to be the proverbial 'elephant in the room'. It pertains to the problem of the predication of existence (*ḥaml al-wujūd*), discussed by me above and ubiquitous in the earlier chapters of the *Maṣāriʿ*. Ṭūsī has been presented as a 'conceptualist' for his characteristic stress on the purely considerational (*iʿtibārī*) status of the objects of reason, constituting the true subject-matter of ratiocination. Shahrastānī, for his part, takes it that our mental concepts hold correct because they correspond to something truly outside the mind. His strong trend is to interpret correspondence (*al-muṭābaqa*) as a verificatory bridge between the extramental and the mental: 'Concepts in the mind are only correct due to their correspondence (*muṭābaqa*) with something outside the mind . . . the universal within the mind corresponds to every single individual amongst what is particular in the external world.'[87] It is very striking in Ṭūsī's response that he refutes this model of correspondence and replaces it with a verificatory bridge between two things *neither* of which is extramental. Correct

[87] Quoted Ṭūsī, *Maṣāriʿ*, pp. 67–68.

concepts (*mafhūmāt*) in the mind correspond to the intellectual universal, which for its part is something in some sense correlated with what is held in common between extramental individuals but which, in itself, is apprehended in the intellect with the meaning of generality. It is a telling detail that although in this passage Ṭūsī takes care to observe that one meaning of 'universal' is the natural universal (*al-kullī al-ṭabīʿī*) present in individuals outside the mind, he is quite firm on the point that the natural universal is not the focus in the issue of correspondence. In his model of correspondence there is, in effect, a sequestration from the extramental and strictly speaking, only the correspondence of the mental concept with the intellectual universal (*al-kullī al-ʿaqlī*).[88]

This conceptualism has a major impact in the case of existence itself. Ṭūsī's emphatically held view is that existence, insofar as it functions as a cohesive (albeit 'ambiguous', *mushakkak*) basis of inferential reason in metaphysical science, is strictly *only* a considerational reality and a mental concept. It follows from this that he rejects the presence of a unified reality of existence in the world *outside* the mind. Extramentally, there are in fact only innumerable specific existences (*al-wujūdāt al-khāṣṣa*). Given that Shahrastānī does take the concept of existence to correspond to something extramental, his teaching that it is radically equivocal, commensurate with all its subjects, is by no means far removed, on scrutiny, from Ṭūsī's view. Both hold that, in extramental reality, there are only discrete, specific existences. The prime difference here (certainly not to be played down) between Shahrastānī and Ṭūsī is that the former's stance on the issue of the predication of existence intentionally threatens the entire Avicennan science of being qua being, and the rational theology it implies,

---

[88] 'That thing [held in common] is sometimes grasped in the intellect with the meaning of generality, and sometimes with the meaning of specificity. When it is grasped with the meaning of generality it comes to be a species or genus, or some other such thing and it is called the intellectual universal (*al-kullī al-ʿaqlī*) – it not being extramentally existent but inscribed in the intellect (*murtasim fi'l-ʿaql*), and for that reason it is called "intelligible". If whatever is inscribed in minds (*mā yartasimu fi'l-adhhān*) corresponds with that, it is "knowledge", otherwise it is ignorance.' Ṭūsī, *Maṣāriʿ*, p. 68.

whereas the latter's stance formally, i.e., in *conception*, aims to preserve it intact. We can, nevertheless, read Ṭūsī's pointedly conceptualist way of approaching existence within Avicennism as, in practice, accommodating a state of affairs in extramental reality which in many respects is akin to Shahrastānī's approach in Ismailism. The most indicative case is, of course, that of the Necessary Being, the godhead itself. I suggested above that Shahrastānī understood the Ismaili parlance in which God is 'beyond existence' to correspond to the idea, formulated in terms of the equivocity of existence, that God is a uniquely transcendental existence. Ṭūsī, while conceptually including God in an existence that is held in common with others, views Him as, extramentally, a uniquely necessary 'special existence' (*wujūduhu'l-khāṣṣ*). For him, the Avicennan formula according to which His existence is identical with His quiddity, is simply a way of articulating what occurs in the extramental order as this 'special existence' characterised by radical necessity. Ṭūsī declares bluntly: 'The First (exalted is He) is distinguished from other than Him, and other than Him is distinguished from Him, on the grounds of the intrinsic reality in question (*bi'l-ḥaqīqa al-dhātiyya*).'[89] We might be forgiven for asking: quelle différence? Some large part of the attraction to Ṭūsī of the doctrine of existence's considerationality may thus have been that it functioned similarly to support an ultra-transcendental theology, as found in Shahrastānī's Ismaili teaching, while maintaining, in view of existence's ambiguity, the formal operativity of Aristotelian metaphysics.

Conclusion

The polemical stridency marking almost every page of Ṭūsī's repost to Shahrastānī's critique of Ibn Sīnā is, surely, partly attributable to the author's highly exigent situation when writing it. He had newly entered the retinue of Hülagü who had been delegated by the Great Khan Möngke from as early as 650/1252 to extirpate the Nizārī state with which Ṭūsī had long been personally linked. Its destruction was duly carried out in 654/1256, together with the slaughter of a large

[89] Ṭūsī, *Maṣāri'*, p. 210.

proportion of its adherents. In 655/1257 alone, the year in which the last resident Nizārī Ismaili imam was put to death, the Mongol commander in Khurāsān, Ötegü-China, massacred some 12,000 of the Nizārīs of Quhistān.[90] It is precisely such events, then, which seem to be the immediate background to Ṭūsī's writing of the text. While the imperative for him to distance himself from the community is also evidenced by his retrospective disclaimers and substitutions, added to works which had been written and spread during his Nizārī period, it is the *Maṣāri*ʿ which comes the closest to being an outright recantation of Ismailism. Despite the technicality and abstraction of much of the discussion that it contains, the *Maṣāri*ʿ is philosophical discourse at its most heated and personal. The stinging assurance of Ṭūsī's arguments may sometimes be attributed to his having once subscribed, himself, to the teachings in question, whose problematic character he has only come to acknowledge in the course of time. A case in point is his harsh dismissal of Shahrastānī's recurring bid to raise the godhead above all relations of contrariety, as discussed above. It is to be noted that this is a reflex of Ismaili theology which Ṭūsī had himself displayed and apparently sincerely promoted in his Nizārī period.[91]

Though he bore responsibility for seminal texts in both the Nizārī Ismaili and Twelver Shiʿi traditions, strong consistency can be rescued from the outward turbulence of the Khwāja-i Ṭūs's religious

---

[90] Daftary, *The Ismāʿīlīs*, p. 429.

[91] See e.g., Ṭūsī, *Contemplation and Action*, § 27, p. 37. Note that even in advocating the principle here he underscores the extreme difficulty of upholding it – as if already sensitive to the failure of figures like Shahrastānī to do so truly. Ṭūsī thus subordinates even the *origination* of contrariety to God and attributes it to the Command (unlike Shahrastānī, for whom the origin of contrariety is God per se). He thus states that God is 'more glorious and exalted than the origin of opposites' [amended translation] (*aʿazz wa aʿlā az mansha'-i mutaqābilayn*). Ṭūsī commensurately stresses the total inaccessibility of the godhead itself to all frames of human analysis, even the model which declares God's transcendence of contraries. Thus transcendence itself must be purged of any untoward connotation of theological comprehension – in line with an Ismaili teaching of 'double transcendence', to which Shahrastānī never (to my current knowledge) had recourse. God, according to Ṭūsī is 'transcendental and transcends *even* this transcendence!' [amended translation] (*munazzah wa az īn tanzīh ham munazzah*).

alignments through noting the staunchness of his dedication to the Greek sciences and the Avicennan school of philosophy – the undoubted hub of his career and worldview.[92] Though hardly extensive, the *Maṣāriʿ* is a key example of that part of his corpus which defines Ṭūsī as a committed Avicennist, one of the series of works which involve his systematic defence of Ibn Sīnā's thought against one or other would-be challenger. Juxtaposing these texts allows the overall patterns and trends marking his defensive interpretation of Ibn Sīnā's philosophy to come into clearer focus. As exemplified in the relevant section above, the *Maṣāriʿ* is typical of Ṭūsī's distinctive approach to Ibn Sīnā's system, notably in its invocation of predicational ambiguity (*tashkīk*), the more specific invocation of the ambiguity of existence (*tashkīk al-wujūd*), and also the role reserved in it for 'considerations', especially in view of their intellectual, versus extramental, status (*iʿtibārāt ʿaqliyya*). The ambiguity of existence in particular is centrally significant to Ṭūsī's defence of Ibn Sīnā against Shahrastānī, since it counters the latter's teaching that existence is predicated equivocally – a stance incompatible with the whole Aristotelian metaphysical project as a rational science of being qua being. By adapting and extending these ideas, bequeathed him by Ibn Sīnā himself, Ṭūsī seems to have gained a wondrous instrument to defend, from many angles, the great philosopher's system against any criticism. Both his doctrine of ambiguous predication and his strong conceptualism in effect seal off Ibn Sīnā's formal system from its critics, while maintaining its definite claim to be constituted by judgements co-ordinate with the objective universe.

Finally, the *Maṣāriʿ*'s most buried element seems the most surprising and telling. It is seen that, instead of the usual dismissal of Shahrastānī's arguments as rooted in a *taʿlīmī* teaching unworthy of comparison with Avicennism and as more akin to the talk of poets and sermonisers, Ṭūsī sometimes prefers – principally in defending the cosmogonic principle 'only one proceeds from the One' – to

---

92 See e.g., Wilferd Madelung, 'Naṣīr al-dīn Ṭūsī's Ethics between Philosophy, Shiʿism and Sufism', in R.G. Hovannisian (ed.), *Ethics in Islam: Ninth Giorgio Levi della Vida Biennial Conference* (Malibu, 1985), pp. 85–101.

protest in favour of the *compatibility* of *taʿlīmī* teaching with that of Ibn Sīnā. It is striking, even bizarre, to find such a line of argument in this, of all Ṭūsī's texts and it is clearly a legacy here of his older agenda. In his decades as a scholar working within the Nizārī fold, he had been involved in precisely such a co-ordination of Avicennan and Ismaili ideas. This cut both ways: it has been shown that there are definite Ismaili features which intrude on his commentary on Ibn Sīnā's *Ishārāt*[93] and also other philosophical texts from his Nizārī period;[94] commensurately, there are also many pronouncedly Avicennan features in the Ṭūsian interpretation of Ismaili teaching in the *Taṣawwurāt*.[95] This second trend, represented by the *Taṣawwurāt*, has

---

[93] Landolt, 'Khwāja Naṣīr al-Dīn al-Ṭūsī (597/1201-672/1274), Ismāʿīlism, and *Ishrāqī* Philosophy'. See above, note 84.

[94] Madelung, 'Naṣīr al-dīn Ṭūsī's Ethics between Philosophy, Shiʿism and Sufism'. The article points out that a variety of Nizārī doctrines leave their trace on *Akhlāq-i Nāṣirī*, such as the alternation of *satr* (veiling) and *qiyāma* (resurrection), imamate, the divine support (*ta'yīd*) of the imam, the terminology of *nāṭiq* (speaker) and *asās* (foundation), society's perpetual need for the imamate, the idea of the successors to the prophets, the central notion of 'authoritative instruction' (*taʿlīm*), the love which is the due of the instructor (*muʿallim*) from the instructed individual (*mutaʿallim*), etc. Note however that the *Akhlāq-i Nāṣirī* is primarily indebted to Miskawayh rather than Ibn Sīnā.

[95] The *Taṣawwurāt* or *Rawḍa-yi taslīm* was apparently a record of Ṭūsī's lectures compiled by his associate Ḥasan-i Maḥmūd Bīrjandī (author of the *Dīwān-i qā'imiyyāt* and probably of *Haft bāb*) (see Ḥasan Maḥmūd Kātib, *Dīwān-i qā'imiyyāt*, ed. and tr. S.J. Badakhchani (Tehran, 2011), English preface, p. 11). The *Taṣawwurāt* is suffused with implicit allusions to Ibn Sīnā's thought, such that it is hard to disentangle the latter from the presentation of Nizārī Ismaili teachings. See Badakhchani, *Paradise of Submission*. The following could be mentioned amongst very numerous examples. In *Taṣawwur* 1, of the two approaches to affirming God's existence one is Avicennan and one Ismaili (p. 16); of the two arguments for God's unity one is Avicennan and one Ismaili (pp. 17–18); *Taṣawwur* 2 uses conceptualism and the intermediate, mental (i.e., *iʿtibārī*) status of 'contingency', which can thus function as a 'cause of receptivity for emanation' despite lacking extramental reality (p. 24); the principle 'only one proceeds from the One' is referred to, especially in *Taṣawwur* 3 (p. 29); *Taṣawwur* 8 declares that the human soul comprehends its essence without the mediation of any physical organ, thus hinting at Ibn Sīnā's famous 'flying man' argument (p. 35); *Taṣawwur* 9 employs the stock terminology of Avicennan noetics (pp. 38–39); *Taṣawwur* 15 promotes an Avicennan interpretation of posthumous reward and punishment as, respectively, the

a far-reaching significance, as in his next phase the Khwāja-i Ṭūs would go on to interpret Twelver teachings in a similarly heavily Avicennising manner, thereby constituting the arguable inceptor of this direction taken in Twelver theology which, having hitherto rejected it, now came so deeply to be characterised by it in its subsequent development. Ismailism, by contrast, was arguably *already* a form of Shiʿism which viewed itself as a 'philosophical religion' and was thus naturally predisposed to foster Ṭūsī's co-ordinative project earlier in his career.[96] Although in itself it remained the same fundamental impulse, circumstances now compelled Ṭūsī to promote and explore the agenda within Twelver Shiʿism, a reversion to the religious milieu of his birth and upbringing. The most intriguing prospect raised by the evidence in the *Maṣāriʿ* that some notions lingered from Ṭūsī's earlier Ismaili-Avicennan project is as follows. Despite the dramatic substitution of Twelver Shiʿism for Nizārī Ismailism in the period relevant to the text, it appears that Ṭūsī in fact had committed himself to certain ideas which could be taken to constitute the core of his own 'philosophical

---

result of the habit, acquired in life, of contemplating intelligibilia and engrossment in stimulation by perceptibilia (p. 59); *Taṣawwur* 16, in keeping with Avicennan modal ontology, reformulates incipiency (*ḥudūth*) in terms of intrinsic contingency (*imkān*), and thus urges that there is no real contradiction between the proposition that the world is incepted (*muḥdath*) in consideration of itself and pre-eternal (*qadīm*) in consideration of God (p. 67); *Taṣawwur* 23 proposes that within 'the order of the intellectual existent' (*kawn-i mawjūd-i ʿaqlānī*), in which all indistinct realities come to be seen as clear ones (*mutabāyanāt*), the 'degrees extend to infinity' (*dar ānjā darajāt nāmutanāhī mī shud*) (p. 107) – a proposition which apparently alludes to the ambiguity of existence qua rationate reality (*tashkīk al-wujūd*). Many other cases of the Avicennising direction of the text could doubtless be found.

96 This accords with a standard view of Ṭūsī's impact on Twelver thought. E.g.: 'From the point of view of [Twelver] Shiʿism his most important achievement was to incorporate philosophical concepts, from his study of Avicenna and other philosophers, into Shiʿi theology. Until this time philosophy had been viewed with suspicion as it was closely associated with Ismaili thought. But Naṣīru'd-Dīn, who had spent many years in the Ismaili stronghold of Alamūt, revolutionised Twelver Shiʿi theology (*kalām*) by expressing it in terms of concepts introduced from philosophy.' Moojan Momen, *An Introduction to Shiʿi Islam: The History and Doctrines of Twelver Shiʿism* (Oxford, 1985), p. 94.

religion', of which his formal exoteric identity, representing one or another form of Shiʿism, was in turn epiphenomenal. Although this nucleus of Ṭūsi's teachings was, post-1256, cut adrift from Nizārī Ismailism even to the point of expressing itself in a purportedly intensely hostile statement like the *Maṣāriʿ*, it was, ironically, unmistakably informed by Ismaili teachings as it had largely been generated in his Nizārī years.[97]

---

[97] It is noteworthy that the reverberation of certain Nizārī Ismaili ideas continues to be felt till the very end of Ṭūsī's career. It has been pointed out that in commenting, as late as 669/1271 (some three years before his death), on Fakhr al-Dīn al-Rāzī's *Muḥaṣṣal*, Ṭūsī is still evidently concerned to counter the author's supposedly distorted account of the doctrine of *taʿlīm*. Moreover, he even rejects there the Twelver doctrine of *badā'* (a divine retraction or 'change of mind' in regard to the succeeding imam's nomination by the preceding imam) – in line with the Ismaili denial of the possibility of such a retraction. Ṭūsī, *Contemplation and Action*, translator's introduction, p. 8, and note 33, p. 61.

PART TWO

AUTHORITY AND LAW

5

Ismaili and Sunni Elaborations of the Sources of Law: The *Kitāb al-Majālis wa'l-musāyarāt* by al-Qāḍī Abū Ḥanīfa al-Nuʿmān and the *Risāla* of al-Shāfiʿī: A Comparative Study

Agostino Cilardo
(Università degli Studi di Napoli 'L'Orientale')

Introduction

The *Kitāb al-Majālis wa'l-musāyarāt*[1] by al-Qāḍī al-Nuʿmān (d. 363/974) contains material on four of the Fatimid imams, al-Mahdī bi'llāh (r. 297–322/909–934), al-Qā'im bi-amr Allāh (r. 322–334/934–946),

[1] *Kitāb al-Majālis wa'l-musāyarāt*, ed. al-Ḥabīb al-Faqī, Ibrāhīm Shabbūḥ and Muḥammad al-Yaʿlāwī (Beirut, 1996). For a description of this work, see Carl Brockelmann, *Geschichte der arabischen Litteratur*, 2 vols (Weimar, 1898–1902); 3 Supplementband (Leiden, 1937–1942); Suppl., vol. 1, p. 325; Fuat Sezgin, *Geschichte des arabischen Schrifttums*, Band I (Leiden, 1967), p. 577, no. 6: *al-Majālis wa'l-musāyarāt wa'l-mawāqif wa'l-tawqīʿāt*; Asaf ʿAlī Asghar Fyzee, 'Qadi an-Nuʿman. The Fatimid Jurist and Author', *Journal of the Royal Asiatic Society* (1934), pp. 1–32, pp. 18, 30–31; Wladimir Ivanow, *Ismaili Literature. A Bibliographical Survey* (a second amplified edition of *A Guide to Ismaili Literature*, London, 1933) (Tehran, 1963), p. 35, no. 79; Muʿizz Goriawala, *A Descriptive Catalogue of the Fyzee Collection of Ismaili Manuscripts* (Bombay, 1965), p. 35; Ismail K. Poonawala, *Biobibliography of Ismāʿīlī Literature* (Malibu, CA, 1977), pp. 61–62, no. 23. An MS, in two parts, is held at The Ismaili Institute; *Muqaddima* to *Kitāb al-Majālis wa'l-musāyarāt*, p. 19; Delia Cortese, *Ismaili and other Arabic Manuscripts. A Descriptive Catalogue of Manuscripts in the Library of the Institute of Ismaili Studies* (London, 2000), p. 52; Farhad Daftary, *Ismaili Literature. A Bibliography of Sources and Studies* (London, 2004), p. 144.

al-Manṣūr bi'llāh (r. 334–341/946–953) and al-Muʿizz (r. 341–365/953–975), as well as on their domestic and foreign policies, and their adherents and agents. But it is not only a work of history (*kitāb ta'rīkh*) and a biography (*kitāb sīra*), including lectures, anecdotes and accounts of the lives of the Fatimid caliphs and the organisation of the Fatimid state; it is also a work dealing with articles of faith (sg. *ʿaqīda*) and ethics (*adab*). In sum, it is a work of an encyclopaedic nature, not a strictly legal work. Thus, we hardly find in this work a legal reasoning based on the Qur'an and *sunna*, rather it includes apodictic statements grounded on the moral and legal authority of the imam himself.

In the Introduction to the *Kitāb al-Majālis*, al-Nuʿmān declares that he has already compiled many books on the authority of the Fatimid caliphs al-Mahdī, al-Qā'im and al-Manṣūr.[2] For instance, he also composed the *Sīrat al-Muʿizz li-Dīn Allāh*,[3] which covers a period from the time when al-Muʿizz attained the supreme authority of the imamate up to the time of writing. Al-Nuʿmān specifies the contents of this new book, which includes what he has heard from al-Muʿizz, and what he has recorded either during sessions or on other occasions. Moreover, al-Nuʿmān says that he wishes to refer to what he learned from various written sources, such as reports or letters. He states that even if he is not transmitting this information literally, he remains true to its meaning, neither adding nor removing anything.

As far as one can tell, the content of the *Kitāb al-Majālis* has been little studied so far. Farhat Dachraoui[4] was interested in a single historical event discussed in this work, while Y.S. Taherali[5] only provides a brief summary of its subject-matter. Therefore, the *Kitāb al-Majālis* deserves a closer study. The focus of attention here will be on the following issues, in a comparative perspective: who the *ūlu'l-amr* were; the concepts of wisdom (*ʿilm*) in the work, as well as those of *ʿāmma*

---

[2] *Majālis*, pp. 43–48.

[3] Al-Nuʿmān discusses this *Sīra* in more detail in another passage. See *Majālis*, pp. 462–463, no. 241.

[4] Farhat Dachraoui, 'La captivité d'Ibn Wāsūl, le rebelle de Sidjilmassa, d'après le Cadi an-Nuʿmān', *Cahiers de Tunisie*, 4 (1956), pp. 295–299.

[5] Y.S. Taherali, '"Kitab al-Majalis wa al-Musairat" of Qadi Numan', *Sind University Research Journal, Arts Series, Humanities and Social Sciences*, I (1961), pp. 5–15.

and *khāṣṣa*; the sources of law; the qualifications necessary for caliphs and imams; the role of the *faqīh*; and the analysis of three case-studies.

The ideas expressed in the *Kitāb al-Majālis* should be compared with those elaborated by al-Nuʿmān in his work specifically devoted to the sources of law, *Kitāb Ikhtilāf uṣūl al-madhāhib*.[6] An outline of the Ismaili legal theories expressed in this latter work was briefly presented by Fyzee,[7] and more broadly by Lokhandwalla.[8] The *Kitāb Ikhtilāf* has been recently edited and translated by Devin J. Stewart.[9]

The Ismaili theories will be compared with the elaboration of the sources of law by Abū ʿAbd Allāh Muḥammad al-Shāfiʿī (d. 204/820), in his *Risāla*,[10] which in general represents the Sunni view. Al-Shāfiʿī's *Risāla*, Majid Khadduri points out, constitutes 'a novel work in the literature of Islamic law'; for this al-Shāfiʿī is given 'a name as the founder of the science of *uṣūl al-fiqh* (roots or sources of the law)'.[11] According to Khadduri, 'The *Risāla* appears to be the first complete and well-organised survey of the *uṣūl*, their interrelationship, and how the detailed rules and decisions were derived from the authoritative sources.'[12] The *Risāla* had a great influence on later jurists. As Khadduri says, 'The originality of the book lies in its new departure in the

---

6 Al-Qāḍī al-Nuʿmān, *Kitāb Ikhtilāf uṣūl al-madhāhib*, edited with a critical introduction by S.T. Lokhandwalla (Simla, 1972); ed. Muṣṭafā Ghālib (3rd ed., Beirut, 1983).

7 A.A.A. Fyzee, 'Shīʿī Legal Theories', in M. Khadduri and H.J. Liebesny (ed.), *Law in the Middle East*, vol. 1 (Washington, DC, 1955), pp. 113–131.

8 S.T. Lokhandwalla, Introduction to his edition of the *Kitāb Ikhtilāf uṣūl al-madhāhib*, pp. 42–133.

9 *The Disagreements of the Jurists. A Manual of Islamic Legal Theory* (New York – London: New York University Press, 2015). On the relationship between this work and the analogous work of Ibn Dāʾūd, see Devin J. Stewart, 'Muḥammad b. Dāʾūd al-Ẓāhirī's Manual of Jurisprudence, *al-Wuṣūl ilā Maʿrifat al-Uṣūl*', *Studies in Islamic Law and Society*, 15 (2002), pp. 99–142.

10 Abū ʿAbd Allāh Muḥammad al-Shāfiʿī, *al-Risāla*, ed. Aḥmad Muḥammad Shākir (Cairo: Maṭbaʿat Muṣṭafā al-Bābī al-Ḥalabī, 1357/1938); English trans. by Majid Khadduri as *Risāla fī uṣūl al-fiqh. Treatise on the Foundations of Islamic Jurisprudence* (2nd ed., Cambridge, 1997).

11 Trans. Khadduri, *Treatise*, p. 40.

12 Khadduri, *Treatise*, p. 41.

study of jurisprudence. From Shāfiʿī's time onward, the *Risāla* became a textbook for students of Muslim jurisprudence. It was carefully studied by Shāfiʿī's followers as well as by the followers of other schools of law.'[13]

Who are the *ūlu'l-amr* (the Ones in Authority)?

The origins of the division between Sunnis and Shiʿis concerns the question of who was entitled to succeed Muhammad as the head of the community: 'O ye who believe! Obey God and obey the Messenger and those charged with authority (*ūlu'l-amr*) among you' (Q. 4:59).[14] God and Muhammad obviously are the supreme authorities and any dispute must be solved by having recourse to them. This implies that any dispute should be referred to God and settled on the basis of the commandment of God corresponding to this case, if this commandment is known. If the divine commandment is not known, then the Prophet Muhammad should be asked: 'If ye differ in anything among yourselves, refer it to God and His Messenger' (Q. 4:59).[15] The question is: Who are the *ūlu'l-amr*?

The Sunni View

Divergences existed about the identity of the 'the Ones in Authority'. Following al-Shāfiʿī, some scholars held that this expression referred

[13] Khadduri, *Treatise*, pp. 41–42. There are valuable works on the Sunni concept of the sources of law. See, for instance, Wael B. Hallaq, *Law and Legal Theory in Classical and Medieval Islam* (Brookfield, VT, 1995); and his *A History of Islamic Legal Theories: An Introduction to Sunni Usul al-Fiqh* (Cambridge, 1999). Hallaq also published books devoted to the early Islamic period, including some references to the sources of law. See, for instance, *The Formation of Islamic Law* (Aldershot, 2004); *The Origins and Evolution of Islamic Law* (Cambridge, 2005); *Sharīʿa: Theory, Practice, Transformations* (Cambridge and New York, 2009); and *An Introduction to Islamic Law* (Cambridge, 2009).

[14] Here and below the translations of the Qur'anic text follow Abdullah Yusuf Ali, *The Holy Qur'an*.

[15] *Risāla*, pp. 80–81, no. 264; trans. Khadduri, *Treatise*, p. 113.

to the commanders of Muhammad's army.[16] In a more general sense, 'the Ones in Authority' were those appointed for a specific office.[17] Power was exercised in various regions by the governors dispatched by Muhammad.[18] Obviously, Muhammad sent men to the provinces who were well known for their veracity.[19] The same applies to the commanders of the Prophet's military expeditions.[20] Muhammad was careful to choose well-known men both as his representatives and as commanders.[21]

The obedience of governors was ensured by the fact that Muhammad sent them orders of permission and prohibition on a continuous basis, and none of them failed to carry them out because the Prophet sent only messengers who were known as truthful, and whose veracity could be certified by the local people.[22]

A more sensitive issue concerns the transmission of power after Muhammad's death and the question of who would then be head of the community. In al-Shāfiʿī's view, Muhammad and his successors are on equal footing with regard to the exercise of power.[23] This means that power belongs to the community as a whole and is exercised by those who are appointed for this purpose. Thus, al-Shāfiʿī argued, this is how Abū Bakr was chosen to be caliph; then Abū Bakr designated ʿUmar; in his turn ʿUmar appointed a council charged with the task of selecting a man whose specific object was to designate the next caliph. Abd al-Raḥmān b. ʿAwf was selected by the council and he chose ʿUthmān b. ʿAffān to be the next caliph.[24] The authority of governors, of judges, and other officials as well, derived from the caliph. Therefore, they handed down decisions, had their decisions executed, and imposed penalties. Their decisions were carried out after them, and

---

16 *Risāla*, p. 79, no. 260; trans. Khadduri, *Treatise*, p. 112.

17 *Risāla*, p. 80, no. 263; trans. Khadduri, *Treatise*, p. 113.

18 *Risāla*, p. 416, no. 1137; trans. Khadduri, *Treatise*, p. 258.

19 *Risāla*, p. 417, no. 1143; trans. Khadduri, *Treatise*, p. 259.

20 *Risāla*, p. 417, no. 1144; trans. Khadduri, *Treatise*, p. 259.

21 *Risāla*, p. 418, no. 1149; trans. Khadduri, *Treatise*, p. 259.

22 *Risāla*, p. 419, no. 1151; trans. Khadduri, *Treatise*, p. 260.

23 *Risāla*, p. 419, no. 1154; trans. Khadduri, *Treatise*, p. 260.

24 *Risāla*, pp. 419–420, no. 1155; trans. Khadduri, *Treatise*, p. 260.

these decisions were transmitted as narratives handed down from them.[25]

The Ismaili View

The transmission of authority at Muhammad's death is seen in a quite different way by the Ismailis. The Companions and Successors are not even mentioned in the *Majālis*. Instead, many passages of this work highlight the primacy and prerogatives of the imams. The imams claim their direct descent from Muhammad through his daughter Fāṭima and his cousin and son-in-law ʿAlī b. Abī Ṭālib. They also claim their right to inherit their ancestors' property and their imamate as well. Even if they are ready to give up their rights over property, the imams require their claim to imamate to be recognised. This was the view of al-Muʿizz with reference to the expropriation of the oasis of Fadak that belonged to Fāṭima by Abū Bakr. In fact, al-Muʿizz, while pointing out his right to inherit from Muhammad, considered the acknowledgement of the transmission of the imamate from Muhammad to ʿAlī and the leadership of imams after ʿAlī as the fundamental principle of the tradition. But – al-Muʿizz observed – the Ismailis' opponents usurped the right of the imams and took their place. These opponents care about material possessions, such as Fadak, and fail to mention the most important issue for the Ismailis, that is, the foundation of the Fatimid claim to the imamate.[26]

In any case, according to al-Muʿizz, the pre-eminence of the imams cannot be equated with the honours attributed to kings. In fact, when al-Nuʿmān kissed the ground in front of Imam al-Manṣūr, al-Manṣūr reprimanded him. When al-Nuʿmān referred this episode to al-Muʿizz, he told him not to follow the orders of al-Manṣūr, and explained his decision saying that kissing the ground in this case is not an act of worship, as it is for the kings of Ethiopia, whom he called Mazdeans.[27]

---

25 *Risāla*, p. 420, no. 1156; trans. Khadduri, *Treatise*, p. 260.

26 *Majālis*, p. 431, no. 228.

27 *Majālis*, pp. 57–60, no. 6.

Reactions of al-Muʿizz on two Contrasting Occasions

A Sunni Scholar Recognises the Supremacy of the Imams

In a speech in the *Majālis* on the persistence of unjust people in supporting falsehood, al-Muʿizz highlights how 'our' (i.e. the imams') right is not hidden from the people, because the imams act with justice towards them; but the religious behaviour of the imams is veiled from their opponents. Only ignorance can cause this situation. However, some opponents are more willing to listen to their reasons, as an interesting debate about their supremacy between al-Muʿizz, al-Nuʿmān and an anonymous Sunni scholar shows. This dialogue is a masterpiece which demonstrates, better than any other theoretical discourse, the social behaviour and the inter-confessional context of the age.

Al-Muʿizz presents himself to his opponent as an open-hearted individual and constantly pressurises him to recognise the rights of the imams. The interlocutor admits their rights and al-Muʿizz does not doubt that it is a true admission, not flattery or dissimulation. Al-Muʿizz then asks him, 'What now prevents you from rejecting your view and accepting what you have recognised?' The Sunni scholar does not reply.

Al-Nuʿmān undertakes to explain why the Sunni scholar was not able to openly accept the pre-eminence of the imams. As regards his community, social conditioning has a preponderant relevance for him. In fact, the Sunni scholar was one of the leaders of it, and he is renowned for his knowledge. This knowledge brought him an eminent position among the Sunnis. If he became one of the supporters of the imams, the Sunnis would reject and despise him, and he would lose his social standing. As regards the Ismailis, the Sunni scholar's knowledge of Ismaili doctrine was not yet at a satisfactory level. In fact, he has only recently been introduced to it. Al-Nuʿmān's discourse indicates that there were other Sunnis who had previously embraced the Ismaili faith, because al-Nuʿmān, addressing the anonymous scholar, says that he is not like those Sunnis who preceded him. In fact, he is still hesitating over his decision. He is neither in the position of the one who actually belongs to Ismailism nor has retained his rank among the Sunnis.

The response of the Sunni scholar is instructive. It reveals his fear of the Umayyads, who followed the Mālikī doctrine, thus disclosing his identity as a Mālikī scholar. In fact, he replied, 'God save me from the tongues of the Banū Hāshim!' So in spite of this discussion with al-Muʿizz, and in spite of his long association with the imams and the abundant grace that they granted him, that man died with only a limited understanding of the knowledge proper to the imams. The proof of God convinced him only slightly. The bitter conclusion of al-Nuʿmān was that, despite any statement made by the imam, who is the *walī* of God, faith comes only from God.[28]

The Supremacy of the Imams Contested

Al-Muʿizz harshly criticised those who, although appointed by the imams to exercise authority, do not accept their pre-eminence. He also denounced those who blamed the imams for having crossed the limit of the rank set by God, thus departing from the creed of their ancestors, compromising the mission entrusted to them by God aimed at reviving truths corrupted by falsehood and the traditions modified by innovators.[29]

The charges against the imams were enunciated by the North African rebel *dāʿī* Ibn Wāsūl when he was brought before al-Muʿizz as a prisoner.[30] The rumours circulating in North Africa, as Ibn Wāsūl confirms, were that the imams had rejected the prophethood of Muhammad and claimed it after him for themselves; they rejected his Prophetic *sunna* and the *sharīʿa* and invited others to do the same.

Al-Muʿizz cursed those who said this and denied this rumour. Al-Muʿizz identified those responsible for these rumours as the Umayyads calling them Banū ʿAbd al-Shams. Al-Muʿizz says, 'They treat us as enemies and loathe us on the grounds that one of them said, "We . . . behaved friendlily as you did, until you said, 'A prophet came out from us!' But, for God's sake, we will not accept it and will not acknowledge [this claim]".'

Al-Muʿizz obviously rejects these rumours. He refuses to link the claim of imamate to the rejection of the *sharīʿa*. He believes, in fact,

---

[28] *Majālis*, p. 365, no. 191. Al-Muʿizz claims the central role among the imams; cf. *Majālis*, p. 500, no. 259.

[29] *Majālis*, pp. 548–550, no. 285.

[30] cf. *Majālis*, pp. 214, 217, 591.

that the task of the imams is precisely to apply the religious law. Al-Muʿizz wonders, 'If we were to invite [people] to withdraw from the *sharīʿa* of our ancestor Muhammad, who else can be called on to preserve it and to adhere to it?'

Another question concerns the right of the imams to succeed Muhammad as leaders of the *umma*. Al-Muʿizz points out precisely what the role of imams is: God made them inherit the honour, glory and dignity of Muhammad and has established them leaders of the *umma* after him. God made it compulsory for people to obey the imams after Muhammad just as it was mandatory to obey Muhammad during his life. The imams certainly tell the truth, according to the word of God: 'Obey God and obey the Messenger and those charged with authority among you' (Q. 4:59). Al-Muʿizz continues to affirm that 'we are those charged with authority whom God has ordered the human beings to obey; we are the guardians of memory to whom God has commanded [the people] to ask questions, despite those who deny it.' The special rank of the imams is justified by al-Muʿizz as a favour from God to them and His grace to them, which can only be obtained with God's help. Al-Muʿizz recognises that this is God's decree. For this, the imams thank God. Only an arrogant impostor would attempt to reach this degree, and only an unbeliever could wish to take it from the imams. This conception of the role of imams is, according to al-Muʿizz, in line with the most authentic tradition of 'our ancestor Muhammad'.[31]

Wisdom

The term 'wisdom' (*ḥikma*) is mentioned several times in the Qurʾan: 'He sent down to you the Book and Wisdom (*ḥikma*), for your instruction' (Q. 2:231); 'God hath sent down to thee the Book and Wisdom' (Q. 4:113); 'And recite what is rehearsed to you in your homes, of the Signs of God and His wisdom' (Q. 33:34); 'to instruct them in Scripture and Wisdom' (Q. 62:2). In the Qurʾanic context, what does the word wisdom refer to? The interpretation of this term is relevant in highlighting the issue of the sources of law.

---

31 *Majālis*, pp. 414–417, no. 216.

The Sunni View

The reasoning of al-Shāfiʿī (d. 204/820) adheres strictly to the wording of the Qurʾan. On the one hand, he notes that God has placed Muhammad in relation to His religion, His commands and His Book, in a position made clear by Him as a distinguished standard of His religion by imposing the duty of obedience to Him as well as prohibiting disobedience to Him.[32] On the other hand, al-Shāfiʿī points out that the term 'wisdom' appears next to the word 'Qurʾan' in different Qurʾanic verses. The word Qurʾan is mentioned first then the word wisdom. Al-Shāfiʿī's conclusion is that wisdom must be identified with the prophetic *sunna*. 'Thus', al-Shāfiʿī continues, 'it is not permissible for Wisdom to be called here anything else but the *sunna* of the Apostle of God. For Wisdom is closely linked to the Book of God, and God has imposed the duty of obedience to His Apostle, and imposed on men the duty to obey his orders. So it is not permissible to regard anything as a duty save what is set forth in the Qurʾan and the *sunna* of His Apostle.'[33]

The Companions (*ṣaḥāba*) and Successors (*tābiʿūn*) in the Sunni System of Law

If wisdom is identified by al-Shāfiʿī with the Prophetic *sunna*, what is then the role of the Companions and Successors (the first and second generations after Muhammad)? In other words, what value has their *sunna* as a source of law? The *ṣaḥāba* and *tābiʿūn* played a substantial part in the formation of the Sunni system of law, as is emphasised in a speech made by ʿUmar at al-Jābiyya, a village on the outskirts of Damascus, in 17/638. This *ḥadīth* is particularly important from the Sunni point of view, because in it Muhammad himself gives support to the idea that it is the duty of all Muslims to follow the legal views of the Companions and Successors.

> ʿUmar said: 'Muhammad stood among us by an order from God, as I am now standing among you, and said: "Believe my Companions, then those who succeed them [the Successors], and after that those who succeed the Successors [the Successors of

32 *Risāla*, p. 73, no. 236; trans. Khadduri, *Treatise*, p. 109.

33 *Risāla*, p. 78, nos. 252–255; trans. Khadduri, *Treatise*, pp. 111–112.

> Successors, the third generation]; but after them untruthfulness will prevail when people will swear [in support of their saying] without having been asked to swear, and will testify without having been asked to testify.'"[34]

Quite apart from the polemical nature of this tradition, it implies that traditions transmitted on the authority of Companions are regarded as a source of law. However, the opinion of a Companion would be accepted if anything related to it is found in the Qur'an, or in the established *sunna* or in consensus (*ijmāʿ*), or any analogical deduction (*qiyās*).[35] But al-Shāfiʿī notes, one seldom finds an opinion of one Companion that is not contradicted by that of another.[36] This observation brings out some basic questions. One of them is: What happens if the Companions disagree?[37] Al-Shāfiʿī's solution leaves much room for the exercise of personal choice by the scholar. In fact, those opinions which agree with the Qur'an, the *sunna* or consensus, or which are the soundest according to the rules of analogy, should be accepted.[38] According to what criteria is this choice made? Undoubtedly, the jurist plays a key role here.

Another basic question arises concerning the opinion of a Companion, with which it is not known whether any of the other Companions agreed or disagreed. Is there any evidence for accepting it, based on the Qur'an or a *sunna* or a ruling, such that the evidence constitutes a narrative (*khabar*)?[39] Al-Shāfiʿī points out that nothing is found concerning this matter in the Book or in any established *sunna*, but he notes that scholars can accept the opinion of a single Companion on one occasion and reject it on another. Scholars also differ concerning some of the opinions of a single Companion.[40] This implies that a scholar is free either to agree or disagree with such opinions, based on his own sound judgement.

---

34 *Risāla*, pp. 473–474, no. 1315; trans. Khadduri, *Treatise*, p. 286.

35 *Risāla*, p. 598, no. 1810; trans. Khadduri, *Treatise*, p. 350.

36 *Risāla*, p. 598, no. 1811; trans. Khadduri, *Treatise*, p. 350.

37 *Risāla*, p. 596, no. 1805; trans. Khadduri, *Treatise*, p. 349.

38 *Risāla*, p. 597, no. 1806; trans. Khadduri, *Treatise*, p. 349.

39 *Risāla*, p. 597, no. 1807; trans. Khadduri, *Treatise*, p. 350.

40 *Risāla*, p. 597, no. 1808; trans. Khadduri, *Treatise*, p. 350.

Problems relating to traditions going back to the Successors are even more sensitive. Al-Shāfiʿī accepts interrupted traditions from Muhammad transmitted on the authority of one of the Successors who saw one of the Companions, although the tradition has to be scrutinised in three ways. Firstly, one should examine the manner of the transmission of a tradition. If the *isnād* was formed of trustworthy traditionists who had related from Muhammad traditions with a similar meaning, this would have been an indication of the soundness of the tradition. Secondly, even if a Successor is the only one to relate a tradition and no one else is found to support him with a similar one, the tradition related by a single Successor should be accepted. Thirdly, whether or not another trustworthy traditionist, who is not included in the *isnād* of a tradition under consideration, agrees with him should also be considered. This would be, in fact, an indication of the soundness of the tradition, although this sort of indication is weaker than the former ones. In case such an indication is not found, the traditions from the Successors are considered as a mere information, which may or may not be accepted.[41]

The binding force of a tradition dating back to a Successor also depends on the degree of closeness that he had with the Companions. Al-Shāfiʿī distinguishes between well-known Successors who knew many Companions and those Successors who knew only few Companions. He observes that such a distinction is required because it was impossible for those who had never met most of the Companions to relate traditions on their authority.[42] Lastly, as far as those who came after the leading Successors who often saw some of the Companions of Muhammad are concerned, al-Shāfiʿī does not grant them any value as a source of law.[43]

In sum, according to al-Shāfiʿī, what has been summarised above is the normative framework within which traditions transmitted on the authority of Muhammad, the Companions, the Successors, and the Successors' Successors, can be either accepted or rejected as sources of

41 *Risāla*, pp. 461–463, nos. 1264–1269; trans. Khadduri, *Treatise*, p. 279.

42 *Risāla*, p. 467, nos. 1285–1286; trans. Khadduri, *Treatise*, p. 281.

43 *Risāla*, p. 465, no. 1277; trans. Khadduri, *Treatise*, pp. 280–281.

law.[44] As it is easy to see, there is a wide range of scholarly discretion in this elaboration.

The Ismaili View

While al-Shāfiʿī confines wisdom to Muhammad, the Ismailis extend its validity to the imams.[45] Al-Muʿizz establishes the theological grounds in order to justify the special rank of the imams and their superiority over ordinary human beings. The origin of their learning and wisdom lies in the fact that they were in the mind of God before the creation of Adam. When God created Adam, Adam looked up and saw written on the support of the Throne: 'There is no god but God, Muhammad is His Messenger.' Then God confirmed it to ʿAlī and his successors. For this reason, the imams are of pious and noble descent, chosen and excellent, the progeny of Muhammad, the Lord of the Prophets and the Seal of the Messengers. 'Our right', al-Muʿizz says, 'is not denied except by the obstinate; it is not rejected except by a presumptious; it is not unknown except to the ignorant; only an unjust person can deny this right. We have been privileged because of the Prophet and we are his legatees (sg. *waṣī*); we inherited the imamate and we have been given dignity (*karāma*).'[46]

On these theological grounds, al-Qāḍī al-Nuʿmān sets the following basic hermeneutic principle:

> The one who hears a statement from the Friends of God (*awliyāʾ Allāh*, i.e. the imams) must consider it a rule (*ḥaqq*) to follow; he should not avoid following it and should not disregard it. In fact, there is wisdom in everything they say. For those whom God guides to the knowledge of the real meaning of these words, for those to whom God shows his face, to whom He grants His knowledge and whom He lets take advantage of it there is a benefit in every word they say.[47] Every statement of the Friends of

[44] *Risāla*, pp. 459–460, no. 1254; trans. Khadduri, *Treatise*, p. 278.

[45] The imams occupy a special rank in the field of wisdom; cf. *Majālis*, pp. 501–503.

[46] *Majālis*, pp. 209–210, no. 103.

[47] *Majālis*, pp. 54–55, no. 4; p. 55.

> God is in agreement with the statements of God and His Messenger, for those who can understand it and reflect on it.[48]

Al-Muʿizz emphasises the pre-eminence of the imams as the Friends of God, as the custodians and the true interpreters of the Qurʾan and the *sunna*.[49] Al-Muʿizz tells al-Nuʿmān:

> We are the doors to God and the means to reach Him. Anyone who approaches us will have a favourable reception; anyone who solicits our favour will obtain it; anyone who pleads for our intercession will receive it; anyone who asks for our forgiveness, his sin will be forgiven. However, the one who committed a sin and the one who did not commit it cannot be equated. For this, there are degrees in the afterlife. God punishes the sins in this world as He wants, and this is His lighter punishment.[50]

Al-Muʿizz draws a direct line from revelation and Muhammad to the imams. In fact, if the decisions of the imams acquire a binding force it is because, as al-Muʿizz states, 'The words of the Friends of God (*awliyāʾ Allāh*) are derived from the Book of God and the statements of His Messenger. Whoever hears something of their speech cannot find in it anything different from the words of the Qurʾan and those of the Prophet.'[51]

Knowledge (*ʿilm*)[52]

The Sunni View

Al-Shāfiʿī focuses exclusively on the knowledge which Muslims should possess. The different levels of knowledge only depend on the recipients, who, however, do not possess any special prerogative.

---

48 *Majālis*, pp. 55–57, no. 5; p. 57.

49 *Majālis*, pp. 69–72, no. 8.

50 *Majālis*, pp. 72–75, no. 9; p. 72.

51 *Majālis*, pp. 72–75, no. 9; p. 75.

52 Al-Shāfiʿī devotes a chapter to this issue titled *Bāb al-ʿilm* ('On Legal Knowledge'), pp. 357–369, nos. 961–997; pp. 81–87, nos. 29–53. The subject-matter of this chapter is dealt with more fully in Shāfiʿī's *Kitāb al-Umm*, vol. 7, pp. 250–265.

He distinguishes between three degrees of *ʿilm*. Thus, people are divided into three classes. Their status in learning is determined according to their rank in knowledge.[53]

The first degree of *ʿilm* pertains to common people, and no one who is adult and sane should ignore it. It includes general provisions, such as the duty of the five daily prayers, fasting during the month of Ramaḍān, performing the pilgrimage, paying the legal alms, the prohibition on interest/usury (*ribā*), on unlawful intercourse (*zinā*), on murder, theft and drinking wine. Such knowledge is obligatory for all Muslims. This kind of knowledge may be found textually in the Qurʾan, or may be generally known among Muslims. People will transmit this knowledge to each other and ascribe it to Muhammad without questioning this ascription or its binding force upon them. It is a kind of knowledge which admits to no error neither in its transmission nor in its interpretation; questioning it is not permitted.[54]

The second kind of *ʿilm* consists of the detailed duties and rules that are obligatory for men, concerning which nothing is said either in the Book of God or in the *sunna*. Whenever a *sunna* exists in this case, it is of the kind related by only a few authorities, not by people in general, and it is subject to different interpretations derived from analogy.[55] These kinds of duties are not obligatory for everyone, but the one who fulfils them performs a supererogatory act, and the one who neglects them does not fall into error. One instance is the fulfilment of *jihād*, which can be obligatory for all able-bodied believers, exempting no one (*farḍ ʿayn*), just like prayer, the pilgrimage and payment of alms, if it is a defensive *jihād*. However, *jihād* is a collective duty (*farḍ kifāya*) if it is an offensive *jihād*. Those who perform *jihād* in the war against the polytheists will fulfil the duty and receive the supererogatory merit.[56]

The third kind of *ʿilm* derives from a narration (*khabar*) or from analogy. The common people have no access to this kind of

---

53 *Risāla*, p. 19, no. 44; trans. Khadduri, *Treatise*, p. 65.

54 *Risāla*, pp. 357–359, nos. 961–965; trans. Khadduri, *Treatise*, pp. 81–82.

55 *Risāla*, p. 359, no. 967; trans. Khadduri, *Treatise*, p. 82.

56 *Risāla*, p. 361, no. 973; trans. Khadduri, *Treatise*, p. 84.

knowledge, nor is it available to all specialists. But those who do acquire it should not neglect it. If one person acquires it, then others can be relieved from the duty of acquiring it; but those who acquire it will be rewarded.[57]

The Ismaili View

The Ismailis have a quite different concept of *ʿilm*. It pertains to the imams and is transmitted from one imam to another.[58] This enables each imam to authentically teach knowledge. So, al-Muʿizz, while speaking about the urgency to search out knowledge (*ṭalab al-ʿilm*), turned to a group of *walī*s who were silent, urging them to pose questions related to religion, and said, 'We have an appropriate response and unequivocal knowledge for everything you ask.'

What is more, the imams possess both the exoteric and esoteric knowledge which was derived from Muhammad, and then was transmitted to ʿAlī and his successors. Al-Muʿizz insists that knowledge comes only from the imams,[59] because they see what others do not see (*innā la-nanẓuru min ḥaythu lā yanẓurūna*).[60] God has reserved to the imams knowledge and wisdom.[61] They are also the source of the secular sciences, like mathematics.[62] It is reported that al-Manṣūr was an expert in astrology (*najāma*), though al-Muʿizz was not.[63]

Thus, the unique holders of all knowledge are the imams, who have the special prerogative of infallibility, although they are human beings.[64] People want to learn the religious knowledge from al-Muʿizz,[65]

---

57 *Risāla*, pp. 359–360, nos. 968–971; trans. Khadduri, *Treatise*, p. 82.

58 On the knowledge transmitted from an imam to another and their claim to the imamate, see also *Majālis*, pp. 220–225. Books were transmitted from al-Manṣūr to al-Muʿizz; cf. *Majālis*, pp. 239–240.

59 *Majālis*, pp. 303–305, no. 157.

60 *Majālis*, pp. 251–252, no. 124.

61 *Majālis*, pp. 312–313, no. 162.

62 *Majālis*, pp. 295–296, no. 154.

63 *Majālis*, pp. 131–132, no. 72.

64 *Majālis*, p. 286, no.145.

65 *Majālis*, pp. 343–344, no. 177.

who is happy to see that the people are in search of it.[66] Al-Muʿizz states that knowledge must be taken only from the imams; and al-Nuʿmān sets down this knowledge in writing only after the imam has given his approval.[67] In another passage, where al-Muʿizz reiterates that knowledge comes only from the imams, al-Nuʿmān mentions *Daʿāʾim al-Islām*, and says that this work was read and commented on by the imam.[68]

> Verily, al-Muʿizz says, the proofs, the evidence, the strength and the confirmation are to be found in the proofs (*ḥujaj*) during the life of the [imams] Friends of God (*awliyāʾ*) . . . they will gradually increase to the state of perfection. As the appointed time of an imam approaches, the reasons of his proof strengthen and his signs are manifest. This is based on what was related by Jaʿfar b. Muhammad, who said, "Alī was the scholar of this *umma*, and we transmit from each other his knowledge in a hereditary way.'

This prerogative gives al-Muʿizz the certainty that no one will ever destroy the imams as long as there is someone from the family of Muhammad who has knowledge similar to Muhammad's.[69]

However, the imams never laid claim to the prophetic mission, as they were accused of doing by extremists and the ignorant. Al-Muʿizz points out that he has never made this claim for himself and no one has never heard it from him. Al-Muʿizz, using a plural 'we' on behalf of all the imams, pointed out that the imams are created as human beings having authority (*marbūbūn*) over other human beings; they possess only the knowledge that they have been taught, and which came to them through their forebear, Muhammad, pertaining to what God entrusted him with and let him inherit, then entrusted to his successors. The imams divulge Muhammad's knowledge and what is hidden only to those people that Muhammad likes and those whom he wants to know it. The imams do not claim the prophethood and the

---

66 *Majālis*, pp. 344–345, no. 179; pp. 351–353, no. 182.

67 *Majālis*, p. 297, no. 155.

68 *Majālis*, pp. 305–307, no. 158.

69 *Majālis*, pp. 265–268, no. 133; p. 267.

Prophetic mission, but they are in charge of the imamate; what is allowed and forbidden is established in the Qur'an, and in its provisions obedience to the imams is enjoined upon human beings. Those who know the imams, know God; those who are ignorant of them, are ignorant of God. The imams are the evidence of His wisdom and are in charge of exercising His power over His servants.[70]

All knowledge is concentrated in the persons of the imams, so much so that al-Muʿizz asks, 'What should one expect of the knowledge except what has been transmitted by our forefathers and ancestors through those Friends of God (*awliyā'*) and servants who are intermediaries between God and people.'

The furthest from knowledge and the closest to ignorance are those who take as knowledge whatever has not been certified by the imams and who assume wisdom to be whatever has not been taken from them.

> How great is the perdition of those who contradict us, but only admire themselves, which prevents them from addressing questions to us, just as God clearly commanded them to do: 'And before thee also the messengers We sent were but men, to whom We granted inspiration: if ye realise this not, ask of those who possess the Message' (Q. 16:43). However, they do not do this, but follow their inclinations and resort to their own points of view. For this reason, they make many people lose their way and they err on an evil path.[71]

Proof (ḥujja)

If the Ismailis believe that the teachings and the lives of the [imams] Friends of God (*awliyā'*) constitute proofs (*ḥujaj*), in contrast, al-Shāfiʿī links the term 'proof' (*ḥujja*) to its strict legal meaning as a piece of evidence on which a ruling can be established. This means that any 'proof can vary in strength. Of course, the strongest proof is the one based on a clear text of the Qur'an or a generally accepted *sunna*, for

---

70 *Majālis*, pp. 523–525, no. 270.
71 *Majālis*, p. 276, no. 139.

there is no doubt concerning either of them. In this case, no one shall be excused for discarding something that is supported by either of them.

A proof is less strong if a *sunna* is derived from a narrative handed down by only a few individuals and there is disagreement concerning it because the tradition is open to different interpretations and it came originally from a single source; in this case, it should be compulsory for those who are informed about it. The one who casts doubt upon it is excused. But, if he is a learned man he should not doubt.[72]

ʿĀmma wa Khāṣṣa

The Ismailis call the Sunnis *ʿāmma* (common believers) and their scholars *ʿulamāʾ al-ʿāmma*, while they call themselves the *khāṣṣa*, that is to say, those who accept what the imams say and establish, and are therefore superior to common believers.[73] This is how these terms are employed in *Kitāb al-Majālis*.

In contrast, al-Shāfiʿī uses these terms respectively for a general (*ʿāmma*) and a particular (*khāṣṣa*) rule. His premise is that God addressed His Book to the Arabs in their tongue in accordance with the meanings known to them. Thus, it is God's divine disposition to make manifest His Book, part of which is 'literally general', which means that the concept of the particular is included in the general.[74]

Al-Shāfiʿī devotes several paragraphs to this issue, considering different options:

- 'General Declaration of the Book intended to be general in which the particular is included',[75] for instance, Q. 11:8 ('He it is Who created the heavens and the earth') and Q. 39:62 ('God is the

---

72 *Risāla*, pp. 460–461, nos. 1256–1261; trans. Khadduri, *Treatise*, pp. 278–279.

73 *Majālis*, pp. 511–514, no. 265.

74 *Risāla*, pp. 51–52, no. 173; trans. Khadduri, *Treatise*, pp. 94–95. M.A.J. Beg ('al-Khāṣṣa wa'l-ʿĀmma', in *EI2*, vol. 4, pp. 1098–1100) examines the two terms, but neither in the meaning given by Ismailis nor in their legal sense as explained by al-Shāfiʿī.

75 *Risāla*, pp. 53–55, nos. 179–187; trans. Khadduri, *Treatise*, pp. 96–97.

Creator of all things, and He is the Guardian and Disposer of all affairs'), which include everything (heaven, earth, things having living spirit, trees and the like) and God is responsible for the sustenance of each creature and He knows their places.

- 'The explicit general Declaration of the Book in which the general and the particular are included',[76] for instance, Q. 4:103 ('For such prayers are enjoined on believers at stated times'), where it is evident that general and particular declarations are included in the Revelation.
- 'The explicit general Declaration of the Book intended to be particular',[77] for instance, Q. 22:73 ('O men! Here is a parable set forth! Listen to it! Those on whom besides God, ye call cannot create (even) a fly, if they all met together for the purpose! And if the fly should snatch away anything from them, they would have no power to release it from the fly: feeble are those who petition and those whom they petition!'). The meaning commonly implied by the word *nās* (meaning 'people') is general, applying to all people. But it is clear for scholars learned in the Arabic tongue that the meaning implied here refers to some of the people, excluding others. This Revelation was addressed only to those who worship gods other than God since there are among the believers those who are lunatics and minors but who do not worship other gods than Him.
- 'General Declaration which the *sunna* specifically indicates is meant to be particular',[78] for instance, Q. 11:12 ('[The distribution in all cases is] after the payment of legacies and debts'). Muhammad made it clear that bequests must not exceed one third of the deceased's estate, and the heirs must receive the two-thirds; and he also made it clear that debts take precedence over bequests and inheritance and that neither the bequest nor the inheritance should be distributed until the creditors have been paid. Thus, if it were not for the evidence of the *sunna* and the consensus of the people, there would be no inheritance until after the bequest was

[76] *Risāla*, pp. 56–58, nos. 188–196; trans. Khadduri, *Treatise*, pp. 97–99.
[77] *Risāla*, pp. 58–62, nos. 197–205; trans. Khadduri, *Treatise*, pp. 99–101.
[78] *Risāla*, pp. 64–73, nos. 214–235; trans. Khadduri, *Treatise*, pp. 103–108.

paid and the bequest would not fail to take precedence over the debt, or be on equal footing with the debt.[79]

Sources of Law

The Sunni View

Al-Shāfiʿī contends that, as a general principle, that no one should give an opinion on a specific matter by merely saying: 'It is permitted or prohibited', unless he has the requisite legal knowledge, which should be based on the Qur'an and *sunna*, or derived from *ijmāʿ* (consensus) and *qiyās* (analogy, analogical deduction).

Al-Shāfiʿī indicates that there is a priority in the order of the sources of law. Decisions are made on the basis of the provisions of the Qur'an and the generally accepted *sunna*, concerning which there is no disagreement; such decisions are sound according to both the explicit and the implicit meaning of these two sources. However, decisions can also be made on the basis of a single individual tradition on which there is no general agreement; such a decision is correctly made only according to its explicit meaning. Decisions are made also on the basis of consensus and analogy, although the latter is weaker. A source other than the *sunna* can be used only if there is no *sunna*.[80]

Consensus (ijmāʿ)[81]

According to al-Shāfiʿī, the consensus of the people must be accepted on matters where no explicit Qur'anic provision or no Prophetic *sunna* can be found. The historical and sociological grounds for this are that, when the Islamic community spread out into new territories because of the conquests, the Muslims dispersed and mixed with other peoples. So it was impossible for them to have knowledge of all the legal rulings, except those which the entire community regarded as

---

79 *Risāla*, p. 207, no. 558; trans. Khadduri, *Treatise*, p. 171.

80 *Risāla*, pp. 598–600, nos. 1812–1818; trans. Khadduri, *Treatise*, pp. 350–351.

81 Al-Shāfiʿī devotes a chapter to the subject of consensus; cf. *Risāla*, pp. 471–476, nos. 1309–1320; trans. Khadduri, *Treatise*, pp. 285–287.

lawful or unlawful. In the community as a whole there is no error concerning the meaning of the Qur'an, the *sunna*, and analogy.[82] According to a tradition related on the authority of Sufyān b. ʿUyayna, the order of Muhammad to follow the consensus of Islamic community is proof that the *ijmāʿ* of the Muslims is binding.[83]

Analogy (qiyās)[84]

Analogy is defined as the method of reasoning through which indications are sought from parallel precedents in the Qur'an or *sunna* in order to solve a new case. Thus, it is strictly forbidden to apply analogy if explicit orders or prohibitions are to be found in the Qur'an and the Prophetic *sunna*.

If either the Qur'an or the *sunna* have prohibited a certain act by an explicit text or permitted it by an implied reason, and such Qur'anic or Prophetic reason is common to the new case to be solved, the new act should be prohibited or permitted in conformity with the implied reason of permission or prohibition. This means that the new case is similar to the original meaning of the precedent. If, however, a given act may be found analogous to only one aspect of a given precedent (or is similar to several precedents) and analogous to another aspect of another precedent, but neither the latter nor the former provides a close analogy, then analogy should be applied to the precedent nearest in resemblance and most appropriate to the new case.[85]

Al-Shāfiʿī does not find any binding text either in the Qur'an or the Prophetic *sunna* justifying analogical deduction. After all, as al-Shāfiʿī

---

[82] *Risāla*, pp. 471–476, nos. 1309–1320; trans. Khadduri, *Treatise*, pp. 285–287. On *Ijmāʿ*, see M. Bernand, 'Idjmāʿ', *EI2*, vol. 3, pp. 1023–1026.

[83] *Risāla*, pp. 401–403, nos. 1102–1105; trans. Khadduri, *Treatise*, pp. 252–253.

[84] Al-Shāfiʿī devotes a chapter to analogy; cf. *Risāla*, pp. 476–503, nos. 1321–1455; trans. Khadduri, *Treatise*, pp. 288–294.

[85] *Risāla*, pp. 39–40, nos. 120–125; trans. Khadduri, *Treatise*, pp. 78–79. See M. Bernand – G. Troupeau, 'Ḳiyās', *EI2*, vol. 5, pp. 238–242. Analogy is of various kinds, and all of them are included under the term 'analogy' (*qiyas*). They differ from one another in the antecedence of the analogy of either one of them, or its source, or the source of both, or the circumstance that one is clearer than the other (*Risāla*, pp. 512–513, no. 1482; trans. Khadduri, *Treatise*, pp. 307–308).

observes, if an analogy is found to be in the text of the Book or the *sunna*, such a text should be called either God's command or the Muhammad's order rather than an analogy.

To all appearances, the use of analogy leaves a great deal of room for the personal intellectual activity of a single jurist, and so the recourse of scholars to their personal reasoning might cause divergences between them. Al-Shāfiʿī admits that divergences are possible, and that the conclusions of those who apply analogy are likely to be in disagreement.[86]

Istiḥsān[87]

To the verb *istaḥsana* al-Bukhārī attributes the meaning 'to make a decision for a particular interpretation of the law as a result of one's own deliberation'; and both Mālik and Abū Yūsuf use *istiḥsān* to refer to something decided according to their own opinion. *Istiḥsān* means, therefore, a juristic preference. It implies a man initiating something by himself, not basing his decision upon a parallel example but on the principle of equity.

Al-Shāfiʿī is categorically against the use of *istiḥsān*, in this sense,[88] meaning that an opinion that is not based on the Qur'an or the *sunna*, nor on an analogy, is not permissible. However, al-Shāfiʿī identifies *istiḥsān* with analogy. Thus, *istiḥsān* is submitted to the same rules as analogy. This implies that one has to have recourse to *ijtihād* in order to seek to know the right answer to a specific issue, and such an issue must be something definite that can be determined by means of evidence or resemblance to an established case.[89]

---

86 *Risāla*, pp. 476–477, nos. 1321–1326; trans. Khadduri, *Treatise*, p. 288; *Risāla*, p. 479, nos. 1333–1334; trans. Khadduri, *Treatise*, p. 290. Cf. also *Risāla*, pp. 217–219, nos. 592–599; trans. Khadduri, *Treatise*, pp. 182–183.

87 Al-Shāfiʿī devotes a chapter to *istiḥsān*; cf. *Risāla*, pp. 503–559, nos. 1456–1670; trans. Khadduri, *Treatise*, pp. 304–332. This subject is also discussed in a separate treatise entitles *Kitāb Ibṭāl al-Istiḥsān*; see al-Shāfiʿī, *Kitāb Umm*, vol. 7, pp. 267–270, 270–277.

88 *Risāla*, p. 25, no. 70; trans. Khadduri, *Treatise*, p. 70. See R. Paret, 'Istiḥsān and Istiṣlāḥ', *EI2*, vol. 4, pp. 255–259.

89 *Risāla*, pp. 503–505, nos. 1456–1459; trans. Khadduri, *Treatise*, pp. 304–305.

Divergence of Legal Opinions (ikhtilāf)[90]

The system of sources outlined by al-Shāfiʿī has caused and still causes disagreement between scholars. Al-Shāfiʿī distinguishes two categories of divergence. In so far as it concerns what is provided by God as clear textual evidence in the Qurʾan or a *sunna* uttered by the Prophet, disagreement is unlawful. But, as for matters that are liable to different interpretations or derived from analogy, disagreement does not constitute a problem.[91] For instance, disagreement cannot exist regarding a well-authenticated *sunna*, while it is possible in case of an interrupted tradition from Muhammad.[92]

The Ismaili View

The Ismaili hierarchy of the sources of law is very simple. A *qāḍī* should decide in accordance with the Qurʾan. In respect of what he does not find in the Qurʾan, he should decide according the Prophetic *sunna* and the views of the guiding imams from the progeny of Muhammad.

This obviously implies the rejection of any other source of law. Thus, in his work *Kitāb Ikhtilāf al-madhāhib*,[93] al-Nuʿmān refuted al-Shāfiʿī's doctrines on *ijmāʿ*, *qiyās*, *istiḥsān*, *istidlāl* and *ijtihād*.

The Ismaili concept of the sources of law does not refer either to Companions or to Successors, or the Successors of the Successors. The only authorities, besides the Qurʾan, are Muhammad and the imams recognised by the Ismailis.

Qualities Required of Caliphs and Imams

The personal and functional qualities required of caliphs and imams are not the same: a caliph is a servant of the law, while the imam is the

---

90 Al-Shāfiʿī devotes a chapter to *ikhtilāf*; cf. *Risāla*, pp. 560–600, nos. 1671–1821; trans. Khadduri, *Treatise*, pp. 333–352.

91 *Risāla*, p. 560, nos. 1671–1675; trans. Khadduri, *Treatise*, p. 333.

92 *Risāla*, p. 470, nos. 1306–1307; trans. Khadduri, *Treatise*, p. 283. On *ikhtilāf*, see J. Schacht, 'Ikhtilāf', *EI2*, vol. 3, pp. 1061–1062.

93 Al-Qāḍī al-Nuʿmān, *Kitāb Ikhtilāf al-madhāhib*, ed. Ghālib: *Ijmāʿ*, pp. 81–136; *Qiyās*, pp. 155–184; *Istiḥsān*, pp. 185–192; *Istidlāl*, pp. 193–202; *Ijtihād*, pp. 203–228.

interpreter and master of the law; a caliph is, nominally at least, elected by people, while the imam is appointed by the previous imam (*naṣṣ*); a caliph is removable, while the imam appointed by divine designation cannot be deposed by men; it is possible though reprehensible, that a caliph might commit sinful acts, while the imam is sinless and infallible; there may or may not be a caliph, given that the Sunni *umma* obeys the law even in the absence of a caliph, while the presence of the imam is an absolute necessity.[94]

The Impeccable Nature of the Imams

When interpreting Q. 19:59 ('But after them there followed a posterity who missed prayers and followed after lusts: soon, then will they face Destruction'), al-Muʿizz, pointed out that

> God, by His grace and beneficence towards me, safeguarded me from desiring anything that He forbade me. No, by God's sake! I look at things forbidden by God with the eye of one who despises them and I am not inclined towards any of them, to the praise of God and by His grace. But praise be to God, who bestowed upon us sinlessness and infallibility (*ʿiṣma*); He ensures that we do not long after what He has forbidden.[95]

The Imams Condemn Ghuluww (Exaggeration/Extremist Views)

However, the imams defended themselves against those *ghulāt* (exaggerators) who wanted to attribute extraordinary qualities to them. Al-Qāḍī al-Nuʿmān related an episode he heard from al-Muʿizz concerning the way in which the Fatimid caliph al-Qāʾim reacted against a group of extremist *duʿāt*, who affirmed that he and his forefathers had knowledge of divine secrets.

On the one hand, al-Qāʾim exalts the true prerogatives of the imams; on the other, he is mainly concerned with the social consequences of the extremist propaganda. He cursed the extremists and said:

---

94 A.A.A. Fyzee, 'Shīʿī Legal Theories', pp. 121–122.

95 *Majālis*, pp. 417–418, no. 217.

> They are turning away from us; they lie about us; based on how they describe us, they want nothing but to attribute to us a lie and make people withdraw from us, because, if they describe us as we are not and people do not see this and do not find it in us, people will not believe that we are the imams.

Al-Muʿizz, for his part, specifies that the secrets known by the imams concern the knowledge kept secret from the people, the knowledge that God granted to them, and that God has asked them to keep secret. But, as far as the secrets mentioned in the Qurʾan ('Say: None in the heavens or on earth, except God, knows what is hidden: nor can they perceive when they shall be raised up [for Judgment]' (Q. 27:65) are concerned, only God knows them.

Moreover, al-Muʿizz compares al-Qāʾim's statement with what Jaʿfar b. Muḥammad (d. 148/765)[96] said when he learned that Abu'l-Khaṭṭāb al-Asadī (d. ca. 145/762)[97] had uttered similar extremist statements.

> One day (al-Mufaḍḍal)[98] came in to Jaʿfar b. Muḥammad and found him depressed and shedding tears. I asked him: 'What has happened to you? Oh, could I but sacrifice myself for you!' Jaʿfar replied: 'This unbeliever and false person claims that I know secrets, God be praised! There is no god but He. He is my Lord and the Lord of my forefathers; He created us [. . .] Therefore, we are the signs of the right guidance and the supreme evidence! Go

---

[96] Jaʿfar al-Ṣādiq, sixth imam of the Shiʿa; M.G.S. Hodgson, 'Jaʿfar al-Ṣādiq', *EI2*, vol. 2, pp. 374–375.

[97] See M. A. Amir Moezzi, 'Ḳaṭṭābiya', *EIr*; Wilferd Madelung, 'Khaṭṭābiyya', *EI2* and Hassan Ansari, 'Abū al-Khaṭṭāb', *EIs*. See also Mushegh Asatryan, *Controversies in Formative Shiʿi Islam: The Ghulat Muslims and their Beliefs* (London, 2017), p. 1.

[98] Wilferd Madelung, 'Ḳaṭṭābiyya', *EI2*, vol. 4, pp. 1132–1133: 'A further subsect of the Khaṭṭābiyya are the Mufaḍḍaliyya, followers of al-Mufaḍḍal b. ʿUmar al-Djuʿfī the moneychanger. They agreed with the other Khaṭṭābiyya sects in deifying Djaʿfar and claiming prophethood for themselves, but diverged from them by repudiating Abu'l-Khaṭṭāb. According to an Imāmī report, al-Mufaḍḍal was appointed by the Imam Djaʿfar to guide the followers of Abu'l-Khaṭṭāb after the condemnation of the latter. Although some negative statements of Djaʿfar are reported about him, al-Mufaḍḍal, unlike the other Khaṭṭābī leaders, was never excommunicated. He became a trusted agent of the Imām Mūsā b. Djaʿfar (148–83/765–99), during whose lifetime he died.'

> to them, who are the companions of Abu'l-Khaṭṭāb, and tell them: "We are beings created and servants submissive to God, but God has given us a degree that no one else has other than us, and it is proper only to us. We are light from the light of God and our party is from us [shares our nature], while other creatures are of fire [are created from fire]."'[99]

Infallibility, Mediation and Imitation of the Imam

On the one hand, al-Muʿizz exhorts people to obey his orders because all that he commands is right. Obedience to his orders leads to happiness and brings benefits in this life and the next. If, on the contrary, a deficiency happens because of the obedience, there will be no negative consequences and effects for those who have obeyed, neither in this world nor in the afterlife. On the other hand, the Ismaili imams consider their behaviour to be a *sunna*. Their life constitutes a model of behaviour; therefore the imams must be imitated. The legacy (*waṣiyya*) of al-Manṣūr to al-Muʿizz at his death was in fact: 'I sum up all the recommendations to you in one single word. Imitate my actions as you have seen me accomplish them, and abandon any action you have seen me abandon. After my death, perform whatever you have seen me performing during my lifetime. What an excellent forebear I am for you!'[100]

Sometimes the imams diverged on particular issues. However, their *ikhtilāf* depends on the fact that the qualities of each imam are adequate for their time.[101]

---

99 *Majālis*, pp. 84–85, no. 18. The imams claim their prerogatives against extremists who attribute to them qualities which they do not possess; cf. *Majālis*, pp. 419–420, no. 219.

100 *Majālis*, pp. 240–241, no. 115; p. 241.

101 *Majālis*, pp. 283–284, no. 141. *Kitāb al-Majālis* reports some divergences among the imams. For instance, al-Manṣūr and al-Muʿizz gave different solutions concerning the treatment of rebels (*Majālis*, pp. 232–234, no. 109). Al-Qā'im and al-Manṣūr came to different conclusions about the killing of rebels; al-Muʿizz explains why this divergence was possible (*Majālis*, pp. 277–279, no. 140). In a specific case al-Manṣūr and al-Muʿizz think differently, but al-Nuʿmān points out that both of

However, the imams are not only the source of knowledge and *sunna*, they also grant their forgiveness, their grace, their beneficence, their favour and their protection if the actions of the people are not appropriate. If the people come to the imam, asking God to forgive them, the imam will ask forgiveness for the people, as Muhammad also did, according to the command of God: 'If they had only, when they were unjust to themselves come unto thee and asked God's forgiveness and the Messenger had asked forgiveness for them, they would have found God indeed Oft-Returning, Most Merciful' (Q. 4:64).

The conclusion of al-Nuʿmān, addressing al-Muʿizz, is instructive: 'You are the successor of the Messenger of God among us and our refuge when seeking forgiveness for our sins, our failure and our iniquities.' Al-Muʿizz replies saying that this is possible provided that the intentions of the people are sincere. Otherwise, it is as with a group which sought Muhammad to ask forgiveness, but without any good intentions. Regarding this episode the Qur'an says:

> The desert Arabs who lagged behind will say to thee: 'We were engaged in (looking after) our flocks and herds, and our families; do thou then ask forgiveness for us.' They say with their tongues what is not in their hearts. Say: 'Who then has any power at all (to intervene) on your behalf with God, if His will is to give you some loss or to give you some profit?' But God is well acquainted with all that ye do (Q. 48:11).[102]

The Role of the *faqīh*

The differences between Sunni and Ismaili ideas regarding the sources of law imply a different role for jurists.

---

them found their solutions in the Qur'an and the statements of the Prophet. In the end they only presented a different interpretation, but they did not diverge (*Majālis*, pp. 75–77, no. 10). The solutions to another question given by al-Manṣūr and al-Muʿizz also diverge (*Majālis*, p. 258, no. 129). In yet another case, al-Manṣūr was specific about a response given by al-Muʿizz (*Majālis*, p. 265, no. 132).

102 *Majālis*, pp. 272–275, no. 136.

The Sunni View

After Muhammad's death disputes came to be decided in accordance with the Qur'an and Prophetic *sunna*. But, in this approach, if there is no relevant text, the matter is decided by analogy on the strength of a precedent sought either in the Qur'an or the *sunna*.[103] However, this raises the question of who the person is who is able to apply analogy.

A Muslim must consider everything that God has revealed in the Qur'an as a mercy from Him and evidence of His existence. Thus, it is obligatory for someone who seeks knowledge to exert his utmost energy in increasing his knowledge, whether it can be found in the Qur'an or obtained by *istidlāl* (deductive/inductive reasoning).[104] However, God endows men with knowledge to any degree and in any way He wants.[105] This implies that there are various levels of legal knowledge.

The first level of knowledge, of which nobody is allowed to be ignorant or doubtful regarding its certainty, consists of the rules drawn from the literal reading of the scriptural sources and consists of the implied meanings of Qur'anic provisions or generally known Prophetic *sunna*.

These are the two sources by virtue of which the lawful is to be established as lawful and the unlawful as unlawful.

The second level concerns legal knowledge that is derived from the traditions related by the reliable transmitters, on the authority of Muhammad, but known only to scholars; the common people are under no obligation to be familiar with it. This kind of knowledge is binding on scholars.

The third level is the legal knowledge derived from *ijmāʿ* (consensus).

The last level is the legal knowledge derived from *ijtihād* (personal reasoning) through *qiyās* (analogy). The jurists, who possess legal knowledge and are qualified to exercise *ijtihād*, are entrusted with the task of

---

103 *Risāla*, p. 81, no. 266; trans. Khadduri, *Treatise*, p. 113.

104 *Risāla*, p. 19, nos. 43–46; trans. Khadduri, *Treatise*, p. 65. On *faqīh*, see D.B. Macdonald, 'Faḳīh', in *EI2*, vol. 2, p. 756.

105 *Risāla*, p. 485, no. 1371; trans. Khadduri, *Treatise*, p. 293.

acquiring and deploying this knowledge. Their decisions are right only to the person who applies analogy, not to the majority of scholars.[106]

Ijtihād[107]

The exercise of *ijtihād* is justified on the basis of a tradition related on the authority of ʿAmr b. al-ʿĀṣ, who heard Muhammad say: 'If a judge makes the right decision through *ijtihād*, he shall be doubly rewarded; if he errs, he shall be rewarded only once.'[108]

However, *ijtihād* is equated to analogy. Thus, it must not be considered as a form of free thinking, since it can only be exercised on the basis of the Qur'an, the *sunna* and consensus. It is the duty of those who have legal knowledge only to express an opinion that is based on certainty.[109] For this reason, al-Shāfiʿī requires the *mujtahid* to follow stringent rules. First of all, nobody should apply analogy unless he is competent to do so as a result of his profound knowledge of the Qur'an. Then, the ambiguous rules in the Qur'an should be interpreted in the light of the Prophetic *sunna*; if no *sunna* is found, one has recourse to the consensus of the Muslims; it is only when there is no consensus that the jurist applies analogical deduction.[110]

Given that *ijtihād* requires profound legal knowledge, no one except a well-informed scholar, fully acquainted with the binding traditions, should apply analogical reasoning. For this, al-Shāfiʿī requires a scholar to possess the following qualifications in order to be regarded competent:

---

106 *Risāla*, pp. 478–479, nos. 1327–1332; trans. Khadduri, *Treatise*, pp. 289–290.

107 Chapter on *ijtihād*: *Risāla*, pp. 487–503, nos. 1377–1455; trans. Khadduri, *Treatise*, pp. 295–303.

108 *Risāla*, p. 494, no. 1409; trans. Khadduri, *Treatise*, p. 299. See also the debate about this tradition, *Risāla*, pp. 494–497, nos. 1410–1420; trans. Khadduri, *Treatise*, pp. 299–300. On *Ijtihād*, see J. Schacht, 'Idjtihād', *EI2*, vol. 3, pp. 1026–1027.

109 *Risāla*, p. 41, nos. 131–132; trans. Khadduri, *Treatise*, p. 80.

110 *Risāla*, pp. 509–910, nos. 1469–1470; trans. Khadduri, *Treatise*, p. 306. It is evident that, given a Qur'anic provision and a Prophetic *sunna*, these provisions are binding. Hence the obligation of everyone who has heard anything from Muhammad, or anything related on his authority, to transmit what he has heard for the information of others (*Risāla*, p. 234, no. 654; trans. Khadduri, *Treatise*, pp. 191–192; *Risāla*, p. 238, no. 657; trans. Khadduri, *Treatise*, p. 194.)

- he must be competent in the established *sunna*, the opinions of his predecessors, consensus (*ijmāʿ*) and disagreement (*ikhtilāf*)
- he must have an adequate knowledge of the Arabic tongue
- he must be sound of mind, able to distinguish between closely parallel precedents
- he must not be hasty in expressing an opinion unless he is certain of it
- he must not refrain from listening to the opinions of those who may disagree with him
- he must not be more preoccupied with the opinion he has given than with the one with which he disagrees.

Al-Shāfiʿī also considers cases when one of the previous qualifications is lacking:

- the one who possesses a mature mind but lacks the other qualifications should not be permitted to express an opinion based on analogy, for he might not know the precedent by which he applies analogy
- the one who possesses the legal knowledge solely as a result of memorisation, and is uncertain of its correctness, should not be permitted to express an opinion based on analogy, for he may not comprehend the meaning of that knowledge
- if a scholar has a good memory but is lacking either in comprehension or knowledge of the Arab tongue, he should not be permitted to apply analogy, for he would be lacking the tool by means of which he applies analogy.[111]

The Ismaili View

Kitāb al-Majālis presents a precise picture of the relationship between the state jurist, al-Nuʿmān, and the political and spiritual guides of the Ismailis, the imam-caliphs.

First of all, books written by al-Nuʿmān were not the result of his independent initiative, but produced on the authority of the imams.

---

[111] *Risāla*, pp. 507–511, nos. 1465–1479; trans. Khadduri, *Treatise*, pp. 305–307.

In general, he depended on their directives[112] and composed his works under their supervision.[113] In the first period of the Fatimid imamate, during the reign of al-Manṣūr, al-Nuʿmān mainly devoted himself to collecting and copying other works.[114] These books were transmitted from one imam to another. So al-Nuʿmān tells us that al-Manṣūr gave a book had belonged to al-Mahdī to al-Muʿizz.[115]

More detailed information about al-Muʿizz is provided by al-Nuʿmān. He says that he wrote a book on the orders of al-Muʿizz; the imam revised it and also made suggestions.[116] Al-Muʿizz asked al-Nuʿmān to find a solution to a question; he did so, then he submitted his solution to the imam.[117] But it is al-Muʿizz who explains to al-Nuʿmān how the Sunnis must be rebutted.[118] Al-Nuʿmān also wrote a book at the request of some *qāḍī*s and scholars; then he submitted his work to al-Muʿizz for approval; the imam analysed the text, revising it as well. Al-Nuʿmān entitled his work *Kitāb al-Dīnār*; but al-Muʿizz advised him to call it *Kitāb al-Ikhtiṣār*.[119]

The relationship between al-Muʿizz and al-Nuʿmān can be summed up by the following sentence by al-Nuʿmān: 'After having explained a question, I submit it to him [al-Muʿizz] in order to obtain his agreement and to make sure that he regards it as correct (*fa-baʿda an basaṭtu shayʾan min-hu rafaʿtu-hu ilay-hi wa-rtaḍā-hu wa-staḥsana-hu*).'[120]

---

112 *Majālis*, pp. 351–353, no. 182.

113 *Majālis*, pp. 301–303, no. 156.

114 *Majālis*, pp. 80–81, no. 13.

115 *Majālis*, pp. 130–131, no. 70.

116 *Majālis*, p. 401, no. 210. Al-Nuʿmān refers to the books he wrote at the request of al-Muʿizz: a book on the history of imams, another on the qualities of Banū Hāshim and one on the faults of the Banū ʿAbd Shams (Banū Umayya); cf. *Majālis*, pp. 117–118, no. 57. Al-Muʿizz takes care to compose a text on lexicography; cf. *Majālis*, p. 134, no. 76. Al-Manṣūr asked al-Nuʿman to write a book on those elements of the Qurʾan that the Sunnis (*ʿāmma*) reject or deny; cfr. *Majālis*, p. 135, no 78. Al-Muʿizz asks al-Nuʿmān to write a book; al-Nuʿmān describes how the imam gives his *nulla osta* (permission, clearance); cf. *Majālis*, p. 545, no. 281.

117 *Majālis*, pp. 357–358, no. 183.

118 *Majālis*, p. 430, no. 227.

119 *Majālis*, pp. 359–361, no. 186.

120 *Majālis*, pp. 135–137, no. 79; p. 137.

However, the activities of al-Nuʿmān as a jurist were not limited to writing legal works. He also carried out the role of *muftī*, and read out his legal works on Fridays.[121]

Case Studies

Three examples can show the dialectic relationship between al-Muʿizz and al-Nuʿmān.

(1) Al-Mahdī, al-Muʿizz and al-Nuʿmān agree on the same doctrine: the inheritance of relatives, both on the father's and mother's side (all blood relatives) (*dhawū al-arḥām*).

Al-Nuʿmān reminds al-Muʿizz of an episode, which involved his predecessor al-Mahdī, concerning the inheritance of the *dhawū al-arḥām*. An anonymous individual advised al-Mahdī to follow 'what the Sunnis (*ʿāmma*) do'. They exclude the *dhawū al-arḥām* from inheritance and most of the Sunni schools give much of the estate of the deceased to the Treasury (*bayt al-māl*). The reason is that this will increase the revenues of the state. In actual fact, only Mālikīs and Shāfiʿīs agree on this doctrine, but the Shāfiʿī school derived it from the Mālikīs. Thus, al-Mahdī's interlocutor presumably belonged to the school prevailing in North Africa, that is, the Mālikī school.

Al-Mahdī rejected this advice for both political and doctrinal reasons. Politically, he believed that the person who gave him this advice wanted to defame him. From the doctrinal point of view, and as a consequence of the previous assumption, al-Mahdī reproached the man for trying to make him take a decision that conflicts with the revelation of God. Indeed, al-Mahdī insisted that God has established the imams only in order to make plain his religion for His servants, not to increase what is unlawful to their advantage, taking from the temporal possessions of the people!

Imam al-Muʿizz confirms the doctrine of his predecessor, stating that 'al-Mahdī is proved to be right!' And he basically repeats the same arguments as al-Mahdī. That is: 'We will not decide for the servants of

[121] *Majālis*, pp. 545–547, no. 282; pp. 547–548, no. 283.

God other than in accordance with what God has revealed, whether they like it or not, whether they agree with it or not. We will not invite them to transgress the provisions of God, since God has put us in His service for this purpose.' Politically, al-Muʿizz reproaches the majority of the people, presumably belonging to the Mālikī school, for thinking about their worldly interests without any care for the establishment of religion. But God ordered the imam to establish His religion, make straight the path of His servants, shield them from judgement and direct their behaviour accordingly.[122]

(2) Al-Muʿizz adapts a rule to special circumstances: The inheritance of slaves.

Not surprisingly, al-Nuʿmān entitles this section: 'The ratification (validation) of the pre-eminence of the Friends of God [imams]' (*tawqīʿ bi-tafḍīl ahl al-walāya*), as if to emphasise that the source of law is the imam, and also with reference to original solutions imposed by special circumstances.

Two cases were submitted to al-Nuʿmān: one concerned the inheritance of some slaves of al-Muʿizz, who left both slave and free relatives; the second case regarded the witness of certain slaves in favour of other slaves. Al-Nuʿmān wished to solve both cases, but he did not find any definite rule (*ḥadd*) established by al-Muʿizz and the imams before him that could be applied to this issue. However, al-Nuʿmān noted that most slaves actually inherit from each other. The *qāḍīs* let slaves inherit and permit a slave to give witness in defence of another slave.

Al-Nuʿmān says briefly that this really should not be the case, because the property of a slave belongs to the master and none of the slaves' relatives should inherit from them except what the master bestows upon them as a benefit. Likewise, a slave giving witness in defence of another slave is unlawful. Al-Nuʿmān correctly attributes

---

122 *Majālis*, p. 97, no. 31. See al-Qāḍī al-Nuʿmān, *The Early History of Ismaili Jurisprudence. Law under the Fatimids. A critical edition of the Arabic text and English translation of al-Qāḍī al-Nuʿmān's* Minhāj al-farāʾiḍ, ed. and tr. A. Cilardo (London, 2012), pp. 43–49 (of the English text).

the same doctrine to the Sunnis (*ʿāmma*). Nevertheless, al-Nuʿmān shows himself doubtful in this regard, because he is not aware whether or not *qāḍīs* in the past have asked the imams whether they considered slaves free persons and whether the *qāḍīs* used the command of the imams according to its evident (*ẓāhir*) meaning.

Then al-Nuʿmān reminds al-Muʿizz of what happened at the time of al-Qāʾim; that is, one of his slaves, who held an administrative office (*dīwān*), died. His heirs made a complaint to the judge and some of them asked al-Nuʿmān for a legal opinion about a legacy the imam made in favour of the deceased slave. Al-Nuʿmān answered that, given that the deceased subject was a slave, a legacy in his favour was not licit and none of his relatives could inherit from him. In fact, what a deceased slave has left belongs to his master, who can freely dispose of it. Al-Qāʾim maintained that the legal opinion given by al-Nuʿmān was correct.

When the case of the inheritance of a slave belonging to al-Muʿizz was presented to al-Nuʿmān, he offered the same solution, but the imam replied: 'Those of our slaves who were engaged in our *daʿwa*, you will treat their affairs as if they were free people; thus, they must be considered the owners of their affairs regarding their inheritance, their witness, their deeds, and in all other cases, of which they can freely dispose. Conversely for the one who is not included in this category, his affairs follow the path of slaves, who cannot dispose of their goods, except what their masters (*mawālī*) grant to them.'

The innovative solution given by al-Muʿizz goes against a basic rule of Islamic law. This astonished al-Nuʿmān. His comment was that he saw this as an order he could never have conceived of and that had never occurred to him before. Faced with this strange new rule, al-Nuʿmān sought to justify it on a legal basis, stating that the benevolence of al-Muʿizz towards those slaves must be regarded as their emancipation. However, al-Nuʿmān obediently accepted the decision of al-Muʿizz, departing from a rigid Islamic rule for political reasons.

After that, al-Nuʿmān asked al-Muʿizz about the legal status of certain slaves who were called to the *daʿwa* in the past, but then they erred, their condition became bad and their shortcomings evident; for this reason, al-Muʿizz no longer called them to the *daʿwa*. Al-Muʿizz decided to apply the provisions concerning slaves in this case. Al-Muʿizz agreed with the legal justification given by al-Nuʿmān to the effect that departing from the Islamic rule must be regarded as emancipation, which, however, is effective only for those who execute his order, that is, commitment to *walāya* and the service of the *daʿwa*. For those who opposed his command the rule was to be applied according to their original state of slavery.[123]

(3) Al-Nuʿmān rectifies the legal definition of *yatīm* given by al-Muʿizz.

Al-Muʿizz explains the term *yatīm* (orphan) as meaning one who does not have a testamentary guardian. The latter takes the place of his father; thus, a minor could no longer be called an orphan. Al-Nuʿmān, instead, points out that, according to Q. 4:6 ('Make trial of orphans until they reach the age of marriage', etc.), an orphan is a minor (*ṭifl*) whose father has died, whether or not he has a testamentary guardian.[124]

Conclusion

The analysis of *Kitāb al-Majālis wa'l-musāyarāt* permits us to concretely perceive the Ismaili theory of the sources of law as elaborated by al-Nuʿmān in his work *Kitāb Ikhtilāf uṣūl al-madhāhib*. In fact, all the episodes considered above are entirely in accordance with Ismaili legal theory.

A comparative analysis of *Kitāb al-Majālis* and the *Risāla* shows a completely different view of the normative sources of Islamic law. The central point of divergence is the role of the imam. For the Ismailis the only *ḥujja* is the imam. As for the Qurʾan, only the imam is its authentic interpreter. As regards the *sunna*, only the Prophetic traditions and those related on the authority of the imams recognised by the Ismailis are authentic. For this reason, if divergences exist between the imams, they are justified by the circumstances of the age.

---

[123] *Majālis*, pp. 393–394, no. 204. On the inheritance of slaves, see A. Cilardo, *Minhāj*, pp. 69–71.

[124] *Majālis*, p. 107, no. 46.

Al-Shāfiʿī outlines a completely different idea of the sources of law. According to his interpretation, the scholar is the interpreter of the Qurʾan. As well as this, the Prophetic *sunna* is submitted to the scrutiny of scholars, because it is contradictory on specific points. In addition, the *sunna* of the Companions and the Successors can be a source of law.

In this context, the different role of jurists in the Sunni and Ismaili view is clear. A Sunni jurist is a *conditor iuris*, a lawmaker. This necessarily implies that he has recourse to his personal judgement. A Sunni jurist is completely free in his elaboration. He claims his absolute independence from the political power of the age. In contrast to this, the Ismaili jurist is at the service of the imams; he is the technician of law, the adviser of the imams; he composes books under the supervision of the imam of the age.

Ultimately, the Ismaili view of the sources of law places it within the sphere of revelation; it has, therefore, a theological basis, and so, because of this, it offers certainty, authenticity and uniformity. However, the Sunni system relies on a human element; that is, the personal reasoning of scholars. For this reason, since the early days of Islam, there were divergences and many schools were formed, meaning many interpretations of the Qurʾan and *sunna*, and finally only four Sunni schools remain extant today.

6

Sacrifice, Circumcision and the Ruler in the Medieval Islamic West: The Ismaili-Fatimid Legacy*

Maribel Fierro
(Higher Council for Scientific Research (CSIC – Spain))

Shiʿi doctrines spread in North African territory in the early period before the establishment of the Ismaili-Fatimid caliphate in Ifrīqiya (Tunisia) in the year 296/909, but only a few records have been left by the limited number of individuals and groups that followed them.[1] The territories of al-Maghrib al-aqṣā (what is now Morocco) saw the emergence of polities governed by descendants of the Prophet's progeny, the Idrisids (Ḥasanids), who were acknowledged as rulers by some Berber groups and whose claims to religious and political authority were informed by Shiʿi ideals as reflected in the inscriptions on some of their coins. However, the evidence for their adoption of Shiʿi rituals and their conceptions of power is scarce again given the absence of an Idrisid historiography.[2]

---

* I wish to thank Aurora González Artigao, David Hollenberg, Orkhan Mir-Kasimov and Luis Molina for their valuable comments and assistance in writing this paper.

[1] Such evidence has been reviewed by Wilferd Madelung, 'Some notes on non-Ismāʿīli shiʿism in the Maghrib', *Studia Islamica*, 44 (1976), pp. 87–97.

[2] Mercedes García Arenal and Eduardo Manzano, 'Légitimité et villes idrissides', in P. Cressier and M. García-Arenal, *Genèse de la ville islamique en al-Andalus et au Maghreb occidental* (Madrid: Casa de Velázquez/CSIC, 1998), pp. 257–284, pp. 266–268; Chafik T. Benchekroun, 'Les Idrissides: l'histoire contre son histoire', *Al-Masaq. Islam and the Medieval Mediterranean*, 23, 3 (2011), pp. 171–188, and 'Rāšid et les Idrissides: l'histoire "originelle" du Maroc entre marginalisation et idéalisation', *Al-Qanṭara*, 35, 1 (2014), pp. 7–37.

As regards al-Andalus, Shiʿism was almost completely absent.[3] The main reason for this was the establishment of Umayyad rule in the region which determined the construction of an identity that was deeply anti-Shiʿi.[4] The interlude of the Ḥammūdī caliphate, under descendants of the Idrisids, after the collapse of the Umayyads in the early fifth/eleventh century might have developed into a full-fledged Shiʿi polity but it lasted for too brief a period and has only left some tantalising bits of evidence.[5] During the reign of Umayyads, Ismaili missions arrived in al-Andalus,[6] and they may have contributed to the Mahdist rebellion of the Umayyad pretender Ibn al-Qiṭṭ in the year 288/900.[7] The establishment of the Fatimid caliphate was a crucial factor in ʿAbd al-Raḥmān III's (r. 300–350/912–961) decision to proclaim himself caliph in the year 316/929, in his expansionist policies in North Africa and in the support given to the Khārijī revolt led by Abū Yazīd (d. 335/947) against the Fatimids. The polemics of the Umayyads of Cordoba against the Fatimids went hand in hand with religious, intellectual and political developments in al-Andalus that would not have taken place otherwise.[8] Ritual was one of the domains where

---

[3] Maḥmūd ʿAlī Makki, 'Al-tashshayyuʿ fī l-Andalus', *Revista del Instituto Egipcio de Estudios Islámicos*, 2 (1954), pp. 93–149.

[4] Gabriel Martínez Gros, *L'idéologie omeyyade. La construction de la légitimité du Califat de Cordoue (Xe-XIe siècles)* (Madrid, 1992) and *Identité andalouse* (Paris, 1997); Maribel Fierro, 'Espacio sunní y espacio šīʿī', *El esplendor de los omeyas cordobeses. La civilización musulmana de Europa Occidental. Exposición en Madīnat al-Zahrā' 3 de mayo a 30 de septiembre de 2001* (Granada, 2001), pp. 168–177.

[5] Almudena Ariza, *De Barcelona a Orán. Las emisiones monetales a nombre de los califas Ḥammūdíes de al-Andalus* (Grenoble, 2015).

[6] Farhat Dachraoui, 'Tentative d'infiltration šīʿite en Espagne musulmane sous le règne d'al-Ḥakam II', *Al-Andalus*, 23 (1958), pp. 97–106; Paul Walker, 'The identity of the Ismaili *dāʿīs* sent by the Fatimids to Ibn Ḥafṣūn', *Al-Qanṭara*, 21 (2000), pp. 387–388.

[7] Maribel Fierro, 'The battle of the Ditch (*al-Khandaq*) of the Cordoban caliph ʿAbd al-Raḥmān III', in Asad Q. Ahmed, Behnam Sadeghi and Michael Bonner (ed.), *The Islamic Scholarly Tradition. Studies in History, Law, and Thought in Honor of Professor Michael Allan Cook* (Leiden/Boston, 2011), pp. 107–130.

[8] Maribel Fierro, 'La política religiosa de ʿAbd al-Raḥmān III', *Al-Qanṭara*, 25 (2004), pp. 119–156, and 'Crossing words and swords: Umayyads and Fatimids in the tenth century', in Miriam Alí-de-Unzaga, Patrice Cressier and Maribel Fierro (ed.), *Fatimids and Umayyads: Competing Caliphates* (forthcoming). For the general polemical context, see Corrado la Martire, *La polemica tra sunniti e ismāʿīliti* (Venezia, 2017).

Sunnis and Shiʿis, and more specifically Ismailis, confronted each other, and the ways in which the Fatimids shaped celebrations such as the *ʿid al-aḍḥā* left an enduring legacy in the religious and political culture of the medieval Islamic West. These ways were developed by the Fatimids to address certain specific historical situations and were subject to change and even abandonment, especially when, after the revolutionary early period, the Fatimids decided not to devote any major effort to converting the Sunni population over which they ruled.[9]

The celebration of the nativity of the Prophet Muhammad (*mawlid al-nabī*) is generally considered to have started as a Fatimid innovation at some point in the beginning of the fifth/eleventh century,[10] that is, after the Fatimid imam-caliphs had moved to Egypt, and it was one that enjoyed great success in the different polities of the late medieval Islamic West, for instance the Azafids, the Marinids, and the Nasrids.[11] Being an innovation, that is, lacking a precedent in the Qurʾan and in the Prophet's Tradition (*sunna*), although this practice was supported by some as praiseworthy and commendable, others subjected it to criticism and even prohibition.[12] This latter view did not stop rulers resorting to it in official celebrations in order to enhance their legitimacy through connecting themselves to the figure of the Prophet

[9] Wilferd Madelung, 'The religious policy of the Fatimids toward their Sunni subjects in the Maghrib', in Marianne Barrucand (ed.), *L'Egypte Fatimide. Son art et son histoire. Actes du Colloque organisé à Paris les 28, 29 et 30 mai 1998* (Paris, 1999), pp. 97–104; Najam Haider, *Shīʿī Islam: An Introduction* (New York, 2014), pp. 123–44.

[10] N. J. G. Kaptein, *Muhammad's birthday festival: early history in the central Muslim lands and development in the Muslim west until the 10th/16th century* (Leiden, 1993), p. 24. See also Marion Holmes Katz, *The birth of the prophet Muhammad: devotional piety in Sunni Islam* (London and New York, 2007).

[11] A recent study on this topic is James A.O.C. Brown, 'Azafid Ceuta, Mawlid al-Nabī and the Development of Marīnid Strategies of Legitimation', in Amira K. Bennison (ed.), *The Articulation of Power in Medieval Iberia and the Maghrib* (Oxford, 2014), pp. 127–151.

[12] Kaptein, *Muhammad's birthday festival*, p. 112; Aviva Schussmann, 'The legitimacy and nature of *mawlid al-nabī*: analysis of a fatwa', *Islamic Law and Society*, 5, 2 (1998), pp. 214–234.

Muhammad. The rise of Sharifism in the Maghrib, that is, the claim that descent from the Prophet Muhammad implied entitlement to rule, was helped by the spread of such a ritual innovation as has been studied by a number of scholars.[13] Having first been supported by those in power, the *mawlid al-nabī* eventually became a popular celebration especially after Sufis and saints seeking to legitimise their own authority sponsored it.[14]

There were many other rituals supported by the Fatimids, whose proclivity for urban ceremonials as well as for a proliferation of sacred spaces and times, and whose inventiveness in devising sacred ceremonial especially after their move to Egypt, have also been analysed by a number of scholars.[15] Among such rituals, some were not 'new' as the *mawlid al-nabī* was, but they were nevertheless labelled as innovations in order to discredit them. Robert Brunschvig devoted a study to analysing the ritual divergences between Ismailis and Sunnis, focusing on the period of Fatimid rule in Ifrīqiya before the Fatimids moved to Cairo.[16] For each ritual, Brunschvig discussed what the Ismaili position was and how it diverged from that of the Sunnis while also taking care to indicate intra-Sunni divergence of opinion (*ikhtilāf*) on the matter. In fact, one of his sources, the fourth/tenth century geographer al-Muqaddasī, specified three different types of ritual practice among

---

[13] A. Sebti, 'Au Maroc: sharifisme citadin, charisme et historiographie', *Annales*, 2 (1986), pp. 433–57; Mohammed Kably, *Société, pouvoir et religion au Maroc à la fin du Moyen Âge (XIVe-XVe siécle)* (Paris, 1986).

[14] Kaptein, *Muhammad's birthday festival*, pp. 123 and 129.

[15] Marius Canard, 'Le cérémonial fatimide et le cérémonial byzantin: essai de comparaison', *Byzantion*, 21 (1951), pp. 355–420; Paula Sanders, *Ritual, politics, and the city in Fatimid Cairo* (Albany, 1994); Irene A. Bierman, *Writing signs: the Fatimid Public Text* (Berkeley and Los Angeles, 1998); Jonathan M. Bloom, *Arts of the City Victorious: Islamic Art and Architecture in Fatimid North Africa and Egypt* (New Haven and London, 2007); Paul Walker, 'Islamic ritual preaching (*khutbas*) in a contested arena: Shiʿis and Sunnis, Fatimids and Abbasids', *Anuario de Estudios Medievales*, 42, 1 (2012), pp. 119–140.

[16] Robert Brunschvig, 'Fiqh fatimide et histoire de l'Ifriqiya', in *Mélanges d'histoire et d'archéologie de l'Occident musulman. Hommage à G. Marcais* (Algiers, 1958), pp. 13–20 (repr. in R. Brunschvig, *Études d'islamologie*, 2 vols (Paris, 1976).

the Fatimids: a) those on which there was *ikhtilāf* among the Sunnis, such as the *qunūt*; b) those that involved the return to the practices of the first Muslims, such as the double *iqāma* in the call to prayer that the Umayyads had reduced to one; c) the practices that were particular to the Fatimids and that went against those of the Sunnis while lacking any clear precedent, such as the prayer of the eclipse with five inclinations (*rakʿas*) and two prostrations in each *rakʿa*. The practices mentioned by Brunschvig relate to purification, the fast and most especially to prayer, such as the *adhān* and *iqāma*; the hours for the obligatory prayers; the use of the *basmala* and other formulas; the *qunūt*;[17] the supplementary night prayers, and the prayers for the dead, and for rain.

The fact that the Fatimids eventually gave up any idea of converting the population of the lands they had conquered to their form of Islam does not mean that they renounced impressing on their subjects what they stood for. The Fatimid practices listed above were all public rituals and thus they were susceptible to rejection from those sectors of the urban population in Ifrīqiya who as Sunni Muslims had been taught to behave otherwise. This public aspect of their rule was of fundamental importance to the Fatimids since by performance or prohibition of rituals or aspects of rituals they made it clear who was in power. One such case was the *ṣalāt al-tarāwīḥ*, the night prayers of Ramadan, a ritual closely linked to the second caliph ʿUmar b. al-Khaṭṭāb who had given them his support against those who interpreted the Prophetic precedent differently. The fact that ʿUmar qualified his decision in favour of the *ṣalāt al-tarāwīḥ* as an 'innovation' (*bidʿa*) gave rise to different interpretations: either such 'innovation', coming from a Companion, had to be necessarily good, or it was not in fact a true innovation from a legal point of view, as though what ʿUmar did was to act as the Prophet would have done. The Fatimids completely rejected the practice of the night prayers of Ramadan. By doing so they sent a powerful message implying that

[17] The term *qunūt* refers to different practices as documented by A. J. Wensinck, 'Ḳunūt', *EI2* online. However, it usually refers to an invocation during prayer in which enemies are cursed.

ʿUmar b. al-Khaṭṭāb had in fact not been a 'rightly guided' caliph because he had allowed the Muslims – and even incited them – to perform something that was an innovation. This reinforced the Fatimid's critical view of the Prophet's Companions who had not supported the claim of ʿAlī b. Abī Ṭālib and his descendants.

The Sunnis, and more specifically, the Mālikīs, reacted to the Ismaili ban on the ritual performance of the *ṣalāt al-tarāwīḥ*, and they did so in different ways: by supporting it so that it became a symbol of Sunnism, and by defending it from the charge of being an innovation. The Fatimids forbade the *ṣalāt al-tarāwīḥ* in Qayrawan to the extent that people stopped performing it, as documented by the Eastern geographer, al-Muqaddasī. For his part, the North African historian al-Mālikī says that it was Muḥammad b. ʿUmar al-Marrūdhī, the judge of the first Fatimid caliph, who prohibited the performance of these prayers in Ifrīqiya. When the amir of Fez, who had formerly paid allegiance to the Fatimids, became an ally of the Umayyads of Cordoba, the Umayyad caliph al-Ḥakam II (r. 350–366/961–976) demanded the *ṣalāt al-tarāwīḥ* be performed in his lands. The Fatimids continued to oppose the practice when they moved to Egypt. The performance of the *ṣalāt al-tarāwīḥ* was then forbidden by the fourth imam-caliph al-ʿAzīz (r. 365–386/975–996) and a man was executed for performing them.[18]

Although there was intra-Sunni disagreement regarding the performance of the *ṣalāt al-tarāwīḥ*, these prayers became well established in Sunni North Africa precisely because the Ismailis had opposed them. The need to clearly outline the boundaries between Sunnis and Ismailis led a Sunni author like al-Ṭurṭūshī (d. 520/1126) while living in Fatimid Alexandria to actively stress the rejectionist views in Sunnism of certain ritual practices that were close to those of the Fatimids. Among these there were the intentional visiting of certain places and buildings considered to be religiously significant, the lamentation over the dead, the celebration of the nights of the

[18] The section on the *ṣalāt al-tarāwīḥ* is taken from Maribel Fierro, 'Al-Ṭurṭūshī and the Fatimids', in Farhad Daftary and Shainool Jiwa (ed.), *The Fatimid caliphate. Diversity of traditions* (London), pp. 118–162, at pp. 141–142.

middle of Rajab and Sha'ban and certain practices in the call to prayer (*tathwīb*), practices that were among those favoured by the Fatimids and on which there was *ikhtilāf* among the Sunnis – a situation that had already been highlighted by al-Muqaddasī in the early Fatimid period as we have seen.[19] The appreciation shown by the Fatimids for mathematical methods in resolving astronomical issues such as determining the end of Ramadan and correctly determining the *qibla* may have also strengthened a tendency among Mālikī jurists to avoid employing these methods.[20] In direct opposition to the Shi'i understanding of the day of 'Āshūrā', its joyful celebration became widespread in the Western Islamic lands.[21] On the other hand, and as mentioned, a Fatimid innovation, the *mawlid al-nabī*, became a powerful instrument for political and religious legitimisation among Sunnis, as was also the case with the Fatimid celebration of *'īd al-aḍḥā*.

In Ifrīqiya, it was the Fatimid imam-caliph himself who publicly sacrificed a she-camel (*nāqa*)[22] during *'īd al-aḍḥā*, a practice that started with the third imam-caliph Ismā'īl al-Manṣūr (r. 335–341/946–953). In 334/946, the second Fatimid imam-caliph al-Qā'im had designated his son Ismā'īl as his heir.[23] Al-Qā'im died in 335/946 and his son succeeded him, adopting the regnal title al-Manṣūr, 'The Victor', once he had managed in 336/947 to put an end to the rebellion of the

---

19 Fierro, 'Al-Ṭurṭūshī and the Fatimids', pp. 140–146.

20 Heinz Halm, *The Empire of the Mahdi: The Rise of the Fatimids*, tr. M. Bonner (Leiden, 1996), pp. 123, 127, 372–373; Mònica Rius, *La Alquibla en al-Andalus y al-Magrib al-Aqṣà* (Barcelona, 2000), p. 88 and cf. p. 57 on the dislike of the Fatimids.

21 Maribel Fierro, 'The celebration of 'Āshūrā' in Sunnī Islam', *Proceedings of the 14th Congress of the Union Européenne des Arabisants et Islamisants, The Arabist*, 13–14 (1994), pp. 193–208.

22 In Taqī al-Dīn Aḥmad al-Maqrīzī, *Itti'āẓ al-ḥunafā' bi-akhbār al-a'imma al-fāṭimiyyīn al-khulafā'*, ed. Jamāl al-Dīn al-Shayyāl, 3 vols (Cairo, 1416/1996) there are references to she-camels as gifts (vol. 1, pp. 121, 249), riding animals with a *qubba* (vol. 1, p. 133, vol. 2, p. 3), as animals sacrificed by the imam-caliph 'Alī al-Ẓāhir (r. 411–427/1021–1036) (vol. 2, p. 167), as well as to the Qur'anic 'Camel of God' and the nickname of *ṣāḥib al-nāqa* given to one of Zīkrawayh's sons that will be mentioned below (vol. 1, p. 169; vol. 3, p. 93).

23 Halm, *The Empire of the Mahdi*, p. 310.

Berber leader Abū Yazīd, known as *ṣāḥib al-ḥimār*, because he always rode a donkey, an action with Messianic connotations. This Zanāta (Ifrān) Berber, called Abū Yazīd Makhlad b. Kaydād, was a Khārijī who had rebelled around the year 332/944. He managed to conquer Qayrawān, where he had coins struck in his name. But he did not manage to conquer Mahdiyya, the fortress-city built by the Fatimids at the beginning of their reign, and the place where the Fatimid caliph al-Qā'im had taken refuge.[24] When Ismā'īl came to power, it was not clear who would eventually have the upper hand, but in the year 335/946 he managed to inflict a defeat on Abū Yazīd, who had to abandon Qayrawān. His defeat was transformed in a proof of the legitimacy of the Fatimid dynasty and of the truth of the Fatimid doctrine. In a reversal of his claims to messianic status, Abū Yazīd was now portrayed as the Dajjāl, the Anti-Christ who would cause upheaval before the appearance of the Messiah or Mahdi who would eventually defeat him. By being identified with the eschatological figure of the Dajjāl, Abū Yazīd was not merely a rival who supported an alternative view of Islam and who sought to gain political power. He was the Great Enemy, whose defeat opened the way for the completion of the divine plan. The ignominious parading of Abū Yazīd's corpse after his death publicly proclaimed his evil and by contrast the righteousness of those who had defeated him. On the day he died (29 Muḥarram 336/19 August 947), Ismā'īl – who had kept his father al-Qā'im's death a secret – proclaimed himself imam-caliph with the title al-Manṣūr bi-Naṣr Allāh. Having vanquished al-Dajjāl, the imam-caliph Ismā'īl al-Manṣūr himself became a Messianic figure: he was the vanquisher of evil who inaugurated a new age in which the Fatimid dynasty would rule until the last Day.[25] It is worth noting that Abū Yazīd was called *ṣāḥib al-ḥimār*, and that the last Umayyad caliph Marwān II, whose defeat signalled the end of the

---

[24] Halm, *The Empire of the Mahdi*, pp. 298–325, and Michael Brett, *The Rise of the Fatimids. The world of the Mediterranean and the Middle East in the tenth century CE* (Leiden, 2001), pp. 165–175.

[25] Brett, *The rise of the Fatimids*, pp. 170–171; Halm, *The Empire of the Mahdi*, pp. 322, 324.

eastern Umayyad dynasty and the triumph of the Abbasids, had also been called *al-ḥimār*.[26]

The Fatimid Ismāʿīl had pursued Abū Yazīd when the latter fled Qayrawān and took refuge in his fortress of Kiyāna (afterwards Qalʿat Banī Ḥammād). Ismāʿīl besieged him there in Shaʿbān-Ramaḍān 335/ March 947, and on 25 April he preached a sermon on the occasion of *ʿīd al-fiṭr* in a festival square which had been set up specifically for this purpose (in this sermon he continued to uphold the fiction that his father was still alive). On 2 July, *ʿīd al-aḍḥā* was held:

> Ismāʿīl appeared on the festival square in festive robes; clad in splendid red, with a yellow turban and a long train hanging from his turban, he led the prayer under a yellow pavilion, preached the sermon, and then sacrificed a she-camel with his own hands.[27]

There is no evidence of this personal involvement of the Fatimid caliph in the celebration of *ʿīd al-aḍḥā* in the reigns of Ismāʿīl's predecessors, al-Mahdī (r. 297–322/909–934) and al-Qāʾim (r. 322–334/934–946).[28] The first two imam-caliphs had stressed the eschatological dimensions of the Ismaili doctrine, an approach that started to wither away at the same time that the Fatimid state was taking shape.[29] The fourth imam-caliph, al-Muʿizz (r. 341–365/953–975), became more concerned with the establishment of the state, with legal codification and with the conquest of Egypt. The personal performance of the sacrifice is recorded also in his case, and again the imam-caliph wore red, sacrificed several she-camels himself, and gave a banquet.[30]

---

[26] Part of this section is based on Maribel Fierro, 'Emulating Abraham: the Fāṭimid al-Qāʾim and the Umayyad ʿAbd al-Raḥmān III', in Christian Lange and Maribel Fierro (ed.), *Public violence in Islamic societies: Power, discipline and the construction of the public sphere (7th-19th centuries CE)* (Edinburgh, 2009), pp. 130–155.

[27] Halm, *The Empire of the Mahdi*, p. 320, quoting Ibn Ẓāfir and al-Maqrīzī.

[28] Halm, *The Empire of the Mahdi*, pp. 160 and 220.

[29] Sumaiya A. Hamdani, *Between Revolution and State: The Path to Fatimid Statehood* (London, 2006); Jamel Velji, *An Apocalyptic History of the Early Fatimid Empire* (Edinburgh, 2016).

[30] Halm, *The Empire of the Mahdi*, p. 354.

The practice is also attested after the Fatimids moved their capital from Ifrīqiya to Egypt, where they founded the city of Cairo. Descriptions of *ʿīd al-aḍḥā* inform us that the celebrations usually lasted three days, corresponding to the *ayyām al-tashrīq* of the pilgrimage. The caliph would sacrifice at both the *muṣallā* and the ritual slaughterhouse (*manḥar*).[31] The meat of the sacrificed she-camel was distributed among those who had attended the ceremony, i.e., members of the closed circle around the imam-caliph.

The practice of personally conducting the sacrifice was also followed by the ʿAlawī dynasty that ruled Morocco from 1078/1668 onwards. These rulers claimed the title *amīr al-muʾminīn.*[32] The practice started during the reign of Mawlāy Ismāʿīl (r. 1082–1139/1672–1727) and has continued until today. In her study, the anthropologist M. E. Combs-Schilling presents an analysis of the role of the sacrifice in the religious legitimisation of political power in Morocco:

> The king emerges from a mosque, white robes gleaming. Robed men close in around him, encircling him in a great body of white. Briefly the circle breaks open to give entry to a ram; its fleece is pure white, its horns are mighty, its dark eyes are boldly encircled in black. Often the ram tosses its head grandly as it is led to the center. Two men seize the ram, force it on its back, turn its head toward Makka, and hold it fast. The king takes a knife in his right hand, utters God's name, and plunges the knife deeply into the ram's throat. The blood spurts, the ram struggles, then in a surge

[31] Sanders, *Ritual, politics and the city in Fatimid Cairo*, pp. 79–80, with indication of the great quantities of animals sacrificed, not only she-camels but also cattle and water-buffalo. Marius Canard, 'Le cérémonial fatimite et le cérémonial byzantin', p. 403, had already pointed out the personal involvement of the Fatimid caliph in *ʿīd al-aḍḥā*. See also Heinz Halm, *Die Kalifen von Kairo: die Fatimiden in Ägypten 973–1074* (München, 2003); Shainool Jiwa, *Towards a Shiʿi Mediterranean empire: Fatimid Egypt and the Founding of Cairo. The reign of the Imam-caliph al-Muʿizz from al-Maqrīzī's Ittiʿāẓ al-ḥunafāʾ* (London, 2009).

[32] The use of the parasol (*miẓalla*) by the ʿAlawīs has a precedent with the Fatimids, and before them with the Abbasids; before the ʿAlawīs, another Sharifian dynasty, that of the Saʿdids, employed it: Sanders, *Ritual, politics and the city in Fatimid Cairo*, p. 49; C.E. Bosworth and P. Chalmeta, 'Miẓalla', *EI2*.

> of life manages to stand up, only to collapse on its side in a pool of blood, heart still pounding. The whole of the nation watches this bleeding ram, for in its dying lies their hope.[33]

In the study from which this quotation is taken, the anthropologist M. E. Combs-Schilling analysed the role of the sacrifice in the religious legitimisation of political power in Morocco:

> Through the innovation, the ʿAlawi monarchs became the sacrificial link between God and nation, the means by which God could see the collectivity's faith and grant his favor. Through the performance, the Moroccan monarchs inserted themselves into the single most powerful canonical ritual in Islam and into the mythic foundations upon which it rests.
>
> Muslims throughout the world participate in the Great Sacrifice. Each year Muslims on pilgrimage in the Arabian Peninsula and Muslim heads of household throughout the lands take a knife in their hands and slay an animal on behalf of their families. But the ʿAlawi monarchs instituted a new level of sacrifice, a national level, which they personally performed. Morocco's sharifi caliph became the only head of any major Muslim state to himself slit a ram's throat on behalf of the political community he leads . . . It seems likely that Mawlay Ismaʿil began the practice, though it is plausible that he reinstituted a practice that earlier Moroccan monarchs had performed, a practice for which documentation is obscure or nonexistent . . . It is . . . the most powerful ritual support of the Moroccan monarchy. It bolsters the king's legitimacy by having him perform the most dramatic action in which humans can engage for the most noble of purposes, the causing of earthly death in order to overcome the limits of earthly life, in order to connect with the divine.[34]

---

[33] M. E. Combs-Schilling, *Sacred Performances: Islam, Sexuality, and Sacrifice* (New York, 1989), pp. 268–275. See also Jocelyn Dakhlia, *Le divan des rois. Le politique et le religieux dans l'Islam* (Paris, 1998), pp. 268–275. A picture of King Hassan II performing the sacrifice can be seen at http://news.bbc.co.uk/2/hi/in_pictures/4611370.stm [accessed 12 May 2017].

[34] Combs-Schilling, *Sacred Performances*, p. 223.

Combs-Schilling thinks that the practice of having the Moroccan king sacrifice the ram on behalf of the community of believers as a whole was an innovation by the ʿAlawīs, but we have seen that the ʿAlawī rulers were not the first in publicly performing the ritual sacrifice on 10 Dhu'l-ḥijja, as the Fatimids did it before them. Since the ʿAlawīs' claim to rule was mainly based on their descent from the Prophet, the precedent for this role would seem to derive from the Fatimids, although the ʿAlawīs are not Shiʿis. It should perhaps also be noted that both in the Fatimid and the ʿAlawī case, the ruler who started the practice of personally performing the sacrifice bore the name Ismāʿīl which underlines the connection of the festival with Abraham's attempted sacrifice of his son, identified in the Islamic tradition with Ismāʿīl and not with Isḥāq.

The Fatimids' sacrifice was carried out in the *muṣallā*, which during the Egyptian period lay near the northern walls of Cairo. Paula Sanders records how the imam-caliph al-ʿAzīz (r. 365–386/975–996) ordered the construction of benches along the route from the palace to the *muṣallā* and commanded the Ismailis to sit on them according to rank, and repeat the phrase *Allāhu akbar* as a way of sacralising the procession route. The prayer at *ʿīd al-fiṭr* and *ʿīd al-aḍḥā* was not preceded by the first call nor the second call to prayer; thus uttering *Allāhu akbar* was simply the beginning of the prayer: the procession itself was now part of the prayer. But there was more to it, as Sanders explains[35]:

> The allegorical interpretation (*ta'wīl*) of the festival in Ismaili thought makes the connection among the procession, the prayer, the construction of the ritual city, and the centrality of the imam even more plausible. Two works of the Fatimid jurist and ideologue al-Qāḍī al-Nuʿmān (d. 363/974), *The Pillars of Islam* (*Daʿā'im al-Islām*) and *The Allegorical Interpretation of the Pillars* (*Ta'wīl al-daʿā'im*), designate three festivals, which are Friday prayer (*al-jumʿa*), the Festival of Fast Breaking *(ʿīd al-fiṭr)* and the Sacrificial Festival (*ʿīd al-aḍḥā*). Each festival has an esoteric (*bāṭin*) paradigm: that of the Friday prayer is the call or mission (*daʿwa*) of Muhammad, which is also the call to the hidden

[35] Sanders, *Ritual, Politics and the City in Fatimid Cairo*, pp. 49–50.

> imams; of the fast of Ramaḍān, concealment (*al-kitmān wa'l-satr*); of the breaking of the fast, the *mahdī* (rightly guided one) and the revealing of the hidden mission; of the sacrificial feast, the *qā'im* (riser). These ritual observances thus symbolised the imam himself.
>
> In his *Allegorical Interpretation*, al-Qāḍī al-Nuʿmān makes explicit the connection between the festivals and their paradigms of the *mahdī* and the *qā'im*. In the *Pillars*, he prescribes that the prayer for the two festivals should be neither in a house nor in a mosque but in an open place, and he says that one should bring out arms (*silāḥ*) to the prayer. The paradigm (*mathal*) of going out to prayer (*al-khurūj li'l-ṣalāt*) and taking out arms (*ikhrāj al-silāḥ*) is striving against the enemies (*jihād*). He explained it further by requiring that the prayer be held in an 'open field' (*al-baraz*), that is, the *muṣallā*. These ideas were current even in the North African period of the caliphate and are probably the appropriate intellectual climate in which the story of the master of the ass (*ṣāḥib al-ḥimār*, i.e., the Kharijite Abū Yazīd) should be viewed.

This connection of the *muṣallā* with Abū Yazīd needs some explanation. Shortly after the Fatimids took power in Ifrīqiya in the year 296/909, in 303/916 they had started building a city by the sea, al-Mahdiyya, to serve them as refuge against disturbances from the Sunni population and other possible enemies. The uncultivated stretch of land between the land wall of the city and the suburb of the Zawīla – on the narrow area connecting the peninsula with the mainland – served as a festival and prayer square (*muṣallā*) on the two highest festivals, *ʿīd al-fiṭr* and *ʿīd al-aḍḥā*. This *muṣallā* was more than simply a site for festival prayer. When al-Mahdī built his capital city al-Mahdiyya, he ordered an arrow to be shot from the wall of the city westwards.

> He then ordered a *muṣallā* to be build where it landed, saying: 'The master of the ass (*ṣāḥib al-ḥimār*) will arrive here', referring to the Kharijite rebel, Abū Yazīd, an avowed enemy of the North African Fatimid state. The prophecy was fulfilled when Abū Yazīd was stopped at the *muṣallā* when he attacked al-Mahdiyya. Given the amuletic power attributed to the *muṣallā* in this historicised legend, it is probably no coincidence that the *muṣallā* at Cairo

> was built outside Bāb al-Naṣr, the gate that was the city's most vulnerable point of attack.[36]

The *muṣallā* was therefore for the Fatimids an eschatological battleground (*malḥama*) connected with the memory of Abū Yazīd's defeat and the festivals were the moments when battle took place, so that participants were expected to bring their weapons. At *ʿīd al-aḍḥā* associated with the Fatimid victory over the Man of the Donkey, the esoteric (*bāṭin*) paradigm of the caliph was the eschatological figure of the Riser (*al-qā'im*). But the most evident association was with the figure of Abraham.

Through the prophet Abraham, Ibrāhīm in Arabic, the Prophet and the Arabs as a whole entered Biblical sacred genealogy: the Arabs were considered to be the descendants of Ismāʿīl, the son Abraham had with his slave concubine Hagar, and who was his first-born.[37] This ancestry and precedence involved a polemical stance against the Jews, who considered themselves the descendants of Isaac (Isḥāq), the son Abraham had with his wife Sarah.[38] In the Biblical and Islamic stories told about Abraham, when he received the good news that his son would be born, he vowed to sacrifice his son. Muslim sources record two divergent views regarding who was Abraham's son intended to be sacrificed (*al-dhabīḥ*) and eventually ransomed (*al-mufaddā*).[39]

---

[36] Sanders, *Ritual, Politics and the City in Fatimid Cairo*, p. 45.

[37] Khalil Athamina, 'Abraham in Islamic Perspective. Reflections on the Development of Monotheism in Pre-Islamic Arabia', *Der Islam*, 81 (2004), pp. 184–205, at pp. 203–204.

[38] René Dagorn, *La geste d'Ismaël d'après l'onomastique et la tradition arabe* (Paris, 1981); Sahri L. Lowin, *The making of a forefather: Abraham in Islamic and Jewish exegetical narratives* (Leiden, 2006).

[39] Among the studies devoted to this issue, see Norman Calder, 'From Midrash to scripture: the sacrifice of Abraham in early Islamic tradition', *Le Muséon*, 101 (1988), pp. 375–402; Reuven Firestone, 'Abraham's son as the intended sacrifice (*al-dhabīḥ*, Qur'an 37:99–113): issues in Qur'anic exegesis', *Journal of Semitic Studies*, 34 (1989), pp. 95–131; Suliman Bashear, 'Abraham's sacrifice of his son and related issues', *Der Islam*, 67 (1990), pp. 243–77; F. Manns (ed.), *Sacrifice of Isaac in the three monotheistic religions* (Jerusalem, 1995). A preference for Isḥāq rather than Ismāʿīl was favoured by Sunni authors in the Islamic West such as Qāḍī ʿIyāḍ, al-Suhaylī and al-Qurṭubī: Bashear, 'Abraham's sacrifice of his son', p. 276.

As Bashear and others before him have indicated, this and other connected issues played a crucial role in the emergence and formation of Islam as an Arab religion linked to Abraham's monotheism through his son Ismāʿīl, father of the Arabs, and of Mecca as a holy place 'connected with the Abrahamic ritual of sacrifice which is symbolically repeated by Muslims during the *ḥajj* ritual'.[40]

Why did the third imam-caliph start the practice of personally performing the sacrifice on the day of *ʿīd al-aḍḥā*? When Ismāʿīl al-Manṣūr did it in the year 335/947 at a moment when victory over the Man of the Donkey was imminent and when his father al-Qāʾim had died (a death then kept secret), he seems to have intended to present himself as Abraham, in Islamic tradition the founder of the pilgrimage rituals in Mecca, including the sacrifice.[41] The Ismailis understood history as a series of cycles, in which the first six had been initiated by a speaker-prophet following the order Adam, Noah, Abraham, Moses, Jesus and Muhammad. Each speaker-prophet was accompanied by a legatee (*waṣī*), who became the speaker-prophet's successor as leader of the community, and disclosed the secret interpretation of the laws brought by the speaker-prophets. The *waṣī*s are followed by the imams the line of which culminates with the appearance of the *qāʾim*.[42] Ismaili *taʾwīl* contains many examples in which prophetic figures are read in a way that promotes the Ismaili understanding of the imamate, reflects the experience of the partisans of ʿAlī and his family and 'impart lessons relevant to contemporary circumstances or the (relatively) recent past'.[43] As David Hollenberg has explained, *taʾwīl* was the lens through which the Ismaili proselytisers and those who followed them saw the

---

40 Bashear, 'Abraham's sacrifice of his son', p. 244. The article is a detailed discussion of those issues.

41 Snouck Hurgronje, *The Meccan Pilgrimage Festival: Its Emergence and Early Development*, tr. Lawrence I. Conrad and Petra Sijpesteijn (Princeton, 2004) (the original work in Dutch was published in 1880).

42 David Hollenberg, *Beyond the Qurʾān: early Ismāʿīlī taʾwīl and the secrets of the prophets* (Columbia, 2016), p. 108.

43 Michael Pregill, 'Measure for measure: prophetic history, Qurʾanic exegesis, and anti-Sunnī polemic in a Fāṭimid propaganda work (BL Or. 8419)', *Journal of Qurʾanic Studies*, 16 (2014), p. 21.

world, having learned that the Qur'an and rituals contained a secret meaning and that the disclosure of such secret meanings would enlighten them and enlarge their understanding of the divine revelation, while at the same time this interpretive endeavour strengthened the links that bound them together.[44]

David Hollenberg has also shown that the first Fatimid imam-caliph ʿAbd Allāh al-Mahdī was represented as Adam in an early Ismaili source, Jaʿfar b. Manṣūr al-Yaman's *Sarāʾir al-nuṭaqāʾ*.[45] Is it too far-fetched to speculate that the second imam-caliph al-Qāʾim, the one who took refuge in Mahdiyya (the Ark?) when the Man of the Donkey seemed in the verge of victory, could then have been linked to Noah? If so, the third imam-caliph was bound to be linked to Abraham and the fourth imam-caliph, al-Muʿizz – known for his legislative activity and his move to Egypt – would have been linked to Moses.

The sacrifice of an animal is an important element of the pilgrimage rituals and, as already indicated, while it takes place in Minā, it is also performed in the rest of the Islamic world.[46] The animal chosen is usually a ram, although no animal is specified in the narrative recorded in Qur'an 37:101–7[47]:

> Then We gave him the good tidings of a prudent boy; and when he reached the age of running with him, he said, 'My son, I see in a dream that I shall sacrifice thee; consider, what thinkest thou?' He said, 'My father, do as thou art bidden; thou shalt find me, God willing, one of the steadfast.' When they had surrendered, and he flung him upon his brow, We called unto him, 'Abraham, thou hast confirmed the vision; even so We recompense the good-doers. This is indeed the manifest trial.' And we ransomed

---

44 Hollenberg, *Beyond the Qurʾān*, p. vii. See also Habib Feki, *al-Taʾwīl: Usūsuhu wa-maʿnīhi fiʾl-madhhab al-ismaʿīlī* (Tunis, 1979); and chapters 5, 6 and 8 in A. Keeler and S. H. Rizvi (ed.), *The Spirit and the Letter: Approaches to the Esoteric Interpretation of the Qurʾan* (London and New York, 2016).

45 Jaʿfar b. Manṣūr al-Yaman, *Sarāʾir wa-asrār al-nuṭaqāʾ*, ed. Muṣṭafā Ghālib (Beirut, 1404/1984). For the work see Hollenberg, *Beyond the Qurʾān*, p. 48.

46 M. Esperonnier, 'La sunna du sacrifice: les recommandations d'Ibn al-Hâjj al-ʿAbdarī', *Revue des Études Islamiques*, 50 (1982), pp. 251–255.

47 The translation is by A. J. Arberry. For a general treatment, see Y. Moubarac, *Abraham dans le Coran* (Paris, 1958).

> him with a mighty sacrifice (*dhibḥ ʿaẓīm*), and left for him among the later folk 'Peace be upon Abraham!'

According to al-Ṭabarī, what was meant by Qur'an 37:107 was not only the ransom on that specific occasion, but sacrifice according to Abraham's religion, 'which is the *sunna* until the day of resurrection', to be followed by the believers.[48] A Muslim tradition describes how Abraham sacrificed the ransom animal – an antelope – and states that it was done in Minā 'where beasts are (ritually) slaughtered today.'[49] The ransom animal, also said to have been a billy goat (*tays*), eventually became the standard 'white, prime, horned' ram (*abyaḍ, aʿyan, aqran*) mentioned in Combs-Schilling's quotation, with a further development identifying it with the same one sacrificed by Adam's son which had been since then stored in Paradise.[50] Why therefore did the Fatimid Ismāʿīl choose a she-camel?

In the entry on Abraham in *Sarā'ir al-nuṭaqā'* no mention is made of a she-camel, only of a ram (*kabsh*) as the animal that was sacrificed by Abraham.[51] It has not been possible to discover an explanation for the choice of the animal to be sacrificed by the Fatimid imam-caliphs, only the insistence that the best animal for sacrifice – because it is the most worthy of what brings the believer to God – was a she-camel.[52] The Prophet Muhammad, according to a report attributed to the first Umayyad caliph Muʿāwiya, was called 'son of the two sacrifices' (*ibn al-dhabīḥayn*): ʿAbd al-Muṭṭalib, the Prophet's grandfather, would have vowed to sacrifice one of his sons and the choice fell on ʿAbd Allāh, who was ransomed by one hundred camels.[53] Given their size, camels could seem to correspond better to the Qur'anic 'mighty sacrifice' (*dhibḥ ʿaẓīm*) than other animals. More importantly, camels were

---

48 Bashear, 'Abraham's sacrifice of his son', pp. 268–269.

49 Bashear, 'Abraham's sacrifice of his son', pp. 251, 261; see also pp. 263, 264–265, 267–268.

50 Bashear, 'Abraham's sacrifice of his son', pp. 262, 254, 260, 268–270.

51 Jaʿfar b. Manṣūr al-Yaman, *Sarā'ir wa-asrār al-nuṭaqā'*, p. 70.

52 Paul Walker, *Orations of the Fatimid caliphs. Festival sermons of the Ismaili imams* (London, 2009), p. 80 and *khuṭbas* numbers 6 and 8, both by Ismāʿīl al-Manṣūr (the term used is *ināth al-ibil*).

53 Bashear, 'Abraham's sacrifice of his son', p. 245.

linked to the Arabs and thus to Ismāʿīl. Perhaps on that first occasion when a she-camel was sacrificed by a member of the dynasty, what the would-be third imam-caliph tried to emphasise was that Ismāʿīl and not Isḥāq was Abraham's son chosen for sacrifice.[54] This concern can be connected with the need to counteract Umayyad propaganda against the Fatimids in which they were called Jews,[55] and this at a moment when the Man of the Donkey – the enemy that the Fatimid Ismāʿīl was fighting against – was being helped by ʿAbd al-Raḥmān III with an Umayyad fleet attacking al-Mahdiyya in the year 335/946. It should also be remembered that, according to the Ḥanbalī Ibn Baṭṭa (d. 387/997), the Jews forbade eating the meat of the camel ritually sacrificed (*jazūr*), in spite of its consumption being allowed by God, and that the Rāfiḍa (that is, the Shiʿis) followed this same prohibition.[56] By eating the meat of the she-camels they sacrificed, the Fatimid imam-caliphs were again proclaiming that they were not Jews, while at the same time differentiating themselves from other Shiʿis as they had also done in the case of the *mutʿa* marriage that they completely rejected. Ibn Baṭṭa adds that the sacrifice of a she-camel is one of the best acts that can be performed to get near God: this is the reason that

[54] The issue of which son was the intended sacrificial victim is discussed in Jaʿfar b. Manṣūr al-Yaman, *Sarāʾir wa-asrār al-nuṭaqāʾ*, pp. 67–89. In my article quoted in note 26 I dealt with the possible connection between the Fatimid practice and the story told about the Umayyad caliph in Cordoba, ʿAbd al-Raḥmān III, that he sacrificed his son ʿAbd Allāh on *ʿīd al-aḍḥā*. The story originated in a pro-Fatimid source.

[55] Ibn Ḥayyān, *al-Muqtabas*, vol. V, ed. Pedro Chalmeta, Federico Corriente and Mahmud Sobh (Madrid, 1979); Spanish trans. by Federico Corriente and María Jesús Viguera (Zaragoza, 1981), 221/247 and 237/263. In *Kitāb al-Istibṣār*, ed. S. Zaghlūl ʿAbd al-Ḥamīd (Casablanca, 1985), p. 117 it is said that when Abū ʿAbd Allāh al-Dāʿī broke with ʿAbd Allāh al-Shīʿī (i.e., the first Fāṭimid imam-caliph) the former tried to convince the shaykhs of the Kutāma that the latter was a pretender, saying that he was really a Jew whom he had presented himself as *al-ʿalawī al-fāṭimī* in substitute for the real one. On the accusation by Sunni polemicists that Maymūn al-Qaddāḥ was the originator of Ismailism see S. Wasserstrom, *Between Muslim and Jew. The problem of symbiosis in early Islam* (Princeton, NJ: Princeton University Press, 1995), pp. 157–158.

[56] Henri Laoust, *La profession de foi d'Ibn Baṭṭa* (Damascus, 1958), pp. 135–137. There seems to be no basis for attribution of such prohibition to the Shiʿis (I would like to thank Devin Stewart for pointing this out).

when a pilgrim does not abstain from sexual intercourse he can compensate for his misdeed by sacrificing a she-camel. Camels were the animals sacrificed by the Prophet Muhammad both at al-Ḥudaybiyya and at the Farewell pilgrimage, on this occasion helped by ʿAlī b. Abī Ṭālib.[57]

However, there are other possible explanations for the choice of the animal. A she-camel plays an important role in the Qurʾanic story of the pre-Islamic Arab prophet Ṣāliḥ active among the Thamūd tribe. The Thamūd asked for a miracle and a she-camel (*nāqat Allāh*) was sent to them, although eventually they killed her and they were subsequently destroyed.[58] This story was one of the best known of the Qurʾan. It is quoted for example by John of Damascus, who mentions that the *nāqat Allāh* left behind a small she-camel that cried out for God and He took her up to Himself, and uses it to debate with the Muslims pointing out that the story posed as many problems as those that Muslims claimed Christ's crucifixion and ascension to the heavens had.[59] That the Qurʾanic story was of significance for the Ismailis is reflected in the nickname adopted by Yaḥyā b. Zikrawayh, *ṣāḥib al-nāqa*. He was one of the sons of the Ismaili *dāʿī*, Zikrawayh b. Mihrawayh, who were sent in 289/902 to the Syrian desert in order to proselytise among the Banū Kalb. Their mission was successful. Yaḥyā b. Zikrawayh adopted an Ismaili genealogy and 'asserted to them . . . that the she-camel he was riding was blessed and if they followed her wherever she went, they would be victorious . . . A number of the Banū l-Aṣbagh flocked to him. They showed sincere devotion to him, called themselves Fatimids and adopted his religion' (*wa-tasammaw*

[57] Brannon Wheeler, 'Gift of the Body in Islam: the Prophet Muhammad's Camel sacrifice and distribution of hair and nails at his Farewell pilgrimage', *Numen*, 57 (2010), pp. 341–388. For Wheeler, these episodes are to be understood with sociogonic more than cosmogonic meaning, as they refer to the end of chaos and disorder, and the construction of society (pp. 365, 372).

[58] The She-Camel of God (*nāqat Allāh*) and the accompanying narratives can be found in Qurʾan 7:73–79, 11:61–69, 15:80–84, 26:141–158, 54:23–31, 89:6–13, 91:11–15. See also Sara Tlili, *Animals in the Qurʾan* (Cambridge, 2013).

[59] Daniel J. Sahas, *John of Damascus on Islam. The 'Heresy of the Ishmaelites'* (Leiden, 1972), pp. 139–141. I owe this information to Christian Sahner.

bi'l-fāṭimiyyīn wa-dānū bi-dīni-hi).[60] On the other hand, among the Shiʿis, Ṣāliḥ was associated with ʿAlī as they shared many similarities, for example, they will both ride a she-camel in Paradise.[61] Finally, camels in Ismaili thought were associated with Jesus: the name ʿĪsā was considered to be the name of the physical and material form of Jesus because the word *ʿīs* means camels.[62] In Ismaili *ta'wīl* camels correspond to the imams.[63]

She-camels were also associated with the Berbers. The Arab paternal ancestor of the Berbers, Barr b. Qays, went to live with his mother's relatives (i.e. the Berbers) because he was following a female camel that had escaped and led him to where they lived.[64] Among the Berbers popular tales circulate that situate in their lands those who killed and ate the She-Camel of God.[65] In the Jāhiliyya, *sā'iba* referred to an unfettered camel that roamed freely and was considered to be untouchable,

---

60 Al-Ṭabarī, *Ta'rīkh*, ed. M.J. de Goeje, 3 series (Leiden, 1879–1901), vol. 3, p. 2219; F. Rosenthal, *The History of al-Ṭabarī, vol. XXXVIII: The return of the caliphate to Baghdad* (Albany, NY, 1985), pp. 113–115; Ibn al-Athīr, *al-Kāmil fī'l-ta'rīkh* (Beirut, 1965–1967), vol. 7, p. 512. On these events, see W. Madelung, 'Karmaṭī', *EI2*; Heinz Halm, 'Die Sohne Zikrawaihs und das erste fatimidische Kalifat (290/903)', *Die Welt des Orients*, 10 (1979), pp. 30–53; Maribel Fierro, 'On al-fāṭimī and al-fāṭimiyyūn', *Jerusalem Studies in Arabic and Islam*, 20 (1996), pp. 130–161.

61 Khalid Sindawi, 'The Prophet Ṣāliḥ and ʿAlī b. Abī Ṭālib', *Ancient Near Eastern Studies*, 49 (2012), p. 211. According to Ṣāʿid al-Ṭulayṭulī (d. 462/1070), the ancient Arabs believed that if a she-camel (*nāqa*) was sacrificed on the grave of a deceased man, he would come back to life mounted on that same she-camel: *Ṭabaqāt al-umam*, ed. L. Cheikho (Beirut, 1912), p. 44; tr. R. Blachère (Paris, 1935), pp. 92–93.

62 Antonella Straface, 'An Ismāʿīlī interpretation of *šubbiha lahum* (Qur. IV, 157) in the *Kitāb šağarat al-yaqīn*', *Orientalia Lovaniensia Analecta*, 148 (2006), pp. 95–100, at p. 96.

63 Hollenberg, *Beyond the Qur'ān*, p. 66.

64 Helena de Felipe, 'Leyendas árabes sobre el origen de los beréberes', *Al-Qanṭara*, 11 (1990), p. 387.

65 Vermondo Brugnatelli, 'L'islamizzazione dei Tuareg alla luce dei dati linguistici', in P. Branca and V. Brugnatelli (ed.), *Studi arabi e islamici in memoria di Matilde Gagliardi* (Milan, 1995), pp. 63–74. The negative image of the Berbers in Arabic sources includes their description as the nation to whom God sent a prophet but they killed him, cooked him and ate him: Mabrouk Mansouri, 'Cynophagy, homosexuality and anthropophagy in medieval Islamic North Africa as signs of hospitality', *The Journal of North African Studies*, 20, 2 (2015), pp. 128–142.

protected from being milked, ridden or slaughtered. Such beliefs were abolished with the advent of Islam (Qurʾan 5:102).[66] The term *al-sība*, especially in the expression *bilād al-sība*, became a metaphor for the untamed and unsubdued, signifying dissidence, rebellion, lawlessness, ungovernability, statelessness, anarchy, chaos, civil war.[67] It can be argued that the sacrifice of a she-camel was a means of symbolising the taming of the rebel Berbers who had threatened Fatimid rule under al-Qāʾim and who had been subdued by Ismāʿīl al-Manṣūr. Ritual sacrifice in Ismaili *taʾwīl* stands for the oath of allegiance.[68] In relation with this possible meaning of subduing the Berbers, the mantle of the Norman king of Sicily Roger II (r. 1130–1154) depicting two lions killing two camels has been interpreted in connection with his North African expansionist policies and his control of former Zirid territories.[69] The colours of the mantle are red and yellow, the colours worn by the first two Fatimid imams who publicly sacrificed a she-camel. The imagery of Roger II's mantle, of which different interpretations have been given, can therefore also be connected to the Fatimid practice analysed here.

Whatever the reason for the choice of she-camels, Ismāʿīl al-Manṣūr's personal performance of the sacrifice clearly established a link with the prophet Abraham within a general Ismaili tendency to look back to salvation history as commentary on present circumstances. The prophet Abraham is also considered to have instituted the practice of circumcision,[70] and in this regard again the Fatimid

---

66 A. J. Wensinck, 'Baḥīra', *EI2*.

67 D. Rivet, 'Sība', *EI2*, where it is mentioned that the expression *bilād sāʾiba* appeared, probably for the first time, in a work by the Mālikī North African jurist Abū ʿImrān al-Fāsī (d. 430/1039) who lived in Qayrawān during the period when the Zirids still kept their allegiance to the Fatimids in Cairo.

68 Hollenberg, *Beyond the Qurʾān*, p. 66.

69 Jeremy Johns, 'Leone che caccia un cammello', in his, 'Le pitture del soffitto della Cappella Palatina', in B. Brenk (ed.), *La Cappella Palatina a Palermo* (Mirabilia Italiae 17) (Modena, 2010), vol. 4, *Schede*, pp. 451–452.

70 'The circumcision ceremony is considered the most important act of purification in Islamic tradition. When God commanded Abraham to purify himself, he went to perform ablution (*wuḍūʿ*), an act of purification performed by Muslims before a prayer. God commanded him to purify himself again, and he removed his impurities. When God commanded him a third time, he went and was circumcised', Athamina, 'Abraham in Islamic Perspective', p. 198.

imam-caliphs established a connection with him. By the year 349/960, especially after having established control of the central Maghrib, al-Muʿizz 'could . . . justly maintain that from the Atlantic to the Indus, believing followers were heeding his every word and waiting for his appearance in the East'. It was then that muezzins were ordered to use only the Shiʿi call to prayer and other Ismaili practices considered innovations by the Sunnis. Al-Muʿizz also – with the help of al-Qāḍī al-Nuʿmān – produced the Ismaili legal code. A great festival, celebrated throughout the empire in the spring of 351/962, marked the successful conclusion of the ventures in the Maghrib. The sons of the imam-caliph had to be circumcised and the occasion was chosen for all the children in the realm to be also circumcised. Despite the heavy cost incurred, ten pavilions were raised in the great court of the palace; every day, with the imam attending the ceremony, between 5,000 and 10,000 boys were circumcised. The purpose of this great circumcision festival was to weld together the entire Muslim population of the empire, Sunni and Ismaili, into one single community (*umma*) under one *imām*. Al-Muʿizz saw himself, as he expressly stated to al-Qāḍī al-Nuʿmān, as the successor to Abraham and the Prophet Muhammad. In view of his success, he could now think himself very close to his goal, the unification of Islam. Counting his three predecessors in Salamiyya, he was indeed the seventh successor (*khalīfa*) of Muḥammad b. Ismāʿīl, whom the Ismailis of the East expected to be the last before the reappearance of the Mahdi-*qāʾim*; perhaps al-Muʿizz himself harboured similar hopes.[71] Ismaili *taʾwīl* equates circumcision to the discovery of the interior sense:[72] the public celebration of that ceremony could also be understood as proclaiming the new period ushered in by al-Muʿizz's reign with its legislative production including both the external and the internal, i.e., the *Daʿāʾim al-Islām* and the *Taʾwīl Daʿāʾim al-Islām*.[73]

---

71 Here I have followed Halm, *The Empire of the Mahdi*, p. 403.

72 Jaʿfar b. Manṣūr al-Yaman, *Sarāʾir wa-asrār al-nuṭaqāʾ*, p. 131; Hollenberg, *Beyond the Qurʾān*, p. 66.

73 Al-Qāḍī al-Nuʿmān, *Daʿāʾim al-Islām*, ed. A.A.A. Fyzee, 2 vols (Cairo, 1952–1961) and *Taʾwīl Daʿāʾim al-Islām*, ed. Muḥammad Ḥasan al-Aʿẓamī, 3 vols (Cairo, 1967–1972).

This sort of public circumcision accompanying that of the son/s of the ruler does not seem to have been performed before Fatimid times. There are examples in Ottoman times, while involvement of the rulers in the circumcision of the children of their subjects is also attested under the Mamluks,[74] as well as is in Morocco under the Saʿdīs. On the 10th of Muḥarram, the day of ʿĀshūrāʾ, the Saʿdī ruler Aḥmad al-Manṣūr (r. 986–1012/1578–1603), the conqueror of the western lands of *bilād al-sudān*, the Sahel regions of Africa, and a claimant to the caliphate, offered free circumcision for children and donations to their families if they were poor.[75] Before him, another al-Manṣūr had done the same. From 368/978 to 392/1002, the vizier and then chamberlain Ibn Abī ʿĀmir al-Maʿāfirī became *de facto* the real ruler of al-Andalus profiting from the minority of Hishām II who had succeeded his father al-Ḥakam II (r. 350–366/961–976) as Umayyad caliph in Cordoba. Ibn Abī ʿĀmir al-Manṣūr is said to have ordered a circumcision ceremony for his sons together with 500 male children of his courtiers and many poor children, with a total cost of 500,000 gold pieces. While this information is only found in a late Eastern source, and therefore its historicity can be doubted,[76] it adds to what we know of Ibn Abī ʿĀmir al-Manṣūr's efforts to build his political and religious legitimacy in a complex process that involved assuming the symbols of caliphal power while maintaining his obedience to the Umayyad

---

[74] Derin Terzioğlu, 'The Imperial circumcision festival of 1582: an interpretation', *Muqarnas*, 12 (1995), pp. 84–100; Adam Sabra, *Poverty and charity in Medieval Islam. Mamluk Egypt, 1250–1517* (Cambridge, 2000), p. 54; Amy Singer, *Charity in Islamic Societies* (New York, 2008), p. 82.

[75] Mohamed El Mansour, 'Hospitality, Charity and Political Legitimacy in Pre-modern Morocco', in Amira K. Bennison (ed.), *The articulation of power in Medieval Iberia and the Maghrib* (Oxford, 2014), p. 188. On Aḥmad al-Manṣūr see Stephen Ch. Cory, *Reviving the Islamic caliphate in early modern Morocco* (Surrey, 2014).

[76] Al-Nuwayrī (d. 732/1332), *Nihāyat al-ʿarab*, ed. and tr. Mariano Gaspar Remiro, *Historia de los musulmanes de España y África por En-Nuguairí* (Granada, 1917), ed. pp. 66–67, trans. 60–61. See Ana María Carballeira, 'The Use of Charity as a Means of Political Legitimization in Umayyad al-Andalus', *Journal of the Economic and Social History of the Orient*, 60, 3 (2017), pp. 233–262.

caliph.[77] In this case, and if the information is to be trusted, he would have adopted a practice of the rival caliphs, the Fatimids, in order to give support to his need for legitimisation. Similar imperatives lay behind the decision of al-Maʾmūn, the Berber Taifa king of Toledo, to celebrate at considerable cost the circumcision of his grandson in the year 455/1063 along with that of the sons of his courtiers.[78] The presence in his court of a scholar, Ibn Sharaf al-Qayrawānī (d. 460/1068 or 470/1077), who had served the Zirids in Ifrīqiya, and who must thus have been aware of the Fatimid precedent may have been instrumental in the performance of such ceremony.[79]

In this chapter, specific practices associated with sacrifice and circumcision under the Fatimids and their possible influence on practices performed by other North African dynasties, especially those claiming Prophetic descent, have been analysed. A comparative analysis of how rulers through the history of Islamic societies have made use of religious ceremonies and rituals to cover for different needs and with different aims is an area of study which will repay further investigation, yielding new insights into the construction and legitimisation of political power.

---

[77] On this process see Pierre Guichard, 'Al-Manṣūr or al-Manṣūr bi-Llāh? Les laqab-s des ʿĀmirides, d'après la numismatique', *Archéologie islamique*, 5 (1995), pp. 47–53; Laura Bariani, *Almanzor* (San Sebastián, 2003).

[78] Ibn Bassām (d. 543/1148), *al-Dhakhīra fī maḥāsin ahl al-jazīra*, ed. Iḥsān ʿAbbās, 8 vols (Libya/Tunis, 1975), vol. 8, p. 128.

[79] 'Ibn Šaraf al-Qayrawānī, Abū ʿAbd Allāh', *Biblioteca de al-Andalus*, vol. 5: *De Ibn Saʿada a Ibn Wuhayb*, ed. Jorge Lirola Delgado (Almería, 2007), 5, 247–256, no. 1120 [P. Lirola Delgado].

7

Human Action, God's Will: Further Thoughts on the Divine Command (*amr*) in the Teachings of Muḥyī al-Dīn Ibn al-ʿArabī (560–638/1165–1240)

Michael Ebstein
(The Hebrew University of Jerusalem)

Mysticism, contrary to a widespread misconception among educated circles and New Age groups in the West, is by no means divorced from politics. Not only have mystical movements in different cultures been involved in politics throughout the ages, but often their very origins and formative history have also been embedded in a political setting. This is especially true in Islam, a religion in which the relationship between spirituality and politics has always been an intimate one. In the Shiʿi world, from a relatively early stage (the first half of the second/eighth century), esoteric and mystical tendencies went hand and hand with political developments.[1] Similarly, as various studies have shown, many Sunni mystics and Sunni mystical movements in the history of Islam did not shy away from politics, but rather chose to operate within the public domain and influence society.[2] In fact, the history of Islamic societies, at least from the sixth–seventh/twelfth–thirteenth centuries onwards, cannot be understood without taking into account

[1] See, for example, M. A. Amir-Moezzi, *The Divine Guide in Early Shiʿism: the Sources of Esotericism in Islam* (Albany, 1994); Amir-Moezzi, *The Spirituality of Shiʿi Islam: Beliefs and Practices* (London, 2011).

[2] To cite but two studies: V. J. Cornell, *Realm of the Saint: Power and Authority in Moroccan Sufism* (Austin, 1998); I. Weismann, *The Naqshbandiyya: Orthodoxy and Activism in a Worldwide Sufi Tradition* (London, 2007).

the tremendous impact of mystical ideas and organisations on social and political processes.[3]

It comes then as no surprise to find in the mystical literature of Islam articulations of political theories or at least discussions of and references to political ideas. Ibn al-ʿArabī, the focus of the current article, serves as a good example: his writings abound with political terminology, and it seems that al-Shaykh al-akbar, 'the greatest Shaykh' as he is known in the Islamic tradition, had much to say about political issues – on for instance, the figure of the ideal ruler, the use of violence, the social-political role as well as the historical mission of *al-insān al-kāmil*, 'the perfect human being', the mystic's attitude towards society and his involvement in the mundane affairs of this world, and so forth. Unfortunately, these and similar aspects of Ibn al-ʿArabī's thought have yet to be studied in a satisfactory and comprehensive manner.[4] In what follows I shall attempt to elucidate a central concept in al-Shaykh al-akbar's teachings, namely, the Divine command (*amr*). As will become clear, this concept has both a spiritual-mystical and political dimension to it; these two dimensions and the relation between them merit close examination.

---

[3] See, for example, J. S. Trimingham, *The Sufi Orders in Islam* (Oxford, 1998); D. Ephrat, *Spiritual Wayfarers, Leaders in Piety: Sufis and the Dissemination of Islam in Medieval Palestine* (Cambridge, 2008); N. Hofer, *The Popularization of Sufism in Ayyubid and Mamluk Egypt, 1173–1325* (Edinburgh, 2015); and more.

[4] See for now M. Chodkiewicz, 'The Esoteric Foundations of Political Legitimacy in Ibn ʿArabī', in S. Hirtenstein and M. Tiernan (ed.), *Muhyiddin Ibn ʿArabi: a Commemorative Volume* (Shaftesbury, 1993), pp. 190–198; J. W. Morris, 'Freedoms and Responsibilities: Ibn ʿArabī and the Political Dimensions of Spiritual Realisation', *Journal of the Muhyiddin Ibn ʿArabi Society*, 38 (2006), pp. 1–21 and 39 (2006), pp. 85–110. On Ibn al-ʿArabī's life and thought see C. Addas, *Quest for the Red Sulphur: the Life of Ibn ʿArabī*, tr. Peter Kingsley (Cambridge, 1993); W. C. Chittick, *The Sufi Path of Knowledge: Ibn al-ʿArabi's Metaphysics of Imagination* (Albany, 1989); Chittick, *The Self-Disclosure of God: Principles of Ibn al-ʿArabī's Cosmology* (Albany, 1998); M. Chodkiewicz, *Seal of the Saints: Prophethood and Sainthood in the Doctrine of Ibn ʿArabī*, tr. Liadain Sherrard (Cambridge, 1993); see also http://www.ibnarabisociety.org/.

The Concept of the Divine Command in the Ismaili Tradition and its Impact on Andalusī Thought

'The Divine command' (*al-amr al-ilāhī*), 'God's command' (*amr Allāh*), or simply 'the command' (*al-amr*) occupies a prominent place in Shiʿi and especially Ismaili teachings. According to the Ismaili worldview, the Divine command is an expression of God's will (*irāda*, *mashīʾa*) and is the source for the high status of the prophets and their heirs, the legatees (*awṣiyāʾ*) and imams, in society. The prophets and their heirs implement the *amr* on earth, and at the same time derive their knowledge and unique powers from it. The implementation of the *amr* is carried out by means of the *sharīʿa*, which is delivered to mankind by the speaker-prophets (*al-nuṭaqāʾ*), and through its esoteric interpretation, the *taʾwīl*, which is the responsibility of the legatees and imams; the *taʾwīl* yields a secret and sacred body of knowledge that is divulged solely to the true believers or initiates, i.e. to the members of the Ismaili community. Obeying the prophets and their heirs is therefore tantamount to obeying God, while disobeying them is equivalent to defying God. Accordingly, the *amr* stands at the very core of religion, and it is against this background that one should understand the fundamental Islamic principle of *al-amr bi'l-maʿrūf wa'l-nahy ʿan al-munkar* (commanding right and forbidding wrong).[5] Since the Divine will never changes, its earthly manifestation in the form of the *amr* bestows continuity on sacred human history: the *amr* passes from one prophet or legatee/imam to the next, thereby linking together all prophets and legatees/imams throughout the generations and securing the spiritual leadership of mankind at all times. The significance of the *amr* for sacred human history likewise stems from its central role in cosmogonic and cosmological processes. In Ismaili teachings, whether of a mythic nature or inspired by Neoplatonic philosophy, the *amr* serves as an essential tool in the Divine creation of the world and in its maintenance; it is perceived as descending from the uppermost levels of the universe through the various cosmic echelons down to the world of man, where it assumes its religio-historical function described above. Hence the special knowledge and unusual powers of the prophets and

5 On this principle see M. Cook, *Commanding Right and Forbidding Wrong in Islamic Thought* (New York, 2000).

their heirs: they originate together with the *amr* in the upper, spiritual worlds and ultimately in Divinity itself. All in all, the *amr* grants unity to creation in its physical and spiritual dimensions, encompassing the cosmos and permeating it from the highest to the lowest levels of existence.[6]

In the Ismaili tradition, the cosmogonic-cosmological and historical functions of the *amr* are inextricably bound with the issue of political legitimacy, as the main goal of Ismaili authors in their speculations on the Divine command was to legitimise the political rule of the imams and to justify the revolutionary activities of the Ismaili *daʿwa* or missionary organisation. Significantly, the concept of *amr* resurfaces in Andalusī writings of the fourth–sixth/tenth–twelfth centuries – composed by Sunni and Jewish thinkers alike – testifying to the impact that various Ismaili notions had on the intellectual scene in medieval Spain and in the Islamic West in general.[7] To be sure, the Andalusī authors differ in their interpretation or adaptation of the Ismaili *amr*; some incorporated all three aspects delineated here, viz., the cosmogonic-cosmological, the historical, and the political aspect, while others adopted only one or two of them. Thus, the Sunni mystic and rebel Ibn Qasī (d. 546/1151) emphasised both the cosmogonic-cosmological and historical functions of the *amr*; and like the Ismailis, he employed the notion of *amr* in order to justify his own messianic aspirations to political power.[8] The political dimension of the *amr* is also evident in the ideology of the Almohads, who seem to have incorporated the concept of the Divine command along with a few other Ismaili-Fatimid ideas.[9] In contradistinction, the Sunni mystics Ibn Masarra (269–319/883–931) and Ibn Barrajān (d. 536/1141), who kept themselves aloof from any

[6] For a full discussion and the relevant sources see M. Ebstein, *Mysticism and Philosophy in al-Andalus: Ibn Masarra, Ibn al-ʿArabī and the Ismāʿīlī Tradition* (Leiden, 2014), pp. 33–76, especially pp. 57–60; to the studies cited there add C. Baffioni, 'The Role of the Divine Imperative (*Amr*) in the Ikhwān al-Ṣafā' and Related Works', *Ishraq*, 4 (2013), pp. 46–70.

[7] See Ebstein, *Mysticism and Philosophy*.

[8] M. Ebstein, 'Was Ibn Qasī a Ṣūfī?', *Studia Islamica*, 110 (2015), pp. 198, 212–215.

[9] See S. Peña, 'El término de origen coránico *Amr Allāh* («disposición de dios») y el linguocentrismo trascendente islámico, en torno al siglo XII', *Anaquel de Estudios Árabes*, 22 (2011), pp. 197–224; M. Fierro, 'The Almohads and the Fatimids', in B. D. Craig (ed.), *Ismaili and Fatimid Studies in Honor of Paul E. Walker* (Chicago, 2010), pp. 161–175.

revolutionary activity, chose to focus on the cosmogonic-cosmological and historical aspects of the *amr*, while disregarding its political implications.[10] Finally, the Jewish thinker Judah Halevi (d. 1141), in whose famous work *The Kuzari* the term 'the Divine command' figures prominently, avoided both its cosmogonic-cosmological aspect (which did not fit his anti-philosophical agenda)[11] and its political dimension. Halevi was obviously not aiming at a political revolution, but rather intended to rehabilitate the status of the Jews from a strictly theological point of view. This he accomplished, *inter alia*, by linking the Divine command with Jewish history and with the destiny of the Jewish people.[12]

Amr in Ibn al-ʿArabī's Oeuvre: From Cosmogony and Cosmology to God's Elect on Earth

In Ibn al-ʿArabī's writings, as in Ismaili sources, God's will and command are indissolubly connected to His word (*kalima*) and creative fiat, 'Be!' (*kun*); the Divine will, command and word are essential for the creation of the worlds as well as for their physical preservation and spiritual wellbeing. The Divine command and word grant unity to existence; in Ibn al-ʿArabī's eyes, creation is a manifestation of God's words (*kalimāt*), it is produced from the very 'material' of His speech. Moreover, similar to the Ismaili Neoplatonic cosmological scheme, Ibn al-ʿArabī envisions the source of God's creative speech – which he often refers to as 'the breath of the All-Merciful' (*nafas al-raḥmān*) or 'the all-merciful/Divine breath' (*al-nafas al-raḥmānī*, *al-nafas al-ilāhī*) – as standing above and encompassing the universal intellect and the remaining strata of the universe that emanate from it. According to Ibn al-ʿArabī, and once again reminiscent of Ismaili speculations – particularly those of the Ikhwān al-Ṣafāʾ, 'the Pure Brethren' – the Divine *amr*/*kalima* descends from the hypostasis of God's creative

[10] See Ebstein, *Mysticism and Philosophy*, p. 61; Y. Casewit, *The Mystics of al-Andalus: Ibn Barrajān and Islamic Thought in the Twelfth Century* (Cambridge, 2017), pp. 280–294.

[11] E. Krinis, *God's Chosen People: Judah Halevi's* Kuzari *and the Shīʿī Imām Doctrine* (Turnhout, 2014), pp. 166, 211, 295–296.

[12] Ibid., pp. 189–223.

speech through the various echelons of the universe down to the world of man.[13] The *amr/kalima* undergoes significant changes during this process of descent: at the level of the cosmic footstool (*kursī*), the differentiation and multiplication of Divine unity intensify and the *amr/kalima* splits into 'rulings' (*aḥkām*) and 'reports' (*akhbār*). The 'rulings' refer to the legal aspects of religion that are established by the messengers and prophets. These rulings become further divided into the *amr* and *nahy* (the commandments and prohibitions) and consequently into the five categories of actions recognised by Islamic law (obligatory, desirable, permitted, disliked, forbidden). Conversely, the term 'reports' alludes to the Divine knowledge that is shared by the messengers/prophets and their heirs, 'God's friends' (*awliyā'*), the mystics.[14] Thus, akin to the Ismailis, Ibn al-ʿArabī viewed the *amr* as the source for both

---

[13] On the Ikhwān al-Ṣafāʾ, an anonymous group of Neoplatonic philosophers who seem to have lived in Iraq during the fourth/tenth century and were affiliated in one way or another with the Shiʿi-Ismaili world, and on the reception of their corpus in al-Andalus, see G. de Callataÿ, 'Brethren of Purity (Ikhwān al-Ṣafāʾ)', *EI3*, and his articles, 'Magia en al-Andalus: Rasāʾil Ijwān al-Ṣafāʾ, Rutbat al-Ḥakīm y Gāyat al-Ḥakīm (Picatrix)', *Al-Qanṭara*, 34, 2 (2013), pp. 297–343, 'Philosophy and Bāṭinism in al-Andalus: Ibn Masarra's *Risālat al-iʿtibār* and the *Rasāʾil Ikhwān al-Ṣafāʾ*", *Jerusalem Studies in Arabic and Islam*, 41 (2014), pp. 261–312, and 'Again on Maslama Ibn Qāsim al-Qurṭubī, the Ikhwān al-Ṣafāʾ and Ibn Khaldūn: New Evidence from Two Manuscripts of *Rutbat al-ḥakīm*', *Al-Qanṭara*, 37, 2 (2016), pp. 329–372; Y. Casewit, *The Mystics of al-Andalus*, index, s.v. 'Brethren of Purity'; Ebstein, *Mysticism and Philosophy*, pp. 28–32, 235–238; Ebstein, 'Was Ibn Qasī a Ṣūfī?'.

[14] Note that according to Ibn al-ʿArabī, the messengers and prophets likewise enjoy 'friendship with God' (*walāya*) as well as what we would call 'mystical' experiences. At the same time, certain high-ranking mystics may enjoy 'general' or 'absolute prophecy' (*al-nubuwwa al-ʿāmma/al-muṭlaqa*), as opposed to 'legislative prophecy' (*nubuwwat al-tashrīʿ*). On Ibn al-ʿArabī's theory of *walāya* and the relation between *walāya* and prophecy, see Chodkiewicz, *Seal of the Saints*; Addas, *Quest for the Red Sulphur*, pp. 76–81; cf. G. T. Elmore, *Islamic Sainthood in the Fullness of Time: Ibn al-Arabi's Book of the Fabulous Gryphon* (Leiden, 1999), pp. 109–162. Nevertheless, for the purposes of the current discussion I will employ the terms 'God's friends' and 'mystics' as designating the heirs of the messengers/prophets. On the difference between prophets (*anbiyā'*, sing., *nabī*) and messengers (*rusul*, sing., *rasūl*), see Ibn al-ʿArabī, *al-Futūḥāt al-makkiyya*, ed. ʿAbd al-ʿAzīz Sulṭān al-Manṣūb (Tarim, 2010), vol. 4, p. 482 (chapter 73, question 53).

the legal-external aspect of religion (messengers/prophets alone) and its esoteric-inner dimension (messengers/prophets and mystics alike).[15]

Based on the teachings of earlier mystics, al-Shaykh al-akbar likewise differentiates between *al-amr al-takwīnī* (the existentiating command) or *amr al-mashīʾa* (the command of volition), on the one hand, and *al-amr al-taklīfī* (the imposing command) or *al-amr biʾl-wāsiṭa* (the command through mediation), on the other. *Al-amr al-takwīnī/amr al-mashīʾa* signifies the command that creates everything in accordance with the Divine will, while *al-amr al-taklīfī/al-amr biʾl-wāsiṭa* indicates the command that is the source of religio-legal duties of the *sharīʿa.*[16] *Al-amr al-taklīfī* and the aforementioned 'rulings' are under the sole jurisdiction of the messengers

---

[15] For a full discussion see the reference above in n. 6; to the sources cited there add Ibn al-ʿArabī, *al-Futūḥāt*, vol. 5, p. 45 (chapter 73, question 153), pp. 418–419 (chapter 160), vol. 6, p. 283 (chapter 198, *faṣl* 19), pp. 321–322, 324 (chapter 198, *faṣl* 31), p. 618 (chapter 262), vol. 7, pp. 417–421 (chapter 307), vol. 8, pp. 355–356 (chapter 351, *waṣl al-amr al-ilāhī*), vol. 10, pp. 424–425 (chapter 469). Ibn al-ʿArabī seems to have derived the notion that the *amr* splits at the level of the footstool from Ibn Barrajān; see Casewit, *The Mystics of al-Andalus*, pp. 281, 283. Note, however, that Ibn al-ʿArabī's cosmology and the exact location of the *kursī* within it differ considerably from Ibn Barrajān's worldview and are much closer to the Ismaili-Ikhwānian Neoplatonic model; see Ebstein, *Mysticism and Philosophy*, p. 62 n. 107, p. 95; and Casewit, *The Mystics of al-Andalus*, pp. 280–282. A description of the *amr*'s descent through the different levels of a cosmic hierarchy that is structured in accordance with Neoplatonic philosophy is likewise found in the oeuvre of Ṣadr al-Dīn al-Qūnawī (d. 673/1274), Ibn al-ʿArabī's foremost disciple; see R. Todd, *The Sufi Doctrine of Man, Ṣadr al-Dīn Qūnawī's Metaphysical Anthropology* (Leiden, 2014), p. 80.

[16] Ibn al-ʿArabī apparently derived this double typology of Divine commands once again from Ibn Barrajān, who had already distinguished between *amr kawn* and *amr sharʿ*; see Ebstein, *Mysticism and Philosophy*, p. 63; Casewit, *The Mystics of al-Andalus*, p. 282. Ibn al-ʿArabī may have also been inspired by Abū Ṭālib al-Makkī (d. 386/996) and other Eastern thinkers (Sufis and theologians alike) who differentiated between God's all-encompassing will and decree, on the one hand, and the legal obligations of the *sharīʿa*, on the other. According to this line of thought, even sinful deeds or transgressions against the *sharīʿa* are ultimately committed in accordance with God's will. See al-Makkī, *Qūt al-qulūb fī muʿāmalat al-maḥbūb*, ed. S. N. Makārim (Beirut, 2007), vol. 1, pp. 266–268 (the end of *faṣl* 30); F. Meier, *Abū Saʿīd-i Abū l-Ḫayr (357–440/967–1049): Wirklichkeit und Legende* (Leiden, 1976) (*Acta Iranica* 11), pp. 73–77; cf. al-Ghazālī (?), *Maʿārij al-quds fī madārij maʿrifat al-nafs* (Beirut, 1975), p. 177 (on this work see F. Griffel, *al-Ghazālī's Philosophical Theology* [Oxford, 2009],

and prophets; only they may receive and issue such legal orders from God. However, as explained above, both the messengers/prophets and their God-chosen heirs, the mystics, obtain 'reports' and, what is more, can gain knowledge of *al-amr al-takwīnī/amr al-mashī'a*. In fact, the non-legal Divine command accompanies the mystics (and of course the messengers/prophets) in virtually all aspects of their life; it ensures their continuous communication with God and guarantees that their actions are performed in complete conformity with the Divine will. According to Ibn al-ʿArabī, the true mystic witnesses the Divine command as it descends from the heavens to the earth and is thereby able to foretell future events that will occur as a result of that command. Furthermore, the mystic can uncover the different cosmic levels through which the Divine command has descended and trace its ultimate source in Divinity itself; eventually the command returns and ascends back to God with the specific spiritual form (*ṣūra*) with which the mystic has adorned it.[17] We may say therefore that in Ibn al-ʿArabī's eyes, the *amr* serves as a Divine medium that facilitates the mutual relationship between God and His chosen one; by means of the *amr*, the mystic becomes acquainted with the Divine plan and consequently is capable of influencing his own destiny or the destiny of others by sending back the *amr* with the 'form' of his good action and intention. Although knowledge of future events is also ascribed to the imams in the Shiʿi-Ismaili tradition, the upward return of the *amr* to the Divine world and the mystic's ability to affect this world by means of God's command

---

p. 301, n. 183 and the references given there). The distinction between God's existentiating will or command (*irāda kawniyya, amr kawnī*) and His legislative will or command (*irāda dīniyya, amr dīnī*) resurfaces later in the writings of Ibn Taymiyya (d. 728/1328) and his school, who may have been inspired in this context by Ibn al-ʿArabī. See the references and discussion in L. Holtzman, *Predestination (al-Qaḍā' wa'l-qadar) and Free Will (al-ikhtiyār) as Reflected in the Works of the Neo-Ḥanbalites of the Fourteenth Century*, PhD dissertation (Ramat Gan, Bar-Ilan University, 2003), pp. 243–254 (in Hebrew; I am grateful to Prof. Holtzman for this reference).

[17] Ibn al-ʿArabī, *al-Futūḥāt*, vol. 7, pp. 421–422. Elsewhere Ibn al-ʿArabī seems to identify God's command with the Divine 'face' (*wajh*) that runs through the cosmic echelons and connects each created being to its Lord; see Ibid., vol. 6, p. 191 (chapter 198, *tawḥīd* 32); on the concept of *al-wajh al-khāṣṣ* (the unique/specific face) see Chittick, *Self-Disclosure*, pp. 91–120, 135–155.

are unique to al-Shaykh al-akbar's thought and in this respect set him apart from most Shiʿi-Ismaili thinkers.[18]

Ideally, the mystic's behaviour vis-à-vis God and his fellow-man in any given situation should accord with a Divine command that is received in the form of an inner address from God (*khiṭāb*) relevant to the particular situation. In principle, a command that truly originates in God – rather than in the lower self, the *nafs* – cannot contradict the Islamic *sharīʿa*.[19] Even the decision to undertake a journey – whether for spiritual or mundane purposes – is the result of a Divine command.[20] Similarly, entering into a theological disputation (*jidāl*), which many Sufi authorities (including Ibn al-ʿArabī himself) disapproved of,[21] is dependent on God's command:

> A Muslim who affiliates himself with God must not engage in any disputation unless it concerns something that he has verified on the basis of an unveiling (*kashf*), not on the basis of thought or reflection. Accordingly, if the matter over which the disputation takes place becomes an object of his mystical vision (*kāna mashhūdan lahu*), it is then that he is obliged to engage in the disputation 'in the way that is best' [see sura 16:125], if he is [so] commanded by a Divine command (*bi-amr ilāhī*). If he is not commanded, he has the choice: if the benefit that the other side might derive from this [disputation] becomes clear to him, [disputing] is then desirable for him. However, if he has no hope that his listeners will accept [his opinion], he should remain silent and not engage in any dispute, for if he does engage in a dispute, he will have strived for their perdition in the eyes of God.[22]

---

[18] On the ability of the mystic to influence Divinity see M. Ebstein, '"In Truth You Are the Polytheist!": Mythic Elements in Ibn al-ʿArabī's Teachings on the Divine Names', *Intellectual History of the Islamicate World*, 6 (2018), pp. 359–387.

[19] See Ibn al-ʿArabī, *al-Futūḥāt*, vol. 5, pp. 359–361 (chapter 146), pp. 362–363 (chapter 147), vol. 7, p. 130 (chapter 283).

[20] Ibid., vol. 8, p. 441 (chapter 355).

[21] See M. Ebstein, '"Religions, Opinions and Beliefs Are Nothing but Roads and Paths . . . While the Goal Is One": Between Unity and Diversity in Islamic Mysticism', in C. Adang et al. (ed.), *Accusations of Unbelief in Islam: A Diachronic Perspective on* Takfīr (Leiden, 2016), pp. 488–523.

[22] Ibn al-ʿArabī, *al-Futūḥāt*, vol. 9, p. 80 (chapter 366).

Not only the conduct of the mystic, but also his Divine knowledge (*maʿrifa*, *ʿilm*) – which, more than any other asset or quality, elevates him above ordinary men – is the fruit of Divine commands.[23] Ibn al-ʿArabī states that he himself wrote his treatise entitled *Mawāqiʿ al-nujūm* 'following a Divine command' (*ʿan amr ilāhī*).[24] Whether to divulge or conceal a mystical secret, which God entrusts as a 'deposit' (*amāna*) in the hands of the mystic, equally is dependent on receiving a Divine command.[25] In general, mystical experiences, which yield special knowledge, and even mystical 'madness' or 'foolishness', all result from Divine commands. In contradistinction, ecstatic utterances (*shaṭaḥāt*) are usually condemned because those who pronounce them have not been granted a Divine command, regardless of their high rank or advanced position on the mystical path.[26]

Ibn al-ʿArabī likewise held that miraculous deeds (*karāmāt*), which always posed a challenge for Sufi thought,[27] must only be performed if the mystic received a relevant command from God.[28] In fact, a Divine command is what distinguishes the miracles of messengers/prophets (*muʿjizāt*) and the miraculous deeds of mystics from sorcery (*siḥr*). This is best exemplified, according to al-Shaykh al-akbar, in the Qurʾanic description of the encounter between Moses and the sorcerers of Pharaoh (*saḥara*; see suras 7:103–126; 20:17–21, 56–73):

---

[23] Ibid., vol. 7, pp. 159–161 (chapter 287).

[24] Ibid., vol. 11, p. 407 (chapter 558, *ḥaḍrat al-sakhāʾ*); cf. Ibn al-ʿArabī, *Fuṣūṣ al-ḥikam*, ed. Abu'l-ʿAlā ʿAfīfī (Cairo, 1946), p. 47.

[25] Ibn al-ʿArabī, *al-Futūḥāt*, vol. 6, p. 417 (chapter 210), vol. 7, pp. 145–147 (chapter 285); see also M. Ebstein, 'Secrecy in Ismāʿīlī Tradition and in the Mystical Thought of Ibn al-ʿArabī', *Journal Asiatique*, 298, 2 (2010), p. 333.

[26] See Ibn al-ʿArabī, *al-Futūḥāt*, vol. 6, p. 115 (chapter 195), pp. 517–518 (chapter 226; the term *amr ilāhī* in this passage can perhaps also be translated as 'a Divine affair'), p. 552 (chapter 236). On ecstatic utterances in the Sufi tradition see C. W. Ernst, *Words of Ecstasy in Sufism* (Albany, 1985).

[27] See, for instance, *bāb karāmāt al-awliyāʾ* in al-Qushayrī's *al-Risāla al-Qushayriyya* (Beirut, 2000), pp. 342–376; and R. Gramlich, *Die Wunder der Freunde Gottes: Theologien und Erscheinungsformen des islamischen Heiligenwunders* (Wiesbaden, 1987).

[28] Ibn al-ʿArabī, *al-Futūḥāt*, vol. 6, p. 81 (chapter 186), pp. 510–512 (chapter 224; one should probably read *taḥakkum* rather than *taḥkīm* throughout the chapter), p. 535 (chapter 231).

> Moses threw his staff on the ground following a command of the Truth (*ʿan amr ḥaqq*), a command of his Trustee (*muwakkalihi*). [God] said to him, 'Throw your staff on the ground' [sura 7: 117], and it became a snake in his eyes and consequently he was afraid. [In the Qurʾan, God] informed that the sorcerers did not throw their ropes and staffs on the ground following a Divine command, but rather following the authority of the Divine names that they possessed (*ʿan ḥukm asmāʾ kānat ʿindahum*). These names have a special property (*khāṣṣiyya*) that causes those who are looking to look at what the sorcerer wants to manifest; and so, by means of those names [the sorcerer] may transform the vision, not the object of the vision. In contradistinction, by means of a Divine command one transforms the very object of the vision, and then the vision follows suit. . .[29]
>
> The [sorcerers] realised that the greatest miraculous sign in this context was that the [snake]-forms [of their staffs] were swallowed up from the eyes of those who were looking, whereas the snake-form of Moses's staff remained as it was in their eyes, although the situation in both cases was the same to their mind. So they realised that Moses spoke the truth concerning that to which he was summoning them. They recognised that what he delivered is beyond the forms and tricks known from sorcery; it is a Divine command/affair untouched by the personal labouring of Moses (*fa-huwa amr ilāhī laysa li-Mūsā fīhi taʿammul*). Accordingly, they believed in his message on the basis of clear sight (*ʿalā baṣīra*).[30]

Judah Halevi, too, employs the motif of the Divine command in his interpretation of the encounter between Moses and Pharaoh's magicians: God's command is what sets the miracles that Moses performed apart from the magic of Pharaoh's wizards.[31] The resemblance in this context between Ibn al-ʿArabī and Halevi should come as no surprise; both seem to have been ultimately inspired by the Ikhwān al-Ṣafāʾ, who wrote in the same vein regarding the essential difference between Moses and Pharaoh:

---

29 Ibid., vol. 8, p. 538 (chapter 360, *niyāba* 10).

30 Ibid., vol. 1, p. 445 (chapter 16); see also Ibid., pp. 652–659 (chapter 40).

31 Krinis, *God's Chosen People*, pp. 203–209.

> Equally, [God] granted His assistance (*ayyada*) to Moses, peace be upon him, through His speech and command (*bi-kalāmihi wa-amrihi*).[32] [Moses] thus subdued Pharaoh as well as the people of his kingdom and the men of his state, while Pharaoh's sorcerers responded to [the summoning of Moses]. These sorcerers were the astrologers and diviners of the time; they were the ones who managed [Pharaoh's] dominion by what they had been able to learn and gain knowledge of. Yet when they witnessed from Moses [an act] whose light overcame them and realised that his work would not be corrupted nor would that which he has delivered be impaired; [when they saw] that the affair/command (*amr*) of Pharaoh that they were involved in is entirely transitory and will dwindle away; [when] they saw that prosperity [originating in celestial phenomena, *al-sa'ādāt*] has become wholly directed and subjugated to Moses and Aaron, peace be upon them – 'they said: we believe in the Lord of the worlds, the Lord of Moses and Aaron' [sura 7: 121-122]; and [when they saw] that the universal assistance (*al-ta'yīd al-kullī*) and the Divine command are what direct that prosperity to Moses and his brother – they responded and submitted themselves to him.[33]

The Divine command is the basis for the miraculous powers and for the high status of God's chosen ones – the messengers/prophets and their heirs, whether legatees and imams (in the case of the Ikhwān), mystics (in the teachings of Ibn al-'Arabī), or the Jewish people as a whole (Halevi).

The Ideal Ruler and the Political Aspect of the *Amr*

As in the Ismaili tradition, in Ibn al-'Arabī's oeuvre the concept of *amr* entails an important political aspect. This aspect is related to the terms

---

[32] The term *ta'yīd* (Divine assistance) in Shī'i and especially in Ismaili literature is closely connected to the concept of *amr* and resurfaces in Andalusī mystical works, including those written by Ibn al-'Arabī; see Ebstein, *Mysticism and Philosophy*, pp. 64–72.

[33] See Ikhwān al-Ṣafā', *Rasā'il ikhwān al-ṣafā' wa-khullān al-wafā'* (Beirut, 1957), vol. 4, p. 375.

khalīfa (here meaning, God's vicegerent on earth) and *al-insān al-kāmil* (the perfect human being).[34] According to al-Shaykh al-akbar, the ideal ruler is either a messenger, prophet, or 'friend of God' who has been granted *khilāfa* (the office or function of *khalīfa*), that is to say, God has appointed him (*istikhlāf*) to execute His will on earth and implement the *sharīʿa* by political means and, if necessary, by force. The *khalīfa* therefore enjoys *taḥakkum* – he may 'have his own way' in the world or 'judge as he sees fit' among human beings. *Khilāfa* in this context requires perfection (*kamāl*) and the ideal *khalīfa* is inevitably a 'perfect human being', given that he serves as a locus for the full manifestation of the Divine names; his violent actions, aimed at pursuing justice and maintaining order, reflect the harsh and wrathful attributes of God, while his benevolent conduct mirrors the merciful aspects of Divinity.[35] Even the *awliyāʾ* who hold no governmental offices and possess no visible political power may still be *khulafāʾ* and perfect human beings if, following their primordial election by God, they are able to fully manifest the Divine names. These *awliyāʾ* may also enjoy the privilege of *taḥakkum*, which in their case means to manipulate God's creation by wondrous means and through miraculous deeds. Accordingly, the existence of the *khalīfa* – be he a messenger, prophet, or *walī*, whether he possesses political power or not – is essential for the full self-disclosure of Divinity in creation; God needs the perfect human being in order to reveal Himself to the world. This mutual relationship between God and His chosen ones is sustained and is properly managed by means of the *amr*:

> If someone is granted *taḥakkum* in the world, this is *khilāfa*. If he wishes, he may perform *taḥakkum* and manifest himself like ʿAbd al-Qādir al-Jīlī, or if he wishes, he may submit like Abū'l-Suʿūd b. al-Shibl, allowing only his Lord to act freely (*al-taṣarruf*) among His servants, though he too is inevitably able to act freely.[36]

[34] For a more detailed discussion of these terms, see Ebstein, *Mysticism and Philosophy*, pp. 157–188.

[35] On the opposing attributes of God in Sufi thought see S. Sviri, 'Between Fear and Hope: On the Coincidence of Opposites in Islamic Mysticism', *Jerusalem Studies in Arabic and Islam*, 9 (1987), pp. 316–349.

[36] On the two Sufi figures mentioned here and their relation to Ibn al-ʿArabī see Addas, *Quest for the Red Sulphur*, p. 241.

However, if a Divine command is attached to him (*yaqtarinu bihi amr ilāhī*) as in the case of David, peace be upon him [see sura 38:26], then there is no way to reject God's command (*amr Allāh*), for this is precisely the lower inclination (*al-hawā*) obedience to which was forbidden [sura 38: 26]. Similarly, ʿUthmān [b. ʿAffān], may God be pleased with him, did not divest himself of the robe of *khilāfa* till he was murdered, because he knew what share the Truth had in it/him (*li-ʿilmihi bi-mā li'l-ḥaqq fīhi*); after all, the messenger of God, may God's prayers and blessings be upon him, forbade him to divest himself of the robe of *khilāfa*. So, if a Divine command is attached to someone's *taḥakkum*, he must manifest himself by means of it and subsequently will not cease to be Divinely assisted (*mu'ayyadan*). On the other hand, anyone to whom a Divine command is not attached has the choice of either manifesting himself by means of [*taḥakkum*], in which case he justly manifests himself (*ẓahara bi-ḥaqq*), or not manifesting himself, in which case he justly conceals himself (*fa-statara bi-ḥaqq*). Not manifesting oneself is better.

The friends of God join the prophets specifically in *khilāfa*, not in the latter's capacity as messengers and prophets, for the gates of both functions are shut.[37] The messenger has the authority to [issue] rulings (*fa-li'l-rasūl al-ḥukm*), and if he is appointed as a *khalīfa* by God (*fa-in ustukhlifa*) he may also perform *taḥakkum*.[38] If he is a messenger, his *taḥakkum* is in accordance with the law he himself has established; if he is not a messenger, his *taḥakkum*, following God's command, is in accordance with the ruling of his time which is the Divine law of his age, for it is in accordance with [this] ruling that either justice or wrongdoing are attributed to him.[39]

---

[37] That is, after Muhammad there can be no more legislative prophets, let alone messengers.

[38] In other words, all messengers issue Divine laws or introduce Divine legal codes. However, they are not necessarily given the right to implement these laws or codes by political means and if necessary by force.

[39] Ibn al-ʿArabī, *al-Futūḥāt*, vol. 5, p. 558 (chapter 177, *al-nawʿ al-rābiʿ*); see also Ibid., pp. 484–485 (chapter 167, *waṣl fī faṣl al-kamāl*), vol. 6, pp. 613–614 (chapter 260), vol. 8, pp. 106–114 (chapter 336), vol. 11, pp. 134–135 (chapter 541), p. 287 (chapter 558, *ḥaḍrat al-iʿzāz*).

The God-chosen *khalīfa*s mentioned in this passage – messengers, prophets (David), *awliyā'* who are rulers of the Islamic community ('Uthmān), and *awliyā'* bereft of political power who either manifest their magical abilities, like al-Jīlī, or choose not to do so, like Ibn al-Shibl – these figures are all perfect human beings who act in accordance with God's will as expressed in His command.[40] True, in Ibn al-ʿArabī's eyes, the most perfect human being and the ideal ruler or messenger-*khalīfa par excellence* was Muhammad, after whom no messengers/prophets can appear. In addition, the majority of Muslim rulers in the eras after Muhammad's death were neither *awliyā'* nor true *khalīfa*s in the sense explained above. As to the *awliyā'*, in the absence of an explicit Divine command, even those among them who are perfect individuals and are capable of performing miraculous deeds (= *taḥakkum, taṣarruf*) ought to abstain from such actions and conceal their magical powers, primarily out of *adab* (courtesy) vis-à-vis God.[41] Still, there is no doubt as to the tremendous power that Ibn al-ʿArabī attributes to the mystics, regardless of whether or not this power is actually manifested in the domains of politics and miracles. The potential power of the mystics, ultimately originating in God and mediated through His command, elevates them (as it does the messengers and prophets) above all other human beings. It is clear then why, like the Shiʿis, Ibn al-ʿArabī declares that in defying the messenger of God and 'those who uphold the affair/command' (*ūlu'l-amr*, see sura 4:14, 59) – presumably both the political rulers of the Islamic community and the perfect human beings, viz., the supreme mystics – one is in fact defying God Himself, 'for by disobeying them one disobeys God's command'.[42]

---

[40] On the political and even financial conduct of the ideal ruler and its conformity with the Divine command, see Ibid., vol. 5, pp. 270–271 (chapter 117).

[41] See D. Gril, 'Adab and Revelation or: One of the Foundations of the Hermeneutics of Ibn 'Arabi', in S. Hirtenstein and M. Tiernan (ed.), *Muhyiddin Ibn 'Arabi: a Commemorative Volume* (Shaftesbury, 1993), pp. 228–263; and F. Chiabboti et al. (ed.), *Ethics and Spirituality in Islam: Sufi Adab* (Leiden, 2017).

[42] Ibn al-ʿArabī, *al-Futūḥāt*, vol. 7, p. 488 (chapter 315).

Historical Continuity and the Role of the Mystic in Society

In Ibn al-ʿArabī's view, the presence of the *amr* in sacred human history is essential for the spiritual wellbeing and salvation of mankind. The Divine command guarantees the proper communication between God and His chosen ones, whether messengers/prophets or their heirs, the mystics. This communication in turn ensures that the Divine will is revealed to the world at all times:

> In the age of messengers, the perfect one is a messenger; and when the office of messengers has ceased [to exist], the perfect one is an heir (*wārith*).[43] The heir cannot manifest himself while the messenger exists, since an heir becomes an heir only after the death of him from whom he inherits. Accordingly, a companion (*al-ṣāḥib*) is not able to possess this level as long as the messenger exists.[44] For the command descends (*yanzilu*) from God continuously, it never ceases; only the messengers receive it specifically on the basis of perfection, and when they are gone, it is then that this preparedness (*al-istiʿdād*) is found in [figures] other than the messengers. These [figures] receive this Divine revelation (*al-tanzīl al-ilāhī*) in their hearts, and are named: 'heirs' (*waratha*). They are not given the name 'messengers', though they impart knowledge on the authority of God by means of a Divine revelation (*bi'l-tanazzul al-ilāhī*). If the latter contains a ruling, its recipient accepts it and rules by it. This is what the superficial scholars (*ʿulamā' al-rusūm*) call a *mujtahid*, one who in their view deduces (*yastanbiṭu*) the ruling . . .[45] This is the share of legislation that people nowadays

[43] On the concept of spiritual inheritance in the teachings of Ibn al-ʿArabī, see Chodkiewicz, *Seal of the Saints*, pp. 74–88.

[44] This statement echoes Shiʿi-Ismaili notions regarding the relationship between a living prophet or imam and his heir; see, for instance, F. Daftary, *The Ismāʿīlīs: their History and Doctrines* (Cambridge, 2nd ed., 2007), pp. 83, 86, 131–132.

[45] 'Superficial scholars' – i.e. scholars who concentrate solely on the exterior-legal aspect of religion, its *ẓāhir* or *rusūm* (prescriptions, customs). A *mujtahid* – literally: 'one who strives, makes an effort'; in Islamic jurisprudence, one who employs his own judgement regarding legal issues. On *istinbāṭ* see S. Sviri, 'The Countless Faces of Understanding: On *Istinbāṭ*, Mystical Listening and Sufi Exegesis', in A. Keeler and S. H. Rizvi (ed.), *The Spirit and the Letter: Approaches to the Esoteric Interpretation of the Qur'an* (London and New York, 2016), pp. 51–85.

> possess following [the death of] the messenger of God, may God's prayers and blessings be upon him. We claim the same, but do not say that *ijtihād* [the act of the *mujtahid*] is what the superficial scholars claim it is, but rather, in our opinion, *ijtihād* is to do your utmost in obtaining the inner preparedness (*al-istiʿdād al-bāṭin*) by which you may receive this specific revelation. In the age of prophets and messengers, only a prophet or a messenger receives such a revelation. In any case, there is no way to contradict a firm ruling that has been established by the Messenger, may God's prayers and blessings be upon him, concerning the same matter.[46]

Although neither messengers nor legislative prophets can appear after the death of Muhammad, and despite the fact that a true mystic must be firmly committed to the Islamic *sharīʿa* and cannot change its established rulings, the channel of communication between God and His chosen ones continues to function in the era after the death of Muhammad – until Judgment day, to be precise – in the form of Divine commands that descend on the hearts of the supreme *awliyāʾ*.[47] For this reason, such *awliyāʾ* have the ability and right to interpret and develop the *sharīʿa* according to their mystical experiences and understanding (*ijtihād*).

As recipients of the Divine command, the elite mystics are also responsible for the spiritual wellbeing and salvation of mankind. 'Know', writes Ibn al-ʿArabī, 'that in the same way that it is said concerning the doctor that he serves nature, it is also said of the messengers and heirs that they serve the Divine command in a general sense'; 'The messenger and the heir are otherworldly doctors of the souls (*ṭabīb ukhrawī li'l-nufūs*) who obey God's command when he commands them. . .'.[48] In other words, the prophets and the mystics are in charge of summoning

---

[46] Ibn al-ʿArabī, *al-Futūḥāt*, vol. 8, pp. 498–499 (chapter 359).

[47] In certain passages, Ibn al-ʿArabī refers to the chain of prophets and their heirs from the beginning of sacred human history to its eschatological end as *amr*; see Ibid., vol. 4, pp. 421, 423 (chapter 73, questions 13 and 15) and vol. 7, p. 10 (chapter 270); note, however, that in these passages, the primary meaning of *amr* is 'affair'. Cf. vol. 8, p. 281 (chapter 347).

[48] Ibn al-ʿArabī, *Fuṣūṣ al-ḥikam*, pp. 97–98.

and inspiring human beings to follow the *sharīʿa*, which is an expression of God's legal command or *al-amr al-taklīfī* (see above).[49] One may note that viewing the prophets and their heirs as spiritual doctors who perform their 'medicinal' work on the basis of the Divine command and in order to implement it is a notion familiar from Ismaili writings, particularly from the Epistles of the Ikhwān.[50] Moreover, in one of the poems contained in his *Dīwān*, Ibn al-ʿArabī celebrates his elevated spiritual state and election by God, declaring that he is 'an heir of Muhammad's knowledge and spiritual state (*anā wārith lā shakk ʿilm Muḥammad wa-ḥālatahu*)'. It is apparent from the content of the rest of the poem that Ibn al-ʿArabī is here referring to his messianic function as 'the seal of Muhammadan friendship with God' (*khātam/khatm al-walāya al-muḥammadiyya*), the first of the three 'seals' that are meant to bring sacred human history to its eschatological end.[51] Ibn al-ʿArabī adds that this was revealed to him 'by means of a Divine command that came to me during the *dhikr*'.[52] Thus, through His command, God assigns historical and even messianic missions to His chosen ones, the supreme *awliyāʾ* – chief among them Ibn al-ʿArabī himself.[53]

---

49 On the summoning of human beings to God (*daʿwa*) by means of or based on the Divine command see also Ibn al-ʿArabī, *al-Futūḥāt*, vol. 10, p. 385 (chapter 463, *al-quṭb al-thānī*).

50 For references see Ebstein, *Mysticism and Philosophy*, pp. 63–64.

51 For detailed discussions of these three figures, see the references above in n. 14.

52 *Dīwān Ibn ʿArabī* (Cairo, 1855), p. 332; see also Addas, *Quest for the Red Sulphur*, p. 119. Note also the fifth line of the poem in which Ibn al-ʿArabī writes that the Truth had informed him that he is 'the sealing of the affair' (*khitām al-amr*). See also p. 334: 'I do not care if I am neither Moses nor Jesus nor their likes, for I comprise the whole affair (*innanī jāmiʿ al-amr*) / Indeed I am the seal of the *awliyāʾ* [of] Muhammad'; see also above n. 47.

53 Note also the messianic insinuation in Ibn al-ʿArabī, *al-Futūḥāt*, vol. 8, p. 289 (chapter 348): 'The Divine command/affair is more complete and perfect in that which follows (*al-tālī*) than in that which precedes (*al-matluww*) and comes before, given that it has what the first one has and more'. On the eschatological function of the elite mystics see also M. Ebstein, 'Spiritual Descendants of the Prophet: al-Ḥakīm al-Tirmidhī, Ibn al-ʿArabī, and Ikhwān al-Ṣafāʾ on *Ahl al-Bayt*', in M. A. Amir-Moezzi et al. (ed.), *L'Esotérisme Shiʿite: ses racines et ses prolongements* (Turnhout, 2016), pp. 539–571.

Conclusion

Amr occupies a central place in the teachings of Ibn al-ʿArabī. Although the concept itself appears already in the Qurʾan and resurfaces in post-Qurʾanic Islamic discourse,[54] the specific contexts in which Ibn al-ʿArabī employs this concept – cosmogony and cosmology, sacred human history, and the social-political role of the perfect human being – point to the Ismaili tradition as the main background against which the Akbarian use of *amr* should be understood. Further evidence for this hypothesis may be gleaned from the writings of Ibn Masarra, Ibn Qasī, Ibn Barrajān, and Judah Halevi as well as from Almohad ideology (see above); all seem to have incorporated the Ismaili notion of the Divine command in their respective teachings.

To be sure, the impact of Ismaili ideas such as *amr* on the evolution of Andalusī thought does not mean that the Ismaili tradition simply 'influenced' thinkers like Ibn al-ʿArabī; nor does it mean that these thinkers were Shiʿis, Ismailis, or crypto-Shiʿis/ Ismailis in any way. Ibn Masarra, Ibn Qasī, Ibn Barrajān, Ibn al-ʿArabī and the Almohad religious leaders were sincere Sunnis, and Judah Halevi a devout Rabbinical Jew. Yet in elaborating and formulating their teachings, these figures could not disregard the religious-political discourse of one of the most powerful and influential movements of the time – the Ismāʿīliyya, which, via the Fatimid empire, had exerted a tremendous influence on the whole western part and on many other regions of the medieval Islamic world. The Ismailis posed a great challenge to Sunni ideals and beliefs; by incorporating Shiʿi-Ismaili conceptions in their Sunni worldviews, Ibn al-ʿArabī and his fellow Andalusīs were in fact addressing and responding to this grave challenge. At the same time, Shiʿi-Ismaili conceptions likewise served these figures in their conflicts with non-Shiʿi foes who contended with them for religious authority and at times for political power too – the exoteric religious establishment (Ibn Qasī, Ibn al-ʿArabī), the waning regime of the Almoravids (Almohads), or the Christian and Islamic communities as a whole (Judah Halevi). Shiʿi-Ismaili notions like *amr* offered such individuals and groups, who were outside the mainstream majority, a perfect theological weapon, a means

---

[54] See the references above in n. 6.

of establishing their own status as God's chosen ones who were to lead mankind, whether politically or spiritually, to its final salvation.

The originality of Ibn Masarra, Ibn Qasī, Ibn Barrajān, Ibn al-ʿArabī, the Almohads, and Judah Halevi is evident in the way in which they employed the Ismaili *amr* and in the specific meanings that this concept acquired in their respective teachings. For instance, and as explained above, some chose to adopt the political-revolutionary and messianic aspect of *amr* (Ibn Qasī, the Almohads), while others focused either on its cosmogonic-cosmological and historical dimensions (Ibn Masarra, Ibn Barrajān) or solely on its theological significance for sacred human history (Judah Halevi). Ibn al-ʿArabī can be viewed as a confluence of these various tendencies: in his writings, one may find the cosmogonic-cosmological, the historical, and the political aspect of the *amr* all intertwined, as is the case in Ismaili writings and in the work of Ibn Qasī. However, contrary to the latter, Ibn al-ʿArabī was careful not to utilise the concept of the Divine command in order to legitimise any personal political ambitions he might have entertained. Although al-Shaykh al-akbar viewed himself as the most supreme spiritual heir of the Prophet Muhammad and conceived of his own destiny in messianic terms, as one of the three figures who were to conclude sacred human history, he never sought a governmental office, nor did he aspire – in contradistinction to Ibn Qasī (and perhaps following the tragic failure of Ibn Qasī's rebellion)[55] – to any position of concrete political power. Moreover, in Ibn al-ʿArabī's eyes, the complex hierarchy of God's friends and the numerous mystics who occupy its many echelons are by and large hidden from the eyes of most human beings. The spiritual actions of the *awliyāʾ* and, when ordered to do so, their wondrous and miraculous deeds – activities that are essential for the very existence of creation – are secret and should be carried out clandestinely.[56] The majority of the *awliyāʾ* remain therefore unknown, veiled by their own anonymity; only a select few – headed by al-Shaykh al-akbar himself – are obliged to manifest themselves to the world, in accordance with the Divine command.

[55] See Ebstein, 'Was Ibn Qasī a Ṣūfī?'.

[56] See M. Chodkiewicz, 'Les *malâmiyya* dans la doctrine d'Ibn Arabî', in N. Clayer et al. (ed.), *Melâmis-Bayrâmis. Études sur trois mouvements mystiques musulmans* (Istanbul, 1998), pp. 15–25.

PART THREE

THE IKHWĀN AL-ṢAFĀʾ, THEOSOPHICAL AND PHILOSOPHICAL TRENDS

8

Onto-cosmology and Hierohistory in the Manuscript Tradition of the *Rasāʾil Ikhwān al-Ṣafāʾ*

Carmela Baffioni
(The Institute of Ismaili Studies)

Introduction

This paper deals with a version of Epistle 50 'On the Various Kinds of Administration' in the encyclopaedia of the Ikhwān al-Ṣafāʾ that is entirely different from the available printed texts and from the new version that I have recently established for the Institute of Ismaili Studies.[1] It can be found in MS Marsh 189, n.d., Oxford: Bodleian Library, whose content and stylistic characteristics[2] suggest that it is

[1] The new established text of the Epistle with English translation and commentary is in *Epistles of the Brethren of Purity. On God and the World: An Arabic Critical Edition and English Translation of Epistles 49–51*, ed. and tr. Wilferd Madelung & Cyril V. Uy II; Carmela Baffioni; and Nuha Alshaar (London: OUP–IIS, 2019).

[2] Such as a great number of unique readings, the fact that it provides different versions of some of the Epistles (for instance, the version of Epistle 10 'On the *Isagoge*', though shared with the much later Bodleian MS Laud Or. 260, 1560 CE; cf. Carmela Baffioni (ed. and tr.), *On Logic: An Arabic Critical Edition and English Translation of Epistles 10–14* [New York and London, 2010], pp. 167–179), and the fact that it indicates every epistle as a *kitāb*. On the ancientness of this title rather than *rasāʾil* see already Susanne Diwald, *Arabische Philosophie und Wissenschaft in der Enzyklopädie. Kitāb Ihwān aṣ-ṣafāʾ (III) Die Lehre von Seele und Intellekt* (Wiesbaden, 1975), pp. 16–17. Otherwise, one should postulate the copyists may have relied on sources not

fairly old.[3] The manuscript, 29 lines per page, has a double Western (Latin) pagination and foliation, with the higher figure smaller, and the lower faded and often even invisible. The text extends from fol. 719/366b to fol. 728/371a.[4]

The contents of the version of Epistle 50 in MS Marsh 189 are very varied. It can somehow be considered to be a sort of 'summary' of a great part of the encyclopaedia. Several themes are discussed in an unusual way; these include some of the topics developed in the 'current' version of Epistle 50.

In Chapter 1 a human and a divine administration are distinguished, with the latter hidden from human intellect. In Chapter 2, four types of administration are introduced, of which the first three are characterised by quality and quantity:[5]

> [1.] The first type is the administration of the mass [*siyāsat al-ʿāmma*]. It is divided into [various] types of administrations, such as the administration of builders, carpenters, blacksmiths, and of those who act in all crafts and arts that a single man can represent in himself before producing them . . ., as we have mentioned in the *Book on the Practical Arts* . . .
>
> The second type is the administration of the elect [*siyāsat al-khāṣṣa*]. It has a quantity and a quality, and is divided into

affected by other traditions. My conjecture was also strengthened by Godefroid de Callataÿ, *Ikhwan al-Safa'. A Brotherhood of Idealists on the Fringe of Orthodox Islam* (Oxford, 2005), p. 3. Note, however, Halflants' contrary opinion in Godefroid de Callataÿ and Bruno Halflants (ed. and tr.), *On Magic I: An Arabic Critical Edition and English Translation of Epistle 52a* (New York–London, 2011), p. 70, n. 2. See also Bruno Halflants, 'Considérations ecdotiques et linguistiques à propos de quelques manuscrits des *Rasāʾil Ikhwān al-Ṣafāʾ*', in Johannes Den Heijer, Paolo La Spisa, and Laurence Tuerlinckx (ed.), *Autour de la langue arabe. Études présentées à Jacques Grand'Henry à l'occasion de son 70e anniversaire* (Louvain-la-Neuve, 2012), pp. 207–218.

[3] The whole text of the Marsh 189 version is provided as Appendix B in the volume mentioned in note 1 above, and entirely translated into English.

[4] I thank Professor Wilferd Madelung and Dr Walid Ghali for their suggestions in some readings of the manuscript text discussed in this article.

[5] The mention of the kinds of administration authenticates the text as a version of Epistle 50.

> [various] types of administrations, such as imamate, amirate and ministry, as well as secretariat, Qur'an reading, *fiqh* practice, high education and the like, as we have mentioned in the *Book on the Theoretical Arts* . . .
>
> The third administration is the administration of the elect among elect [*siyāsat khāṣṣat al-khāṣṣa*], and it is the prophetic administration, helped through revelation, inspiration and the divine humanity [*al-nāsūt al-ilāhī*].[6] It has a quantity and a quality, [by which] the prophet is able to put together an ensemble [constituted of] the main part of people according to his doctrine [*madhhabihi*] and revelation [*sharʿihi*, here and later] thanks to the subtlety of his administration, the beauty of his belief, the wondrous [*gharīb*] of his speech, the sweetness of his eloquence, the beauty of his constitution, his sincere speech and his sincere acts in which there is no confusion, adulteration, deceit or make-believe, [and] afterwards thanks to his straightness and perseverance in establishing his revelation that he acknowledged, in setting forth the good habit to people and the praiseworthy way of life [*sīra*], and in establishing one's right in front of another, with the subtlest conduct [*sīra*] and the best administration.
>
> The fourth type is the divine administration in which there is neither quantity nor quality, and none of the humans is able to know its secret or its concealed [part], except a Messenger whom He has chosen[7] . . . Human administration [is] a part of it, because of the substance of the Intellect and of the Soul that [are] in mankind . . . (fols 367a11–367b3)

The first theme addressed after the two introductory chapters is cosmology, considered several times – in Chapters 3, 4 and 7. Chapters 5 and 6 concern the creation of Man; Chapters 8 and 11 deal with his superiority over all other creatures, and with the human soul.

Chapter 9 states that divine administration is evident in the death of the human body, whereas the Soul is eternal – an idea on which religious law and philosophy agree. This topic is also addressed in Chapters 10 and 11.

---

6 Possible allusion to the imam, who has to keep God's revelation and inspiration alive.

7 Cf. Qur'an 72:27.

Chapter 12 deals with the making of talismans as a kind of 'rational administration'; other examples of administration are given to urge the initiate to practice the 'administration' of self-improvement.

Chapter 13 lists questions about the relationship between different kinds of administration and their different purposes, with brief answers in the form of sapiential statements.

Chapters 14 and 15 provide more examples of administration with religious and moral duties, also expressed in gnomic terms.

Onto-cosmology in the MS Marsh 189

The Marsh 189 version often foreshadows 'esoteric' doctrines. One of these is onto-cosmology, which will be addressed in this paper. Immediately after the enunciation of the long title, the text opens with cosmology because the author introduces creation as a form of divine administration:

> [2.] Know that the first originated and the first invented [thing] that the Creator, blessed and exalted be He, originated and invented through His Word that is a Word of Truth [was] the Active Intellect. He said to him,[8] *Be*, and he was.[9] He said, blessed be His name, 'and the Pen [be, too]'.[10] Then He originated the Soul from the emanation of the Intellect.[11] Then He created from the two of them all creatures as [God] said, honoured and glorified be He, *O mankind! Reverence your Guardian-Lord, who created you from a single Person, created, of like nature, his mate, and*

---

[8] The personal masculine and feminine pronouns are used for the Active Intellect and the Universal Soul since, being heavenly hypostases, they can be regarded as concomitant causes of being.

[9] The formula '*Kun fa-kāna*' recalls the divine Imperative, expressed in the Qur'an as '*Kun, fa-yakūn*'; cf. Qur'an 3:47 and 59; 6:73; 16:40; 19:35; 36:82; 40:68.

[10] This says that the Active Intellect is given the Qur'anic name *qalam*, 'Pen'.

[11] The Arabic actually says *min fayḍi al-nafsi al-ʿaqla*, which appears to be inconsistent with the general doctrine of emanation; it may be a scribal error consisting of inversion of the words. The text does not mention the other name for the Universal Soul, *lawḥ*, 'Tablet'.

> *from the two of them scattered (like seeds) countless men and women* ...[12] This is [what is] called by philosophers the 'marriage' [*al-nikāḥ*] and the 'first', and these two [are] for them the first Adam and the first [*al-awwal*][13] Eve, those to whom [God] said [*al-mukhāṭabāni*], ... *approach not this tree, or ye run into harm and transgression [fa-takūnā min al-ẓālimīn]*.[14]
>
> The first generated being [*mawlūd*] born from this marriage [was] administration, and from administration the heavens, the earth and what [*man*] is in them [*fīhinna*] came.[15] Some philosophers call them 'nature' ... (fols 366v28–367a6)

After the introductory remarks, the link of onto-cosmology with Divine administration is made clearer in Chapter 3:

> [3.] Know, O my brother, that God, blessed and exalted be He, with the subtlety of His administration administered the Intellect, set him as a circle [made] of unmixed, complete, perfect and pure light, and inscribed in him all the creatures till the day of the Great Resurrection. Afterwards, He originated from the emanation of justice the knowing and active Soul, and set her[16] as a circle of light, with a middle and two extremities.[17] To the first extremity the limit of the Intellect [belongs], and through it [the Soul] looks at the inscriptions that [are] in the Intellect, and settles them in Nature. By the second extremity [there is] a third [being, tending] to Nature – to Matter – namely the Absolute Body, and [the Soul] completes [it] (fol. 367b8–12)

---

[12] Quotation of the first part of Qur'an 4:1 taken from Abdullah Yusuf Ali's translation, *The Holy Qur'an*.

[13] If it is not another scribal error, the masculine *al-awwal* could be explained in that Eve is here considered a 'category' – the feminine principle.

[14] Quotation of the second part of Qur'an 2:35.

[15] Usually, the Qur'an says, *wa-mā baynahumā*. Here, all the beings mentioned are personified. The 'Heavens' and the 'earth' are feminine, unlike the other creatures. The masculine singular pronoun *man* might refer to Adam (but this issue is postponed and will be dealt with on another occasion).

[16] See above, n. 8.

[17] Obviously, circles are here to be conceived one inside the other – what makes it possible to speak of their 'middle' and 'extremities'.

Divine administration, the Active Intellect, the Universal Soul and Nature are called the *ʿanāṣir* – the four original components preached by philosophers, whence the generation process began. Then the text goes on as follows:

> [4.] From these [original components] the four constituents [*ʿanāṣir*] came, called by philosophers heat, coldness, humidity and dryness. From these four constituents, God willing, four elements [*usṭuqusāt*] came, and they are the four basic principles [*arkān*] – the second marriage[18] and the second birth [*al-wilāda*][19] and, according to others, the third marriage and the third birth[20] . . . From these basic principles all creatures were created (fol. 367b12–16)

The *arkān* are compared to the four birds in Qurʾan 2:260, of which God spoke to Abraham when he asked Him to show how He gave life to the dead: '"Show me how thou givest life to the dead." He said: "Dost thou not then believe?" He said: "Yea! But to satisfy my own understanding." He said: "Take four birds; tame them to turn to thee; put a portion of them on every hill".'[21] Three of the elements are presented through references to Qurʾanic verses: water through part of Qurʾan 11:7 ('and His Throne – was over the Waters.'); air, possibly through the first part of Qurʾan 4:11 ('Moreover He comprehended in His design the sky, and it had been (as) smoke'), whence the author concludes that 'smoke and vapour do not come but from earth'; and earth through part of Qurʾan 30:20 ('created you from dust'). No Qurʾanic verse is quoted to explain fire, probably because the subject is dealt with later in the discussion on the nobility of man compared with angels.

18 Namely, the marriage of the four constituents – the qualities.

19 Namely, the birth of the four elements – fire, air, water and earth.

20 As if the four original components counted as a marriage and a birth in themselves. This is also an allusion to the natural world, both heavenly and sublunar.

21 Quotation of Qurʾan 2:260, apart from the first and the last words and some difference from the *vulgata*. Likewise, thanks to God's omnipotence, all creation comes from four principles.

Then the process continues as follows:

> [5.] And when He created, with the subtlety of His administration, the lowest like [*min*, here and later][22] the highest and the highest like the lowest, and the second marriage and the third birth occurred; the sphere rotated, and the stars rotated with it . . . ; He set them [as] seven heavens in strata . . . ; He set the noblest of those seven, movable, journeying lights[23] [as] the Honourable and Pious and Just angels[24] that are the cream of His creation who put their trust in His face;[25] afterwards, He divided the sphere into four parts and ordered it according to the best order, and set in it [beings] similar to the seven journeying [planets] and mansions[26] for the chosen angels . . . Philosophers call that conjunction [*al-ijtimāʿ*] a *qirān* [= junction].[27] When the sphere rotated, the stars came in conjunction, and the inferior, physical constituents came into relationship with one another, the natures mingled and mixed, the rarefied mingled with the dense depending on the position of the stars . . . and on the rotation of the sphere . . . according to a certain junction and a certain time – time is the movement of the sphere;[28] the natures were assembled and became related in marriage; and a generated being was born from them, namely, minerals (fol. 367b20–29)

Chapter 4, which explains that minerals were generated from water and earth, deals more with plants as the result of a new marriage of the rarefied with the dense, which may well be a lacuna in the text. Plants are used as a proof of the existence of a Creator:

---

[22] See infra, p. 213.

[23] The term *maṣābīḥ* is found in Qur'an 41:12 and 67:5.

[24] These adjectives are mentioned in Qur'an 80:16 with reference to the angelic scribes.

[25] Or, 'on His design'. I read, *amannā' wajhihi*.

[26] The allusion is obviously to the lunar mansions, mentioned also infra, in text [17.].

[27] The term means also 'wedding', but the passage seems to rather have an astronomical-astrological relevance.

[28] Time, 'the movement of the sphere' in the well-known Platonic definition in *Timaeus*, 10.37c–38b, also came into existence in this phase.

> [6.] Of these five genera of plants, the first that sprouted in the air [did so] for the rotation of the sphere and the position of the stars, because the sphere and the angels that are in it [are], with respect to the wise Maker, at the [same] level as servants and helpers with respect to kings, and it [= the sphere] is at the [same] level as the wheel [used by] potters . . . The wheel is moved only because the potter sets it in motion, and likewise the sphere is moved only by the administration of its Mover and Creator . . . , and He is much beyond what heretics say! (fol. 368a6–11)

A 'fourth birth' is mentioned in Chapter 5, foreshadowing the creation of man. Here, the same process described in text [5.] above is repeated in similar terms:

> [7.] Afterwards, the stars were assembled, God willing, and connected in [their] journeying, and the spiritual constituents set the physical constituents in motion; so, they were moved and mixed, and the mixture was good and the marriage perfect; they entered into each other, and that composition was the fourth birth. Some philosophers know it as the 'first', the 'second' and the 'third' birth, and do not agree on it, except that each of their speech[es] is correct according to the doctrinal school of each of them (fol. 368a13–17).

After having continued with the discourse on man, Chapter 6 returns to cosmology by mentioning rest: [8.] 'Every physical, earthly, heavy body is made of coldness – namely, of the rest that fits the bodies that return to destruction, corruption, annihilation and ruin' (fols 368a27–28).

This text means that heat was created before cold. This pair was also called 'light and darkness' or 'soul and body', but they are not 'the highest administrators': this role belongs to God.

Anthropology and Hierohistory in the MS Marsh 189

We have, therefore, four ontological levels: the level including the first two hypostases originally introduced by Neoplatonics; the level of the four qualities and elements; the level of the heavenly and the sublunar worlds; and the level of mankind.

Chapters 5–9 address the creation of man and his superiority over other animals. In Chapter 5, Qur'an 2:30 on the appointment of mankind as 'caliph of God' is quoted as a proof of the distinction of mankind from the other created beings, in terms of an opposition between the stars (that here substitute for the angels) and Adam:

> [9.] After that composition there was no [other] composition like it, because the natures and the stars do not get assembled [any longer] as they had assembled in the constitution [*khilqa*, here and later] of man: after that composition they differed, came into contrariety, showed enmity to each other and came into opposition. By getting assembled together, the stars regretted the constitution of the physical Adam, and said to their Creator, *Wilt Thou place therein one who will make mischief therein and shed blood? – whilst we do celebrate Thy praises and glorify Thy holy (name)?* He said to them, 'That has been clarified in the highest before I created you; I know what ye know not'[29] (fols 368a17–21).

Quite interestingly, cosmological enmity, which implied eternal barrenness, is associated with the dispute between God and Iblīs with regard to Adam, when Adam's ontological nobility was opposed to his moral evilness. The ontological perfection of man as well as the ontological process are addressed together in Chapter 7:

> [10.] Know, O my brother, that the first of the created beings [was] heat, then cold – and the two [are] those that are called 'light and darkness', and 'soul and body'.[30] They were diverse, then were harmonised with each other, and their diversity was due to motion. From heat humidity [*līn*] was generated that made it fertile, and from cold dryness was generated that made it fertile, so that the two became four. Indeed, first, at the beginning of creation they were two; then, two [more] were generated from them, and the two became four, two of them living and moving, and two at rest.
>
> From the combination of these four all creatures came. Some living beings [*al-ḥayawān*, here and later] belong to

---

[29] The last words resemble the last part of Qur'an 2:30.

[30] See also above, p. 200.

> life – namely, to motion – like angels; some living beings belong to death – namely, to rest – like minerals and plants; and some living beings belong both to life and death – like animals and man. Nevertheless, the soul of man [is set at] the middle of the circle; he is the top of the [living beings], and the noblest of substances is [his] heart. The disposition in the creation of all creatures was like this, so consider, O my brother, this administration (fol. 368b2–10).

After having said that man is the noblest creature because his soul is in the median circle, the author continues:

> [11.] Natures came from the four substances that are like the four constituents;[31] natures joined to their shapes – shape being closeness to and relationship with something – hence all these things came from the four natures, the four natures were generated from the four [above] mentioned substances, the four substances were generated from motion and rest, rest from motion, and motion from the eminent, prime substance to which nothing is similar, which is the beginning – namely, the Prime Motion that [can] be neither described nor characterised, nor [can] intellects arrive to its description, definition and substance (fols 368b12–17).

In all these passages an ascending hierarchy is established: things ← natures ← substances (namely, the *ʿanāṣir*) ← motion and rest ← motion and ← Prime Motion that is beyond every description and comprehension. Contrary to what we have remarked with regard to the text [9.] above, here the 'way upwards' of onto-cosmology foreshadows the spiritual rising of man, described in Chapter 6:

> [12.] Know, O my brother, that the relationship of man with animals is like the relationship of the head with the body; that man among animals is God's caliph on His earth,[32] and before him He made His angels prostrate themselves; that an intelligent man [capable of] administrating himself [*al-musa'yyis*] does not cease,

[31] See text [4.] above.
[32] Cf. Qur'an 2:30 and 38:26.

> through his administration, to rise degree by degree until he comes into the ensemble of the Friends, then from the Friends to the Pure, until he becomes an angel by [God's] saying to something: Be, and it is (fol. 368a22–25).

The advance of man to the point of becoming an angel in potentiality reflects the current version of Epistle 50. This passage implies that man becomes an angel in potentiality thanks to a new divine creation. In Chapter 8 we read:

> [13.] God said, blessed and exalted be He, *We have indeed created man in the best of moulds. Then do We abase him (to be) the lowest of the low.*[33] Of his nobility with reference to Him [is] that He created him by his hand and breathed in him [something] of His spirit, set him as a harmonious human being,[34] then as a satisfying king,[35] and set him as His caliph on His earth, and made his angels prostrate themselves before him.[36] He created him similar to Himself, as was said in the *ḥadīth*, 'I shall create something similar to Me', [like something] not being in a body – God is much beyond being in direct contact with bodies![37] And He created him, among all natures, of the most perfect substance and of the most beautiful aspect. He is the strongest and the most balanced of substances, and his soul is permanent and eternal among the souls of all animated beings, because his soul [is set at] the middle of the circle,[38] and the middle is the most balanced of things. . . . Defective and weak [as he can be], nevertheless all animals obey man, and it suffices for you [to know] that all [of

---

33 Quotation of Qur'an 95:4–5.

34 Cf. Qur'an 32:9; 15:29; 38:72. The expression *basharan sawiyan* appears in Qur'an 19:17, in a different sense (Yusuf Ali's translation: 'a man in all respects').

35 Cf., for a similar expression, Qur'an 19:6.

36 Cf. Qur'an 15:30 and 38:73.

37 This is the same statement developed in some of the natural epistles. See Epistle 19 'On Minerals', Chapters 12 and 13, and Epistle 21 'On Plants', Chapter 1, in Carmela Baffioni (ed. and tr.), *On the Natural Sciences: An Arabic Critical Edition and English Translation of Epistles 15–21* (New York–London, 2013), pp. 276, 280 and 321 respectively.

38 See above, p. 202.

> them] are nourishment for him and [that] in some of them there is [even] healing for him[39] (fols 368b21–369a10)

A sort of 'evolution' is described here, and the 'double creation' marks the passage from the natural to the heavenly level.

Later, the nobility of man is addressed from the gnosiological standpoint:

> [14.] Then [God] characterised him with the vision through intellect, which is the noblest of things, and He did not characterise any other [animal] with that. So He composed the noblest with the noblest, then He taught him with [the use of] intellect,[40] where to write with pen on paper, so that he encompassed with that the world, as He said, blessed and exalted be He, *Proclaim! And thy Lord is Most Bountiful, He Who taught (the use of) the Pen, Taught man that which he knew not*[41] (fol. 369a10–12)

However, it seems that the mention of the Pen sets man in relationship with the ontological process as well. The words 'He composed the noblest with the noblest' may in fact hint at the Active Intellect, the noblest ontological hypostasis, and at man, the noblest of creatures.

The peculiar 'evolutionism' highlighted above is better clarified in Chapter 9, which addresses themes already mentioned:

> [15.] The soul of man is the subtlest [*alṭaf*, here and later] and the most elevated of souls, and his body [comes] from the subtlest and the most regulated of the [physical] constituents, and he is compound of the subtle[st (*laṭīf*, here and later]) parts] of the

---

[39] These lines recall the contents of Epistle 22 'On Animals', variously referred to in Epistle 40 'On Causes and Effects'. See Carmela Baffioni and Ismail K. Poonawala (ed. and tr.), *Sciences of the Soul and Intellect, Part III: An Arabic Critical Edition and English Translation of Epistles 39–41* (New York and London, 2017), pp. 118, 120, 213–221. See also infra, p. 212.

[40] We have here the same construction of the verb as in sura 96:4, *'allama bi'l-qalam*.

[41] Quotation of Qur'an 96:3–5. So this chapter ends in the same way as it had begun, by providing Scriptural proofs of the nobility of man.

> [various] substances – of the hot of earth, the cold of water, the thin of fire and the subtle of air –, and comes from these contrary things according to the decree of the Wise Administrator. Afterwards he became balanced and subtle thanks to the movement that is the spirit of life, when [*wa*] the spirit began to settle in him [while] he was not yet claimed [to be] subtle but was a dense mass, as He said, exalted be He, *Has there not been over Man a long period of Time, when he was nothing – (not even) mentioned?*[42] And when the substance was established in him, he became subtle and balanced, and became a man, whom philosophers called 'the median, balanced substance', as He said, exalted be He, *Thus have We made of you an* umma *justly balanced*,[43] in the sense of 'just'. The median is the most balanced of things, because his soul [is set at] the middle of the circle, as we have already recalled[44] (fols 369a22–369b1)

Therefore, the last lines approach human perfection from a third standpoint, the moral one. Nonetheless, the author confirms the vision of man as a microcosm of the entire creation, bringing him back again to onto-cosmology:

> [16.] His soul [comes] from the quintessence of motion, and he is the compendium of his knowledge[45] [that is] preserved [in the Tablet]; in him [there is] the property [*ṣifa*, here and later] of the seven heavens, of the seven planets [*al-kawākib*], of the twelve mansions and of the twenty-eight stations;[46] and in him there is the property of the rivers, the trees and the fruits of Paradise [*al-jinān*]. He who wants to see the macrocosm in its entirety should reflect on the form of man. Consider then, O my brother, this administration, and reflect on the disposition of this wisdom of the Lord [*al-rabbāniyya*]! (fols 368b26–369a1)

---

42 Quotation of Qur'an 76:1.

43 Quotation of the beginning of Qur'an 2:143.

44 See above, pp. 202 and 203.

45 Cacography in the text.

46 For which see Qur'an 10:5 and 36:39.

And again:

> [17.] Know that your Creator breathed in you [something] of His spirit, made you a compendium of His world, and explained to you in the structure [*khulq*, here and later] of your body and of your soul the realms of heavens and earth, therefore, be among the certain.[47] He said, exalted be He, about your souls, *Will ye not then see*[48] the reign of heavens and earth in the structure of man? For this [reason] philosophers called him a 'microcosm' (fol. 370a7–10)

The opposition between the ontological perfection of man and Adam's fall is a relevant feature of our text, but the esoteric meaning of Adam's story[49] is the main subject of an addition to Epistle 50 found in the MS Esad Efendi 3638, probably dating to 685-86/1287, Istanbul: Süleymaniye library, one of the oldest extant manuscripts of the *Rasā'il*. I have discussed this elsewhere.[50] The focus here is on the onto-cosmological passages that are found in that addition.

In paragraph 4 of my edition, the text deals with the first ontological level, concerning the hypostases of Neoplatonic origin:

> [18.] If the issue [*dhālika*] is like that, the only [possible] demonstration with regard to the faculty of the [Active] Intellect [*al-quwwa al-ʿaqliyya*] propagated in the faculty of the [Universal] Soul [*al-quwwa al-nafsāniyya*] [and] joined to the purity of

---

[47] Cf. Qur'an 6:75, which in its entirety runs as follows: 'So also did We show Abraham the power and the laws of the heavens and the earth, that he might (with understanding) have certitude'. Verses 76–82 of this sura describe Abraham's rejection of astrolatry.

[48] I quote here Yusuf Ali's translation of the last words of Qur'an 51:21. The question *A-fa-lā-tubṣirūn* is found also in Qur'an 28:72 and 43:51, translated differently by Yusuf Ali. The following words of the text do not belong to the Qur'an, presenting one of the numerous examples of the Ikhwān's personal *tafsīr* of the Holy Book.

[49] The text and complete translation of this addition are provided as Appendix A in the volume mentioned in n. 1 above.

[50] In the paper titled 'The Esoteric Meaning of the Sin of Adam in the Manuscript Tradition of the *Rasā'il* Ikhwān al-Ṣafā'', presented at the International Conference *The Problem of Evil: A Challenge to Shiʿi Theology and Philosophy in Islam* (Palermo, 26–28 October 2016), (forthcoming).

> the substance of the human nature[51] [is] that the roots [have] a first[52] [one] that branches off and comes to be from them, and that the [roots] precede them[53] in examination and closeness to their places [*maḥallihā*] (fol. 280a29–30)

Paragraph 7 of my edition deals with the third level – the sub-lunar world – and with the disposition of the world in couples in particular:

> [19.] Know, O my brother, that God, honoured and glorified be He, created the world in couples harmonised with each other, perfected them by His wisdom, assessed them through His work and reported to them the names of what was to come from them and appear from them. He posed the spiritual rarefied and settled for it the physical dense. The Imperative preceded them; in it [= the Imperative] was the power of some of them over others. Therefore, to it [= the Imperative] [belongs] the encompassment of each of them, according to its closeness to the Imperative and to the investigation of [the Imperative] of what is given to it to understand from the circle of what encompasses it and is disposed above it (fol. 280b9–12)

These ideas, which are similar to those expressed in the MS Marsh 189, are explicitly connected by the author of the addition to Epistle 49 of the encyclopaedia, 'On the Acts of the Spiritual Beings'. Paragraph 8 continues:

> [20.] Afterwards [God] set the beginning in the prime roots as a perfect creation, provided [it] with the form of perfection, placed for it the instrument of duration, set the form of the things preserved in it in potentiality – since it [= the first beginning and the first creation] was the preserved Tablet,[54] and traced its circle with the Pen of the Imperative . . . [He] Who encompasses the

---

[51] These lines should be taken to be an allusion to the onto-cosmology described in paragraph 11 of that addition.

[52] *Al-awwal* is Adam, the first ramification after the heavenly hypostases.

[53] Namely, the faculties of the Active Intellect and the Universal Soul that, according to the author of the addition, come after the roots.

[54] Cf. Qur'an 85:22.

> circles of what appeared from His Imperative in highness, glory, loftiness and exaltation over [the fact] that what is in the wideness of His omnipotence is forever in the universality of His creation.[55] Indeed, He predetermines forever the images [*al-amthāl*] of what appeared and the coming-to-be of what was in doubles [*aḍʿāfan*], which is neither encompassed by the numbering of the [Active] Intellect [*al-ʿadad al-ʿaqlī*], nor reached through perception by the imagination of the [Universal] Soul [*al-wahm al-nafsānī al-kullī*]. After [that], He did not acquire [benefits] for what is by Him, since He does not draw [anything] from any essence different from His own essence: He is good, graciously disposed, confers favours and prolongs [His favour] because of the wideness of His omnipotence over what He has emanated (fol. 280b12–17)

The following hierarchies are recognisable in these cosmogonic descriptions. The first establishes the succession: God → Imperative/*qalam* → All-encompassing circle/*lawḥ* → Beings in couples/names → the entire creation. The second gives: God (the model of the couples that, if my understanding of the passage is correct, are beyond the Active Intellect and the Universal Soul) → the principles/*lawḥ*, and → the 'circle'. The third gives: Imperative/*qalam* → First creation/beginning/*lawḥ* → Motion → Couples → Active Intellect → Universal Soul. The text subsequently notes that the last element of creation was the form of the particular Adam, the noblest creature whose noblest part is the human heart – 'the place in which the movements of the "mothers" are concentrated'.

Proto-Ismaili and Ismaili Doctrines in the MS Marsh 189

The onto-cosmological ideas expressed in the MS Marsh 189 reflect proto-Ismaili and Ismaili doctrines. The identification of the Active

---

55 These lines (that state that God has no reciprocal relationship with any of the lower hypostases: in this representation, He bestows His gifts almost 'by dictate of His omnipotence') mean that the existence of something similar to the eternal God is impossible.

Intellect and the Universal Soul with God's 'Pen' and 'Tablet' is found in the earliest instances of Ismaili doctrines, which developed a cosmological description in terms of light as well. The divine Imperative, too, plays an important role in onto-cosmologies of Ismaili origin, and it can be identified with the 'Prime Motion' of text [11.] above. The qualities connected to the Prophet in text [1.] are also a commonplace in Ismaili texts, above all the references to his speech and eloquence. To further support this point, a couple of examples related to onto-cosmology can be given.

The following ontological description by the Ismaili philosopher and missionary Abū Yaʿqūb al-Sijistānī (active in the second half of the fourth/tenth century) may be considered to be a summary of the doctrines reported above:

> When God . . . originated by His Imperative the two roots that are the Pen and the Tablet, and made them the two roots of all creatures, what there was and what there would have been appeared in them. The Imperative of both of them ultimately turned into [*istaqarra ʿalā*] Matter and Form, in such a way that the natural world [may] be formed [*li-takawwun*] from them . . . What came to be formed of [*al-ḥāṣil min*] the natural world reached its climax with [*balagha ilā*] the rational, mortal animal that is man, <and> from what [*mimmā*] was emanated to the originated [being] – namely, His Imperative – there cannot be [*lā yaṣluḥ*] subsistence for humanity [*qiwām al-bashar*] in the natural world unless by succession in it of death after life. A part of the emanation [*al-ifāḍa*, here and later] from the Intellect was emanating [*mufīḍa*] on its Follower, and such emanation from the Intellect was [also] emanated [*mufāḍa*] – I mean the succession in humanity of death after life. This emanation from God's Imperative was on the Pen, and from the Pen on the Tablet as an angel [*malakan*] charged with the death of humanity, which is not possible to attain by senses, and the Power accorded that emanation for [*aʿṭā al-qudra bi-tilka'l-ifāḍa ʿalā*] the seizing [*qabḍ*] of spirits as a surprising event [*baghta*[56]] outside [*bilā*]

[56] This is a Qur'anic word, cf. 6:31, 44 and 47; 7:95 and 187; 12:108; 21:40; 22:55; 26:202; 29:53 and 55; 43:66; 47:18.

> time and an upturn [*ṭafra*] outside [*bilā*] space. Likewise from the emanation of God's Imperative . . . on the Pen happened that [*jarā . . . an*] the cream of humanity ultimately got to [*tantahī ilā*] he who receives inspirational help [*ta'yyid*] without intermediary or through a spiritual intermediary. The emanation flew [*jarat*] from it to the Follower, and that emanation from God's Imperative . . . became [*ṣārat*] an angel charged with the transmission [*tablīgh*] of the message to messengers. Therefore, in the world of the Intellect and the Soul [there are] angels charged with the completion of wisdom, whom number cannot count, they speak not before He speaks, and they act [in all things] by His Imperative.[57] The faith in angels of he who knew them by these signs is a faith that suits the faith [*yaṣluḥ li*] in God purified [*al-mukhlaṣ*] from attributes and relations (*Sullam al-najāt* ['The Ladder of Salvation'], pp. 27, 10–30, 3)[58]

The apparently contradictory statement in text [10.] above (which refers to the constant immobility of minerals and plants, – whereas plants grow, hence move, though not in space)[59] suggests that minerals have an embryonic form of life even though they do not move and their development is not immediately perceived. This idea will be fully developed by the other great Ismaili thinker and missionary Ḥamīd al-Dīn al-Kirmānī (d. after 411/1020). He called minerals '*al-nafs al-ṭabī'iyya*',[60] and explained life in them as a means that makes them reach their

---

57 These two are Qur'anic expressions, see sura 21:27.

58 Abualy Alibhai Mohamed (ed.), *Abū Ya'qūb al-Sijistānī and* Kitāb sullam al-najāt. *A Study in Islamic Neoplatonism* [PhD Dissertation] (Cambridge, MA, 1983). Cf. also *Tuḥfat al-mustajībīn* ('The Gift for Them Who Answer [the Call]'), p. 14, 24–25 in 'Ārif Tāmir (ed.), *Thalāth Rasā'il Ismā'īliyya* (Beirut, 1403/1983). The names 'Pen/*qalam*' and 'Tablet/*lawḥ*' attributed to the Intellect and the Soul are counted by Sijistānī among the 'shara'itical' names, and are explained in his *Kitāb al-Iftikhār* ('The Book of Boasting'). See Ismail K. Poonawala (ed.), *Kitāb al-Iftikhār by Abū Ya'qūb Isḥaq b. Aḥmad al-Sijistānī (Died After 361/971)* ([Beirut], 2000), pp. 110–115; they are also stated to be the same as Neoplatonic entities, see pp. 114–115.

59 These ideas are expressed in Epistle 21 'On Plants'; see Baffioni, *On the Natural Sciences*, p. 328. In general, the Ikhwān al-Ṣafā' maintain that plants are living creatures, and that even minerals have an embryonic form of life.

60 Ḥamīd al-Dīn al-Kirmānī, *Rāḥat al-'aql* ('The Rest of the Intellect'), ed. Muṣṭafā Ghālib (Beirut, 1984), p. 414, 2.

perfection according to their mixture, besides preserving them in existence.[61]

Chapter 5 of the MS Marsh 189 summarises an esoteric interpretation of Qur'an 2:30. In Chapter 11, prophecy and the spirit of God breathed into man are a further proof of his nobility; as a result of it, angels prostrated themselves before Adam:[62]

> [21.] On that demonstration both prophecy and philosophy agreed – that the soul is living, eternal, permanent, [that it] illuminates bodies like a lamp does, without weight or sensation, and that the soul of man is nobler and higher than the souls of animals, because the soul of man is [made] of the Noble Substance, as He said, exalted be He, *and breathed into him something of His spirit*[63] (fols 369b26–370a1)

And again:

> [22.] To the nobility of man [belongs the fact] that he is characterised by prophecy and by the divine spirit.[64] Because of that the Prophet brought the clear verses and the inimitable peculiarities [*al-gharā'ib al-mu'jizāt*, of his speech],[65] and because of that some of the excellent divine [*al-khiyārīna al-rubūbiyya*] claimed that they[66] are [part of] the lot [*qisma*] of man because of [his] divine, eternal, permanent soul. I shall expound this [issue] with a commentary in the *Book on Spells and Charms*.[67] Because of this honoured substance by which man is characterised God made

[61] Ibid., p. 414, 5–12.

[62] However, the author maintains the point that man can become like the angels only when he performs angelic acts.

[63] Quotation of part of Qur'an 32:9.

[64] Namely, the spirit of God He breathed in him.

[65] On the 'miracle' [*mu'jiza*] of the Prophet's language, broadly addressed in the encyclopaedia in Epistle 31 'On the Causes of the Diversity of Languages', see Carmela Baffioni, 'The "Language of the Prophet" in the Iḫwān al-Ṣafā'', in Daniel De Smet, Godefroid de Callataÿ and Jan M.F. Van Reeth (ed.), *Al-Kitāb. La sacralité du texte dans le monde de l'Islam*. Actes du Symposium International tenu à Leuven et Louvain-la-Neuve du 29 mai au 1 juin 2002 (Bruxelles, Louvain-la-Neuve and Leuven, 2004), pp. 357–370.

[66] Namely, prophecy and the divine spirit.

[67] With this title, the author refers to Epistle 52 'On Magic'.

> His angels prostrate themselves before him and made them obedient to him. Then He made him such that he ate animals and rendered them subservient to what he wanted. Then He characterised him with intellect; and God, exalted be He, did not create in His lower world anything endowed with intellect except man, and if it were not for his heavy body he would be an angel, but he is linked to [*ʿāqid ilā*] angels when his acts are like the acts of the angels, in fact he resembles the thing towards which he is attracted[68] (fol. 370a10–16)

The last lines recall the allusion to the 'Pen' in text [14.] above.

The Influence of Balīnūs on the MS Marsh 189

My main concern in this article, however, is to show the interesting similarities noticeable between the MS Marsh 189 and *Sirr al-Khalīqa* attributed to the Arabic Apollonius of Tyana – Balīnūs; a text dating probably back to the beginning of the third/ninth century.

Parts of this work have been edited and translated by Silvestre de Sacy and Julius Ruska. Ruska also proved that the famous alchemist text known as *Tabula Smaragdina* has its original place at the end of this book; Paul Kraus has shown that the entire book is a commentary on that text. Kraus's analysis led to its dating in the time of the caliph al-Maʾmūn, and demonstrated its close relationship with the Syriac *Book of Treasures* by Job of Edessa (ca. 817 CE) and with the *Perì fyseos anthropou* by Nemesius of Emesa (fifth century CE), as well as its influence on Jābir b. Ḥayyān.[69] After the capital research by Ursula Weisser, it is worth quoting here Daniel De Smet's recent judgment: 'L'emploi du *Kitāb Sirr al-khalīqa* dans la littérature ismaélienne mérite une étude à part entière'.[70] It is hoped that what follows will provide some further elucidation of this complex and intriguing issue.

---

68 This confirms what stated in n. 62 above.

69 M. Plessner, 'Balīnūs', *EI2*, vol. 1, pp. 994–995.

70 Daniel De Smet, 'L'auteur des *Rasāʾil Ikhwān al-Ṣafāʾ* selon les sources ismaéliennes ṭayyibites', *Shii Studies Review*, 1 (2017), pp. 151–166, at p. 164, note 39.

To begin, the *coincidentia oppositorum* established in text [5.] above between the lowest and the highest reminds us of the *Tabula Smaragdina* found by Balīnūs in the cavern in the hands of Hermes Trismegistus, where we read, almost in the same terms:

> It is true, without doubt in it and sound, that the highest [is] like [*min*, here and later] the lowest and the lowest like the highest, an accomplishment of prodigies [*ʿajāʾib*] from a sole [principle], just like all things come from one, according to a sole organisation. The Sun is its father, the Moon its mother, the wind brought it in its womb [*baṭn*], and the earth nurtures it.[71]

The 'rarefied' and the 'dense' are mentioned as well at p. 524, 11 (the Arabic for 'dense' in the whole work being, however, *ghalīẓ* rather than *kathīf*).

After having emphasised the uniqueness of the Creator in opposition to the duality of His creation (pp. 100, 11–101, 4 Weisser), Balīnūs says that the Creator 'produced [*aḥdatha*] all things by His power [*qudra*]' (p. 101, 6), and continues: 'The first [thing] that was created [was] His speech, as He said: 'Be so and so!' And that Word came to be – the cause [*ʿilla*] of the whole creation, and the rest of creation [is] an effect; that [was] the beginning of the couples – namely, of creation' (p. 101, 8–9). God cannot be the cause of anything because a cause somewhat resembles its effect (p. 102, 1–6). God's word is beyond any nature, substance or quality; it is not perceived, and everything comes through it (p. 102, 6–8): it is 'God's will [*idhn*], and His Imperative' (p. 102, 8–9).

These lines are very close to text [2.] above, where God's Word precedes the Active Intellect, originated first by God through the Imperative, 'Be'. The Intellect and the Soul constituted the first couple, from which all creatures came. Thus, they are the 'marriage' and the first stage of the process of coming-to-be. In Balīnūs, creation is the same

71 Balīnūs al-ḥakīm/pseudo-Apollonius of Tyana, *Sirr al-khalīqa wa-ṣanʿat al-ṭabīʿa, Kitāb al-ʿilal/Buch über das Geheimnis der Schöpfung und die Darstellung der Natur (Buch der Ursachen)*, ed. Ursula Weisser (Aleppo, 1979), p. 524, 4–10; the complete text is found at pp. 524, 4–525, 6.

as *'ibtidā' al-izwāj'*. The personification of the two hypostases with Adam and Eve links ontology to hierohistory.

As to the first fruit of that marriage, called in the MS Marsh 189 'administration', it looks the same as the *fi'l* of which Balīnūs speaks immediately afterwards, by saying: 'The first [thing] that was produced [*ḥadatha*] after God's Word, honoured and glorified be He, much beyond [everything else], is the act – namely [*dulla bi*, here and later] motion, namely heat' (p. 103, 2–3). This is the principle of creation. Action is the same as motion, that is to say, the same as heat. Afterwards, defect of heat brings rest – namely, coldness (p. 103, 4–5). Balīnūs, too, identifies the cosmological principle motion/heat with 'the spirit of our father Adam' (p. 103, 5). Heat produced all other things, among which man is the most perfect (p. 103, 6–11).

The MS Marsh 189 recognises four different stages (or levels) in the process of production of being from God. These stages are called in Balīnūs *taqṭī'*; more precisely, he mentions a *taqṭī'* (division) without composition (*tarkīb*) in the Prime Substance, similar to the *wilāda al-khafiyya* (hidden birth), and a *taqṭī'* endowed with composition, similar to the *wilāda al-ẓāhira* (manifest birth). The second *tarkīb* produced the *wilāda al-khilqa* (p. 109, 3–6). In our manuscript, these may correspond to the second marriage – the marriage of the four qualities – the second birth – the birth of fire, air, water and earth – and the third marriage and the third birth – the coming-to-be of the natural world – mentioned in text [5.].

When heat was attached to (*'aṭafa 'alā*) coldness, that was a single thing – heat at the beginning, cold at the end; coupling (*izdiwāj*) was produced with this attachment as well, in the sense that heat functioned as an active male, and cold as a passive female (p. 109, 7–10). From their coupling two *mawlūd* came – humidity, called *līn*, and dryness (p. 109, 10–11). These lines resemble the description given in text [10.] above.

Humidity and dryness in their turn felt attraction (*intaza'a*) for those similar to themselves – dryness for cold and humidity for heat –, and entered them. Another coupling – a 'second marriage' – was then produced (pp. 109, 11–110, 2). Earth derived from dryness and coldness, and air from humidity and heat. Dryness, therefore, was like a male for the cold (that is female) – 'made it fertile', the MS Marsh 189 would say. Contrariwise, however, Balīnūs adds that humidity was like a female for heat and heat like a male for humidity. Heat, in fact, is always male, and coldness always female (p. 110, 2–7). As neither a male combines (*dhahaba ilā*) with a male, nor a female with a female, after these new combinations – one cold and dry the other hot and humid – there was no more birth (*wilāda*), because their coupling (now called *tazwīj*) is sterile (*ʿaqīm*) (p. 110, 7–11). Their coupling was, instead, fertile when the four qualities came *min sūs wāḥid* ('from a single root', p. 111, 1–2).

From the combination of the heat and humidity with the coldness and dryness two children (*waladāni*) came, one cold and humid and the other hot and dry (p. 112, 4–7). This indicates the formation of water and fire. Afterwards, the qualities and their coupling were separated [*infaṣalā*], and there was no more division (*taqṭīʿ*), because coupling was complete: coldness with humidity (here, *ruṭb*), heat with dryness, coldness with dryness and heat with humidity (pp. 112, 9–113, 2). In sum,

> The principle of creation was from the one. Then the two came – namely, heat and coldness. Then the three came – namely, the combination [*ijtimāʿ*] of the two. Then the four came – namely, heat, coldness, humidity [*līn*] and dryness. Then the generation process [*wilāda*] came to a rest [*istaqarrat*], and nothing more was added, or separated and added [again], because from the four the perfection of all contraries [come]. And when it is paired [*izdawajat*], and the natures are four . . . reciprocal enmity began (p. 113, 3–8)

These considerations can be compared with text [9.] above.

Elsewhere, this process is summarised as follows. The four natures come from two powers (*quwwa*) – heat and coldness. From heat comes humidity (*līn*), and from coldness dryness; from their mixture (*imtizāj*) four compound natures come – fire (from heat and dryness), water (from coldness and humidity), air (from heat and humidity) and earth (from coldness and dryness) (p. 187, 2–9). These natures (now, air is called *rīḥ* and earth *turāb*) are later named *usṭuqusāt* and *ummahāt*, as well as 'the single roots (*al-uṣūl al-afrād*)' that exist without composition – heat, coldness, humidity and dryness (pp. 187, 10–188, 1). Another composition came from those natures in composition, called 'the macrocosm' (*al-ʿālam al-akbar*), whence the four basic principles (*arkān*) of the world came: heat and dryness prevail on the eastern *rukn*, heat and humidity on the southern *rukn* (called *al-jarbī*), coldness and humidity on the western *rukn*, and coldness and dryness on the northern *rukn* (called *al-taymī*) (p. 188, 1–7). Here we see that Balīnūs distinguishes the four natures (those mentioned in text [4.] above) from the fire, air, water and earth existing in the sublunar world.[72]

Let us now come to man, on whom the MS Marsh 189 says:

> [23.] Know, O my brother, that the head of man was created in the air and his feet [were created] in the earth, because to the property of an ascending, rising [being] it does not [belong] his heavy body, but his ascending soul, as it – namely, the soul – [is] in the body according to the form of the body, but it is spiritual whereas the body envelops it like the peel of a compound [being] and similar [things]. Among the created beings, others [have] the head reversed, like plants, and the head turned upside down, as the animals that walk on four [paws], for causes we have already expounded in the *Book on Animals*.[73]
>
> So reflect, O my brother, on the nobility of man above the other animals. Indeed, man is like that because of the balance of the four natures in him – namely, fire, air, water and earth. Fire and air attract his upper parts, and cause[74] his head to rise in the air; earth is not excessive in him because of their [= of the natures] balance in relation to him: it[75] [tries to] attract him with its strength and to prostrate him like the animals endowed with four [paws] or like plants in the earth, but he is the most balanced in structure and the most perfect [of animals] in nature. Likewise

---

72 Note that the terms *al-jarbī* and *al-taymī* are also found in Epistle 18 'On Meteorology', Chapter 7. Cf. Baffioni, *On the Natural Sciences*, p. 200.

73 The author refers to Epistle 22 that brings this title. See Lenn E. Goodman and Richard McGregor (ed. and tr.), *The Case of the Animals Versus Man Before the King of the Jinn: An Arabic Critical Edition and English Translation of Epistle 22* (New York and London, 2009), pp. 70 and 109.

74 Here the text shifts from a plural to a dual form of the verb.

75 The earth which is considered feminine in this context, though diacritical dots are not always perspicuous.

> [is] his property with regard to his Creator when he turns to Him, and no other among animals [can do so] (fol. 369a1–9)

Balīnūs deals with man in the sixth part of *Sirr al-khalīqa*. He says that he is 'the most perfect of natures in substance, the most beautiful in aspect (*manẓaran*), the highest in importance (*khaṭaran*) and the strongest and most balanced among substances as well, so that he reigns over everything' (p. 424, 3–6). With his head upwards – because it is light – and tending downwards because of his weight, he is 'in the middle (*bayna*) among animals, in balance' (p. 424, 7–10).

Conclusion

On the one hand, the comparisons with *Sirr al-khalīqa* may confirm the antiquity of the MS Marsh 189 – and, consequently, that it contains a version of Epistle 50 that predates the printed versions and the other manuscripts I examined; but it could also be a collection of materials assembled from older versions of different epistles as well. On the other hand, so far, we are in no position to ascertain when or by whom the addition in MS Esad Efendi 3638 was composed.

The only possible conclusion is that there were two parallel traditions concerning the *Rasāʾil* earlier than the MS ʿĀtif (Atif) Efendi 1681, 1182 CE, Istanbul: Süleymaniye library, the oldest available, on which the new edition of the encyclopaedia published by the IIS is based. One of these traditions connects the Brethren to proto-Ismaili and Ismaili philosophical doctrines.

An example is MS Marsh 189, where the origin of the world is described attributing an important role to the divine Imperative; the supralunar hypostases (Active Intellect and Universal Soul) are compared to God's Tablet and Pen; and man is introduced as the king of the universe. One relevant feature is the relationship between the perfection of man and the fall of Adam which is also the subject of the addition to Epistle 50 contained in MS Esad Efendi 3638 in which the esoteric meaning of the story is communicated to the elect.

The version of Epistle 50 in MS Atif Efendi 1681 is evidence of the opposite tradition. Almost all the passages leading to 'radical' interpretations of the feasts discussed, which are provided in the Beirut edition of the *Rasā'il* (1957), have been expurgated from it.[76] The MSS containing additions similar to those extant in the Beirut edition are MSS Esad Efendi 3637, n.d., but ca. thirteenth century, Istanbul: Süleymaniye library – among the oldest extant MSS of this epistle; Köprülü 871, 820/1417 CE, Istanbul: Süleymaniye library; Ar 2303, 1611 CE, Paris: Bibliothèque nationale; and Laud Or. 255, n.d., Oxford: Bodleian library. The MSS closest to the Atif versions are, instead, MSS Esad Efendi 3638 and Feyzullah 2131, AH 704, Istanbul: Süleymaniye library.

The gap between the dates of the *Rasā'il* and the Atif MS prevents us from knowing whether the latter contains the 'original' version written while the Brethren were in *taqiyya* and hence made public without the 'esoteric' passages, or they were added later to increase the 'esoteric' meaning of the treatise. Be that as it may, the discovery of a 'purged' version suggests an interpretation very different from the one proposed by Henry Corbin with regard to Epistle 50,[77] and we may only speculate as to the reasons why such a different version circulated in the milieu of the Brethren.

It is necessary to advise the reader, however, that this situation does not diminish the complexity of the manuscript tradition of the *Rasā'il*, because in other cases MS Atif Efendi 1681 also provides additions to individual epistles that are close to proto-Ismaili and Ismaili ideas and doctrines.[78]

---

[76] I have discussed the impact of these different versions of Epistle 50 on the interpretation of the rites described in it in 'The Three Kinds of Rituals in Epistle 50 of the Ikhwān al-Ṣafā'', paper presented at the 28th Conference of the UEAI (Palermo, Sept. 12-16, 2016), in A. Pellitteri et al. (ed.), *Re-defining a Space of Encounter. Islam and Mediterranean: Identity, Alterity and Interactions*. Proceedings of the 28th Congress of the Union Européenne des Arabisants et Islamisants, Palermo 2016 (Leuven: Peeters, forthcoming), pp. 427–436.

[77] H. Corbin, 'Rituel sabéen et exégèse ismaélienne du rituel', *Eranos Jahrbuch*, 19 (1950), pp. 181–246.

[78] Cf. Baffioni, *On Logic*, pp. 157–165; and Baffioni, *On the Natural Sciences*, pp. 359–392. The Appendix A at pp. 359–369 deals with Balīnūs' influence.

9

Extra-Ismaili Sources and a Shift of Paradigm in Nizārī Ismailism

Daryoush Mohammad Poor
(The Institute of Ismaili Studies)

Introduction

Referring to the sophisticated system of doctrines produced by various Ismaili communities as 'Ismaili philosophy' may require some clarification. In a recent article, Daniel De Smet has noted how Henry Corbin has been mainly responsible for introducing what he called 'Shi'i philosophy' into the existing literature. What Corbin was referring to was clearly different from the academic philosophical activity of European philosophers, be they continental or analytic philosophers. Corbin basically called this literature 'theosophy' or *ḥikmat-i ilāhiyya*. De Smet provides a neat description of what this 'philosophy' entails and I will not repeat those here.[1] Apart from De Smet's articulations of this system of thought, one can make a strong case for calling this body of literature 'Ismaili philosophy' by explaining it in terms of the epistemological framework of critical rationalism. In Karl Popper's opinion, theories developed in response to genuine problems form a valid philosophical activity, no matter if they are critical or uncritical.[2] In this sense, what is here described as Ismaili philosophy is a set of theories developed in response to genuine and existential problems

[1] See D. De Smet's Introduction to Part VIII, 'Philosophy and Intellectual Traditions', in F. Daftary and G. Miskinzoda (ed.), *The study of Shi'i Islam: History, Theology and Law* (London, 2014), pp. 545–547.

[2] See K. Popper, *In Search of a Better World*, tr. Laura J. Bennett (London and New York, 1992), pp. 173–188.

faced by Ismailis. Looking at the development of this philosophy from the perspective of growth of knowledge,[3] we can identify developments, revisions and re-assessments of these theories whose central drive, according to those who developed them, was the pursuit of truth. These revisions resulted in what is known as a 'paradigm shift' – to borrow a term from Thomas Kuhn.

Therefore, my first submission is that the body of literature which may be called Ismaili philosophy is a set of theories provided as solutions to genuine problems – at the heart of which is the issue of the tension between reason and revelation. There are significant areas of philosophical activity which can also be categorised under 'theological' sciences, with the awareness that we must not conflate and confuse philosophy and theology. These areas or themes include theories about the knowledge of God, generally categorised under divine unity (*tawḥīd*), theories about prophethood (*nubuwwat*), the imamate and theories on eschatology.[4] For Ismailis – almost for every known Ismaili community in history – one can safely argue that these theories are closely connected with how Ismailis understand the doctrine of imamate and how they proceed to defend the legitimacy of the line of Ismaili imams.

Now to the second proposition to be discussed here, which deals with the diversity of interpretations and articulations of these doctrines. Returning to the initial comments about Ismaili philosophy above, in making a case for Ismaili philosophy we must note the use of the abstract term philosophy here. For far too long, scholars who have been writing in the field of Ismaili studies, have used the singular abstract form. This style of reference to the diverse body of literature produced by different Ismaili communities in the form of their doctrines obscures a critical observation. There is a tendency to refer to Ismaili philosophy in a broad and unifying manner by identifying certain elements which sometimes cover a limited span of the history

---

[3] See also D. Miller, *A Pocket Popper* (Glasgow, 1983), pp. 171–180.

[4] It is important to note that the term 'theory' is used in the critical rationalist sense of it and must not be confused with the common usage of the term. The term theory here is used instead of 'doctrine' to indicate the role of human agency in developing these theories/doctrines and the historicity of them.

of these doctrines and then extending them to other periods. Articulations of the doctrine of imamate among Ismailis in the early years of the genesis of Ismailism are not the same as articulations produced in the early and later Fatimid period (fourth–sixth/tenth–twelfth centuries). These articulations found an entirely new orientation during the Nizārī episode of Ismailism before the fall of Alamūt in 654/1257. Then further layers were added in the post-Alamūt period, when the Nizārī Ismailis were affiliated with Sufi groups and identified more closely with them, up to the modern period. Throughout all these periods, there was a continuum which was significantly highlighted in defending the legitimacy of the line of imams and the very concept of imamate itself. Yet, there were also visible shifts and changes in these articulations. A notable example of this can be seen in how Ismailis came up with different articulations of the concept of *qiyāmat* and the *qāʾim*. This point is noted by Paul Walker referring to Wilferd Madelung's assessment of these articulations:

> Surely, if any single concept brought all of the Ismailis together, it was their fundamental attachment to the line of imams they accepted. Yet, when Wilferd Madelung, the first modern investigator with access to a substantial range of the early Ismaili literature, attempted to verify the doctrine of the imamate and the messiah in each of the successive phases of the history of the movement, he found that the literature produced by the *daʿwa* offered no consistent teaching on these issues. In fact, the doctrine appeared to change over time, evolving according to circumstances. He discovered, moreover, that at any given time there were important variations between the views of one faction and another.[5]

There is a general perception among scholars and the laymen alike that Ismailism is characterised by Neoplatonic philosophy. Despite certain strong and valid instances which partially support this claim, nothing could be further from the truth. It is true that Ismaili writers – or missionaries (*dāʿīs*) – were open to employing most forms

---

[5] Paul E. Walker, *Early Philosophical Shiism: The Ismaili Neoplatonism of Abū Yaʿqūb al-Sijistānī* (Cambridge, 1993), pp. 9–10.

of learning current in the particular era in which they lived when articulating their doctrines. This approach inevitably embraced the literature produced following the translation movement that took place during the second to fourth/eighth to tenth centuries. But the Ismailis were not exceptionally interested in appropriating and adapting this knowledge, even though we have plenty of evidence to show that Ismailis were profoundly interested in these methods in the early years of their history. But can we characterise Ismaili philosophy as Neoplatonic? Can we reject any system of thought which does not bear the visible signs of the Neoplatonism of certain Ismaili writers as being non-Ismaili?

Ismaili Philosophy and Neoplatonism: Myths and Realities

Identifying the key elements of Ismaili thought is not merely a taxonomical endeavour. It serves a much broader purpose. Without knowing the specific junctures at which Ismaili philosophy turned in a new or different direction, we will not be able to locate the kind of problems that gave rise to these shifts. These junctures cannot be viewed merely in historical terms. Their intellectual and philosophical content is also critical. Among these junctures, there is a theme which is widely regarded as an integral part of Ismaili philosophy. The theme is none other than Neoplatonism.

The history of embracing philosophical doctrines, such as Neoplatonism among Muslims in general and Ismailis in particular, goes back to the translation movement in which works of Greek origin were translated into Arabic and then extensively used by Muslim philosophers and some of the *mutakallimūn* in their engagements with the revelation.[6] As such, the core element of such an openness to the so-called 'foreign' philosophical doctrines relied heavily on how autonomous human reason is located in the epistemological framework of the sources of knowledge and more specifically the

[6] See F. Daftary, 'The Iranian School of Philosophical Ismailism', *Ishraq: Islamic Philosophy Yearbook*, 4 (2013), pp. 13–24.

knowledge of God. How does one know God? What are the attributes and epithets of God? How does God speak? How does God create? These kinds of questions are perennial and early on in Islamic history engaged the minds of philosophers and *mutakallims*. In the Ismaili context, the question of creation and knowledge of God was a central theme in the literature produced by Ismaili *dāʿī*s and also by philosophers with similar tastes and approaches. The case of the Brethren of Purity (*Ikhwān al-Ṣafāʾ*) is, of course, a prominent one. Briefly put, Ismailism shares a concern with these issues with various other Muslim communities. There is, however, one significant difference in the doctrines of the Ismailis which is the belief in a living present imam, a belief which is central to Ismaili cosmology.

It can be argued Ismaili *dāʿī*s actively propagated a refined version of Neoplatonism which included certain aspects of the Neoplatonism of al-Fārābī (d. 339/950) and Ibn Sīnā (d. 428/1037), but which was distinct from it due to their articulation of the doctrine of imamate. Indeed, Neoplatonism is not a permanent theme in Ismaili cosmology; it was only dominant in the Fatimid period reaching its peak in the writings of Ḥamīd al-Dīn al-Kirmānī (d. after 411/1020); later Ismaili communities, specifically the Nizārī Ismailis, moved away from this Neoplatonic emanational cosmology. This shift effectively began with the articulation of the doctrine of *taʿlīm* by Ḥasan-i Ṣabbāḥ (d. 518/1124) and was clearly formulated in the doctrine of *qiyāmat* initially by Muḥammad al-Shahrastānī (d. 548/1153), then by Ḥasan II (561/1161), the first Nizārī Ismaili imam, and subsequently by Ḥasan-i Maḥmūd-i Kātib (d. 644/1246)[7] and Naṣīr al-Dīn Ṭūsī (d. 672/1274), who is credited with compiling and writing some of the seminal Nizārī doctrinal texts.[8]

Making a distinction between different eras in the history of Ismaili doctrine is particularly significant because a lack of historical understanding of the shifts which have occurred can lead to grave errors in

---

[7] For further details, see S. J. Badakhchani, *Spiritual Resurrection in Shiʿi Islam: An Early Ismaili Treatise on the Doctrine of Qiyāmat* (London, 2017).

[8] See Badakhchani's introduction in Naṣīr al-Dīn Ṭūsī, *Contemplation and Action: The Spiritual Autobiography of a Muslim Scholar*, ed. and tr. S. J. Badakhchani (London, 1998).

properly situating their evolution in the broader context of Muslim doctrines. In order to illustrate this point, the case of al-Shahrastānī, the famous heresiographer, will be considered here. Hitherto he has been generally regarded as an Ashʿarī theologian but, as a result of recent scholarship, we now know of his intimate affiliations with and considerable influence on the Nizārī Ismailis.[9] The Neoplatonism of Ismailis *dāʿīs* such as Abū Yaʿqūb al-Sijistānī (d. after 361/971) and Ḥamīḍ al-Dīn al-Kirmānī, two of the most prominent Ismaili *dāʿīs*, will only be briefly touched upon in consideration of certain reflections of scholars who properly identify such elements in their doctrinal articulations.

In his meticulous study of al-Sijistānī, Paul Walker notes:

> Al-Sijistānī simply did not consider himself a member of the *falāsifa* (philosophers). He never tells his readers that Greek Neoplatonism is essential to his arguments, nor does he even admit, except rarely, that important works of such philosophy already exist and thus provide a background for his statements. Yet, by many ordinary criteria he was thoroughly imbued with philosophical and scientific attitudes, and these were of a fairly sophisticated sort.[10]

Poonawala, in his introduction to his edition of the *Kitāb al-Maqālīd* is more specific about this:

> The *Kitāb al-Maqālīd al-malakūtiyya* represents a refined stage of earlier attempts by the author/s of the *Rasāʾil Ikhwān al-Ṣafāʾ* (Epistles of the Brethren of Purity) and al-Nasafī to adapt Neoplatonism to Shiʿi Ismaili doctrine and align it with the Islamic doctrine of *tawḥīd* (belief in the divine unicity).[11]

He proceeds to provide the genealogy of the introduction of Neoplatonism in Ismaili doctrines by tracing it back to Muḥammad al-Nasafī (d. 332/943), the chief Ismaili *dāʿī* of Khurāsān and al-Sijistānī's predecessor. Referring to al-Nasāfī's *Kitāb al-Maḥṣūl*, he writes:

---

9 See G. Monnot, 'al-Shahrastānī', *EI2*, vol. 9, pp. 214–216.

10 Walker, *Early Philosophical Shiism*, p. 322.

11 I. K. Poonawala, *Kitāb al-Maqālīd al-malakūtiyya* (Tunis, 2011), pp. 5–6.

> In addition to expounding the pre-Fatimid Ismaili teachings, the author had inherited from his predecessors, the pre-Fārābian (Fārābī, d. 339/950) version of Neoplatonism which was introduced by al-Nasafī and disseminated among the followers of al-Kindī (d. ca. 252/866).
>
> In the aforecited book, al-Nasafī introduced the three hypostases of Plotinus, viz., the One, the Intellect, and the Soul, and the theory of creation (i.e., a series of gradual procession) of the universe from One (i.e., God) into the Ismaili cosmology and tried to adapt it to the Islamic principle of monotheism and Ismaili teaching.[12]

Poonawala continues to record the reactions and criticisms these doctrines faced in the Ismaili *daʿwa*. We know of al-Kirmānī's sharp critique of both al-Sijistānī and al-Nasafī with Abū Ḥātim al-Rāzī being the other prominent *dāʿī* opposing these doctrines. The history of the evolution and introduction of Neoplatonism is not clear-cut. There are all kinds of reactions to it along the way. Even al-Sijistānī, in his so-called Neoplatonist narrative of the *tawḥīd* and creation, both in the *Kashf al-Maḥjūb* and the *Kitāb al-Yanābīʿ*, tried to move beyond Plotinus and surpass his limitations. Some philosophers asserted that God is the cause of creation; al-Sijistānī refuted this claim in the 8th *Iqlīd*. As we shall see shortly, this adaptation or refinement of Neoplatonism is later further refined among Nizārī Ismailis to the extent that it hardly resembled the typical Fatimid version which was developed by al-Kirmānī. Al-Sijistānī asserted that the knowledge of 'pure origination' is even beyond the reach of the spiritual entities, let alone the human intellect. In order to remove God further from the universe, al-Sijistānī stated that the cause of origination (or creation) is not God but His Command or Word. And it was here that among Nizārīs the doctrine was refined and revised, representing a shift a few centuries later under the influence of al-Shahrastānī.

Before moving on to the Nizārī phase of Ismailism, it is important to say a few words about al-Kirmānī. He was probably the most outstanding Ismaili *dāʿī*, endowed with a sophisticated philosophical

---

12 Ibid., p. 30.

mind and so responsible for revising Ismaili cosmology inspired by al-Fārābī and Ibn Sīnā, the only differences being that he constructed a decadic system of hierarchies corresponding to the ranks of the Fatimid *daʿwa*. As Paul Walker notes:

> Al-Kirmānī's purpose in the *Riyāḍ* is to replace the Neoplatonism of the several older generations with doctrines that he and Ibn Sīnā, his contemporary, have taken from al-Fārābī. To undermine those who formulated an Ismaili version of Neoplatonism, he marshals the opposing opinions of its great exponents and exposes their rancorous arguments about its specific problems and failings. But in so doing it appears that he must approach this goal delicately. It is likely that al-Sijistānī, whom he would like to replace as the chief spokesman of philosophical Ismailism, was long recognised as the pre-eminent theologian of the *daʿwa*. This eminence predates al-Kirmānī by several decades.[13]

By now, just how problematic and challenging the introduction of Neoplatonism into Ismaili doctrines was can be clearly envisaged. The Neoplatonic cosmology underwent such radical modifications that by the time of Ṭūsī it had lost its attraction and was no longer a key component of Ismaili doctrine, even though Ṭūsī himself who was an ardent protagonist of Ibn Sīnā made every effort to preserve certain elements of it. This shift is one of the hallmarks of Nizārī doctrine.

Nizārī Doctrine and its Further Shifts

After the schism between the Mustaʿlian and Nizārī branches of Ismailism, it was mainly the Mustaʿlian communities who preserved the sophisticated cosmology of al-Kirmānī. The Persian school of Ismailism quickly reverted to reviving the refined doctrine of al-Sijistānī but this time with far-reaching consequences. At the heart of the doctrine of the authoritative teaching of the imam (*taʿlīm*) introduced by Ḥasan-i Ṣabbāḥ is the knowledge of God or *tawḥīd*, and it is in the context of articulating this doctrine that he placed the

13 Walker, *Early Philosophical Shiism*, p. 61.

Ismaili imam at the centre of a slightly revised cosmology connecting it with creation. His discussion about *tawḥīd* and creation is reminiscent of al-Sijistānī, however al-Sijistānī does not mention the imamate in his articulation of the doctrine of *tawḥīd* and creation. So, the element prominently added here is the imamate. The first instance of a systematic assessment of the doctrine can be found in the *Chahār faṣl* by Ḥasan-i Ṣabbāḥ.

Following Ḥasan-i Ṣabbāḥ (d. 518/1124) al-Shahrastānī, who lived shortly after Ḥasan-i Ṣabbāḥ, became central to the Nizārī Ismaili *daʿwa*. Discussing the details of how al-Shahrastānī was connected with Ismailism is beyond the scope of this chapter but very briefly al-Shahrastānī's views were sharply at odds with those of al-Kirmānī, a point which has been a source of confusion for some scholars who have come across his writings in the context of his affiliation with the Ismailis. Looking for Neoplatonic elements in the writings of al-Shahrastānī,[14] which are conspicuously lacking, has led to a belief that al-Shahrastānī could not have had anything to do with Ismailis. There are specifically two works of al-Shahrastānī which are of interest here and to discussions about Ismaili doctrines and Neoplatonism: his *Majlis-i maktūb-i munʿaqid dar Khʷārazm*[15] and his commentary on the Qur'an, the *Mafātīh al-asrār wa-maṣābīḥ al-abrār*.[16] In the *Majlis* which is a short treatise – or more accurately a 'sermon' – in Persian, al-Shahrastānī provides an account of creation which shares many elements with those of al-Sijistānī. In articulating his positions on creation and command, he sharply criticises the Ashāʿira, the Muʿtazila, the Karrāmīs and the philosophers and considers the narratives of all these groups not just flawed but also at odds with the Qur'an and the tradition of the Prophet: 'And all of this is neither the language of the Qur'an, nor the words of the book and the tradition.

[14] See M. Farmānīyān, 'Shahrastānī: Sunnī-yi Ashʿarī yā Shiʿi-yi bāṭinī', *Haft āsimān*, 7 (2000), pp. 135–182.

[15] Which I have recently edited and translated it is awaiting publication.

[16] See T. Mayer, *Keys to the Arcana: Shahrastānī's esoteric commentary on the Qur'ān: a translation of the commentary on Sūrat al-Fātiḥa from Muḥammad b. ʿAbd al-Karīm al-Shahrastānī's Mafātīḥ al-asrār wa-maṣābīḥ al-abrār* (Oxford, 2009).

We are the people who say "God said so and the Messenger of God said so"'.[17]

The approach in these segments of the *Majlis* is conspicuously similar to the way in which Ḥasan-i Ṣabbāh articulates the doctrine of imamate.[18] The sum of the positions of al-Shahrastānī and Ḥasan-i Ṣabbāḥ is later formulated in Ṭūsī's *Sayr wa sulūk*. This short treatise by Ṭūsī is incidentally one in which al-Shahrastānī is introduced with the title *dāʿī al-duʿāt* thus producing extensive speculations about the Ismaili affiliations of al-Shahrastānī.[19] In the *Sayr wa sulūk*, after critically assessing the arguments of philosophers who depict God as the prime cause (*ʿillat-i ūlā*) and the first intellect as the first effect (*maʿlūl-i awwal*) with no intermediary between the first cause and the first intellect, Ṭūsī then lays out the Nizārī doctrine of *taʿlīm*. The revision proposed by Nizārīs, as articulated by Ṭūsī, suggests that it is wrong to attribute creation directly to God because God is beyond any attribute. Such a doctrine would be far from pure *tawḥīd*. Instead creation is attributed to God's command rather than God himself. The command – the *amr* or the *kalima* – becomes the originator of the First Intellect or the Universal Intellect. What distinguishes Nizārīs from their predecessors is that the imam now became the manifestation of God's command. The imam is not God. He is not God's command either. He is the manifestation of that command. In the process of this articulation, what happened was that the typical Neoplatonic emanation was driven into the shadows and then gradually disappeared from Nizārī Ismaili doctrine.

---

17 See M. R. Jalālī Nā'īnī, *Du Maktūb az Muḥammad b. ʿAbd al-Karīm Shahrastānī* (Tehran, 1990), p. 119. All references to the text of the *Majlis* are from this edition. Translations are all mine. Jalālī Nā'īnī's edition appears on pages 95 to 143 of this volume. Henceforth referred to as *Majlis* only.

18 See S. J. Badakhchani, 'Shahrastani's Account of Hasan-i Sabbah's Doctrine of Taʿlim', in M. A. Amir-Moezzi (ed.), *Islam: Identité et altérité. Hommage à Guy Monnot* (Turnhout, 2013), pp. 27–55. In particular, the end of paragraph 2 of the treatise written by Ḥasan-i Ṣabbāḥ conveys the same message.

19 Naṣīr al-Dīn Ṭūsī, *Contemplation and Action: The Spiritual Autobiography of a Muslim Scholar*, ed. and tr. S. J. Badakhchani (London, 1998). Persian text, p. 3, trans., p. 26.

There is, however, one caveat to this narrative. Ṭūsī who became the chief proponent of Ismaili doctrine during his association with Nizārī Ismailis, happened to be an ardent believer in Ibn Sīnā's cosmology and his philosophical system. Despite his purely Nizārī articulation of creation and command in the *Sayr wa sulūk*, one can discern his discomfort in the early chapters of *Rawḍa-yi taslīm*[20] where he is visibly in favour of Ibn Sīnā's cosmology and his emanational narrative. This is, however, the only instance where one finds some resistance to the marginalisation of Neoplatonic emanationism. Of course, Ṭūsī displayed a sharper criticism of this marginalisation when he wrote the *Maṣāriʿ al-muṣāriʿ* which is a critique of al-Shahrastānī's *Kitāb al-Muṣāraʿa.*[21] In the latter, al-Shahrastānī sharply criticised Ibn Sīnā for his cosmological doctrines and in particular for his emenationist theory of creation. Such disagreements with the typical philosophical narrative of creation are evident both in his *Majlis* and in the *Mafātīḥ*. In his introduction to the English translation of the *Muṣāraʿa*, Madelung notes how Ismaili doctrines are interwoven in this text and others by arguing that 'in his *Majlis* and the *Muṣāraʿa* his Ismaili thought prevails more consistently. Al-Shahrastānī can thus be described as Sunni socially and communally, but as Shiʿi and Ismaili in some of his core beliefs and religious thought.'[22] Ṭūsī's later criticisms of al-Shahrastānī's disagreements with Ibn Sīnā must be understood in their historical context. The *Maṣāriʿ* was written at a time when the Ismaili fortress state had collapsed under the Mongol assault and Ṭūsī had already made every effort to exonerate himself of the accusation of being an Ismaili. In this situation, refuting al-Shahrastānī who was widely believed to be an Ismaili, incidentally suggested so by Ṭūsī himself, would have been an ideal means of dispelling any suspicion of a continuing sympathy for the Nizārī Ismailis.

---

[20] Naṣīr al-Dīn Ṭūsī, *Paradise of Submission: A Medieval Treatise on Ismaili Thought*, ed. and tr. S. J. Badakhchani (London, 2005). Henceforth referred to as *Rawḍa*.

[21] T. Mayer, *Struggling with the Philosopher: A Refutation of Avicenna's Metaphysics* (London, 2001).

[22] Ibid., p. 4.

Following the destruction of the Nizārī fortresses and the subsequent concealment of Nizārī Ismailism under the guise of Sufism, the remaining traces of philosophical Neoplatonism were now repudiated. The Nizārīs only retained whatever was left of that cosmology as a result of their later connection with Sufism which became their second identity.

In light of the above, it is now clear that Neoplatonism was only the hallmark of the language of the Ismaili *daʿwa* for a limited time. And this Neoplatonism reached its peak at the time of Ḥamīd al-Dīn al-Kirmānī fading away completely during the Nizārī phase of Ismaili history. This critical point solves the mystery of how someone like al-Shahrastānī could be a foundational figure for the reorientation of Ismaili doctrines.

Three Cases of Interaction: A Humanistic Intersection

A very broad glance at the vast literature produced by the different Ismaili communities reveals that the Ismailis, or at least the Nizārī Ismailis, constantly revised their theories in response to the problems which they encountered. What now follows presents a comparative overview of the doctrines held by three specific figures with whom the Ismailis were either closely affiliated or with whom they had intellectual interactions. The historical timeframe of these three figures spans the years from 437/1045 to 525/1131, the first year being that of the birth of Sanāʾī Ghaznawī and the second being that of the death of both Sanāʾī Ghaznawī and ʿAyn al-Quḍāt Hamadānī, two of the figures who will be discussed. Both Sanāʾī[23] and

[23] Abu'l-Majdūd b. Ādam Sanāʾī Ghaznawī, the prominent poet and mystic of the fifth–sixth/eleventh–twelfth centuries, was born in Ghazna ca. 467/1075. He died and was buried ca. 529/1135 in Ghazna and his mausoleum is to be found there. He was a vocal anti-rationalist poet who was highly critical of the Hellenistic philosophy and its influence among Muslims. There are disagreements over his dates of birth and death. Dates here are according to Shafīʿī Kadkanī's narrative in his *Tāziyānahā-yi sulūk: naqd wa taḥlīl-i chand qaṣīda az ḥakīm Sanāʾī* (Tehran, 1372 Sh./1993).

ʿAyn al-Quḍāt[24] were prominent Sufi figures who lived during the early years of the Alamūt era of Ismaili history. In between these years, we have the period of the life of al-Shahrastānī,[25] the other important figure who will be discussed.

The articulation of the doctrine of *qiyāmat* after its declaration by Ḥasan II, the fourth ruler of Alamūt and the first Ismaili imam in the line of Nizārī imams in Persia, in 559/1165, that is to say over thirty years after the death of Sanāʾī, is critical for making sense of such interactions. The existing literature speaking about the content and purpose of the declaration of *qiyāmat* belongs mainly to the period of Muḥammad III, during which period Ṭūsī played a vital role in organising and polishing these articulations. One of the major sources for them is the sayings or writings of Ḥasan II known as *Fuṣūl-i muqaddas* which is lost except for fragments preserved in the works of Nizārī literature. Close examination of how the Nizārī Ismailis understood and articulated this doctrine reveals traces of the powerful influence of or engagement with the ideas and doctrines put forward by the three figures in question. They will be examined one by one.

A) Al-Shahrastānī

Al-Shahrastānī's writings, and particularly his last two works, namely his *Majlis-i Khʷārazm* and his *Mafātīḥ* can now be safely regarded as Ismaili works. They delineate Ismaili doctrines in unequivocal terms and serve as a guiding template for extrapolating the trajectory of the

---

24 ʿAyn al-Quḍāt Hamadānī (490–525/1097–1131) is another mystical figure who was a disciple of Aḥmad al-Ghazālī and, indirectly, Muḥammad al-Ghazālī (apart from some relatively unknown Sufi *Pīrs*). He was put on trial and then executed on charges of claiming to be a prophet and being an Ismaili, believing in the *imām-i maʿṣūm*. For a detailed account of his life and thought, see Hamid Dabashi, *Truth and narrative: The untimely thoughts of ʿAyn al-Quḍāt al-Hamadhānī* (London, 1999) and Nasrollah Pourjavady, *ʿAyn al-Quḍāt wa ustādān-i ū* (Tehran, 1374 Sh./1995).

25 Muḥammad b. ʿAbd al-Karīm al-Shahrastānī (d. 548/1153), the prominent heresiographer and the author of the *Kitāb al-Milal waʾl-niḥal* was often until recently known as an Ashʿarī theologian and chronicler of Muslim sects. Recent scholarship is now increasingly considering him a senior figure on the Nizārī Ismaili *daʿwa*.

revision of Nizārī Ismaili doctrines. Without going into too much detail, it can be said that al-Shahrastānī was responsible for providing a coherent narrative of the new orientation of Nizārī Ismaili thought in which the doctrines of *taʿlīm* and *qiyāmat* were central features – and this is what al-Shahrastānī himself described as *al-daʿwa al-jadīda* in his *Milal*. This point is rarely noted for the simple reason that contemporary scholarship has not yet located al-Shahrastānī's place in these debates, despite recent discoveries.

In whatever we find in the literature between the time of Ḥasan-i Ṣabbāḥ and Ḥasan II, we can always establish a link with how al-Shahrastānī prepared the foundations of the doctrines of Nizārī Ismailism. Al-Shahrastānī's last two works provide us with ample evidence to demonstrate this point. Building on a comparison of the works of al-Shahrastānī and extant Nizārīs sources, one can conjecture that al-Shahrastānī had indeed been an Ashʿarī theologian in his youth and then converted to Ismailism, disguising his identity until the final years of his service at the court of the Saljūq sultan Sanjar – the period in which he wrote his earlier works including the *Milal*, the *Nihāya* and the *Muṣāraʿa*.

There are two important observations here. First of all, acknowledging al-Shahrastānī's Ashʿarī background, one can argue that he continued to adhere to some of the theological elements of his earlier Ashʿarī manifestation and these were later fully embedded in Nizārī imamology mirroring a kind of 'ethical voluntarism' pervasive in Ashʿarism, the difference being that in Nizārī Ismailism, the question of ethics is closely interconnected with knowledge of and submission to the Ismaili imams. Secondly, bearing in mind al-Shahrastānī's critique of Ibn Sīnā's philosophy and Ṭūsī's – rather hasty and harsh – response to it written in the aftermath of the fall of Alamūt, al-Shahrastānī seems to have played a critical role in reshaping the doctrines of the new *daʿwa*. After al-Shahrastānī, Nizārī Ismaili thought no longer resembled the typically Neoplatonic style of doctrine that the Fatimids and their later branches adhered to after the Nizārī-Mustaʿlian schism (even though one can always find traces of it here and there). Indeed, in the Nizārī context, Neoplatonism is pushed so much into the shadows that one finds the ideas of al-Kirmānī are only dominant among Mustaʿlians. This point is not only demonstrated in al-Shahrastānī's works but also in almost every doctrinal work produced by the Nizārīs.

A case in point is Ṭūsī's *Aghāz wa anjām* which is a peculiarly Ismaili work of hermeneutical exegesis. Comparing this short treatise with the typical Fatimid-style of *ta'wīl* in al-Qāḍī al-Nuʿmān's *Asās al-ta'wīl* demonstrates this point.

In short, setting aside the new arguments made in favour of al-Shahrastānī being a senior figure in the Nizārī *daʿwa*, he seems to have been responsible for a) providing a new theological-philosophical orientation for Ismaili doctrines and removing prominent Neoplatonic forms of terminology; and b) providing a coherent narrative of the doctrines of *taʿlīm* and *qiyāmat* distinct from the Fatimid version of them. Moreover, he also served as a kind of conduit for adapting certain Ashʿarī elements to fit Ismaili doctrine (despite his sharp and explicit criticism of Ashʿarism in his later works). In what follows are some examples of how al-Shahrastānī's narrative became integral to the Nizārī understanding of the doctrines of *qiyāmat* and imamate.

In the *Majlis*, explaining the evolution of the *sharīʿat*, al-Shahrastānī writes:

> Beware! You must not consider the abrogation (*naskh*) of the ritual laws their nullification (*ibṭāl*); it is a perfection. If the sperm were to be destroyed, where would the clotted blood rest? If letters were to be destroyed, where would meanings reside? All religious laws have an origin and a perfection; the lord (*ṣāḥib*) of the origin is different from the lord of the perfection. In each *sharīʿat*, the origin and the perfection are different – and in this *sharīʿat*, the *lā ilāha illā Allāh* is the progeny of faith; worship and transactions are the body of faith; knowledge (*ʿulūm*) and truths (*ḥaqā'iq*) are the soul of faith. And in the same manner that all parts and members of a corporeal person exist in the progeny of the person as a potential capable of coming into actuality, all the laws of the *sharīʿat* exist in the *lā ilāha illā Allāh* potentially capable of coming to actuality. Therefore, the phrase *lā ilāha illā Allāh* is in a sense the universal of faith, in the same manner that the progeny is in a sense the universal of the person. Hence, once you utter the *kalima*, you will have uttered the universal [concept of] religion.[26]

[26] See *Majlis*, pp. 103–104.

In the *Rawḍa*, we read:

> The legal statutes of each prophet who succeeded the prophet who preceded him were all aimed at perfecting those previous laws, not their abrogation. But that perfection has, from the exoteric and formal point of view, appeared like abrogation not perfection, because until something is changed from one state to another it cannot be given the form which is the aim of the perfection of that thing. For example, until the sperm changes its state through alteration and modifications, it will not move on from the form in which it is and pass through the stages of coagulated blood, embryo, flesh and bone – in attaining to each of which it moves closer to the soul – and so it will not attain the completeness of the human form.
>
> One must understand the process of perfecting and abrogating (*ibṭāl*) religious laws in the same manner. If, [for instance], a religious statute instituted by one prophet remains unchanged and is not followed by another edict instituted by the prophet who succeeds him, then in the end, the lord of the Resurrection (*qāʾim-i qiyāmat*) will be unable to exercise his [proper] spiritual authority, and consequently, those who are subject to this [outdated] religious edict will never be able to progress from the way to the aim, from the letter to the spirit, from deceptive similitudes (*mushābahat*) to what is distinctly clear (*mubāyanat*), from relativity to reality, and from legalistic religion (*sharīʿat*) to the Resurrection (*qiyāmat*).[27]

In the *Majlis*, we read:

> It is the scent of prophecy that one smells from these words said by the progeny of the Prophet: 'God created his religion on the basis of his creation' – this is the same foundation of creation and the command. The command and *dīn* belong to one category; creation and the *sharīʿat* belong to another category.[28]

---

27 Ṭūsī, *Rawḍa*, pp. 139–140 (paras. 417–418).
28 See *Majlis*, p. 110.

And we read the same narrative in the *Rawḍa* as follows:

> He [the Prophet] has been called the 'Seal of the Prophets' because [as has been said], 'God, the Blessed, the Exalted, has based His religion on the likeness of His creation, so that they might find His creation a sign indicating His religion, and His religion a sign indicating His unicity (*waḥdāniyyat*).'[29]

This particular tradition is cited first by Nāṣir-i Khusraw in the *Jāmiʿ al-ḥikmatayn*[30] and it is attributed to the Prophet, as can also be seen in the *Rawḍa*. There are no traces of this particular tradition in this form in sources other than Ismaili ones. This tradition and the explanations we saw earlier, all pertain to how Ismailis, and in particular the Nizārīs, understood the doctrine of *qiyāmat*.

With regard to imamate, the Nizārīs started using a term for the imam which also encapsulates their perception of truth. The imam is referred to as the *muḥiqq* or as someone with whom truth is identified. In contrast, the opponent of the Nizārī imam is referred to as the *mubṭil* or as someone who is the embodiment or personification of falsehood. In the *Majlis*, when al-Shahrastānī presented his narrative of creation, he said:

> O Angels! For a long time, your direction (*qibla*) was either the throne or the earth, either above or below! Now, it is time for you to turn your face towards a person (*shakhṣ*) to whom time and space are but mere modest servants at his door: 'Bow down to Adam' (2:34). The throne is the universal [concept] for space; the aeon (*dahr*) is the universal for time; and Adam is the universal for mankind.[31]

Comparing this passage, and similar passages in the *Majlis*, with Nizārī sources demonstrates not just parallels in the use of terms but also in developing concepts to articulate obedience to the Imam of the Time. In a paragraph cited from Ḥasan II's *Fuṣūl-i muqaddas*, in the *Haft bāb*, we read:

---

[29] Ṭūsī, *Rawḍa*, p. 138.

[30] Nāṣir-i Khusraw in *Jāmiʿ al-ḥikmatayn*, see E. Ormsby, *Between Reason and Revelation: Twin Wisdom Reconciled* (London, 2012), p. 145.

[31] See *Majlis*, p. 107.

> Since in the qiyāmat God is known and manifest, what else remains to be known or hidden? [But in the realm of the] *sharīʿat* which is imaginary and fanciful, what else remains there which is not imaginary or fanciful? In other words, the commandment of God's reality is never imaginary or fanciful, but in the realm of the *sharīʿat* people find it imaginary.[32]

One of the key themes of the doctrine of *qiyāmat* as articulated by Ḥasan II was the personification of truth, which is turning one's face from the celestial *qibla* to the personified one, and the personification of the *qibla* – towards which believers prostrate in the realm of truths and resurrection – is the imam or the *muḥiqq*. This point is presented in unequivocal terms in al-Shahrastānī's *Mafātīḥ*, which also distinguishes him from other denominations including the Twelvers:

> Just as Iblīs did not acknowledge the present, living, current imam, the commonalty are the same as that, while the expectant Shiʿa only acknowledge the awaited, hidden imam. And God has blessed servants on earth who do not get ahead of Him in speaking and they act on His Command, servants who are the purified servants of God, over whom Satan has no authority.[33]

In the passage in question as noted by Toby Mayer:

> Adam is significantly presented here as the original 'mediator of the Command' (*mutawassiṭ-i amr*), that is, the functional archetype of the imam in Shiʿism. It is vital in this connection that al-Shahrastānī claims that the group he himself espouses is alone in its true commitment to what God and His Messenger said.[34]

This approach to creation and the *tawḥīd* is peculiarly Nizārī and this is what Ṭūsī described as *tawḥīd-i ṣirf* and *tanzīh-i mahḍ* in the *Sayr wa sulūk*.[35] This narrative of creation and the story of Adam and Iblīs is

---

[32] See Badakhchani, *Spiritual Resurrection*, p. 76.

[33] Al-Shahrastānī, *Mafātīḥ*, p. 280. Translation from T. Mayer, *Keys to the Arcana*, p. 18.

[34] T. Mayer, *Keys to the Arcana*, p. 18.

[35] 'There is no doubt that no one maintains such pure unity (*tawḥīd-i ṣirf*), such unconditioned absoluteness (*tanzīh-i mahḍ*) [of God], except the Taʿlimiyān.' Ṭūsī, *Contemplation and Action*, p. 37.

also found in *Taṣawwūr* 16 of the *Rawḍa*.[36] These similarities and on occasion the almost identical articulations of Ismaili doctrines leave no doubt that al-Shahrastānī played a critical role in establishing the basis for the reorientation of Nizārī doctrines and they also demonstrate the way in which he achieved this.

B) Sanāʾī Ghaznawī

The case of Sanāʾī is particularly important because, first of all, like al-Shahrastānī, he was also given the title *dāʿī al-duʿāt* in Nizārī works. One can easily trace the powerful influence of Sanāʾī on the poetry of Nizārīs in the *Dīwān-i qāʾimiyyāt* (which is where he is called a *dāʿī*).[37] Whether Sanāʾī had indeed been an Ismaili nor not is both beyond the scope of this paper and irrelevant to the point being made here. In all likelihood, the title may have been an honorary one, displaying a degree of tolerance and openness by Nizārīs for certain Sufi ideas.

What is important in this context is how and in what way Sanāʾī's poetry is used by Ismailis. In almost every single case when his poetry is referenced and used by Nizārīs, whether in their poetry or in prose writings, it is used to articulate the doctrine of *qiyāmat*. Indeed verses from one of his famous and most powerful *qaṣīda*s, On the Station of the People of Divine Unity (*qaṣīda dar maqam-i ahl-i tawḥīd*), are often found in important Nizārī works when it comes to explaining the doctrine of *qiyāmat*. We do not have any solid historical details connecting Sanāʾī with the Ismailis as someone who had joined their community. Unlike al-Shahrastānī, who in his later works was remarkably transparent about his Ismaili doctrines, we do not have any such clear indications in Sanāʾī's works. Yet, his poetry was held in the highest regard by the Nizārīs. There are indications in Sanāʾī's poetry, however, of a deep attachment to Sunni Islam in devotional terms, for example when speaking about the caliphs. His praise for the Prophet's household and indications of a Shiʿi leaning do not reveal much that might connect him with Ismailism, but his verses happened to emerge in a doctrine which

---

36 Ṭūsī, *Rawḍa*, pp. 65–71.

37 Ḥasan-i Maḥmūd-i Kātib, *Dīwān-i qāʾimiyyāt*, ed. S. J. Badakhchani (Tehran, 2011), p. 287.

bears a prominent Nizārī mark. The only conjecture we can entertain is that the Ismailis happily and comfortably resorted to writings by the Sufis of Khurāsān to articulate their own doctrines.[38] This was, of course, not limited to Sanā'ī. One can occasionally find verses from 'Aṭṭār in various Nizārī manuscripts to bolster the ethical content of the doctrine of *qiyāmat*. In the section on 'Ayn al-Quḍāt Hamadānī, specific examples will be provided, but put very briefly, the key message of the doctrine of *qiyāmat* once stripped from the Nizārī terminology is that ritual practices are not sufficient in and by themselves for securing salvation and unity with God. In other words, adherence to rituals alone does not make one an ethical person; indeed formalism and ritualism can veil salvation thus losing their ethical content.

In this context, Sanā'ī's narrative is important in the sense that his poetry constitutes an acute critique of ritualism among his contemporaries. In the *qaṣīda* beginning with: *Musalmānān Musalmānān! Musalmānī Musalmānī*, Sanā'ī writes:

> O Muslims! O Muslims! Islam! Islam (*musalmānī*)! Repent! Repent from this faith of faithless ones!
>
> Islam is today nothing but a name used for rituals and habits! Alas for Islam! Alas! Where is Islam?
>
> The sun of faith has set, the day of faithless ones has dawned! What happened to the anguish of *Būdardā*? What happened to the Islam of *Salmān*?!
>
> Drink the wine of religious wisdom (*ḥikmat-i shar'ī*) in the realm of faith; because the Greek ones who speak through whims (*hawas-gūyān-i yūnānī*) are deprived of this feast!
>
> If you seek the path of truth, purify yourself from your own self, because the truth and creation cannot live together on the divine path!
>
> For taking this path, there were two chivalrous ones who set foot on this road out of purity; one of them said: 'I am the truth!' (*ana al-ḥaqq*) and the other said: 'Glorified be my status!' (*subḥānī*).[39]

---

38 For an extensive narrative on the Sufism of the Khurāsān, see M. R. Shafī'ī Kadkanī, *Zabān-i shi'r dar nathr-i Ṣūfiyya* (Tehran, 1392 Sh./2013).

39 See M. Shafī'ī Kadkanī, *Tāziyānahā-yi sulūk: naqd wa taḥlīl-i chand qaṣīda az ḥakīm Sanā'ī* (Tehran, 1372 Sh./1993), p. 220.

There are two key themes in these verses. First of all, he expresses his dissatisfaction that Islam is now reduced to a name referring only to rituals and habits and this is the critical component of the doctrine of *qiyāmat*. The second theme is a critique of the philosophers ('Greek ones who speak through whims'). Strangely enough, this critique which is a prominent theme in Sanā'ī's poetry was written in the same spirit in which al-Ghazālī wrote his *Tahāfut* against philosophers, but it also overlaps with the way in which al-Shahrastānī criticised Ibn Sīnā in particular and philosophers in general (as notes in earlier citation from the *Majlis*). The last verse in the above lines directly refers to the ecstatic claims of al-Ḥallāj and Bāyazīd Bisṭāmī. Such ecstatic claims were then reformulated by the Nizārī's in their own terminology when they spoke of *waḥdat*.

Sanā'ī's verses are cited in the *Rawḍa* on three occasions. The first instance comes in the opening chapters:

> Infidelity and religion, both are trotting along Thy path,
> Ever-repeating 'He is the One who has no partners'.[40]

The verse in question is from Sanā'ī's *Ḥadīqa al-ḥaqīqa*. The second and third occasions are in the context of explaining the doctrine of *qiyāmat*. While criticising the practicing of 'Islam' without caring for its esoteric content, Sanā'ī also points out that one cannot reach that higher level of spiritual unity without first passing through the stages of the *sharī'at*.[41] This is the second part of a verse from Sanā'ī's *qaṣīda*. A paraphrase of this verse is cited in *Taṣawwur* 24[42] and the entire verse is cited in the annex to the *Rawḍa* which is the report of a conversation with Muḥammad III[43] (although in the current edition of these Nizārī works, none of these are flagged up as verses by Sanā'ī).

This is precisely the point expressed by Ṭūsī in his *Maṭlūb al-mu'minīn*. Sanā'ī is not the only Sufi whose views resonate with the *qiyāmatī* penchant of the Nizārīs. As mentioned earlier, 'Aṭṭar is another. An earlier figure whose ideas bear striking similarity with

---

[40] Ṭūsī, *Rawḍa*, p. 13.

[41] *Bi ma'nī kay rasad mardum guzar nākardah bar asmā.*

[42] Ṭūsī, *Rawḍa*, p. 109.

[43] Ṭūsī, *Rawḍa*, p. 173.

how the *qiyāmat* was understood by the Nizārīs is Abū Saʿīd b. Abi'l-Khayr (357–440/967–1049).[44] A close comparison of Abū Saʿīd's tolerant and open understanding of faith and the manner in which he challenged the formalist and ritualist approaches of orthodox Muslims with what we find in Nizārī doctrines assists the quest to find the parallels between Nizārī doctrine and that of the Sufis of Khurāsān. It also reflects a more critical point. The Nizārī Ismailis were not the only Muslims who were in favour of rethinking the relationship between the *sharīʿat* and its deeper inner meanings – what Nizārīs called the *qiyāmat*. Many Sufis shared the same ideas and even expressed them as boldly, and sometimes in more explicit terms, as did the Nizārīs. The intellectual and doctrinal atmosphere of Muslim communities was a fertile one for such encounters with rituals. The Ismailis were not peculiarly unique in this approach.

This brings us to the third and last case, which concerns another Sufi figure: ʿAyn al-Quḍāt Hamadānī.

C) ʿAyn al-Quḍāt Hamadānī

ʿAyn al-Quḍāt Hamadānī lived during a period of intensive intellectual and doctrinal activity by the Nizārīs. It was in the decade before his birth and in his early youth that Muḥammad al-Ghazālī wrote his famous polemical works against the Ismailis, and in particular the Nizārīs. ʿAyn al-Quḍāt was a direct disciple of Aḥmad al-Ghazālī and an indirect disciple of the polemicist/Sufi, his brother Muḥammad. He even recounted a dream in which the Prophet named ten scholars who are 'firmly grounded in knowledge' (*al-rāsikhūn fi'l-ʿilm*) and the tenth was revealed to him as al-Ghazālī.[45] The narrative reflects the degree

---

[44] Abū Saʿīd is another of the prominent Sufis who are generally known to belong to the school of Khurāsān in the mystical tradition. The most important source for his biography is the hagiographical work written by his grandson, Muḥammad b. Munawwar. For a full account of his life and thought, see Shafīʿī Kadkanī's introduction to Muḥammad b. Munawwar Mīhanī, *Asrār al-tawḥīd fī maqāmāt al-shaykh Abī Saʿīd* (4th ed., Tehran, 1376 Sh./1997).

[45] See ʿAyn al-Quḍāt Hamadānī, *Tamhīdāt* ed. ʿAfīf ʿUsayrān (4th ed., Tehran, 1994), p. 280.

of respect he had for al-Ghazālī. Yet, ʿAyn al-Quḍāt wrote a lengthy letter in which he examines the Nizārī doctrine of *taʿlīm* and challenges al-Ghazālī's account of their doctrines. In short, he believes that al-Ghazālī failed to engage with the real problem Nizārīs were addressing with regard to the knowledge of God. The letter in question, letter no. 75, is not only important because he criticised al-Ghazālī in it. It is also peculiarly interesting because he quoted verses from a famous *qaṣīda* by Nāṣir-i Khusraw to corroborate his point. These verses and other verses he quoted in other places in his writings reflect his remarkable familiarity with the Ismailis and their thought.[46]

We know that one of the pretexts for killing ʿAyn al-Quḍāt was the accusation that he was a *taʿlīmī*. While it is difficult to argue for ʿAyn al-Quḍāt having converted to Ismailism, there is one area in his writings which is of interest in the context here. ʿAyn al-Quḍāt's interest in a non-orthodox version of eschatology and his particular narrative of *qiyāmat* bears a striking resemblance to the doctrine articulated by the Nizārīs who wrote after the imamate of Ḥasan II. The conclusion is that his writings appear to have been among the Sufi works that were widely circulated among the Nizārīs.

We know that Ṭūsī, during his affiliation with Ismailis, translated ʿAyn al-Quḍāt's *Zubdat al-ḥaqāʾiq* into Persian along with commentaries on it. This should not be confused with his *Tamhīdāt* which is also known as *Zubda*: the *Tamhīdāt* is in Persian anyway and there would have been no point in Ṭūsī translating it into Persian (before 632/1234). But as regards the *Zubdat* the question is why the Ismailis were interested in a Persian translation and commentary of the work, whether it was merely a result of their general interest in scholarship or if they took the further step of using these Sufi ideas in their own doctrine. The evidence suggests the latter.

As noted earlier in the case of Sanāʾī, the Ismailis regularly referred to mystical poetry in articulating their doctrines. We also know that the language used by ʿAyn al-Quḍāt resembled the language used by

46 See H. Landolt, 'Early Evidence for the Reception of Nāsīr-i Khusraw's Poetry in Sufism: ʿAyn al-Quḍāt's Letter on the Taʿlīmīs', in O. Alí-de-Unzaga (ed.), *Fortresses of the Intellect: Ismaili and Other Islamic Studies in Honour of Farhad Daftary* (London, 2011), pp. 369–386.

Ismailis. In the *Tatimma*, al-Bayhaqī noted that "Ayn al-Quḍāt mixed mysticism with Greek philosophy'.[47] This is precisely the reason why some of the contemporaries of al-Shahrastānī suspected him of being an Ismaili. What is rather vague here is what these authors meant by 'Greek philosophy'. This cannot be simply Neoplatonic philosophy (neither al-Shahrastānī nor ʿAyn al-Quḍāt are known as Neoplatonists). At least, as can be seen in al-Shahrastānī's *Muṣāraʿa*, there is a clear divergence from the typical Neoplatonism found among philosophers and Fatimid writers. What people like al-Bayhaqī – who said similar things about al-Shahrastānī – had in mind is a rational approach to faith and the style of argumentation which does not exclusively rely on *naql* or *samʿ* which is basically transmission from authoritative sources. This approach is particularly evident in the eschatological approach of ʿAyn al-Quḍāt Hamadānī. First of all, he did not believe in physical resurrection – a doctrine shared by all Ismailis and some philosophers – and secondly his narrative of the evolution of religions and how their esoteric meanings are lost over time fully resonates with the Nizārī doctrine of *qiyāmat*.

ʿAyn al-Quḍāt is critical of rituals reducing the content of faith to habit:

> O dear friend! Your actions are ruled by your intentions. So, examine what motivates your actions and see that your intention is proportionate to your knowledge. If your knowledge and actions all lead to worldly pleasures, then you have no idea about the pleasures of the hereafter. Therefore, any intention rising from within you will be for this world and you are unaware of it; if you pray or fast or give alms, your motivation for them is nothing but habit. And the Prophet – peace be upon him – said, 'I was raised to reject habits' (*buʿithtu bi rafḍ al-ʿādāt*). If seeking permanent pleasures motivates you to action, then this is the love of the hereafter. You love worldly pleasures but these are ephemeral pleasures and those are permanent ones; that is why you seek them so passionately.[48]

---

[47] ʿAlī al-Bayhaqī, *Tatimmat ṣiwān al-ḥikma*, ed. Muḥammad Shafīʿ (Lahore, 1351/1932), p. 123.

[48] ʿA. Munzawī and ʿA. ʿUsayrān (ed.), *Nāmaha-yi ʿAyn al-Qūḍat Hamadānī* (2nd ed., Tehran, 1362 Sh./1983), vol. 1, p. 26 (author's translation).

This familiar theme is not only a Sufi one, shared with people like Sanāʾī, but it is also a critical Nizārī doctrine. This is precisely the theme of the concluding paragraphs of Ṭūsī's *Maṭlūb al-muʾminīn*.[49] The same theme is repeated in Muḥammad III's responses to Ṭūsī in the annexes of the *Rawḍa* in a section which is found in S. J. Badakhchani's PhD thesis.[50]

The following citation from his *Zubdat* is even more telling:

> And recognise this point before anything: that the Final Day (*al-yawm al-ākhir*) is different from the days known by the rising of the sun because on the day of resurrection, the sun shall become darkened. The term Final Day has been used for lack of any other term, as the Prophet – peace be upon him – has described it when he said, 'The time has turned around in the same manner as the day God created the heavens and the earth.' And as the Qur'an has termed it in saying, 'Surely your Lord is God, who created the heavens and the earth in six days' (7:54). And until such time that the heavens and the earth turn into something else than what they are now, it is impossible for the wayfarer to reach the day of resurrection (*yawm al-dīn*). If you have now comprehended this point, then you should know that the human soul has many stages which cannot be enumerated. And the soul constantly moves through its stages. It is said that the soul constantly evolves in this world from one stage to another: in the grave, because the grave is the first station of the stations of the hereafter and in that stage too, it evolves. And also in the stages of resurrection it evolves and it is said that this shall also continue in the hereafter.[51]

This passage combines discussions of physical resurrection with *qiyāmat* where the true wayfarer reaches unity (*waḥdat*).

49 Ṭūsī, *Shiʿi Interpretations of Islam: Three Treatises on Islamic Theology and Eschatology* (London, 2010), pp. 42–52.

50 S. J. Badakhchani, *The Paradise of Submission: A Critical Edition and Study of Rawzeh-i Taslīm commonly known as Taṣawwurat* (PhD thesis, University of Oxford, 1989), p. 240.

51 ʿAyn al-Quḍāt Hamadānī, *Zubdat al-ḥaqāʾiq*, ed. ʿA. ʿUsayrān (Tehran, 2000), p. 79.

The next passage is from his *Tamhīdāt*:

> Wait, O friend, until such time when the meaning of this *ḥadīth* becomes clear to you that, 'The Prophets pray in their tombs'. Then you will realise why 'the sound of the cockerel is his prayer' is the same as 'and [he] mentions the Name of his Lord, and prays' (87:15). And for God's sake, heed this point: one day, Shiblī rose to perform the *namāz*. He waited for a long time and then he performed the prayer. Once he was done he said, 'Woe to me! By God, if I pray, I will be in denial and if I do not pray, I will become a disbeliever.' Do you imagine that Shiblī was not among the people who are described as those 'who are constant at their worship?'[52]

In an earlier section in the same part of *Tamhīdāt*, he again draws attention to the issue of worship being reduced to habit:

> [Where the Qur'an says] 'And who observe their prayers. And continue at their prayers' (23:9; 70:23), it is not the same prayer of yours and mine consisting of rising and bowing and prostrating. This prayer is the one of which 'Abd Allāh Yunāji [sic][53] reports: 'Seeking pleasure from worship is the result of turning away from God'; pleasure should be sought in the one who commands it, not in the worship itself.[54]

These passages are all from a section in the *Tamhīdāt* titled 'Exposition of the five pillars of Islam (*Sharḥ-i arkān-i panjgānah-yi Islām*). In the *Rawḍa* and the *Maṭlūb*,[55] Ṭūsī considered the subject of the seven pillars of the *sharī'at* (with *ṭahārat* and *jihād* being the different ones) then proceeded to provide their esoteric interpretation in a manner resembling that of 'Ayn al-Quḍāt.

---

[52] 'Ayn al-Quḍāt Hamadānī, *Tamhīdāt*, ed. 'Afīf 'Usayrān (4th ed., Tehran, 1994), pp. 81–82.

[53] The name as recorded by 'Ayn al-Quḍāt (or the editors) seems incompatible with other recordings of this name. Al-Kalābādhī gave this name as Abū 'Abd Allāh al-Nabājī citing the same quote. See A. Al-Kalābādhī, *al-Ta'arruf li-madhhab ahl al-taṣawwuf*, ed. A. Shamsuddin (Beirut, 2001), p. 160.

[54] 'Ayn al-Quḍāt Hamadānī, *Tamhīdāt*, pp. 80–81.

[55] Ṭūsī, *Rawḍa*, pp. 142–155; *Maṭlūb*, in *Shi'i Interpretations of Islam*, pp. 40–43.

As we can see, these doctrinal articulations, which are specifically related to the Nizārī interpretations of the *qiyāmat*, are closely related to how a Sunni Sufi elaborates on them, giving further texture to the argument made here.

Conclusion

The cases of Sanāʾī Ghaznawī, al-Shahrastānī and ʿAyn al-Quḍāt Hamadānī reflect a pattern in the activity of the Nizārī Ismaili *daʿwa*. The Nizārīs would openly borrow ideas, terminologies and categories when seeking to articulate their doctrines. Apart from al-Shahrastānī whose Ismaili affiliations are now beyond doubt and who openly defended the imamate, there is no sense of a doctrinal closeness to the Nizārī concept of imamate. Yet, there are many areas in their thought which are not just shared with the Ismailis but which the Nizārīs used liberally in order to articulate their beliefs. Comparing paragraphs and verses from the writings of these three figures with the extant material from the Nizārī literature, including those surviving fragments from Ḥasan II, gives us a sharper and more focused image of the doctrine of *qiyāmat*. While it is improbable – and possibly highly unlikely – that Sanāʾī and ʿAyn al-Quḍāt had actually joined the Ismailis, their ideas and thoughts were undoubtedly widely used among the Nizārīs. This episode of Ismaili history also displays the earliest signs of interaction between the Nizārīs and the Sufis, paving the way after the fall of Alamūt for their future affiliations with Sufis – who were then of a rather different disposition than people like Sanāʾī and ʿAyn al-Quḍāt. There are other figures who may be studied with the same approach, possibly Shihāb al-Dīn Suhrawardī (d. 587/1191) and Ibn al-ʿArabī (d. 638/1240), but these three figures are among the most prominent examples demonstrating a vibrant intellectual interaction between Nizārīs and other Muslim communities. Examining this literature opens up the possibility of reviewing intellectual interactions beyond political divisions and polemical refutations.

10

Nature according to Ḥamīd al-Dīn al-Kirmānī (d. after 411/1020–1021) and Mullā Ṣadrā (d. 1050/1640): Ismaili Influence on a Twelver Thinker or Dependence on Common Sources?[1]

Janis Esots
(The Institute of Ismaili Studies)

The Concept of Nature in Greek Philosophy

'Nature' (*φύσις*) was already an important philosophical concept for the Presocratics, who typically treated it either as the prime matter, or as a process (of genesis), or as the yield/result of such a process.[2] Plato used the term extensively[3] but the concept of nature is not the central theme of any of his dialogues. In the *Philebus*, Socrates treated the study of nature as the field of research that investigates the causes of being and becoming (*Phil* 59a). In the *Timaeus*, the term 'nature'

[1] An earlier stage of my research on the subject is reflected in a short article 'Ḥamīd al-Dīn al-Kirmānī's Teaching on Nature and Parallels to It in the Thought of Mullā Ṣadrā' (*Islamic Philosophy Yearbook Ishrāq*, 4 (2012), pp. 262–271), in which I limit myself to a comparison of a few selected passages from al-Kirmānī's and Ṣadrā's works, without making an attempt to consider their doctrines in the context and against the background of Greek and Arabo-Islamic natural philosophy. Some of the quotations (usually in my own translation) are taken from that previous article, with either minor or substantial revisions.

[2] See e.g. Gérard Naddaf, *Le concept de nature chez les Présocratiques*, tr. Benoît Castelnérac (Millau, 2008), pp. 31, 35 ff.

[3] See e.g. *Phaedo*, 96a6 ff, *Phaedrus*, 270a ff, *Sophist*, 265c–e, and *Laws*, X 891b8–892c7.

typically refers to the things which are subject to generation and corruption.

Aristotle treated the concept at length in the first four books of his *Physics*. In broad terms, he equated nature with form.[4] He offered several (partially overlapping) definitions, some of which pertain to the universal aspect of nature, and others to the particular one. In the first case, the concept refers to a universal form of becoming.[5] In the second, it designates the substance of a natural thing.[6]

Aristotle's ideas were further developed by his commentators, in particular Alexander of Aphrodisias and John Philoponus. Like Aristotle, Alexander denied that natural things come to be in reference to an idea (or form, in its Platonic sense) as a model/paradigm.[7] Instead, he viewed universal nature as the power or influence which the celestial (supralunar) bodies exert on the sublunar ones ('**the power from the divine [i.e. celestial] bodies**[8] is the cause of the [difference] between the simple [elemental] bodies and of their coming-to-be, **itself coming to be their form and nature**').[9] He described this celestial nature as the cause of the unity and order of the world that 'pervades the whole world and holds its parts together'.[10] Elsewhere – in

---

4 See e.g. Aristotle, *Physics*, II.1 193a9–17; idem, *Meteorology*, XII.3 1070a11–12.

5 Aristotle, *Physics*, II.1.

6 Aristotle, *Metaphysics*, V.4.

7 Alexander of Aphrodisias, Commentary on [Aristotle's] *Metaphysics*, 103, 4–104, 18, English translation in Richard Sorabji, *The Philosophy of the Commentators, 200 – 600 AD: A Sourcebook*, vol. 2. Physics (Bristol, 2012 [1st ed. 2004]), pp. 33–34.

8 The celestial bodies are divine because/insofar as they are animated by the divine soul(s), which give them life and make them self-moving. The soul, in turn, is divine because/insofar as it participates in the divine intellect, which, in turn, participates in the One. On the divinity of the celestial bodies in Greek thought, from Alexander of Aphrodisias to Simplicius, see Philippe Hoffmann, 'Science théologique et Foi selon le Commentaire de Simplicius au *De Caelo* d'Aristote', in Elisa Coda and Cecilia Martini Bonadeo (ed.), *De l'Antiquité tardive au Moyen Âge. Études de logique aristotélicienne et de philosophie grecque, syriaque, arabe et latine offertes à Henri Hugonnard-Roche* (Paris, 2014), pp. 296–307.

9 Alexander of Aphrodisias (?), *Quaest.* 2.3, 49, 29–50, 7, the English translation in Sorabji, *The Philosophy of the Commentators*, vol. 2, p. 41.

10 Alexander of Aphrodisias, *On the Cosmos*, ed. and trans. Charles Genequand (Leiden: Brill, 2001), pp. 112–113. Cf. Damien Janos, '"Active Nature" and Other

his commentary on the *Meteorology* IV.7.9–14 – he put it even more explicitly, defining nature as 'the eternal movement of the divine (i.e., celestial. – J.E.) bodies and the power that comes to be in these sublunary bodies as a result of their proximity to those [celestial ones]'.[11] In the aspect and to the extent in which nature aims to produce a certain physical/corporeal form, it can be treated as a manifestation of providence.[12]

Philoponus, in his commentary on Aristotle's *Physics*, describes nature as 'a life or a power which has descended into bodies and which moulds and manages them'.[13] Notably, in his commentary on *Physics*,[14] Philoponus used the term 'productive nature' (ἡ ποιοὺσα φύσις) (which, as Damien Janos justly remarks, may have been the Greek prototype of Abū Bishr Mattā b. Yūnus al-Qunnāʾī's (d. 328/940) 'active nature' (*al-ṭabīʿa al-faʿʿāla*).[15] Philoponus believed that both God and nature create but (according to Simplicius' account), he underlined the point that nature 'creates (ποιεῖν) what is generated out of what exists . . . while God does so out of what does not exist'[16] – to

Striking Features of Abū Bishr Mattā b. Yūnus's Cosmology as Reconstructed from His Commentary on Aristotle's *Physics*', in Damien Janos (ed.), *Ideas in Motion in Baghdad and Beyond: Philosophical and Theological Exchanges between Christians and Muslims in the Third/Ninth and Fourth/Tenth Centuries* (Leiden, 2016), p. 161.

11 Alexander of Aphrodisias, *Commentary on [Aristotle's] Meteorology* 47, 9–14, the English translation in Sorabji, *The Philosophy of the Commentators,* vol. 2, pp. 41–42. Cf. Janos, '"Active Nature"', p. 162.

12 The original Greek text of Alexander's treatise is lost, but it survives in Arabic translation – see the relevant passage (in which Alexander, to a certain extent, identifies nature with providence) in Alexandre d'Aphrodise, *Traité de la providence*, version arabe de Abū Bišr Mattä ibn Yūnus, ed. and trans. Pierre Thillet (Lagrasse, 2003), p. 20 (of the Arabic text), l. 21 – p. 21, l. 3; cf. the English translation by P. Adamson in Sorabji, *The Philosophy of the Commentators*, vol. 2, *Physics*, p. 42.

13 [Philoponus,] *Ioannis Philoponi in Aristotelis Physicorum libros tres priores commentaria*, ed. Hieronymus Vitelli (Berlin: Georg Reimer 1887), p. 197, l. 32–35. Cf. Janos, '"Active Nature"', pp. 164–165.

14 [Philoponus,] *In Aristotelis Physicorum libros tres priores commentaria*, p. 317, l. 18.

15 Janos, '"Active Nature"', p. 165.

16 Simplicius, *On Aristotle Physics 8.1–5*, tr. István Bodnár, Michael Chase and Michael Share (London, 2014 [1st ed. 2012]), p. 44 (1145, 7–11).

put it differently, the creative activity of nature is exercised in the realm of becoming, whereas that of God is exercised in the world of being.

In turn, Plotinus described nature as the formative principle, *λόγος* (reason), acting in a visible form. In his understanding, it was the last of the *λόγοι* and, therefore, a dead one (if considered *per se*; if viewed in relation to the soul which sustains it, it is, or at least seems to be, alive), incapable of producing another *λόγος* and, for that reason, producing only visible forms or bodies.[17] According to Plotinus, nature is generated by (the universal) soul and is the product of soul's contemplation of the intellect (whereas the product of nature's (or the vegetative faculty's) contemplation of the soul (i.e., of its rational part/faculty) is natural bodies).[18] Nature is 'the offspring of a prior soul with a stronger life . . . [which] quietly holds contemplation in itself, not directed upwards or even downwards, but at rest in what it is, in its own repose and a kind of self-perception, and in this consciousness and self-perception it sees what comes after it, as far as it can, and seeks other things no longer.'[19] Elsewhere, Plotinus calls nature 'an image of intelligence (or reflection)' (*ἴνδαλμα γὰρ φρονήσεως ἡ φύσις*), which 'has the last ray of the rational forming principle which shines in it',[20] thus identifying it with the lowest part of the universal soul.

For Proclus, nature is a hypostasis (i.e., ontological degree or level of reality) between the soul and the natural/material body (and, thus, separate from the soul).[21] He believed that nature is not only related to

[17] Plotinus, *Enn.* III. 8 (30) 4.1–14. Cf. Linguiti, Alessandro, 'Physics and Metaphysics', in Paulina Remes and Svetla Slaveva-Griffin (ed.), *The Routledge Handbook of Neoplatonism* (London, 2014), p. 350.

[18] Plotinus, *Enn.* III. 8 (30) 2,19–34, 3 and 4, the English translation by A. H. Armstrong in Plotinus, *Enneads*, vol. 3. *Enneads III.1–9* (Cambridge, MA and London, 1980 [1st ed. 1967]), pp. 365–371.

[19] Plotinus, *Enn.* III. 8 (30) 4, 14–21, English trans. by Armstrong in Plotinus, *Enneads*, vol. 3, *Enneads III.1–9*, p. 371.

[20] Plotinus, *Enn.* IV. 4 (28) 13, 3–6, English trans. by Armstrong in Plotinus, *Enneads*, vol. 4, p. 171.

[21] Martijn, Marije, *Proclus on Nature: Philosophy of Nature and Its Methods in Proclus' Commentary on Plato's* Timaeus (Leiden, 2010), p. 24.

bodies, but also **immersed** in them – and, for that reason, it lacks self-sufficiency.[22] Elaborating on Plato's distinction between being and becoming, he introduced two intermediate categories, 'being-and-becoming' (*τὸ ὄν χαι γινόμενον*) and 'becoming-and-being' (*τὸ γινόμενον χαι ὄν*),[23] and attributed nature to the latter. Furthermore, he described it as 'an incorporeal essence, inseparable from bodies, in possession of their *λόγοι*, incapable of contemplating itself'.[24] (In other words, nature is the sum of its *λόγοι*, the rational principles of all physical entities. It acts, through them, either **in** its essence or **from** its essence. The first action ensures its permanence as a principle; the second fills bodies with physical powers.)[25] Remarkably, Proclus identifies nature with the 'fate' (*εἱμαρμένη*) of the body[26] (and not with providence, *πρόνοια*).

Simplicius of Cilicia, probably the last major Greek Neoplatonist, elaborating on certain of Aristotle's remarks,[27] emphasised the **passive** aspect of nature (for more on this aspect see the section on al-Kirmānī),[28] describing it as a passive power, or propensity, of being moved, while treating the soul (which he defined as the first actuality of the body possessing organs) as the **agent** of motion[29] (which was a typically

---

22 Proclus, *In Tim.* I. 10.24–11.5. Cf. Martijn, *Proclus on Nature*, p. 29.

23 Proclus, *In Tim.* I. 257.5–6.

24 Proclus, *In Tim.* I. 12.26–30.

25 Proclus, *Théologie platonicienne*, ed and trans. H. D. Saffrey and L. G. Westerink, vol. V, book V (Paris, 1987), p. 64 (V.18.64.15–18). Cf. Linguiti, '*Physis* as *Heimarmene*: On Some Fundamental Principles of the Neoplatonic Philosophy of Nature', in Riccardo Chiaradonna and Franco Trabattoni (ed.), *Physics and Philosophy of Nature in Greek Neoplatonism. Proceedings of the European Science Foundation Exploratory Workshop (Il Ciocco, Castelvecchio Pascoli, June 22–24, 2006)* (Leiden, 2009), pp. 185–186.

26 Proclus, *On Providence*, tr. Carlos Steel (London, 2014 [1st ed. 2007]), pp. 46–47 (§12). Cf. Linguiti, '*Physis* as *Heimarmene*', p. 178, idem, 'Physics and Metaphysics', p. 354, n. 30.

27 Aristotle, *Physics* 8.4, 2555b30–31; cf. also ibid., 2.1, 192b13, 22.

28 Simplicius, *In Physica* 287, 24–25, English trans. in Sorabji, *The Philosophy of the Commentators*, vol. 2, p. 50.

29 Simplicius, *In Caelo* 387, 12–19, English trans. in Sorabji, *The Philosophy of the Commentators*, vol. 2, p. 49; Simplicius, *In Physica* 287.

Platonic view).[30] He also believed that, rather than being identical with the vegetative soul, nature was inferior to it, pertaining to the simple elements only.

To conclude this sketchy outline, it must be added that, in broad terms, the Greek Neoplatonists viewed nature first and foremost as a universal principle, which primarily governed the physical world (both its sublunar and supralunar realms) **as a whole**, and only secondarily and by extension – the individual entities. In turn, the Aristotelians typically understood nature as an **individual nature of each entity**.[31]

The Concept of Nature in Islamic Philosophy

The early Muslim philosophers typically, following Aristotle, treated nature as the essential first principle of motion and rest. Thus, Abū Yūsuf Yaʿqūb al-Kindī (d. ca. 252/866) defined it as the 'beginning (or principle) (*ibtidāʾ*) of motion and rest after motion'.[32] A remarkably original interpretation of nature was given by Abū Bishr Mattā b. Yūnus, who, as mentioned above, on the basis of certain insights of Alexander of Aphrodisias and John Philoponus, developed the concept of the 'active nature' (*al-ṭabīʿa al-faʿʿāla*), which he believed to be disseminated in all natural things.[33] Although Abū Bishr's treatment of nature includes some core elements of Aristotle's teaching (thus, nature is the innate principle of motion and rest of natural/physical things, which actualises them and moves them towards a certain end),[34] he, nevertheless, introduces important new features. Thus, Abū Bishr appears to attribute to nature some degree of intellect, or at least a shadow of it.[35] Even more importantly, he

---

[30] See e.g. Plato, *Phaedrus* 245c8–9, where Socrates describes soul as 'the origin and principle of motion'; cf. *Timaeus* 34b10–35a1 and 36e2–4.

[31] Linguiti, '*Physis* as *Heimarmene*', p. 175.

[32] Al-Kindī, *al-Rasāʾil al-falsafiyya*, ed. Abū Riḍā (Cairo, 1950), vol. 1, p. 169, quoted from Roger Arnaldez, 'Ḥaraka wa sukūn', *EI2*, vol. 3, 169 b.

[33] Arisṭūṭālīs, *al-Ṭabīʿa*, tr. Isḥāq b. Ḥunayn, ed. ʿA. Badawī (Cairo, 1964), vol. 1, p. 147, l. 19.

[34] For more details, see the discussion in Janos, '"Active Nature"', p. 149.

[35] Arisṭūṭālīs, *al-Ṭabīʿa*, vol. 1, p. 135, l. 3–10.

argues that active nature is neither form, nor matter (and, thus, neither formal, nor material cause), but an **agent and a productive principle** (i.e., an efficient cause). Like Alexander of Aphrodisias, Proclus, Philoponus and Simplicius, Abū Bishr clearly separates nature from the soul, treating them as two different hypostases.[36] The autonomy of nature is particularly evident during the early stages of the development of the embryo, he argues. However, it is important to note that, while, according to Abū Bishr, nature is autonomous in its efficiency, the end and goal of its action is not determined by itself, but by the transcendent final cause. In a way, Abū Bishr's active nature can be identified as (or reduced to) the influence (*ta'thīr*) of the celestial bodies (and their motion) upon the terrestrial ones.[37] Ultimately, this motion of the celestial bodies is caused by the Creator, conceived by Abū Bishr, in an Aristotelian vein, as the prime mover.[38] (In this way, the active nature bears certain providential traits.) Janos has shown that Abū Bishr had access to certain parts of Philoponus on Aristotle's *Physics*, concluding that 'the latter work represented perhaps the main source of inspiration for his concept of active nature'.[39] Hence, it can be argued that this concept emerged as the result of the synthesis of Aristotelian, Alexandrian and Philoponian elements. In turn, the Ismaili thinker Ḥamīd al-Dīn al-Kirmānī, as will be discussed below, probably had access to Isḥāq b. Ḥunayn's Arabic translation of Aristotle's *Physics*, with Abū Bishr's commentary, and/or to the likely sources of the latter's teaching on active nature – such as Alexander of Aphrodisias' *On the Principles of the Cosmos* (translated as *Fī mabādī' al-kull*), the Pseudo-Aristotelian *De mundo*,[40] and, in particular, Philoponus' commentary on Aristotle's *Physics*.[41]

---

[36] Arisṭūṭālīs, *al-Ṭabī'a*, vol. 1, p. 151, l. 14–5. Cf. Janos, '"Active Nature"', pp. 149, 152.

[37] Arisṭūṭālīs, *al-Ṭabī'a*, vol. 1, p. 151, l. 5–6; cf. English trans. in Janos, '"Active Nature"', p. 142.

[38] Arisṭūṭālīs, *al-Ṭabī'a*, vol. 1, p. 151, l. 7–8; cf. the English trans. in Janos, '"Active Nature"', p. 142.

[39] Janos, '"Active Nature"', p. 167.

[40] The Arabic text and English translation of which was prepared by David A. Brafman in his PhD dissertation. See David A. Brafman, *The Arabic* De mundo: *An Edition with Translation and Commentary* (PhD dissertation, Duke University, 1985).

[41] See the detailed arguments in favour of this hypothesis in Janos, '"Active Nature"', pp. 171, 173.

The Ikhwān al-Ṣafā' appear to have trod the middle path between Platonists and Aristotelians: they retained the concept of the universal (celestial) soul, and interpreted nature as its power that flows in all sublunary bodies, moves and governs them, and delivers them to their (natural) ends.[42] Hence, the universal soul can be described as the spirit of the world, nature as the action of the soul, and the four elements as its prime matter.[43]

In turn, Ibn Sīnā (d. 428/1037), in his treatment of nature, seems, by and large, to have followed Aristotle. Many of his remarks on the subject represent paraphrased passages from Aristotle's *Physics*. E.g. in the *'Uyūn al-ḥikma* he said:

> Nature is an occasioner (*sabab*) in that it is a certain essential principle (*mabda'*) of motion and rest of that in which it is inherent essentially, not by accident.[44]

Elsewhere in the *'Uyūn*, Ibn Sīnā restated the same idea, replacing 'motion' (*ḥaraka*) with 'change' (*taghayyur*) and 'rest' (*sukūn*) with 'stability' (*thubūt*):

> Nature is the essential first principle (*al-mabdā' al-awwal*) for the essential movement of that in which it is present, in short, for every essential change (*taghayyur*) and every essential immutability (*thubūt*).[45]

A more careful examination of the relevant passages in Ibn Sīnā's works allows us to conclude that nature occasions motion only in a body which is not in its natural state and/or position (perhaps this was apprehended already by al-Kindī, who spoke of nature as 'the way that leads to rest', *al-ṭarīq ilā al-sukūn*).[46] In the *Najāt*, this point is explained by Ibn Sīnā in the following way:

---

[42] [Ikhwān al-Ṣafā'], *Rasā'il Ikhwān al-Ṣafā' wa-khillān al-wafā'*, ed. Khayr al-Dīn al-Ziriklī (Cairo, 1928), vol. 2, p. 112.

[43] Ibid., p. 113.

[44] Ibn Sīnā, "Uyūn al-ḥikma', in Fakhr al-Dīn al-Rāzī, *Sharḥ 'Uyūn al-ḥikma*, ed. A. al-Saqā (Tehran, 1373 Sh./1994), vol. 2, p. 35. Cf. David E. Pingree and Syed Nomanul Haq, 'Ṭabī'a', *EI2*, vol. 10, p. 25 a.

[45] As A.-M. Goichon points out, this statement represents a free translation of a passage from the second book of Aristotle's *Physics* (see Arnaldez, 'Ḥaraka').

[46] See Arnaldez, 'Ḥaraka'.

> If nature requires the motion of a certain thing, this thing is not in its natural state, and nature moves it [only] in order to return it to its natural state and to reach the latter. When the natural state is reached, the necessitator (*mawjib*) of the motion disappears, and the [natural] motion of the thing becomes impossible . . . Every motion through nature is a natural flight from a [certain] state, and whenever such a flight occurs, it is a flight from a disagreeable state.[47]

Nature tries to return the body to its natural state by the nearest way possible. In case of local motion, this attempt is manifested in the straightness (*istiqāma*) of motion. As soon as the natural state is fully achieved and actualised, the natural motion comes to an end (probably this motivated al-Kindī to describe the state of rest as the 'realisation of actuality and the last fulfilment').[48]

In the *Taʿlīqāt*, Ibn Sīnā argued that nature is not the agent (*fāʿil*) and the cause (*ʿilla*) of the thing, namely that it is capable neither of bringing a thing into existence, nor of sustaining it. Its function comes down to creating preconditions for imposing a certain form upon matter, that is to say, to perfecting and refining the predisposition (*imkān istiʿdādī*):

> In reality, nature is incapable of more than setting [matter] in motion (*taḥrīk*) and preparation (*iʿdād*), through which the matter which is moved by it [i.e., nature] can receive the form, towards which it (matter) is moved, and nature is neither the agent, nor the effuser (*mufīd*) of existence. Rather, the effuser is the bestower of forms (*wāhib al-ṣuwar*), whereas nature is the mover of the thing, which moves it towards what is effused upon it by the bestower of forms. It performs no other act except moving the thing towards its furthest limit (*ghāya*) – that, through which it (the thing) is presented to the first agent, and it [nature] seems to perform this function unwillingly, as if it were being compelled.[49]

---

[47] Ibn Sīnā, *al-Najāt min al-gharq fī baḥr al-ḍalālāt*, ed. M.T. Dānishpazhūh (2nd ed., Tehran, 1379 Sh./2000), pp. 212–213.

[48] Al-Kindī, *Rasāʾil*, vol. 1, p. 86; cf. Arnaldez, 'Ḥaraka'.

[49] Ibn Sīnā, *al-Taʿlīqāt*, ed. ʿAbd al-Raḥmān al-Badavī (Qumm, 1379 Sh./2000), p. 209.

Nature is presented here as the innate organising principle of matter, a dim 'consciousness of the unconscious'. Like matter, it is passive and inert in itself and seems to perform its function 'as if it were being compelled' (this enigmatic expression probably led Ṣadrā to suppose the existence of two different natures, one of which obeys the soul willingly (because it is a part and a level of the soul), but the other does it unwillingly and under compulsion, see on this below).[50]

Ḥamīd al-Dīn al-Kirmānī on Nature

Is there a specifically Ismaili teaching on nature? In order to answer this question let us examine, as an example, Ḥamīd al-Dīn al-Kirmānī's treatment of the subject. At a quick glance, we can already establish that his definition of nature combines the elements of the definitions of Aristotle and Plotinus. In an Aristotelian vein, he first described nature as the principle of movement and rest of the thing in which it essentially inheres. But, following Plotinus, he then stated that the essence of this moving principle consists of life which flows from the world of divinity/lordship (*rubūbiyya*), and which is referred to as the form (which can perhaps be equated with the soul here) that receives its existence through the emanation from the world of primordial creation, together with the prime matter which necessarily accompanies it, so that one of them is active, and the other – passive.[51]

Daniel De Smet in his *Quiétude de l'intellect* lists three important points where al-Kirmānī's treatment of nature differs from the Aristotelian one and coincides with that of Plotinus: 1) nature emanates from the celestial world; 2) the difference between animated and

---

[50] Ṣadr al-Dīn al-Shīrāzī (Mullā Ṣadrā), *al-Ḥikma al-ʿarshiyya*, ed. G. Āhanī (Isfahan, 1341 Sh./1962), p. 233.

[51] Ḥamīd al-Dīn al-Kirmānī, *Rāḥat al-ʿaql*, ed. Muṣṭafā Ghālib (Beirut, 1983), p. 296. Cf. Daniel De Smet, *La Quiétude de l'intellect: Neoplatonisme et gnose ismaélienne dans l'oeuvre de Hamîd ad-Dîn al-Kîrmânî (X^e/XIe s.)* (Leuven, 1995), p. 324, n. 62. Notably, Plotinus often treats nature as the active element of bodies, their form, life and soul, viewing these three terms almost as synonyms ('the realm of nature, which is life, [also] named "the soul"'). See De Smet, *Quiétude*, p. 324.

unanimated nature disappears, all sublunar creatures possessing a soul; 3) nature is understood as a pure form, synonymous with the soul and life, and not as an entity composed of form and matter.[52] Al-Kirmānī's most important point is that nature is two-fold in its essence and manifests itself simultaneously in its active and passive aspects, i.e., as the moving form of everything and as matter which receives that form. As matter, nature gives the thing its corporeality, i.e., body; as form, it gives it the soul and prepares it for the receipt of effusion of the agent intellect.[53] He wrote:

> It was explained earlier that, when the thing which is known as the 'prime matter' (*hayūla*) came into existence, this [coming] happened without an intention on the part of the primordial creation,[54] so that prime matter would find its cause in the latter. And it lacked the excellence that was in the possession of the other, namely the actual intellects, which emanated from the noblest relation – the one which [is found] in the primordial creation, (which [creation simultaneously] is the first created), but divine providence (*ʿināya*), which pervades everything, turned towards it [the prime matter], and from the blinding radiance (*suṭūʿ*) of its [providence's] lights was engendered the one whose engendering in it [the prime matter] was possible, in keeping with its [the engendering's] ranks in excellence.
>
> And we say: this existent, which is the prime matter, is one thing, but its essence, through which it exists, consists of two parts. Each of these two parts is [in turn] divided into [many] parts, which have one common name and many [particular] names, each of which is the proper name of one of these [specified] parts. Furthermore, every part has two relationships: 1) the relation to what is the source of its existence in the world of primordial creation, which is the first created, and in this relation it is one. This relation is established in the aspect of its [the relevant part's] substance and through this relation its quiddity is known;

52 See De Smet, *Quiétude*, p. 324, n. 63. Cf. Plotinus, *Enneads*, III.8.2.

53 See al-Kirmānī, *Rāḥat*, pp. 269–273.

54 Or creation from nothing (*ibdāʾ*), which, in al-Kirmānī's system, is identical to the first created thing or the first intellect.

2) the relation to the existents that exist through it. In this relation it is multiple, and this relation is established in the aspect of its acts in these existents.

As for the first part, when it is related to what is the source of its existence, attempting to establish its quiddity, [we find that] it is life *in actu*, emanating from the world of holiness, [which life is] not essentially independent in its existence and is not separated from that on which its existence depends, because its existence [arises] from the non-separated relation, and it permeates the world of body. The heavens and the earth are full of it; nothing is void of it and nothing is hidden from it. [This life-nature] acts in the corporeal world, giving everything its first perfection – the one which pertains to its existence.

When it is related to the existents that exist through it, [then,] generally, scrutinising its encompassing action, [we establish that] it is the mover of everything in which it resides and the perfection of the existence of the latter through its own existence, while [when considered] particularly, it is that which, in respect to its actions, [is present] in every part. When it moves bodies by circular motion, it is the orbit; when it moves fire and air up, it is lightness; when it moves water and something heavy down towards its centre, it is heaviness; when it moves the plant to grow, it is the vegetative soul; when it moves the animal to seek pleasure, it is the animal soul; [finally,] when it urges the human being to grasp the existents [by his knowledge (?)], it is the rational soul. All this, in the aspect of its being the agent, is one nature, but through its actions in different matters, in which it acts, it is multiple . . .

When the second part of the prime matter is considered in relation to what is the source of its existence, and, as such, encompasses its quiddity, it is perceived as life *in potentia*, emanating from the world of holiness, not essentially independent in its existence of the first part (that which is the life *in actu*) and not free from the need in it. It is the source of the existence of the world of body, and, in it, becomes the object of the action of life *in actu*, giving, together with the latter, to every existent its first perfection – that which pertains to its being existent.

When it is related to the existents, the source of whose existence it is, in a general way, it is a three-dimensional body, but [when it is related to them] in a particular way, that is, in accordance with the manner in which each part of it receives the action

> of the agent, [then,] if it moves by a circular motion, it is celestial spheres and luminaries; if it moves by a rectilinear motion, it is fire, air, water and earth; if it moves in all directions (up, down, right, left, forwards, backwards), without leaving its place, it is the plant; if it moves in all directions, leaving its place and being transferred [to a different one], it is the animal, and all this is one nature and one body, which, if considered in accordance with the manner of its receiving the effects of the agent, becomes multiple.[55]

Thus, al-Kirmānī treated nature as the fundamental life-giving principle of the corporeal universe, in which he distinguishes the active and passive parts. Such treatment, certainly, is much closer to the Platonic understanding of nature than to the Aristotelian one: according to Plato, the bodily cosmos, which is originated, has two causes – the agent (or demiurge, *bāri'*) and the prime matter; according to Aristotle, the eternal corporeal world has one cause – its prime mover. However, al-Kirmānī's treatment of nature is not identical to the Neoplatonic one: much like Aristotle, al-Kirmānī considered nature (more precisely, its active component) to be the mover of the corporeal universe – in its totality and in its parts.

Al-Kirmānī's understanding of nature seems to be much broader than Ibn Sīnā's: while Ibn Sīnā treated nature as the occasioner (*sabab*), responsible for predisposition (*imkān istiʿdādī*) and for the bestowal of motion (more specifically, that kind of motion whose purpose is the achievement of rest) on the body, al-Kirmānī considered it to be both motion and rest, mover and moved (body), action and affection (*infiʿāl*), actuality and potentiality and, perhaps most importantly, actual and potential life (both of which have emanated from the world of holiness).

Al-Kirmānī viewed nature as the by-product and the secondary result of the first emanation (the primary issue of which is the second intellect). In one aspect, nature is the potential intellect which unites in itself prime matter and form.[56] In another aspect, al-Kirmānī

[55] Al-Kirmānī, *Rāḥat*, pp. 269–271.

[56] See al-Kirmānī, *Rāḥat*, p. 80.

seemed to identify it with prime matter which is animated through the act of immaterial intellects.[57] It relates to what ranks below it in the cosmic hierarchy as the separated intellects relate to itself – i.e., acting upon the existents of a lower rank, it leaves in them traces and effects which are essentially similar to those left in itself by the pure intellects, as this passage seems to testify:

> . . . so that it would be known that **providence (ʿ*ināya*) flows in every existent [pervading it] from above and, in this act, it acts as nature**, in keeping with its status of a power flowing in the world of bodies from the world of divinity, which [power sympathetically] inclines towards what is actualised by the intention of pure intellects, namely [towards] the [celestial] bodies which precede it [i.e. nature] in excellence (*sharaf*), [manifesting itself as] ordering in levels (*tartīb*) [those] bodies [that are] formed from such matters which cannot be used for the creation of higher [celestial] bodies and creating from these matters the noble animals and placing what is incapable of producing higher incorruptible bodies among the existents through a sort of creation, in conformity with what suits it, in a way which is similar to the act of the pure intellects upon what was actualised by the intention of the primordial creation . . . namely upon the prime matter, which does not have a degree of that which transcends it in excellence, that is, of the actual intellect, and it is not in conformity with its [actual] waystation so that they [the pure intellects] would make it, through what flows in it, namely [through] their lights, similar to their essences *in actu* and [make that prime matter] an occasion of the existence of other than it, and would give it forms that suit it, such as [those of] the celestial spheres, luminaries and the others.[58]

When the prime matter is acted upon by the immaterial intellects, their lights and energies permeate it, thus making it similar – but **only in act not** in essence – to these intellects. Namely, the prime matter becomes capable of acting as the life-giving and animating principle

[57] See al-Kirmānī, *Rāḥat*, p. 167.
[58] Al-Kirmānī, *Rāḥat*, pp. 224–225.

which pervades every part and level of the corporeal world. But, in its passive aspect, nature itself is this corporeal world in its entirety, ranked in degrees and levels. Therefore, it would not be wrong to say that nature acts upon itself, actualising its own potentiality. Although al-Kirmānī preferred to describe nature as **life** – or, more precisely, as **that kind of life which permeates and sustains the world of the bodies**, one can maintain it is also possible, using a slightly different term, to call it **the principle of corporeal existence**. To put it in the terms of Mullā Ṣadrā, **when existence descends from the level of pure intellects to the level of natural bodies, it manifests itself as nature**. Regardless of their particular concerns and different terminology, on this principal point the positions of al-Kirmānī and Ṣadrā (but not that of Ibn Sīnā!) seem to coincide. This coincidence does not explicitly testify to Ṣadrā's acquaintance with this particular work by al-Kirmānī. However, it testifies to Ṣadrā's awareness of **this particular perspective of thought** that opens up as soon as one apprehends that in the bodily world life manifests itself as nature (and not otherwise). The novelty of Ṣadrā's approach lies in considering the issue in the context/against the background of the principle of the analogical gradation of existence (*tashkīk al-wujūd*).

In spite of its novel elements, al-Kirmānī's cosmological doctrine remains partially dependent on the teachings of his Ismaili predecessors, in particular those of Abu'l-Yaʿqūb al-Sijistānī, who dealt with cosmological issues in detail in his *Kitāb al-Yanābīʿ* ('Book of the Sources'). The potential entity which emanates from the first creation (*al-mubdaʿ al-awwal*) is called by al-Sijistānī 'the universal soul' (*al-nafs al-kulliyya*). From the universal soul, according to al-Sijistānī, emanate prime matter and form, which become intermediaries for the origination of the material world.[59] Postulating the existence of a common originating principle of prime matter and form, i.e., nature (*ṭabīʿa*), al-Kirmānī probably followed the approach of al-Sijistānī. In turn, Ṣadrā's cosmology, as far as it is recognises two fundamental existential levels – the world of primordial creation/being proper and

[59] See Farhad Daftary, *A Short History of the Ismailis: Traditions of a Muslim Community* (Edinburgh, 1998), p. 95.

the world of nature/becoming – follows the trend which, in Islamic philosophy, was established by the Ismaili thinkers, in particular by al-Kirmānī.

Ibn al-ʿArabī on Nature

Ibn al-ʿArabī talked about two natures, the first of which, according to him, relates to the second as mother to daughter. The first nature is the one which receives the traces and effects of God's names. This nature is, in fact, the cloud (*ʿamā*) and the breath of the Merciful:

> Nature is more worthy to be attributed to the Real than anything else, because everything else becomes manifest only in that which becomes manifest from **nature, that is, the breath, which permeates the cosmos** . . . And look at the inadequacy of the property of the **[first] intellect, for in reality it is one of the forms of the cloud and the cloud is one of the forms of nature.**[60]

According to Ibn al-ʿArabī, nature manifests itself to the cosmos only in and through its traces, remaining forever unseen and hidden in its essence.

> Nature is the highest, greatest mother of the cosmos, of whom the cosmos never sees the entity, only the effects, just as it never sees anything of the Real but its effects, never its entity.[61]

Ibn al-ʿArabī called this nature the 'highest and greatest mother' (*al-umm al-ʿāliyāt al-kubrā*),[62] which William Chittick interprets as 'the receptivity that allows the existent thing to become manifest' (thus treating it as the passive/receptive cosmic principle).[63]

---

[60] Ibn al-ʿArabī, *al-Futūḥāt al-makkiyya* (Beirut, n.d.), vol. 3, p. 420, English trans. in William C. Chittick, *The Sufi Path of Knowledge: Ibn al-ʿArabi's Metaphysics of Imagination* (New York, 1989), p. 140.

[61] Ibn al-ʿArabī, *Futūḥāt*, vol. 4, p.150, English trans. in Chittick, *Knowledge*, p. 141.

[62] See e.g. Ibn al-ʿArabī, *Futūḥāt*, vol. 4, p. 150.

[63] Chittick, *Knowledge*, p. 140.

The second nature receives the traces and effects of the first intellect. Ibn al-ʿArabī calls it 'the second mother' and the 'daughter of the greatest nature'. It acts as an intermediary between the universal soul and dust (*habāʾ*) (i.e., the prime matter).[64]

In a number of places, Ibn al-ʿArabī discussed the relationship between God's command and universal nature. He saw this relationship as like that between a man and a woman:

> A woman in relation to a man is like nature in relation to the divine command, since the woman is the locus of the existence of the entities of the children, just as nature in relation to the divine command is the locus of the manifestation of the entities of the corporeal bodies. Through it they are engendered and from it they become manifest. So there can be no command without nature and no nature without command. Hence, the engendered existence depends upon both.[65]

One notices that Ibn al-ʿArabī saw the main difference between command and nature in activity and passivity/receptivity, peculiar to each of them respectively. Therefore, he perceived the world of command as meaning the world in which activity dominates over passivity and the world of nature – the world in which passivity has the upper hand over activity. This domination, however, does not depend on the intensity of existence as such (as is the case with Ṣadrā).

In all likelihood, Ṣadrā would have agreed that nature is the breath of the Merciful. But he would have added that not everything that can be qualified as breath of the Merciful is nature. He understood nature as typifying the lowest kind of existence, the one which lacks permanence and stability altogether and, therefore, is forced to perpetually renew and reproduce itself.

Ṣadrā on Nature

In his *Risāla fī ḥudūth al-ʿālam* ('Treatise on the Origination of the World'), Ṣadrā provided the following definition of nature: '[Nature is]

---

[64] Ibid.

[65] Ibn al-ʿArabī, *Futūḥāt*, vol. 3, p. 90, English trans. in Chittick, *Knowledge*, p. 141.

a thing, whose reality consists in self-renewal (*tajaddud*) and flow (*sayalān*).'[66]

In the *Asrār al-āyāt*, we find a more expanded version of the same definition:

> Inevitably, among the existent substances must exist a flowing substance, self-renewing in its essence, the mode of whose existence consists in passing (*inqiḍā'*) and self-renewal, in such a way that it is impossible to conceive of fixity and continuance (*istimrār*), neither in respect of its existence, nor in respect of its non-existence . . . and this substance cannot be an immaterial and incorporeal one – otherwise the potency of preparedness [or predisposition] (*al-quwwa al-isti'dādiyya*) would not be [present] in it. On the contrary, it is a material substance, in which some sort of potency and some sort of act are present.[67]

In the first definition, nature is treated as a habitude of action, while in the second one it is the principle and source of change. The novelty of Ṣadrā's approach can be apprehended if we recollect that before him most philosophers believed the principle of change and renewal to be either motion or time, but not nature (which, however, was treated as the principle of motion). According to Ṣadrā, his predecessors (whom he does not name) failed to apprehend that motion is an attribute of nature and a concomitant of its existence, and that time is the measure of the self-renewal of the essence of nature. More importantly, they were unable to understand that, in its low-intensity spectrum, existence does not manifest itself otherwise than as, in and through this flowing affair (i.e., nature), whose 'marks' (*'alāmāt*) time and movement are.

> A gradual transition (literally: coming out) (*khurūj*) from potentiality to actuality constitutes the meaning of motion and [that of] its existence in mind, in conformity with the outside. That through which the transition from potentiality to actuality takes

---

[66] Ṣadr al-Dīn al-Shīrāzī, *Ḥudūth al-'ālam*, ed. M. Khājavī (Tehran, 1366 Sh./1987), p. 206.

[67] Ṣadr al-Dīn al-Shīrāzī, *Asrār al-āyāt*, ed. M. Khājavī (Tehran, 1981), pp. 84–85.

> place, is nature. The thing which receives [i.e., serves as the receptacle for] the transition, is matter. The transitioner (*makhraj*) [i.e., the maker of transition, its efficient cause] is another terrestrial or celestial substance. The measure of transition is time, whose [true] reality is nothing else than the measure of self-renewal and passing.[68]

To explain his point, Ṣadrā compared movement to an individual (*shakhṣ*) whose spirit is nature, and time to an individual whose spirit is perpetuality (*dahr*). He understood that nature relates to the soul, or rather to the intellect, as a ray relates to the sun, the former being individuated through the individuation of the latter.[69]

In a passage, crucial for the understanding of Ṣadrā's views on natural existence, he described the latter as a self-renewing and gradual (*tadrījī*) affair:

> An essentially self-renewing entity [which is the nearest agent of motion] is the kind of the existence of bodily nature, which has an intelligible reality with God and a gradual continuous ipseity in matter (which is a [purely] potential entity). In the same way as, according to the common belief of philosophers, existence itself is differently actualised in things in the aspect of strength and weakness, independence and need, priority and posteriority, some [individual] existences are gradual (*tadrījī*) in their essence and ipseity, not due to any attribute which is predicated to them. Such, for example, is the existence of bodily nature. And this kind of existence, because of its inability to perpetually last in its ipseity, is gradually actualising and self-renewing.[70]

Apparently, Ṣadrā believes that lasting and continuous persistence of an individual existence has something to do with its strength and intensity. Depending on the degree of the latter, this existence displays different properties. Low-intensity existences cannot actualise themselves at once and become fully present here and now. Instead, they require temporal and spatial continuity in order to actualise

68 Ṣadrā, *Ḥudūth*, p. 208.
69 Ibid., p. 228.
70 Ṣadrā, *Ḥudūth*, p. 253.

themselves and to display their properties. Or perhaps low-intensity existence itself generates tempo-spatial continuity, in which case time and space are nothing but concomitants of the said existence? If so, the reason for Ṣadrā's tacit dismissal of Mīr Dāmād's theory of perpetual creation is evident: in all likelihood, he considered time and perpetuity to be concomitant properties of the different spectra of the intensity of existence. Upon the decrease or increase of intensity, these properties convert one into another (time becoming perpetuity, and vice versa. And, more importantly, becoming turning being, and contrariwise).[71]

According to Ṣadrā, the border region between the act of nature and the act of soul is the 'beginning of the horizon of the animal' (*awā'il ufuq al-hayawān*). This border region, in his opinion, also separates material sensible engendered existents from immaterial formal imaginal ones.[72] Can this sensible material perpetually self-renewing entity, namely nature as understood by Ṣadrā, be described as a dead *λόγος*? In other words, is Ṣadrā's definition of nature compatible with that of Plotinus? The latter's vision of the world in general, and nature in particular, rests on a focused contemplation of the One, while Ṣadrā's intuition is that of perpetual flow of the natural being towards perfection. To Plotinus, the sensible universe comes into existence due to the impurity and alloying of contemplation. When the contemplating subject purifies itself, the sensible world disappears. In turn, to Ṣadrā, nature is a flow which brings the lower up and makes the unaware and unconscious aware and conscious. But, very much like Plotinus, Ṣadrā admitted that our need for sense experience is confined to the initial stages of perception and held that on higher stages the soul does not require the intermediacy of a sensible object in order to perceive the intelligible form/paradigm. Thus, Plotinus and Ṣadrā were in agreement that the realm of nature is one of semi-conscious and alloyed contemplation, wherefore the soul must leave it, making spiritual ascent to the intelligible. However, unlike Plotinus, Ṣadrā stressed

---

[71] I am not discussing here whether and/or how this conversion is possible. This issue will be dealt with in my forthcoming monograph on the school of Isfahan.

[72] Ṣadr al-Dīn al-Shīrāzī, *al-Ḥikma al-muta'āliyya fī al-asfār al-'aqliyya al-arba'a*, ed. R. Lutfī, I. Amīnī and F. Ummīd (3rd ed., Beirut, 1981), vol. 5, p. 347.

the positive aspect of nature: it is the gate that opens towards the realm of divinity and the principle of the flow which brings the unconscious towards consciousness.

Conclusion: An Attempt of Comparison

Does al-Kirmānī's teaching on two natures have anything in common with an outwardly similar theory of Ṣadrā? If yes, what exactly? The Ṣadrian theory apparently applies only to the higher animals, in particular, to human beings. According to it, there are two natures inherent in human beings, one of which emanates from the essence of the soul, being its level and faculty, whereas the other inheres in the elements and members of the body. The first obeys the soul willingly and spontaneously, while the second does it unwillingly and under compulsion.[73] Some similarity between al-Kirmānī's and Ṣadrā's teaching is evident: both thinkers discerned the active and the passive aspects of nature. However, in al-Kirmānī's system, nature represents an extension of the **universal** soul, whereas for Ṣadrā it is one of the lower levels of the **particular** soul or the particular soul in the aspect of its dependence on the particular body.[74]

In view of the above, is there detectable and provable evidence of the influence of al-Kirmānī on Ṣadrā, via Ibn al-ʿArabī or directly, as far as their views on nature are concerned? Or were they merely using common sources and depended on them?

If there was either a (direct or indirect) influence, or dependence on common sources, it should, most likely, be sought in the division of nature into the active and passive aspects and the elaboration on the role and function of each of them – the doctrine, which, as we have learnt, based on some scattered remarks made by Aristotle, was developed by Alexander of Aphrodisias, Philoponus and Simplicius, and later, in Islamic philosophy, elaborated by Abū Bishr Mattā b. Yūnus and, in particular, by Ḥamīd al-Dīn al-Kirmānī.

---

[73] Ṣadrā, *ʿArshiyya*, p. 233.

[74] Ṣadrā, *Asfār*, vol. 3, p. 67.

Not only was the latter surprisingly well informed about the teachings on nature of the Greek and the earlier Muslim philosophers (which is no wonder, given that he must have had access to the academic libraries of both Cairo and Baghdad),[75] but he also made significant contributions to them. His treatment of the problem of nature – and, indeed, the importance he assigned to it – was apparently dictated by the shift of the Ismaili cosmological paradigm from Platonism towards Aristotelianism, for which al-Kirmānī himself was primarily responsible (one can assume that al-Kirmānī's decision was influenced not only – and probably not so much – by his belief in the philosophical superiority of (the Arabic) Aristotle to (the Arabic) Plato but by his faith in its better suitability to the current ideological needs of the Fatimid empire, which was experiencing a certain degree of political and religious turbulence during al-Ḥākim's reign). This shift implied, among other changes, the attribution of the role of the principle of motion in the sublunar world to nature, instead of soul.[76] Remarkably, al-Kirmānī would sometimes identify nature with soul (and life),[77] but at other times treat them as two different hypostases[78] – which might

---

[75] On the Fāṭimid libraries in Cairo, see Daniel De Smet, 'Les bibliothèques ismaéliennes et la question du néoplatonisme ismaélien', in Cristina D'Ancona, (ed.), *The Libraries of the Neoplatonists. Proceedings of the Meeting of the European Science Foundation Network "Late Antiquity and Arabic Thought. Patterns in the Constitution of European Culture" held in Strasbourg, March 12–14, 2004* (Philosophia Antiqua 107) (Leiden, 2007), pp. 481–492. On the philosophical libraries in early Abbasid Baghdad, see Gerhard Endress' article in the same volume: 'Building the Library of Arabic Philosophy. Platonism and Aristotelianism in the Sources of al-Kindī', pp. 319–350.

[76] As shown by Johansen, Aristotle does not treat the world as a single ensouled/animated being. However, he appeared to believe that the circle which defines the motions of the stars is ensouled, as are all planets. The ultimate physical source of motion, according to Aristotle, is the motion of the outer celestial sphere. See Thomas K. Johansen, 'From Plato's *Timaeus* to Aristotle's *De Caelo*: The Case of the Missing World Soul', in Alan C. Boven and Christian Wildberg (ed.), *New Perspectives on Aristotle's* De caelo (Leiden, 2009), pp. 9–28, in particular pp. 17 and 26–27.

[77] Al-Kirmānī, *Rāḥat*, p. 277, l. 11; cf. De Smet, *Quiétude*, p. 324.

[78] E.g., in Ḥamīd al-Dīn al-Kirmānī, *Kitāb al-Riyāḍ fi'l-ḥukm bayna al-ṣādayn ṣāḥibayn al-iṣlāḥ wa'l-nuṣra*, ed. 'Ārif Tāmir (Beirut, 1960), p. 126, l. 9–10; cf. De Smet, *Quiétude*, p. 251.

testify to his awareness of the difficulties the aforementioned shift involved. It seems that when he identified nature with soul, he meant the active aspect of the former; conversely, when he equated it with prime matter, he referred to its passive aspect.

Ṣadrā's hypothesis of two different natures, one of which obeys the soul willingly (because it is part and level of the soul), but the other unwillingly and as if by compulsion (since it is part of the body), can be viewed as a particularisation of al-Kirmānī's theory on the active and passive aspects of the universal nature. In our present state of knowledge, it cannot be proved that Ṣadrā had either direct or mediated access to the *Rāḥat al-ʿaql* (where al-Kirmānī's theory is found in its most detailed form), or any of other his texts. As we know, the Ismaili community guarded its manuscripts closely. However, some of al-Kirmānī's works, or their paraphrases/summaries may have found their way outside the Ismaili community. According to some scholars[79] when, due to his conflict with the Twelver jurists in his native Shīrāz, Ṣadrā had to leave the city and go into hiding, he may have sought refuge with the Ismailis in Kahak or Anjudān, and may have had access to some Ismaili texts there.[80]

Alternatively, he may have acquired his information from some source, which was also used by al-Kirmānī. I would venture to say that, in that case, it is likely to have been the Arabic translation or paraphrase of Alexander of Aphrodisias or Philoponus' commentary

---

[79] Ibrāhīm Dihgān, *Ta'rīkh-i Arāk*, with the assistance of A. Hudā'ī and a preface by Īraj Afshār (Tehran, 1386 Sh./2007), p. 326.

[80] The hypothesis demands further investigation. We possess no detailed information about the nature of the conflict. According to the oral tradition (which for generations persisted, e.g., among the descendants of Ṣadrā's commentator, Mullā Ismāʿīl al-Iṣfahānī Darb-i Kūshkī 'Wāḥid al-ʿAyn' (d. 1277/1860)), the conflict resulted in Ṣadrā's flight from his native city and his going into hiding in a remote mountain area (rather than in a formal exile). He is said to have resided for a while in the village of Kahak. There are several villages bearing this name is central Iran. However, the large village of this name in the agricultural area near Qum is by no means suitable as a hiding place. Hence, it is more likely that Ṣadrā sought refuge in another Kahak, a remote village in the mountainous area near Maḥallāt, populated by the Ismailis which was for a while the seat of the Ismaili imam.

on Aristotle's *Physics*, or some other work which relies on these commentaries/paraphrases.

If we accept Alessandro Linguiti's basic criterion for the distinction between the Neoplatonic and Aristotelian approaches to the problem of nature (namely, that the Neoplatonists treat nature as a universal principle, which primarily governs the physical world **as a whole**, and only secondarily the individual entities, while the Aristotelians typically view nature as an individual nature of each entity),[81] we have to conclude that Ṣadrā moved his teaching on nature much closer to textbook Aristotelianism than al-Kirmānī did – probably because he believed the latter to provide a convenient starting point for the introduction of his most original (and, simultaneously, most controversial) doctrine, of substantial motion (by means of which motion we, human beings, can allegedly travel from the realm of becoming to the realm of pure being).

81 Linguiti, '*Physis* as *Heimarmene*', p. 175.

PART FOUR

MYSTICAL TRENDS

11

Early Ismailis and Other Muslims: Polemics and Borrowing in *Kitāb al-Kashf*[1]

Mushegh Asatryan
(University of Calgary)

Introduction

Kitāb al-Kashf is considered one of the earliest sources of Ismaili literature.[2] Attributed to the Ismaili *dāʿī* Jaʿfar b. Manṣūr al-Yaman (d. ca. 346/957), it is one of the very few surviving texts composed before the rise of the Fatimids. Still, its peculiar, uneven structure has led many scholars to conclude that it was either the work of numerous authors, or that it was not written as a single work, and that its various parts were probably only later combined and edited to form a single text.[3]

---

[1] I would like to express my gratitude to Fârès Gillon, who generously shared with me his knowledge of *Kitāb al-Kashf* while I was working on this article. My thanks are due to Daniel Beben, Geoffrey Moseley, Rodrigo Adem, Necati Alkan and Christopher Anzalone for their kind advice and help with acquiring research materials. I also wish to thank the anonymous reviewers for their invaluable suggestions. Finally, I am grateful to Orkhan Mir-Kasimov for his careful reading of an earlier draft of this article and for his valuable comments.

[2] It was edited twice: first by Rudolf Strothmann in 1952 from two manuscripts, and for a second time in 1984 by Muṣṭafā Ghālib, from one manuscript. In this article I will be using a reprint of the first edition (London, 2010), while referring to Ghālib's edition where it offers valuable insights.

[3] H. Ansari, 'Chand matn-i muhimm az ṭayf-hā-yi mukhtalif-i Shīʿī dar bārah-yi qā'imiyyat: Kitāb al-Kashf wa māhiyyat-i ān', available online at http://ansari.kateban.com/post/2174 (accessed on 4 June 2017); F. Gillon, 'Aperçus sur les origines de l'ismaélisme à travers le *Kitāb al-Kašf*, attribué au dâʿî Ǧaʿfar ibn Manṣūr al-Yaman', *Ishraq*, 4 (2013), pp. 90–92; for some of the textual peculiarities of the text, see idem, 'Une version ismaélienne de *ḥadīṯs* imamites. Nouvelles perspectives sur le traité II du *Kitāb al-Kašf* attribué à Ǧaʿfar ibn Manṣūr al-Yaman (Xe s.)', *Arabica*, 59 (2012),

What complicates the possible attribution or dating of the text even further is the existence of numerous elements that echo the teachings of other currents within Shiʿism, namely the teachings of the so-called Shiʿi 'extremists' of Iraq, known in Arabic as *ghulāt* (henceforth Ghulat), and of their successors in Syria, the Nuṣayrīs, who inherited much of the latter's textual heritage and ideas.[4] Finally, Epistle Four of the book contains no mention of any specifically Ismaili ideas, and bears no thematic or formal continuity with other parts of *Kitāb al-Kashf*, suggesting a copying and an insertion from an altogether different text. In its turn, part of the same chapter, almost identically occurs in a text stemming from the Nuṣayrī-Ghulat tradition, *Kitāb al-Haft wa'l-aẓilla* (Chapter 59), where it also seems to be a quite unexplained insertion.[5]

In the pages that follow two of the features of *Kitāb al-Kashf* will be studied which will provide some clarity as to the origin of certain of its parts, and will clarify some of its references and terminology. First, the possible connection between the author of *Kitāb al-Kashf* and the Ghulat will be examined through a close reading of the seemingly Ghulat ideas that it contains. Second, the provenance of the enigmatic Fourth Chapter of *Kitāb al-Kashf* will be considered along with its possible connection to various kinds of Ghulat and Nuṣayrī literature. For ease of reference, the Appendix provides a critical edition of Chapter 59 of *Kitāb al-Haft*, where the differences between it and Epistle Four of *Kitāb al-Haft* are marked. Each section of this chapter concludes with a discussion of the possible historical routes that have led to these two yet unexplained features of *Kitāb al-Kashf*. Because the Ghulat and the Nuṣayrīs shared much in common, when discussing texts and ideas that belong to both traditions, they are referred to as 'Ghulat-Nuṣayrī'.

---

pp. 486–487; W. Madelung, 'Das Imamat in der frühen ismailitischen Lehre', *Der Islam*, 37 (1961), p. 53; H. Halm, *Kosmologie und Heilslehre der frühen Ismaʿīlīya: eine Studie zur islamischen Gnosis* (Wiesbaden, 1978), pp. 18–52; D. Hollenberg, *Beyond the Qur'ān: Early Ismāʿīlī Ta'wīl and the Secrets of the Prophets* (Columbia, 2016), pp. 45–46.

[4] Cf. Ansari, 'Chand matn-i muhimm'; Halm, *Kosmologie*, pp. 149–153.

[5] To my knowledge, none of the scholars who have studied the text have noted this commonality, and it was brought to my attention by Rodrigo Adem, whom I sincerely thank. I briefly discuss the place of this chapter in *Kitāb al-Haft wa'l-aẓilla* in my *Controversies in Formative Shiʿi Islam: The Ghulat Muslims and their Beliefs* (London, 2016), pp. 38–39.

The discussion of the Ghulat elements in *Kitāb al-Kashf* aims to go beyond the study of just one Ismaili text, however. Its aim is to demonstrate a fruitful way of approaching the notion of influences in the religious and intellectual history of Islam. Hitherto, the existence of the elements of one school or religious group in the texts of another has been mostly interpreted as a matter of either borrowing, influence, or of a surviving substratum. In either case, systems of thought have been treated as self-contained entities which interact with one another, sometimes contaminating each other, sometimes not. The discussion here aims to show that it is much more fruitful to look at texts and ideas as the products of human agents interacting with one another, and that they often reflect their political orientations rather than simply their personal convictions.[6]

Kitāb al-Kashf and Polemics Against the Ghulat

Anyone acquainted with the texts of the Ghulat-Nuṣayrīs will detect in *Kitāb al-Kashf*, especially in Epistles One and Three, numerous elements that recall Ghulat-Nuṣayrī terminology and ideas. For example, the text discusses certain *aytām* (sg. *yatīm*, literally meaning 'unique'), the first two of which are the Prophet's famous companions Abū Dharr and Miqdād.[7] The author does not explain what the term means, but in numerous texts of the Ghulat-Nuṣayrī tradition *yatīm* denotes one of the degrees of the spiritual hierarchy of believers and the two persons most commonly associated with the position are Abū Dharr and Miqdād.[8] Further, the term *ḥijāb* denotes in *Kitāb al-Kashf* a veil,

---

[6] For a critique of the 'influence paradigm' in Islamic Studies, see H. Abdulsater, *Shi'i Doctrine, Mu'tazili Theology: al-Sharīf al-Murtaḍā and Imami Discourse* (Edinburgh, 2017), p. 6; more broadly, see Q. Skinner, 'Meaning and Understanding in the History of Ideas', *History and Theory*, 8, 1 (1969), pp. 3–53.

[7] *Kitāb al-Kashf*, p. 62.

[8] E.g., Muḥammad b. Sinān, *Kitāb al-Ḥujub wa'l-anwār*, in *Silsilat al-turāth al-'alawī*, ed. Abū Mūsā and Shaykh Mūsā (Lebanon, 2006), vol. 6, p. 22; *Umm al-kitāb*, ed. Wladimir Ivanow, *Der Islam*, 23 (1936), para. 198; Ḥusayn b. Ḥamdān al-Khaṣībī *al-Risāla al-Rastbāshiyya*, in *Silsilat al-turāth al-'alawī*, ed. Abū Mūsā and Shaykh Mūsā (Lebanon, 2006), vol. 2, p. 27.

wherein the inner (*bāṭin*) part of God's knowledge is hidden.[9] This vaguely recalls the usage of the term in Ghulat-Nuṣayrī texts, denoting the physical bodies into which God enters, thereby 'veiling' himself.[10] Finally, the several references to famous Shiʿi 'extremist' and the alleged author of numerous texts of Ghulat provenance, Mufaḍḍal b. ʿUmar al-Juʿfī (active in the late second/eighth century), suggest another possible connection between the Ismaili text and the milieu in which the Ghulat texts were produced.[11] However, beyond these occasional uses of terminology and personal names, no firm evidence exists that the author or authors of *Kitāb al-Kashf* may have 'borrowed' terminology from Ghulat-Nuṣayrī writings, and their occurrence may be an instance where a common inventory of themes and terms was shared by various early Shiʿi groups.

There are, however, two ideas found in *Kitāb al-Kashf* that betray a rather direct connection with the Ghulat tradition. The first is the notion of the reincarnation of souls, which in Arabic, and especially in the Ghulat-Nusayrī tradition, is mainly expressed by two terms, each denoting a slightly different form of the concept. One is *tanāsukh*, referring to the rebirth of human souls into other *human* bodies; the other is *maskh* or *masūkhiyya*, indicating the rebirth of human souls into sub-human forms, such as animals, plants, and inanimate objects.[12] And the second is the idea of God taking on a 'body'. Not only does the discussion in *Kitāb al-Kashf* closely resemble the ones

---

9 *Kitāb al-Kashf*, pp. 144–145.

10 E.g., *Kitāb al-Ashbāḥ wa'l-aẓilla*, ed. Mushegh Asatryan as 'An Early Shiʿi Cosmology: *Kitāb al-Ashbāḥ wa'l-aẓilla* and its Milieu', *Studia Islamica*, 110 (2015), paras. 4, 6–8; Muḥammad b. ʿAlī al-Jillī, *Ḥāwī'l-asrār*, in *Silsilat al-turāth al-ʿalawī* (Lebanon, 2006), vol. 2, p. 164.

11 For a brief discussion of the possibly Ghulat elements, see Ansari, 'Chand matn-i muhimm'.

12 The references in the Ghulat literature are too numerous to list all, for some examples, see *Kitāb al-Ashbāḥ*, paras. 11, 13, 45, et passim; *Kitāb al-Ṣirāṭ*, ed. al-Munṣif b. ʿAbd al-Jalīl (Beirut, 2005), pp. 129, 138; for a general discussion, with a list of references, see Asatryan, *Controversies*, pp. 149–154. Some sources offer a more elaborate terminology for the types of rebirth or transformation, depending on the type of creatures one turns into, see al-Khaṣībī, *al-Risāla al-Rastbāshiyya*, p. 65.

found in the Ghulat-Nuṣayrī tradition, but there is even a direct reference to the fact that the ideas come from among the 'extremists among Muslims' (*al-ghulāt min al-muslimīn*).[13] Still, as clear as the connection between the occurrence of the idea and terminology in the Ismaili text is to that found among the 'extremists among Muslims', just what exactly this 'connection' indicates must still be determined. In his *Kosmologie und Heilslehre*, Heinz Halm implies that the occurrence of the originally Nuṣayrī idea of *Seelenwanderung* in this Ismaili text is simply the trace of an earlier layer that has survived 'despite the Ismaili redaction'.[14] A close reading of the passages on metempsychosis and God's bodily forms, found mainly in the first, but also in the third and fifth Epistles of *Kitāb al-Kashf*, however, betrays not the remnants of an unsuccessfully erased Ghulat-Nuṣayrī influence, but instead a polemic against the Ghulat-Nuṣayrīs who articulate both notions in rather direct, physical ways.[15] Let us examine the passages in *Kitāb al-Kashf* more closely.

The first fragment discussing metamorphosis is found almost at the very beginning of the text, in Epistle One. After the encomium that opens the text, the author proceeds to admonish the reader to be faithful to God and to His friends (*awliyā'*, sg. *walī*), and to keep the secrets of God within the circle of the elect and not to divulge them among the undeserving.[16] Slightly later,[17] he goes on to quote Q 2:6: 'As for those who disbelieve, it makes no difference whether you warn them or not: they will not believe',[18] explaining that these are the adversaries (*aḍdād*, sg. *ḍidd*) and their followers. The idea of metempsychosis comes up after the author quotes the next verse of the same sura, Q 2:7: 'God has sealed their hearts and their ears, and their eyes are

13 *Kitāb al-Kashf*, p. 56.

14 Halm, *Kosmologie*, p. 150; I myself have mistakenly viewed the instances of Ghulat-related terminology in *Kitāb al-Kashf* as indicating that they are possibly of Ghulat provenance (*Controversies*, p. 32).

15 Cf. the references above.

16 *Kitāb al-Kashf*, pp. 51–52.

17 *Kitāb al-Kashf*, p. 53.

18 Here and henceforth, the Qur'anic translations are by Abdel Haleem (Oxford, 2004).

covered. They will have great torment'. This torment, the author explains, comes in the form of metamorphosis (*bi'l-masūkhiyya*, lit. 'as metamorphosis') and of the numerous bodies (*tarākīb*, sg. *tarkīb*) and the levels of hellish suffering.[19] The punishment is meted out specifically on those who reject the truth after becoming aware of it, those who enlist in the propaganda for truth (*daʿwat al-ḥaqq*) but are enticed to leave it, thus becoming 'like animals' (*mithl al-bahāʾim*) who have no knowledge of truth or religion, and are deprived of its benefits.

What of metamorphosis and the 'degrees'? The author henceforth continues to explain that *masūkhiyya* refers to the loss of the lofty position of knowledge and to descent into ignorance. And to underscore the correctness of his own explanation of the term (and, as we shall see later, to juxtapose it to alternative, 'incorrect' explanations), the author ends with the phrase: 'and this is the correct meaning of the reference to *masūkhiyya*'.[20] In Epistle Five, the idea is explained in very similar terms, and the author stresses the point that transformation into subhuman forms (in this case, into dogs and swine) is just a simile.[21] A similarly immaterial description of *masūkhiyya* concludes Epistle Three, where it is said to be a person's:

---

19 The phrase that expounds on the Qur'anic verse 2:7 is slightly ambiguous, but it is likely that it refers to the levels of suffering in hell (*Kitāb al-Kashf*, p. 53; ed. Ghālib, p. 25). Thus, after the sentence promising that the damned will 'have great torment', *wa-lahum ʿadhābun ʿaẓīm*, the author explains: *yaʿnī bi'l-masūkhiyya wa'l-tarākīb bi'l-ṭabaqāt bi-alīm al-adrāk*. The first part (*yaʿnī bi'l-masūkhiyya wa'l-tarākīb*) may be translated as 'He [i.e. God in the Qur'an] means [their torment will be] in metamorphosis and in bodies'. The word *adrāk* (both editors mistakenly transliterate it as *idrāk*, which does not fit the context; interestingly, Ghālib corrects this in a footnote, p. 53, n. 4, but his explanation does not sufficiently clarify the term) is the plural of *darak* or *dark*, which refers to one of the levels of Hell (cf. *Lisān al-ʿArab*, s.v. *d-r-k*; cf. also Q 4:145). Given its position, the phrase *bi'l-ṭabaqāt bi-alīm al-adrāk* modifies *bi'l-masūkhiyya wa'l-tarākīb*, specifying how exactly the torment 'in metamorphosis and in shapes' occurs: 'in the stages, in the painful levels (of Hell)'. And given that *adrāk* refers particularly to the levels of Hell, *ṭabaqāt* must also refer to the stages of Hell specifically. Having been placed immediately after *ṭabaqāt*, which has a more general meaning, and may refer to the degrees of anything, *alīm al-adrāk* comes to specify exactly what stages (of Hell), and what *types* of levels (painful, *alīm*).

20 *Kitāb al-Kashf*, p. 54.

21 Ibid., p. 136.

> departure from one stage (*ṭabaqa*) to another; that is, now he is considered a Muslim and a friend of God's Prophet, God's blessings upon him and his family, then he leaves that stage for the stage of the ignorant, and they push him from the territory of knowledge to the level of infidels (*kuffār*); who push him from the territory of obedience and belief to the level of idolaters (*mushrikīn*), for he has considered his own choice equal to God's command, and he saw the devil, who led him astray and went astray with him. This is the meaning of the reference to metamorphosis (*maskh*), which is the change from a laudable (*maḥmūda*) condition to these blameworthy (*madhmūma*) ones.[22]

Now, in all of said cases, the stress is that the correct interpretation of metamorphosis is not actual rebirth from one physical form to another, but a person's passage from a loftier standing to a baser one and his deprivation of the true knowledge of God. Earlier the idea of metamorphosis as one of the teachings of the Ghulat was mentioned, and although they are not named in the passages on *masūkhiyya*, the part that describes God's appearance to human beings names them directly, while very accurately describing their teachings about it and rejecting their view. The author approaches the theme through an interpretation of Q 24:35, 'God is the light of the heavens and earth', where he quotes Jaʿfar al-Ṣādiq as explaining that God's miracles (*āyāt*) brought forth ten domes (*qibāb*, sg. *qubba*)[23] of light, seven of which are the *nāṭiq*s, and three are the *kālī*, the *raqīb*, and the *bāb* (all of which are Ismaili terms). These ten, the author further explains, are the veil for God's concealed knowledge (*sutrat ʿilm Allāh al-maknūn*),

> He indicated them with this name; it is not the way the Christians say, [namely,] that the body of Jesus is a frame (*haykal*), in which the Creator has descended onto the earth, walking among his servants – God is much higher than that! Similar is what the extremists (*ghulāt*) among Muslims say about the imams and the prophets, [namely,] that their bodies are likewise frames

[22] Ibid., p. 128.

[23] This term occurs in Ghulat texts as well, but there it denotes the cycles of history, which bears no similarity to the usage here, see, e.g., *Kitāb al-Ṣirāṭ*, p. 203.

> (*hayākil*), in which the Creator veils Himself and descends upon earth. [Rather], they are domes (*qibāb*) and positions (*maqāmāt*), which enclose (*taḥwīhi*) Him on earth, and He dwells (*yaqūmu*) in the body of each one of them in His time. God is glorious and much loftier than how the unjust speak of him![24]

Here the author of the lines does not specify how exactly his vision of God's descent into the ten *qibāb* differs from the Ghulat (and Christian) idea of God's descent into human flesh, but for our purposes it is sufficient to point out that he is quite clearly engaged in a polemic against their teachings and is at pains to distance his own teachings from theirs. And while the Ghulat are directly named only in the discussion of God's dwelling in human shape, it is safe to assume that the discussion of metamorphosis is likewise directed against their version of the teaching. For one thing, his description of the idea as professed by them is rather accurate. For another, the passage about God's dwelling in human shape, where the Ghulat are mentioned by name, together with the passages on *masūkhiyya*, are situated close to each other in Epistle One of *Kitāb al-Kashf*, suggesting they are part of a single discussion.[25] Finally, an interesting detail immediately preceding the discussion of *masūkhiyya* closely echoes the way in which some of the early heresiographers described the Ghulat.

After the solemn opening of Epistle One, the author says that the first thing that a believer needs, pertaining to religion and the knowledge of truth, is fidelity (*amāna*) to God and His friends (*awliyā'*). He then tells the reader that he takes the covenant (*mīthāq*) of God from him, and forbids that which God has forbidden to

---

[24] *Kitāb al-Kashf*, p. 56. Another instance where God takes on human form is found in Epistle Five, which states that 'God shows (*yuẓhir*) Himself to His creation in seventy frames (*sab'īna haykalan*)', *Kitāb al-Kashf*, p. 141. And although there is no polemic against, and no direct reference to the Ghulat, both the term denoting the bodies that God takes on, and the idea itself, recall the Ghulat teachings about God dwelling in human shape, also frequently termed *haykal*, e.g., Muḥammad b. Nuṣayr, *Kitāb al-Akwār al-nūrāniyya wa'l-adwār al-rūḥāniyya*, in *Silsilat al-turāth al-'alawī*, ed. Abū Mūsā and Shaykh Mūsā (Lebanon, 2006), vol. 1, p. 162; *Kitāb al-Ṣirāṭ*, pp. 159–178.

[25] *Kitāb al-Kashf*, pp. 53–56.

His prophets, apostles, gates (*abwab*), and proofs (*ḥujaj*).[26] He then continues:

> Likewise your father, who has given you drink, and your brother, who has been breastfed together with you, [both forbid] things such as carrion, blood, and pork, [and] the divulging of it [. . .] and the writing it down except for a truthful deserving believer.[27]

The discussion of how the believers should not divulge the truth to those undeserving of it continues for another page, then the passage about *masūkhiyya* begins. The notion that true knowledge must be kept secret from the undeserving is rather common in Ismailism, connected to the idea of the two levels of truth, the external (*ẓāhir*), available to all, and the esoteric, hidden (*bāṭin*), which is the preserve of the elite.[28] What further reaffirms the idea that the passage on *masūkhiyya* that follows this discussion is directed specifically against the Ghulat is the passing enumeration of the things that the author forbids to his reader (just as God has forbidden to His chosen one): carrion, blood, and pork (*al-mayta al-dam wa-laḥm al-khinzīr*).

These three items are prohibited in three Qurʾanic verses (Q 16:115; 2:173; 5:3), where they are mentioned in the same order. And one of the most commonly recurring accusations against the Ghulat in the early Islamic heresiographies is that they considered these three things, together with some others prohibited by Islam, as permissible. Three of these heresiographers, al-Nawbakhtī (d. between 300/912–13 and 310/922–22), Abu'l-Ḥasan al-Ashʿarī (d. 324/935–36), and Saʿd b. ʿAbd Allāh al-Qummī (late third–early fourth/tenth century), repeat the phrase verbatim, in their descriptions of the beliefs of, respectively, the early second/eighth century Shiʿi 'extremist' Muʿammar b. Rashīd,

---

[26] Ibid., pp. 51–52.

[27] Ibid., p. 52; a question that is beyond the scope of this essay, but nonetheless an interesting one, is whether the 'father' and the 'brother' mentioned in the passage are used in the literal sense or whether they denote spiritual ranks of some kind.

[28] Hollenberg, *Beyond the Qurʾān*, pp. 16, 64; F. Daftary, *The Ismāʿīlīs: Their History and Doctrines* (Cambridge, 2nd ed., 2007), p. 129.

his roughly contemporary 'extremist' Abū Manṣūr al-ʿIjlī, and their contemporaries, a group known as Ḥarbiyya.

1. [Muʿammar] declared permissible (*aḥalla*) adultery, theft, the drinking of wine, carrion, blood pork, sex with one's mother.[29]
2. [Abū Manṣūr al-ʿIjlī] declared permissible (*istaḥalla*) women and things that are forbidden (*al-maḥārim*), and declared this permissible for his friends and claimed that carrion, blood, pork, wine, gambling (*maysir*) and other forbidden things are permissible.[30]
3. They [the Ḥarbiyya] claimed that he [ʿAbd Allāh b. Muʿāwiya] declared as permissible (*aḥalla*) carrion,[31] blood, pork.[32]

In various combinations, these three items are found in other accounts by these authors as well, together with some other of the abominations that the Ghulat allegedly viewed as permissible.[33]

To sum up, it is now clear that the author of (some parts of) *Kitāb al-Kashf* describes some of the beliefs that he himself endorses, namely,

---

29 Al-Nawbakhtī, *Firaq al-Shīʿa*, ed. Hellmut Ritter (Istanbul, 1931), p. 39.

30 Al-Ashʿarī, *Maqālāt al-islāmiyyin*, ed. Hellmut Ritter (Wiesbaden, 1980), p. 10.

31 Here it is phrased as *laḥm al-mayta*, lit. 'the flesh of carrion', as opposed to simply *mayta*.

32 Saʿd al-Qummī, *Kitāb al-Maqālāt wa'l-firaq*, ed. Muḥammad Jawād Mashkūr (Tehran, 1963), p. 41.

33 ʿAbd al-Qāhir al-Baghdādī, *al-Farq bayn al-firaq* (Beirut, 1402/1982), p. 244; al-Ashʿarī, *Maqālāt*, 6; al-Qummī, *Kitāb al-Maqālāt*, p. 53. For a discussion of references to the Ghulat's antinomianism in the accounts of the heresiographers, and in original Ghulat works, see Asatryan, *Controversies*, p. 161; Asatryan, 'Of Wine, Sex, and Other Abominations: Accusations of Libertinism in Early Islamic Iraq' (forthcoming). Another case of Ghulat-related terminology (but not necessarily of Ghulat 'influence') is the use of *muqaṣṣira*, 'those who fall short', to denote those Shiʿis who fall short of the knowledge of truth. As we know, the Ghulat called those Shiʿis who did not accept their teachings (and perhaps in response to their charges of extremism) as *muqaṣṣira*. True, the author of *Kitāb al-Kashf* uses this term to denote those who fall short of accepting *his own* version of truth, not that of the Ghulat, but the use of a specific term such as this, in conjunction with what was discussed above, is another indication that the author is dealing here with ideas pertaining to the Ghulat-*muqaṣṣira* polemics, see pp. 54, 159, 161; cf. Ansari, 'Chand matn-i muhimm'; on the term *taqṣīr*, see M. H. Gerami, *Nakhustīn munāsibāt-i fikrī-yi tashayyuʿ: bāzkhānī-yi mafhūm-i ghuluw dar andīsha-yi jarayānhā-yi mutaqaddim-i imāmī* (Tehran, 2012), pp. 189–194.

the idea of God's human representatives on earth, and the notion of *masūkhiyya*. In both cases he is adamant that these are not physical phenomena – whereby God descends upon earth in human flesh, or the human soul is reborn, moving from one physical body to another – but spiritual ones. And in both cases, it is clear that the people the author is trying to distance his group from are those whom early Muslim heresiographers called Shiʿi 'extremists' (*ghulāt*), for some of their 'extreme' ideas. In the discussion of God's human representatives, this becomes clear after the author directly names the group ('the extremists among Muslims'). And in case of the discussion of *masūkhiyya*, it becomes apparent, on the one hand, from the close similarity (though without naming) between the beliefs of the Ghulat and how *Kitāb al-Kashf*'s author describes the 'incorrect' perception of the idea, including both the content and the wording. Finally, the passage preceding the discussion of *masūkhiyya* and God's human forms lists, among the forbidden things, the chief sins that the heresiographers had attributed to the Ghulat, further indicating that the group the author has in mind is precisely this one.

It has already been noted that according to some scholars, *Kitāb al-Kashf* is not a unified text but that its six different epistles were composed by different persons, or by the same person but on different occasions. This, of course, raises legitimate concerns about the relationship between the passages discussed above that are found in different parts of the text, namely, Epistles One, Three and Five. Still, the possibility of the different origins of *Kitāb al-Kashf*'s various epistles notwithstanding, there are, it can be argued, grounds to view these passages as the work either of the same author, or, at the very least, as having been subjected to later editorial interference by the same editor. For not only do they contain similar vocabulary to refer to the process of metamorphosis (*maskh*, *masūkhiyya*) and the bodies into which one is 'reborn' (*haykal*, pl. *hayākil*);[34] but what is more, the second and third mentions of *masūkhiyya*, in Epistles Three and Five, are accompanied with the expressions, respectively, 'an explanation of this [i.e. *masūkhiyya*] has already preceded . . .', and 'as already explained

34 Apart from the abovementioned passages, see also p. 141, which discusses God's appearance in human *hayākil*.

above'.[35] This either means that all three passages are penned by the same author, who refers back to his earlier discussions of the same subject; or, that an editor inserted this feature, noting the earlier occurrences of the idea. And although speculations about the overall structure and history of *Kitāb al-Kashf* are beyond the scope of this essay, this feature may be indicative of the history of the composition of the text. As such, it strongly suggests the common origin of the three chapters where the anti-Ghulat polemic is found.

Despite the rather thin historical evidence for the history of early Ismailis, and of their relations with other Shiʿi groups, it is possible to offer a historical contextualisation of the anti-Ghulat polemic found in *Kitāb al-Kashf*. Whether it is the work of Jaʿfar b. Manṣūr al-Yaman or not, many of the scholars who have studied this text agree that it is likely it was composed in pre-Fatimid times, i.e. before the fourth/tenth century. This was a period when the Ghulat as a group were still active in Iraq,[36] and so were some of the early Ismaili agents. Going back a century, there is evidence of contact between Ismāʿīl b. Jaʿfar, the sixth Shiʿi imam Jaʿfar al-Ṣādiq's son and the eponym of the Ismailis, and some of the Ghulat of his time.[37] Whether these episodes of contact, or stories about them, were the cause of the anxiety of the author of *Kitāb al-Kashf* regarding his group being associated with the Ghulat, is impossible to ascertain. Still, during the time when the Ismaili propaganda (*daʿwa*) in Iraq began, i.e. in the second part of the third/ninth century, the Ghulat were very present here and many of them were prominent members of the Shiʿi community.[38] If indeed

---

[35] *Kitāb al-Kashf*, pp. 128, 136.

[36] Asatryan, *Controversies*, pp. 79–135; H. Abdulsater, 'Dynamics of Absence: Twelver Shiʿism during the Minor Occultation', *ZDMG*, 161, 2 (2011), pp. 312–331; L. Massignon, 'Recherches sur les Shiʿites extrémistes à Baghdad à la fin du troisième siècle de l'Hégire', in *Opera Minora*, Youakim Moubarac (ed.), vol. 1 (Paris, 1969), pp. 523–526; on the dynamics within the Shiʿi community at that time, see M. A. Amir-Moezzi, 'Knowledge is Power: Interpretations and Implications of the Miracle in Early Imamism', in his *Spirituality of Shiʿi Islam* (London, 2011), pp. 225–227.

[37] Abū Ḥātim al-Rāzī, *Kitāb al-Zīna*, in ʿAbd Allāh al-Sāmarrāʾī, *al-Ghuluww wa al-firaq al-ghāliya* (Baghdad, 1972), p. 289; Daftary, *The Ismāʿīlīs*, pp. 91–92. For a recent discussion, see my *Controversies*, pp. 51–52.

[38] Asatryan, *Controversies*, pp. 79–82.

Kitāb al-Kashf was composed during pre-Fatimid times, the author's strong emphasis that certain teachings of his group are certainly distinct from those of the Ghulat, may be explained by the fact that the two groups, the Ismailis and the Ghulat, lived in proximity to each other in Iraq. And because the teachings of the Ghulat were widely known and criticised,[39] the author of the Ismaili treatise was at pains to show that his own use, e.g., of terms such as *masūkhiyya*, has nothing to do with that of the Ghulat. Conversely, the anti-Ghulat polemic may serve as a further indication that *Kitāb al-Kashf*, or certain of its parts, were indeed composed in pre-Fatimid times. It furthermore suggests the place of their composition, namely in Iraq, where the Ghulat were active, and where the early Ismaili propaganda was then unfolding.

The Letters of the Alphabet and Epistle Four: Nuṣayrī Borrowing?

If the description of metamorphosis and God's representation in human form turned out to be not an influence by, but a polemic against, the Ghulat, there is an instance in *Kitāb al-Kashf* that suggests direct borrowing from another text. This is in Epistle Four,[40] which drastically departs from the remaining parts of the text both in its content and in its style of exposition.

One difference between Epistle Four and the rest of *Kitāb al-Kashf* is the use of *isnād*s, which open the two stories comprising this chapter. No other part of *Kitāb al-Kashf* contains any use of transmitter chains. Only in a handful of cases are the names of Jaʿfar al-Ṣādiq, Mufaḍḍal al-Juʿfī, Jābir b. Yazīd al-Juʿfī, and an anonymous 'sage' (*al-ḥakīm*) evoked to lend credence to this or that statement,[41] but even in this case, the use of a single name does not resemble a real *isnād*. The main difference, however, setting this chapter apart from all the other parts of *Kitāb al-Kashf*, and suggesting separate authorship, is its content.

---

[39] Some of the heresiographic works mentioning the Ghulat are noted above, p. 7.

[40] *Kitāb al-Kashf*, pp. 130–132.

[41] Ibid., pp. 56, 61, 77, 80, 114, 119, 121, 122.

Unlike the remaining parts of *Kitāb al-Kashf*, which consist mostly of theological discussions on various themes, such as the 'speaking imams' or the degrees of believers, the two reports that comprise Epistle Four focus on the letters of the alphabet. The first, shorter report (henceforth, 'Letters 1'), deals with them only in passing. It opens with the phrase: 'The first thing that God created was the letters of the alphabet' (*awwalu mā khalaqa Allāhu ḥurūf al-muʿjam*), which is repeated twice with two different transmitter chains. Then it continues, for several lines, to praise God's oneness, eternity, His absolute transcendence, His absolute knowledge, and so forth.[42]

The second report (henceforth, 'Letters 2') is longer, one to one and a half pages long, depending on the edition,[43] and it is far more detailed, while its *isnād* is more rudimentary, simply stating that 'some of the companions of Abū ʿAbd Allāh, on the authority of al-Ḥasan, on the authority of Abū ʿAbd Allāh [Jaʿfar al-Ṣādiq] have told us etc'.[44] The story itself gradually reveals the importance of the letters of the alphabet, then proceeds to discuss the anatomy of their pronunciation. (In classical Arabic, the word *ḥarf* signified both a letter and the sound that it denoted.) What is most curious about this story, which, as noted, takes up most of Epistle Four, is that it occurs almost verbatim in another text, namely, as Chapter 59 of *Kitāb al-Haft wa'l aẓilla* (henceforth '*Kitāb al-Haft* 59'), a multi-layered text of Ghulat origin that was preserved by the Nuṣayrīs of Syria, who have added to it some textual layers.[45] Interestingly, in *Kitāb al-Haft*, too, this chapter seems to be inserted, as it has nothing to do with the rest of the text.

We thus have two treatises, one from the Ismaili, one from the Ghulat-Nuṣayrī tradition, both of which contain the same textual fragment almost verbatim, and in both of which this fragment stands in stark contrast to the remaining text. Two questions arise here. Is the text in one of the fragmments copied from the other, and if yes, which is copied from which? If no, then from where did both texts copy it?

---

[42] *Kitāb al-Kashf*, p. 131.

[43] Strothmann's edition is smaller, and the second story is spread over a page and a half, pp. 131–132. In Ghālib's edition it occupies just a page, pp. 91–92.

[44] *Kitāb al-Kashf*, p. 131.

[45] See my *Controversies*, pp. 13–42.

By this I mean, from which of the two textual traditions does the fragment come, the Ismaili or the Ghulat-Nuṣayrī one? Or does it come from an altogether unrelated source? (In the case of *Kitāb al-Kashf*, this includes both the common fragment, i.e., Letters 2, and the short story that precedes it, i.e. Letters 1.)

In what follows, an answer to these questions will be posited through a close reading of the two different versions of the fragment (Letters 2 and *Kitāb al-Haft 59*), and by looking at the discussions of letters in other texts from the early Ismaili and the Ghulat-Nuṣayrī traditions.

Let us begin with the textual differences between Letters 2 and *Kitāb al-Haft 59*. The Arabic text presented in the Appendix clearly marks the two variants one against the other, and in the discussion, the paragraph numbers of the Arabic text will be used to refer to the relevant passages.

The text begins smoothly in both variants. Para. 1 does not seem to present any major problems for either, and both are rather similar. Para. 2 contains a passage that is missing in *Kitāb al-Haft 59*, but still reads rather logically in Letters 2. The content of paras. 3 and 4, however, and the way they connect to one another, begin to pose problems for Letters 2. As found in *Kitāb al-Haft* 59, the passage presents a rather smoothly flowing narrative concerning the function of the letters of the alphabet and the role they play as a collective:

> [Jaʿfar] al-Ṣādiq said: 'The division (*maqṭaʿ*) of letters[46] is twenty-eight letters, through which the connected ones[47] become known.' Mufaḍḍal said: 'How is it, lord, may God sacrifice me for you?' He said, may peace come from him: 'Do you not know, Mufaḍḍal, that speech consists of twenty-eight letters, [which are a means for] expression among the creatures, teaching them what they do not know. If we say to a man "alif", he will not understand a thing, or if someone says to him "lām", he will not understand a thing, or if it is said "hā", he will not understand a thing from it either.'

---

[46] In the discussion that follows, the Arabic *ḥurūf* denotes, both, the letters and the sounds they indicate. When translating the Arabic word, I will use 'letters' to indicate both of its meanings.

[47] The 'connected ones' are the words that are formed by connecting the letters, see paras. 4 and 5.

The beginning of the above passage sets the stage for the later discussion (to follow in paras. 4 and 5) of the 'connected ones' (*al-mawṣūlāt*), i.e. the letters of the alphabet that are connected to one another, which serve as a means of expression (*ʿibāra*) and knowledge (lit., 'those that make them know', *muʿarrifa*). In *Kitāb al-Haft 59*, when asked what he means, the narrator (Jaʿfar al-Ṣādiq) shows how meaningless each letter is when uttered just by itself. By contrast, in Letters 2, which is a truncated version of paras. 4 and 5, the entire discussion is distorted beyond recognition. And whereas the first sentence (para. 3) makes sense when read alone, the second sentence (para. 4) is utterly meaningless, and is clearly a badly copied version of the same passage in *Kitāb al-Haft 59*: 'and if it is said that someone ALF,[48] nothing is understood by it'.

Kitāb al-Haft 59 continues the discussion in para. 5, telling the reader how the letters/sounds work when joined up, and this quite logically completes the preceding discussion of how the letters do *not* work when uttered alone.

> But if they are brought together, they will be united, made into a bounded piece, and into a syntactical relationship – through the putting together of information. So [if] it is said to him 'God is all-knowing, He is God', do you not see that there is an adjective and a noun modified by the adjective?[49]

---

48 Given the structure of the sentence, this root could be read in any number of ways, most probably as a verb, but even then this does not make sense, whereas in *Kitāb al-Haft 59* the passage smoothly connects with what follows.

49 The passage sounds rather awkward in English, but the Arabic makes sense as it contains references to the preceding and following discussions. Thus, the idea of the letters being 'brought together' (*jamaʿat jamīʿan*), contrasts with the previous discussion of how meaningless the letters/sounds are when taken separately; the idea that they will be 'be collected into a composition' (*taʾallafat taʾlīfan*) continues the idea, stressing, furthermore, that the collecting together of the letters will result in a composition, as *allafa*, in addition to denoting mere collection, also implies bringing unity to the object gathered; and the mention of the making of the letters into a 'relation' (*nasaban mansūban*) refers to the relation between the noun and its adjective in the next sentence. Of course, the word *nasab* is used in a more general sense of 'relation', but in the sentence that follows, the type of relationship that is described, between a noun and an adjective, is a syntactical one.

The passage in Letters 2, meanwhile, makes little sense, as it merely contains some of the words from *Kitāb al-Haft 59*'s variant, but the sentence it presents is ungrammatical and unfinished: 'If they are unified, collected, brought together, and related to one another through the putting together of information'. The Qur'anic verse that is quoted immediately after, furthermore, shows no connection to the context. The problems of Letters 2 continue in para. 7:

> Do you not know that spelling is impossible without letters, whether in Syriac or in other languages? He said: 'I said, "And why is that?" He responded: "Because Syriac became established during the time of Abraham, God's prayers upon him – as Hebrew, as Syriac, as Persian, and as Arabic".'

Not only is there a logical disconnection between the mention of Syriac, and then the successive listing of the four languages; and not only is there a grammatical inconsistency between the first mention of Syriac as feminine (*al-suryāniyya*) and the subsequent listing of languages all as masculine (*'ibrāniyyan*, etc.). The discussion of Syriac springs from nowhere (the earlier discussion implicitly revolved around Arabic), and the subsequent mention of the four languages seems out of place in general. Finally, the narrator's response ('Because Syriac. . .') does not answer the question.

On the other hand, *Kitāb al-Haft 59* presents a logical succession of topics, which may be summarised as follows: speech and writing are impossible without spelling (*hijā'*, para. 6). Spelling is impossible without letters/sounds (*ḥurūf*, para. 7). Finally, speech consists of twenty-eight letters, which are the letters of the alphabet, but this is only true for Arabic. During Abraham's time languages became intermixed (para. 8).[50] All of this information is compressed in Letters 2 into just two sentences which are very loosely connected, and which do not form a coherent narrative (and para. 8 is missing from it

[50] In *Kitāb al-Haft 59*, after this passage only Hebrew is specifically mentioned as one of the languages resulting from the mixing during Abraham's time. It is likely that the four languages mentioned in Letters 2 have belonged here but were deleted and only Hebrew remained: i.e., after 'the languages became intermixed', people began speaking 'Hebrew, Syriac, Persian and Arabic'.

altogether). Paras. 9-11 likewise consistently show a more coherent text in *Kitāb al-Haft 59* and a distorted one in Letters 2.

What can we infer from the preceding? The only thing that can be stated with certainty is that Epistle Four, comprising the two stories about letters, is a later addition to the text. And whereas there are doubts about the identity of the author (or authors) of the other parts, or about their relationship to one another, their overall focus and style allow for the possibility of a single authorship. Not so with Epistle Four. For not only is it drastically different from the rest of the book in its focus, as it touches upon none of the themes discussed in other parts of the book, but the state of the text itself, abounding in inconsistencies and mistakes, betrays rather careless copying from elsewhere.[51]

In the case of *Kitāb al-Haft wa'l-aẓilla*, despite the much more coherent passage found in this text, the chapter on letters (*Kitāb al-Haft 59*) also seems to have been inserted, as it bears no stylistic or thematic similarity to the other parts of the book. (Of course, *Kitāb al-Haft* in general is a multi-layered text, and this chapter is not the only fragment that stands out.)

The next question that arises is the origin of Epistle Four, i.e. what other text it was copied from? Or, if the exact text may not be determined, what religious tradition does it originate from? It is highly unlikely that the person who inserted it into *Kitāb al-Kashf* copied it from Chapter 59 of *Kitāb al-Haft*. Firstly, because all of the available editions of the latter text lack the first short fragment about letters that opens Epistle Four (Letters 1). And secondly, because in *Kitāb al-Haft* itself this chapter is a later insertion.

Further, was Epistle Four copied from an Ismaili text or from a Nuṣayrī one? There are no themes specific to the Ismaili tradition in it, and the reading of early Ismaili accounts about letters – including the discussion of letters in Epistle Two of *Kitāb al-Kashf* – contain nothing

---

[51] This is not to say, of course, that some of the changes introduced in Letters 2 to the Urtext may not have been intentional.

sufficiently similar to it.[52] As to Nuṣayrī ones (the occurrence of Letters 2 in a Ghulat-Nuṣayri text might suggest this), the only two elements reminiscent of Ghulat-Nuṣayrī ideas are the mention of *aẓilla* (shadows) in Letters 1, and of *shabāḥ* (form or apparition) in Letters 2. As is well known, according to Ghulat and Nuṣayrī writings, the *aẓilla* and *ashbāḥ* (pl. of *shabaḥ*) were luminous spiritual entities that had been created by God before all else.[53] The contexts where the two terms are mentioned, however, are too broad to indicate direct Ghulat-Nuṣayrī provenance with any certainty. The first term appears in the context of the praise to God: 'No shadow covers Him, but He covers the heaven with all of its shadows' (*lā ẓill yumsikihu wa-huwa yumsiku al-samā'a bi-aẓillatihā*). The second term is used in an even more general way: 'God has not created a name without making a meaning for it, He has not made a meaning for it without making a form (*shabaḥ*) for it, He has not made a form for it without making boundaries for it'.[54] The instances in Nuṣayrī texts that do discuss the letters likewise do not show any substantial similarities to this passage, as they are

52 *Kitāb al-Kashf*, pp. 92–94; for a survey of letter symbolism in early Ismaili writings, see M. Ebstein, *Mysticism and Philosopy in al-Andalus: Ibn Masarra, Ibn ʿArabī, and the Ismāʿīlī Tradition* (Leiden, 2014), pp. 77–122; the chief Ismaili accounts that discuss the letters are the following: Abū Ḥātim al-Rāzī, *Kitāb al-Iṣlāḥ*, ed. Ḥasan Manūchihr and Mahdī Muḥaqqiq (Tehran, 1383 Sh./2004), pp. 204–205; al-Ḥāmidī, *Kanz al-walad*, ed. Muṣṭafā Ghālib (Beirut, 1416/1996), pp. 27–28; *Kitāb Ta'wīl ḥurūf al-muʿjam*, ed. Stanislas Guyard in *Fragments relatifs á la doctrine des ismaélis* (Paris, 1874), pp. 19–26. Guyard's edition does not provide a title, but one is supplied by another, unpublished manuscript of the same text, see D. Hollenberg, '*Anta anā wa-anā minka* ("You are me, and I am from you"): A Quasi-Nuṣayrī Fragment on the Intellect in the Early Ismāʿīlī Treatise *Kitāb Ta'wīl ḥurūf al-muʿjam*', in Joseph Lowry and Shawkat Toorawa (ed.), *Arabic Humanities, Islamic Thought: Essays in Honor of Everett Rowson* (Leiden, 2016), pp. 51–52; Jaʿfar b. Manṣūr al-Yaman, *Kitāb al-ʿĀlim wa'l-ghulām*, ed. and trans. James Morris as *The Master and the Disciple: An Early Islamic Spiritual Dialogue* (London, 2001), paras. 85, 87, 437, 440.

53 References to this are legion, see a discussion of the idea and of the texts that refer to it in my *Controversies*, pp. 64–78; among the primary sources see, e.g. *Kitāb al-Ashbāḥ*, paras. 1–3; *Kitāb al-Haft*, pp. 16–18.

54 *Kitāb al-Kashf*, pp. 130–131.

mostly concerned with the symbolic meaning of letters.[55] Thus, while a borrowing *from* a Nuṣayrī text is possible, there is not enough evidence to ascertain this, and this possibility ought to remain just a hypothesis.

We are thus left with very little that would enable us to explain in what circumstances the textual fragment on the letters of the alphabet was embedded into two different texts from two different traditions, the Ismaili and the Ghulat-Nuṣayrī ones. Certainly, there were numerous contacts between the Nizārī Ismailis and the Nuṣayrīs after the former conquered the Nuṣayrī fortresses in Northern Syria in the sixth/twelfth century, thus coming into possession of the Nuṣayrī written lore, so that the manuscripts of some of the currently known Ghulat-Nuṣayrī texts come from Nizārī Ismaili collections.[56] These contacts are reflected, for example, in the fact that passages with Ismaili content are inserted into Nuṣayrī works, and vice versa.[57] One can thus imagine an environment in medieval Syria where Nizārī-Ismaili authors read and copied texts from both traditions. The fact that most, if not all of the known manuscripts of *Kitāb al-Kashf*

---

[55] Letter symbolism is discussed in numerous Ghulat and Nuṣayrī texts, see, e.g. the opening of *Kitāb al-Aẓilla*, quoted in al-Jillī, *Ḥāwī al-asrār*, p. 207; Ḥasan al-Ḥarrānī, *Ḥaqā'iq asrār al-dīn*, in *Silsilat al-turāth al-ʿalawī* (Lebanon, 2006), vol. 4, pp. 71–72; al-Jillī, *Risālat al-ḥurūf*, in *Silsilat al-turāth al-ʿalawī*, ed. Abū Mūsā and Shaykh Mūsā, vol. 2, pp. 335–341. An interesting case is *Risālat al-tawḥīd*, nested in three different Nuṣayrī sources. One is *Kitāb al-Mithāl wa'l-ṣūra*, in *Silsilat al-turāth al-ʿalawī*, vol. 1, pp. 209, 225–226, attributed to the eponym of the Nuṣayrīs, Muḥammad b. Nuṣayr (d. after 254/868); and the second and the third are *Ḥawī al-asrār*, p. 202, and *Ḥaqā'iq asrār al-dīn*, pp. 44–45 and 77–78, written by, respectively, Muḥammad b. ʿAlī al-Jillī (d. after 399/1009) and Ḥasan b. Shuʿba al-Ḥarrānī (fl. second half of the fourth/tenth century). Curiously, a more complete version of the same text, without the title and framed as a tradition narrated on the authority of Jaʿfar al-Ṣadiq, is quoted by Ismaili author Abū Ḥātim al-Rāzī in his *Kitāb al-Zīnā*, ed. Saʿīd al-Ghānimī (Beirut, 2015), vol. 1, pp. 95–97.

[56] Some of the manuscripts of *Kitāb al-Haft*, e.g., come from the collections of Syrian Ismailis.

[57] E.g., see the introduction to *Kitāb al-Haft*, pp. 10–11, which contains an Ismaili fragment and is clearly a later addition; or some of the passages in *Kitāb Ta'wīl ḥurūf al-muʿjam*, p. 22; for a discussion, see Hollenberg, '*Anta anā*', pp. 55–57.

originate in India[58] does not preclude the possibility of the book's circulation in medieval Syria, as many works produced (or transmitted) by the Ismailis in Syria have been preserved in the collections of the Indian Bohra community. For example, the text known as *Kitāb al-Ashbāḥ wa'l-aẓilla*, composed by the Ghulat probably in Iraq before the fourth/tenth century and then transported to Syria by the Nuṣayrīs,[59] has survived in two manuscripts, at least one of which comes from a Bohra collection (and the other one also comes from India).[60] And an Ismaili work entitled *Kitāb Ta'wīl ḥurūf al-muʿjam*, containing passages (possibly insertions) of Nuṣayrī content, hence possibly of Syrian provenance, has survived in two manuscripts, one of which is of a probable Syrian provenance, and the other, again, has been preserved by the Indian Bohras.[61] How this transmission of texts between various medieval Ismaili centres happened is beyond the remit of this paper, but it is indicative that Ismaili texts produced in various centres did eventually find their way into Indian Bohra collections.[62]

There are alternative possibilities too, of course, and just because *Kitāb al-Kashf* shares a common passage with a text composed or compiled in medieval Syria, this does not necessarily indicate that it was composed in Syria as well. Texts (and not just Ismaili ones)

---

58 I. Poonawala, *Bibliography of Ismāʿīlī Literature* (Malibu, 1977), p. 73, mentions several manuscripts of the work in Indian Bohra collections. Of the two manuscripts used by Strothmann for his edition, one came from the collection of Asaf Fyzee, an Indian Bohra scholar, and the other from Berlin, but its origin is unknown. And the manuscript used by Ghālib came from the collection of the Pakistani Ismaili scholar, ʿAzīz ʿAlī.

59 For a list of the Nuṣayrī works that quote this text, see Asatryan, 'An Early Shiʿi Cosmology', p. 10.

60 Poonalawa, *Bibliography*, p. 339; A. Gacek, *Catalogue of the Arabic Manuscripts in the Library of the Institute of Ismaili Studies*, vol. 1 (London, 1984), p. 7.

61 On this text, see Hollenberg, '*Anta anā*', pp. 51–52; idem, *Beyond the Qur'ān*, p. 46; M. Bar-Asher, 'Outlines of Early Ismāʿīlī-Fāṭimid Qur'ān Exegesis', *Journal Asiatique*, 296, 2 (2008), p. 264.

62 Cf. Hollenberg, *Beyond the Qur'ān*, pp. 50–51; on this transfer of texts between the Nuṣayrī and the Ismaili traditions, see D. De Smet, 'Les racines docétistes de l'imamologie shiʿite', in M. A. Amir-Moezzi, et al. (ed.), *L'Ésoterisme Shiʿite: ses racines et ses prolongements* (Turnhout, 2016), pp. 90–91.

travelled all across the medieval Islamic world, and the fragment about letters, which was most likely copied into *Kitāb al-Haft* in Syria, could have been inserted into *Kitāb al-Kashf* in any one of the other centres where Ismaili texts were produced and circulated, such as Yemen, North Africa, or, again, India.[63]

Conclusion

The foregoing pages have raised as many questions as they have provided answers, but it is hoped that some further light has been shed on the history of *Kitāb al-Kashf*. What can be said with a great degree of certainty is, first, that the passages reminiscent of Ghulat-Nuṣayrī content in this Ismaili text are not the result of 'influence' or 'contamination' of one textual tradition by another, but an attempt by an early Ismaili author to distance his group from the Shiʿi Ghulat through a polemic against them. Second, it can be demonstrated that Epistle Four of *Kitāb al-Kashf* was inserted into the text after all of its parts were already in place. These findings could be indicative of the history of the early and medieval Ismaili movement – but only after more information about the history of this text, and the history of the literature of other Shiʿi groups, comes to light.

Appendix

A Critical Edition of Kitāb al-Haft *59, and its Difference from Letters 2*

The following is a critical edition of *Kitāb al-Haft 59*, based on three of the four available editions of *Kitāb al-Haft wa'l-aẓilla*.[64] As noted above, Letters 2 almost verbatim corresponds to this text, but in

---

[63] On the transfer of Ismaili manuscripts to India, see I. Poonawala, 'Ismāʿīlī Manuscripts from Yemen', *Journal of Islamic Manuscripts*, 5 (2014), pp. 1–25.

[64] I have omitted the edition found in volume 6 of *Silsilat al-turāth al-ʿalawī* as it corresponds to Ghālib's edition and adds nothing to the text.

several places it significantly departs from it. In noting the variants between *Kitāb al-Haft 59* and Letters 2, only those passages that show substantial differences are marked – such as misplaced sentences, added passages, or missing phrases – and minor differences are ignored since they do not alter the overall meaning of the text, and are probably the result of scribal choices or errors, such as added pronouns, conjunctions, differences in number, incorrect gender, etc. Ultimately, the aim is to show that *Kitāb al-Haft 59* is closer to the Urtext than Letters 2, and that the text has been significantly distorted in the latter.

The critical apparatus supplied below in the footnotes thus focuses only on the variants of *Kitāb al-Haft 59* – except for a few cases where Letters 2 supplies a valuable, or a more meaningful, reading; or when noting the variants between the two editions of Letters 2 (the latter are only noted when both readings make sense; otherwise, the reading the best fitting is selected without noting the variant). In order to make the incongruences of Letters 2 readily visible, the differences between *Kitāb al-Haft 59* and Letters 2 are marked as follows:

– Brackets designate
   a. a phrase that is found in Letters 2 but is missing in *Kitāb al-Haft 59* (either completely or in that particular place).
   b. a phrase the variant of which is found in *Kitāb al-Haft 59* in the same place, but which differs from it to such a degree as to render a completely different meaning. In this case, the alternative reading of the phrase supplied by Letters 2 will immediately follow that of *Kitāb al-Haft 59*.
– Underscore designates
   a. Those passages that occur in *Kitāb al-Haft 59* but are missing in Letters 2 (again, either completely or in that particular place).
   b. Those passages in *Kitāb al-Haft 59* which have similar, but distorted, variants in Letters 2. In this case, the latter will immediately follow the former and will be enclosed in brackets.

Original punctuation has been simplified where possible. For ease of reference, the relevant passages in the text below have been numbered, and the numbers are given in angle brackets.

Sigla

Kitāb al-Haft wa'l-aẓilla, Chapter 59 (*Kitāb al-Haft 59*)

ت: ed. Arif Tamer and Ignace Khalifé

غ: ed. Muṣṭafā Ghālib

تا: ed. Arif Tamer

Kitāb al-Kashf, Epistle Four (Letters 2)

ش: ed. Rudolf Strothmann

غا: ed. Muṣṭafā Ghālib

<١> قال الصادق[65]: لم يخلق الله اسماً إلا وجعل له معنىً ولم يجعل له معنىً إلا وجعل له شبحاً ولم يجعل له شبحاً إلا وجعل له حدوداً ولم يجعل له حدوداً إلا وجعل له فطراً[66] ولم يجعل له فَطراً[67] إلا وجعل له فصلاً ووصلاً. ولم يعرف المفصول إلا بالموصول ولو كلّم الناس في المفصول لما عقلوه.[68] قال المفضل[69]: يا مولاي كيف ذلك؟ ولما عرف الناس الكلام ومعانيه؟[70]

<٢> [قال: أوما تعلم أن الكلام العربي على ثمانية وعشرين حرفاً وأربعة أُخر فالأربعة الأخر توجد في حرف واحد مخلص.
[قلت: وما ذلك؟

<٣> فقال الصادق[71]: مقطع الحروف ثمانية وعشرون[72] حرفاً عقلو بها الموصولات.
قال المفضل[73]: وكيف ذلك يا مولاي؟ جعلني الله فداك.
قال منه السلام: أما تعلم يا مفضل أنّ الكلام ثمانية وعشرون[74] حرفاً عبارةً بين الخلائق ومعرفة لهم فيما أنكروه.

---

65 غ: العالم منه السلام
66 .ت غ س، تا ش غا: قطراً
67 .ت غ س، تا ش غا: قطراً
68 .عقلوا" غ: عقلوا به موصولا"
69 .قال المفضل" غ: قلت"
70 أضاف غ: قلت وما ذلك؟
71 .فقال الصادق" غ: قال"
72 .تا، ت غ: عشرين
73 .قال المفضل" غ: قلت"
74 .تا، ت غ: عشرين

<۴> فلو قلنا للرجل ”ألف“ ما فهم منها شيئا أو قيل للرجل ”لام“ ما فهم منها شيئاً أو قيل له ”هاء“ ما فهم منها شيئاً أيضاً[75] [فلو قيل إن أحداً ألف[76] ما فهم بها شيء].

<۵> وإذا جمعت جميعاً تألّفتْ تأليفاً وحداً[77] محدوداً ونسباً منسوباً باجتماع المعرفة [فإذا ألفت وجمعت وحدت ونسبت باجتماع المعرفة. قال الله ”فاعلموا إنه لا إله إلا هو“[78]]. فقيل له ”الله عليم[79] إنه الله“ أولَا ترى أن ههنا صفة واسم موصوف بصفة؟

<۶> ألا ترى أن الاسم غير الهجاء والتفصيل غير الموصول [ألا ترى بأن الاسم عم الهجاء غير التفصيل]؟ أما تعلم أن الكلام نسخة الكتاب والكتاب لا يجوز إلا بالهجاء؟

<۷> أما تعلم أن الهجاء لا يجوز إلا بالحروف [إما بالسريانية وإما بغيرها؟ قال: قلت ولمَ ذلك؟ قال: لأن السريانية ثبتت على عهد ابراهيم صلوات الله عليه عبرانياً وسريانياً وأعجمياً وعربياً]؟

<۸> أما تعلم أن الكلام هو كله يخرج من ثمانية وعشرين حرفاً وهي الحروف المعجمة؟

قال المفضل: يا مولاي فهل بهذا تمت المعرفة؟

قال منه السلام: فأما العربية فتمت وأمّا غيرها فلا.

قال المفضل: يا مولاي وما ذلك؟

فقال: لأن الألسن يا مفضل تبلبلت على عهد ابراهيم فصار الكلام في العبرانية.

<۹> وإن دعائم الكلام أربعة وزاد في الكلام الصفير[80] والزجر والنقر والهتف[81] من الحروف.[82] فمن عرف[83] توصيلها[84] وتفصيلها والكلام بها عرف جميع الألسن المتبلبلة ونُطْقَ[85] كل طائر أدقّ نطق. فمن عرف ذلك فقد عرف نطق كل طائر وكل ذي[86] أربع من البهائم[87] [وكانت دعائم فزادت في الكلام الصفير والزجر والنقر والهتف، فمن عرف تفصيلها وتوصيلها فإن الكلام بها يعرف وبها عرف منطق الطير ومنطق البهائم ونطق كل ذي نطق أربع].

---

[75] ”أو قيل للرجل . . . أيضاً“ ساقطة من غ.

[76] ش: ألّف.

[77] ”وحداً“ تا غ: واحداً.

[78] راجع سورة 11:14.

[79] ت: أعلم.

[80] ش، ت تا غ ش: الصغير.

[81] أضفت هذه الكلمة من متن كتاب الكشف ولعلها قد كانت في هذا الموضع في متن كتاب الهفت نظرا لما تقدمها في الجملة، وقد شُطبت.

[82] تا، ت غ: حروف.

[83] ”فمن عرف“ ساقطة من ت غ.

[84] ت غ: وتوصيلها.

[85] أضاف تا: مع.

[86] ”وكل ذي“ تا: وإلى كل طائر، ت: وإلى كل طائر دق، غ: وإلى كل طائر ذو.

[87] ”أربع من البهائم“ ت غ، تا: نطق أربع وهكذا للبهائم.

<١٠> ألا[88] تعلم أنك إذا صفرت في الطير صفر وتهتف بالحمام والبهائم فتنزجر. فلولا إنّك أفهمتها[89] ما لم تفهم [ولولا أنك قد أفهمتها شيئا لم تزدجر، فقد أفهمتها ما لم تفهمه] بالزجر والهتف والنقر والصفير والنبح والنهيق والعوي. [قال: والهتف مما خرج حتى تبلبلت ألسن الناس من الثمانية والعشرين حرفاً.]

<١١> وما يفتح به الفم[90] فهو الزجر وما يلزم من الفم فهو من الصفير وما رددته إلى الهواء فهو من النقر وما فتحت به الفم ويخرج من الحلق فهو من الهتف [وما يفتح به قال فما خرج من الحلق فهو من الهتف]. فافهم ذلك إن شاء الله عليه توكلنا وإليه أنبنا وسلام على المرسلين والحمد لله رب العالمين.[91]

88 ت غ: وليس.

89 تا، ت غ: افتهمتها.

90 تا ت غ: فهم.

91 وسلام . . . رب العالمين" ساقطة من غ".

12

The Intellectual Interactions of Yemeni Ṭayyibism with the Early Shiʿi Tradition

Daniel De Smet
(CNRS (France) - PSL - LEM, UMR 8584)

Ibrāhīm b. al-Ḥusayn al-Ḥāmidī (d. 557/1162), the second Ṭayyibī *dāʿī muṭlaq* in Yemen, is generally considered to be the founder of the esoteric doctrine (the so-called *ḥaqāʾiq* or 'truths') of Ṭayyibī Ismailism. In his *Kitāb Kanz al-walad*, a work that served as a model for later authors dealing with the *ḥaqāʾiq*, he integrated the legacy of the Ikhwān al-Ṣafāʾ - both the *Rasāʾil* and the *Risāla al-Jāmiʿa* - into the philosophical system developed by the Fatimid *dāʿī* Ḥamīd al-Dīn al-Kirmānī (d. after 411/1020), whose *Kitāb Rāḥat al-ʿaql* is extensively quoted as a highly authoritative source.[1] Furthermore, he sought to link al-Kirmānī's worldview to the quite different cosmology developed by the Fatimid *dāʿī al-duʿāt*, al-Muʾayyad fi'l-Dīn al-Shīrāzī (d. 470/1078).[2]

---

[1] Daniel De Smet, 'La *Risāla al-Ǧāmiʿa* attribuée aux Iḫwān al-Ṣafāʾ: un précurseur de l'ismaélisme ṭayyibite?', in A. Straface, C. De Angelo and A. Manzo (ed.), *Labor limae. Atti in onore di Carmela Baffioni,* vol. 1 (Studi Magrebini, 12) (Naples, 2018), pp. 269–298; Daniel De Smet, 'L'auteur des *Rasāʾil Ikhwān al-Ṣafāʾ* selon les sources ismaéliennes ṭayyibites', *Shii Studies Review*, 1 (2017), pp. 151–166. On Ṭayyibī doctrine in general, see Daniel De Smet, *La philosophie ismaélienne: un ésotérisme chiite entre néoplatonisme et gnose* (Paris, 2012).

[2] The influence of al-Muʾayyad, who after al-Kirmānī is the most often quoted Fatimid author in Ṭayyibī sources, still needs investigation. This is hampered by the fact that we lack an integral and critical edition of al-Muʾayyad's *Majālis*, along with a thorough study of his thought.

Besides the Ikhwān al-Ṣafāʾ and the literature of the Fatimid *daʿwa*, Ṭayyibī authors used a third type of source, including traditions about 'the apparitions and the shadows' (*al-ashbāḥ wa'l-aẓilla*), the pre-existence of Muhammad and ʿAlī (sometimes extended to the other 'People of the Cloak', Fāṭima, al-Ḥasan and al-Ḥusayn), along with the distinction between the 'divinity' (*lāhūt*) and the 'humanity' (*nāsūt*) of the prophets and the imams, who appear on earth in a bodily 'envelope' (*ghilāf*) or 'garment' (*libās*), serving as a veil (*hijāb*) for the divine principle they are manifesting. These traditions, which are attributed to the Prophet and the first Shiʿi imams, are transmitted by authorities such as Jābir b. ʿAbd Allāh al-Anṣarī, Jābir b. Yazīd al-Juʿfī, al-Mufaḍḍal b. ʿUmar al-Juʿfī or Muḥammad b. Sinān, who are well known in the so-called *ghulāt* literature.[3]

The present investigation will undertake a preliminary exploration of the intellectual interactions of Yemeni Ṭayyibism with this *ghulāt* tradition that is characteristic of early Shiʿism. But, first of all, it is necessary to determine its relationship with Ismailism in general.

The 'Mufaḍḍal Tradition' and Ismailism

During the second and third/eighth and ninth centuries, Shiʿi circles from Iraq, mainly based in Kūfa and surroundings, as well as from Persia, issued a set of doctrines presented as the 'secret revelations' of the first imams to some of their chosen disciples. Prominent among these 'revelations' is the esoteric teaching of the sixth imam Jaʿfar al-Ṣādiq (d. 148/765) as conveyed to al-Mufaḍḍal b. ʿUmar al-Juʿfī. This 'Mufaḍḍal tradition' consists of a large number of *ḥadīth* often transmitted as stemming from al-Mufaḍḍal by Muḥammad b. Sinān, a contemporary of the imams Jaʿfar al-Ṣādiq, Mūsā al-Kāẓim (d. 183/799) and ʿAlī al-Riḍā (d. 203/818). Quoted by heresiographers,

---

[3] The terms *ghuluww* (exaggeration, extremism) and *ghālī/ghulāt* (exaggerator[s], extremist[s]) are of course in scholarly, academic terms inadequate, as they are labels used by heresiographers and polemicists in order to stigmatise movements they consider as 'heretical'. They are only used here for the sake of convenience; at the end of this paper, we will see what exactly the Ṭayyibī authors meant when speaking themselves about *ghuluww*.

they are often included in Imāmī collections, even when they are usually rejected as *ghuluww* by mainstream Twelver Shiʿism. Above all, they were incorporated into books and treatises now belonging to the literature of the Nuṣayrīs, mainly the *Kitāb al-Haft al-sharīf* (or *al-Haft wa'l-aẓilla*) and related texts, such as *Kitāb al-Ṣirāṭ*, *Kitāb al-Ashbāḥ wa'l-aẓilla* and *Kitāb al-Aẓilla*.[4] Similar traditions were collected in the *Umm al-kitāb* and are supposed to reflect the secret teachings of the fifth imam Muḥammad al-Bāqir (d. ca. 114/732) to another member of the Juʿfī clan, Jābir b. Yazīd al-Juʿfī.[5]

One of the most characteristic features of the 'Mufaḍḍal tradition' is the notion of the shadows and apparitions. According to the *Kitāb al-Haft*, Jaʿfar al-Ṣādiq taught al-Mufaḍḍal that the generation of our terrestrial world is the result of a long process of degradation, caused by a series of revolts of the creatures against the commands of their Creator. The first thing that God, as a pure light, created out of his will (*mashīʾa*) was shadowy light (*al-nūr al-ẓillī*) which gave rise to a great number of shadows (*aẓilla*). These shadows were dressed (*libās*) in 'apparitions' (*ashbāḥ*): corpses of light animated by souls or spirits (*arwāḥ*). Seven heavens, each ruled by a figure called Adam, were inhabited by these 'apparitions'. Hidden behind a veil (*ḥijāb*) of light, God transmitted his commands and teachings directly to these 'apparitions'. Nevertheless, the 'apparitions' disobeyed the divine orders, so that their light was transformed into obscurity. Endowed with a material body, they fell down into this world of generation and corruption,

---

[4] The seminal study on the 'Mufaḍḍal tradition' is Heinz Halm, 'Das "Buch der Schatten". Die Mufaḍḍal-Tradition der *Ġulāt* und die Ursprünge des Nuṣairiertums' (I), *Der Islam*, 55 (1978), pp. 219–266; (II), *Der Islam*, 58 (1981), pp. 15–86. Halm's pioneering work has been updated with new material by Mushegh Asatryan, *Controversies in Formative Shiʿi Islam. The Ghulat Muslims and their Beliefs* (London and New York 2017); Mushegh Asatryan, 'An Early Shīʿi Cosmology. *Kitāb al-ashbāḥ wa l-aẓilla* and its Milieu', *Studia Islamica*, 110 (2015), pp. 1–80; Mushegh Asatryan, 'Shiite Underground Literature Between Iraq and Syria. "The Book of Shadows" and the History of the Early Ghulat', in Y. Tzvi Langermann and Robert G. Morrison (ed.), *Texts in Transit in the Medieval Mediterranean* (Pennsylvania, 2016), pp. 128–161.

[5] For an overview of the research on this important text, see Sean Anthony, 'The Legend of ʿAbd Allāh Ibn Sabaʾ and the Date of *Umm al-kitāb*', *JRAS*, Series 3, 21 (2011), pp. 2–4.

deprived of direct contact with God. Out of mercy for his fallen creatures, God sent a series of messengers to them, the first of which was Muhammad. Originally, these messengers were apparitions, covered successively with a 'ghostly veil' (*al-ḥijāb al-shabaḥī*) and a 'spiritual veil' (*al-ḥijāb al-rūḥī*), before manifesting themselves in a human body. The human body of the messengers – prophets and imams – is thus described as a veil (*ḥijāb*, *satr*), a 'mould' (*qālab*), a 'shirt' (*qamīṣ*) or an 'envelope' (*ghilāf*), being at the same time hiding, receiving and manifesting their divine nature, the 'apparition' or 'shadow' proceeding from the light of the Creator.[6]

Closely linked to this conception is the idea, widespread in early Imāmī *ḥadīth*, about the pre-existence of Muhammad and the imams. Before the creation of the world, they were shadows and apparitions of light proceeding from the light of God.[7] According to another version, fully developed in the *Umm al-kitāb*, five luminous limbs (*jawāriḥ*) proceeded from God's light long before the generation of the world: Muhammad, ʿAlī, Fāṭima, al-Ḥasan and al-Ḥusayn. During the successive cosmic eras, this pentad took different forms, before entering into human bodies at the moment that our material world was generated. The bodies of the prophets and imams resemble statues (literally 'temples', *hayākil*) or moulds (*qawālib*), housing the divine essence of the different members of the pentad.[8]

---

[6] Al-Mufaḍḍal al-Juʿfī (attrib.), *Kitāb al-Haft al-sharīf*, ed. Muṣṭafā Ghālib (Beirut, 1964), pp. 15–24, 27–28. On the *aẓilla wa'l-ashbāḥ*, see Asatryan, *Controversies*, pp. 64-71; Asatryan, 'Early Shīʿī Cosmology', pp. 6–7; Patricia Crone, *The Nativist Prophets of Early Islamic Iran. Rural Revolt and Local Zoroastrianism* (Cambridge, 2012), pp. 209–215; Daniel De Smet, 'Les racines docétistes de l'imamologie shiʿite', in Mohammad Ali Amir-Moezzi, Maria De Cillis, Daniel De Smet and Orkhan Mir-Kasimov (ed.), *L'ésotérisme shiʿite, ses racines et ses prolongements* (Turnhout, 2016), pp. 92–95.

[7] Uri Rubin, 'Pre-existence and light. Aspects of the concept of *Nūr Muḥammad*', *Israel Oriental* Studies, 5 (1975), pp. 62–119; idem, 'Prophets and Progenitors in the Early Shīʿa Tradition', *Jerusalem Studies in Arabic and Islam*, 1 (1979), pp. 41–65; Mohammad Ali Amir-Moezzi, *Le guide divin dans le shīʿisme originel* (Lagrasse 1992), pp. 81–83.

[8] *Umm al-kitāb*, ed. Wladimir Ivanow, *Der Islam*, 23 (1936), § 39–42, 70–72, 81–83, 101–103, 116–118; German translation in Heinz Halm, *Die islamische Gnosis. Die extreme Schia und die 'Alawiten* (Zurich and Munich, 1982), pp. 132–134, 142, 145, 150–151, 154.

The 'Mufaḍḍal tradition' and the *Umm al-kitāb* are connected with the second/eighth century Shiʿi movements of the Khaṭṭābiyya and the Mukhammisa.[9] Both are considered to be precursors of the Ismāʿīliyya, which only appeared in the next century.[10] Nevertheless, it is commonly thought today that the doctrines exposed in the *Kitāb al-Haft*, the *Umm al-kitāb* and related texts have nothing to do with Ismailism.[11]

Of course, these doctrines are not those of 'standard' Ismailism as it would be developed in the Qarmaṭī and Fatimid traditions. Muḥammad al-Nasafī (d. 332/943), for instance, in his *Kawn al-ʿālam* mocked the speculations about the shadows and the apparitions, ascribing these 'nonsensical stories' (*khurāfāt*) to a 'demented fool'. In the eyes of the learned Qarmaṭī *dāʿī*, Neoplatonic philosophy was without a doubt a more rational and 'scientific' way to explain the generation of the universe.[12] On the other hand, elements belonging to the 'Mufaḍḍal tradition', including the quotation of Chapter 59 of the *Kitāb al-Haft*, appear in the *Kitāb al-Kashf*, attributed to the Fatimid *dāʿī* Jaʿfar b. Manṣūr al-Yaman (d. ca. 346/957).[13]

Beside these two contradictory attitudes of rejection and adoption, the speculations of the second and third/eighth and ninth century

---

[9] Halm, 'Buch der Schatten (II)', pp. 19–25, 58–64; Halm, *Islamische Gnosis*, pp. 69–78, 199–230; Asatryan, *Controversies*, pp. 47–53, 154–156.

[10] Al-Nawbakhtī, *Firaq al-Shīʿa*, ed. M. Ṣ. Āl Baḥr al-ʿUlūm (Najaf 1936), p. 69: 'The Ismailis are the Khaṭṭābiyya, the disciples of Abu l-Khaṭṭāb'; *Umm al-kitāb*, ed. Ivanow, §52–53, p. 97: 'The Ismaili doctrine was founded by the disciples of Abu l-Khaṭṭāb'; cf. Farhad Daftary, 'The Earliest Ismāʿīlīs', *Arabica*, 38 (1991), pp. 216–226.

[11] Thus, according to Heinz Halm, *Kosmologie und Heilslehre der frühen Ismāʿīlīya. Eine Studie zur islamischen Gnosis* (Wiesbaden, 1978), p. 167, the 'Mufaḍḍal tradition' had not the slightest importance ('*ohne Bedeutung*') for the development of Ismaili doctrine; cf. Farhad Daftary, *Ismaili Literature. A Bibliography of Sources and Studies* (London and New York, 2004), p. 163: '[The *Kitāb al-Haft*] does not contain any Ismaili ideas'; ibid., p. 165: 'The *Umm al-kitāb*, which does not contain any Ismaili doctrines'; cf. Anthony, 'The Legend of ʿAbdallāh Ibn Saba'', p. 3.

[12] Wilferd Madelung, '*Kawn al-ʿĀlam*: The Cosmogony of the Ismāʿīlī *dāʿī* Muḥammad b. Aḥmad al-Nasafī', in Bruce D. Craig (ed.), *Ismaili and Fatimid Studies in Honor of Paul E. Walker* (Chicago, 2010), pp. 28–29.

[13] Halm, 'Buch der Schatten (II)', pp. 83–84; Asatryan, 'Shiite Underground Literature', pp. 140, 156 n. 102.

ghulāt influenced later Ismaili thought, although they were often reformulated and hidden under the guise of Neoplatonism. For instance, the role of Muhammad as first created being to whom God delegated the governing of the universe – the doctrine of *tafwīḍ*, held by the Mufawwiḍa, a movement close to the Khaṭṭābiyya and the Mukhammisa – was taken by the cosmic Intellect, to which the Creator delegated his power, a position that was accepted by the Ismaili Abū Yaʿqūb al-Sijistānī (d. after 361/971).[14] The five 'wings' of the deity distinguished by the Mukhammisa survive in the Ismaili pentad of Intellect, Soul, al-Jadd, al-Fatḥ and al-Khayyāl,[15] whereas the old theme of the cosmic rebellion and subsequent fall once again surfaces in some Ismaili texts from the Fatimid period, to be fully elaborated in the dissident Druze literature.[16] A similar continuity also exists concerning the nature of the prophets and the imams, or the succession of different Adams and pre-adamite peoples.[17] In short, the doctrinal boundaries between the second and third/eighth and ninth century Shiʿi movements of the so-called *ghulāt* and fourth to fifth/tenth to eleventh century Ismailism are not so clear-cut as is commonly believed.

The *Kitāb al-Haft* and related texts were adopted by the Nuṣayrīs, who introduced them into Syria during the fourth/tenth century.[18] Two centuries later, the Nizārī Ismailis, led by Rāshid al-Dīn Sinān,

---

[14] Compare the exposition of the doctrine of the Mufawwiḍa by Saʿd b. ʿAbd Allāh al-Qummī, *Kitāb al-Maqālāt wa'l-firaq*, ed. M. Jawād Mashkūr (Tehran, 1963), p. 61, with Abū Yaʿqūb al-Sijistānī, *Kitāb Ithbāt al-nubuwwāt*, ed. Wilferd Madelung and Paul Walker (Tehran, 2016), pp. 2–3. On the links between the 'Mufaḍḍal tradition' and the Mufawwiḍa, see Asatryan, *Controversies* (passim).

[15] Daniel De Smet, 'La fonction noétique de la triade al-Jadd, al-Fatḥ et al-Khayāl. Les fondements de la connaissance prophétique dans l'ismaélisme', in Hinrich Biesterfeldt and Verena Klemm (ed.), *Differenz und Dynamik im Islam. Festschrift für Heinz Halm zum 70. Geburtstag* (Würzburg, 2012), pp. 319–336.

[16] Halm, *Kosmologie*, pp. 75–90.

[17] De Smet, 'Les racines docétistes', pp. 87–112; Daniel De Smet, 'Le mythe des préadamites en islam chiite', *Intellectual History of the Islamicate World*, 6 (2018), pp. 252–280.

[18] Asatryan, *Controversies,* pp. 123–135; Asatryan, 'Shiite Underground Literature', pp. 143–147.

took possession of fortresses such as Maṣyāf, Qadmūs and al-Kahf, ruling over a region with a major Nuṣayrī population. In the nineteenth century, an American missionary, Henry de Forest, acquired a Syrian Nizārī manuscript and sent it to the Orientalist Edward Salisbury for translation. At almost the same time, the French consul Jean-Baptiste Rousseau obtained another manuscript in Maṣyāf; deposited in the *Bibliothèque nationale* in Paris, it was edited and translated by Stanislas Guyard in 1874.[19] René Dussaud, the founder of modern research about the Nuṣayrīs, discovered in some of the Nizārī fragments published by Guyard strong affinities with Nuṣayrī doctrine and attributed it to the influence of the Syrian Nuṣayrīs on Rāshid al-Dīn Sinān.[20] The presence of the 'Mufaḍḍal tradition' in Syrian Nizārī writings (including the texts translated by Salisbury) was finally confirmed by Heinz Halm, who explained it as the result of a 'Nuṣayrī-Ismaili syncretism' going back to the sixth/twelfth century.[21] Direct contacts between the two communities would also account for the fact that manuscripts of the *Kitāb al-Haft* and related texts seem to be preserved in Syrian Nizārī libraries.[22] Although the *Umm al-kitāb* does not belong to the Nuṣayrī literature, the Nizārīs are supposed to have discovered this book in Syria; they subsequently introduced it into Central Asia, where it was translated into Persian.[23]

---

19 Edward Salisbury, 'Translation of Two Unpublished Arabic Documents Relating to the Doctrines of the Ismāʿilis and Other Bāṭinian Sects, with an Introduction and Notes', *JAOS*, 2 (1851), pp. 257–324; Edward Salisbury, 'Translation of an Unpublished Arabic Risāleh by Khālid ibn Zeid al-Juʿfy with Notes', *JAOS*, 3 (1852), pp. 165–193; Stanislas Guyard, *Fragments relatifs à la doctrine des Ismaélis* (Paris, 1874).

20 René Dussaud, 'Influence de la religion noṣairī sur la doctrine de Râchid ad-Dîn Sinân', *Journal Asiatique*, 9, 16 (1900), pp. 61–69.

21 Halm, 'Buch der Schatten (I)', pp. 263–265.

22 Asatryan, *Controversies*, pp. 134–135; Asatryan, 'Shiite Underground Literature', pp. 130, 153 notes 24 and 25. Unfortunately, the private libraries of the Syrian Nizārīs, inaccessible to outsiders, have never been catalogued.

23 Halm, 'Buch der Schatten (II)', p. 42 and note 115; Anthony, 'The Legend of Abdallāh Ibn Saba'', p. 9. In fact, the exact circumstances of the adoption of the *Umm al-kitāb* by the Nizārīs remain unknown; see Wladimir Ivanow, 'Notes sur l'Ummu'l-Kitab des Ismaëliens de l'Asie Centrale', *Revue des Études Islamiques*, 6 (1923), pp. 419–426.

Without denying the possibility that Nuṣayrī doctrine influenced Syrian Ismailism, the interest of the Nizārīs in these texts and the ideas they contain could also be due to the fact that they still belonged to a living tradition among the Ismailis in the Fatimid period preceding the emergence of the Nizārīs. This could explain the otherwise puzzling phenomenon that in the same sixth/twelfth century a similar revival of the 'Mufaḍḍal tradition' occurred in the rival branch of the Ṭayyibiyya in Yemen, far remote from Syria and from any possible Nuṣayrī influence, and also that 'Mufaḍḍal books' were kept in Bohra collections in India.[24] This is, for instance, the case with the *Kitāb al-Ashbāḥ wa'l-aẓilla*.[25] David Hollenberg recently discovered that one of the texts published by Guyard from a Syrian Nizārī manuscript, in which Hollenberg recognised a 'quasi-Nuṣayrī' doctrine, is also preserved in an Indian manuscript belonging to the collection of the Ṭayyibī scholar Zāhid ʿAlī (now in the Institute of Ismaili Studies, London, Arab. MS. 1283).[26] Rather than postulating an improbable Nuṣayrī influence on Ṭayyibism or contacts between Syrian Nizārīs and Yemeni or Indian Ṭayyibīs, the common interest for 'Mufaḍḍal books and ideas' can be explained by the fact that both communities share a common Ismaili heritage including the early Shiʿi traditions of the so-called *ghulāt*.

Ṭayyibī Intellectual Interactions with the 'Mufaḍḍal Tradition'

Heinz Halm noted the importance of the 'Mufaḍḍal tradition' in Ṭayyibī literature, including sayings of the first imams transmitted by

---

24 Halm, 'Buch der Schatten (I)', pp. 221–222.

25 Adam Gacek, *Catalogue of Arabic Manuscripts in the Library of The Institute of Ismaili Studies*, vol. I (London, 1984), p. 7; Ismail K. Poonawala, *Biobibliography of Ismāʿīlī Literature* (Malibu, 1977), p. 339. It is interesting to note that Ivanow, working in Indian Ṭayyibī libraries, described it as "a work definitely belonging to the Yamanite period" (Wladimir Ivanow, *Ismaili Literature. A Biographical Survey* (Tehran, 1963), p. 97 n° 370).

26 David Hollenberg, '*Anta anā wa-anā minka* ('You are me, and I am from you'): A Quasi-Nuṣayrī Fragment on the Intellect in the Early Ismāʿīlī Treatise *Kitāb Ta'wīl ḥurūf al-muʿjam*', in Joseph E. Lowry and Shawkat M. Toorawa (ed.), *Arabic Humanities, Islamic Thought. Essays in Honor of Everett K. Rowson* (Leiden and Boston, 2017), pp. 50–66, in particular pp. 51–53, 65.

al-Mufaḍḍal and other *ghulāt*.[27] However, the question of Ṭayyibī interaction with this early Shiʿi tradition has never been investigated. In the following pages, three main doctrines and the way Ṭayyibī authors integrated them in their own system will be examined: (1) the shadows and the apparitions; (2) the five aspects of the deity and their pre-existence; (3) the relation between the divinity, the humanity and the bodily envelope of the imam. Finally, there will be an endeavour to understand what exactly Ṭayyibī authors mean when claiming that their doctrine about the imams has nothing to do with *ghuluww*.

a. *The Shadows, the Apparitions and their Fall*

In accordance with the plea for continuity between Ismailism and early Shiʿi traditions, as expressed in the first part of this paper, al-Ḥāmidī introduces the notion of the 'apparitions and the shadows' in his *Kanz al-walad* by quoting Abū Yaʿqūb al-Sijistānī's *Kitāb al-Bishāra*, a work that seems to be lost today.[28] In the quoted passage, al-Sijistānī develops the Ismaili topic of the heptads, presented as seven concentric circles moving around a central point. The Creator (who manifestly remains outside the system) produces the Command (*al-amr*), located in the centre of seven circles representing its seven attributes: the unity (*al-waḥda*), the first (*al-awwal*), the cause (*al-ʿilla*), the eternal (*al-azal*), the thing (*al-shayʾ*), the word (*al-kalima*) and the intellect (*al-ʿaql*), the latter forming the outer circle encompassing all the others. In its turn, the intellect is the centre of a new set of seven circles: the soul (*al-nafs*) or the spiritual lights (*al-anwār al-rūḥāniyya*), the shadows (*al-aẓilla*), the apparitions (*al-ashbāḥ*), the forms (*al-ṣuwar*), the persons (*al-ashkhāṣ*) and the species (*al-ajnās*), the latter

[27] Halm, 'Buch der Schatten (I)', p. 265; ibid. (II), p. 80; Halm, *Kosmologie*, p. 166.

[28] On *Kitāb al-Bishāra*, mentioned by al-Sijistānī in *Kitāb al-Iftikhār*, ed. Ismail Poonawala (Beirut, 2000), pp. 193, 201 and *Kitāb al-Maqālīd*, ed. Ismail Poonawala (Tunis, 2011), p. 205, see Paul Walker, *Early Philosophical Shiism. The Ismaili Neoplatonism of Abū Yaʿqūb al-Sijistānī* (Cambridge, 1993), pp. 20–21, 164; Poonawala, *Biobibliography*, p. 86. For the interest Ṭayyibī authors took in *Kitāb al-Bishāra*, see François de Blois, *Arabic, Persian and Gujarati Manuscripts. The Hamdani Collection in the Library of The Institute of Ismaili Studies* (London and New York, 2011), p. 90 (the *Risālat rawḍat al-ḥikam* by ʿAlī b. Ḥātim al-Ḥāmidī).

enveloping the other circles. The species are identified with Adam, who is at the centre of a heptad of prophets (*nuṭaqā'*), ranking from Adam to the Resurrector (*qā'im*). All these circles are moving; just as the prophets succeed each other the spiritual lights become (*ṣāra*) shadows, the shadows become apparitions, the apparitions become forms, the forms become persons, and the persons become species.[29]

This progression, from the most luminous to the more compact substances, recalls the cosmology described in the *Kitāb al-Haft*. Moreover, the passage from *Kitāb al-Bishāra* associates the members of the different heptads with letters of the alphabet (*ḥurūf*), organised in sets of seven, following an early Shiʿi tradition widespread in Ismaili literature.[30] A similar doctrine can be found in the *Kitāb al-Fatarāt* attributed to Jaʿfar b. Manṣūr al-Yaman, a source often quoted in Ṭayyibī literature. After stressing the role of the letters in the generation of the universe and the emanation of the 'letters of the prophets' from the Pen and the Tablet, each of the seven prophets having his own set of seven letters, the author cites and approves a tradition transmitted by the adepts of transmigration (*ahl al-tanāsukh*) from Jaʿfar al-Ṣādiq, who is supposed to have said:

> God Most-High created shadows. The first of the shadows was Adam, who was the first to respond. Then [comes] the second until the seventh [. . .] and from them were produced the seven letters: the letter of the legatee (*waṣī*) of Adam, the letter of the legatee of Noah, the letter of the legatee of Abraham, the letter of the legatee of Moses, the letter of the legatee of Jesus, the letter of the legatee of Muhammad and the letter of the proof (*ḥujja*) of the *qā'im*. Then were produced from them the seven letters of the imams of Adam.[31]

---

29 Ibrāhīm b. al-Ḥusayn al-Ḥāmidī, *Kitāb Kanz al-walad*, ed. Muṣṭafā Ghālib (Wiesbaden, 1971), pp. 258–261. The text continues with another series of heptads: every prophet is the centre of seven concentric circles representing the seven imams of his cycle. As is often the case with Ṭayyibī authors quoting from otherwise unknown sources, it is difficult to establish where the fragment from *Kitāb al-Bishāra* ends and where al-Ḥāmidī's comments and elaborations start.

30 Halm, *Kosmologie*, pp. 38–52.

31 Jaʿfar b. Manṣūr al-Yaman, *Kitāb al-Fatarāt*, passage published in Halm, *Kosmologie*, pp. 219–220.

Al-Ḥāmidī's cosmic system is based on the theory of the ten Intellects borrowed from al-Fārābī by the Fatimid philosopher Ḥamīd al-Dīn al-Kirmānī.[32] Claiming to reveal the true meaning (*ḥaqīqa*) of al-Kirmānī's *Rāḥat al-ʿaql*, al-Ḥāmidī introduced the notion of the 'primordial error' (*al-khaṭī'a al-ūlā*) made by the third Intellect (or second emanated being, *al-munbaʿith al-thānī*). Out of inadvertence and confusion, the third Intellect worshipped the first Intellect or first created being (*al-mubdaʿ al-awwal*) as the Creator (*al-mubdiʿ*) and refused to acknowledge the role of the second Intellect or first emanated being as an intermediary between the first Intellect and itself. In other terms, the third Intellect professed the *tawḥīd* in an erroneous way, so that it no longer received the divine influx (*mādda*) necessary for its actualisation. After the emanation of seven other Intellects in actuality out of the second Intellect, it remained an Intellect in potentiality at the tenth and last level of the cosmic hierarchy.[33]

This cosmic drama and the subsequent fall (*hubūṭ*) due to an error or an act of insubordination to the divine commands, are well known from early Shiʿi literature (for instance *Kitāb al-Haft* and *Umm al-kitāb*); it left traces in Fatimid Ismailism and was fully elaborated in the Druze writings.[34] Following al-Ḥāmidī's interpretation of *Rāḥat al-ʿaql*, Muḥammad b. Ṭāhir al-Ḥārithī (d. 584/1188) introduced in the theory of the ten Intellects a terminology which recalls the ancient 'Mufaḍḍal tradition'. The 'radiating divine light' (*al-nūr al-shaʿshaʿānī al-ilāhī*) of the first Intellect is hidden behind a veil (*ḥijāb*). The nine Intellects emanating from the first are qualified as 'pure luminous and formal apparitions' (*ashbāḥ ṣūriyya maḥḍa nūrāniyya*), bearing inside (*fī ḍimn*) their essence a plurality of 'formal apparitions' (*ashbāḥ ṣūriyya*). After the error and subsequent fall of the third Intellect, followed by the latter's repentance, the first Intellect organised a *daʿwa*, summoning the 'formal apparitions' inside the different Intellects to

[32] On this theory, see Daniel De Smet, *La Quiétude de l'Intellect. Néoplatonisme et gnose ismaélienne dans l'œuvre de Ḥamīd al-Dīn al-Kirmānī* (Leuven, 1995).

[33] Al-Ḥāmidī, *Kanz*, pp. 65–69, 83–89, 295–296; De Smet, *Quiétude*, pp. 248–251; De Smet, *Philosophie ismaélienne*, pp. 82–88.

[34] Halm, *Kosmologie*, pp. 75–90.

profess *tawḥīd* in a correct way. All responded positively, except the 'formal apparitions' belonging to the fallen tenth Intellect. They continued their rebellion, fell further down and became forms (*ṣuwar*) mixed with matter (*hayūlā*). Nevertheless, there was a gradation in the disobedience of these apparitions, so that they split in three groups: those who were close to repentance and correct *tawḥīd*, those who were half on the way to it, finally those who rejected the call and were guilty of pure *kufr*. Out of the first two groups and their corresponding matter, the tenth Intellect formed the celestial bodies and spheres, whereas the third group served as material for the generation of the four elements and their mixtures, causing the appearance of the three natural reigns: minerals, plants and animals. The tenth Intellect, acting as demiurge (*mudabbir*), generated the sense perceptible world in order to save the 'spiritual apparitions' (*ashbāḥ rūḥāniyya*) mixed with matter. Their redemption (*khalāṣ*) is only possible through the production of the '*alif*-like persons' (*ashkhāṣ alifiyya*), meaning the human species whose upright position is similar to the form of an *alif*. Directed by the 'eminent person' (*shakhṣ fāḍil*) of the prophet or the imam, the process of purification allows the tenth Intellect to save the 'formal apparitions' that were lost during its fall from their admixture with matter, in order to reintegrate them into its essence, thus returning gradually to its initial third position in the cosmic hierarchy. This final return will be achieved with the formation of the most eminent of the eminent persons: the 'perfect child' (*al-walad al-tāmm*), the *qā'im* inaugurating the final resurrection.[35]

Notwithstanding the absence of the shadows (*aẓilla*), al-Ḥārithī's *Kitāb al-Anwār al-laṭīfa* describes a succession of entities similar to those we find in texts related to the 'Mufaḍḍal tradition': 'radiating divine light' hidden behind a veil, 'pure luminous and formal appari-

35 Muḥammad b. Ṭāhir al-Ḥārithī, *Kitāb al-Anwār al-laṭīfa*, ed. Ḥussām Khuḍūr (Salamiyya, 2011), pp. 46–64, 76–77. The Ṭayyibī system as revealed by al-Ḥāmidī and al-Ḥārithī is close to Manichaeism; see Daniel De Smet, 'La colonne de lumière, une notion manichéenne dans l'ismaélisme ṭayyibite', in Anna Van den Kerchove and Luciana G. Soares Santoprete (ed.), *Gnose et manichéisme. Entre les oasis d'Égypte et la Route de la Soie. Hommage à Jean-Daniel Dubois* (Turnhout, 2017), pp. 349–375.

tions', 'formal apparitions', 'forms' mixed with matter, 'persons' incorporated in the prophets and the imams.[36]

b. The Five Aspects of the Deity and their Pre-existence

Echoing Shiʿi traditions about the apparition of the imams as apparitions of light (*ashbāḥ nūr*) long before the creation of the world,[37] Idrīs ʿImād al-Dīn (d. 872/1468) explained a saying of Muḥammad al-Bāqir by stating that the friends of God (*awliyāʾ Allāh*) manifest themselves to mankind 'as apparitions and in their human natures' (*biʾl-ashbāḥ waʾl-nawāsīt*), so that people can see them and receive their guidance. However, only the friends of God are able to perceive these apparitions as they really are, 'with their subtle, luminous and noble forms' (*bi ṣuwarihim al-laṭīfa al-nayyira al-sharīfa*), and this in accordance with the purity of their own forms and the radiance of their essence.[38]

Following the creation of the luminous apparitions of Muhammad, ʿAlī, Fāṭima, al-Ḥasan and al-Ḥusayn, God created the angels out of light. As He remained hidden behind these apparitions, the angels erroneously held them to be God himself and glorified them. Thereupon, God put the angels to the test by sending clouds of obscurity, so that they were no longer able to see any of the apparitions. Thus, they addressed a new glorification to God, asking him to remove these veils while recognising the fact that He is the real agent (*al-faʿʿāl*) who does what He wants.[39] In other terms, the deity manifests himself in a pentad of apparitions, five entities of light, which are created by and subjected to the uncreated, hidden (*ghayb*) God.

The story about the glorification of the angels is part of a long *ḥadīth* reporting the teachings of the Prophet Muhammad to his uncle

---

[36] The *Risālat al-Mabdaʾ waʾl-maʿād* by al-Ḥusayn b. al-Walīd (d. 667/1268) (ed. with French translation by Henry Corbin, *Trilogie ismaélienne* (Tehran and Paris, 1961)) is in fact a summary of al-Ḥārithī's *al-Anwār al-laṭīfa*. However, for some reason the author avoids using this terminology, for instance replacing *ashbāḥ* with *ṣuwar* (thus pp. 102–104 of Corbin's edition).

[37] Amir-Moezzi, *Guide divin*, pp. 81–83.

[38] Idrīs ʿImād al-Dīn, *Kitāb Zahr al-maʿānī*, ed. Muṣṭafā Ghālib (Beirut, 1991), p. 182.

[39] Idrīs, *Zahr*, p. 177.

al-ʿAbbās b. ʿAbd al-Muṭallib, as transmitted by Jābir b. ʿAbd Allāh al-Anṣarī.[40] In response to al-ʿAbbās' question about the superiority of the Ahl al-Bayt over his own family, the Prophet said:

> God created me and He created my brother ʿAlī when there was no heaven, no earth, no Paradise, no Hell, no Tablet and no Pen. When He wanted to create us, He uttered a word (*kalima*) and it became a light and a soul (*nūran wa-rūḥan*). He mixed them together and created me and ʿAlī from it. From my light He created the Throne – I am superior to the Throne – and He created from ʿAlī's light the light of the heaven, as ʿAlī is superior to the heavens. From the light of al-Ḥasan He created the light of the moon and He created from the light of al-Ḥusayn the light of the sun, establishing both [the sun and the moon] as a light for the inhabitants of the earth [. . .].[41] From the light of Fāṭima God Most-High created something resembling the form of the candlestick and He suspended it at the ring (*qurṭ*) of the Throne, so that it illuminates (*azharat*) the heavens and the earth. For this reason, Fāṭima was named 'the radiant' (*al-zahrā'*).[42]

According to another tradition quoted by Idrīs ʿImād al-Dīn, Jaʿfar al-Ṣādiq responded to a question about the Lord (*al-rabb*) by saying, 'The five words of God are one.' He then appeared to the person who had asked this question successively in the forms of the moon (ʿAlī), Fāṭima, Muhammad, al-Ḥasan and al-Ḥusayn, declaring, 'They are all

[40] This companion of the Prophet (d. ca. 77–78/696–697), favourably disposed towards ʿAlī and the first imams, was a prolific transmitter of *ḥadīth*, including *ghulāt* traditions; he appears, for instance, as the first authority in the *isnād* of *ḥadīth*s transmitted by Jābir al-Juʿfī from al-Bāqir or in traditions transmitted by al-Mufaḍḍal al-Juʿfī and Muḥammad b. Sinān (Etan Kohlberg, 'An Unusual Shīʿī isnād', *Israel Oriental Studies*, 5 (1975), pp. 143–149; cf. Amir-Moezzi, *Guide divin*, p. 63 n. 130). He is mentioned in the *Umm al-kitāb*, where he is sometimes mixed up with Jābir b. Yazīd al-Juʿfī, and in *isnād*s of Nuṣayrī texts (Halm, *Islamische Gnosis*, pp. 125, 128, 134–137, 155, 164, 188, 190–191, 320; Anthony, 'The Legend of Abdallāh Ibn Saba'', pp. 13–14).

[41] Follows the passage about the glorification of the angels.

[42] Idrīs, *Zahr*, pp. 176–177.

one; they speak with one tongue and take the form they want, with the power of God, the Lord of the worlds.'[43]

In a similar way, ʿAlī manifested himself to Jābir b. ʿAbd Allāh al-Anṣarī under the form of the letter *mīm*, then he took the form of the letter *fā'*, two times the form of the *ḥā'*, before returning to the form of the *ʿayn*:

> This is the noble, magnificent, eminent and apparent form under the veils, the form by which are established the true meanings (*maʿānī*) of the books. He said, 'Jābir, these are my veils and my garments in which I appear in every age and at any time.'[44]

In another version of this tradition, also quoted by Idrīs, the imam (in this case ʿAlī Zayn al-ʿĀbidīn) after accomplishing the 'miracle of the letters' (*muʿjizat al-ḥurūf*), said, 'Jābir, they are shirts (*qumuṣ*) for every age and any time. The shirts change, but I do not change.'[45]

These traditions accord to ʿAlī and the corresponding letter *ʿayn* a certain prominence over Muhammad and 'his' letter *mīm*. However, this *ʿayniyya* trend does not seem to be a theological issue for Ṭayyibī authors, as they also quote *mīmiyya* traditions, which present Muhammad as the first created being manifesting himself through the other members of the pentad.[46] Thus, in the same chapter, Idrīs mentions a

---

43 Idrīs, *Zahr*, p. 167. This tradition recalls the so-called 'school anecdote' in the *Umm al-kitāb* (§ 39–43) where Muḥammad al-Bāqir appeared to his teacher ʿAbd Allāh b. Saba' successively in the forms of the five of the Ahl al-Bayt, each time proclaiming his divinity; see a German translation of the passage in Halm, *Islamische Gnosis*, pp. 132–134, and an English one in Antony, 'The Legend of Abdallāh Ibn Saba'', pp. 12–30.

44 Idrīs, *Zahr*, p. 254; cf. Ibid., pp. 167, 216–217 (here, it is the fourth imam ʿAlī Zayn al-ʿĀbidīn who appears to Jābir b. ʿAbd Allāh al-Anṣarī).

45 Idrīs, *Zahr*, pp. 216–217; for similar traditions, see De Smet, 'Racines docétistes', pp. 95–99.

46 Al-Shahrastānī, *Kitāb al-Milal wa'l-niḥal*, ed. Muḥammad Kīlānī (Beirut, n.d.), vol. 1, pp. 175–176: 'Some believe in the divinity of both [ʿAlī and Muhammad], but give precedence to ʿAlī concerning the prerogatives of divinity; they are called *al-ʿayniyya*. Others believe also in the divinity of both [ʿAlī and Muhammad], but consider Muhammad as superior in divinity; they are called *al-mīmiyya*. Yet others believe in the divinity of all the members of the Companions of the Cloak, Muhammad, ʿAlī, Fāṭima, al-Ḥasan and al-Ḥusayn. They consider these five as one single

tradition of al-Bāqir transmitted by Jābir b. Yazīd al-Juʿfī. The imam, in response to a question about the real essence (*ḥaqīqa*) of the Prophet, said that his rank corresponds to the 'Preceder' (*sābiq*), the first created being, the first Intellect, directly generated by Gods command (*amr*). This essence is hidden 'in the cave' (*fī ghār*) of the body and cannot be seen. Muhammad's person (*shakhṣ*) in reality never ceased to exist; it did not disappear, it never fled, and no harm overtook it: all this only happened in appearance (*tashbīh*). At the other hand, his humanity (*nāsūt*) is subjected to pain and suffering, as is the case with every human body. The same is true for Fāṭima, al-Ḥasan, al-Ḥusayn, and supposedly also for ʿAlī (although he is not named here): their essence is one and the same, inalterable and hidden in a corporeal envelope, which is corruptible.[47]

c. The Divinity (lāhūt), the Humanity (nāsūt) and the Bodily Envelope (ghilāf) of the Imam

The distinction between the 'divinity' (*lāhūt*) and the 'humanity' (*nāsūt*) of the imam is treated in most Ṭayyibī doctrinal works, in contrast with the earlier Fatimid literature, which generally avoided this sensitive issue.[48] In his *Kanz al-walad*, al-Ḥāmidī devoted a *faṣl* to the question, piling together sources belonging to different Shiʿi traditions.

As is often the case, he started from al-Kirmānī's *Rāḥat al-ʿaql*, with its clear distinction between the Creator (*al-Mubdiʿ*) and the act of creation (*ibdāʿ*), the latter being identical with the first created being (*al-mubdaʿ al-awwal*), the first Intellect.[49] However, he introduced a

---

thing; the spirit (*rūḥ*) inheres in each of them in an equal way, and no one of them is superior to the others'. These are exactly the doctrines reflected in the different traditions quoted side by side in Idrīs' *Zahr al-maʿānī*.

47 Idrīs, *Zahr*, pp. 179–180. I suppose that Khālid b. Zayd al-Juʿfī in Ghālib's edition is a mistake for Jābir b. Yazīd al-Juʿfī.

48 Habib Feki, *Les idées religieuses et philosophiques de l'ismaélisme fatimide* (Tunis, 1978), pp. 205–209; Daniel De Smet, 'La naissance miraculeuse de l'imam ismaélien. Nourritures célestes et corps camphré', *Acta Orientalia Belgica*, 28 (2015), pp. 323–333.

49 On the identification of the act of creation with the first created being, see De Smet, *Quiétude*, pp. 148–150.

third level to al-Kirmānī's system, 'the manifest spiritual form' (*al-ṣūra al-rūḥāniyya al-ẓāhira*), and claimed that these three levels are connected by a chain (*silsila*). Thus, the Creator is linked to the act of creation or first created being and the latter is linked to the spiritual form.[50]

What al-Ḥāmidī intends to prove is that the *ibdāʿ–mubdaʿ* or first Intellect represents the divinity (*lāhūt*) of the imam, and that the 'manifest spiritual form' is his humanity (*nāsūt*). In order to make this point, he provides a quote introduced by the phrase, *qāla al-ḥakīm* ('the sage says')[51]:

> Know that the Hidden (*al-ghayb*) – may He be praised! – is united with his act of creation (*ibdāʿ*), speaks through it and is veiled by it. It [the *ibdāʿ*] is his greatest name and the greatest named thing, that which is named by all the existents; it summons (*al-dāʿī*) to its essence by its essence; it is the first before everything and the last after everything; it transfers the designation (*al-nāṣṣ*) from the past imam upon the next imam [. . .]; it is not hidden by a twinkling of an eye, being eternal, everlasting and perpetual, manifesting itself with what it wants and how it wants, by the most outstanding of its temples of light, bringing them closer with the assistance of its spiritual dignitaries (*ḥudūdihi al-rūḥāniyya*).[52]

In other terms, the transcendent hidden Creator manifests himself through the first created being (*ibdāʿ – mubdaʿ*) or first Intellect, God's representative to whom He has delegated all his powers, and who is at the same time the principle of the imamate. In its turn, the first Intellect manifests itself in the 'temples of light', the uninterrupted chain of imams assisted by the dignitaries of their *daʿwa*.

---

50 Al-Ḥāmidī, *Kanz*, p. 193. This notion of a 'chain' is alien to al-Kirmānī and contrary to his thought, as he would never have accepted the notion that the Creator remains linked to his creature after the act of creation is accomplished; for al-Kirmānī, there is a gap between the Creator and his creation (De Smet, *Quiétude*, pp. 101–110).

51 In *Kanz al-walad* and other Ṭayyibī sources, *al-ḥakīm* often (but not exclusively) refers to the imam who is supposed to be the author of the *Rasāʾil Ikhwān al-Ṣafāʾ* and the *Risāla al-Jāmiʿa* (De Smet, 'L'auteur des *Rasāʾil Ikhwān al-Ṣafāʾ*", p. 156). However, this passage does not occur in Ghālib's edition of the *Risāla al-Jāmiʿa*.

52 Al-Ḥāmidī, *Kanz*, p. 193.

Al-Ḥāmidī further specifies this doctrine by distinguishing three levels in the divine manifestation, each level serving as a veil hiding the higher level: (1) the Hidden is manifested as well as veiled by the first Intellect, the principle of the imamate; (2) the first Intellect is manifested as well as veiled by the 'separated luminous form' (*al-ṣūra al-mujarrada al-nūrāniyya*) or temple of light, which is the imamate; (3) this separated form is manifested as well as veiled by the 'envelope' (*ghilāf*), which is the imam in his corporality, being a man from flesh and blood.[53]

Then there follows a quote taken from Jaʿfar b. Manṣūr al-Yaman, who is supposed to have said 'somewhere' (*fī baʿḍi awḍāʿihi*), glorifying God Most-High, that his inward aspect (*bāṭin*) is hidden and not perceptible, whereas his outward aspect (*ẓāhir*) is the imamate.[54]

Al-Ḥāmidī has now all the elements he needs to formulate his doctrine about the *lāhūt* and the *nāsūt* of the imam. The Creator remains hidden in his essence, inaccessible to his creatures. He manifests himself through his act of creation, the first created being, the first Intellect, which is the principle of the imamate, corresponding to the divinity (*lāhūt*) of the imam. This *lāhūt* remains hidden to the believer, but manifests itself through its spiritual form, which is the humanity (*nāsūt*) of the imam. In order to make this manifestation possible, the spiritual form or *nāsūt* appears in the *ghilāf*, the bodily envelope of the imam.[55]

> Praised be his [the imam's] divinity which is veiled for us, whereas he manifests himself to us by his humanity. He appears to his creature by his creature in so far that he is his creature. This

---

[53] Al-Ḥāmidī, *Kanz*, pp. 193–194. 'Separated' (*mujarrad*) means here separated from matter, incorporeal.

[54] Al-Ḥāmidī, *Kanz*, p. 194.

[55] The distinction between these three levels is not al-Ḥāmidī's invention, as it is already present in the beginning of the fifth/eleventh century in the writings of the Druze *dāʿī*, Ḥamza b. ʿAlī: God remains hidden in his *lāhūt* but reveals himself through his *nāsūt*, which took the bodily appearance of al-Ḥākim. There is much confusion about this matter in modern scholarship on the Druze doctrine, as the person of Caliph al-Ḥākim is often incorrectly identified with the *nāsūt* of God; see Daniel De Smet, *Les Épîtres sacrées des Druzes* (Leuven 2007), pp. 39–40.

> means that his veiled divinity is the act of creation (*ibdāʿ*), which is the [first] created being (*mubdaʿ*); his humanity appearing to us is this separated form; his appearance to his creature by his creature means 'by the envelope' (*bi'l-ghilāf*), as it falls inside the limits of creation.[56]

As a final legitimation of this doctrine, al-Ḥāmidī quotes Jaʿfar al-Ṣādiq who said, 'Our outward aspect is the imamate, our inward aspect is hidden and cannot be perceived' (*ẓāhirunā imāma, bāṭinunā ghayb lā yudrak*),[57] followed by a tradition reported on the authority of Jābir b. ʿAbd Allāh al-Anṣarī: ʿAlī appeared to Salmān and Abū Dharr 'in his luminous form' (*bi'l-nūrāniyya*), whereas al-Ḥusayn appeared in the same way to Jābir. Asked about such apparitions, Muḥammad al-Bāqir warns his disciples:

> Do not invoke us as gods, but say about our excellence what your minds can bear. All this is only a part of the signs of your Lord. Do not say about God what pertains to us, and do not say about us what belongs to the most eloquent of our party.[58]

Manifestly in order to honour 'the most eloquent' of the Shiʿa, al-Ḥāmidī then cites some verses describing the 'spiritual form' (*ṣūra rūḥāniyya*) and the 'envelope form' (*ṣūra ghilāfiyya*) of the imam, verses that are taken from a *Kitāb al-Ibtidāʾ wa'l-intihāʾ* which might belong to the 'Mufaḍḍal tradition'.[59]

As a matter of fact, the Ṭayyibī doctrine about the *lāhūt* and the *nāsūt* of the imam is based on the *ḥadīth*: 'Our outward is the imamate, our inward is hidden and cannot be perceived', as interpreted and transmitted by the 'Mufaḍḍal tradition'. This is particularly clear from Idrīs's *Zahr al-maʿānī*. The author reports that Jaʿfar al-Ṣādiq was

---

[56] Al-Ḥāmidī, *Kanz*, p. 195.

[57] This *ḥadīth* is also quoted in al-Ḥāmidī, *Kanz*, p. 165; Idrīs, *Zahr*, p. 254.

[58] Al-Ḥāmidī, *Kanz*, p. 195.

[59] Al-Ḥāmidī, *Kanz*, pp. 195–196. Ghālib (p. 195, note 7) remarks that several works bearing this title are kept in Ismaili libraries, one of them being attributed to al-Mufaḍḍal al-Juʿfī; see Halm, 'Buch der Schatten (I)', p. 222; Halm, *Kosmologie*, p. 166.

questioned by Muḥammad b. Sinān, 'a man belonging to the elite of his friends' (*khāṣṣat awliyā'ihi*),[60] about Muhammad and 'Alī.

Ja'far answers that since Muhammad proceeds from God's light, he is indicative of *Allāh*. As such, Muhammad is the inward divinity (*al-lāhūt al-bāṭin*), hidden but manifested by the name of 'Alī, the latter referring to the apparent form (*al-ṣūra al-ẓāhira*). Muhammad and 'Alī are the two faces of the same reality: the *bāṭin* manifested in the *ẓāhir*, the *lāhūt* manifested through the *nāsūt*. This is the esoteric meaning of the *ḥadīth* of Ghadīr Khumm: Muhammad is the friend (*walī*) of 'Alī and 'Alī is the friend of Muhammad. Hence *Allāh* or Muhammad is hidden in his *bāṭin*, but manifest in his *ẓāhir*: his friend 'Alī, representing the *nāsūt* or the imamate. Although it is not explicitly stipulated one may extrapolate that, in this instance, the use of the Arabic word *Allāh* refers to the first created being, the first Intellect, and not to the Creator as such, to which no name can be attributed.[61]

The fourth imam 'Alī Zayn al-'Ābidīn declared in the presence of Jābir b. 'Abd Allāh al-Anṣarī: 'I am the house of the Merciful' (*anā bayt al-raḥmān*) or, on another occasion, 'We [the imams] are the faces of the Merciful' (*naḥnu wujūh al-raḥmān*). God dwells in the imams and manifests his hidden essence through them.[62]

d. 'No Exaggeration (ghuluww) and no Reduction (taqṣīr)'

Heinz Halm considered paradoxical the fact that Ṭayyibī authors transmitted a set of ideas and even whole books belonging to the 'Mufaḍḍal tradition' of the *ghulāt*, although they vehemently rejected *ghuluww*.[63]

---

[60] Muḥammad b. Sinān is a well-known transmitter of traditions from al-Mufaḍḍal and other members of the Ju'fī group; see Halm, 'Buch der Schatten (I)', pp. 236–240; Asatryan, *Controversies*, pp. 62–64.

[61] Idrīs, *Zahr*, pp. 163–164. According to the Imāmī heresiographer Sa'd b. 'Abd Allāh al-Qummī, *Kitāb al-Maqālāt wa'l-firaq*, ed. Muḥammad Jawād Mashkūr (Tehran, 1963), pp. 56–57, the Mukhammisa professed that the *bāṭin* of God is Muhammad, whereas his *ẓāhir* is the imamate. For the use of the word Allāh as referring to the first created being, see De Smet, *Quiétude*, pp. 177–180.

[62] Idrīs, *Zahr*, pp. 189–190.

[63] Halm, 'Buch der Schatten (I)', p. 265 n. 281: 'Trotz grundsätzlicher Ablehnung des *ġuluww* hat die ṭayyibitische Lehre eine Reihe von Vorstellungen und Begriffen, ja sogar ganze Mufaḍḍal-Bücher der *ġulāt* rezipiert'.

Indeed, the central issue in Ṭayyibī Ismailism is how to determine the right way to profess *tawḥīd*, an obligation incumbent on the whole of creation, from the first Intellect to the lowest being in the sublunary world. Attesting to God's unity and uniqueness implies avoiding the two extremes of 'exaggeration' (*ghuluww*) and 'reduction' (*taqṣīr*). According to al-Ḥāmidī, the 'primordial error' of the third Intellect, causing its fall and provoking the 'drama in heaven', was due to its faulty *tawḥīd*, which was at the same time corrupted by *ghuluww* and *taqṣīr*. The third Intellect acted as a *ghālī*, an 'extremist', when it identified the first Intellect or first created being with the Creator (*mubdiʿ*); it behaved as a *muqaṣṣir* when rejecting the role of the second Intellect as a necessary intermediary. In other words, as a Shiʿi *ghālī* would have done, the third Intellect assimilated the *lāhūt* with the Creator, and, resembling a Sunni Muslim, it rejected the *nāsūt* or the imamate.[64]

Al-Ḥāmidī describes the *ghulāt* as people who believe in the divinity of man (*ilāhiyyat al-bashar*). They claim that God, the Creator, is present in the world of generation and corruption, incorporated in a human body; at every moment, He needs water and food, He may become ill, suffer pain and die, or be killed by his enemies.[65] In this perspective, the traditions about the Prophet Muhammad and the imams, transmitted by Jābir b. ʿAbd Allāh al-Anṣarī, al-Mufaḍḍal, Muḥammad b. Sinān and others who are generally considered as *ghulāt*, have in fact nothing to do with *ghuluww*, as the divine principle or *lāhūt* manifested through the prophets' and the imams' *nāsūt* and *ghilāf* does not refer to the Creator, but to his first creature, the first Intellect. Despite their divine character, the prophets and the imams are distinct from God or, at the most, they can be considered as 'created divinities' to which God has delegated a large part of his powers. On the other hand, considering that the prophets and the imams are deprived of divinity means 'reducing' their nature as divine messengers: this is *taqṣīr*.[66]

According to al-Ḥāmidī, the *ghulāt* misunderstood expressions such as: 'The Commander of the faithful [ʿAlī] is the creator of the

---

64 Al-Ḥāmidī, *Kanz*, pp. 65–68, 88–89, in particular p. 67.

65 Ibid., p. 31.

66 Ibid., pp. 204, 293, 299; Idrīs, *Zahr*, p. 280.

forms of religion; he produces them, gives them life and lets them grow; he forms them with the eternal, everlasting form of the second perfection, that gives life to the intellects and the souls; he actualises them with the supreme elixir which never ends'. For the *ghulāt*, this means that ʿAlī is the Creator and God, the Ultimate reality, whereas in fact the sentence refers to the imam as representing the Intellect responsible for the actualisation of the human soul.[67]

Al-Ḥāmidī accuses the Nuṣayriyya of holding such *ghulāt* beliefs about ʿAlī's divinity.[68] Along with the related sect of the Isḥāqiyya (the followers of Isḥāq al-Aḥmar) the Nuṣayrīs were already depicted in al-Kirmānī's *Kitāb Tanbīh al-hādī* as incorporating *kufr* or *ghuluww par excellence.* Although, as a representative of moderate Fatimid Ismailism, al-Kirmānī abstains from quoting traditions about the *lāhūt* and the *nāsūt* of the imam, he has exactly the same conception of *ghuluww* as al-Ḥāmidī.[69]

Conclusion

Ṭayyibī authors, starting with al-Ḥāmidī's *Kanz al-walad*, included in their version of the Ismaili doctrine a set of notions going back to early Shiʿi movements which appeared in al-Kūfa and surroundings during the second/eighth and third/ninth centuries, in particular the Khaṭṭābiyya and the Mukhammisa. Themes such as the shadows and

---

67 Al-Ḥāmidī, *Kanz*, p. 221. The imam as a manifestation or incorporation of the Agent Intellect (the tenth Intellect in al-Kirmānī's system) giving the human intellect its second perfection (its complete actualisation) is a standard doctrine in Fatimid Ismailism; see De Smet, *Quiétude*, pp. 151–159, 355–360.

68 Al-Ḥāmidī, *Kanz*, p. 225, where the doctrine of the Nuṣayriyya is qualified as *kufr*. Elsewhere (*Kanz*, p. 286), al-Ḥāmidī distinguishes different 'erring sects': the *ghulāt*, the *muqaṣṣira*, the Nizāriyya, the Ḥākimiyya and the Ithnā ʿashariyya. If the Ḥākimiyya refers to the Druze, this would mean that al-Ḥāmidī did not regard them as part of the *ghulāt*.

69 Daniel De Smet, '*Kufr* et *takfīr* dans l'ismaélisme fatimide. Le *Kitāb Tanbīh al-hādī* de Ḥamīd al-Dīn al-Kirmānī', in Camilla Adang, Hassan Ansari, Maribel Fierro and Sabine Schmidtke (ed.), *Accusations of Unbelief in Islam. A Diachronic Perspective on* Takfīr (Leiden and Boston, 2016), pp. 92–97.

the apparitions, the cosmic drama and the subsequent fall, the five aspects of divinity, or the distinction between the divinity and the humanity of the imam, although not totally unknown to Fatimid Ismailism, were introduced into al-Kirmānī's system, expanded by the heritage of the Ikhwān al-Ṣafā'. A large number of *ḥadīth* reporting the sayings of Muhammad, ʿAlī and the first imams, transmitted by Jābir b. ʿAbd Allāh al-Anṣarī, Jābir b. Yazīd al-Juʿfī, al-Mufaḍḍal b. ʿUmar al-Juʿfī and Muḥammad b. Sinān, are quoted as authoritative sources. These transmitters, along with the doctrines they attribute to the Prophet and the imams, are usually suspected of *ghuluww* by mainstream Shiʿism. Some of the works containing this type of *ḥadīth* (for instance the *Kitāb al-Haft*) have been adopted by the Nuṣayrīs. However, for the Ṭayyibī authors, the traditions in question have nothing to do with *ghuluww*; it is only their interpretation by *ghulāt* sects such as the Nuṣayriyya that deserves the label of *kufr*. As far as the author of *Kanz al-walad* was concerned, the *ghulāt* mixed together the different levels of manifestation of God, ascribing to the Creator what belongs to the imam, considering the imam as the Creator or confusing the divinity of the imam with his humanity.

The intellectual interactions of Yemeni Ṭayyibism with the early Shiʿi tradition, of which the present paper only gives some examples, deserve further research. A more systematic exploration of Ṭayyibī literature, including many still unpublished works, is necessary in order to assess the influence of the *Kitāb al-Haft* and related 'Mufaḍḍal texts', some of which are kept in Ṭayyibī libraries. The striking presence of Mukhammisa traditions, close to those found in the *Umm al-kitāb*, a book that was at some point introduced into the Nizārī community, raises the question of the parallel transmission of this text in Ṭayyibī circles.

Although much work remains to be done, it is clear that the intellectual interactions between the different branches of Shiʿi Islam are much more complex than was once thought.

13

The Nizārī Ismaili Theory of the Resurrection (*Qiyāma*) and Post-Mongol Iranian Messianism

Orkhan Mir-Kasimov
(The Institute of Ismaili Studies)

Islamic mystical messanism, based on the expectation of a Saviour who will purify the faith and usher in a golden age of justice, constitutes an important factor of change and reform which has been part of the Islamic religious and socio-political landscape from the inception of Islam to the present day.[1] Several scholars have argued that Islam started as a messianic movement and Muhammad viewed himself as a

[1] There are several Arabic terms used to refer to messianic figures and which can express various kinds and degrees of messianic expectation. For example, Mujaddid al-Dīn, the 'renovator of religion', is a title attributed to several historical figures, such as Muḥammad al-Ghazālī (d. 505/1111), who were believed to be in possession of a divine mandate for periodical purification and rectification of the religious spirit and practice, especially at the turn of each century. The term Mahdi, the 'rightly guided one', can designate a historical rectifier of religion, similar to Mujaddid or, more specifically, the eschatological Saviour. The term *qā'im* (the one who rises) is used mostly in the Shiʿi context, and refers particularly to the eschatological role of the last imam in the Twelver and Ismaili branches of Shiʿi Islam. For a more detailed analysis of these and other terms expressing various aspects of messianic idea in the Islamic context see Y. Friedmann, *Prophecy Continuous: Aspects of Aḥmadī Religious Thought and Its Medieval Background* (Berkeley, Los Angeles and London, 1989), pp. 105–118. The discussion of semantic fields covered by each of these terms is beyond the scope of this article, but it is worth noting that the term 'messianism' applied to Islamic context does not refer only to the eschatological Saviour and does not necessarily imply the imminent end of the world; it can express a broad spectrum of ideas related to reform, change and modification aiming at the revivification and purification of religion and a return to the 'true' Islam of the prophetic age.

herald of the coming Saviour. I will not enter into the ongoing discussion about the validity of this hypothesis,[2] but it is known that the idea of the imminent coming of the Saviour was one of the sources of inspiration for the Shiʿi revolts against the Umayyad rulers during the first centuries of Islam, when apparently the term Mahdi acquired its meaning of 'eschatological Saviour'.[3] The coming of the Saviour and restoration of just rule was one of the central narratives that legitimised the Abbasid revolution, and it was later exploited by the Abbasids and their opponents alike, becoming an important political factor during the Abbasid period.[4] A similar role for messianic ideas in legitimising the change is observable in the western part of the Islamic world. Two out of three Berber revolutions that shaped the geopolitical configuration of the Maghrib, namely the Fatimid and the Almohad ones, were based on forms of messianic ideology which enabled them to contest the authority of the Abbasid caliph and to create alternative caliphates.[5] The Umayyad rulers in al-Andalus also used messianic symbolism to consolidate their legitimacy.[6] The intense search for a new conception of religious and political authority in the post-caliphal period was substantially informed by mystical and messianic doctrines and led to the consolidation of the new geopolitical configuration of the Islamic world, including the Ottoman, Safavid and

---

[2] An excellent summary and relevant bibliography can be found in M.A. Amir-Moezzi, 'Muḥammad le Paraclet et ʿAlī le Messie. Nouvelles remarques sur les origines de l'islam et de l'imamologie shi'ite', in M.A. Amir-Moezzi, M. De Cillis, D. De Smet and O. Mir-Kasimov (ed.), *Shiʿi Esotericism: Its Roots and Developments* (Turnhout, 2016), pp. 19–54; Fred Donner argued against the thesis of messianism in primitive Islam. See his 'La question du messianisme dans l'islam primitif, *Revue des Mondes Musulmans et de la Méditerranée*, 91–94 (2000), pp. 17–28.

[3] Wadad al-Qadi, 'The Development of the Term *Ghulāt* in Muslim Literature with special reference to the Kaysāniyya', in A. Dietrich (ed.), *Akten des VII. Kongresses für Arabistik und Islamwissenschaft* (Göttingen, 1976), pp. 295–319.

[4] H. Yücesoy, *Messianic Beliefs and Imperial Politics in Medieval Islam: The ʿAbbāsid Caliphate in the Early Ninth Century* (Columbia, SC, 2009).

[5] For a comprehensive study of the Western Islamic messianism see M. Garcia-Arenal, *Messianism and Puritanical Reform: Mahdis of the Muslim West* (Leiden, 2006).

[6] Garcia-Arenal, *Messianism*, pp. 92–95.

Mughal empires, where various interpretations of the figure of king as spiritual and/or messianic leader played an important role.[7]

The history of Islamic mystical messianism cannot be analysed in any detail within the limits of this chapter, but I would like to emphasise two important points. First, messianism does not necessarily imply the idea of an *imminent* coming of the Saviour or an imminent end of time. Obviously, the condition of imminence would have been a vulnerable point if the predicted event did not happen, and would have compromised any messianic claim as means of religious or political legitimisation. The most developed and influential Islamic messianic doctrines do not mention the immediate end of the world. Instead, they claim to usher in a new messianic era, during which mankind will be led by specially initiated figures. This idea is expressed, in various forms, in such intellectual trends as Twelver and Ismaili Shiʿism and the Sufism of Ibn Arabī (d. 638/1240).

According to the Twelver doctrine of occultation, the last imam, the Saviour (*qāʾim*) will return at some indefinite point in the future.

[7] The Safavids are perhaps the most salient example of spiritual leaders who founded an important royal dynasty. But the role of mystical and messianic/millenarian ideas in legitimising the Mughal emperors is also clearly visible. See A. Moin, *The Millennial Sovereign: Sacred Kingship and Sainthood in Islam* (New York, 2012). On the idea of a divine mandate for the rule of Muḥammad Shaybānī Khān (d. 916/1510), founder of the Uzbek polity in Transoxania, see A.J.E. Bodrogligeti, 'Muḥammad Shaybānī Khān's Apology to the Muslim Clergy', *Archivum Ottomanicum*, 13 (1993–1994), pp. 85–100. The Ottoman case is probably less obvious because the idea of spiritual or messianic leadership was not at the forefront of Ottoman legitimisation narratives. However, a connection with dervishes and saintly Friends of God, who informed Othman (d. after 1326), the eponym and founder of the Ottoman dynasty, that a divine mandate for universal rule had been bestowed on him and his descendants, was part of Ottoman legitimisation strategies. See C. Imber, 'The Ottoman Dynastic Myth', *Turcica*, 13 (1987), pp. 7–27. Still more important are the messianic and millenarian motives behind the state-building and legislative activities of Sulaymān the Magnificent (r. 926–974/1520–1566), one of the central figures in Ottoman history. On this, see C. Fleischer, 'The Lawgiver as Messiah: the Making of the Imperial Image in the Reign of Süleyman', in G. Veinstein (ed.), *Soliman le Magnifique et son temps* (Paris, 1992), pp. 159–177; and his 'Mahdi and Millenium: Messianic Dimensions in the Development of the Ottoman Imperial Ideology', in K. Çiçek (ed.), *The Great Ottoman-Turkish Civilization* (Ankara, 2000), vol. 3, pp. 42–54.

Although it has been stipulated that the imam will have no representatives during his major occultation, the clergy progressively assumed the prerogatives of the hidden imam in order to position themselves as a privileged class entitled to rule the Twelver community during the period of occultation.

Ismaili Shiʿism does not have an exact analogy for the major occultation, which explains the fact that messianic manifestations have been more apparent in this branch of Shiʿism throughout its history. But the immediate character of messianic expectations was regularly downplayed as they adapted to the perspective of the long-term practical requirements of government, and it was placed in a historical perspective. This happened when the Fatimids modified the early Ismaili concept of the imamate stating that the Imam-caliphs of their dynasty now collectively represented the Saviour, and then again later, when the development of the Nizārī Ismaili theory of Resurrection (*qiyāma*) re-interpreted the event of the proclamation of the *qiyāma* by Ḥasan *ʿalā dhikrihiʾl-salām* in 559/1164, placing it in the indefinitely long sequence of alternating periods of manifestation (*kashf*) and occultation (*satr*) that would lead ultimately to the final Resurrection.[8]

Similar to the Shiʿi doctrines, according to which the new era leading to the eschatological revelation has already been prefigured by the last imam (the seventh imam of their line, Muḥammad b. Ismāʿīl, for the Ismailis and the twelfth imam of their line, Muḥammad b. Ḥasan al-ʿAskarī, for the Twelvers), Ibn ʿArabī's theory of the seals of sainthood (*khatm al-walāya*) entailed that the era of the seal of Muhammadan sainthood had already begun in the time of Ibn ʿArabī (who probably suggested that he was himself that Seal). During this era,

[8] On the Fatimid reform of the theory of imamate, see F. Daftary, *The Ismāʿīlīs, their History and Doctrines* (Cambridge, 2nd ed., 2007), pp. 116 ff., 164 ff. On the Nizārī re-interpretations of the theory of the *qiyāma* during the later Alamūt period, especially on the 'routinisation' of *qiyāma*, admitting to the possibility of several periods of 'resurrection' in the course of history alternating with the periods of 'dissimulation' until the great final Resurrection (*qiyāmat al-qiyāmāt*) see Daftary, *Ismāʿīlīs*, p. 381; Naṣīr al-Dīn al-Ṭūsī, *Rawḍa-yi taslīm*, ed. and trans. by S.J. Badakhchani as *Paradise of Submission* (London and New York, 2005), paras 174–175, p. 69 (English) and p. 80 (Persian).

mankind would be placed under the spiritual leadership of the saints who had attained the highest degree of divine Friendship (*walāya*), to whom belonged the supreme religious (and therefore political?) authority in the Islamic community.[9]

It was this adaptation to a long-term historical perspective, and placed under the authority of a messianic figure, that made Islamic messianism such an efficient instrument of change in Islamic history.

The second point that I would like to underscore with regard to the understanding of Islamic messianism concerns its relationship with mysticism. Just as a link with a source of spiritual inspiration is essential for any form of mysticism, a messianic figure derives legitimacy from his/her claim to be linked to the divinely inspired eschatological knowledge that will be fully revealed by the Mahdi or *qā'im* at the end of time. The idea of an authoritative and divinely inspired spiritual leader is essential to the mystical vision of Islam, both Shiʿi and Sufi. Such a leader, called the imam in Shiʿi Islam and the *quṭb* (head of the spiritual hierarchy) or the Perfect Man in the Sufism, was believed to have direct access to this divine knowledge and to convey it to the community in order to ensure the living presence of the prophetic revelation and the right guidance of the community in the era after the death of the Prophet. The divine knowledge concentrated in the figure of the Shiʿi imam or the Sufi *quṭb* is fundamentally the source of salvation, both for individual believers and for the community as a whole. From this point of view, there is no significant difference between the authoritative spiritual leader and the messianic Saviour. The only difference is that the messianic leader ushers in a period which prepares a universal disclosure of this salutary knowledge, while an ordinary Shiʿi imam or Sufi *quṭb* would communicate it only to a limited circle of disciples. This similarity between authoritative spiritual leader and messianic Saviour is also expressed in the identification of two technical terms, *qiyāma* and *ḥaqīqa*, on which there is a particular emphasis

[9] M. Chodkiewicz, *Le Sceau des saints: prophétie et sainteté dans la doctrine d'Ibn Arabî* (Paris, 2012), pp. 134–150; Elmore, *Islamic Sainthood in the Fullness of Time: Ibn al-ʿArabī's Book of the Fabulous Gryphon* (Leiden, Boston and Köln, 1999), pp. 131–162.

in the Nizārī Ismaili theory of Resurrection. The truth (*ḥaqīqa*) revealed by the messianic Saviour at the time of the Resurrection (*qiyāma*) is the same as the truth accessed and conveyed by a Shiʿi imam or a Sufi *quṭb*. It is for this reason, it can be argued, that a messianic dimension is inherent in mysticism as such, being more or less latent or apparent depending on the historical circumstances.

In other words, from this perspective, messianism can be described as a particular case of mysticism. Therefore, it is not surprising that some Sufi shaykhs came close to making messianic claims.[10] Messianic ideas were arguably present in Sufi doctrines, in particular after the Mongol invasions when Sufism adopted a more active socio-political stance. Influential Sufi orders such as the Kubrawiyya and Naqshbandiyya produced messianic offshoots, the Nūrbakhshiyya and Mujaddidiyya respectively,[11] and Shāh Niʿmat Allāh Walī (d. 834/1430–1431) apparently entertained views that were close to the messianic outlook.[12] Expressions such as 'mystical messianism' or 'mystico-messianic (tendency or milieu)' in this paper refer to this close relationship between mysticism and messianism.

---

[10] See Devin DeWeese, 'Intercessory Claims of Ṣūfī Communities during the 14th and 15th Centuries: 'Messianic' Legitimizing Strategies on the Spectrum of Normativity', in O. Mir-Kasimov (ed.), *Unity in Diversity: Mysticism, Messianism and the Construction of Religious Authority in Islam* (Leiden and Boston, 2014), pp. 197–220.

[11] On these movements and their founders, Muḥammad Nūrbakhsh (d. 869/1464) and Aḥmad Sirhindī (d. 1034/1624), see S. Bashir, *Messianic Hopes and Mystical Visions: The Nūrbakhshiya between Medieval and Modern Islam* (Columbia, SC, 2003), and Y. Friedmann, *Shaykh Aḥmad Sirhindī: An Outline of his Thought and a Study of his Image in the Eyes of Posterity* (Montreal and London, 1971).

[12] Shāh Niʿmat Allāh Walī was the founder of the influential Niʿmat Allāhī Sufi order. Certain verses of his *Dīwān* suggest that Shāh Niʿmat Allāh believed he possessed a universal religion (*madhhab-i jāmiʿ*) and was divinely guided in it. See K.M. al-Shaybī, *al-Ṣila bayna'l-taṣawwuf wa'l-tashayyuʿ* (Beirut, 1982), vol. 2, p. 221. According to the *Rasāʾil* of one of his closest disciples, the dervish Muḥammad Ṭabasī, Shāh Niʿmat Allāh maintained that true kingship belonged to the spiritual leader who had attained the highest degree of perfection (the role that he probably attributed to himself), while worldly kings should be subordinated to such a spiritual leader. See N. Pourjavady and L. Wilson, *Kings of Love: The Poetry and History of the Niʿmatullāhī Sufi Order* (Tehran, 1978), pp. 21 and 41–42.

As mentioned, the mystico-messianic movements of the Mongol and post-Mongol periods (seventh–tenth/thirteenth–sixteenth centuries), such as the Ḥurūfīs, Musha'sha' and Nūrbakhshīs, played an important role in elaboration of the new conception of religious and political authority which made possible the survival of Islamic rule in the Eastern part of the Islamic world and its transition from the structures of the Abbasid caliphate based in Baghdad to new geopolitical formations. Situated at the confluence of esoteric Shi'ism and Sufism, these movements possessed elaborate and highly sophisticated doctrines combined with more or less clear socio-political agendas. They entertained complex relationships with the political rulers of the day and developed efficient mechanisms to spread their ideas and attract followers. Some of them were even able to establish independent polities, as the Musha'sha' state which existed in Khuzistān (south-western Iran and eastern Iraq) between the middle of the ninth/fifteenth century and beginning of the tenth/sixteenth, the dynasty itself surviving into the nineteenth century, being a rival to and, in a sense, anticipating the similar, but even more successful movement of the Safavids.[13]

By the seventh/thirteenth century, in the period immediately preceding the Mongol invasions, messianic ideas had crystallised within two major theoretical developments: in the Nizārī Ismaili doctrine of Resurrection (*qiyāma*) such as presented in the works of the Alamūt period, including the *Haft bāb* by Maḥmūd-i Kātib[14] and the *Rawḍa-yi taslīm* by Naṣīr al-Dīn Ṭūsī, and in the monumental thought of Ibn 'Arabī. While the influence of Ibn 'Arabi's doctrines and that of Twelver Shi'i messianic beliefs can be more easily discerned in the messianic doctrines of the Mongol and post-Mongol periods, the Ismaili input remains more discreet and can rarely be unambiguously identified. This can be partly explained through deployment of the

---

13 On the Ḥurūfīs, see O. Mir-Kasimov, 'Astarābādī, Faḍlallāh' and 'Ḥurūfiyya', *EI3*. On the Musha'sha' and their similarity to the Safavids see M. Mazzaoui, 'Musha'sha'iyān: A Fifteenth Century Shī'ī Movement in Khūzistān and Southern Iraq', *Folia Orientalia*, 22 (1981–1984), pp. 139–162, and his *The Origins of the Safawids: Šī'ism, Ṣūfism and the Ġulāt* (Wiesbaden, 1972).

14 Maḥmūd-i Kātib, *Haft bāb*, ed. and trans. by S.J. Badakhchani as *Spiritual Resurrection in Shi'i Islam: An Early Ismaili Treatise on the Doctrine of Qiyāmat* (London and New York, 2017).

strategy of *taqiyya*, when the Ismaili doctrines were dissimulated under a Sufi or Twelver Shiʿi appearance.[15]

However, it is also difficult to conceive that such an advanced and elaborated messianic doctrine as that of the *qiyāma* did not play any role in the formulation of the messianic doctrines of the eighth/fourteenth and ninth/fifteenth centuries. And it seems that, at least in one case, we have the evidence of a distinctively Ismaili substratum in the doctrine of an influential Iranian mystical and messianic movement. This movement was founded in the second half of the eighth/fourteenth century by a profound and original thinker named Faḍl Allāh Astarābādī (d. 796/1394), and came to be known under the name of al-Ḥurūfiyya. The Ḥurūfis were one of the influential Iranian, and later Anatolian, mystical and messianic movements of the time.[16]

In the remaining part of my paper I would like to compare the Ismaili texts relating to the *qiyāma* doctrine with the works of Faḍl Allāh Astarābādī. The object is not to produce a decisive proof of the *qiyāma* doctrine's influence on post-Mongol Iranian messianism. But since the similarities between these texts arguably go beyond accidental parallelisms, this comparison might provide new material for consideration of the possible impact of the *qiyāma* doctrine.

Before starting to analyse the textual evidence, it could be useful to recall a few general points of similarity between the Nizārī Ismaili texts

---

[15] The possibility of Ismaili influence on the Iranian and Anatolian mysticism is regularly mentioned in the scholarly literature. See, for example, A. Yaşar Ocak, *La révolte de Baba Resul ou la formation de l'hétérodoxie musulmane en Anatolie au XIIIe siècle* (n.p., 1989), pp. 33, 43, 63, 76 (Ismaili influence on the Bābā'ī movement in Anatolia) and E. Gezik, 'How Angel Gabriel Became Our Brother of the Hereafter (On the Question of Ismaili Influence on Alevism)', *British Journal of Middle Eastern Studies* (online publication, 2015), pp. 56–70. M.G.S. Hodgson, *The Order of Assassins: The Struggle of the Early Nizârî Ismâʿîlîs Against the Islamic World* (The Hague, 1955), p. 276, and H. Landolt, "Aṭṭār, Sufism and Ismailism', in L. Lewisohn and C. Shackle (ed.), *ʿAṭṭār and the Persian Sufi Tradition: The Art of Spiritual Flight* (London, 2006), pp. 3–26, mention the possibility of connection between the Ismaili tradition and Persian mystical poetry, in particular with reference to Farīd al-Dīn ʿAṭṭār (d. 618/1221) and Jalāl al-Dīn Rūmī (d. 672/1273). However, it seems that favourable circumstances for a systematic scholarly exploration of Ismaili influence on Mongol and post-Mongol Islamic mysticism and messianism have not yet developed.

[16] See n. 13.

and the doctrine of Faḍl Allāh Astarabādī.[17] Probably the most important of these is the central importance of the *ta'wīl* understood as a universal process in the course of which every entity of the created world returns to its ontological origin in the creative divine Word. Faḍl Allāh's doctrine of the Word (*kalima*) as the direct emanation of the divine Essence stands as an argument in favour of Ismaili influence. The description of the human being and human form as the most perfect locus of manifestation of the divine Word, containing all the divine attributes, and its connection with some kind of doctrine of imamate is one of the central lines in both Nizārī Ismaili literature and the work of Faḍl Allāh. The cosmogonical and cosmological role ascribed to the language and, more specifically, to the letters of the alphabet, central for Faḍl Allāh, is a topic that was particularly developed in Ismaili literature from early on. Finally, there are also a few direct Ismaili references in the works of Faḍl Allāh. The records of dreams attributed to him contain a mention of the Ismaili strongholds of Rūdbār-i Astarābād and Ḥiṣār-i Gird-i Kūh; and in one place in his voluminous *Jāvidān-nāma*, Faḍl Allāh fleetingly refers to the idea that the prophets are manifested by series of seven (*kashf-i anbiyā bi-haft wa bi-haft*, fol. 99b). And it should not be forgotten that Faḍl Allāh's native Astarābād is close to the major Ismaili fortresses of Gird Kūh and Soru. These similarities led several scholars, including Edward Browne and Vladimir Ivanow, to conclude that Faḍl Allāh and his followers represented a previously unknown branch of the Ismailis, and Henry Corbin also regarded Ḥurūfism as one of the forms of post-Mongol Iranian Ismailism.

While a closer examination of Faḍl Allāh's thought shows that it is somewhat exaggerated to claim that the Ḥurūfīs were a branch of the Ismailis, comparison of the texts of these two groups reveals some close parallels, examples of which are provided below. On the Ismaili side, I have used the texts belonging to the Iranian Nizārī Ismaili tradition of the *qiyāma*, such as *Haft bāb* by Ḥasan-i Maḥmūd-i Kātib, *Rawḍa-yi taslīm* by Naṣīr al-Dīn al-Ṭūsī, and *Haft bāb-i Abū Isḥāq* by Abū Isḥāq Quhistānī. These are abbreviated as follows:

[17] For a more detailed discussion and further references see O. Mir-Kasimov, *Words of Power: Ḥurūfī Teachings between Shiʿism and Sufism in Medieval Islam* (London and New York, 2015), pp. 406 ff.

HB = Ḥasan-i Maḥmūd-i Kātib, *Haft bāb,* ed. and tr. Jalal Badakhchani as *Spiritual Resurrection in Shiʿi Islam: An Early Ismaili Treatise on the Doctrine of Qiyāmat,* London and New York, 2017.

HBAI = Abū Isḥāq Quhistānī, *Haft bāb-i Abū Isḥāq,* ed. and tr. Wladimir Ivanow, Bombay, 1959.

Rawḍa = Naṣīr al-Dīn al-Ṭūsī, *Rawḍa-yi taslīm,* ed. and tr. Jalal Badakhchani as *Paradise of Submission: A Medieval Treatise on Ismaili Thought,* London and New York, 2005.

I use Badakhchani's translation for the HB and the *Rawda,* and Ivanow's translation for the *HBAI,* possibly with some minor modifications.

Page numbers separated by a slash refer respectively to the English translation and to the original text.

These Ismaili texts are compared with Faḍl Allāh's magnum opus, the *Jāvidān-nāma-yi kabīr,* which is still unpublished. I used my own partial editions and translations of this work based on the available manuscripts. The folio numbers provided below correspond to the manuscript of the British Library Oc.Or.5957.

The first selection of texts is focused on the idea of the imam as the personification of the divine Word. It is worth noting the similarity of scriptural material, including the Qurʾanic verses, the *ḥadīths* and biblical citations, used in the Ismaili texts and in the *Jāvidān-nāma,* which can be observed in several excerpts in this and following selections.

ISMAILI TEXTS	JAVIDAN-NAMA-YI KABIR
1. The manifestation of the sublime Word is the Imam – may salutations ensue upon mention of him – [whose reality] is beyond all human thought and imagination, and above all	'The Qur'an is the Word, and the Word is Imam, and Jesus is the Word' (177a). 'The Qur'an is my Imam.'[18] [. . .] The Imam is the person [referred to by the expressions]: 'I am the

[18] For the identification and references of the traditional material cited in the *Jāvidān-nāma,* see Mir-Kasimov, *Words of Power,* 'Inventory I: *Ḥadīths* and Sayings', pp. 463–474.

description, whether it be positive or negative. *Rawḍa* paragraph 330 (p. 113/139) In the Qur'an it is stated: '*On the day when we call all men through their Imam*' [Q. 17:71]. In another place it is said: '*All things will be reckoned in a manifest Imam*' [Q. 36:12]. In the Qur'an, the word [imam] appears in many places and proves that it is the name of God. HB paragraph 11 (p. 52/12)	speaking Word of God' and '*His Word that He committed to Mary*' [Q. 4:171]. Therefore, the Word is Imam, and whosoever is dead without having known the Word dies the death of the ignorant. This means that whosoever does not know the Word of his time is an unbeliever (*kāfir*). 'I am the speaking Word of God', '*All things will be reckoned in a manifest Imam*' [Q. 36:12], that is, 'in the manifest Word' (189a–b).

The next selection underscores the idea that the human form is the perfect form of the manifestation of the divine names and attributes, that is, of the knowable aspect of God:

ISMAILI TEXTS	JAVIDAN-NAMA-YI KABIR
2. All prophets and Imams (*anbiyā' wa awliyā'*), referred to the Divine and Divinity (*khudā wa rubūbiyyat*) using [the concept of] man and have said that He, the Almighty and High, always appears among mankind in human form, and this unique form is specifically His form. In a tradition, the Prophet [Muhammad], peace be upon him, says: 'Verily God created man in His own image.' In another place he says: 'In the form of the Most Merciful'. HB paragraph 8 (p. 51/11).	'God created Adam in His form.' The form of God is an attribute of God, and [each] divine attribute [consists of] the 32 divine 'words'. The original nature (*khilqat*) of Adam was created in accordance with this attribute [of form]. The form of Adam is [therefore] really the form of God (139a).

For this reason, the human form leads to the knowledge of God:

ISMAILI TEXTS	JAVIDAN-NAMA-YI KABIR
3. It is impossible for one to know anything so long as he knows nothing about the form or properties of that thing. Whatever has no affinity with the properties of that person, must remain absolutely unknowable to him, and it is absolutely impossible to find a way to knowing the unknowable. It was the wish of God that He should be recognised and worshipped. He chose [for this] man, from all creation, and favoured him with His own form and attributes, and this [man's] form is His personal form. All the prophets and saints indicated this. It is mentioned in the *ḥadīth* that the Prophet said: 'Verily God created Adam in resemblance of His own form.' It is not said that God manifested Himself in the form of Adam. Therefore that form is His own form. Similarly, it is said in the Torah: 'We wanted to produce man after the form and image of Ourselves so that he would recognise and worship Us.' HBAI (p. 37/36).	'God created Adam in His form.' The form of God is an attribute of God. . . The original nature of Adam was created in accordance with this attribute [of form]. The form of Adam is [therefore] really the form of God (139a). It is said in the Torah: 'Let Us make man in Our image, after Our likeness, and let them have dominion over the fish of the sea, and over the fowl of the air. . . So God created man [Adam].' [. . .] Adam, peace be upon him, was shaped in the form of God [. . .] Whosoever reaches [the knowledge of the innermost meaning] of the form of Adam, attains [the knowledge] of God and of all prophetic [revelations] (396b–397a). God manifested Himself to the Messenger in the most beautiful form, so that [Muhammad] became aware that his [bodily] form is the form of God and the form of Adam, and that he knew why the Essence of God came into this form. [. . .] [God speaks in the first person]: 'Because when you know [the innermost meaning of] your own bodily form and of your face, you know

My Face and Myself: "Whosoever knows himself knows his Lord." Because I have written on My Face the 32 "words",[19] which are the signs of My Word, you are My Word and My writing [. . .] When you read My form [. . .] [only then] will you know me, you [can] not know Me otherwise [. . .] Adam is My vicegerent in the sense that he has My form: "God created Adam in His form and in the form of the All-Merciful." Truly, this form of Adam is My form [. . .] Know your own form in order to know Mine. All objects and beings are annihilated within My form. All objects, beings, stars and heavens [. . .] move within My form. Every one of them, at the moment of its creation, manifests something from My form [. . .] This form, I gave it to Adam, I clad him in it' (221b–222a).

Just like the human form, the universe expresses the totality of the knowable aspect of God. But while this knowledge is dispersed in an infinite variety of forms of objects and beings constituting the universe, it is concentrated in the human form. Therefore, the human form is a representation of the universe, and the universe is identical to the human form as the sum of the divine knowledge:

---

[19] According to the *Jāvidān-nāma*, the original divine Word has 28 and/or 32 aspects, called 'words' (*kalimāt*). This detail of Faḍl Allāh's doctrine is not essential for the purpose of the present paper, but more information on this topic can be found in O. Mir-Kasimov, *Words of Power*, pp. 437–438.

ISMAILI TEXTS	JAVIDAN-NAMA-YI KABIR
4. That divine energy which is scattered in the skies, which are like a father, the elements which are like a mother, and the phenomena of the physical world which are like children – all are synthesised in man. And for the reason that all these forces become [thus] synthesised in a form, it is obvious that that form is God's own. As the world implies the scattered properties of man, man therefore means a synthesis of those properties. Therefore in reality man is Macrocosmos. Those elemental properties of man, which are scattered, each returns to its proper place and these scattered elemental properties of man we call the world of things in existence. HBAI (p. 45/45) Thus, in relative terms, mankind is scattered [all over] the Universe and, as such, the universe is said to be the macrocosm (*insān-i kabīr*) and mankind the microcosm (*insān-i ṣaghīr*). But in reality the universe is the microcosm and mankind the macrocosm. Thus, universe is the human being dispersed, and the human being is the sum of the entirety of the universe. When the dispersed world is assembled, it is called the living human being, and when humans die and become dispersed, this is called the dispersed world. HB paragraph 61 (pp. 73–74/32).	God brought together all the named [objects] [. . .] and established them as counterparts of the 32 'words', and made of 32 'words' the names of all [named objects]. He created Adam in accordance with the number of these [32 'words'], and wrote them on the face of Adam by the hand of His power. He [made these 'words' so that they] expressed themselves from the 32 teeth, from the tongue and face [of Adam] [. . .]. When all things are bound together by the line of balance, they [produce] the science[20] of the divine Word. Adam and Eve are, each of them, the locus of manifestation of all 32 divine [ontological] 'words'. Their bodies are bound to all things, as everything is part of them, and [their bodies represent] the totality. All the heavens and planets with their effusions are turned in direction of the earth, and they [Adam and Eve] are the spiritual direction of the all. Eve is the foundation and the Mother. During the prayer over the dead and the Resurrection everybody is called back to the Mother, because it is through the original nature of the face (*khilqat-i wajh*) of Eve that the original nature of the face of Adam and the science of the 32 [ontological] 'words' manifests itself. Adam, Eve and the 32 'words' shine

[20] *ʿilm* is not translated as 'knowledge' here because, in this context, it designates a sign, a visible form which potentially leads to the knowledge of the divine 'words'. 'Science' should be understood here as a means leading to knowledge.

The divine power by which all creatures exist, attains in man its complete development and manifestation. This means that all divine ideas which are scattered in nature are concentrated in man. Therefore, as regards his substance and properties, he is perfect. HBAI (p. 27/27).	from behind the soot and the smoke [of the ink] of the conventional writing. They are the divine Books, [the letters of which] shine through their faces and their bodies. They are the divine Word [. . .]. All things are bound to their bodies [i.e., of Adam and Eve] from six [spatial] directions, and thus also [included into] the divine Book [. . .]. The six [spatial directions] are bound to the bodies [of Adam and Eve] and form their members. All that face them from the six directions is [part of] their members and of their bodies. All things are one body of Adam, and the names of all things come from him. The innermost meaning and secret of all things manifests itself in him (91a–b). The human being is the locus of manifestation of the 32 [ontological] 'words' [. . .] because God made manifest the distinctive signs of the 32 'words' in the original nature of the humans. Other objects [and beings] are not enabled to such a manifestation, and the science cannot be manifested in them in its entirety (162a). The power is the support and the source of all. The voice and the letters are rooted in the power, while the power without beginning is rooted in its own essence [. . .]. The voice, the letters, single and compound, which is the human spirit, come from the power and return to the power (472b–473a).

The following citations express the idea that, at the end of time, the capacity of speech, which is inherent in every existent entity, will be explicitly manifested and everything will be able to speak. This passage is better understood in the light of the idea, expressed in the previous citations, that the human being is a macrocosm which contains the whole created universe. Since the human being is endowed with speech, every part of the human macrocosm, that is, every existing thing, participates in this capacity. In addition, since every existing entity is the locus of manifestation of a certain number of the elements of the original divine Word – this idea is particularly developed in the *Jāvidān-nāma* – at the moment of the final revelation, these elements of the Word, by which things were created, will be explicitly manifested each in their locus of manifestation, and thus the original source of everything existing will be revealed in its speech:

ISMAILI TEXTS	JAVIDAN-NAMA-YI KABIR
5. The Prophet says that in the hereafter [even] stone and dried clay will be able to speak. But no extant thing can speak except for human beings. This therefore means that in the hereafter everything will return to its original source. Therefore it follows that everything will return to its original source through human beings, and the origin of human beings is this, their created form. HBAI (p. 47/47).	Everything is endowed with speech and will [possess this quality] in the future, because all objects are the remains of the members of Adam's [body]. 'God gave us speech, as He gave everything speech' [Q. 41:21]: [this verse] refers to [the fact] that all things will be speaking [by virtue of] his [Adam's] unity and [within his] single body [. . .] Look at the bodily form of Adam, and at the structure of the universe. All that you can observe [is an expression of the] unity, and Adam is the locus of manifestation of the Speech. Therefore, the speech of Adam is potentially in everything, and each thing is brought into existence [by] the speech of Adam. 'God gave us speech, as He gave everything speech', because the speech is the distinctive feature of Adam (25b).

The following passages display similar interpretations of the apocalyptic Qur'anic verse, 14:48. Since everything in the created universe is ultimately a manifestation of the divine truth, which is identical with the divine Word, this truth will be eventually manifested in the heavens and in the earth:

ISMAILI TEXTS	JAVIDAN-NAMA-YI KABIR
6. [From the statement attributed to Ḥasan 'alā Dhikrihi al-Salām] We have spread the earth and the skies of the religion of Absolute Truth, as is said in the Coran (14:48): '*On the day when the earth shall be changed for another earth, and the heavens too*'. HBAI (pp. 39/38–39).	All existing objects and beings are the 'words' of God, as is mentioned [in the verse]: '*God gave us speech, as He gave everything speech*' [Q. 41:21]. '*Upon the day the earth shall be changed to other than the earth, and the heavens*' [Q. 14:48] [means that] when the heavens and the earth will be changed to other than heavens and earth, they will be substituted for by the divine Word (411a).

The interpretation of Jesus' role in the *Jāvidān-nāma* has many common points with that in the Nizārī Ismaili texts. One example of this similarity is the commentary on Jesus' saying concerning the missions of the previous prophets, the commentary which is in line with the Nizārī Ismaili theory according to which the laws of the previous prophets are not abrogated but brought to a higher degree of perfection by the subsequent prophets, and this process of progressive perfection culminates in Resurrection[21]:

[21] See al-Ṭūsī, *Rawḍa-yi taslīm*, paragraphs 417–418, pp. 139–140, Persian text pp. 173–174.

ISMAILI TEXTS	JAVIDAN-NAMA-YI KABIR
7. [God] in the beginning brings a canon law and religious injunctions in order that humanity may be separated from the sheep and quadrupeds which live as nature has created them, and in order that their life should be spiritual, and they may reach [the position of human beings]. After this they are told that there is a [higher] degree, and this is reason, which is the abode of intellect, so that their life may become intellectual. Therefore the former is left out for the sake of the perfection of the other. Jesus says: 'I have not come to cancel Torah, but for perfecting it'.[22] HBAI (p. 67/67)	Jesus said: 'I have not come to make the religions of the [previous] prophets deficient, I have come to complete them.' He said: 'I am the Word of God' [. . .] Jesus will come in order [to complete] this Word, [all] the 32 'words' of which were given to Adam, and of which every prophet received some 'words'. [Jesus] said: 'I will come in order to complete them and to reveal the secret of their fullness. I have not come to make them deficient.' (426a).

The following citations link the imperfect revelations with the requirement to use allusive and figurative language. The final revelation, that of the Resurrection (*qiyāma*), brings the revelation process to its perfection. Since the metaphysical truths of the divine Word can now be observed directly, there is no further need to use parables and figures of speech. Both the *Jāvidān-nāma* and the Ismaili texts attribute the task of the final revelation to Jesus. In one of the Ismaili citations a similar role is also attributed to ʿAlī, and a similar parallelism between Jesus and ʿAlī can be observed in some passages of the *Jāvidān-nāma* which cannot be cited here for the sake of space.[23]

The interpretation of the second birth in the *Jāvidān-nāma* also has close parallels in Ismaili texts, referring to the same Gospel verse. In the

[22] For this saying, cf. Matthew 5:17, 'Do not think that I have come to abolish the Law or the Prophets; I have not come to abolish them but to fulfil them.'

[23] For the parallels between Jesus and ʿAlī in the *Jāvidān-nāma* and in the broader Shiʿi context see O. Mir-Kasimov, *Words of Power*, pp. 342–343 and n. 8 p. 343; see also still broader Islamic textual evidence related to this topic studied by M.A. Amir-Moezzi, 'Muḥammad le Paraclet et ʿAlī le Messie', p. 41 ff.

ISMAILI TEXTS	JAVIDAN-NAMA-YI KABIR
8. He [Jesus] said: 'I will return in the *Qiyāmat* and divulge the Father's task.'. . . [In the era of the *Qiyāmat*] he [Jesus] will speak unambiguously and unite knowledge of the *ẓāhir* (exoteric) with [knowledge of] the *bāṭin* (esoteric). HB paragraphs 20–21 (p. 57/15). As the Prophet used only figurative language, and had not brought his community out of that [backward] stage, the 'debt' that is the duty to do that, remained on him. And Mawlānā ʿAlī paid that debt, bringing his community from the state of being dependent on allegories, and being lost in the letter of *sharīʿat,* to the world of clarity and absolute reality. HBAI (p. 32/32).	Jesus did not express his [knowledge fully] at the time [of his first coming]. He possessed the science of the 32 'words' of the divine [Word] on his face, as well as 32 and 28 teeth,15 which [represent] the science of the 32 divine 'words'. But these 32 'words', in accordance with which his face had been created, were not actualised on his tongue. [This is why] he said: 'I will come [back] in order to explain' (423b). O Christian, be aware that the prophets who came before the manifestation of Jesus foretold that a virgin will give birth to a son, who will be named 'God is with us'. When he comes, idolatry will be uprooted and there will be only one religion, one nation and one confession, and every human being will have the knowledge of God. The Jews say that Jesus of the Christians is not the [Messiah] foretold by the prophets because he did not unify all religions, nations and confessions, and all humans did not attain the knowledge of God. One could answer that Jesus said: 'O apostles! I speak to you by symbols, signs and allusions. I will come again and explain their meaning.' He also said: 'I will not come to make the religions of the [previous] prophets defective, but I will come to complete them.' The Messenger, peace be upon him, testified that he [i.e., Jesus] was [the person] foretold by the [previous] prophets. He had come and he is gone, but he is the divine Word, which will come again. His [second] coming is one of the signs of the Resurrection (*nishān-i qiyāma*). O Christian, according to Jesus, when he said: 'All that I have told you, I told by symbols and signs, and I will come again in order to clarify them', you will not [fully] understand his words before he [comes again and] explains them (396a).

Ismaili text, the second birth mentioned by Jesus means a birth in the world of spiritual hermeneutics (*ta'wīl*). The *Jāvidān-nāma*'s interpretation of the second birth is exactly the same. It is described as awareness of the original divine Word, which is the ultimate goal of the *ta'wīl*:

ISMAILI TEXTS	JAVIDAN-NAMA-YI KABIR
9. [HBAI 67] Physical birth takes place in the world of revelation (*tanzīl*), and spiritual birth takes place in the world of *ta'wīl.* If one does not know what is *tanzīl* and *ta'wīl,* what is *ẓāhir* and *bāṭin,* he will not find his way to salvation (*ma'ād*). Jesus says: 'Who does not become born twice, will not attain the Kingdom of Heaven'.[24] HBAI (p. 67/67)	Whosoever possesses a bodily form cannot enter the kingdom of heaven which is the [invisible] Word, unless he or she is born anew. Indeed, the Messiah said: 'Except a man be born again, [he cannot see the kingdom of God]' (387b).

Mention of the Hindu deity called Nāran or Nārīn is probably a minor detail, but it is all the more telling because it is not very usual in an Islamic context:

ISMAILI TEXTS	JAVIDAN-NAMA-YI KABIR
10. As for the Hindus, they sculpt two idols, one real (*ḥaqīqī*) [named *Nāran*], that is [their Lord], and the other is called *Bahrā*, that is, the false pretender (*dajjāl*). HB paragraph 25 (p. 58/16).	When the Hindus say that Nārīn has four hands this means that he is the lord of the four 'words' (367b).[25]

[24] Cf. John 3:3.

[25] In Faḍl Allāh's theory of ontological language, 'four words' refer to four primary sounds which connect the series of 28 and 32 primary sounds (28+4=32). They also represent the four natural elements (fire, air, water and earth).

Both the Nizārī Ismaili texts and the *Jāvidān-nāma* emphasise the similarity between the structure of the universe and time, on the one hand, and the structure of the human body, on the other. The only difference between the Ismaili and Ḥurūfī texts is that the former has only the number seven as the basis of this structure, while the latter uses seven, eight, and their combinations. Four times seven equals 28, four times eight is 32, 28 and 32 is 60, six times 60 is 360[26]:

ISMAILI TEXTS	JAVIDAN-NAMA-YI KABIR
11. [HBAI 60] Therefore the basis of numbers is seven. We may say: there are seven skies which contain seven planets. There are... seven days in the week. Man has seven parts of the body . . . hair, skin, flesh, bones, veins, fat, blood. HBAI (p. 60/59).	Why has God divided the heavenly spheres in 32 and 28 parts, in accordance with the number of His 28 and 32 'words'? Because, according to *aḥadīth*, the human being has 360 bones, every one of which has a degree [of the heavenly sphere] as a counterpart. [The human body] is thus [structured exactly] as a [heavenly] sphere, [in accordance with the measure of] six times 60. Every 60 [from this measure are composed of] 28 and 32. [The human body is divided into] 360 [parts of] fat, 360 [parts of] blood vessels, 360 [parts of] flesh and 360 [parts of] skin. Every bone has thus a part of fat, a blood vessel, a part of flesh and of skin as a [*cont.*]

[26] With regard to the importance of the number seven, in another passage (f. 99b), the *Jāvidān-nāma* says that 'the prophets are manifested in series of seven' (*kashf-i anbiyā bi-haft wa bi-haft*). This statement could constitute an important argument in favour of the Ismaili influence, but the idea of prophetic heptads is not developed elsewhere in the *Jāvidān-nāma*.

ISMAILI TEXTS	JAVIDAN-NAMA-YI KABIR
	counterpart, and [every one of these parts of the human body] faces a degree from the 360 degrees of the sphere of constellations. All heavenly spheres are divided in accordance with the 360 parts of bones, flesh, skin, fat and blood vessels [of the human body] (451b). The 360 degrees . . . are the shape, the form and the garment of Adam. The parts of his body are divided [in accordance with the constellations and the phases of the moon]: 'By the heaven of the constellations' [Q. 85:1], 'And the moon – We have determined it by stations' [Q. 36:1]. [These verses] refer to the 28 and 32 [degrees, repeated] until they attain [the number of] 360 (351b–352a). 'By the heaven of the constellations' [Q. 85:1], which contains 12 constellations. Every constellation [occupies] 30 degrees, so that together they cover 360 degrees, or six times 60 degrees. Every 60 degrees are [composed of] 28 and 32 degrees: 'his height is 60 cubits in Heaven'. The heavens, just as the time of a week, are created in accordance with the face of Adam (97b).

Finally, another telling, albeit fleeting mark of possible Ismaili influence is the *Jāvidān-nāma*'s mention of the term *ta'līm* which, in the Ismaili context, and especially in the context of Nizārī doctrine, designates the initiatory teachings of the imam.[27] More specifically, echoing the Ismaili text, the *Jāvidān-nāma* repeats the idea that at the moment of final revelation (identified with the Resurrection in the Ismaili text and with the second coming of Jesus in the *Jāvidān-nāma*) there will be no need for the *ta'līm*:

ISMAILI TEXTS	JAVIDAN-NAMA-YI KABIR
12. But at the *Qiyāmat* God Himself will be His own *dalīl,* guide [to His substance]. In the *Qiyāmat* there will be no [need of either] *naẓar,* direct observation, nor of *ta'līm,* learning from others, one will have to know God directly. HBAI (p. 65/65).	When he (Messiah) comes, all religions, confessions and beliefs will be unified all over the world. All the created beings and the people of the Book will be unified. The divergences between the scriptures [of the different religions] will be levelled, and babies in their cradles will have [perfect] knowledge of God. After [the coming of the Messiah] there will be no need for education (*ta'līm*) (421b).

Conclusion

As mentioned, the goal of this paper is not to prove that the *Jāvidān-nāma-yi kabīr* of Faḍl Allāh Astarābādī is an Ismaili or even a pseudo-Ismaili work. The *Jāvidān-nāma* creatively combines many elements from various currents of Islam. But it seems likely that some Ismaili doctrines, and more particularly the Nizārī Ismaili theory of *qiyāma,* were among its main sources of inspiration. If this is true then, through

[27] On *ta'līm* as the authoritative teachings of the Shi'i imams, especially in the Nizārī Ismaili context, see Daftary, *The Ismā'īlīs*, pp. 339–342.

the intermediary of influential eclectic mystical and messianic movements such as the Ḥurūfīs, the Nizārī Ismaili theory of the *qiyāma* might have played a role far beyond the limits of the Nizārī Ismaili community, contributing to the processes that eventually led to the formation and consolidation, in the ninth/fifteenth and tenth/sixteenth centuries, of the new geo-political configuration of the eastern Islamic world in the form of the Ottoman, Safavid and Mughal empires.

Appendix

Original text of the citations:

ISMAILI TEXTS	JAVIDAN-NAMA-YI KABIR
مظهر کلمهٔ اعلی امام لذکره السّلام، منزه از تصور و تصویر و متعالی از وصف و تنزیه. و در قرآن است که «یوم ندعوا کلّ اناس بامامهم» (17:71) و جای دیگر می فرماید «وکلّ شئ أحصیناه فی إمام مبین» (36:12) و در قرآن نام امام بسیار است که دلیل می کند [امام] نام خدا است.	1. قرآن کلمه و کلمه امام است و عیسی کلمه القرآن امامی [. . .] پس اماما آن کسی بود یعنی انا کلام الله النّاطق و کلمة القاها الی مریم پس کلمه امام بود و هر کس که بمیرد و کلمه نداند جاهل مرده بود من مات و لم یعرف امام زمانه فقد مات میته جاهلیة یعنی کلمهٔ زمانی خوشتنه نداند کافر بود انا کلام الله النّاطق و کلّ شیء احصیناه فی امام مبین ای فی کلمة مبین.
همه انبیاء و اولیاء اشارت [خدا و ربوبیت] به مردی کرده‌اند و گفته‌اند که او عزّ و علا همیشه در میان خلق بصورت مردی باشد و این صورت خاص صورت اوست. [چنان که در خبر است از پیغمبر علیه‌السلام که فرمود: اِنّ الله خلق آدم علی صورته و جای دیگر میگوید علی صورة الرّحمن.]	2. خلق الله تعالی آدم علی صورته صورت خدا صفة خداست و صفة خدا 32 کلمهٔ خداست که خلقة آدم بران صفة مخلوقست بحقیقة صورت آدم صورت خداست.

ISMAILI TEXTS	JAVIDAN-NAMA-YI KABIR
محال است که کسی راه بچیزی برد مادامی که بر صورت و صفت آن چیز واقف نباشد و هر چه بهیچ وجهی بر صورت و صفت این کس نباشد مجهول مطلق این کس باشد و راه بردن بمجهول مطلق محال است و ارادت باری آن بود که او را بشناسند و بپرستند از همه موجودات انسان را برگزید و بصورت و صفت خاصّ خودش گرامی کرد، و این صورت خاصّ حضرت اوست، و همه انبیا و نیکان اشارت بآن کرده‌اند چنانچه در خبر پیغمبر می‌آید که انّ الله خلق آدم علی صورته و در خبر دیگر علی صورت الرّحمن یعنی بدرستی که خدای تعالی آدم را بیافرید بر صورت خویش، نمیگوید خدا ظاهر شده (است) بر صورت آدم پس این صورت صورت خاصّ او باشد و همچنین در عبارت توریت میخواستیم ما که پیدا کنیم انسانرا بر صورت و هیئت خود تا مارا .بشناسند و بپرستند	3. خلق الله تعالی آدم علی صورته صورت خدا صفة خداست و صفة خدا 32 کلمهٔ خداست که خلقة آدم بران صفة مخلوقست .بحقیقة صورت آدم صورت خداست و در توریة آمده است که من که خدا ام میخواستم چیزی بیافرینم بشکل خود و هیئاة خود و صورت خود که پاذشاه مرغان هوا و ماهیان دریا باشد آدم را بیافریدم [. . .] بباید دانستن که آدم علیه السلام چون بشکل خدا و صورت خدا و هیئات خدا برآمده است اکنون بدان که شکل و صورت ازان صورت است هرگاه که صورت آدم را ره دانسته باشی بخدا برده باشی و جمیع انبیاء را دانسته بدان که ره بسخن خدا و نطق خدا که مسیح گفت .من نطق خدا ام برده باشی آنکه خدا باحسن صورت خوشتنه برسول نمود ازان جهة بود که صورت خود را صورت خدا و صورت آدم دانه و بزانه که ذات خدا چرا باین صورت برآمد [. . .] که هرگاه که صورت خود را و وجه خود را بزانی وجه مرا و مرا بدانی که من عرف نفسه فقد عرف ربّه براء آنکه بر وجه خود 32 کلمة نوشته ام که کلام منست باشارة و تو کلام منی و کتاب منی [. . .] آن زمان که صورت مرا بخوانی که کتب علی نفسه الرّحمة مرا بشناسی و الّا نشناسی [. . .] آدم باین معنی که صورت من دارد خلیفهٔ من است که خلق الله تعالی آدم علی صورته و علی صورة الرّحمن بحقیقة آن صورت آدم صورت منست [. . .] صورت خود را بدان تا صورت مرا بدانی و همه اشیاء و موجودات در صورت من محوست و همه اشیاء و مخلوقات و انجم و افلاک

ISMAILI TEXTS	JAVIDAN-NAMA-YI KABIR
	سیر در صورت من دارند و هر [. . .] یکی را چون بخلقة برسی نموداری از بعض صورت من اند [. . .] و آن صورترا بآدم دادم و درو پوشانیدم. و این قوّت الهی که پراکنده است در آسمانها که پدر اند و عناصر که مادر اند و موالید که فرزند است همه در انسان جمع میشود و بواسطهٔ آنکه همه قوتهائی که جمع کرده است بصورت ظاهر میشود که آن صورت خاصّ خدای است، و چون عالم عبارت از تفصیل معانی انسان است و انسان عبارت از جمع او معانی، پس بحکم حقیقت انسان عالم کبیر باشد و اجزای انسان که پراکنده شود هر یکی با مرکز خود رود و او پراکنده اجزای انسانرا عالم موجودات خوانیم.
پس به حکم اضافه مردم در عالم پراکنده است و از این رو است که عالم را به اضافه انسان کبیر می گویند و مردم را انسان صغیر گویند. و از روی حقیقت، عالم را انسان صغیر خوانند و مردم را عالم کبیر. پس عالم است که تفصیل جمع مردم است و [مردم است] که جمع تفصیل عالم است. عالم پراکنده چون مجتمع شود زندگی باشد و مردمش خوانند و مردم زنده چون بمیرند و پراکنده شوند، عالم پراکنده خوانند. و قوت الهی که همه موجودات بآن قائم است در مرتبهٔ انسان تمام میشود، پس او بحسب ذات و صفات کامل باشد.	4. حضرت احدیّة جمیع مسمّیات را اعّم ازانکه ذات او باشند و نباشند در ازاء 32 کلمة نهاد و آورد و 32 کلمة را اسماء ایشان کردانید و خلقة آدم و آدمی که کی بعدد آ کلمة کی و در وجه آدم بکتابة ید قدرة خود نبوشت و از 32 دندان و زبان و وجه آنرا ظاهر کرده [. . .] که همهٔ اشیاء که با همدیگر بر خطّ استواء چون در آیند علم کلمهٔ خدائی اند آدم و حوّا هر یک بتمامی مظهر جمیع 32 کلمهٔ آلهی اند و وجود ایشان متّصل است بهمهٔ اشیاء بجهة آنکه همه اشیاء جزو ایشانند و ایشان کلّ اند و آسمان و سیّارات با فیض خود همه رو در زمین دارند و خنان قبلهٔ همه بند و حوّا براء آ اصلی و امّی و در تلقین گور و قیامة همه را بامّ واخوانند که از خلقة وجه خو خلقة وجه آدم و علميّة 32 کلمة ظاهر ببو آدم و حوّا و 32 کلمة همازن که از پس

ISMAILI TEXTS	JAVIDAN-NAMA-YI KABIR
	سیاهی و دوده اصطلاحی و کتابة می درخشد ایشان کتب خدائی آلهی اند از وجه خنان و اندام خنان می درخشد و کلمهٔ آلهی اند انّما المسیح عیسی ابن مریم رسول الله و کلمته انا کلام الله النّاطق و همه اشیاء که متّصل بوجود خنانند از شش جهة همازن کتاب خدائی اند که نور علی نور شش جهات خنان متّصل بوجود خنان هستند و اجزاء خنان بند هر چه از شش جهات رو پدیشانن دارند اجزاء ایشانند و وجود ایشان اند پس همهٔ اشیاء یک وجود آدم بود هستی و اسماء همه اشیاء سر از خو برآوی برای این معنی و سرّ همهٔ اشیاء بدو ظاهر شدن. چون مظهر 32 کلمة انسان خواهد بودن و قابل آن خدا علامة 32 کلمة در خلقة انسان ظاهر کرد و چون اشیاء دیگر قابلیّة ظاهر بودن در ایشان نبود علم در ایشان همچنین تمام ظاهر نبود. قرارگاه و مبداء همه قوّة است و صوت و حروف بقوّة قائمند و قوّة ازلی بذات خود قائمست [. . .] صوت و حروف و مفرد و مرکّب روح انسان است و از قوّة بدر آمده است و باز گشت هم بقوّة باشد.
پیغمبر میگوید که در آخرت سنگ و کلوخ سخنگوی باشند و سخنگوی الا مردم نتواند بود و می آید که در آخرت همه چیزها بمعاد رسند پس باید که همه چیز بواسطهٔ مردم بمعاد خود رسند و مبدأ مردم این صورت خلقی است.	5. همه اشیا را معلوم شد که ناطق اند و خواهند بود که بقیّهٔ جزو آدم اند انطقنا الله الّذی انطق کلّ شیء دالّست که همه اشیا ناطق خواهند شد بوحدانیّت او و یک وجود [. . .] و در صورت آدم نظر کن و در نظم اشیا و هرکه را مشاهده کنی و توحید را و آدم مظهر نطقی پس بالقوّة در اشیا و همهٔ اشیا نطق آدم موجود بو که انطقنا الله الّذی انطق کلّ شیء باین معنی گفت که نطق مخصوص بآدم است.

ISMAILI TEXTS	JAVIDAN-NAMA-YI KABIR
و بزمین و آسمان دین حقیقت بگستراندی چنانچه در قرآن میآید «یوم تبدّل الارض غیر الارض و السموات» (14:48).	6. پس لازم آمد که همه اشیاء کلمهٔ آلهی باشند که گفت انطقنا الله الّذی انطق کلّ شیء یوم تبدّل الارض غیر الارض و السّماوات چون آسمان و زمین بغیر آسمانها و زمین مبدّل شوند کلمهٔ آلهی قائم مقام گردد.
هم باوّل شریعتی و احکام بیاورد تا مردم از انعام و بهائم که حکایت طبیعی کنند جدا شود تا حکایت ایشان نفسانی شود و در آن چیز آیند، پس از آن گویند (که) مرتبهٔ دیگر هست و آن عقل است و محلّ صواب تا حکایت ایشان عقلانی شود، پس ابطال آن یکی بهر کمال آن دیگری باشد، مسیح گوید «ما جئت لابطال توراة و لیکن لاکملها».	7. مسیح گفت که نیامده ام که دین انبیاء نقصان کنم بدان آمده ام که تمام کنم چون گفت سخن خدا ام [. . .] پس مسیح خواهد آمدن تا آن سخن را که بآدم آمده است که 32 است و بهر نبیّ ازان چند کلمة آمده است فرمود که خواهم آمدن که آنرا تمام کنم و سرّ تمامئ آنرا آشکار کنم و نیامدم که نقصان آن کنم. گوید من به قیامت باز آیم و کار پدر آشکارا کنم . . . و علم ظاهر و باطن یکی کند و آشکارا بگوید.
چون نبی سخن متشابه گفته بود و امّت را از آن بیرون بیاورده ادای وام بود در گردن او، و مولانا علی ادای آن وام کرد و مردم را از کون مشابهت و گم بودگی در ظاهر شریعت بدر آورد و بعالم پیدائی در حقیقت رسانید.	8. دران وقت بجهة آن مسیح اظهار خود نکرد که علم 32 کلمهٔ آلهی بر وجه داشت و 28 دندان و 32 دندان که علم 32 کلمهٔ آلهی بود داشت امّا بر زبان او 32 کلمه که وجه او بران خلقة بود روان نبود گفت خواهم آمدن و بیان خود کردن. اکنون ای ترسا بزان که انبیاء آمدند پیش از ظهور مسیح و واتند که دختری پوری بزا که نام او خدا با ما بو وقتی که او بیاسه شرک از دنیا برود مرتفع شود دین و ملّت و مذهب یک ببو مجموع آدمی زاد خدا شناس ببند یهود هوا مسیحه که ترسایان او را میدانند این نیست که انبیاء وعده کیند براء آ دین و ملّت و مذهب همه یک نشدند و همه خلق خداشناس نشدند جواب اوی که مسیح واتی ای حواریون من با شما سخن برمز و اشارة و کنایة گفته ام این بار بیایم

ISMAILI TEXTS	JAVIDAN-NAMA-YI KABIR
	و معنئ آنرا بیان کنم و گفت که من نیامدم که دین انبیاء را ناقص کردانم بلکه آمدم تمام کردانم پیغمبر عم گواهی بدی که خو بو آ که انبیاء خبر داده بودند آمد و برفت و او کلمهٔ خدا باز خواهد آمدن و نشان قیامة یکی آمدن اوست اکنون بقول مسیح ای ترسا آن سخن که مسیح گفت من هرچه با شما گفته ام برمز و اشارة گفته ام باز خواهم آمدن تا آنرا آشکاره کنم پس بقول مسیح شما سخنهاء او را تا او بیان نکند فهم نخواهد کرد.
ولادت جسمانی در عالم تنزیل، ولادت روحانی در عالم تأویل، و اگر تنزیل و تأویل که ظاهر و باطن است نداند راه با معاد نبرند، مسیح گوید من لم یولد مرّتین لم یبلغ ملکوت السماء.	9. تا دو بار نزاید یکی از شکل و صورت بوده باشد در ماکوت آسمانی که کلمه و کلام است نرود همچنان که مسیح گفت: من لم یولد مرّتین.
و هندوان دو بُت می‌تراشند یکی حقیقی [که آن را نارن] خوانند، و اعنی مولانا قائم قیامت و دیگری را بهرا [سائین] اعنی دجال.	10. پس آن که هند گفتند که نارین خداوند چهار دست بود یعنی خداوند چهار کلمه بود. و هندوان دو بت می‌تراشند یکی حقیقی
گوئیم هفت آسمان است که کواکب سیارهٔ هفتگانه دارد . . . و هفت روز هفته است و انسان را هفت عضو است . . . موی و پوست و گوشت و استخوان و رگ و پیه و خون.	11. اکنون چرا حضرت احدیّة افلاک را بر 32 و 28 قسمة بعدد 28 و 32 کلمهٔ خود کرد بجهة آنکه انسان که بحدیث سیصد و شصت استخوان دارد هر یک در مقابلهٔ درجة تا همچو فلک شش بار شصت باشد هر شصت 28 و 32 همچنین سیصد و شصت پی و سیصد و شصت رگ و سیصد و شصت گوشت و سیصد و شصت پوست بجهة آنکه تا هر استخوان در مقابلهٔ پی و رکی و گوشتی و پوستی هست همچنانکه در محاذاة فلک البروج که سیصد و شصت درجة است جمیع افلاک منقسم شوند در مقابلهٔ سیصد و شصت پاره استخوان و گوشت و پوست و پی و رگ منقسم شوندد.

ISMAILI TEXTS	JAVIDAN-NAMA-YI KABIR
	سیصد و شصت درجة و غیره شکل و صورت و کسوت او که آدم است و اجزاء آدم است مقسوم است و السّماء ذات البروج و القمر قدّرناه منازل که عبارة است از 28 و 32 28 و 32 تا سیصد و شصت تمام شد. و السّماء ذات البروج که دوازده برج است و هر برجی سی درجه تا سیصد و شصت درجه بود تا شش بار شصت درجه بود و هر شصت درجه 28 و 32 درجه بود که طوله ستّون ذراعا فی السّماء تا آسمانها همچنان که زمان هفته بوجه آدم مخلوق شد.
بحکم قیامت خود خدا دلیل است بر خود، آنجا نه نظر است و نه تعلیم، او را خود باو باید شناخت.	12. و چون او بیاید در جهان دین و مذهب و اعتقاد یکی شود و همه خلایق و اهل کتاب یکی شود و اختلاف کتاب برخیزد و پچه در کهواره خداشناس شود بعد ازان بتعلیم احتیاج نباشد.

PART FIVE

ISMAILI-SUFI RELATIONSHIPS IN BADAKHSHĀN

14

Ismaili-Sufi and Ismaili-Twelver Relations in Badakhshān in the Post-Alamūt Period: The *Chirāgh-nāma*

Nourmamadcho Nourmamadchoev
(The Institute of Ismaili Studies)

Introduction

In 1959 Wladimir Ivanow, the pioneer of modern Ismaili studies, published the text of the *Chirāgh-nāma* in the *Revue Iranienne d'Anthropologie*. In the introduction to the published text, Ivanow briefly discusses Ismaili-Sufi relations. Expressing his joy at finding this valuable source that allowed him to elaborate his proposed theory of Ismaili-Sufi relations, he remarks:

> I was therefore very glad when some pilgrims from Central Asia brought a very interesting document, fully vindicating the proposed theory. It is called 'Chiragh-Nama,' an opuscule of what may be called the purely darwish nature. It may be explained that wandering religious mendicants, who go under the general name of darwishes in the Islamic world, vary very much in their ways, habits and traditions.[1]

According to the local oral tradition the performance of the ritual of *Chirāgh-rawshan,* lighting or kindling the lamp, was passed down from generation to generation and is linked to the figure of Nāṣir-i Khusraw

---

[1] W. Ivanow, 'Sufism and Ismailism: *Chiragh-nama*', *Revue Iranienne d'Anthropologie*, 3 (1959), p. 15; See also, N. Nourmamadchoev, *The Ismāʿīlīs of Badakhshan: History, Politics and Religion from 1500 to 1750* (PhD thesis, SOAS, London, 2014), pp. 215–242.

(394–481/1004–1088), who is known in the region as Pīr Nāṣir or Pīr Shāh Nāṣir-i Khusraw.[2] The oral tradition draws our attention to the traditions of *Chirāgh-rawshan* and *madāḥ-khānī*, which were an integral part of religious assemblies. The tradition of *madāḥ-khānī*, singing devotional and didactic poetry, is as old as the tradition of *Chirāgh-rawshan* and, in many cases, these two traditions are intimately connected.

The term *Chirāgh-rawshan* consists of two linguistic elements: the *chirāgh* (or *charāgh*), which stems from a Syriac word *shrag* or *shragh*, meaning a lamp,[3] and the Persian term *rawshan* (or *rawshan kardan*), which literally means 'to light' or 'to kindle.' Thus, *Chirāgh-rawshan* means a shining or luminous lamp. It is one of the oldest surviving Ismaili religious traditions practised among the inhabitants of mountainous Badakhshān. It is also a custom prevalent among the Ismailis of the northern areas of Pakistan, some parts of modern Afghanistan, and the Xinjang province of modern China.

The following discussion is a textual analysis of the intricate nature of the text of the *Chirāgh-nāma*. The text is a unique example of intellectual interaction between Ismailis, Sufis and Twelver Shiʿis in Badakhshān. I shall discuss the infiltration of various terminology in the text of the *Chirāgh-nāma* which is recited by a *khalīfa*, a local Ismaili religious leader, during the performance of the *Chirāgh-rawshan*.

What is the *Chirāgh-rawshan*?

The *Chirāgh-rawshan* is a *majlis*, a gathering of believers, where a lamp is kindled and verses from the Qur'an are recited for the eternal peace

[2] F. Daftary, *The Ismāʿīlīs: Their History and Doctrines* (Cambridge, 2nd ed., 2007), p. 207; A. Nanji, 'Nāṣir-i Khusraw', *EI2*, vol. 7, pp. 1006–1007; A. Shokhumorov, 'Ṭarzi Daʿwat-i Fāṭimī va Peshvāyāni Barjasta-i Mazhabi Ismāʿīlīya', in H. Farmand (ed.), *Dānā-i Yumgān: Majmuʿa-i Maqālat-i Seminār-i Bayn al-Milalī* (Kabul, 1987), pp. 152–153; A. Bertel's, *Nasir Khusraw i Ismailizm* (Moscow, 1959), pp. 186–190; Nourmamadchoev, *The Ismāʿīlīs of Badakhshan*, pp. 142–147.

[3] J. P. Smith, *A Compendious Syriac Dictionary Founded upon the Thesaurus Syriacus of R. Payne Smith* (Oxford: Clarendon, 1903), p. 597.

of a departed soul. The recitation of the Qur'anic verses is followed by the singing of didactic and devotional poetry, *madāḥ-khānī*, until dawn – the time when the ritual of *Chirāgh-rawshan* is performed. Then the *khalīfa* reads the text of the *Chirāgh-nāma* and the participants chant a choral praise to God, the Prophet Muhammad and the imams from the Ahl al-Bayt.

The local tradition informs us that the tradition of *Chirāgh-rawshan* also consisted of several other religious rituals, namely, *daʿwat-i baqā* and *daʿwat-i fanā*.[4]

Chirāgh-rawshan, as one of the parts of the funeral ceremony, is performed on the second or third night. This usually takes place after the burial of the body. The burial is usually preceded by various rituals such as bathing and shrouding of the body followed by the prayer. There is a similarity in the practice of *Chirāgh-rawshan* among the Ismailis of Badakhshān and the northern areas of Pakistan. The core of this tradition is intrinsically connected to the Qur'anic notion of light (*nūr*). Thus, when the *chirāgh* or lamp is kindled, the religious ritual starts, consisting as has been said of several inter-related rituals, such as reciting verses from the Qur'an and reciting some other important religious prayers known as *duʿā*. This is followed by the singing of religious and didactic poetry (*madāḥ-khānī*) in praise of the Prophet Muhammad and the imams from the Ahl al-Bayt. Prior to the lightning of the *Chirāgh*, the *khalīfa* prepares the wick (Per. *fatīla*) for the lamp and inserts it in the oil specially prepared from the fat of a sacrificial animal – a ram.[5]

The Ismailis of Badakhshān, Afghanistan, China and the northern areas of Pakistan are of the opinion that the practice of *Chirāgh-rawshan* has a philosophical meaning, which, in one way or another, is linked to the figure of Nāṣir-i Khusraw. Nonetheless, no precise evidence has thus far been produced to prove this assertion.

---

4 A. Najib, 'Nazare ba Marāsimi '*Charogh-rawshan*' dar Osiyo-i Markazi', in U. Shozodamuhammad (ed.), *Sources of the Tradition of 'Charoghrawshan'* (Dushanbe, 2009), pp. 77–84.

5 I. Zarubin, *Shugnanskaia Ėtnografiia* (Arkhiv Vostokovedov AN SSR, Moscow, n.d.), f. 12, op. 1, no: 242, fols 123–156.

The Practice of *Daʿwat-i Baqā* and *Daʿwat-i Fanā*

The *daʿwat-i baqā* and *daʿwat-i fanā* mentioned above are two religious rituals performed by the local Ismaili *khalīfas* in Badakhshān and neighbouring regions. The *daʿwat-i baqā* is performed for the elders of the community during their lifetime. *Daʿwat-i fanā*, unlike *daʿwat-i baqā* is performed for the soul of a deceased person.[6]

The term *fanā* literally means *to pass away* or *to perish.*[7] This term in Sufi provenance means to die in God. Therefore, in the Sufi context, *fanā* is the passing away of the self, which is the essential prerequisite for the survival (*baqā*) of the selfless divine qualities placed in man by God.[8] The combination of the Sufi term *fanā* and an Ismaili term *daʿwat* produces a new meaning. As a generic term, *daʿwat-i fanā* (symbolically means 'a gathering of believers bidding farewell to the departed soul') thus refers to the religious rite which is part of the funeral practice among the Ismailis of Badakhshān. The performance of this rite, as a compulsory element of the *daʿwat* ceremony or funerary rites, previously took place on the third night.[9] Traditionally, neighbours bring food for the members of the bereaved family for three days.[10]

The term *baqā* literally means *to survive, subsist* or *to remain*[11] and is used to refer to life. Like the term *fanā*, the term *baqā* is also of Sufi origin and in combination with the term *daʿwat* it refers to religious

---

[6] M. Khan, *Living Tradition of Nāṣir Khusraw* (Unpublished report submitted to Central Asian Unit at the IIS, London, 2004); E. Hojibekov, 'Roje' ba yak Sunnatii Mazhabii Mardumi Badakhson', in S. Niyozov, and R. Nazariev (ed.), *Nāṣir Khusraw: Yesterday, Today, Tomorrow* (Khujand, 2005), pp. 605–610.

[7] H. Wehr, *A Dictionary of Modern Written Arabic* (Beirut and London, 1980), p. 729.

[8] A. Wilcox, 'The Dual Mystical Concept of Fanā' and Baqā' in Early Ṣūfism', *BJMES*, 38, 1 (2011), pp. 95–96.

[9] *Daʿwat-i fanā* or *shab-i daʿwat* was performed on the third night. In modern times it is performed on the second night.

[10] I. Zarubin, *Shugnanskaia Ėtnografiia*, fols 123–156; J. Biddulph, *Tribes of the Hindoo Koosh* (Calcutta, 1880), p. 123; A.Z. Lashkariev, *Pokhoronno-Paminalnaia Obriadnost' Bartangtsev* (Unpublished Thesis: Institute of Ethnology and Anthropology, Moscow, 2007); A. Saidula, '*Chirogh rawshan*: Shiʿi Ceremonial Practiced by the Ismaili Communities of Xinjiang, China', in F. Suleman (ed.), *People of the Prophet's House: Artistic and Ritual Expressions of Shiʿi Islam* (London, 2015), pp. 232–241.

[11] H. Wehr, *A Dictionary of Modern Written Arabic*, p. 69.

rituals and rites practised by the Ismailis of Badakhshān. The term *daʿwat-i baqā* (symbolically means 'to celebrate life or subsistence') refers not only to physical but to spiritual subsistence as well. The body, according to Ismaili teaching as well as to the local tradition, is transitory while the soul is eternal.

The *Chirāgh-nāma*: Reflections on the Texts and Their Authorship

A copy of the text of the *Chirāgh-nāma* can be found in the collection of religious texts of any Ismaili *khalīfa* in Badakhshān, the northern areas of Pakistan and Xinjiang province of China. The manuscripts consulted for this study show that the text can be divided into two parts. Part One consists of various prayers and background discussion and Part Two is the text used during the *daʿwat* or *Chirāgh-rawshan*.

Part One of the text varies in length and in content. For example, the text of the *Chirāgh-nāma* collated from various manuscripts by Qudrat Allāh Beg has a short treatise as an introduction called *Rūḥ-nāma* ('A Treatise on the Soul').[12] Although Qudrat Allāh Beg's compilation is not dated, it is clear that it consists of compilation of the same text drawn from various sources. The total length of the text including the *Rūḥ-nāma* is in excess of 95 folios. By contrast the text of the *Chirāgh-nāma* found by Ivan Zarubin in Gorno-Badakhshān consists of 43 folios.[13] This text is dated 1334/1915 and it is evident that it was copied from an older manuscript. Part Two of the *Chirāgh-nāma* consists of 15 or 20 texts, which are Qurʾanic verses, various prayers, poems in praise of the Prophet Muhammad and imams from the Ahl al-Bayt. The texts are linked together by an invocation – *ṣalawāt* (lit. prayer, praise or benediction). When the *khalīfa* performs the

---

12 MS Q *Chirāgh-nāma* (no date, private collection, Northern area of Pakistan. A copy of the text was kindly provided to me by Dr Faquir Muhammad Hunzai for which I am very grateful. Unlike Qudrat Allāh Beg's copy, the manuscript of *Chirāgh-nāma* in the collection of the IIS, however, does not have the text of *Rūḥ-nāma*. See: MS 31 *Chirāgh-nāmah*, no date. IIS collection.

13 I. Zarubin, *Latin Transcription of the Text of Chirāgh-nāma* (Institute of Oriental Studies, St. Petersburg, The Zarubin Collection, f. 121, op. 1, no: 366).

ritual of *Chirāgh-rawshan*, the participants recite the *ṣalawāt* together in chorus. The author or authors of these texts remain unknown.

The question of the authorship of the *Chirāgh-nāma* opens up a broad spectrum of discourses on the origin of the text as well as of this particular religious rite. A discussion of the pre-Islamic origin of the text of the *Chirāgh-nāma* undoubtedly falls beyond the framework of this article, since no written sources are available to enable its reconstruction. Thus, this short discussion will be confined to the framework of the Islamic tradition in general and the Ismaili tradition in particular. It has already been mentioned that the tradition of *Chirāgh-rawshan* consists of several distinctive inter-related rites – the recitation of Qurʾanic verses, *madāḥ-khānī* and the performance of *Chirāgh-rawshan* – that are fundamentally Islamic in character.

The oral tradition from Badakhshān maintains that the tradition of *Chirāgh-rawshan* originated at the time of Nāṣir-i Khusraw. Sources such as the *Hidāyat al-muʾminīn al-ṭālibīn* of Fidāʾī Khurāsānī (d. 1342/1923) and *Silk-i gawhar-rīz* of Guharrez the son of Khwāja ʿAbd al-Nabī, the son of Khwāja Ṣāliḥ-i Yumgī (fl. thirteenth/nineteenth century) narrate that Nāṣir was sent to Khurāsān and Badakhshān to convert the local population to the Ismaili faith and provide spiritual guidance. According to Abusaid Shokhumorov (d. 1999), a Tajik scholar, Nāṣir produced a work on 'the relation of the body and soul and the survival of the soul after the body's annihilation,' entitled *Miṣbāḥ* ('The Lamp').[14] The work is mentioned in Nāṣir-i Khusraw's *Jāmiʿ al-ḥikmatayn* but unfortunately, no copy has come down to us. Shokhumorov apparently based his argument on the authorship of the *Chirāgh-nāma* on this particular work but it remains difficult to substantiate such an assertion in the absence of the work itself.

Thus the Ismailis of Badakhshān argue that Nāṣir-i Khusraw is the author of the text. Similarly, they argue that the philosophical underpinning of the ritual of *Chirāgh-rawshan* stems from Nāṣir's works, which were propagated during the *majlis*. The *majlis*, in its turn, could be the initial form of this tradition that incorporated the recitation of Qurʾanic verses along with a talk on religious and didactic topics.

---

[14] A. Shokhumorov, 'Charogh-rawshankunī', *Masʿalahoi Pomirshinosī*, 5 (2003), p. 93.

Singing *madāḥ* in this *majlis* lends a purely mystical essence to the ritual of *Chirāgh-rawshan*. It is this tradition, *par excellence*, that is sacred to the local population as, in its spiritual and philosophical dimension it is linked to the figure of Pīr Shāh Nāṣir-i Khusraw.

As outlined above, the text of the *Chirāgh-nāma* is a combination of prose and poetry, 'arranged more or less systematically in such a way that the contents may be used for singing.'[15] Traditionally, author(s) used to give their name or *nom de plume* in the signature line at the end of the text. However, the text of the *Chirāgh-nāma* consists of a range of poems, where we can see only one or two such signature lines. Upon a close reading of the text, we can see that the single signature line is actually a combination of two signature lines with the same rhyming scheme:

Asrār-i mulki jabbār chun rūz-u shab ba takrār,
Gūyim Qāsimī-wār, ṣalawāt bar Muḥammad.
Khūsh guft Niʿmat Allāh ramzīst qul huwa Allāh,
Barkhān bi nām-i Allāh, ṣalawāt bar Muḥammad.

The secrets of the world of the Almighty like night and day repeatedly,
We say as did Qāsim, blessings [be] upon Muhammad.
It was well said by Niʿmat Allāh, 'Say: He is God' is a symbol,
Recite in the name of God, blessings [be] upon Muhammad.[16]

This example alludes to the figure of Qāsim-i Anwār (d. 837/1433) and at the same time to Shāh Niʿmat Allāh Walī (d. 834/1431), which makes it quite odd. The question that presents itself at this point is how a poem can have two signature lines. Surprisingly, this particular case presents a tri-dimensional complexity, the first and second being the

15 Ivanow, 'Sufism and Ismailism: *Chiragh-nama*', p. 15.

16 MS. P. *Chirāgh-nāma* and *Namāzi janāza* (no date; private collection of Umed Shozodamuhammad, v. Kushk, Tajikistan), fol. 19b; Shozodamuhammad, *Sources of the Tradition of 'Charoghrawshan'*, pp. 34–35. The first signature line that quotes the name of Qāsim-i Anwār is missing from Shāh Niʿmat Allāh Walī's *Dīwān*, which leads us to assume that this particular line was added to the text by another scribe. This signature line is also missing in MS 31 *Chirāgh-nāma*, pp. 12–13. For the original signature line, see: Shāh Niʿmat Allāh Walī, *Kulliyāt-i Ashʿār-i Shāh Niʿmat Allāh-i Walī*, ed. Jawād Nurbakhsh (Tehran, 1374 Sh./1995), p. 638 ff.

relationship of Niʿmat Allāh Walī to Qāsim-i Anwār and vice versa, and the third their relationships to the tradition of *Chirāgh-rawshan* and the Ismailis of Badakhshān. It also raises yet another important issue related to the process of textual transmission. We are all aware that minor or sometimes even major errors or additions can creep into a text at the time of its transcription, but this intentional or unintentional addition to the text may perhaps have been made by the scribe under 'an indomitable impulse to seek poetic glory.'[17]

Returning to the question of authorship, it should be pointed out that the text of the *Chirāgh-nāma* contains only one poem by Niʿmat Allāh Walī, which does not prove that he was the author of the entire text. The question that arises, at least from the discursive and logical point of view, is: if the text of the *Chirāgh-nāma* was written neither by Nāṣir-i Khusraw nor by Niʿmat Allāh Walī nor any other of the Ismaili *dāʿī*s, Sufi *Pīr*s and shaykhs, who then wrote it? Unfortunately, we are far from being able to postulate an authorship for the text, as the names of the prophets, imams, saints and Sufi mystics stretch the historical framework of this tradition from the time of Adam up to that of the Sufi Niʿmat Allāh Walī.

What can be said with certainty, however, is that the text of the *Chirāgh-nāma* is of Persian origin, and was written by someone who was well-versed both in the Qur'an and the doctrine of the imamate, which is shared by the Ismaili and Twelver Shiʿis. The text of the *Chirāgh-nāma* is also heavily infiltrated by Sufi mystical symbolism and expressions. Furthermore, the surviving copies of the *Chirāgh-nāma* contain considerable textual evidence that it is a crystallised text dating at least from the end of the ninth/fifteenth century.

Textual Analysis of the *Chirāgh-nāma*

Reading the text of the *Chirāgh-nāma* in its historical, cultural and ritualistic contexts brings to the fore various aspects of Islamic history in

17 A. Roy, *The Islamic Syncretic Tradition in Bengal* (Princeton, 1983), p. 9; A. Asani, *The Būjh Niranjan: A Critical Edition of a Mystical Poem in Medieval Hindustani: With its Khojkī and Gujarati Recensions* (Ph.D. Thesis, Harvard University, 1984), p. 8.

general and Ismaili history in particular. It is, however, through analogy and symbolism that these aspects touch the core of the tradition. To understand the text and its symbolic significance, the context, whether historical or intellectual, in which it was produced should be explored. The historical context, in turn, is framed by reference to the various elements of socio-religious interaction. The text clearly reflects the ever-changing nature of the milieu and the demands for integration, reformulation and acculturation. These processes, which directly or indirectly influenced the text, create a paradigm whereby the text cannot be explained or, most importantly, comprehended without the context or vice versa. As George Steiner, a well-known literary critic, commented:

> When using a word we take into resonance, as it were, its entire previous history. A text is imbedded in specific historical time; it has what linguists call a diachronic structure. To read fully is to restore all that one can of the immediacies of value in which speech actually occurs.[18]

Therefore, the study of *Chirāgh-nāma* as a text highlights a methodological concern. First of all, it is necessary to analyse the content critically in order to understand the entire, or partial, history of the particular ritual through the terms and notions employed within the text. To do this will require a critical methodology in order to move from speculative questioning to a close reading of the text, requiring the adoption of forms of inter-related methodology, comparing and contrasting various parts and sections of the text while at the same time dividing the text up into smaller units in order to comprehend the meaning. These methodologies will allow us to go beyond the context in order to understand the background discussed above.[19]

It should be mentioned that the structural organisation of the various texts, in prose or poetry, presented in the text of the *Chirāgh-nāma* raises some vexing questions regarding the relationship between them. The principal one that emerges from an examination of various sections of the *Chirāgh-nāma* is that of co-existence between Ismailism,

---

18 G. Steiner, *After Babel: Aspects of Language and Translation* (London, 1975), p. 24.

19 G. Shoeler, *The Oral and the Written in Early Islam* (London, 2006); Steiner, *After Babel*, Chapters 1 and 3.

Imāmī Shiʿism and Sufism. These three Islamic communities appear to share certain common ground while directly opposing each other on certain theological and doctrinal issues; at the same time they share the same geographic and ritualistic space. How can Twelver Shiʿi teaching, which is, ideologically, in opposition to Ismaili and Sufi teaching share the same geographical and doctrinal space within the context of the *Chirāgh-nāma*? Does this reflect an imposition, which could only have been possible through political intervention? Or is it an unintentional interpolation and addendum to this religious rite and its text? Or perhaps is it simply another form of the practice of *taqiyya* by local Ismailis which allowed these teachings to become more generally used? Questions about the origin of the work, briefly touched on above, also surface once more. As a consequence, this section is divided into shorter sub-sections that will allow a consideration of certain issues through a closer reading.

One additional point about the text of the *Chirāgh-nāma* must be noted at this point, which is its use of language. It contains certain verses from the Qurʾan (in Arabic) but is mostly written in Persian, the *lingua franca* of the local population, infused with the religious and mystical symbolism, theological issues as well as the ethical teachings of Islam. The structural organisation of the text rotates around the principle of *tawḥīd* (the Oneness of God) and the concepts of *nubuwwat* (Prophetology) and *imāmat* (the imamate), which are the significant elements in Ismaili teaching.

The Qurʾanic References in the *Chirāgh-nāma*: The Symbolism of Light

The Qurʾan is the foundational scriptural text of Islam used in the daily life of Muslims. The text of the *Chirāgh-nāma* is permeated with verses from the Qurʾan. It starts with the glorification of God and professes the Oneness of the Lord – *tawḥīd*.

It is a common, widespread practice that every text and ritual in Islam, whether in Persian or Arabic, opens with a religious formula, the *basmala*, and the *Fātiḥa* the opening verse of the Qurʾan, followed by an invocation and glorification (*takbīr*) of the Almighty. Clearly this standard practice, that refers to the source of the ritual in Islamic scripture, was maintained in all the manuscripts of the *Chirāgh-nāma*. Despite the fact that Andrei Bertel's (d. 1995) detected the possible origin of the ritual of *Chirāgh-rawshan* in Zoroastrianism, he still asserted that 'the source of similitude of "*Chirāgh-rawshan*" is the Holy Scripture, particularly the verse of Light – *Nūr*'.[20] The noun *nūr* in the context of the Qur'an evokes one of the Beautiful Names of God, imbedded in the *ayat al-nūr* and therefore present in all manuscript copies of the *Chirāgh-nāma*. The verse reads:

> God is the Light of the heavens and the earth. The parable of His Light is a niche, wherein is a lamp. The lamp is in a glass. The glass is as a shining star kindled from a blessed olive tree, neither of the East nor of the West. Its oil would well-nigh shine forth, even if no fire had touched it. Light upon light. God guides unto His Light whomsoever He will, and God sets forth parables for mankind; and God is Knower of all things.[21]

It becomes evident from the verse above that the three main components of the ritual of *Chirāgh-rawshan*, namely *nūr* (light), *ramz/mathal* (allegory/symbol) and *chirāgh dān/mishkāt* (niche), are clearly taken directly from the *ayat al-nūr*. The appearance of *nūr* is reflected in the lighting of the *chirāgh* (the lamp), specially made of a wick (*fatīla* or *rīshta*), placed in specially made oil. This is the allegory of the *zaytūn* (olive tree).[22] For the local Ismailis, however, the *chirāgh* or the *nūr* or the light of the *chirāgh* symbolises knowledge or attaining the knowledge of God through the recognition of the Imam of the Time. The *fatīla* or the *rīshta*, on the other hand, symbolises the unbroken chain of the imamate. In the light of this, it can be seen that Nāṣir-i Khusraw's use of these Qur'anic notions in his philosophical poetry find echoes in the text and ritualistic elements of the performance of *Chirāgh-rawshan*.

---

[20] A. Bertel's, 'Naẓariyāt-i barkhe az ʿurafā va shīʿīyāni Ithna ʿAsharī rājiʿ ba arzishi mīrath-i adabī-i Nāṣir-i Khusraw', *Yādnāma-i Nāṣir-i Khusraw* (Mashhad, 1976), p. 117.

[21] Qur'an, 24:35 in S. H. Nasr, *The Study Qur'an: A New Translation and Commentary* (New York, 2015), pp. 878–880.

[22] See also in the Old Testament: You shall charge the sons of Israel that they bring you clear oil of beaten olives for the light, to make lamp burn continually (Exod. 27:20).

For him 'lighting the lamp' is the path to wisdom, which is futile without knowledge and action:

> *Shamʿ-i khirad bar firūz dar dil-u bishtāb,*
> *Bā dil-i rawshan ba suyyi ʿālam-i rawshan.*
> *Chūn ba dil andar chirāgh khāh-i afrūkht,*
> *ʿIlm-u ʿamal bāyadat fatīla wa rawghan.*
>
> Light the candle of wisdom within your heart,
> And hurry, heart aglow, toward the world of light.
> If you would light a lamp within your heart,
> Make knowledge and action your wick and oil.[23]

The poetic and philosophical language of Muslim luminaries allowed these notions to spread throughout Muslim communities. Hence, these notions, expressed in various languages, were accepted. This became possible due to the metaphorical/symbolic expressions from the Qur'an, which were enshrined in the Ismaili devotion to the imam, Sufi *dhikr* (remembrance) as well as in the simple invocation of the Beautiful Names of God by every Muslim. Likewise, it was preached in sessions (*majālis*), such as those pronounced both by Ismaili *dāʿīs* and preachers from other confessions.

The Qur'anic maxim expressed in the verses above is employed in the text of the *Chirāgh-nāma* in the sense of edification and teaching. It is a call to convey religious knowledge to the one who is attending the sermon known as the *daʿwa* (*daʿwat*) or *majlis*.

At the core of the rite of *Chirāgh-rawshan* is the notion of the Light. According to the *Chirāgh-nāma* this special light 'was sent from the Almighty, and it was sent for the sake of Muhammad, [which then] was passed on to ʿAlī.'[24] Thus, it becomes clear that one of the main sources of this religious rite is the Holy Qur'an, particularly the *ayat al-nūr*. The core of this light, as the Qur'an puts it, is kindled from the light that 'no fire touched' (Qur'an, 24:35).

---

23 Nāṣir-i Khusraw, *Dīwān*, 78:15–16; A. Hunsberger, *Nāṣir Khusraw: The Ruby of Badakhshan* (London, 2000), p. 78.

24 MS. N. *Chirāgh-nāma* (Incomplete copy, no date, in the private collection of the author, London), fol. 2a. This short extract is present in all of the copies of the *Chirāgh-nāma* I have studied. The Persian rendering of the text is as follows: *Īn chirāgh az jabbār-i ʿālam āmad az barāyi Muḥammad āmad, az Muḥammad ba ʿAlī āmad.*

Elements of Sufism in the Text of the *Chirāgh-nāma*

Badakhshān witnessed the arrival of Sufis from Iran and Central Asia most probably in the second half of the eighth/fourteenth century or perhaps even earlier. The life and missionary activities of Sayyid ʿAlī Hamadānī (d. 786/1385), a Kubrawī Sufi, who was also known as ʿAlī-yi Thānī, may shed new light on the historical development of Sufism in Badakhshān.[25] Jaʿfar-i Badakhshānī, his student and biographer, in his work *Khulāṣat al-manāqib* depicts the details of his life and activity in the region.[26] The *Manqabat al-jawāhir* of a certain Ḥaydar-i Badakhshī, who was affiliated to the Kubrawī-Hamadānī line as well as Khalīl Allāh Badakhshānī's *Jāmiʿ al-salāsil*, an unstudied text reflecting a lineage traced to Ḥusayn-i Khwārazmī are also important for this study.[27]

The history of the *Chirāgh-nāma* in subsequent centuries saw the presence of Sufi mystical symbolism in the religious literature, most likely brought to the region in the seventh/thirteenth and eighth/fourteenth centuries and, in some cases, possibly even much earlier. The local inhabitants transcribed and preserved Sufi sources in their private collections as sacred sources of their religion. This phenomenon is unique and raises questions about Ismaili-Sufi and Ismaili-Twelver Shiʿi relations. The first intricate question is how these ideas found their way to this remote mountainous region. Were the texts brought to the region intentionally or was it an unintentional move by the learned to transcribe and preserve these sources? While this

---

[25] G. Böwering, "Alī b. Sehāb al-Dīn b. Moḥammad Hamadānī', *EIr*, vol. 1, pp. 862–864. For more details, see D. DeWeese, 'The Eclipse of the Kubravīyah in Central Asia', *Iranian Studies*, 21, 1–2 (1988), pp. 45–83; D. DeWeese, 'Sayyid ʿAlī Hamadānī and Kubrawī Hagiographical Traditions', in L. Lewisohn (ed.), *The Heritage of Sufism*, vol. 2: *The Legacy of Mediaeval Persian Sufism (1150–1500)* (Oxford, 1999), pp. 121–158; J. Elias, 'A Second ʿAlī: The Making of Sayyid ʿAlī Hamadānī in Popular Imagination', *The Muslim World*, 90, 4 (2000), pp. 395–420.

[26] Nūr al-Dīn Jaʿfar Badakhshī, *Khulāṣat al-manāqib: Dar manāqib-i Mīr Sayyid ʿAlī-i Hamadānī*, ed. S. A. Zafar (Islamabad, 1995); J. K. Teufel, *Eine Lebensbeschreibung des Scheichs ʿAlī-i Hamadānī (gestorben 1385): Die Xulāṣat ul-Manāqib des Maulānā Nūr ud-Dīn Caʿfar-i Badaxšī* (Leiden, 1962).

[27] For details of *Jāmiʿ al-salāsil*, see DeWeese, 'Sayyid ʿAlī Hamadānī and Kubrawī Hagiographical Traditions', pp. 121–158.

phenomenon must remain a topic for a future separate study it should be emphasised that relationships between Ismailis and Sufis in post-Mongol Iran were facilitated by the uniting of the Sufi lexicon and Ismaili terminology.[28]

The infusion of Sufi terms and terminology throughout the text of the *Chirāgh-nāma* is very clear and it reflects the technical and terminological spectrum of interchange between these two esoteric movements. The use of Sufi terms, such as *silsila* (brotherhood), *pīrān-i ṭarīqat* (masters or saints of the path), *ʿāshiq-i ṣāḥibnaẓar* (insightful lover), *arkān-i ṭarīq* (pillars and principals of the path), and *ʿārif* (gnostic), *faqīr* (ascetic renouncing material wealth) and *darwīsh* (lit. itinerant or Sufi), along with others provide examples of this interaction.

Although the *Chirāgh-nāma* is permeated with Sufi terminology, it does not mention the names of the Sufi mystics, since quoting their specific teachings could have changed the general frame of the ritual. It is also impossible to define clearly either the timeframe or the milieu in which the text was produced on the basis of the mystical symbolism alone. The clearest example of Sufi influence in the *Chirāgh-nāma* can be found in one of the poems of Niʿmat Allāh Walī, where he calls upon his followers to praise the Prophet Muhammad:

Khūsh raḥmatest yārān, ṣalawāt bar Muḥammad,
Gūyim az dil-u jān, ṣalawāt bar Muḥammad.
Gūyim az dil-u jān bā ʿārifān-i Kirmān,
Shādī-i ruyyi yārān, ṣalawāt bar Muḥammad.

O my friends, it is such a mercy, praise [be] upon Muhammad,
Let us recite it from our heart, praise [be] upon Muhammad.
We're reciting from our heart with the Gnostics from Kirmān,
It is a happiness in face of our friends, praise [be] upon Muhammad.[29]

---

28 L. Lewisohn, 'Sufism and Ismāʿīlī Doctrine in the Persian Poetry of Nizārī', *Iran*, 41 (2003), pp. 229–251.

29 MS. Ch. R. *Khushnawīs – Chirāgh-nāma* (no date, private collection of Khalīfa Shohi Kalon Shozodamuhammad, v. Kushk, Tajikistan), fols 17a–20a; See also, Ivanow, 'Sufism and Ismailism: Chiragh-nama', pp. 67–68; Shāh Niʿmat Allāh Walī, *Kulliyāt-i ashʿār-i Shāh Niʿmat Allāh-i Walī* (Tehran, 1374 Sh./1995), p. 638.

Comparing the text of this poem in the *Kulliyāt-i ashʿār-i Shāh Niʿmat Allāh-i Walī* with the manuscript copies of the *Chirāgh-nāma*, it is clear that the poem of Shāh Niʿmat Allāh Walī, which initially consisted of eleven distiches, has been tripled in length. This raises the question of the role of the scribe. Was it the poet or scribe who eloquently reproduced and expanded the text or was it the work of an anonymous local poet who combined his own poetry with that of Niʿmat Allāh Walī?

A comparison of the text of this poem from all the available sources would indicate that this particular *ghazal* by Niʿmat Allāh Walī was used as a base for this specific poetic composition, which, under unknown circumstances, crept into the text of the *Chirāgh-nāma*. Some distiches of this poem were incorporated into the text of the *Chirāgh-nāma* and, with the passage of time, other distiches were composed and added to it as well. The theme – *ṣalawāt bar Muḥammad* – which is the core of this poem, is chanted by the gathering of believers as a chorus during the recitation of the *Chirāgh-nāma*. This is the appealing element of this mystical poetry that was absorbed into the Ismaili ritual. The core of both texts of the poem concerns the same theme, which represents a general association with a revered wisdom in the figure of the Prophet.

Another poem, on the same theme but with different wording, occurs at the beginning of the *Chirāgh-nāma* where, instead of *ṣalawāt bar Muḥammad*, the phrase *khūsh gū ṣalawāt Muṣtafā-rā* is used.[30] These two expressions are semantically identical and, in the *Chirāgh-nāma*, they obviously represent the same recurring theme of veneration for the Prophet of Islam and the Ahl al-Bayt.

Another passage in the *Chirāgh-nāma* provides the names of two famous Sufi mystics, Khwāja Aḥmad Yasawī (d. 562/1166) and Farīd al-Dīn Ganj-i Shakar (d. 5 Muharram 664/17 October 1265), as well as that of the eighth Twelver Shiʿi imam – ʿAlī b. Mūsā al-Riḍā (151–203/768–818) together with the name of the Fatimid Ismaili *dāʿī* Nāṣir-i Khusraw. The passage starts with the praise and glorification of God as follows:

[30] MS 31 *Chirāgh-nāma*, pp. 4–8. Ivanow, 'Sufism and Ismailism: Chiragh-nama', pp. 61–63.

> *Ilāhā! Awwal yād kunam buzurgī wa ʿaẓamat wa jalāl-u jamāl-i pāk-i tabārak wa taʿālā-rā... wa imāmān-i ḥaqq-rā... wa ʿulamā-i sharīʿat-rā wa pīrān-i ṭarīqat wa ḥaqīqat wa maʿrifat-rā, wa rāhrawandagān-i rāh-i ḥaqq-rā.. wa awliyā wa anbiyā [wa] muqarribān-i bārgāh-i kibriyārā, yaʿnī sar-i Turkistān Khwāja Aḥmad-i Yasawī-rā, wa sīna-i Khurāsān Imām ʿAlī Mūsā'-i Riḍā-rā, pusht-i Kūhistān ḥaḍrat-i sulṭān Shāh Sayyid Nāṣir-i Khusraw-rā, pāyi Hindūstān Shaykh Farīd-i Shakar Ganj-rā . . .*
>
> O Lord, let me [us] remember the greatness and glory and beauty of the Almighty . . . and the Truthful imams . . . and the scholars of the religion and the masters of the path and truth and knowledge, and the followers of the path of truth, and the saints and the prophets and those close companions who are held in honour at the court of the Almighty – such as 'the head' of Turkistān Khwāja Aḥmad-i Yasawī, and 'the chest' of Khurāsān Imam ʿAlī Mūsā al-Riḍā, and 'the back' of Kūhistān Sayyid Shāh Nāṣir-i Khusraw, and the 'feet' of Hindūstān Shaykh Farīd-i Shakar Ganj.[31]

This short passage presents a strange combination of the names of two Sufi *Pīrs*, a Twelver Shiʿi imam and the name of Nāṣir-i Khusraw – the Ismaili *ḥujjat* of Khurāsān. It even refers to them as the 'head of Turkistān,' the 'chest of Khurāsān,' the 'back of Kūhistān' and the 'leg of Hindustān,' as if they were closely related to each other in terms of their religious affiliation and activity. It is evident from the historical sources that Imam ʿAlī b. Mūsā al-Riḍā was the eighth Twelver Shiʿi imam, while Khwāja Aḥmad Yasawī was the founder of a Sunni Sufi order in Central Asia known as the Yasawiyya. Shaykh Farīd al-Dīn Masʿūd Ganj-i Shakar, on the other hand, was a Chishtī Sufi from South Asia. Although these figures are members of different and, at some points, opposing religious and ideological movements, their names appear along with the name of Pīr Nāṣir-i Khusraw. The reference to these figures in the *Chirāgh-nāma* seems to be based on a Sufi *risāla* by an anonymous author, entitled *Bāb dar bayāni ṭarīqat wa ḥaqīqat* (A Chapter Explaining the Path and the Truth), which is also

---

[31] MS 31 *Chirāgh-nāma*, pp. 1–3. Ivanow, 'Sufism and Ismailism: Chiragh-nama', pp. 60–61.

known as the *Ṭarīqat-nāma*. This particular treatise contains a list of the names of the Prophets from Adam to Muhammad along with those of some well-known Sufi masters and some Ismaili *Pīr*s and *dāʿīs*.[32] It is highly likely that this genealogical chart was compiled by someone who was largely unfamiliar with the nature and history of these movements. Thus, the anonymous *risāla* seems to be the product of a scribe who tied together whatever seemed appealing to him. It also seems plausible to argue that Central Asia, Khurāsān and India in this period, to a certain extent, shared a similar pattern of popular religion and culture. This was probably due to the fact that travel and migration between these regions created an environment of mutual exchange of spiritual and mystical practices as well as religious learning. Thus, an almost similar common heritage ties these regions together, even though each region also has its own distinctive features.

The last relevant example is the appearance in the *Chirāgh-nāma* of the name of Shams al-Dīn Muḥammad of Tabrīz,[33] the well-known guide of Jalāl al-Dīn Rūmī. The passage, thus, reads:

> *Har ki nām-i Shams-i Tabrīzī shunīd-u sajda kard,*
> *Nām-i ū maʿqūl-i ḥaqq gasht dām az ḥaqq mīzanad.*
>
> Whoever hears the name of Shams-i Tabrīzī and prostrates,
> His name becomes well-linked to God as he calls of the truth.[34]

The appeal of this passage lies in its double meaning. To the ordinary Ismaili believer, this passage seems to be a reference to the Ismaili imam of the post-Alamūt period also known as Shams al-Dīn

[32] A. Bertel's and M. Baqoev, *Alfavitnii Katalog*, p. 31; Elchibekov, 'Obshie Religiozno-Filosofskie i Folklorno-Mifologicheskie Obosnovaniia Ierarkhii Dukhovenstvo v Ismailizme i Sufizme', *Religiia i Obshestvennaia Mysl' Stran Vostoka* (Moscow, 1974), pp. 317–319.

[33] For the biography of Shams of Tabriz, see W. Chittick, *Me and Rumi: The Autobiography of Shams-i Tabrizi* (Louisville, 2004) and his 'The Real Shams-i Tabrīzī', in M. Rustom, A. Khalil, and K. Murata (ed.), *In Search of the Lost Heart: Exploration in Islamic Thought* (New York, 2012), pp. 49–55.

[34] MS. N. *Chirāgh-nāma* (Incomplete copy, in the private collection of the author), fol. 2b; MS 31 *Chirāgh-nāma*, p. 15; Ivanow, 'Sufism and Ismailism: Chiraghnama', p. 69.

Muḥammad (d. ca. 710/1310), who succeeded his father, Imam Rukn al-Dīn Khurshāh (d. 655/1257). The esoteric meaning lies once more in the juxtaposition of different professions of faith. Hence, a kind of un-thought coalescence is achieved, which seems to have originated in the local context and requires further scholarly investigation.

Twelver Shiʿi Influence in the *Chirāgh-nāma*

Although a split after the death of Imam Jaʿfar al-Ṣādiq (d. 148/765) divided the Shiʿi community into rival groups, doctrinally, they still shared much common ground, particularly when it came to the subject of the nature of leadership and the imamate. Imam Jaʿfar al-Ṣādiq was the last imam recognised equally by the Twelver Shiʿis and the Ismailis. From this point onwards, these communities developed distinctive doctrinal and cultural traditions of their own. The Ismailis first established the Fatimid caliphate in Egypt in 297/909, ruled over by imam-caliphs from the Prophet's progeny through his daughter Fāṭima. Later they established the Nizārī state in Alamūt in Iran in 483/1090. The Twelver Shiʿi state was established much later, in 907/1501, by Shah Ismāʿīl Safavi I (r. 907–930/1501–1524).

The coming to power of the Safavid dynasty in Iran heralded an improvement of the condition of Shiʿi-oriented movements and communities. It did, however, become a totally different movement that condemned and persecuted those who did not comply with its religious teaching and rules. It has even been argued by some modern scholars that some originally Sunni-oriented Sufi brotherhoods became Shiʿi *ṭarīqa*s at this time.[35]

Like any other religious and political regime, the Safavids also attempted to spread their new religious ideology, namely the new form of Twelver Shiʿi Islam they espoused, to neighbouring countries. Signs of the Safavid religious and political ideology may be observed in Badakhshān and its adjacent principalities. This is particularly evident

---

[35] N. Pourjavady and L. Wilson, 'The Descendants of Shāh Niʿmatullāh Walī', *Islamic Culture* (1974), pp. 49–57; T. Graham, 'Shāh Niʿmatullāh Walī: Founder of the Niʿmatullāhī Ṣūfī Order', in L. Lewisohn (ed.), *The Heritage of Sufism*, vol. 2 (Oxford, 1999), pp. 173–190.

in the tradition of *madāḥ-khānī*, one of the religious rites performed during *Chirāgh-rawshan*. For instance, an anonymous *qaṣīda*, *Ākhir-zamān-nāma*, wrongly attributed to Nāṣir-i Khusraw, is sung during *Chirāgh-rawshan*. This *qaṣīda* contains the names of some of the Safavid monarchs. For instance, one verse reads:

> *Shāh Ismāʿīl-i Ḥaydar warā khānand khalq,*
> *Khāk-i pāyash dar naẓar ahl-i jahān khāhad girift.*
> *Baʿd az īn shāhī kunad farzand-i ū panjāh sāl,*
> *Baʿd az ānash fayḍ-i raḥmat dar jahān khāhad girift.*

> Shah Ismāʿīl of Ḥaydar's tribe the people call him,
> The inhabitants of the world will take the dust of his feet into account.
> After him, his son will rule the world for fifty years,
> Then the grace of mercy will disseminate and fill the world.[36]

This *qaṣīda*, which is sung during *Chirāgh-rawshan*, talks about Shah Ismāʿīl, the first Safavid ruler. It also implicitly refers to the reign of Shah Tahmāsp, who ruled Iran for fifty-two years from 930/1524 to 984/1576. At the heart of this *qaṣīda* lies the messianic expectation, which constitutes the core of the Twelver Shiʿi teaching. Rather than explicitly referring to the Twelfth Shiʿi imam, Muḥammad al-Mahdī, as the saviour of the world, the *qaṣīda* instead portrays the Safavid shahs as the saviours of the world. This position is very strange, implying as it does that the authority of the ruling shahs overrides the rule of the Hidden Shiʿi imam. It could be asked how such a *qaṣīda* could have entered the Ismaili religious rite in Badakhshān.

Another element of Twelver Shiʿi doctrine present in the *Chirāgh-nāma* is the appearance of the genealogy of imams from Imam Mūsā al-Kāẓim down to Imam al-Mahdī, who went into *ghayba* (occultation). The list of imams included in the *ghazal* of Niʿmat Allāh Walī reflects the state of constant flux in the text of this particular *ghazal* in the *Chirāgh-nāma*. The *ghazal* has absorbed the recurring changes facing the tradition of Nāṣir-i Khusraw. The changing nature of the text also reflects the degree of precaution exercised by the members of the

---

36 G. Berg, 'Ismāʿīlī Poetry in Tajik Badakhshan: A Safavid Connection?', *Persica*, 17 (2001), p. 3.

local *daʿwa*, particularly with the coming of foreign rule that imposed new elements of belief on the members of the mountain-dwelling communities. The following text shows that these are later interpolations in the text, which logically connect the Sufi text to the Shiʿi doctrine of the imamate. Hence, the genealogy of the Shiʿi imams crept into the text of the *Chirāgh-nāma* under obscure circumstances but with clear political and ideological intention:

Zayn al-ʿIbād bihtar Bāqir shinās-u Jaʿfar,
Shāhand ān dū sarwar, ṣalawāt bar Muḥammad.
Mūsā' falak ghulāmat, Shāh-i Riḍā ba nāmat,
Shud ʿarsh-i ḥaqq maqāmat, ṣalawāt bar Muḥammad.
Shāh az Taqī chū khānī, nāmash ʿajab bidānī,
Az jān Taqī bikhānī, ṣalawāt bar Muḥammad.
Man hamchū yak kamīnam, khāk-i rah-i Naqīam,
Muhtāj-i ʿAskarīyam, ṣalawat bar Muḥammad.
Mahdī imām-i dīn ast ham qibla ham yaqīn ast,
Sirr-i shāh-i mubīn ast, ṣalawāt bar Muḥammad.

Know better Zayn al-ʿIbād, Bāqir and then Jaʿfar,
They are both kings these two leaders, praise [be] upon Muhammad.
O Mūsā the sphere is your slave, the king Riḍā is named after you,
Your status has been elevated to the throne of God, praise [be] upon Muhammad.
If you call Taqī the king, you will know his name,
Then call the name of Taqī from your heart, praise [be] upon Muhammad.
I am like a slave on the path of Naqī,
I am in need of ʿAskarī, praise [be] upon Muhammad.
Mahdī is the Imam of the religion, he is the *qibla* and the certainty,
He is the secret of the Manifest King, praise [be] upon Muhammad.[37]

[37] MS BT 175 *Ṣalawāt-nāma*, fol. 2a; See also MS BT 35 *Chirāgh-nāma wa qandīl-nāma*, fol. 11a; Shozodamuhammad, *Sources of the Tradition of "Chiroghrawshan"* (Dushanbe, 2009), pp. 24–25.

Before this passage, the text presents another addendum to the *Chirāgh-nāma*, where the scribe or preacher calls the participants of the *majlis* to the true religion, that is to say, in this instance to Twelver Shiʿism. The passage laments:

Dīn dīn-i duwāzdah imām ast,
Dar sharʿ-i nabī chū ū tamām ast.
Az sharʿ burūn hama ḥarām ast,
Khūsh gū ṣalawāt Muṣṭafā-rā.

The true religion is that of the Twelve imams,
It is completed in the divine law of the Prophet.
Illicit are all those outside the divine law,
Convey eloquent salutation to the Chosen One (i.e. Muhammad).[38]

Historical sources, such as the *Taʾrīkh-i Badakhshān* of Mīrzā Sangmuḥammad Badakhshī and Faḍlʿalībek Surkhafsar and the *Taʾrīkh-i mulk-i Shughnān* of Sayyid Ḥaydar Shāh Mubārakshāhzāda, show that the region was subjugated by foreign rulers. Since it was the sole region populated by the Shiʿis (Ismailis), the Sunni rulers attempted to convert them to the 'true religion,' namely Sunni Islam. What seems surprising is the fact that elements of Twelver Shiʿi doctrine have been promulgated during the *Chirāgh-rawshan* ceremony which was alien even to the Sunni rulers. The reason for such a phenomenon is difficult to ascertain, particularly as local and peripheral sources do not provide direct or indirect reference to this intermix of religious ideas.

Chirāgh-rawshan: An Ismaili Tradition of Badakhshān

As mentioned above, the text of the *Chirāgh-nāma* takes its metaphorical and symbolic expressions from the verse of Light (Qurʾan, 24:35), as interpreted within the context of Ismaili teaching. Unfortunately, the author(s) of the text remain unknown to us; nor do the internal elements of the text provide any clue regarding its authorship.

[38] Ibid., p. 23.

Although the *Chirāgh-nāma* was influenced by both Sufi and Twelver Shiʿi doctrines, its core Ismaili teaching rotates around the notion of light, conceived in three dimensions, particularly the light of God (*tawḥīd*), the light of the Prophet (*nubuwwat*) and the light of the imamate from the Ahl al-Bayt. The Sufi terminology used in the text of the *Chirāgh-nāma* shows the degree of the interaction between these two esoteric movements within the wider context of Islam.

Examination of the various copies of the *Chirāgh-nāma* at our disposal reveals that they are all crystallised texts that accommodate various mystical teachings mingled with the Ismaili doctrine. These latter elements do, however, constitute the core beliefs of the Badakhshānī Ismailis, which is reflected in their reverence for the figure of Pīr Shāh Nāṣir-i Khusraw, the founder of the Ismaili communities in Badakhshān and the adjoining areas. Yet, the term *madhhab-i Nāṣiriyya* (the followers of Nāṣir) is also used to refer to the tradition of Nāṣir-i Khusraw and was probably coined sometime at the end of the ninth/fifteenth or first half of the tenth/sixteenth century.[39]

Returning to the analysis of the text, our attention is next drawn to the peculiar mix of Sufi terminology and Ismaili teaching, which overlap each other. For instance, one passage reads:

Ay ʿāshiq-i ṣāḥib naẓar,
Dar daʿwat-i Nāṣir darā.
Ay muʾmin-i pāk-i gawhār,
Dar daʿwat-i Nāṣir darā.
Nāṣir zi awlād-i nabī,
Ḥaqqā, ki farzand-i ʿAlī.
Gar nāṣirī-rā ṭālibī,
Dar daʿwat-i Nāṣir darā.

O insightful lover, join the mission of Nāṣir!
O pious believer, join the mission of Nāṣir!
Nāṣir is the scion of the Prophet,
He is a true offspring of ʿAlī.
If you're a claimant of Nāṣir's teaching,
Join the mission of Nāṣir.[40]

---

[39] A. Bertel's, *Nasiri Khusraw i Ismailizm* (Moscow, 1959), p. 182.

[40] MS. F. *Chirāgh-nāma* (no date, in the private collection of Dr. Faquir Muhammad Hunzai, London), fols 24–25.

The above example clearly shows that this is a sermon conducted during the *majlis*, which calls upon an 'insightful lover' – a follower of a Sufi *ṭarīqa* – as well a 'pious believer' – a reference to a Sunni Muslim – to join Nāṣir-i Khusraw's mission. The context of this and other similar poems evokes the post-Alamūt *taqiyya* theme, which is totally different from Nāṣir-i Khusraw's Ismaili-Fatimid teaching. Surprisingly, the text of *Chirāgh-nāma* is used as a bridge to link these two teachings and is designed to '*explain the secrets of divine knowledge in prose and poetry*'[41] to those joining Nāṣir's mission. It should be emphasised that the expression *dar daʿwat-i Nāṣir darā* (meaning 'join the mission of Nāṣir') encompasses all the interrelated elements of Nāṣir-i Khusraw's tradition. In other words, the practice of *Chirāgh-rawshan* is a continuation of the Ismaili tradition in the local context despite the fact that, during the period of concealment, access to the imam was limited.

Clearly, some poems in the *Chirāgh-nāma* are of a double provenance and express a double loyalty. They either discuss the lineage of the Twelver Shiʿi imams or present the genealogy of the Ismaili imams, as I have shown above. The controversial nature of these poetic compositions is intricate and difficult to explain. Nonetheless, one's attention is drawn to an interesting passage quoted in the *Taʾrīkh-i Rashīdī*, where the author refers to the Muḥammad-Shāhī imam, Shāh Raḍī al-Dīn II b. Ṭāhir (d. 916/1510), employing the term *Chirāgh kush* (lit. light extinguisher). It seems safe to assume that, due to the practice of *taqiyya*, the Muḥammad-Shāhī imams propagated a 'form of Ismailism in the guise of Twelver Shiʿism'.[42] This hypothesis, proposed by Farhad Daftary in relation to Imam Shāh Ṭāhir Dakkanī – the famous Nizārī Muḥammad-Shāhī imam, seems also to be applicable to the missionary activity of his father, Imam Raḍī al-Dīn II b. Ṭāhir, in the region of Badakhshān. It is highly likely that the new elements that crept into the tradition with the arrival of Imam Raḍī al-Dīn II would have caused a certain degree of distrust and disagreement.

---

[41] Ibid., fol. 24. The original text reads: *Asrar-i ʿilmi man ladun, Dar naẓm-u nathrash gūsh kun. Bishnaw zi jān bāz īn sukhun, Dar daʿwat-i Nāṣir darā.*

[42] F. Daftary, *The Ismailis: Their History and Doctrines* (Cambridge, 2007), pp. 453–454.

It may have been on account of this that he was dubbed *Raḍī al-Dīn-i chirāgh kush.*[43]

Although the text of the *Chirāgh-nāma* is permeated with Sufi and Twelver Shiʿi elements, the ritualistic, spiritual and other internal textual components keep it distinctively Ismaili. Quite striking is the fact that, in the post-Timurid period, when the region was under Sunni rulers, the tradition was still practised, and the local *dāʿīs* openly called 'insightful lovers' and 'pious believers' to join the tradition or the mission of Nāṣir, who is referred to as 'the mercy and proof of Mustanṣir.' The text elaborates it in the following way:

Ū raḥmat-i Mūstanṣir ast, *Ū ḥujjat-i Mustanṣir ast,*
Ū nuṣrat-i Mustanṣir ast, *Dar daʿwat-i Nāṣir darā.*

He is the mercy of Mustanṣir; he is the Proof of Mustanṣir,
He is the victory of Mustanṣir, join the mission of Nāṣir.[44]

This passage above coincidentally includes certain historic facts. First of all, it confirms that Nāṣir-i Khusraw was a contemporary of the imam-caliph al-Mustanṣir biʾllāh (d. 497/1094) and, secondly, it validates the claim that he was granted one of the highest ranks in the hierarchy of initiation, namely that of *ḥujjat* (chief *dāʿī*), before being sent to Balkh, Khurāsān and Badakhshān. The presence of these elements in the text of the *Chirāgh-nāma* implicitly shows that the author(s) was well acquainted with the philosophical teaching of Nāṣir-i Khusraw and the history and doctrines of the Nizārī Ismailis. Thus, it is evident from the practice of this rite among the Ismailis of Badakhshān that it represented a call to join the mission or to join the tradition of Nāṣir-i Khusraw. The following example from the *Chirāgh-nāma* illustrates this point:

Yak shab būdam dar daʿwatash,
Bastam kamar bar himmatash.
Īnjā chirāgh-i Nāṣir ast,

[43] Dughlāt Ḥaydar, *Taʾrīkh-i Rashīdī*, ed. ʿA. Ghafārī-Fard (Tehran: Mīrāth-i maktūb, 1383/2004–2005), p. 146.

[44] MS. F. *Chirāgh-nāma*, fol. 25; See also MS. N209, *Khushnawīs: Chirāgh-nāma* (no date, from private collection of Shohi Kalon Sherzodshoev, Porshinev, copy obtained in 2008), fols 16b–17a; A. Bertel's, 'Naẓari Barkhe az 'Urafā', *Yādnāma-i Nāṣir-i Khusraw* (Mashhad, 1976), p. 110.

Bī-shakk murādat ḥāṣil ast.
Īnjā chirāgh ast jāy-i ḥāl,
Īnjā nagunjad qīl-u qāl.

One night I participated in his summons,
I girded my loins up in his service.
This is the place of Nāṣir's spiritual summons,
Undoubtedly your destiny will be fulfilled here.
This is the lamp – a place of real spiritual experience,
Wherein there is no place for idle chatter.[45]

The passage above is related in the first person and therefore, we might cautiously suggest that it was a 'pious believer' or 'an insightful lover' who would have participated in the *daʿwat-i Nasir*. While the Ismaili connection of this first person narrator is never explicitly mentioned in the text, the passage above shows that the person who engaged with and participated in the *daʿwat-i Nāṣir* found a spiritual satisfaction in the teaching, where any discussion beyond the theme of Ismaili teaching would be of no importance. Hence, one can suggest that the narrator seems to have joined the community.

Conclusion

The *Chirāgh-rawshan* tradition is an old religious rite practised among the Ismailis of Badakhshān. Its symbolic meaning is drawn from the Qur'an while its core rotates around the notion of *nūr*. A house where the lamp is lit alludes to the practice of remembering God's name and offering praise to Him. Yet, in the Ismaili context, it reflects the three aspects of the notion of light, which correspond to the doctrine of *tawḥīd* (oneness), *nubuwwat* (prophethood) and *imāmat* (imamate).

The influence of various Islamic teachings, particularly Twelver Shiʿism and Sufism, on the practice of *Chirāgh-rawshan* is evident in the changing pattern of the text of the *Chirāgh-nāma*. Due to the infusion and amalgamation of various teachings as well as the absence

45 MS. N. *Chirāgh-nāma (Incomplete)*, fol. 4b. The first verse of the poem – This is the lamp of Nāṣir – is an allusion to the *daʿwat-i Nāṣir* or *shab-i daʿwat*.

of further sources, the issue of authorship remains open to further research.

The Sufi terminology incorporated in the text of the *Chirāgh-nāma* demonstrates the relationship between Sufism and Ismailism in the peripheral context of the Islamic community. Although Badakhshān was an isolated, semi-independent country, on the periphery of the Islamic world, the peoples controlling the neighbouring countries, directly or indirectly, influenced its religious landscape. As a result, the purely Ismaili practice of *Chirāgh-rawshan* incorporated certain antagonistic elements from other faiths. What must be counted a really strange phenomenon, however, is the fact that, in the local context of Badakhshān and its mountain principalities of the Pamirs, these antagonistic teachings succeeded in creating a state of equilibrium and peaceful co-existence within Ismaili religious practice.

The case of *Chirāgh-rawshan* and its text represents a unique mixture of Ismaili, Sufi and Twelver Shiʿi teachings. The prevailing element in the *Chirāgh-nāma* is the doctrine of *tawḥīd*, *nubuwwat* and *imāmat*, expressed in the Ismaili context. The text on the other hand, combines the various elements from Ismaili doctrine with post-Alamūt Nizārī Ismaili teaching infused with Sufi terminology, expressing the 'secrets of hidden knowledge' that has kept the light of faith burning in mud-brick houses on the periphery of Islamdom down to the present day.

15

The Concept of *Wilāya* in Mubārak-i Wakhānī's *Chihil Dunyā*: A Traditional Ismaili-Sufi Perspective on the Origins of Divine Guidance

Abdulmamad Iloliev
(The Institute of Ismaili Studies)

Introduction

Mubārak-i Wakhānī (d. 1903) was by far the most productive Persian author of Islamic mysticism in nineteenth-century Badakhshān. Andrey Bertels once observed that Wakhānī was 'the Avicenna of Badakhshan', whose intellectual accomplishments exceeded the limits of his geographic and intellectual environment.[1] As his pen name Wakhānī indicates, he was born and indeed spent his whole life in Wakhan, a remote mountainous area in the Pamirs, which until the early twentieth century was practically isolated from the rest of the world. Examination of Wakhānī's works reveals that he was well grounded in the Persian and Arabic languages, the religious sciences, poetry, astronomy, music and art.[2] His poetic legacy includes over sixteen titles covering a wide array of topics, which seek to establish a state of equilibrium between Ismaili and Sufi ideas expressed in the finest mystical spirit.

This article aims to examine the concept of *wilāya* (the exercise of authority) and its vocalisation *walāya,* which denotes devotion for and

[1] Andrey Bertels, 'The Ismāʿīlīs of Badakhshan', in the Audio Cassettes recorded during Bertels' lectures at the Institute of Ismaili Studies in London, cassette 9 (12. 06. 1984).

[2] See Abdulmamad Iloliev, *The Ismāʿīlī-Sufi Sage of Pamir: Mubārak-i Wakhānī and the Esoteric Tradition of the Pamiri Muslims* (New York, 2008).

allegiance to Shiʿi imams, in Wakhānī's *Risāla-yi Chihil Dunyā* ('The Epistle of the Forty Worlds') in relation to the special role and spiritual authority of ʿAlī b. Abī Ṭālib (d. 40/661) in Shiʿi and Sufi thought.[3] Discussing Wakhānī's perception of *wilāya* as the divinely given spiritual authority of ʿAlī, it seeks to explore how Sufi ideas are used alongside and in conjunction with the Ismaili concept of *imāma*. Arguing for the primordial and prehistorical origin of the *wilāya* of ʿAlī, Wakhānī provides six 'proofs' or testimonies (*shahādat*) on behalf of the six Abrahamic prophets with resolution (*anbiyāʾ-i ūluʾl-ʿaẓm*), viz., Adam, Noah, Abraham, Moses, Jesus and Muhammad, and argues that *wilāya* being the inner meaning (*bāṭin*) of *nubuwwa* is not temporarily or geographically confined. Similarly, it is important to see where Muhammad as the final prophet of God stands in Wakhānī's mystical discourse on the 'second phase' of the prophet's *miʿrāj* (spiritual ascent) to the mysterious Chihil Dunyā (Forty Worlds) – the divine kingdom of the king of *walāya* (*shāh-i walāya*) (i.e. ʿAlī). For it is in this celestial world that Muhammad undergoes an extraordinary spiritual experience and upon his return to the physical world proclaims the *imāma* of ʿAlī.[4]

The Text of the *Chihil Dunyā* and its Major Themes

There are two original manuscripts of the *Risāla-yi Chihil Dunyā* currently preserved in the private collections of Wakhānī's relatives in the village of Yamg in Tajikistan, where they were first discovered by the author of this article in 2002. The manuscripts were compiled in

[3] For the importance of *walāya* in Shiʿi doctrine see Mohammad Ali Amir-Moezzi, *The Spirituality of Shiʿi Islam* (London, 2011), pp. 231–275. See also Mawil Dein and Paul Walker, 'Wilāya', *EI2*. The theme of the spirituality of ʿAlī and his special role in Shiʿi thought is widely discussed among modern scholars of Islamic studies. See, for instance, Amir-Moezzi, *The Spirituality of Shiʿi Islam*; Reza Shah-Kazemi, *Justice and Remembrance. Introducing the Spirituality of Imam ʿAlī* (London and New York, 2006).

[4] MS Mubārak-i Wakhānī, *Risāla-yi Chihil Dunyā*, 1320 AH, Mubārak-i Wakhānī's Museum, fol. 23.

1320/1902 as two separate hand-bound books. The only difference between them is that one of them, in addition to the *Chihil Dunyā*, also contains another mystical work by Wakhānī called *Qaṭrat al-baḥr* ('A Drop of the Ocean'). Composed in a panegyric (*madīḥa*) style, the *Risāla-yi Chihil Dunyā* consists of 747 distiches, of which five are direct quotations from Ḥāfiẓ-i Shirāzī (d. 792/1390) and ʿAbd al-Qādir Bīdil (d. 1132/1720).

It should be noted that belief in the mythological cosmology of the 'Forty Worlds' as the divine kingdom of ʿAlī was popular among the Ismailis of Badakhshān before Wakhānī composed this work. For instance, there is the *Hāḍa Naql-i Chihil Dunyā* ('This is the Tale of the Forty Worlds'), dated 1313/1895, which is the earliest written source found so far on this subject. Written by an unknown scribe, this manuscript consists of two works including the *Chihil Dunyā* and *Āfāq wa Anfus* ('Worlds and Souls' or 'The Esoteric and Exoteric Worlds'). It is currently held in the Institute of Ismaili Studies' Ismaili Special Collection Unit (MS 814). One can safely assume that Wakhānī may have been influenced by this work and most definitely by the local oral tradition about the Chihil Dunyā, however his epistle considerably differs from the *Naql-i Chihil Dunyā* as far as literary form, structural organisation and textual sophistication are concerned. Contrary to the latter, Wakhānī's work is in the poetic form of *mathnawī*, and it is very well organised in the sense of the structural division of its chapters and their thematic implications which logically suit the arguments provided. It consists of six sub-chapters, referred to as 'testimonies' (*shahādat*), numbered from one to six respectively, four chapters (*faṣl*) and two concluding parts (*qism*) each of which deals with a specific topic but flows as a continuation of previous ideas. By dividing the poem into three different categories, Wakhānī draws a fundamental distinction between the importance of the messages conveyed and the styles of literary expression. For instance, the language of the first part, containing the testimonies of the six prophets with resolution or the masters of divine revelation (*ṣāḥib-i waḥy*), is a demonstrative monologue, in which each speaker testifies to the main argument proposed by the author. The six eminent prophets give personal evidence to authenticate the sanctity of ʿAlī as *Shāh-i Walāya*. Wakhānī, however, applies the term *wilāya* to both the spiritual and temporal authority of

ʿAlī in the realms of the *bāṭin* (esoteric) and the *ẓāhir* (exoteric) – two important concepts in Ismaili philosophy. In the first five sub-chapters and the main chapters, the discourse is mainly focused on the *bāṭinī* dimensions of the subject and tends to represent the divine kingdom of ʿAlī in which he is the king. In the prologue to sub-chapter six and the remaining chapters with a *ẓāhirī* agenda, the term stands for the Shiʿi concept of *imāma* as the second (after *nubuwwa*) and eternal phase of the cycle of occultation (*dawr al-satr*) in the religious universe (*ʿālam-i dīn*). Here, therefore, the application of the term *wilāya* is based on the arguments given in the poem. The chapters are mostly composed in the form of allegorical tales in which an expressive discourse is centred on a single theme – the *miʿrāj* or miraculous journey of Muhammad to the Chihil Dunyā. The verbal communication in the final part of the epistle, nevertheless, is evocative of the author's main didactic argument; that is, the significance of *imāma* as an eternal institution of human guidance. Initially, then, the work is a relatively lengthy poem on a specialised subject with narrative elements characterised by considerable unity and compression in all of its parts, namely the theme, plot, structure, character, settings and mood.

Although the *Risāla-yi Chihil Dunyā* touches upon several Sufi themes, however it is the Ismaili dimension of faith that is most clearly illuminated through the form and content of the epistle. At the heart of this dimension lies the Ismaili esoteric doctrine of the six days of the creation of the religious universe (*ʿālam al-dīn*), manifested in the six periods of the cycle of occultation (*dawr al-satr*) on earth, represented by the six law-giving prophets, namely Adam, Noah, Abraham, Moses, Jesus and Muhammad, and its completion on the seventh day (i.e. the day of resurrection) by the imam of the Resurrection (*qāʾim al-qiyāmat*). Wakhānī proposes that ʿAlī, as the symbol of *imāma*, is not merely the representative of the seventh day, but also the core substance (*jawhar*) of the entire cycle of prophecy and the celestial man of the preceding cycle of the epiphany (*dawr al-kashf*) in heaven. Likewise, he stresses the esoteric significance of the *imāma* as the eternal period in the religious universe that was concealed during the temporary phase of *nubuwwa* until the time of Muhammad and unveiled after his death. Although each of the six eminent prophets testified to the sanctity of ʿAlī, it was Muhammad who, through his *miʿrāj* to the

Chihil Dunyā, realised the true essence of ʿAlī as the symbol of the divine secret.[5]

Prophetic Testimonies

The framework for the discussion in the six sub-chapters of the poem is mainly built upon the general Islamic understanding of the Abrahamic religious discourse, in which the idea of the origination, continuation and completion of the divine revelation is approached from a mystical angle. Nevertheless, the content of the discussion has quite a different connotation; it is framed in Wakhānī's local religious context – the context of the *Panj-Tanī* tradition (the Fivers or the followers of the Ahl al-Bayt of the Prophet) – a fusion of Ismaili and Sufi ideas and practices.[6] Distinctive by virtue of certain elements of belief and practice (e.g. veneration of saints, visitation of shrines, *Pīr-murīd* relationship, cult of dead, devotional music and dance), this tradition was strongly characterised by an absolute belief in the spiritual power of ʿAlī and idealisation of his personality by ascribing to him divine attributes. Wakhānī, therefore, aimed to elaborate on this polemical discourse by presenting the testimonies of the six prophets on the divinity of ʿAlī. Each of the six eminent prophets testifies to the unity of the divine unique manifested in the person of ʿAlī as the light (*nūr*) or the spirit (*jān*) of God, preserved in Paradise until the creation of the human being in the form (*jism*) of Adam, as well as one of the most sacred divine names first taught to Adam. Wakhānī argues that it was the divine light of ʿAlī, the Lord (*mawlā*), that made Adam manifest himself (*padid āvard*) in human form, and that it was because of this light that the angels paid tribute to him.[7]

Theorising the traditional approach to the issue of creation, Wakhānī firstly emphasises the light of ʿAlī, sometimes referred to as the light of Abī Ṭālib, as the source of spiritual illumination that is, paradoxically, substituted with the common Islamic idea of the light of Muhammad

---

[5] MS Wakhānī, *Risāla-yi Chihil Dunyā*, fols 17–18.

[6] Abdulmamad Iloliev, *The Ismāʿīlī-Sufi Sage of Pamir*, pp. 59–87.

[7] MS Wakhānī, *Risāla-yi Chihil Dunyā*, fol. 1a.

as the first creation of God. The light of ʿAlī is presented as the symbol of submission to the divine power (*qudrat-i ilāhī*) and to the institution that implements it: *imāma*. In the following verses quoted by Wakhānī from, as he believed, a wise gnostic (*ʿārifān*), he attempts to justify his argument concerning the reason for the angels' submission to Adam:

> The angels had to prostrate to the mortal Adam,
> For the light of ʿAlī b. Abī Ṭālib manifested in his forehead.
> If the light of oneness did not shine in the *wilāya* [of ʿAlī],
> The angels would have not bowed their proud heads to this body.[8]

Secondly, he briefly mentions the process of mystical emanation in which there is God, whose light causes the creation or more correctly appearance (*padīd āmadan*) of Adam as a symbol of the physical world or the commencing point of the six days of creation of the religious universe (*ʿālam-i dīn*) during the cycle of occultation (*dawr al-satr*). The light itself, however, as the essence (*dhāt*) of God, is described as beyond creation or existence. This is because, Wakhānī claims, these factors are inapplicable to the divine essence, but depend solely upon the divine will (*khwāhish*) and command (*amr*); that is, in the words of the Qurʾan: 'Our command is but a single [act] like the twinkling of an eye' (54:50). Nevertheless, as Wakhānī argues, there are six levels of emanation from the appearance to the perfection of the religious universe represented in the six eminent prophets until its completion in the time of the *imāma*. This argument is in line with certain classical Ismaili sources such as al-Ṭūsī's *Rawḍa-yi taslīm*, where the creation of human beings from the physical angle is represented by the six eminent prophets: Adam as semen, Noah as sperm, Abraham as blood, Moses as embryo, Jesus as bone and flesh, and Muhammad as the complete human form.[9]

Proceeding to this, it should be noted that although Adam in the context of the *Chihil Dunyā* is not specified as any of the three known

---

[8] Ibid., fol. 18a. All direct quotations of Wakhānī are Iloliev's translations unless stated otherwise.

[9] Naṣīr al-Dīn Ṭūsī, *Paradise of Submission: A Medieval Treatise on Ismaili Thought: A New Persian Edition and English Translation of Naṣīr al-Dīn Ṭūsī's Rawḍa-yi taslīm*, ed. and trans. S. J. Badakhchani (London, 2005), p. 139.

Adams in Ismaili gnosis namely, the first prophet of the cycle of *nubuwwa*, Adam the Pure (*Ādam-i Ṣafī Allāh*), the universal primordial Adam (*Ādam al-awwal al-kullī*), and the spiritual Adam (*Ādam-i Ruḥānī*) or the angel of humanity, rather, the poem generally refers to Adam as the first prophet as well as the first human being created by God out of divine love and for the purpose of divine recognition.[10] In his *shahāda*, therefore, Adam, as the first apostle of God, demonstrates his (1) knowledge of the divine names among which ʿAlī (lit. the highest) is the most significant; (2) recognition of the uniqueness of *Mawlā* (the Lord) and *Mawlānā* (our Lord, that is to say, ʿAlī); and (3) submission to the divinity of the divine name (i.e., ʿAlī). Wakhānī applies these three points in Adam's testimony throughout his work. According to traditional accounts, each of the six eminent prophets was qualified in a particular area of the divine names.[11] Adam, for instance, was most distinguished in knowing them. Wakhānī asserts that, of the ninety-nine names of God, the most beautiful (*zibā*) and the most real (*ḥaqqānī*) is that of ʿAlī, thus Adam first learned this name from the Almighty and testified to its primordial essence (*dhāt-i qadīm*):

> I swear to the wise God of eternity,
> That the origin of ʿAlī is pure and primordial.[12]

When this is established, Wakhānī attempts to enact a doctrinal foundation of submission to the divinity of that divine name. As explored above, he believes that the only reason why the angels prostrated before the newly created Adam was the manifestation of the light of ʿAlī that they saw in him; a divine light, which not only caused Adam's creation, but also itself became the superlative essence of humanity. Therefore, he argues that, this light has existed transcendently since the time of Adam in all the prophets (in the realm of the *ẓāhir*) and continued until the end of the period of *nubuwwa* which was sealed by Muhammad, and that it exists eternally in the imams (in the realm of the *bāṭin*).

---

[10] For an esoteric history of Adam see Henry Corbin, *Swedenborg and Esoteric Islam* (Pennsylvania, 1990), pp. 110–112.

[11] See for instance Ṭusī's *Rawḍa-yi taslīm*, ed. and trans. S. J. Badakhchani, pp. 136–137. *Kalām-i Pīr*, ed. W. Ivanow, p. 18.

[12] MS Wakhānī, *Risāla-yi Chihil Dunyā*, fol. 1b.

Thus, the divine light, as the sign of the divine presence in human form, was incarnated in Adam and then passed on to Noah and, after him, the light was encircled in the other prophets as it was simultaneously in the Ismaili imams. Here Wakhānī refers to the classical Ismaili belief that during the phase of the prophethood, there were imams or the *ḥujjat*s (proofs) for each of the six law-giving prophets respectively; thus for Adam there was Seth (Shayth), for Noah – Sam, Abraham – Malik al-Salām, Moses – Aaron (Hārūn) and Joshua (Yusha b. Nūn), Jesus – Shamʿūn al-Ṣafā' or Simon the Rock (Simon Peter), Muhammad – ʿAlī. The constant manifestation of God was, therefore, inevitable in the *ẓāhirī* (exoteric) and the *bāṭinī* (esoteric) realms of the religious universe, as represented by the prophets and the imams. In others words, the parallel representation of the divine light in both realms, which by themselves are two of the ninety-nine names of God (al-Ẓāhir and al-Bāṭin), is a sign of the eternity of the divine light, being constantly enhanced by the transformation from one body to another. Thus, Wakhānī's argument implies that submission to God is meant to be a submission to the divinity of the divine names.[13]

Submission is also a key element in Noah's testimony in which, contrary to Adam's testimony, the main character acts as the main speaker of the sub-chapter. The significance of the issue of submission in his testimony is probably justified by the fact that, in the Qur'an (4:163; 26:105), Noah (Nūḥ Nabī Allāh) is portrayed as a faithful messenger of God who preached submission (i.e. Islam) to the divine will. The ultimate consequence of this obedience is the salvation of the soul. Noah accepts the *wilāya* of ʿAlī and, like Adam, testifies to its primordial essence.

In the testimony of Abraham (*Ibrāhim Khalīl Allāh*), for the first time in the poem, Wakhānī explicitly mentions the importance of what is understood in the Ismaili context as spiritual hermeneutics (*ta'wīl*), one of the prophetic qualifications of Abraham. As mentioned earlier, each of the six prophets was qualified in a particular aspect of the divine names; accordingly, Abraham was aware of the inner meanings of the divine names and their interpretations. Abraham's testimony, therefore, is doctrinally significant because of the idea of

---

13 Ibid., fol. 26a.

spirituality, which is associated with his name in the Qur'an (e.g. 6:75) and in the Muslim tradition. This is the basic point upon which Wakhānī tries to build his argument concerning what the names of God imply in the realm of spirituality. According to Wakhānī, what Abraham witnessed – from 'the veil of concealment' – was the existence of the *wilāya* of the king of the spiritual world, on whom human souls depend, and who himself is the necessary being (*wājib al-mawjūd*) because of the soul's dependence on him. Thus Abraham witnessed 'Alī's being as the mysteries of the heart (*asrār-i dil*) and its secrets (*rāz*), which can be disclosed only through the science of the hearts (*'ilm al-qulūb*) and by the possessors of the heart (*ṣāḥib-dilān*). Apart from the clearly intended allegory, however, one must acknowledge the historical – as viewed from the Abrahamic religious perspective – implication of Abraham's testimony in the poem and his role as the father of all monotheistic religions (Judaism, Christianity and Islam) as it is understood in the context of Islam. It is claimed that the chief impact of Abraham's death was the division of his religion between the lineages of his sons, Isaac (Ishāq) and Ishmael (Ismā'īl), who became the forefathers of the later Jews, Christians and Muslims respectively. Likewise, Isaac and Ishmael are regarded as the representatives of God's revelation in the realms of the *ẓāhir* and the *bāṭin* as well as the breaking points in the religion of Abraham. Although Wakhānī admits that the followers of Zoroaster, Moses and Christ do not recognise the *nubuwwa* of Muhammad and the *wilāya* of 'Alī, he insists that they are all the ancestors (*aslaf-u sālifīn*) of the Muslims. As shown by these analyses, many illusions in the poem to *nubuwwa* and *wilāya* are derived from and addressed to the general Muslim traditional belief in the pre-Islamic historical development of a monotheistic religion that later took on a more precise form (i.e. Islam) under Muhammad.[14]

In the fourth *shahāda* Wakhānī refers to Moses (Mūsā Kalīm Allāh) –'the interlocutor of God' – as 'the origin of religion' (*asl-i dīn*), the first prophet, who acquired the knowledge of the *wilāya* of 'Alī through the divine revelation in the form of a divine book (the Torah). Here Wakhānī refers to the traditional story about Moses' receiving the

[14] MS Wakhānī, *Risāla-yi Chihil Dunyā*, fol. 2b.

divine revelation on the mountain of Ṭūr when he prayed to God. His intimate prayers (*munājāt*), consequently, turned into a dialogue (*munāẓira*) with the 'occult voice' (*āwāz-i ghaybī*) of ʿAlī. In the poem, Moses is the speaker as well as the main addressee of the discourse. There are three main points in Moses' testimony that Wakhānī deploys to formulate his statement concerning the essence of Muhammad's *miʿrāj* as a whole. The impact of the *miʿrāj* on Muhammad's further understanding of the divine essence, as argued in the poem, will be examined in more detail below, but first it is necessary to discuss the three main points in Moses' testimony in order to trace Wakhānī's argument about the *miʿrāj*: (1) each concealed voice heard by the prophets was that of ʿAlī; (2) 'everything is vested in the manifested imam'; and (3) ʿAlī is the chosen (*mujtabāʾ*) name by and for God to be recognised by all, the privileged as well as the common people (*khāṣṣ-u ʿāmm*). What is paradoxical about the first point is that it slightly softens Gabriel's role as mediator between God and the prophets during the transmission of the divine revelation, as believed in the general Islamic context, and implies a monistic concept of the essence of ʿAlī by presenting him as the direct speaker of the divine revelation. Wakhānī, thus, suggests that for Moses the imperative call (*nidāʾ*) of ʿAlī was the direct means of receiving the divine revelation, but, referring to the Qurʾan (7:143), Wakhānī admits that Moses was not allowed to see the face of the Lord:

> 'You will not see me' was the call of the Lord,
> He who revealed the divine revelation from the occult.
> Every voice that he heard from the occult,
> Was, undoubtedly, the voice of ʿAlī.[15]

In the fifth testimony presented on behalf of Jesus Christ (ʿĪsā Masīḥ), Wakhānī explicitly elaborates on the esoteric aspect of the issue, especially the creative role of ʿAlī as the holy spirit (*rūḥ al-qudus*), whose 'blessed breath' (*dam*) caused 'the spirit of God' (*Rūḥ Allāh*) to manifest himself in the form of a human being in the physical world by being born of Mary. In the following verses Wakhānī with slight modification refers to the Qurʾan (57:3) as the first confession of ʿĪsā:

---

[15] Ibid., fol. 2b.

When Jesus was born of Mary,
With the breath of Murtaḍā in this world,
He said: 'You are the beginning and the end,
You are the *bāṭin* and the *ẓāhir*.'[16]

The life and death of Jesus Christ, whose name is mentioned several times in the Qur'an, and his total absorption in the life of the spirit, profoundly influenced the works of Sufi poets. Persian poets passionately portrayed Jesus as one of their own, a symbolic representation of 'eternal life'.[17] In a way, Wakhānī sought to pursue a Christ-like life: suffering in this world and unity with the divine in the hereafter. His perception of Jesus resembles that of the Muslim mystics, but he goes further in mystifying his personality. Wakhānī, implicitly referring to the Qur'an (3:39), says that the status of Jesus in the physical world is similar to that of Adam. Nevertheless, the core of his argument, in sharp contrast with the Christian doctrine of Jesus as the Son of God, inclines towards the recognition of Jesus Christ beyond his status as a prophet. He is regarded as the spirit and the physical manifestation of God on earth until his return to the origin, i.e. God. The mysterious personality of Jesus, who is even described by certain Christian mystics as 'fully god and fully man',[18] logically suits Wakhānī's point in highlighting 'Alī's role in the *Panj-Tanī* tradition as the divine supreme authority (in the realm of the *bāṭin*), as well as a human being, the first Shi'i imam from the family of Prophet Muhammad (in the realm of *ẓāhir*). Allusions in the poem to the divinity of Jesus Christ are mainly derived from a Persian mystical concept of *hama ūst* (all is him), an equivalent of *waḥdat al-wujūd* (the unity of being).[19] The traditional

---

16 Ibid., fol. 3a.

17 See Sorour Sorodi, 'On the Jesus' Image in Modern Persian Poetry', *The Muslim World*, 69, 4 (1979), pp. 221–228. See also Annemarie Schimmel, *And Muhammad is His Messenger* (Chapel Hill, NC, 1985), p. 165.

18 See for example Wolfhart Pannenberg, *Jesus: God and Man*, tr. Dauane Priebe and Lewis L. Wilkins (Philadelphia, 1968). Charles Waldrop, 'Karl Barth's Concept of the Divinity of Jesus Christ', *The Harvard Theological Review*, 74, 3 (1981), pp. 241–263.

19 For the doctrine of *hama ūst* and *waḥdat al-wujūd* see William Chittick, 'Rūmī and Waḥdat al-wujūd', in A. Banani, R. Hovannisan, and G. Sabagh (ed.), *Poetry and Mysticism in Islam: The Heritage of Rūmī* (Cambridge, 1994), pp. 70–111. William Chittick, 'Waḥdat al-Shuhūd', *EI2*, vol. 10 (2000), pp. 37–39. See also Hermann Landolt,

Ismaili monist belief, which derives from this thought claims that in the realm of the *bāṭin*, all of the prophets and imams are the same, that is they are the ʿAlī of their times, but in the realm of the *ẓāhir* or the physical world, they act in accordance with their human names and times (*nām-u zamān*).[20] Furthermore, it is claimed by some medieval Ismaili sources, for instance the *Kalām-i Pīr* that there is no difference between God, the Prophet and Imam ʿAlī and that, in reality, there is only one divine substance that appears to be three in the eyes of the ignorant.[21] For Wakhānī, who also bases his argument on the traditional accounts, ʿAlī – either explicitly (*jalī*) or implicitly (*khafī*) – is the symbol (*ramz*) of the manifestation of that divine unity in the form of divine light (*nūr*). Accordingly, this transcendent light has been shining in the world of religion from the time of prophethood to the time of *imāma*. Wakhānī believes that ʿAlī, as the transcendent divine light, is the essence of the religious world (*ʿālam-i dīn*), the core substance (*jawhar*) of its motion (*gardish*) and the principle of its existence (*mawjūdiyyat*). In other words, ʿAlī is the manifestation of both the divine (*lāhūt*) and human (*nāsūt*) natures of God. All the prophets and the imams, therefore, possessing that divine light, are the representatives of God in the physical world through whom God makes himself known to human beings, and through whom God expects to be worshipped.[22]

Furthermore, Wakhānī argues that, if the recognition of ʿAlī is limited only to the realm of his material attributes as is encompassed by titles such as 'Commander of Faithful' (*amīr al-mū'minīn*) or 'Lion of God' (*shīr-i khudā*), then true divine knowledge (*ta'yīd*) will not be obtained. *ʿIlm al-ta'yīd*, therefore, is crucial in the recognition (*shinākht*) of God, and he who has this knowledge can actually comprehend the true nature of God. For Wakhānī, the master of this science and the sign of the unity of the divine is ʿAlī and the pupils of the *ta'yīd* are, of course, the lovers (*ʿāshiqān*) and the gnostics (*ʿārifān*),

---

'Aziz-i Nasafi and the Essence-Existence Debate', in J. Āshtiyānī et al. (ed.), *Consciousness and Reality: Studies in Memory of Toshihiko Izutsu* (Leiden, 2000), pp. 119–125.

[20] See for instance Wladimir Ivanow, *Kalami Pir: A Treatise on Ismaili Doctrine, also (wrongly) called Haft Babi Shah Sayyid Nasir* (Bombay, 1935), pp. 76–78.

[21] Ivanow, *Kalami Pir* (Bombay, 1935), p 76.

[22] MS Wakhānī, *Risāla-yi Chihil Dunyā*, fols 4b, 15b.

who, through love (*ʿishq*) and blessed knowledge (*maʿrifat*), perceive the true vision of the beloved.[23]

The Testimony of the Prophet Muhammad

Unlike the testimonies of the preceding prophets, where the evidence is based on what they heard and learned from the 'occult voice', Muhammad's testimony is firmly supported by the visual substantiations of his own spiritual experience obtained during his Night Journey (*isrāʾ*) and Ascension (*miʿrāj*). The myth about his outward journey, which is believed to have happened on either the twenty-seventh night of Rajab or the seventeenth night of Rabīʿ I in the year before the Hijra, has been a popular subject in Islamic mystical literature for centuries, especially in Persian poetry.[24] Wakhānī also employs this theme to justify his argument concerning the manifestation of the divine sign to Prophet Muhammad, although from a different perspective. Firstly, his recounting of the *miʿrāj* is rather a consequence of the Prophet's spiritual experience in heaven than an actual case of the *miʿrāj* as narrated in the traditional Muslim stories. Secondly, he narrates a new story about another ascent of the Prophet, which we may refer to as the second *miʿrāj*, but, this time, to the mysterious Chihil Dunyā, as the title of Wakhānī's work suggests. The issue of the Prophet's journey to the 'Forty Worlds' will be discussed in more detail below. This section will examine the denouement of his first *miʿrāj* and its doctrinal significance for the *Panj-Tanī* faith, as seen in the sixth testimony.

The sixth testimony in the *Risāla* has the didactic purpose of conveying a message of doctrinal importance to the faithful readers where, in the realm of physical attributes, ʿAlī b. Abī Ṭālib is presented as the first sign of the unveiling of *imāma* during the final phase of

23 Ibid., fol. 4a.

24 See Nazeer al-Azma, 'Some Stories on the Impact of the Story of the *Miʿrāj* on Sufi Literature', *The Muslim World*, 63, 2 (1973), pp. 93–104. Mohammad Ali Amir-Moezzi, *The Spirituality of Shiʿi Islam*, pp. 171–174. Frederick Colby, 'The Subtleties of the Ascension: al-Sulamī on the Miʿrāj of the Prophet Muhammad', *Studia Islamica*, 44 (2002), pp. 167–183. James Morris, 'The Spiritual Ascension: Ibn al-ʿArabī and the *Miʿrāj*', *Journal of the American Oriental Society*, 107 (1987), pp. 629–652.

the *nubuwwa* of Muhammad. The fact that the issue of *imāma* after the death of the Prophet became a key point in the Shiʿi, especially the Ismaili, doctrine of religious authority is what Wakhānī uses as the substructure for his argument to further elaborate on the inner aspect of *imāma*. For he believed that *imāma* is deeply rooted in the essence of ʿAlī, as was discovered and recognised by Prophet Muhammad after his return from the *miʿrāj*. The belief that ʿAlī had unveiled himself and revealed the mysteries of the divine secrets in the time of, and to, Muhammad is a well-known concept in the Ismaili esoteric programme, especially apparent in post-Alamūt literature.[25] What Wakhānī does here, however, is to systematise the idea in the framework of the traditional indigenous narrative by providing it with a sustainable doctrinal background.

The testimony is articulated in the form of a story, in which each episode develops because of its preceding involvement with the three main characters, the Prophet, ʿAlī and Gabriel, and the author. The unity of the testimony's episodic structure may well be segregated into three stages in the Prophet's post-Ascent spiritual state: (1) the Prophet's return to reality and perplexity about his unreal experience; (2) the angel Gabriel and the awakening of the Prophet's inner consciousness; and (3) the removal of his illusion and submission to the divine. As mentioned earlier, the themes of *isrāʾ* and *miʿrāj*, as traditionally narrated and discussed in the Islamic context, are not the concerns of the sixth testimony, but the author's purpose in raising them initially is merely to support the key point of his entire work; that is, to argue for the primordial origin and internal nature of the *wilāya* of ʿAlī. For this reason, the testimony begins by stressing the significance of the *imāma* of ʿAlī, as it is perceived in the realm of its religious universe (*ʿālam-i dīn*) and its physical reality. This reality alone, however, as the author argues, was insufficient to convince the Prophet about the essence of ʿAlī and the importance of the institution of the *imāma*.

---

[25] See for instance Ivanow, *Kalām-i Pīr*: 'O ʿAlī, thou wert hidden with all the Prophets, and thou hast become manifest with me.' 'Thou art the book of God. Thou art the mystery of God because no one knows thy mysterious substance except God. The mystery of God is revealed in his words, which all deal with the exalted position, both mine and thine', p. 78.

He, thus, needed to be shown the signs of divine truth in the *miʿrāj* through his personal spiritual experience. This is what Wakhānī focuses on in the sixth testimony; then, he concentrates exclusively on Muhammad's post-*miʿrāj* states, the first of which is the state of perplexity (*ḥayrat*) which occurs immediately upon his return to earth. His perplexity was caused by the outcome of his initial expectation of the *miʿrāj*, which was to be shown the signs of the divinity, as promised in the Qur'an (41:53). Instead, in heaven, he saw a familiar face: the face of his own cousin and son-in-law with whom he interacted almost every day and who first received and cheered him after the ascent. Furthermore, the Prophet is surprisingly impressed when he hears the whole story of his *isrā'* and *miʿrāj* from ʿAlī. Here, Wakhānī quotes a verse from Ḥāfiẓ, in which he questions how it is possible that the mystery of the divine secret, known only by a spiritually progressed (*sālik*) gnostic (*ʿārif*), could be known to a wine seller (*bāda-furūsh*).[26] Wine, in general Sufi thought, usually symbolises divine love and ecstasy, and the wine seller or cupbearer (*sāqī*) is the guide. Although one cannot dismiss different interpretations of this question in particular and the whole *ghazal* of Ḥāfiẓ in general, the reason for Wakhānī's citation of it appears to be concealed by the very nature of his mystical discourse about ʿAlī's role in the Prophet's mission. As he argues, not only the ignorant (*jāhil*) failed to accept the *wilāya* of ʿAlī, but even Muhammad himself was unaware of it before his second *miʿrāj*.[27]

The next stage in the Prophet's spiritual experience begins with questioning what he saw in the first *miʿrāj*. Wakhānī refers to this stage as *marḥila-yi āgāhī* (the stage of awareness), where he converses with the angel Gabriel – the symbolic manifestation of his inner consciousness. Gabriel provides Muhammad with three explanations about the *wilāya* of ʿAlī. First, speaking on behalf of the angel, Wakhānī argues that God is not an unimaginable distant mystery, but is very close to human piety, and possesses a human form in the realm of the material world in order to be accessible to and directly addressable by human beings. Here he quotes the Qur'an (41: 6) and the famous prophetic *ḥadīth*

[26] For the four lines of Ḥāfiẓ's verse quoted by Wakhānī see M. Bārī, *Kulliyāt-i Shamsiddīn Muḥammad Ḥāfiẓ-i Shīrāzī* (Tehran, 2001), p. 142.

[27] MS Wakhānī, *Risāla-yi Chihil Dunyā,* fols 4b, 21b.

('Verily God created man in His own image') to support his argument. He further argues that the recognition of God in human form is a sign of the divine manifestation in the physical world and the only possible way in which Prophet Muhammad could perceive the beauty of the divine form; otherwise, the image of God is beyond description. Second, the angel tells the Prophet that following his death, the chain of religious guidance will continue through the genetic line (*nasl-i dhurriyyat*) of ʿAlī, and that his role as a Warner (*mundhir*) about God's command (referring to the Qurʾan, 13:7) will cease and that divine guidance will directly flow from the family (*kunyat*) of ʿAlī until the day of the resurrection (*rūz-i qiyāmat*). Furthermore, quoting the Qurʾan (5:67), the angel instructs Muhammad to pass this message on to his community, as this was the key condition for the completion of his prophetic mission. This statement, thus, is intended to justify the general Shiʿi doctrinal argument concerning the inevitability of the end of the prophethood as an intermediate God-human link and the continuation of divine guidance through *imāma*, which will then bridge the gap between divine-human relationships. Third, Gabriel tells Muhammad that his own duty, as the mediator between God and the Prophet, in bringing down (*nuzūl*) the divine revelation (*waḥy*), will also cease with the explicit emergence of ʿAlī's *imāma*. What Wakhānī tries to emphasise here is the importance of the transformation of divine revelation by highlighting the very Ismaili doctrinal point that with the end of the period of the *nubuwwa*, there will be no further need for Gabriel to act as the agent of divine revelation and guidance, and that everything will be vested in the Imam of the Time (*imām-i zamān*).

The World of Chihil Dunyā

The most remarkable point in Muhammad's testimony is his desire to know and discover the secrets of divine mystery, its wonders *(ʿajāʾib)* and peculiarities (*gharāʾib*) hidden in the Chihil Dunyā. Wakhānī describes the Chihil Dunyā as a supra-sensory world located beyond Qāf, a mystical mountain in Islamic cosmology surrounding the terrestrial world to which our topography cannot be applied in the material sense. It is a kind of spiritual space which resembles Henry Corbin's *mundus imaginalis* (or *ʿālam al-mithāl*), an intermediate world of images which stands between the empirical world and the world of abstract understanding.[28] Wakhānī depicts the Prophet's journey to and discovery of the forty abodes of the Chihil Dunyā as the true moment (*laḥẓa*) of divine inspiration (*ilhām*), leading one to imagine oneself in the divine presence. In this connection, when Wakhānī speaks of the 'true moment', he probably refers to one of the famous prophetic *aḥādīth*, often quoted by Sufis, where the idea of time is used to accommodate the duration of the divine presence within oneself and one's spiritual power to be able to live in and gain inspiration from that moment.[29] Such a moment for the Prophet, Wakhānī maintains, occurred during his journey to the Chihil Dunyā and his meeting with its inhabitants, the *chihil tan* (the 'forty men').[30]

Before travelling to the Chihil Dunyā, it is important to understand who the *chihil tan* are and why the number forty is so key in *Risāla-yi Chihil Dunyā*. To begin with the latter, it is worth mentioning that numbers such as forty stand for various elements in the nature and culture of human existence and constitute a system of values for particular societies. As Schimmel puts it, the number forty, having a special symbolic meaning in Islamic mysticism and beyond, is closely associated with the ideas of the preparation, purification, maturity and completion of the human soul and its growth to the stage of the true understanding of the divine essence.[31] It is a very special omnipresent number in the sacred scriptures as well as popular cultures around the world, associated with the forty days in which Buddha attained enlightenment, Moses experienced theophany and the number of hours that the body of Jesus lay in the tomb before his resurrection. According to Muslim tradition, forty was the number of days during which Prophet Muhammad undertook a *khalvat* (retreat or *chilla* in Persian) on the mountain of Hira to receive divine revelation at the age of forty. As far as the Persian term *chihil tan* is concerned, there is no wide doctrinal employment of it in the broad context of Islamic mysticism. Nevertheless, forty as the number of the special category of the hidden Islamic saints, sometimes

---

28 See Henry Corbin, *Swedenborg and Esoteric Islam*, p. 11.

29 The *ḥadīth* says 'I have a time with God to which even Gabriel, who is pure spirit, is not admitted.' See *Kalām-i Pīr*, p. 84.

30 MS Wakhānī, *Risāla-yi Chihil Dunyā*, fol. 11a.

31 Annemarie Schimmel, *The Mystery of Numbers* (Oxford, 1993), p. 245.

referred to as 'hidden men' (*rijāl al-ghayb*), is categorically mentioned in Islamic mystic literature. For instance, al-Hakim al-Tirmizī (d. 292/912), who is regarded as one of the earliest Muslim thinkers to employ the term *walī* in relation to the concept of friendship with God, in his *Khatm al-awliyā'* ('Seal of the Saints'), said that there is a special category of 'forty strictly truthful men' (*ṣiddīqūn*) among the hidden saints in the court of God.[32] Al-Tirmizī's idea was later developed by 'Alī b. 'Uthmān al-Ḥujwīrī (d. 464/1072) in his famous *Kashf al-maḥjūb*, in which he described the hidden saints as the superior (*najīb*) or the divinely chosen category of saints who live among ordinary people and solve their earthly problems.[33] Thus, the believers merely need to seek help from the *rijāl al-ghayb* by undertaking a special process of meditation, which involves the recitation of certain prayers (*du'ā'*) and silent *dhikr*; absolute concentration during the entire process is absolutely essential. The famous medieval Sufi authority and biographer 'Abd al-Raḥmān Jāmī (d. 897/1492), in his *Nafaḥāt al-uns min ḥaḍarāt al-quds*, further elaborated on the issue. He distinguished the forty *abdāl* as one of the most important groups of the hidden saints, who live among human beings, but whose presence is not physically observed or even noticed.[34] The myth about the *chihil tan* is also significantly strong in the popular imagination of Central Asian Muslims; it constitutes the core principle of popular religious belief in the hidden saints and their miraculous powers.[35] They believe that the *chihil tan* constitute a secret society of hidden saints, very close friends of God, who are blessed with supranatural powers and divine knowledge with which they can assist faithful believers as 'guardian angels' without disclosing themselves.

Wakhānī's perception of the *chihil tan* is mainly based on the traditional accounts. However, his aim in his *Risāla* is to unveil their 'true nature' (*fiṭrat-i ḥaqīqī*) as the inhabitants of the world of divine secrets, towards which the Prophet travelled. In contrast to traditional

---

[32] Bernd Radtke and John O'Kane, *The Concept of Sainthood in Early Islamic Mysticism: Two works by al-Hakim al-Tirmidhi* (Richmond, 1996), pp. 68–69, 109.

[33] 'Alī Hujwīrī, *Kashf al-maḥjūb*, tr. R. A. Nicholson (London, 1936), pp. 214–228.

[34] 'Abd al-Raḥmān Jāmī, *Nafaḥāt al-uns min ḥaḍarāt al-quds*, ed. M. Tawḥīdīpūr (Tehran, 1375 Sh. /1996), pp. 145–150.

[35] See for example Mikhail Andreyev, *Chiltani v Sredne-aziatskikh Verovaniiakh* (Tashkent, 1927), pp. 334–348.

accounts, Wakhānī at first tries to disclose the secretive nature of the *chihil tan* and unveils the secret behind their mission by making them accessible to human beings through the example of Prophet Muhammad. Then he goes on to define them as 'the seekers of meaning' (*qism-i dar pay-i maʿnā*). It is in this deeper sense of the *chihil tan*'s essence that the Prophet enters the world of divine secrets and determines the meaning behind his prophetic mission. Wakhānī also calls the *chihil tan* 'the lovers of the *wilāya* and family of ʿAlī'; they truly recognise his *ilāhiyyat* in the realm of the spiritual world. Thus, for the Prophet to understand the truth of the divine secrets and achieve the ultimate goal of his prophetic mission – to establish an institution of human guidance (*imāma*) – it was essential to travel to the land of divine wonders and meet the *chihil tan*.[36]

The Prophet in the Chihil Dunyā

The prophet Muhammad's quest for meaning starts with his questioning the consequences (i.e. surprise and confusion) of his first *miʿrāj*. It is, therefore, a quest for the truth about the mystery behind the divine essence manifested in a human form that prompted the Prophet to accept Gabriel's invitation to undertake the second *miʿrāj* to the *Chihil Dunyā*. Throughout his journey, the Prophet is accompanied by ʿAlī, either 'in person' or in 'other forms' (e.g. an old man, Gabriel, Khiḍr, etc.), in order to discover the reality of ʿAlī. In other words, it is a journey from ʿAlī with ʿAlī and to ʿAlī. Part of the story portrays how ʿAlī, 'in person,' accompanies the Prophet up to the mountain of Qāf and then gives him his ring, as an entry card, to discover the four summits of the first world of the divine wonderland, namely the Ṭurfa-Jāʾ (the place of enjoyment), the Darvāza-yi Shahr (the city gate), the Bāzār (the market) and the Dār al-Salām (the abode of peace). In the Ṭurfa-Jāʾ, the Prophet is shown the natural beauty of the spiritual world (rose gardens with aromatic scents, peaceful rivers of milk, golden mountains, etc.) before he progresses towards the divine. The beauty of spiritual reality, described as if it were perceived in the

---

[36] MS Wakhānī, *Risāla-yi Chihil Dunyā*, fols 11–20.

sensory world, indicates that, in Islamic mysticism, the spiritual or the world hereafter is far better than the physical world. Through the gate, the Prophet enters the city market, a place full of food and commodities, with the active presence of human beings. This is the first and only time in the epistle that the Prophet encounters the *chihil tan* in the course of his heavenly voyage. The story goes on to relate how the Prophet's hunger for the food he sees in the market causes him to reach out for it, but before he is able to take any someone grabs his hand and, seeing he is an outsider, asks him who he is. It is in this moment of anxiety that the conversation between the Prophet and the *chihil tan* starts. They accuse him of being a stranger who has tried to steal ʿAlī's property; the Prophet strives on the contrary to prove his family relationship to ʿAlī. The dispute finally brings both groups to the Dār al-Salām, the court of ʿAlī, to see whether the Prophet is telling the truth. But the truth that the Prophet is about to uncover overlaps his main argument with the *chihil tan*; it is true that he is ʿAlī's relative and that the food that he was about to take was also ʿAlī's property. But the one on the throne, whom the *chihil tan* referred to as ʿAlī, is in fact the face of God which he had seen during his first *miʿrāj*. The idea of the Prophet seeing ʿAlī in the *miʿrāj* and speaking to him as if God was speaking frequently appears in several pre-modern Ismaili sources, including the *Kalām-i Pīr*.[37] Wakhānī goes further and in line with his contemporary, the Iranian poet Fidāʾī Khurāsānī glorifies the divine in the person of ʿAlī, his inner and outer images (*ṣūrat wa sīrat*)[38]:

> As the Prophet looked at the beauty of the *Mawlā*,
> It appeared to him to be Almighty God, whom he saw on the
> Ascent.[39]

---

37 According to the *Kalām-i Pīr* the Prophet is believed to have said: 'When I was taken to the heavens on the night of the Ascension (*Miʿrāj*) . . . I saw an angel who sat on a chair (*minbar*) of light, and other angels were standing around him. I asked Gabriel who this angel was. Gabriel replied, "Come near, and greet him," When I went near and greeted him, I saw that he was my cousin, ʿAlī b. Abī Ṭālib. . . O my Lord dost Thou speak to me, or ʿAlī?' God replied: "I love no one more than ʿAlī b. Abī Ṭālib. This is why I spoke to thee by the tongue of ʿAlī, so that thy heart shall be quiet and not filled with awe." ' See Ivanow, *Kalami Pir*, p. 82.

38 For Fidāʾī Khurāsānī see Alexander Semyonov, 'Ismailitskiy Panegirik Obozhestvennomu Aliyu Fidayi Khurasanskogo', *Iran*, 1, 38 (1928), pp. 51–70.

39 MS Wakhānī, *Risāla-yi Chihil Dunyā*, fol. 14b.

After the *dīdār* (spiritual meeting with the *Mawlā*), the Prophet's quest for meaning (*maʿnā*) continues in the remaining thirty-nine abodes of the Chihil Dunyā, where he is encouraged to discover the custom (*sunnat*) of the divine world and the power (*qudrat*) of its king. Here Muhammad is engaged in a dialogue with a luminous angel (*parī bā nūr pīchīda*), who tells him that the *chihil tan* once heard from ʿAlī that in three thousand years a messenger of God named Muhammad would arrive to complete the divine mission. The Prophet is shocked by this revelation and falls to the ground, unconscious. When he opens his eyes, he sees ʿAlī holding a cup of wine and offering him a drink in order to understand the miracles he has seen and the mysteries he has heard:

> This wine is from the wine-house of my *wilāya*,
> The Universe, including this world, is my *wilāya*.[40]

Wine, in Islamic mysticism, symbolises spiritual ecstasy, which intoxicates the mystic's soul causing it to lose its individual consciousness and find its universal consciousness in the presence of a vision of the Beloved. The Prophet is offered the wine of gnosis (*may-i maʿrifat*) to drink, in order to understand the miracles of the Chihil Dunyā and the true essence of its king. After this his journey to the divine wonderland comes to an end he is sent back to the realm of physical reality, to Medina. Upon his arrival, he goes straight to Fāṭima's house, where ʿAlī is also present but asleep, and gives her the ring that ʿAlī gave him when they were on the mountain of Qāf.

The Prophet's journey to the Chihil Dunyā is depicted by Wakhānī as a moment of true spiritual experience in which Muhammad lived for a thousand years, passing through various stages of discovery (*kashf*) in order to understand the esoteric (*bāṭin*) meaning of divine revelation. This allegory intends to provide basic support for Wakhānī's argument concerning the *wilāya* of ʿAlī and his role as the true interpreter of divine revelation. For this, the Prophet first had to see ʿAlī in the realm of the spiritual world with his own eyes, and then, in the realm of the physical world, convey the message to the community of Muslims to follow ʿAlī and his descendants as religious guides.

[40] Ibid., fol. 21b.

Approaching the matter from the esoteric (*bāṭin*) and exoteric (*ẓāhir*) principles, Wakhānī's presentation of ʿAlī overlaps both his physical and spiritual attributes while discussing the Prophet's spiritual experience in the Chihil Dunyā. ʿAlī is the one whom the Prophet meets before (as a human being), during (as the Lord) and after the journey (again as a human being). In other words, ʿAlī here stands for the sublime manifestation of divine unity, the core principle of the *ẓāhir* and *bāṭin* of the religious universe, the symbol of guidance and the embodiment of all guides.

To conclude his *risāla*, Wakhānī quotes and interprets two of the most important *aḥādīth* in the Shiʿi context concerning the role and importance of the imam. Firstly, 'If the world were devoid of the imam, even for a moment, it would perish with all its inhabitants.' Secondly, 'Whoever dies without recognition of the Imam of the Time, his death would be a death of an ignorant one and the place of the ignorant is hell.' Wakhānī's deployment of these two *aḥādīth* recapitulates his main arguments in the *risāla*. It has the didactic purpose of addressing specific audiences to recognise the essence (*dhāt*) and attributes (*ṣifāt*) of ʿAlī b. Abī Ṭālib. These two *aḥādīth* serve as the means of justification for what follows, whether one recognises or rejects ʿAlī and his *imāma*. In other words, the message that Wakhānī seeks to convey is that there is a reward (*thawāb*) for what is recognised, and a punishment (*ʿiqāb*) for what is rejected. One of the remarkable points in both interpretations is the stress on the knowledge (*maʿrifat*) of the Imam of the Time, whose recognition, in which Wakhānī concurs with prophetic epistemology, begins with the recognition of oneself. Through the *maʿrifat* of the imam, the seeker first recognises himself, the cause of his existence and future destiny, and then he falls in love (*muḥabbat*) with the source of the *maʿrifat* and desires to walk on the path (*ṭarīqat*) in order to determine the truth (*ḥaqīqat*).

Conclusion

The *Risāla-yi Chihil Dunyā*, as a sophisticated presentation of the traditional *Panj-Tanī* belief in the idea of divine authority, its origination, existence and continuation in the *wilāya* of Imam ʿAlī and his progeny, is a remarkable piece of mystical literature, combining Ismaili and

Sufi doctrines produced in Badakhshān in the pre-modern period. Composed in a mystical spirit, the *risāla* is an argumentative religious discourse, where the role of ʿAlī, as the shah of *wilāya* in the realm of spiritual realities – the Chihil Dunyā – is often exaggerated. ʿAlī in the *risāla* stands for the sublime manifestation of divine unity, the core principle of the *ẓāhir* and the *bāṭin* of the religious universe. In order to support his argument about the primordial and pre-historical origin of ʿAlī's divine authority, Wakhānī gives six testimonies on behalf of the six *ūlu'l-ʿaẓm* prophets. These Abrahamic prophets, symbolising the six levels of spiritual emanation from the appearance to the perfection of the religious universe, play a significant role in the Shiʿi understanding of divine guidance embedded in the concept of *nubuwwa* and *imāma*. Islamised Biblical stories are often deployed by the Qurʾan and Muslim tradition to argue for Islam's primordial and prehistoric origin as a monotheistic religion. In these stories the *ūlu'l-ʿaẓm* prophets are described as the predecessors of Muhammad in the chain of prophets starting with Adam. Wakhānī is quite flexible when it comes to crossing theological boundaries between Islam, Judaism and Christianity in order to reach the source of divine inspiration.

Wakhānī specifically emphasises the role of the Prophet Muhammad and his spiritual experience in the Chihil Dunyā. His journey to the world of divine secrets and discovery of its forty abodes is what Wakhānī passionately calls the true moment of divine inspiration, leading one to imagine oneself in the divine presence. Muhammad, as a perfect example of the seeker, through his journey to the Chihil Dunyā finally found the source of divine knowledge and guidance. It was after this journey that the Prophet, on his final pilgrimage from Mecca to Medina proclaimed ʿAlī as his successor and unveiled the *imāma* of ʿAlī in the realm of physical reality as the perpetual institution of a human guide. As a source of guidance, *imāma* will continue in ʿAlī's progeny until the day of resurrection.

PART SIX

THE INTERACTION AND CIRCULATION OF KNOWLEDGE ACROSS RELIGIOUS AND GEOGRAPHICAL BOUNDARIES

16

Beyond Space and Time: The Itinerant Life of Books in the Fatimid Market Place*

Delia Cortese
(Middlesex University)

In the popular science fiction series *Star Trek* Vulcans are famously shown to communicate with each other through mind-melding, a technique that enables interlocutors to merge thoughts, consciousness and ideas without the need for physical contact or verbal interaction. When looked at from today's standpoint, texts produced by early and medieval Muslim thinkers could indeed seem to be the product of some sort of pre-modern mind-melding across the Islamic world. Through the texts that have reached us we can appreciate the outcome of intellectual interaction in the fusion or contrast of ideas, the mutual proliferation of influences and the interpolation of works by certain scholars into those of others. However, authors are mostly silent on the practicalities and modalities that enabled the intellectual interactions they display to take place in the first instance. What was the physical dimension that underpinned intellectual exchange? In which spaces did scholars come together? Which occasions became catalysts for encounters? Which tools did they make use of? Biographical dictionaries and historiographical works are replete with anecdotes of people coming into personal contact in a variety of circumstances, such as for example, while travelling to and from Mecca on the Ḥajj, or meeting up in markets or centres of learning and mosques, or gathering in each other's houses. Sometimes casual walks in the streets of Baghdad,

* I am grateful to Professor Yaacov Lev for his suggestions in writing this paper. I am solely responsible for any shortcomings.

Damascus or Cairo might have been the setting for chance dialogues between high calibre scholars. This information is, however, mostly generic and vague, with the boundary between historical reality and hagiography often blurred. Given that transmission of knowledge – even when orally communicated – depended ultimately on access to and the availability of written material, charting how books as objects changed hands could provide tangible examples of how the material exchange of cultural goods might have ultimately impacted on a literary output marked by the blending of ideas.

The information in Muslim historiographical works on the book trade in the pre-modern Middle East is scanty and fragmentary at best.[1] The reason for this neglect lies in the fact that, in the context of a culture where, from the third/ninth century onwards, social elites became book-obsessed, the modality of production as well as the circulation and distribution of books came to be taken for granted to the point of not requiring any special record except for exceptional episodes concerning exceptional books.[2] By the third/ninth century, the general adoption of paper as a cheaper medium for writing than for instance vellum, helped to make books a commonplace feature of cultural life. It was a given that royal patrons would establish libraries in their palaces and that mosques would house collections of books. Men of learning were often book collectors as well as producers of tomes both as authors and copyists. In the eastern part of the Muslim world by the fifth/eleventh century the *madrasa* had become the obvious gravitational point for book production, trade and circulation.[3]

[1] Comprehensive, in-depth research on this practical aspect of pre-modern Islamic cultural history is non-existent. On the emergence, formation and proliferation of a book culture at the Fatimid court and beyond in this period see Paul E. Walker, 'Libraries, Book Collection and the Production of Texts by the Fatimids', *Intellectual History of the Islamicate World*, 4 (2016), pp. 9–21.

[2] A succinct yet detailed overview of major public and private libraries in the medieval Muslim world can be found in Etan Kohlberg, *A Medieval Muslim Scholar at Work: Ibn Ṭāwūs and his Library* (Leiden, London and Cologne, 1992), pp. 71–74.

[3] On business opportunities generated by the *madrasa* where students and teachers provided a ready market for booksellers, paper makers etc., see Gary Leiser, 'Notes on the Madrasa in Medieval Islamic Society', *The Muslim World*, 76 (1986), pp. 16–23.

The typical mechanisms by which books were purchased, owned and gathered in collections consisted of copying them, presenting them as pious donations and trading in them. Also, since books were generally expensive,[4] they were considered valuable commodities to be passed on through inheritance as family heirlooms.

The *warrāq* is the figure that is most typically associated with all things relating to the production of the medieval Islamic book. Encompassing the role of paper vendor, seller of writing tools, copyist and scholar in his own right at any one time, the *warrāq* could occupy varied positions on the social scale from a marginal who scraped a living through writing for others to a distinguished member of the scholarly elite. To the latter category belonged the celebrated bibliophile Ibn al-Nadīm (d. 385/995) who, indeed, became known as al-Warrāq. Whether produced for a commission or through individual initiative, the ultimate purpose of copying books as a profession was to sell them. For this reason often the activities of the copyist overlapped with that of the *kutubī*, the vendor or broker of volumes already in circulation. This paper will focus on this latter figure, by concentrating on personalities that became primarily famous in Fatimid Egypt because of their bookselling activities. The works circulated via the *warrāq* were mostly the result of personal selection by the copyist and/or the commissioner; they were often influenced by intellectual trends within specific scholarly networks and were produced with a specific project in mind. By contrast, the book vendor, the *kutubī*, had to rely on whatever and whenever stock was available; he had to go out of his way to procure books to sell, a factor that meant he was exposed to or reliant on the contingencies of the time and place in which he lived. In terms of cultural impact, by circulating extant books, the *kutubī* provided greater potential for the popularisation of a broader, random and diverse range of subjects to a broader audience while, at the same time, contributing – deliberately or by default – to the life or death of a particular form of literary tradition.

Fatimid Egypt (358–567/969–1171) offers a distinctive social, religious and cultural context in which to map the function and role that

---

[4] On the value of books see Eliyahu Ashtor, *Histoire des prix et des salaires dans l'orient medieval* (Cairo, 1981), pp. 60, 112, 212.

the book trade played in facilitating intellectual interaction. While defined by activities and events linked to and/or determined by an Ismaili dynasty – except for strictly *daʿwa* literature – the practical means of book exchange transcended Ismailism as a doctrinal entity. Unlike the territories under Abbasid rule, the institution of the *madrasa* was absent in Egypt until towards the very end of the Fatimid era. This meant that Egypt lacked a predictable learning hub where book exchanges would be expected to occur. The Fatimids, as a Shiʿi Ismaili dynasty were a religious minority ruling over a majority Sunni population, a state of affairs that meant that contrasting and competing scholarly traditions were brought into contact. For example, the imam-caliph al-Ḥākim founded in Cairo his 'Abode of Knowledge' or *dār al-ʿilm* ostensibly as an outreach venture intended to serve scholars irrespective of their religious affiliation.[5] In Egypt the Fatimids became the first Muslim dynasty to give their patronage to major libraries located in royal palaces and in the learning institutions they supported. Perhaps with some exaggeration, the royal libraries were said to contain one and a half million volumes.[6] Books were produced for Ismaili *daʿwa* purposes with a very strictly limited circulation; however, books were written on Ismaili law that could be publicly circulated and, outside the doctrinal context, books on all the known fields of learning were written, copied, circulated, collected and praised. The book culture the Fatimids promoted was so infectious that it was embraced by high-ranking officers of state – for example the viziers Ibn Killis (d. 380/991) and al-Afḍal (d. 515/1121) – as well as the wider urban cultural elite. Throughout most of their reign the Fatimids succeeded in rivalling the Abbasids by securing trading routes between India, the Mediterranean and the Middle East which enabled international travellers to combine excellent mercantile opportunities with undertaking the pilgrimage to Mecca. This was because Egypt was uniquely placed between the Red Sea, which led to the Indian Ocean and East Africa, and the Mediterranean. This attracted to Egypt an international traffic of scholars-*cum*-traders[7] who – notwithstanding the boom-and

[5] However, testimonies on the effective use of this facility by visiting scholars are rare.

[6] Walker, 'Libraries', p. 10.

bust crises that marked the economic and political life of the Fatimid period – found Egypt conducive to establishing and reinforcing networks through which goods and learning could be exchanged. The argument in this paper is that it is against the backdrop of these 'fluid' contexts that we can situate the *kutubī* as cultural agent, emerging as he does (it was generally a he) with a sharper focus than the 'mere' copyist in historiographical accounts covering the Fatimid period.

Attitudes to Book Buying and Selling in the Medieval Islamic World

The price of books differed from region to region due to a number of factors, one of many being the fluctuation in currency values in different places and at different times. It is therefore difficult to establish the exact cost of books across the Near and Middle East throughout the medieval period. However, it is generally agreed that books were an expensive commodity. Typically, written sale contracts were drafted when books were purchased, a practice that otherwise was only applied to the purchase of houses, other immobile property, and slaves.[8] With so much at stake, book acquisition would need careful consideration and discernment on the part of the buyer. Ibn Jamāʿa (d. 733/1333) in his *Tadhkira* provides guidelines on how to buy a book. For example, to ensure its quality the buyer should check that it is complete at beginning and end; that there are no missing parts in the middle; that the general state and quality of the paper is consistent with the asking price. The book's editorial qualities would have to conform to certain expectations and conventions.[9] Indeed we can detect a degree of preciousness over the quality of books at the Fatimid court where

7 On the link between trade and scholarship among medieval Muslim savants see Hayyim J. Cohen, 'The economic background and the secular occupations of Muslim jurisprudents', *Journal of the Economic and Social History of the Orient*, 13 (1970), pp. 16–61.

8 Shlomo D. Goitein, *A Mediterranean Society: The Economic Foundation*, vol. 1 (Berkeley, CA, 1999), p. 196.

9 Badr al-Dīn Muḥammad b. Ibrahīm b. Jamāʿa, *Tadhkirat al-sāmiʿ waʾl-mutakallim fī adab al-ʿālim waʾl-mutaʿallim* (Hyderabad, 1353/1934), pp. 172–177.

preference was given to bespoke copies of books to be housed in sponsored libraries. In fact, it appears that the purchase of existing books was not contemplated in the detailed budget of al-Ḥākim's *dār al-ʿilm* where, instead, enormous sums were set aside for paper, scribes, writing tools and book restauration.[10]

The fact that the pre-modern Islamic world became awash with books, whether by means of the *warrāq* or the *kutubī*, does not necessarily mean that trading in books was an unconditionally endorsed practice. In the eastern part of the Islamic world, the establishment of the *madrasa* had led to the professionalisation of the *ʿulamāʾ* who, preserving their scholarly and religious authority, deliberated on what was admissible and non-admissible in matters of the transmission of learning. For example, Ibn Jamāʿa recommended that when possible students should buy the texts they needed and/or copy them to cut costs while facilitating memorisation. At the same time though, he went to some lengths to point out that acquiring books, even large numbers of them, did not by itself promote knowledge and understanding. Private reading and note taking did not in any way relieve the student from checking his reading of a text against that of his teacher or *shaykh*. Ultimately, Ibn Jamāʿa insisted, true knowledge derived only from a learned person not from books.[11] The lack of a professional class of learned men, that is to say of the *ʿulamāʾ* in Fatimid Egypt meant that privatisation of learning was not seen as problematic.[12] Interestingly, the scholar and *ḥadīth*-transmitter, Abu'l-Fatḥ al-Ṣawwāf (374–440/984–1048), arriving in Baghdad from *madrasa*-free Cairo, came across as an oddity for buying books, choosing to study them by himself, ignoring the authority of the *shaykh* and

[10] As noted by Youssef Eche, *Les bibliothèques arabes publiques et semipubliques en Mesopotamie, en Sirie et en Egypte au Moyen Age* (Damascus, 1967), p. 364. For a detailed breakdown of the *dār al-ʿilm*'s budget see Walker, 'Libraries', pp. 14–15.

[11] Ibn Jamāʿa, *Tadhkirat*, pp. 164–167. Cf. also Jonathan Berkey, *The Transmission of Knowledge in Medieval Cairo: A Social History of Islamic Education* (Princeton, 1994), p. 26.

[12] In the Ismaili context public access to religious and sacred literature was under the strict control of the *daʿwa* organisation. There is no evidence however that Ismailis were prevented or forbidden from buying and reading books belonging to traditions and genres outside those produced by and for the community.

transmitting *ḥadīths* he learned about from books without the support of any oral authority.[13]

With the exception of possibly one institution, in Cairo, *madrasas* appeared under the Ayyubids and it was not until the second half of the seventh/thirteenth century that a distinctive and defined class of *ʿulamāʾ* began to establish itself in Egypt. In Alexandria *madrasas* had been established during the last phase of Fatimid rule, following the arrival of prominent foreign Mālikī and Shāfiʿī *ḥadīth*-transmitters who enjoyed patronage there.[14] The most distinguished figure to settle in Alexandria was the greatest Shāfiʿī scholar of the late Fatimid period, Abū Ṭāhir al-Silafī (d. 576/1180) who, over time, amassed an extensive personal library and, as book collector, engaged with the most important booksellers of his time.[15] It is indeed around this personality and his close-knit intellectual network that much of what is known about *kutubīs* in fifth/eleventh and sixth/twelfth centuries Egypt revolves.

Booksellers in Cairo and Alexandria

It is likely that, from at least the middle of the fifth/eleventh century up until the end of the Fatimid period and possibly beyond, the *sūq* of the

---

[13] Taqī al-Dīn Aḥmad al-Maqrīzī, *Kitāb al-Muqaffā al-kabīr*, ed. M. Yaʿlawī (Beirut, 1991), no. 1833.

[14] For a concise overview of the history of *madrasas* in Egypt shortly before and immediately after the demise of the Fatimids see Anne-Marie Eddé, *Saladin* (Paris, 2008), pp. 440–442.

[15] His most celebrated work, *Muʿjam al-safar*, has been the subject of an extensive range of studies and partial as well as complete editions. Among the most important see Umberto Rizzitano, 'Akhbār ʿan baʿḍ muslimī ṣiqilliyya alladhīna tarjama la-hum Abū Ṭāhir al-Silafī', *Annals of the Faculty of Arts, University Of ʿAyn Shams*, 3 (1955), pp. 49–112; I. ʿAbbās, *Akhbār wa-tarājim Andalusiyya al-mustakhraja min Muʿjam al-safar li al-Silafī* (Beirut, 1963); S.M. Zaman, *Abū Ṭāhir al-Silafī al-Iṣbahānī. His life and works with an analytical study of his Muʿjam al-safar* (PhD thesis, Harvard University, Cambridge MA, 1968); Ḥ. Ṣāliḥ, *The life and times of al-Ḥāfiẓ Abū Ṭāhir al-Silafī accompanied by a critical edition of part of the author's Muʿjam al-safar* (PhD thesis, University of Cambridge, 1972); Bahīja Bakr al-Ḥasanī (ed.), *Muʿjam al-safar* (Baghdad, 1978), vol. 1; B. A. Maʿrūf, 'Muʿjam al-safar li-Abī Ṭāhir al-Silafī', *al-Mawrid*, 8 (1979), pp. 379–383. The full text was published by S. M. Zaman, *Muʿjam al-safar* (Islamabad, 1988). For this paper however only al-Ḥasanī's edition and S. M. Zaman's PhD thesis were available to me.

books was in Fusṭāṭ, on the eastern side of the ʿAmr b. al-ʿĀṣ mosque, in the first lane of the lamp vendors by the wall of ʿAmr's house.[16] The Persian Ismaili missionary and poet Nāṣir-i Khusraw who visited Cairo and Fusṭāṭ in 439–441/1047–1050 does not mention the book market in his *Safar-nāma* but, when he describes the ʿAmr mosque, he says that outside it on its four sides there were bazars onto which the doors of the mosque opened. He comments that the courtyard of the mosque was continuously full of scholars and Qurʾan readers,[17] thus confirming that the area by the *jāmiʿ* was the obvious location for booksellers to conduct their trade.

It is indeed in the alleys of this *sūq* that we encounter Ibrāhīm b. Saʿīd al-Ḥabbāl (391–482/1000–1089), arguably the most dominant figure in the Egyptian book trade of the fifth/eleventh century. A Shāfiʿī, connected to the Ismaili elite as a descendant or *mawlā* of the eminent Fatimid jurist al-Qāḍī al-Nuʿmān's family, al-Ḥabbāl was rated as one of the greatest savants of his time having reportedly learned from some 300 *shaykhs*. Among his mentors was ʿAbd al-Ghanī b. Saʿīd whom he listened to in 407/1016. ʿAbd al-Ghanī (332–409/990–1018) occupies a special place at the very heart of the transmission of learning in fifth/eleventh century Egypt: it is indicated that he headed al-Ḥākim's *dār al-ʿilm* on an on-and-off basis and he is indeed one of the very few scholars, irrespective of *madhhab*, to be named as having been formally associated with that institution. ʿAbd al-Ghanī can therefore be regarded as a major figure who bridged the gap between two neighbouring religious, intellectual and cultural realms of Fusṭāṭ and Cairo, complementing as he did his role at the Fatimid centre of learning with his teaching in the ʿAmr mosque.[18]

---

16 Taqī al-Dīn Aḥmad al-Maqrīzī, *al-Mawāʿiẓ waʾl-iʿtibār fī dhikr al-khiṭaṭ waʾl-āthār* (henceforth *Khiṭaṭ*), ed. Ayman Fu'ad Sayyid (London, 2002), vol. 3, p. 338.

17 Nāṣir-i Khusraw, *Sefer Nameh Relation du Voyage de Nassiri Khosrau*, ed. Ch. Schefer (Amsterdam, 1970), p. 148.

18 On ʿAbd al-Ghanī see Delia Cortese, 'Voices of the silent majority: the transmission of Sunni learning in Fāṭimī Egypt', *Jerusalem Studies in Arabic and Islam*, 39 (2012), pp. 345–365 (pp. 353–356).

Many notable scholars named al-Ḥabbāl as one of their informants and several travelled to Cairo to receive their *ijāza* from him.[19] He is known as the author of several collections of *ḥadīth*s, but he is best remembered for *Wafayāt al-miṣriyyīn*.[20] His fame, and the influence that came with it, must have generated anxiety within the Fatimid establishment since al-Ḥabbāl became the target of a rare case of scholarly censorship under this regime. Towards the end of his life the Fatimid rulers forbade him from transmitting *ḥadīth*s, threatened him and controlled his movements. The reason for these restrictions is not known. However, his importance as a figure at the core of the international network of exchange of learning and practical circulation of knowledge during this period lies not only in his reputation but also as having been one of the greatest book wholesalers and bibliophiles of his time.

Information on al-Ḥabbāl's book trading activities comes to us from a reliable source in matters on books, the already mentioned Abū Ṭāhir al-Silafī, whose *Muʿjam al-safar* represents a detailed record of his interactions with all the scholars he met. These include Muḥammad b. Ṭāhir, a customer and friend of al-Ḥabbāl. Al-Silafī relates Ibn Ṭāhir's accounts of his first encounter with al-Ḥabbāl. Intending to meet him while in Cairo, Ibn Ṭāhir went to look for him in the *sūq* by the ʿAmr mosque and spotted him in a perfumer's shop. After approaching him, al-Ḥabbāl read two *ḥadīth*s to Ibn Ṭāhir who, from that moment on kept a daily appointment with the scholar at the ʿAmr mosque all the while he was in Cairo.[21] It is reported that al-Ḥabbāl's stock of

---

[19] See Muḥammad b. Aḥmad al-Dhahabī, *Siyar aʿlām al-nubalāʾ*, ed. Shuʿayb al-Arnaʾūṭ (Beirut, 1410/1990), vol. 18, pp. 496–501; ʿAbd al-Ḥayy b. Aḥmad b. al-ʿImād, *Shadharāt al-dhahab fī akhbār man dhahaba* (Beirut, 1350/1982), vol. 3, p. 366; Taqī al-Dīn Aḥmad al-Maqrīzī, *al-Muqaffā*, no. 147. See also Ibrāhīm b. Saʿīd al-Ḥabbāl, *Wafayāt al-miṣriyyīn*, ed. Maḥmūd al-Ḥaddād (Riyāḍ, 1408/1987), introduction.

[20] The work is an annotated list of obituary entries, which constitute arguably the most systematically compiled directory to date of fourth–fifth/tenth–eleventh century Sunni scholars active in Egypt, written by a contemporary.

[21] Shams al-Dīn Abū ʿAbd Allāh Muḥammad al-Dhahabī, *Taʾrīkh al-islām wa wafayāt al-mashāhīr waʾl-aʿlām*, ed. Bashshār ʿA. Marʿūf (Beirut, 1424/2003), vol. 10, no. 40, pp. 503–505.

volumes amounted to over 500 *qinṭār*s of books (ca. 22,500 kg.).[22] This, according to the testimony of one of his clients, Murshid b. Yaḥyā al-Madīnī, he sold on average at 100 *dīnār*s per 20 *qinṭārs*.[23] According to an anecdote, when some 500 *dīnār*s worth of al-Ḥabbāl's books were spoilt by rain, Ibn Ṭāhir advised him to build a special *khizāna* (repository) to contain his stock. He replied that if he built a *khizāna*, it would have to be of the size of the ʿAmr mosque so big was his collection.[24] Al-Ḥabbāl's reputation as a book expert made him a magnet for bibliophiles in many different ways: when Ibn Ṭāhir came into possession of 20 quires of old paper (*kāghaẓ ʿatīq*) he consulted al-Ḥabbāl who informed him that it was paper that had been brought to the vizier Ibn al-Furāt (d. 391/1001) from Samarqand.[25] Al-Ḥabbāl took advantage of his privileged access to books to hold story-telling sessions for which he became a model. It is reported that in 489/1095 in the ʿAmr mosque Ibrāhīm b. Sulaymān al-Bazzāz (d. after 489/1096) narrated the *Kitāb al-ʿAjā'ib* by al-Ḥasan b. Ismāʿīl al-Ḍarrāb, in the beautiful style of al-Ḥabbāl.[26] Finally, one of his students, the Mālikī jurist Ibn Ḥayḍara al-Kutubī (b. 447/1055) followed in his footsteps and became a renowned bookseller in Alexandria in his own right.[27]

Al-Ḥabbāl built his enviable stock thanks to the extensive network of scholars to which he belonged, through his travels particularly to Mecca where he had prolonged periods of residence, and via supply

---

22 One *qinṭār* in Egypt corresponded to 44.93 kg. Note however that the word used in the edited text could be a misreading of *qimṭār*, a case particularly used to store books. If that is the case the subsequent passage should be understood that the sale of books here went by case rather than by weight.

23 As reported by al-Silafī, who met him, in al-Dhahabī, *Siyar*, vol. 18, p. 499.

24 Al-Dhahabī, *Siyar*, vol. 18, pp. 496–501; Ibn al-ʿImād, *Shadharāt*, vol. 3, p. 366; al-Ḥabbāl, *Wafayāt*, pp. 9–10 of the introduction.

25 Al-Dhahabī, *Siyar*, vol. 18, p. 500.

26 Al-Maqrīzī, *al-Muqaffā*, no. 157. The reporting of daily life events capturing the modalities and occasions for the public dissemination of popular literature in medieval Egypt is rare. See Shoshan Boaz, 'On Popular Literature in Medieval Cairo', *Poetics Today*, 14, 2 (1993), pp. 349–365.

27 Al-Maqrīzī, *al-Muqaffā*, no. 2188. He was known to al-Silafī who wrote about him.

from the *warrāq* families of his time. In his *Wafayāt* he lists eight of them with whom he was in direct contact.[28] Above all, however, al-Ḥabbāl's bookselling enterprise must have been favoured by the massive amount of books that suddenly flooded the Cairo market following the plundering and consequent dispersal of the famous Fatimid caliphal libraries that took place in 460–461/1067–1069.[29] In those years, at the apex of the political, economic and social crisis that hit Egypt during al-Mustanṣir's reign, *al-shidda al-mustanṣiriyya*, angry unpaid soldiers and officials of the Fatimid army ransacked the palaces and the institutions of the regime, including the library in the outer section of the royal palace.[30] In the aftermath of this dispersal of books the book market became so saturated that dealers sent volumes to sell in Alexandria, the Maghrib and even as far as Baghdad.[31] A graphic account of how books found their way out of the palace into private hands relates to an episode involving Muḥammad b. Barakāt al-Naḥwī al-Ṣūfī (420–520/1029–1126), an eminent scholar who lived near the ʿAmr mosque and who was part of a distinguished network of traditionists. Caught up like most people in the famine that hit Egypt, Muḥammad b. Barakāt had the good fortune to be invited for lunch by the head of police in Fusṭāṭ, on the grounds that he was his children's tutor. On that occasion he took away two loaves of bread, one of which he sold to his mentor, Ibn Babshadh. He then sold the other loaf in the market of the lamps for 14 *dirhāms*. With the money,

---

[28] Al-Ḥabbāl, *Wafayāt,* nos 83 (Abu'l-Qāsim Jaʿfar b. Muḥammad b. al-Maristānī al-Warrāq (d. 387/997) who had two sons from whom al-Ḥabbāl heard *ḥadīths*), 142 (Abū ʿAbd Allāh Muḥammad b. al-Warrāq, d. 394/1003), 201 (Abu'l-ʿAbbās Aḥmad b. al-Ḥasan al-Dimashqī b. al-Warrāq, d. 414/1023), 219 (Abu'l-Ḥusayn Muḥammad al-Fārisī al-Warrāq, d. 416/1025), 226 (Abu'l-Qāsim ʿAbd Allāh b. Muḥammad b. Muḥammad b. al-Warrāq al-Kharqī, d. 416/1025), 324 (Abu'l-Ḥasan al-Ḥākimī al-Warrāq, d. 440/1048), 355 (Abu'l-Qāsim Ḥamza b. al-Qāsim b. ʿAfīf al-Warrāq, d. 447/1055), 375 (Abu'l-Ḥasan ʿAlī b. al-Baqā' al-Warrāq, d. 450/1058).

[29] The most detailed accounts on the vicissitudes visited on the Fatimid royal libraries can be found in the works of al-Maqrīzī, *Ittiʿāẓ al-ḥunafā'* and the *Khiṭaṭ*. For a summarised version of his accounts see Heinz Halm, *The Fāṭimids and their traditions of learning* (London, 1997), pp. 81, 91–93.

[30] See Walker, 'Libraries', p. 12.

[31] Ibid., p. 13.

Muḥammad b. Barakāt approached the attendants at the entrance hall of the palace library who sold him books at one for a *dirhām*. Back at his home, Muḥammad b. Barakāt locked the door and hid the books in a hole that he dug in the ceiling.[32] In a topsy-turvy world where bread was more valued than books by ordinary folk, the scholar here is shown to privilege feeding the intellect rather than the body but also having an eye for a long-term investment in durable goods.

In times of cash-flow crises books also entered the book market through being institutionally and formally released from the Fatimid royal libraries to serve as collateral in lieu of monetary payments owed by the regime to government officials. A Cairo Geniza document from the year 537/1142 records, for example, a minute written by al-Ẓāfir (still heir-apparent at this stage) instructing that a medical work by ʿAlī b.ʿĪsā held in the library of his father, the caliph al-Ḥāfiẓ, be issued to the amīr Fakhr al-Dīn Abū Manṣūr. Additional documentary evidence for this period shows that in these instances the books served as financial security rather than as objects of study.[33] There is evidence that books released or liberated from al-Ḥāfiẓ's and al-Ẓāfir's libraries eventually came to be part of the library collection of the Iraqi Shiʿi scholar, Ibn Ṭāwūs (d. 664/1266).[34]

Whether royal or private, no library was spared during those years of chaos and devastation. According to Muḥammad, the son of a Shāfiʿī traditionist and jurisconsult, Abu'l-ʿAbbās Aḥmad b. Ibrāhīm al-Rāzī (d. 491/1097–1098),[35] his family had moved from Cairo to Alexandria because of the *shidda*. While in Cairo, Aḥmad al-Rāzī had systematically collected extensive notes and books as a result of meeting with and attending the lessons of a great number of scholars. According to

---

32 Al-Maqrīzī, *al-Muqaffā*, no. 1903.

33 For the edition, translation and commentary on this document see Geoffrey Khan, *Arabic Legal and Administrative Documents in the Cambridge Genizah Collection* (Cambridge, 1993), document no. 116. For another significant example of books taken in lieu of salary in the Fatimid period see Walker, 'Libraries', p. 12.

34 Cf. Kohlberg, *A Medieval Muslim Scholar*, nos 149, 344 and 352.

35 On him see George Vajda, 'La Mašyaḫa d'Ibn al-Ḫaṭṭāb al-Rāzī. Contribution à l'histoire du Sunnisme en Égypte fāṭimide', in N. Cottard (ed.), *La transmission du savoir en Islam (VIIe-XVIIIe siécles)* (London, 1983), vol. 5, pp. 21–99 [originally published in *Bulletin d'Études Oriéntales*, 23 (1970)], p. 32, no. 1.

his son however, all this material was looted – together with the family belongings – during the family's transfer to Alexandria.[36] Eventually Abū Ṭāhir al-Silafī came to be part of Aḥmad al-Rāzī's scholarly legacy. Al-Rāzī's daughter, Turfa (d. 534/1139–1140), herself an authoritative transmitter of *ḥadīth*s, became al-Silafī's mother-in-law and one of his mentors.[37] He was also close to Muḥammad, whom he wrote about in his *Muʿjam*. In 512/1118 al-Silafī made a selection of his *mashyakha* titled *Intikhāb min mashyakhat al-Rāzī wa thabt masmūʿāti-hi.*[38] Also, al-Silafī expanded his collection of books by buying, upon his death, part of the library of the Alexandrian *muḥaddith* ʿAlī b. al-Musharraf al-Anmāṭī (d. 518/1124) who in turn had been one of Aḥmad al-Rāzī's students.[39]

Once settled in Egypt, al-Silafī only left Alexandria for two years between ca. 515/1121 and 517/1123 when he stayed in Cairo. It must have been during this period in the Fatimid capital that he met the booksellers Abū Ṭāhir al-Muhadhdhab and Abu'l-Ḥasan Aḥmad b. ʿAlī b. Ḥāshim al-Kutubī known as Ibn al-Mawqifī (464–539/1071–1144). The latter was born in Alexandria but traded books in Cairo where he died. Al-Silafī claimed to have bought many books from him and praised him as a memoriser of verses by Egyptian poets.[40] The availability of ready-made books did not prevent al-Silafī adding to his library by frequenting highly respected *warrāq*s whilst he was in Cairo. One was Abū Muḥammad al-Khuzāʿī al-Warrāq (d. 530/1135) whose

---

[36] Vajda, 'La Mašyaḫa', p.22

[37] On Turfa and other female savants in her family circle see Delia Cortese, 'Transmitting Sunni Learning in Fatimid Egypt: The Female Voices', in Farhad Daftary and Shainool Jiwa (ed.), *The Fatimid Caliphate, Diversity of Traditions* (London, 2018), pp. 175–176.

[38] Farhat Nasim Hashimi, *A critical edition of Kitāb al-Wajīz fī dhikr al-mujāz wa al-mujīz by Abū Ṭāhir Aḥmad b. Muḥammad b. Aḥmad b. Muḥammad al-Silafī, al-Iṣbahānī (d. 576/1181)* (PhD thesis, University of Glasgow, Glasgow, 1989), p. 19.

[39] Gary Leiser, *The restoration of Sunnism in Egypt: Madrasas and mudarrisūn 495–647/1101–1249* (PhD thesis, University of Pennsylvania, Philadelphia, 1976), p. 176. See also Halm, *The Fāṭimids*, p. 77.

[40] Al-Silafī mentions them in his *Muʿjam* in paragraphs 63 and 1278 according to Zaman, *Abū Ṭāhir Aḥmad b. Muḥammad al-Silafī*, p. 231. For the entry on Ibn al-Mawqifī see al-Silafī, *Muʿjam*, ed. al-Ḥasanī, no. 344.

calligraphy he admired.[41] Another was the more famous Aḥmad b. al-Hutaya al-Lakhmī al-Fāsī (478–561/1085–1165). A Mālikī Qur'an reciter and briefly a *qāḍī* in 533/1138 al-Fāsī lived near the Rāshida mosque in Fusṭāṭ. With his wife and his daughter, who became renowned for their ability to copy his hand, Ibn al-Hutaya established a cottage industry in book-copying on commission or for sale, specialising in works on *fiqh*, *ḥadīth* and literature. His family's reputation for quality rested on not selling the finished book if it contained just a single error in copying.[42]

Perhaps the most effective way for both booksellers and collectors to lay their hands on superior quality tomes, sometime even at a reasonable price, was through auctions (*nidā'*).[43] At the very end of Fatimid rule the figure who in many ways dominated the auction market and, allegedly, to some extent managed to manipulate it to his own advantage, was the famous late Fatimid-Ayyubid official al-Qāḍī al-Fāḍil (529–596/1135–1200), who along with his brother was arguably among the most voracious and demanding book collectors of the time. Credited with having spent almost a year's worth of his revenues to purchase for over 30,000 *dīnār*s a large *musḥaf* in Kufic script believed to have been one of the Uthmanic codices, al-Qāḍī al-Fāḍil was known to buy books on every subject from everywhere. It is reported that some twenty years before his death his library already contained some 120,000 books.[44] The amassing of this bibliographical fortune coincided with the capitulation of the Fatimid regime. On that occasion, Ṣalāḥ al-Dīn gave al-Qāḍī al-Fāḍil oversight of the dispersal of the royal library, a role that he happily took given his passion for books. Reportedly, in that capacity he picked the most valuable books for himself without paying or asking permission from Ṣalāḥ al-Dīn. An eyewitness to these events, ʿImād al-Dīn al-Kātib, noted that a

---

41 Ibid., no. 138.

42 Al-Maqrīzī, *al-Muqaffā*, no. 495. See also Ibn Khallikān, *Kitāb Wafayāt al-a'yān/Ibn Khallikān's Biographical Dictionary*, trans. W. MacGuckin De Slane (Beirut, 1842), vol. 1, pp. 151–152.

43 Johannes Pedersen, *The Arabic Book* (Princeton, 1984), p. 51.

44 Numbers here vary massively with some biographers indicating 70,000. Cf. Kohlberg, *A Medieval Muslim Scholar*, p. 73. Details of al-Qāḍī al-Fāḍil's book collecting can be found in al-Maqrīzī, *Khiṭaṭ*, vol. 4, part 2, pp. 463–465.

large quantity of these books were then sold. He himself admitted to buying books on this occasion but eventually not paying for them as Ṣalāḥ al-Dīn later gifted them to him. Eventually in 573/1177 he took to Syria eight camel-loads of books from this collection. Al-Qāḍī al-Fāḍil took part in the sale too. Apparently, having examined the collection, he selected the best works. Once he had done that, he then removed their bindings so that the books would look valueless and of poor quality. In that state, the volumes were thrown in baskets the contents of which he would then buy in bulk at very low bids.[45] However, it has been argued that, by acting in this way, al-Qāḍī al-Fāḍil did in fact his best to save as many precious royal books as he could. Indeed the practical handling of the dispersal of the Fatimid palace library had been delegated to the eunuch Qarāqūsh al-Asadī, deemed to know nothing about books.[46] Under his watch the sale, that took place twice a week every week, was open to ordinary buyers who, not unlike al-Qāḍī al-Fāḍil, damaged the copies they were interested in so that they could buy them at discounted prices.[47]

Besides sourcing books directly from the royal collection, al-Qāḍī al-Fāḍil actually bought books from the most prominent Cairo bookseller and broker of the day, Abu'l-Futūḥ Nāṣir b. Abi'l-Ḥasan ʿAlī b. Khalaf al-Anṣārī better known as Ibn Ṣūra (d. 607/1210). He was a Shāfiʿī who had been one of ʿAbd al-Rahman b. Salāma al-Quḍāʿī's students of *ḥadīths*. Brother of the more famous *qāḍī* for the Fatimids, Muḥammad b. Salāma al-Quḍāʿī (d. 454/1062), al-Quḍāʿī was associated with the *qāḍī al-qudāt* ʿAbd al-Malik b. ʿĪsā al-Mārānī. The poet and courtier Usāma b. Munqidh (d. 584/1188) dedicated verses to him thus indicating that the bookseller had already established his

[45] ʿAbd al-Raḥmān b. Ismāʿīl Abū Shāma, *Kitāb al-Rawḍatayn fī akhbār al-dawlatayn* (Cairo, 1287–1288/1870–1871), part 1, p. 200. See also Eche, *Les bibliothèques arabes*, p. 250, who doubts the truthfulness of the account of al-Fāḍil's book vandalism. For an alternative view on the fate of the Fatimid royal libraries following the advent of the Ayyubids see Fozia Bora, 'Did Ṣalāḥ al-Dīn Destroy the Fatimid Books? A Historiographical Enquiry', *Journal of the Royal Asiatic Society*, 25 (2015), pp. 21–39.

[46] About Qarāqūsh as a foolish figure of fun in Muslim medieval lore see Shoshan Boaz, 'On Popular Literature in Medieval Cairo', pp. 356–358.

[47] Abū Shāma, *Kitāb al-Rawḍatayn*, p. 268. See also Eddé, *Saladin*, pp. 69–70.

reputation during the late Fatimid period. Eventually he too, under the supervision of the amīr Muḥammad b. Muḥammad b. Banān, was charged with taking care of the sale of the books in the Fatimid royal library at the time of Ṣalāḥ al-Dīn.[48] As broker (*simsār*) Ibn Ṣūra's role was to find purchasers for other people's books. He used to conduct his business sitting in the vestibule of his house and offering books for sale to men of rank and learning. It was customary for them to assemble there every Sunday and Wednesday and remain there till the trading time was over. His business must have been profitable because his house was noted for its elegance. When it caught fire and burned down the event was commented on in poetry with some glee by one of Ibn Ṣūra's detractors. It is possible that it was Ibn Ṣūra's closeness to the Fatimid regime via his affiliation to the judiciary that caused Ibn al-Munajjim to brand him an infidel, worthy of hell in his verses.[49] An anecdote epitomises the level of al-Qāḍī al-Fāḍil's refinement as a book buyer and Ibn Ṣūra's reputation as a vendor trusted to meet the demands of the most discerning customer. According to Ibn Ṣūra, al-Qāḍī al-Fāḍil asked him to procure a copy of *al-Ḥamāsa*[50] for his son al-Ashraf Aḥmad to read. Knowing how exigent al-Qāḍī al-Fāḍil was, Ibn Ṣūra showed him thirty-five copies of the work from his stock. Al-Qāḍī al-Fāḍil went through each copy one by one recognising the hand of the copyist of each manuscript. Once he had seen them all, however, he concluded that none was of a quality suitable for his child and he ordered Ibn Ṣūra to procure him a copy for a *dīnār*.[51] But Ibn Ṣūra's status as the preeminent sixth/twelfth century Cairo bookseller was secured when, having gone to Alexandria especially for the occasion, he succeeded in adding to his stock possibly one of the most important private book collections of

---

48 Ayman Fu'ad Sayyid, *Ibn Ṭuwayr's Nuzhat al-muqlatayn fī akhbār al-dawlatayn* (Beirut, 1992), p. 127 and note 2.

49 Ibn Khallikān, *Wafayāt*, vol. 1, pp. 178–179.

50 A number of anthologies of Arabic poetry and epics under this name came to be part of the canon of classical Arabic literature. The lack of mention of the author here may indicate that the one referred to is the ultimate *Ḥamāsa* that is the one by Abū Tammām. On this genre see Charles Pellat, 'Ḥamāsa', *EI2*, vol. 3, pp. 110–112.

51 Al-Maqrīzī, *Khiṭaṭ*, vol. 4, part 2, p. 465.

his time, that of Abū Ṭāhir al-Silafī, which Ibn Ṣūra bought following his death.[52]

A survey of the book trade in Fatimid Egypt would be incomplete without mention of the role that the Jews played in that market. Evidence gathered from the Cairo Geniza documents shows that it was typical of physicians to dedicate themselves to this commerce[53] and, more generally, wholesalers included trading in books among a diverse array of products they dealt with, such as flax, silk, olive oil, spices and metals. It is notable that the marketability of a book was mostly based on its intellectual value rather than its value as an object, that is, because of its physical qualities and aesthetic characteristics. Within the context of a small Jewish community, comprising a small pool of readers, the activities surrounding book production and exchange were concentrated in the hands of a closely-knit intellectual elite among the merchant and civil servant classes.[54] There is also reason to believe that the Coptic scholarly elites too had their own networks through which books changed hands through family legacy, copying and trading.

Conclusion

In 2016 Konrad Hirschler published the catalogue of Ashrafiyya library in Damascus.[55] Written in the 670s/1270s this is the earliest-known

---

[52] Ibn Khallikān, *Wafayāt*, vol. 1, pp. 178–179. On Ibn Ṣūra see also Zakī al-Dīn Abū Aḥmad al-Mundhirī, *al-Takmila li-wafayāt al-naqala*, ed. Bashshār ʿA. Maʿrūf (Najaf, 1401/1981), vol. 3, pp. 323–324.

[53] Goitein, *A Mediterranean Society*, vol. 1, pp. 154, 379. For an example of a famous Jewish physician in the Fatimid period who became renowned for his book collecting see Walker, 'Libraries', p. 16.

[54] I am very grateful to Dr Miriam Frenkel for sharing with me the advance copy of her article on the subject 'Book lists from the Cairo Genizah: a window on the production of texts in the middle ages', *Bulletin of the School of Oriental and African Studies*, 80 (2017), pp. 233–252. On book production and the circulation of books among Jews in Medieval Egypt see also Judith Olszowy-Schlanger, 'Cheap Books in Medieval Egypt: Rotuli from the Cairo Geniza', *Intellectual History of the Islamicate World*, 4 (2016), pp. 82–101.

[55] Konrad Hirschler, *Medieval Damascus: Plurality and Diversity in an Arabic Library. The Ashrafiyya Library Catalogue* (Edinburgh, 2016).

extant purposely composed Arabic medieval library catalogue and a rare pre-Ottoman document relating to books. In retracing the steps that led to the formation of this library which came about through the merging of a number of collections, Hirschler identified the presence of books that had previously belonged to al-Ashraf Aḥmad. This is the same person encountered above for whom his father, al-Qāḍī al-Fāḍil, would only buy the best books available in the market. Having brought him up with such a refined taste in books, al-Qāḍī al-Fāḍil eventually bequeathed to him his own collection.[56] Besides narrative accounts, evidence from the Ashrafiyya library catalogue shows that the provenance of al-Ashraf Aḥmad's collection indeed goes right back to the Fatimids, featuring as it does many books that reflect the intellectual life of the Fatimid court.[57] While no Ismaili works are recorded, the Ashrafiyya shows that books that were in circulation in Fatimid Egypt found their way to Syria. Beside the endowment formula, the details of other practical modalities of book circulation that caused some of these volumes to resurface in another library, on another continent, a century later are not known.

However, another *de facto* library catalogue testifying to the world of Muslim bibliophiles in the seventh/thirteenth century, is the one complied by Etan Kohlberg thanks to his analysis of Ibn Ṭāwūs's works. The result is a systematic and annotated reconstruction of a considerable list of books in Ibn Ṭāwūs' personal library. Unlike al-Ashraf Aḥmad, he was an Iraqi Twelver Shiʿi scholar whose books in some cases were explicitly said to have come from the Fatimid royal libraries. Additionally, unlike the Ashrafiyya, Ibn Ṭāwūs' ownership of Ismaili or Ismaili-related works is implied through his selection of quotations from a work by the Fatimid jurist al-Qāḍī al-Nuʿmān and from the epistle on astrology of the Ikhwān al-Ṣafāʾ.[58]

---

[56] Besides building his private collection, al-Qāḍī al-Fāḍil had also furnished with books the *madrasa* carrying his name that he founded in 580/1184–1185. See Walker, 'Libraries', p. 13. This library was however dispersed during the famine of 694/1295 when students sold the books to procure food. Cf. Eddé, *Saladin*, p. 442.

[57] See Hirschler, *Medieval Damascus*, pp. 32–35.

[58] Kohlberg, *A Medieval Muslim Scholar at Work*. The title of the work by al-Nuʿmān is not indicated by Ibn Ṭāwūs but its extracts have been identified as belonging to *al-Majālis wa'l-musāyarāt*. Cf. nos. 335 and 193 for the Ikhwān. Note that Ibn Ṭāwūs attributes the epistles to a single author.

Beyond the intricate, varied and personal vicissitudes that brought about the formation of the two library collections discussed above, this paper is illustrative of some mechanisms through which books changed hands, having looked at the role that booksellers played in facilitating the movement of books in fifth–sixth/eleventh–twelfth centuries in Fatimid Egypt and beyond. Through the activities of these dealers we can appreciate how it might have been possible that books that once belonged to the Fatimid court or their institutions of learning might have ended up in the course of time, thanks in part to booksellers in Cairo and Alexandria, in the hands of prominent scholars such as Abū Ṭāhir al-Silafī; how some copies of books that, thanks to Aḥmad al-Rāzī had 'transited' through Egypt came to rest on al-Silafī's bookshelves; how, in turn, parts of the latter's collection might have resurfaced in the house of Ibn Ṭāwūs or, in the case of al-Qāḍī al-Fāḍil – and later his son, in their possession through the brokerage of Ibn Ṣūra.

These book transfer mechanisms however needed agency in order to be activated as the figure of the *kutubī* did not emerge in a vacuum. Two major events can be identified as having brought about the emergence of a large-scale book market in Fatimid Egypt: one was the *shidda al-mustanṣiriyya*, a crisis that caused the first major movement of books from the royal and other major private libraries into the marketplace. The royal libraries were eventually re-filled only to be dispersed once and for all when the Fatimid regime collapsed at the hand of the Ayyubids. The vicissitudes of books in Egypt in this period tell us how, ultimately, intellectual interactions depended on personal contacts mediated through the exchange of books; on human beings of various ranks and religious affiliations encountering one another irrespective of personal conviction and despite, or because of, the major upheavals that affected their lives.

The anecdotes reported that shed light on the itinerant life of books in medieval Egypt can be hagiographical in that they often contain exaggerations intended to reflect positively on the personalities involved. Notwithstanding this limitation, these accounts are remarkable in providing us with valuable information on the *modus operandi* of booksellers in the Fatimid period. Whether sold by weight, case or camel load, or simply by the copy as in the example given above of Ibn Ṣūra, the sale and purchase of books by and large knew no boundaries, whether geographical, intellectual or religious. With the demise of the Fatimids, however, and the restoration of Sunni Islam as the official religious denomination endorsed by the Ayyubid regime, books that were Twelver Shiʿi and/or Ismaili in content are understood to have been destroyed. The purge nevertheless did not prevent the survival of some Shiʿi and even Ismaili works which resurfaced decades later in libraries such as, for example, those of Ibn Ṭāwūs and the Ashrafiyya.[59]

For all its triumphs and upheavals, it was ultimately the cultural, religious and economic fluidity that characterised Egypt under the Fatimids that transformed that region from a cultural backwater into a centre of intellectual activity serving as a launch pad for books to boldly go where no volumes had gone before.

59 Hirschler, *Medieval Damascus*, pp. 123–125.

17

On the Cusp of 'Islamic' and 'Hindu' Worldviews? The *Ginān* Literature and the Dialectics of Self and Other

*Wafi A. Momin**
(The Institute of Ismaili Studies)

Framing the Problem

Scholars have long sought to make sense of the multi-layered character of the Satpanth tradition. They have examined such aspects as the sacred vision it propounded, the contours of its rich and intricate worldview, the rituals and social practices its followers observed, the varied sources of inspiration behind its evolution, and the factors that have conditioned its growth over time. But whatever aspect they may have chosen to examine, and whatever sources they may have drawn upon in their quest, hardly any scholar has failed to bring into sharp relief the multivalent nature of its religious complexion. This complexion is further envisaged to have been largely shaped by the ideas and practices that are now, in a different setting, readily identified with the reified categories of 'Islam' and 'Hinduism'.[1] To put it differently, the

* This paper is based on a section of my doctoral dissertation. I am grateful to Aziz Esmail, Wendy Doniger and Muzaffar Alam for their perceptive feedback on an earlier incarnation of the paper appearing in the dissertation. I am also grateful to Qudsia Shah and Farouk Mitha for reading an earlier draft of the paper and providing valuable comments.

[1] This point is illustrated by the following remarks of Françoise Mallison, which were made in connection with the method of preaching adopted by the agents of the Satpanth mission, as well as about the *ginān*s, a major literary output of the tradition (see further on): 'The utilization of Hinduism is not limited to points of doctrine but

tradition has now become firmly associated, both in scholarly discourse and popular imagination, with a paradigmatic case of how multiple strands of thought creatively interact and coalesce to form a kind of composite structure, defying the confines of narrowly constituted religious identities.

It is this facet of the legacy of Satpanth that has drawn much public attention and lately caught the interest of the newspapers in India. For instance, amidst the rising wave of communalism that India has experienced in recent times, the tradition (alongside others depicting similar traits) has served as a timely reminder of the country's primordial ethos of tolerance and co-existence – a place where numerous faiths have flourished and lived together in harmony for centuries. In particular, observers have turned to the case of what is known as the Imāmshāhī branch of the larger, organic Satpanth – widely regarded as an offshoot of the Indian Nizārī Ismaili tradition – to point up the evils of communal politics in India, along with the attendant alienation and marginalisation of minority groups, notably Muslims. The shrine of the Satpanthī saint, Imām Shāh, at Pirana (a major centre of the Imāmshāhīs near Ahmedabad in Gujarat), frequented by a large number of Muslim and Hindu devotees, has long symbolised the image of inter-religious harmony – a testament (in popular perception) of Imām Shāh's teachings, amalgamating the best of what the two religions had to offer.[2] Moreover, the shrine's seemingly composite legacy has at times been invoked to infuse an optimistic spirit, for instance, against the backdrop of communal riots of 2002 in Gujarat, as well as to reveal how the polarisation of religious groups in the aftermath of the riots has witnessed the shared space of the shrine

includes the borrowing of metaphors, literary forms and all the ritual and cultural practices, to such an extent that the content of the *ginān* becomes a witness of contemporary Hindu practices and beliefs'; see her 'Hinduism as Seen by the Nizārī Ismā'īlī Missionaries of Western India: The Evidence of the Ginān', in Günther-Dietz Sontheimer and Hermann Kulke (ed.), *Hinduism Reconsidered* (rev. ed., New Delhi, 1997), p. 192.

[2] See, for example, 'In Incredible India, many faiths coexist', *Times of India* (Ahmedabad edition), September 19, 2010, p. 16; and 'Ahmedabad's sufi shrine Pirana shows unique confluence of faith', *Daily News & Analysis*, March 4, 2011.

being subjected to an overriding of what are held to be Islamic traces by similarly regarded Hindu symbols. This has simply turned the space into what is often dubbed a 'mini Ayodhya', evoking one of the painful chapters of Hindu-Muslim conflict in modern India.[3]

The direct ramifications of such an image of the multivalent character of Satpanth are nowhere more evident than in what has been made of the exact contours of its religious identity. With its roots going far back in history, the image has sharply divided scholarly opinion in recent times, producing at least two mutually incompatible viewpoints. The first, and a far more entrenched one, has long envisaged Satpanth as a local, Indic expression of what is known as the Nizārī branch of Ismaili tradition, which (as per this viewpoint) evolved on the Indian subcontinent over the course of many centuries through the work of Nizārī missionaries. By this token, the supposedly 'Hindu' symbols and ideas reflected in the literary and theological experience of the tradition and ritual life of the community, in the final analysis, were but an ingenious means of attracting Hindus to the Ismaili dispensation in the Indian context.[4]

Countering this long-held position, another school of thought has lately crystallised around the second viewpoint which sees the forthright identification of Satpanth with the Ismaili tradition as a more recent demarcation. As per this view, the demarcation was mainly

---

[3] Dominique-Sila Khan, 'Liminality and Legality: A Contemporary Debate among the Imamshahis of Gujarat', in Imtiaz Ahmad and Helmut Reifeld (ed.), *Lived Islam in South Asia: Adaptation, Accommodation and Conflict* (New Delhi, 2004), pp. 209–232; and Dionne Bunsha, *Scarred: Experiments with Violence in Gujarat* (New Delhi, 2006), pp. 262–266.

[4] There is a long list of works espousing this viewpoint. Among the earlier influential studies, see especially Syed Mujtaba Ali, *The Origin of the Khojāhs and their Religious Life Today* (Bonn, 1936); and W. Ivanow, 'Satpanth', in his *Collectanea* (Leiden, 1948), pp. 1–54. The viewpoint was further elaborated by a number of subsequent studies. For its more nuanced articulation in some recent works, see Ali S. Asani, 'From Satpanthi to Ismaili Muslim: The Articulation of Ismaili Khoja Identity in South Asia', in Farhad Daftary (ed.), *A Modern History of the Ismailis: Continuity and Change in a Muslim Community* (London, 2011), pp. 95–128; and Shafique N. Virani, '*Taqiyya* and Identity in a South Asian Community', *The Journal of Asian Studies*, 70 (2011), pp. 99–139.

imposed by the colonial legal apparatus in response to a series of legal disputes that surfaced among the Khojas of Bombay (forming one of the clusters among the followers of Satpanth) around the mid-nineteenth century. Following the logic of this thesis, it was more precisely the well-known Aga Khan Case of 1866 which almost operated like the culprit in what would amount to a plot for redefining the religious identity of the Khojas along different lines. It further holds that so far-reaching were the consequences of the lawsuit that it reshaped the self-image of the Khojas in how henceforth they understood their religious identity as 'Ismaili', an interpretation that was to be sealed by the aforementioned, well-entrenched trend of Satpanth historiography. The logical culmination point of the lawsuit was thus a gradual displacement of multivalent motifs in Satpanth beliefs and practices with a rigid trend of Islamisation during the late nineteenth and the early twentieth century.[5]

At a deeper level what these two positions have sought to unravel is how the putative 'Islamic' and 'Hindu' symbols have interacted in the life of Satpanth, formulating in turn a particular paradigm. A paradigm that represented, from one standpoint, simply an encoded form of Nizārī Ismaili doctrine, while, from the other, little more than one of the many overlapping religious cults in early modern India, which shared popular modes of devotion centred around charismatic figures, and embraced the then prevalent social ideology against the 'orthodoxies' associated with Islam and Hinduism.

In fostering such portrayals of Satpanth, scholars have frequently (if not exclusively) relied upon the corpus collectively known as the *ginān* literature. The *ginān*s are primarily a body of sacred lyrics (together with some prose works), composed in a variety of poetic forms, and in languages as diverse as Gujarati, Hindi, Sindhi and Punjabi. Among the Satpanthī communities they are regarded as literary masterpieces, embodying the teachings of individuals who are now revered in the tradition as *pīr*s and *sayyid*s, the charismatic figures

---

[5] See, in particular, Amrita Shodhan, *A Question of Community: Religious Groups and Colonial Law* (Calcutta, 2001); Teena Purohit, *The Aga Khan Case: Religion and Identity in Colonial India* (Cambridge, MA, 2012); and Iqbal Akhtar, *The Khōjā of Tanzania: Discontinuities of a Postcolonial Religious Identity* (Leiden and Boston, 2016).

believed to have been active as proselytisers in India for a long time. Indeed, it is in the *ginān* literature that we find the earliest expression of the cherished ideals that have gone into the making of the Satpanth *Weltanschauung*.[6] Given their salient role in the religious life of the Satpanthī communities, *ginān*s have been the focus of a number of studies seeking to answer some of the vital questions pertaining to the historical evolution of the tradition.[7]

This paper seeks to problematise the interplay between what are readily postulated as 'Islamic' and 'Hindu' motifs in the formation of the ideals of Satpanth, as seen through the lens of the *ginān*s. By looking at some specific examples from the *ginān* literature, I will demonstrate the complexity behind the aforementioned oversimplification, which portrays the interplay largely in terms of a process that seamlessly amalgamated elements from both the traditions either to facilitate a proselytising project, or to ingeniously formulate a structure that could not be easily identified with a narrowly construed religious identity. I will argue on the contrary that in fact one observes disparate planes of interaction between the ideas and cosmologies associated with the two religions operative on various levels in the corpus. They allow us to observe the manner in which different voices in the *ginān*s understood and negotiated their identity vis-à-vis the categories 'Muslim' and 'Hindu'. It is moreover within these planes that we see the collective self of the tradition being articulated and etched against the backdrop of specific dialectics between self and other. All of these modes of interaction, in short, present a far from unified picture of the encounter, one that can be said to be characteristic of the entire corpus, much less the overall tradition. But before discussing the *ginān*s, it is important to say a few words about the perspective that informs

---

[6] *Sat-panth* literally means the 'True Path'. In the *ginān*s, the idea is also invoked by other (less frequently employed) terms, like *sat-dharam* ('True Religion').

[7] For a discussion of various features of the *ginān*s, see Ali S. Asani, 'The Ginān Literature of the Ismailis of Indo-Pakistan: Its Origins, Characteristics and Themes', in Diana L. Eck and Françoise Mallison (ed.), *Devotion Divine: Bhakti Traditions from the Regions of India* (Groningen and Paris, 1991), pp. 1–18; and Christopher Shackle and Zawahir Moir, *Ismaili Hymns from South Asia: An Introduction to the Ginans* (Richmond, 2000). For a literary appreciation of the compositions, see Aziz Esmail, *A Scent of Sandalwood: Indo-Ismaili Religious Lyrics (Ginans)* (Richmond, 2002).

the approach adopted here towards the compositions in utilising them for the stated purpose of this paper.

Formulating a Perspective

The kind of eclectic vision invariably held to be borne out by the *ginān*s, along with its implications for the identity formation process of the communities that supposedly participated in this vision, has previously been assessed from diverse viewpoints. For example, some scholars have invoked the concept of 'syncretism' in characterising the phenomenon in question, albeit presenting it in a more positive light, rather than as a random amalgamation of disparate elements.[8] Others have questioned or tended to do away with the problematic terminology explaining the phenomenon (including syncretism), and have proposed more neutral formulations, like 'acculturation', 'cultural adaptation' etc., paying closer attention to larger religio-cultural forces at work.[9] Still others have not hesitated to put forward an overarching theoretical proposition, derived from models used elsewhere, to describe groups as having (at times too readily assumed) 'indeterminate' identities. A conceptual category that has lately found much currency in this connection is that of 'liminality', often employed to describe the religious experience of Indian Nizārī Ismailis.[10]

---

[8] Tazim Kassam illustrates the concept through the figure-ground representation of a goblet and two faces to show how diverse elements from Hindu and Muslim traditions were brought together in a *ginān*, *Brahma Prakāsh*, postulated as an ingenious approach adopted for conversion by Nizārī Ismaili preachers in India; see her 'Syncretism on the Model of the Figure-Ground: A Study of *Pīr* Shams' Brahma Prakāśa', in Katherine Young (ed.), *Hermeneutical Paths to the Sacred Worlds of India: Essays in Honour of Robert W. Stevenson* (Atlanta, 1994), pp. 231–242.

[9] Dominique-Sila Khan, *Conversions and Shifting Identities: Ramdev Pir and the Ismailis in Rajasthan* (New Delhi, 1997), pp. 22–25 *passim*. Ali Asani looks at the phenomenon and the evolution of the tradition within 'three overlapping cultural contexts' – Ismaili, Indo-Muslim and Indic; see his *Ecstasy and Enlightenment: The Ismaili Devotional Literature of South Asia* (London, 2002), pp. 3–13. See also Purohit, *The Aga Khan Case*, pp. 9–15, 59–63.

[10] See Dominique-Sila Khan, *Crossing the Threshold: Understanding Religious Identities in South Asia* (London and New York, 2004), pp. 44–50 *passim*.

Indeed, such attempts to question and rethink the conceptual frames deployed to problematise the phenomenon are important and draw attention to many a critical issue that one ought to bear in mind in studying a multi-layered tradition like Satpanth. But a major problem with them is the manner in which they are applied in totality to, and taken as a representative image of, the range of expressions ensuing out of the historical experience of the tradition. For instance, in applying the idea of liminality to the tradition – understood as a threshold position serving as a gateway to multiple worlds – its proponents often overlook the fact that such a conceptual frame necessarily assumes a position halfway between stable, unchanging structures – in this case, the doctrinal systems associated with Hindu and Muslim traditions. When employed for traditions like Satpanth and the processes through which they evolved, the idea is defeated by an inherent logic which seeks to place it in a largely premodern setting, associated with what is seen as a world of fluid religious identities, and contrasted with a colonial/post-colonial epistemic order characterised as representing rigid identities. For what is ignored here is that the presumed stable structure outside the threshold space itself represents a far from fixed condition, in so far as it is formed by different agencies acting within their own set of discursive spaces. The notion of liminality, in short, disregards the fact that the Satpanth tradition (like others) was a product of a long process of negotiation during which certain forms of identity might well have sat (or were believed to have existed) outside the condition of a threshold, even if the logic of the notion (however problematic) were to be accepted. In other words, such forms of identity have constantly been in the making – at best, what has changed is the vantage point whence to assess and understand them.[11]

[11] In presenting this critique, I do not disregard the analytical value of the concept of liminality which has been fruitfully applied by Victor Turner and others in the study of a variety of transition forms, particularly rites of passage; see, for example, Victor Turner, *The Ritual Process: Structure and Anti-Structure* (Ithaca, NY, 1977). What I am simply arguing is that, as a conceptual category, it has very limited relevance (if any) for understanding the experience of the Satpanth tradition for the reasons just stated.

This brings us to a connected issue of how the *ginān*s have been approached by scholars in deducing an image of Satpanth sacrality in premodern times. It is above all symptomatic of an overarching tendency in Satpanth scholarship to seamlessly project the entire spectrum of (roughly) the pre-1840s period (i.e. before the seat of the Nizārī imamate moved to India) as constituting a monolithic temporal space. This space is furthermore seen as reflective of an invariant set of dispositions with respect to the overall character of the tradition. To put it differently, scholars have frequently depicted this premodern Satpanth manifestation as a kind of hybrid of various beliefs that remained unchanged until the rupture following the so-called direct intervention of the Ismaili imams once they settled in India. Moreover, the kernel of this manifestation is believed to have consisted solely in and, therefore, is to be faithfully reconstructed on the basis of, a single literary tradition, namely the *ginān*s, considered to be the product par excellence of the putative Nizārī Ismaili preaching. This attitude and approach take us far away from a much needed differentiated view of the premodern space in the history of Satpanth, a long period that saw many shifts as the tradition encountered many an internal and external challenge, anchored on the issues of authority, legitimacy, and in some cases survival and assimilation, while responding to the exigencies of its immediate and larger socio-political setting.

One finds this tendency amply evident in how the particular dialectics in individual *ginān*s (along with their use of specific terminology and narrative strategy) are taken to form a uniform discourse, presumed to operate coherently throughout the corpus. An apt example of this attitude may be seen in a recent work by Teena Purohit on the Aga Khan Case of 1866 who offers an analysis of the *Das Avatār*, a *ginān* recounting the periodic manifestation of Viṣṇu in bodily form (see the next section) which was a point of discussion and contestation during the trial proceedings. In offering a critique of how Justice Arnould, the presiding judge, viewed (a certain version of) the *Das Avatār* in the lawsuit as an 'Ismaili conversion text', Purohit resorts to deploying a critical reading of the longer version (in particular its tenth section), one that is attributed to Imām Shāh, ignoring completely the question of what prompted Arnould to examine the *Das Avatār* in the first place, as well as the fact that the plaintiffs had sought to manipulate its true character during the proceedings. This question was tied to perhaps the most important issue in the lawsuit reflective of the respective positions held by the plaintiffs and defendants, namely whether the Khojas were Sunni or Shiʿi converts to Islam. Arnould decided this question through an exhaustive enquiry into the history and practices of the Khojas, including what appears to Purohit to be a simplified and problematic reading of the *Das Avatār*, but arguably not of a version (the one ascribed to Imām Shāh) that she juxtaposes against Arnould's reading, but of a different one (attributed to Sadardīn) that configures its own dialectic of the theme. Simply put, the kind of details that the longer version provides and the narrative it weaves together out of them, so vital for the framework Purohit constructs in presenting her arguments, are conspicuously absent in the much shorter, condensed version that Arnould evidently worked with.[12]

In presenting an assessment of the *ginān*s – of how ideas and symbols from many different sources interact in their worldview – I will steer clear of suggesting any new construct that may be applied seamlessly to the corpus as a whole, which may then help us to understand the overall socio-religious evolution of the communities concerned. Instead, I propose to draw attention to a relationship between two notions that mutually inform each other and operate at different levels in the corpus, allowing the exploration of some key variations in *ginān*ic thought overall and beyond. This is the discursive association between the notion of 'identity', a set of markers/symbols used by individuals or social groups to signify the terms of sameness and difference, and that of 'boundaries', the limits set by these agents to ensure the fostering of their identity, and to mark them off from others.[13]

Approaching the *ginān*s and the broader history of Satpanth from the viewpoint of an interaction between these two notions – 'identity' and 'boundary making' – allows us to observe that what is invariably

---

[12] Purohit, *The Aga Khan Case*. There are other important issues pertaining to methodological aspects of approaching the *ginān*s, such as their periodisation, the extent to which their discourses may be taken as the lived reality of the Satpanth communities, which are not discussed here. For a discussion of these issues, see Wafi Momin, *The Formation of the Satpanth Ismaili Tradition in South Asia* (PhD dissertation, The University of Chicago, 2016), especially, pp. 48–52, 113–130.

[13] For some of these observations, I draw upon Fredrik Barth, 'Boundaries and Connections', in Anthony P. Cohen (ed.), *Signifying Identities: Anthropological Perspectives on Boundaries and Contested Values* (London, 2000), pp. 17–36.

posited as the Hindu-Muslim amalgamative character of the tradition is not a stable norm, but a condition constantly in flux, seemingly responding to the evolving circumstances of the groups concerned whereby a new set of boundaries was constantly being forged in response to a given form of identity privileged and fostered by particular agencies at specific times. Moreover, it is important to make a distinction between this process as taking place in the worldview of the *ginān*s, and the one outside it in the actual experience of the communities, for the two were not necessarily mirror images of one another. The *ginān*s at best serve as one of the windows through which this process may be observed. Paying attention to an interaction between these two notions further allows one to focus on particular voices (wherever they are retrievable) and the conditions under which a certain kind of premium was attached to foster a particular facet of an identity. Finally, when viewed from this standpoint, no given form of identity necessarily remains liminal, for the structures against which their liminal state is construed are themselves not stable blocs immune to change – they too are prone to transformations through the same process.

Examining the *Ginān* Archive

Turning to the archive of the *ginān*s, the most familiar and somewhat frequently encountered plane of interaction between what is postulated as the 'Islamic' and 'Hindu' worldviews is one where the compositions seek to present a harmonious vision. So pervasive is this mode of interaction that it has left an indelible imprint on the way the *ginān* literature is commonly envisaged, viz., as sitting on an intermediary terrain between the two religious traditions, with the kind of reductive depiction of Satpanth religiosity as outlined in the beginning of the paper. This form of interaction is more often found in those *ginān*s which deal with cosmo-eschatological and soteriological themes. However, what is important to bear in mind is that even while making use of such wide-ranging ideas from multiple sources as they do, the *ginān*s in question hardly circumscribe them under the Islamic/Muslim or Hindu typology, or for that matter any other strict classificatory categories.

Even a passing glance at the manifold discourses in the *ginān*s would make it plain that cosmo-eschatological and soteriological imaginings constitute a persistent concern which often takes the form of stories about the creation. The vision of such imaginings is, however, not explained in a systematic fashion in any specific set of *ginān*s. Rather, it is complex and multi-layered, enunciated throughout the corpus – a principle that also applies to other discourses in the compositions. There are nonetheless some *ginān*s which dwell exclusively (or predominantly) on such matters, and to illustrate the aforementioned mode of interaction, I will examine here the discourse of one such *ginān*, namely the *Muman Citaveṇī*.[14]

In the *Muman Citaveṇī*, as in many other *ginān*s, the moment of primeval creation is first contrasted with an earlier condition when there was nothing save the Godhead, called here Sāmījī, whose identity is gradually unfolded using different epithets.[15] Out of nothingness, Sāmījī first produced a cosmic egg from his mouth, nurtured it for some time, and then brought forth from it seven levels of earth and ten heavens.[16] From the very onset, the text constantly refers to the twin forces of 'affection' (*het*) and 'pride' (*ahaṁkār*), revealing their saliency in the cosmogonic process, as well as that of 'divine play' (*līlā*/*ramat*), often postulated as the reason why creation happened in the first place. Still a 'formless being' (*nirākār*) or 'eternal light' (*nūr*) – the text frequently alternates these names with others too, such as the 'designer/maker' (*sirajanahār*/*kiratār*) and the 'unstained one' (*niraṁjan*) – the Lord thereafter fashioned four bodies from his light, in addition to forming his own body. From his forehead he created Muhammad,

---

[14] Composed in Gujarati, the *ginān* is conventionally attributed to Pīr Sadardīn. For a detailed analysis of the text, see Momin, *The Formation of the Satpanth Ismaili Tradition*, pp. 132–143 *passim*. References to manuscripts of the *ginān*s housed at the Institute of Ismaili Studies (London) will be provided by 'KH' followed by the manuscript number, and to those housed at Harvard will follow the system of its catalogue, preceded by the prefix 'HC'. For the Harvard manuscripts, see Ali S. Asani, *The Harvard Collection of Ismaili Literature in Indic Languages: A Descriptive Catalog and Finding Aid* (Boston, 1992). The collection at the Institute of Ismaili Studies is currently undergoing a systematic cataloguing.

[15] Sāmī (from the Sanskrit *svāmī*) and Sāheb (from the Arabic *ṣāḥib*) are two of the most frequently used epithets for the Godhead in the *ginān* literature.

[16] *Muman Citaveṇī*, vv. 1–7 (KH 868, ff. 145r–146r); for the printed version, see Pīr Sadaradīn, *To Munīvarabhāi Moṭī yāne Muman Cītaveṇī* (3rd ed., Muṁbai, 1957), pp. 1–2.

from his chest Fāṭima, from his eyes Ḥasan and Ḥusayn, while he himself manifested as ʿAlī. He then created from these luminaries the 'Pole Star' (*qutb tāro*), but no sooner had he raised the star into heaven than the latter began to tremble from its brightness. Taking notice of it, the Lord had the name 'Yā ʿAlī' ('O ʿAlī') written on its four corners and so made it stable. The star, in this way, became the source of light in the universe well before the sun and the moon were created.[17]

The text then takes us through a process of perpetual creative activity on a cosmic scale, spread over hundreds of *yugas* ('cosmic epochs'), with long periods of inaction too, in which numerous other beings and constituent elements of the universe were formed. First, the Lord created the Goddess Śaktī (alternatively referred to as Māyā/Sarasvatī), Brahmā (from the light of Muhammad), Viṣṇu (a manifestation of the Godhead himself) and Mahesar (Maheśvara/Śiva), who is also depicted as Ādam. Ḥawwā' (Eve) was later created from the left part of Ādam's body (*ḍābā aṁg*), and the human race thus came from them. Then followed the four Vedas, the angels, the world (*saṁsār*), living creatures (*jīvs*) – their classification into a fourfold scheme, namely *svedaja* ('sweat-born'), *jarāyuja* ('viviparous'), *aṇḍaja* ('oviparous') and *udbhija* ('sprouting') – and, to account for their deeds, heaven and hell, as well as the sun, the moon, stars, oceans, rivers, vegetation etc.[18] Throughout this process of creation, we constantly witness the divine play at work; for instance, Viṣṇu once makes Śaktī believe that she herself is the proud creator of everything in the universe, the supreme deity, but the text alludes to the notion that human life needs to release itself from the illusion (*māyā*) created by her.[19]

The creative agency of the Godhead (whose identity is unequivocally revealed as Viṣṇu) is clearly brought to the fore in the text, and although he often assures Brahmā that the world order was formed from his (Brahmā's) light, it is Viṣṇu who serves as the *raison d'être* of the cosmos, Brahmā's role in the cosmogonic evolution being subsidiary at best. We also find Brahmā time and again admitting his inability

---

[17] Ibid., vv. 8–13 (KH 868, ff. 146r–147r); printed text, pp. 2–3.

[18] Ibid., esp. vv. 13–49, 112–113, 292–298, 322–329 (KH 868, ff. 147r–152r, 161r–161v, 186v–187v, 191r–192v); printed text, pp. 3–8, 17, 42–43, 47–48.

[19] See, for example, ibid., vv. 107–116 (KH 868, ff. 160v–162r); printed text, pp. 16–17.

to know the secrets of the creation, harbouring doubts and relying frequently on Viṣṇu for comprehending the divine purpose in bringing forth the cosmic order, as well as his ignorance of the Vedas (with which he is entrusted from the onset of their production), whose knowledge Viṣṇu imparts to him.[20]

The most striking feature of the text is the formulation of one-to-one equivalence between the Hindu deities and the Muslim luminaries, popularly known as the 'Five Pure Ones' (*panjtan-i pāk*). Thus, Viṣṇu is equated with ʿAlī, Brahmā with Muhammad, Fāṭima with Sarasvatī, Ādam/Śiva with Ḥasan, while Ḥusayn is depicted as a form of Viṣṇu himself. In this structural typology, whereas one notices a functional similarity, partial as it may be, in (for instance) the roles ascribed to the prophet Muhammad and Brahmā in their respective traditions – both being connected in some ways with acts of creation – one also finds an evidently random association between other mytho-historical figures of the two traditions. Hence, it is hard to find any functional connection in the case of Fāṭima/Sarasvatī and Ḥasan/Ādam or Śiva, except in so far as it serves to make the typology structurally consistent.[21] It is important to note that the text does not introduce any separate deity or mythological figure to form an equivalence for Ḥusayn. He and ʿAlī are the functional other of the Godhead (Viṣṇu), a pattern unmistakably exhibiting the working of some sort of theology in the background, for Ḥusayn is indeed regarded as an imam in the Imāmī Shiʿi tradition, and therefore carries the same functional standing as the other revered imams (Imam ʿAlī included) in the tradition.[22] A functional equivalence is also introduced between

---

[20] For references to Viṣṇu imparting knowledge of the Vedas to Brahmā, see ibid., vv. 32–40 (KH 868, ff. 149v–151r); for Brahmā's ignorance of the creation, and his 'light' being the source of all the created elements, see vv. 238–273 (KH 868, ff. 179r–184r); printed text, pp. 5–7, 35–40.

[21] Ibid., vv. 230–232 (KH 868, ff. 178r–178v); printed text, pp. 33–34 (vv. 227–230). It is the equivalence between ʿAlī/Viṣṇu and Muhammad/Brahmā that is consistently employed in the *ginān* literature, while the others are encountered less frequently.

[22] It must be noted that whereas, in various facets of Ismaili thought, Ḥasan was included in the list of revered imams, among the Nizārīs his name was dropped, affording him the status of a 'trustee' (*mustawdaʿ*) imam as opposed to the 'permanent' (*mustaqarr*) one; see Farhad Daftary, *The Ismāʿīlīs: Their History and Doctrines* (2nd ed., Cambridge, 2007), p. 97.

the four Vedas of the Hindus and the holy books revered by Muslims and others as authoritative scriptures, embodying the divine revelation. Thus, the Ṛg, Yajur, Sāma and Atharva Vedas are corresponded with the Torah, Psalms, Gospels and Qur'an respectively.[23]

The account of creation in the *Muman Citaveṇī* features many other episodes, connecting the threads of a larger cosmic drama, which need not concern us here. Also, there are motifs enunciated elsewhere in the *ginān* corpus which are either missing or not dealt with in greater detail in the *Muman Citaveṇī*. But what is evident from this synopsis is that the narrative is set in the framework of what are now commonly known as Hindu creation myths, especially the Purāṇic ones.[24] Within this overarching framework, different layers of what may be traceable to Biblical/Qur'anic creation themes are carefully integrated into the narrative in order to produce a harmonious worldview of the cosmogonic evolution from the pre-creation state to the eventual eschatological reckoning. This kind of polyphonic vision is vividly depicted in another recurrent motif, in what I term the *Avatāric* paradigm of the *ginān*s, recounting the periodic manifestation of the Godhead in bodily form for the fulfilment of a specific soteriological purpose. The paradigm, broadly speaking, follows closely the well-known account of Viṣṇu's ten incarnations as narrated in the Hindu scriptures, notably the Purāṇas. In the first nine of these forms, he is depicted as destroying the forces of evil, usually epitomised by an arch devil (called *daitya*, *dānava* etc.), in order to establish justice and restore the balance of truth in the world, while in the last, awaited form – often called Nakalaṁkī ('the Immaculate One') in the *ginān* literature – it is predicted he will appear from the west and perform his cosmic victories.[25]

---

[23] *Muman Cītaveṇī*, vv. 234–238 (KH 868, ff. 178v–179r); printed text, pp. 34–35 (vv. 232–236).

[24] For a discussion of creation myths in the Hindu tradition, see Cornelia Dimmitt and J. A. B. van Buitenen (ed./tr.), *Classical Hindu Mythology: A Reader in the Sanskrit Purāṇas* (Philadelphia, 1978), pp. 15–58; and Wendy Doniger O'Flaherty (tr.), *Hindu Myths* (New Delhi, 1994), pp. 25–55.

[25] The *Avatāric* paradigm has been the subject of much discussion, with scholars offering different takes on it. My purpose in drawing attention to it is to highlight the kind of eclectic vision that penetrates through a number of *ginān*s. I suggest a different reading of the paradigm in Momin, *The Formation of the Satpanth Ismaili Tradition*, pp. 141–152 *passim*.

Leaving aside for the moment the question of what exactly inspired this seemingly synthetic vision – whether it was some kind of strategic missionary zeal or other factors – it is quite apparent that the *Muman Citaveṇī* and other *ginān*s that operate within this scheme of interaction do not restrict such ideas to the taxonomy of Hindu or Muslim worldviews. They remain by and large quite indifferent to the precise sources of such ideas – a feature they share with other literary traditions that exhibit a seemingly spontaneous impulse reflective of the premodern performative milieu of India. On the rare occasions that the *Muman Citaveṇī* invokes these categories, it is precisely to stress the harmonious character of the salvific history in which both Hindus and Muslims participate as adherents of different religions, albeit created by the same God towards the same purpose in life – the unconditional recognition of Viṣṇu/ʿAlī as the Lord and Brahmā/Muhammad as the archetypal *guru* and so on.[26] What we find at best, in some rare instances, is that some Hindu scriptures (Vedas and Purāṇas) and the Qur'an are alluded to as the authoritative source for certain ideas expressed in the *ginān* corpus. For example, while the Purāṇas as a source of creation myths are not mentioned in the *Muman Citaveṇī*, their influence on the *ginān*ic accounts of creation is evident beyond the echoes of shared discursive structures, for in some other compositions they are explicitly acknowledged as the 'authority' for certain information included there.[27] But beyond this, we rarely find an attempt to limit such ideas (even when they are traceable to Purāṇic-Vedic, Qur'anic or other scriptures) to any narrowly envisaged classification, much less to a teleologically-oriented conception of Islam and Hinduism.

---

26 *Muman Cītaveṇī*, vv. 285–293 (KH 868, ff. 186r–187r); printed text, pp. 41–43 (vv. 284–292).

27 See, for example, the composition *Ād to alakh agīyā ramīyo* (KH 746, ff. 77r–78r) where the nature of the Divine Being, Brahmā's age and other cosmic matters are authenticated from the testimony of the Purāṇas; for the printed version of the *ginān*, see Pīr Sadaradīn, *Mahān Isamāīlī Saṁt Pīr Sadaradīn Racit Gīnānono Saṁgrah* (Muṁbai, 1952), *ginān* 86, pp. 88–89. On a relevant note, the embodiment of such apparently Purāṇic themes in the *ginān* literature may be approached in terms of reciprocal transformations between the classical Sanskrit Purāṇas and their vernacular adaptations as discussed by Wendy Doniger and others; see Wendy Doniger (ed.), *Purāṇa Perennis: Reciprocity and Transformation in Hindu and Jaina Texts* (Albany, 1993).

In presenting the kind of harmonising discourse sketched above, the *gināns* at times go a step further and in creative ways adopt the iconic figures and popular lore associated with different religious clusters. It is within this plane of interaction that we find a number of Hindu/Indic mythological or other widely venerated figures embodied into the domain of Satpanth sacrality. However, instead of producing mere structural/functional equivalences – the kind of what we find in the *Muman Citaveṇī* and other *gināns* – whereby A of one tradition becomes B of another, the compositions in this case actively engage with the narratives associated with such figures and modify them to suit their own ends, articulating in the process the quintessential ethos of the tradition. A good example of this appropriation is illustrated in the story of king Hariścandra and his wife Tārā, and deserves our attention here.[28]

One night, while the king was fast asleep, Tārā prepared to leave for a place called the 'abode of religion' (*dharam duvār*). She wore religious attire putting aside her royal regalia, took the king's favourite horse, and left the palace, crossing the insurmountable barriers of the palace gate and the Yamuna river through divine intervention. As she reached the designated place, the people who had congregated there rejoiced at her arrival. The queen addressed the audience and conducted religious ceremonies, asking everyone to be quick, for the practice of this faith ought to remain secret from the king. As part of the ceremonies, the king's favourite horse was slaughtered and its meat was distributed among the participants as a divine grace. Once the ceremonies were concluded, however, the horse was brought back to life out of its bones and skin through the collective prayers of the congregation. As Tārā was ready to leave, she realised that one of her

[28] While scattered references to various motifs from the story are found in quite a few compositions, there is one *ginān* that dwells at length on the narrative; see *Sejaḍīye sutore rājā nīṁdrā dharī* (KH 860, ff. 2r–6r). The manuscript version of the *ginān* has fewer verses than the printed one, the latter adding various details to the overall narrative which remains by and large the same in both the versions; for the printed version, see Sadaradīn, *Saṁgrah*, *ginān* 174, pp. 185–193. See also the composition *Amar te āyo more shāhajījo* (HC, Ms Ism K 22, ff. 368v–369r) which presents some of the threads from the story; the printed version appears in Sadaradīn, *Saṁgrah*, *ginān* 189, pp. 206–208.

sandals had gone missing. But it had actually been taken away by the king himself, who had only pretended to be asleep and followed her all the way to this place, noticing her strange behaviour that particular night. The queen nonetheless managed to produce a similar sandal miraculously through the supplication of the congregation to God and returned to the palace. As she entered the room, Hariścandra got up and told her that he had a strange dream in which he saw her leaving the palace. When Tārā denied this unexpected revelation, the king became angry and showed her the sandal as a proof of the claim. He then drew his sword and asked her to show the tray she had brought back, containing meat and other consecrated items. However, when the tray was shown to the king, the meat and other items had become transformed into oranges, grapes etc. which left him totally bewildered as he himself had witnessed the entire scene at the congregation. Upon witnessing this wonder, Hariścandra asked the queen to tell him the mysteries of the *panth* she followed. Tārā warned him that the path is a difficult one, and he would have to sacrifice everything to the *guru* – his own self, his favourite horse, his son, the rule of Ayodhya and so on – before being initiated into it. In spite of this warning, the king remained adamant, and after sacrificing everything, and undergoing certain travails as a testimony to his steadfastness, was eventually initiated into the 'True Path'.

Serving perhaps as a kind of etiological tale, explaining how Hariścandra became an archetypal devotee in the Satpanth imagining – for he is time and again portrayed as an exemplary deliverer of seven crore of souls – the *ginān*ic narrative clearly modifies the well-known account of the king's travails in order to suit its own ends.[29] The most striking modification is the inversion of the main thread – it is not the Brahman Viśvāmitra who is responsible for Hariścandra's ordeal, as we find it in the Sanskrit accounts. Rather, it is the king's own desire to embrace Satpanth and know its mysteries – a transformation that he underwent after witnessing the wonders performed by the queen as an

[29] Aside from the Sanskrit accounts of Hariścandra's ordeal, we find many vernacular versions of the story that correspond closely to the *ginān*ic retelling; see, for example, Kathleen M. Erndl, *Victory to the Mother: The Hindu Goddess of Northwest India in Myth, Ritual, and Symbol* (New York, 1993), pp. 93–96.

adherent of the 'True Path' – that induced him to forsake all the worldly glory and possessions in favour of the True Path's arduous practice.

What we thus observe in many a *ginān* bearing this kind of interaction of ideas is that the collective self of the tradition is subtly formulated through an integration of multiple threads, many of which resonate with Purāṇic/Vedic and Biblical/Qur'anic accounts, without necessarily giving an impression of imposing something alien. The threads are thus not viewed internally as if they formed part of something supervening, in particular that which is now rigidly identified with the taxonomy of 'Hindu' and 'Muslim'. Rather they are infused into the larger world of Satpanth *Weltanchauung* in a manner so as to form its integral part, without creating a demarcation between self and 'other', even when the latter is identifiable with a specific religious strand.

Moving on, another major plane of interaction is to be seen in those *ginān*s which comment on the waning spirit of the socio-religious order of the time, and offer their own assessment with regard to its idealised code of conduct. In other words, we find a number of *ginān*s within this scheme exhibiting an overwhelming concern with the prevalent modes of sacrality and social structure, while offering a sharp criticism of their practices and ideals. It is against this backdrop that we observe how many *ginān*s simply dissociate the path they propound from that followed by either Muslims or Hindus, naming at times sub-clusters within these larger categories. In fact, the 'other' here becomes the very site against which the collective self and quintessential ethos of the tradition are spelt out and formulated in terms of a unique path that promises (among other things) deliverance from the endless cycles of rebirth, as well as alternate solutions to the mundane problems of life. This kind of engagement and criticism reminds us, in many ways, of the Sufis and North Indian poet-saints, known as *sant*s and *bhakta*s – the likes of Ravidās, Kabīr, Guru Nānak, Mīrābāī etc. – who advocated the practice of unmediated, direct devotion to the Divine Being, disregarding the role of any clerical authority, such as the Brahmans and the *'ulamā'*.[30]

[30] For an accessible introduction to the ideas propounded by some of the well-known poet-saints of India, see John Stratton Hawley and Mark Juergensmeyer (tr.), *Songs of the Saints of India* (New Delhi, 2004).

In presenting its criticism, the *ginān* repertoire employs a straightforward, matter of fact language, anchoring the whole discourse around the quest for truth, a property depicted as the core feature of the Satpanth ideology. In this context, a somewhat recurrent denunciation encountered in the *ginān*s is of excessive ritualism, an infatuation with religious practices on the part of Paṇḍits, Brahmans, Mullahs, Qāḍīs, Yogīs and the like, without any realisation of the real intent behind the external form of religious worship. In criticising the superficiality of ritual acts, the *ginān*s at times pose a rhetorical question and ask the audience if such ritual behaviour would yield the intended result. One *ginān* warns the pilgrims frequenting Kāshī as follows:

> Visiting Kāshī and bathing in the Ganges,
> what good is this watery pilgrimage?
> If one were to attain salvation only by bathing,
> fish would be the first one to get it.
> Fish, even while living in the Ganges,
> only stink in time.[31]

The rhetorical device in the *ginān*s is further reinforced by the use of such expressions as *munivar* (saint), *rikhisar* (great sage), *mu'min* (believer) etc. to address their listeners, infusing in them a strange sense of irony, for in spite of being endowed with the qualities of sagacity and piety as these appellations imply, the *ginān*s constantly remind them of the fallacies pervading their acts, as well as their ignorance of reality.[32] Similarly, the target of such criticism is not just mindless preoccupation with ritualism; it is also levelled against those who preach in favour of such acts in the first place, claiming to have attained the ultimate truth, which in *ginān*ic parlance is simply a delusion. Hence, the religious clerics now associated with Muslim and Hindu traditions are often censured for their pretentious learning, which amounts to nothing more than a form of self-deception.

---

[31] See the composition *Dhaṁdhukāranī sāṁkh bhaṇīje*, vv. 4–6 (HC, Ms Ism K 22, ff. 376r–376v), printed version, Sadaradīn, *Saṁgrah*, *ginān* 183, pp. 201–202.

[32] Kabīr used a similar rhetorical strategy by employing the term *sant* to address his audience whom he then assailed for the emptiness of this pretention; see Linda Hess and Shukdeo Singh (tr.), *The Bijak of Kabir* (New York, 2002), pp. xii *passim*.

For example, one *ginān* addresses the pretentions of Paṇḍits and Brahmans in these words:

> Oh brothers! Paṇḍit became weary reading the scriptures,
> yet he couldn't find the secret of the Divine;
> Dismissing God (*Allāh*) and Muhammad from his mind,
> so was Brahman led astray from the true calling.[33]

The alternative that the *ginān*s offer to the prevailing forms of religiosity, when commenting on them, is not too drastically different from the same modes of expressions they criticise. In other words, the overall fabric of the alternative vision draws its basis from some of the religious structures widely prevalent at the time, conventionally associated with the devotional fervour of the medieval *sant*s, *bhakta*s and Sufis. Hence, we often find the corpus cherishing the ideals of Satpanth by comparing them to those of other *panth*s or *darśana*s ('philosophical schools'). In this context, the most important feature that the *ginān*ic vision shares with other traditions is that of an unwavering allegiance to the *guru*, who for the most part remains unidentified. However, we sometimes encounter a conscious effort to draw a functional similarity between the *guru*, on the one hand, and Muhammad/Brahmā or a *pīr*, on the other, depicted in some cases as the archetypal guide (as, for instance, in the *Muman Citaveṇī*). While a distinction is often drawn between the concepts of *guru*/*pīr* and *nar*/*shāh*, seen as referring respectively to the institutions of *pīr*ship and imamate, in an effort to create a neat typology of religious ranking and authority in the Satpanth sacral vision, there is a great deal of overlapping in these ideals too, for even the concepts of *imām* and *nar* are frequently depicted in terms of the 'True Guide' (*satguru*).[34]

It must be noted here that the *ginān*s do not merely criticise the prevalent modes of piety or sacred dispensations. Rather, in pointing out shortcomings in the practices associated with different religious

---

[33] *Pustak paḍī paḍī paṁḍīt thākā*, vv. 1–2, KH 871, p. 37; printed version (with variation) in Pīr Hasan Kabīradīn et al., *Mahān Isamāīlī Saṁt Pīr Hasan Kabīradīn ane Bījā Sattādhārī Pīro Racit Gīnānono Saṁgrah* (Muṁbai, n.d.), *ginān* 29, p. 52.

[34] For the typology, see Shackle and Moir, *Ismaili Hymns from South Asia*, pp. 21–22; for an example of the overlapping between these ideas, see *Muḷabaṁdhano Achoḍo* (attributed to Pīr Shams), vv. 1–10 (KH 831, pp. 1–2).

clusters, they go a step further and comment on what their ideal rules of conduct ought to be. What we see in such cases is not so much a rejection of other socio-religious collectives by plainly declaring the superficiality of their observances, but an effort towards creating affinity between their ethos and values and those of the Satpanth religious ideals. This dialectic vividly manifests itself in an interesting *ginān* called the *Khaṭ Darashan*, apparently taking its name from the well-known six 'orthodox' schools (*saddarśanas*) of Indian philosophy. However, far from being an exposition of the philosophical ideas connected with these schools, as the name might suggest, a better part of the *Khaṭ Darashan* actually provides a kind of didactic commentary on how the self-proclaimed adherents of some of the prevalent religious and social groups ought to conduct themselves so that they might live up to the collective ideals of their fraternities.

In this vein, the *Khaṭ Darashan* touches upon not only the ideal comportment of some social/religious fraternities, like Vairāgī, Vaiṣṇava, Jaṁgam (Lingāyat priest), Jogī (Yogī), Sanyāsī, Munī, Jain, Brahmacārī, Satī, Brahman, Paṇḍit, Sufi, Qāḍī, Mullah, Musalmān, Pativratā (devoted wife), Gharbārī (householder) etc., but even discusses the traits of the Lord (*sāmī*) and his true devotee (*sevak*).[35] For example, the qualities of an ideal Sanyāsī are sketched in these words:

> Sanyāsī, he who praises Śiva,
> forsakes the worldly temptations,
> partakes in nothing but rightful alms,
> being firm upon the posture (*āsan*),
> realises, deep in his heart, what good are ashes?
> True Sanyāsī, so says Gur Sohodev, he is indeed![36]

Elsewhere, the Jogī is admonished in these words concerning the true practice of yoga:

> O ascetic! Make the way [to the divine] your sack, contentment your [begging] bowl, and make your thoughts as strong as a staff;

[35] The text is attributed to Pīr Sadardīn; see *Khaṭ Darashan*, esp. vv. 1–23 (KH 426, ff. 70v–73r).

[36] Ibid., v. 8 (KH 426, ff. 71[a]v–71[b]r). Sohodev is now commonly regarded as an epithet of Pīr Sadardīn, but this may not actually have been the case in the past.

wear the two earrings of endurance and compassion,
and make knowledge your diet;
O ascetic! The true Jogī is one who has no one else in his heart.[37]

I now turn to discuss the final set of *ginān*s to underscore yet another layer of interaction between the ideas and categories associated with the terms 'Hindu' and 'Muslim'. Being subtly present in the corpus, this layer has largely been overshadowed by others discussed above, and hence has escaped the notice of scholars. What we find in these examples is an attitude of distancing from what are regarded as the Hindu practices, and a self-conscious association with a form of what might be described as 'Muslimness'. An interesting example of this dialectic formulation can be seen in a series of *ginān*s ascribed to Imām Shāh and his sister Bāī Buḍhāī, presented in the form of a dialogue (*saṁvād*). The compositions in question are essentially a narrative of Bāī Buḍhāī's initiation to the mysteries of the Satpanth practice. Through the course of the dialogue, she enquires about a number of religious and moral problems. Responding to her questions, Imām Shāh tries to dispel her doubts at each stage and make it possible for the discussion to progress to the next level. Towards the end of their conversation, Bāī Buḍhāī asks about the Hindus: Who are Rām and Kṛṣṇa? And, why do people worship them in the form of idols? In her enquiry, she exhibits a vivid consciousness of being a Muslim, and shows her bewilderment as to why the path she follows is associated with that of the Hindu 'other', whose practice of frequenting temples, worshipping idols etc. she views as 'worthless' (*khoṭā*). Imām Shāh's response, in many ways, is in line with the harmonising attitude towards the two traditions that I have previously discussed. While criticising Hindus for the worship of idols, he makes it plain that all this is in vain, for the real manifestation of Rām and Kṛṣṇa resides in the 'west', in the form of ʿAlī. In revealing the truth about the ten incarnations, he creates the kind of structural/functional equivalences between the mytho-historical figures associated with the two traditions that we see in the *Muman Citaveṇī* and other *ginān*s, Thus,

---

37 *Abadhu jugat jol saṁtosh pātra karo*, v. 1, in Pīr Shams, *Mahān Isamāīlī Saṁt Pīr Shams Racit Gīnānono Saṁgrah* (Muṁbai, 1952), *ginān* 58, p. 63.

Prahlād (a mythical figure) is portrayed as Ibrāhīm (Abraham), Hariścandra as Mūsā (Moses), and Hindus of earlier times as Muslims of today, being reborn in Satpanth as part of their reward for previous deeds.

What is interesting about this dialogue is not just the voice of Bāī Buḍhāī, distancing herself from the Hindus and their practices, or that of Imām Shāh, offering a therapeutic perspective to her anxiety. But what is equally interesting is the voice of the absent composer, moderating the whole dialogue and bringing to the fore, in the voice of a female character, concerns that seem to have prevailed about the nature of the Satpanth practice and its relationship to what are envisaged in this case as Hindu observances and ideals, conceived by the protagonist Bāī Buḍhāī here as undesirable and worthless.[38]

In another set of *ginān*s, narrating the travels of Pīr Shams and his two disciples through various places, we find a similar cognisance of the Hindu other. In one of his sojourns, the *pīr* is said to have encountered a group of pilgrims who had camped near a village to take the ritual bath. His disciples Vīmras and Surbhāṇ (portrayed as young boys) also went to the river and incidentally caused some drops of water to fall on a Brahman, named Devrām. He shouted, 'I am a Brahman and you are Muslims (*musalā*); you have committed a wicked act', and rushed to the village, which was inhabited entirely by the Hindus. The people of the village accordingly gathered to punish Vīmras and Surbhāṇ for their sinful act. One of them approached the boys and enquired about their superior – he was referred to Pīr Shams. The villagers came to the saint and asked about the 'birth-group' (*jāt*) of his disciples who had polluted the Brahman. When the *pīr* asked why what seemed to him a trivial matter was of serious concern, the Brahman replied that he would now have to bathe in the Ganges in order to become purified. The *pīr* at once caused the Ganges to flow

[38] See *ginān*s 59–71 of the 'dialogue', KH 558, ff. 363v–382r; for the printed version, see Sayyid Imām Shāh and Bāī Buḍhāī, *Saiyyad Īmāmashāh tathā Bāi Buḍhāino Saṁvād ane Gīnān 10 Gugarīnāṁ* (2nd ed., Muṁbai, 1926), pp. 40–50. In the manuscripts, I have found two versions of the dialogue, a shorter one with 21 and a longer one with 71 *ginān*s. Though very likely, it is difficult to suggest definitively (at this stage) if the longer version contains *ginān*s incorporated later on. On Bāī Buḍhāī, see also [E. J.] Varatejī, *Satapaṁthanī Devīyo* (2nd ed., Muṁbai, 1926), pp. 6–12.

through the village, and so the Brahman and other (Hindu) villagers bathed and embraced Satpanth.[39]

What is important about this hagiographic tale is the depiction of Pīr Shams and his disciples as Muslims, marking them off from the Hindus, the latter defined with respect to certain customs – the need for ritual purification resulting from pollution, caste affiliation and so forth. This is rather significant, for whereas the *ginān*s are unequivocal in their criticism of external religious observances practiced by both 'Muslim' and 'Hindu' groups, as was seen earlier, this attitude of what would amount to distancing, as ascribed to the revered agents of Satpanth preaching, is largely exhibited towards the Hindus. In other words, whereas the *ginan*s on occasion identify these agents as 'Muslims', one hardly comes across an instance where we see the same agents being identified as 'Hindus', envisaged as a religious group. Hence, within this larger plane of interaction, we observe the collective self of the tradition being carved in terms of a Muslim identity by contrasting it against a Hindu one. This configuration in the *ginān*ic worldview, often overlooked, has major implications when we assess the collective literary heritage of the tradition in dealing with the larger question of the formation of the identities of Satpanth adherents.[40]

Concluding Observations

Although the sources at our disposal (including the *ginān*s) do not always allow us to sketch a neat portrait of varied modes of transformation through which the Satpanth tradition evolved over its long history, the contours of this transformation have nonetheless come to be painted by scholars in broad strokes. They are generally demarcated, rather unsatisfactorily, in a way that the British colonial institutions are seen as the ones that brought about a rupture in how the Satpanthī communities (the Khojas in particular) envisaged their identity in exclusivist terms at a critical juncture in their history, thus departing significantly from the premodern amalgamative texture of the tradition. As some

[39] See the compositions *Pīr shamas sadhāvīyā*, in Shams, *Saṁgrah*, *ginān* 67, p. 71; and *Vaḷatā brāhmaṇ bolīyā*, in Shams, *Saṁgrah*, *ginān* 68, p. 72.

[40] See Momin, *The Formation of the Satpanth Ismaili Tradition*.

recent studies tend to argue, this new way of conceptualising identity was the consequence of a rigid, legal definition of the Khojas as 'Ismailis' around the mid-nineteenth century which was antithetical to an earlier, precolonial mode, harbouring a more assimilative spirit.

It is hard to say with any degree of certainty if the cross-fertilisation of ideas and symbols associated with what have been defined as Muslim and Hindu worldviews – frequently invoked as being characteristic of the *ginān*s, and hence indelible evidence of the standpoint mentioned above – was something that the tradition as a whole invariably experienced, much less in its embryonic stage. For, as I have argued elsewhere, the formation of the tradition, moving from a more organic practice, harbouring multiple streams of thought, to a more bounded structure (expressed in different sectarian terms) is a process that ought to be understood by taking into account the interplay of a multitude of factors and agencies that carved their own discursive spaces within which the ideological basis of the tradition was formulated – a process that is not necessarily, and not in its entirety, self-evident from the *ginān*s.

Nonetheless, the analysis of selected *ginān*s here points to multiple forms of interaction between the cosmologies associated with the categories 'Hindu' and 'Muslim', which do not lend themselves to any kind of overarching, uniform discourse. In many cases, the *ginān*ic attitude towards the prescribed religious ideals is highly amalgamative, displaying a rich cross-fertilisation of putative Hindu and Muslim ideas in a harmonious manner. But there are other configurations of identity too – the dialectics between the collective self of the tradition and the 'other' – which show at one extreme an uneasiness with the presence of what are held to be Hindu elements in Satpanth religiosity and practice, and on the other a disassociation with either Hindu or Muslim forms of faith, transcending in the process any narrowly conceived religious affiliation, and concerned solely with the discipline and purity of the inner self and a commitment towards truth. What this means is that the very roots of what was to transpire in the colonial period, with respect to the religious texture of Satpanth and its communities, was already embodied in the premodern practice of the tradition. To be sure, the colonial period saw the transformation and channelling of this worldview in new directions, but it was not a complete departure from that earlier moment, rather its creative refashioning in a new era by a new set of factors and agencies that closely identified themselves with the tradition.

18

Spring's Equinox: Nawrūz in Ismaili Thought*

Shafique N. Virani
(University of Toronto)

> *God is the One who sends forth the winds to stir up the clouds; then we drive them toward barren lands, giving life to the earth after its death. Thus is the Resurrection.*
>
> *Qur'an 35:9*

Introduction: The Equinox from Earthly Spectacle to Heavenly Knot

For some five thousand years, the Great Sphinx of Giza has fascinated people. Fashioned by the ancient Egyptians to be one of the largest single-stone statues on earth, it is certainly no accident that due to its exact positioning, on the day of the vernal equinox, the first day of spring, the majestic colossus gazes directly toward the rising sun.[1] For a thousand years the setting sun of the equinox casts a dramatic spectacle of undulating light and shadow on the northern stairway of the Mayan architectural and scientific marvel, the Temple of Kukulcan in Chichén Itzá, Mexico.[2] In his most famous work, *Phaenomena*, the ancient Greek poet-astronomer Aratus celebrated the 'beautiful and

---

* This article is dedicated to the memory of the late Alwaez Rai Shamsuddin Bandali Haji.

[1] Manfred Bietak et al., 'Ägypten', *Archiv für Orientforschung*, 32 (1985), pp. 128–184.

[2] Anthony F. Aveni, Susan Milbrath, and Carlos Peraza Lope, 'Chichén Itzá's Legacy in the Astronomically Oriented Architecture of Mayapán', *RES: Anthropology and Aesthetics*, 45 (2004), pp. 123–143.

great star' Alpha Piscium as the singular 'Knot of the Heavens', a tribute to its shining where the equator, the ecliptic, and the equinoctial colure intersect, revealing the precise point of the vernal equinox in the firmament.[3] Similarly, the Japanese have long welcomed the arrival of spring with the ceremony of Higan-e, symbolising spiritual enlightenment.[4]

At the exact moment of the equinox, the sun crosses the celestial equator, marking in the northern hemisphere when day begins to gain ascendancy over night, and light over darkness. The moment has had tremendous symbolic significance throughout history in the art, architecture, ritual and literature of many cultures across the globe.

To the ancient Iranians, the return of spring was an annual symbol of the victory of light, which likely led Zoroaster (fl. perhaps ca. 1000 BCE) to remind his disciples:

> Our 'limited time' will be succeeded by the 'Time of Long Dominion' (virtually eternity), with the world and all that is in it restored to the perfect state in which it was created by Ahura Mazdā . . . [The spring festival] could thus be renamed the '(festival of the) New Day' which will eventually bring everlasting bliss; and so this observance could aid faith and deepen understanding of doctrine.[5]

Similarly, both the Jewish Passover and the Christian Easter are festivals that occur during spring, and the date of the celebration is calculated with relation to the equinox.[6] In Christianity, the coming of

---

[3] Godefroid De Callataÿ, 'The Knot of the Heavens', *Journal of the Warburg and Courtauld Institutes*, 59 (1996), pp. 1–13.

[4] Masao Fujii, 'Maintenance and Change in Japanese Traditional Funerals and Death-Related Behavior', *Japanese Journal of Religious Studies*, 10, 1 (1983), p. 46; Masakazu Watabe, 'Elijah's Promise: An Oriental View', *Brigham Young University Studies*, 44, 2 (2005), p. 156.

[5] Mary Boyce, 'Nowruz i. In the Pre-Islamic Period', *Encyclopaedia Iranica*, at http://www.iranicaonline.org/articles/nowruz-i.

[6] On the calculation of the dates of these festivals and their relationship to the equinox, see Werner Bergmann, 'Easter and the Calendar: The Mathematics of Determining a Formula for the Easter Festival to Medieval Computing', *Journal for General Philosophy of Science/Zeitschrift für allgemeine Wissenschaftstheorie*, 22, 1 (1991), pp. 15–41; J.B. Segal, 'Intercalation and the Hebrew Calendar', *Vetus Testamentum*, 7, 3 (1957), pp. 250–307.

spring is thus intimately connected with the concept of resurrection, a concept shared with the passage from the Qur'an quoted above. Indeed, one of the most common names for Easter in Arabic is *ʿīd al-qiyāma*, feast of the resurrection.

Nawrūz in Muslim Cultures: From the Day of the Covenant to the Day of the Resurrection

Spring is a time of renewed life. The Qur'an thus compared the signs of spring, such as the revivification of barren lands by the life-giving rain clouds, to the Day of Resurrection. Given its natural as well as scriptural symbolism, and its importance in pre-existing religious traditions, the image of spring's arrival also played a powerful role in Islamic cultures and literatures. In addition to festivities common in other celebrations, others more symbolic of the coming of spring or specific to Nawrūz (the Arabic pronunciation of the more classical Nō Rōz) were ubiquitous in many Muslim lands, such as decorating eggs, lighting candles, bonfires, or other types of illumination, growing various grains, sprinkling water or rose essence, and distributing sugar crystals.

To Muslim rulers, the ancient associations of Nawrūz with the glory and sacred power of the royal courts were particularly attractive, and so encouraging its commemoration affirmed their splendour and prestige. While most rulers were not the focal point of strictly religious festivals, a secularised Nawrūz could certainly be harnessed for imperial ends.[7] The Umayyad and Abbasid caliphs celebrated Nawrūz with appropriate pomp and pageantry, as did the Fatimids and indeed

[7] Alireza Shapur Shahbazi, 'Nowruz ii. In the Islamic Period', *Encyclopedia Iranica*, at http://www.iranicaonline.org/articles/nowruz-ii. Shapur Shahbazi's bibliography and references have been particularly useful for this piece. It is important to remember that it is only since the time of the calendar reform under Sultan Malik-Shāh (d. 485/1092) that Nawrūz has regularly marked the vernal equinox. With regard to these shifts, see Simone Cristoforetti, 'Nowruz iii. In the Iranian Calendar', *Encyclopedia Iranica*, at http://www.iranicaonline.org/articles/nowruz-iii; Antonio Panaino, Reza Abdollahy, and Daniel Balland, 'Calendars', *Encyclopaedia Iranica*, at http://www.iranicaonline.org/articles/calendars.

numerous other Muslim dynasties.[8] That merrymakers sometimes went beyond the bounds of what was deemed acceptable behaviour is evidenced by the fact that at various times both the Abbasid and Fatimid caliphs had to rein in their subjects, and to restrict the kindling of bonfires and sprinkling of water traditionally associated with the festival.[9] Certain Muslims, like al-Ghazālī (d. 505/1111), frowned upon the prominence of Nawrūz customs, worried about their pre-Islamic origins.[10] Others, however, cited supportive traditions. For example, al-Maqrīzī (d. 845/1442) connects the celebration of Nawrūz to the Prophet Abraham's miraculous escape when the idolators threw him into a blazing fire (see Qur'an 21:68–69). The confrontation between the Prophet Moses and Pharaoh's magicians is also said to have taken place on this day (20:59), and it is equally claimed that the ring of Solomon was recovered on Nawrūz.[11] In *al-Āthār al-bāqiya* ('Vestiges of the Past') and *al-Maḥāsin wa'l-aḍdād* ('Book of Beauties and Contraries'), after discussing the Prophet's positive opinion of giving gifts that sow love in the hearts of people, al-Bīrūnī (d. 440/1048) records:

> It is reported that the Commander of the Faithful, ʿAlī (upon whom be peace) was approached by a group of Persian chieftains, who presented him with gifts of silver bowls filled with sweets. He asked, 'What are these for?' They replied, 'Today is Nawrūz.' He replied, 'May all of our days be Nawrūz!' They ate the sweets, which he served his sitting companions, dividing the bowls among the Muslims.[12]

---

[8] Shapur Shahbazi, 'Nowruz ii. In the Islamic Period'.

[9] Abū Jaʿfar Muḥammad b. Jarīr al-Ṭabarī, *Ta'rīkh al-rusul wa'l-mulūk*, ed. Michael Jan de Goeje, et al. as *Annales quos scripsit Abu Djafar Mohammed ibn Djarir at-Tabari* (Leiden, 1879–1901), vol. 13, p. 2144; tr. Franz Rosenthal as *The History of al-Ṭabarī: The Return of the Caliphate to Baghdad; the Caliphates of al-Muʿtaḍid, al-Muktafī and al-Muqtadir, A.D. 892–915/A.H. 279–302*, vol. 38 (Albany, 1985), p. 20.

[10] Abū Ḥāmid Muḥammad al-Ghazālī, *Kīmīyā-yi saʿādat*, ed. Ḥusayn Khidīw-jam (Tehran, 1380 Sh./2001), vol. 1, p. 522.

[11] Cited in Boaz Shoshan, *Popular Culture in Medieval Cairo* (Cambridge, 1993), pp. 40–41, who also notes additional sources and references to the 'Biblical' history of Nawrūz.

[12] Jāḥiẓ (pseud., attrib.), Abū ʿUthmān ʿAmr b. Baḥr al-Fuqaymī al-Baṣrī, *al-Maḥāsiṇ wa'l-aḍdād*, ed. Muḥammad Amīn al-Khānjī al-Kutubī (Cairo, 1324/1906),

Perhaps the most striking interpretation tying Nawrūz directly to Muslim religious heritage is one found in Twelver Shiʿi works such as al-Majlisī's (d. 1110/1699) *Biḥār al-anwār* ('Oceans of Lights'), which intimately connects the festival with significant events in the history and eschatology of the Abrahamic tradition and particularly episodes of importance to the Shiʿis. Addressing Muʿallā b. Khanīs, Imam Jaʿfar al-Ṣādiq (d. 148/765) is reported to have said:

> O Muʿallā, the day of Nawrūz is the day God accepted the covenants of his servants to worship Him and not to associate anything with Him and to believe in His Prophets and Proofs and to believe in the imams. It is the first day upon which the sun rose and the winds blew and the splendour of the world was created. It is the day Noah's ark grounded upon Mount Ararat. It is the day God resurrected the thousands who had gone forth from their homes in fear of death: God said to them, 'Die!' then brought them back to life.[13] It is the day on which Gabriel came down to the Messenger of God. It is the day on which the Messenger of God bore the Commander of the Faithful ʿAlī upon his shoulder so that he could throw down and destroy the idols of the Quraysh from atop the Sacred House, and likewise Abraham. It is the day on which the Prophet ordered his companions to pledge allegiance to ʿAlī as Commander of the Faithful. It is the day on which the Prophet turned ʿAlī towards the valley of the jinn to take their pledge of allegiance. It is the day on which the Commander of the Faithful received the second pledge of allegiance. It is the day on which he triumphed over the people of Nahrawān and slew Dhu'l-Thadya. It is the day on which our Resurrector (Qāʾim) shall appear with his deputies. It is the day on which our Resurrector (Qāʾim) shall triumph over

---

pp. 237–238. The narrative in Bīrūnī's work is incomplete, due to a lacuna in the manuscript, Muḥammad b. Aḥmad al-Bīrūnī, *al-Āthār al-bāqiyah ʿan al-qurūn al-khāliyah, Chronologie orientalischer Völker: von Albêrûnî* (Leipzig, 1878), p. 215; ibid., trans. by Eduard Sachau as *The Chronology of Ancient Nations: An English Version of the Arabic Text; Or, "Vestiges of The Past"* (London, 1879), p. 199. See also Ḥasan Taqīzāda, *Gāh-shumārī dar Īrān-i qadīm* (Tehran, 1316 Sh./1933), pp. 153–154.

[13] A reference to Qurʾan 2:243.

> the Antichrist (Dajjāl) and crucify him at the rubbish-heap of Kufa.[14]

Sentiments similar to those found in Twelver Shiʿi texts are equally present in Nuṣayrī texts, such as the *Majmūʿ al-aʿyād* ('Book of Festivals') by Abū Saʿīd Maymūn b. Qāsim al-Ṭabarānī (d. 424/1033), which associates Nawrūz with the theophanic appearance of 'al-Mawlā', i.e., ʿAlī b. Abī Ṭālib, through the ages.[15] Thus, in both these ʿAlid traditions, from the pre-eternal day of the covenant through to the end of times, Nawrūz is inextricably woven into the fabric of trans-historical religious consciousness.

Nawrūz in Ismaili Literature

The symbolism of spring in general, and of Nawrūz in particular, can be found in Ismaili literature spanning virtually every major historical period and is present in the literary heritage of the three principal linguistic groupings: the Arabic of the Islamic heartlands, the Persian of Iranian and Central Asian traditions, and the various South Asian languages of the Indo-Pakistan subcontinent. Intellectual interactions with the regional environment are readily apparent in the literatures, whether the timing of the festival in the Arab world, the vivid imagery and vocabulary of South Asian traditions that draw from the symbolism of wider mystical currents in the Subcontinent, or the metres and metaphors that permeate the Persian works, indelibly rooting them to the birthplace of Nawrūz, and the conventions that sprung from it.

Two prominent uniting themes permeate the three broad traditions, regardless of time period or language: vernal phenomena as metaphors for the blessing of the imam of the time, and the sacralisation of the earth's springtide finery by sublimating these symbols to convey knowledge of a

---

[14] The translation, slightly modified, is from John Walbridge, 'A Persian Gulf in the Sea of Lights: The Chapter on Naw-Rūz in the *Biḥār al-Anwār*', *Iran*, 35 (1997), pp. 88–89.

[15] Abū Saʿīd Maymūn b. Qāsim al-Ṭabarānī, '*Sabīl rāḥat al-arwāḥ wa-dalīl al-surūr wa'l-afrāḥ ilā fāliq al-aṣbāḥ (Majmūʿ al-aʿyād)*', ed. Rudolf Strothmann, *Der Islam*, 27 (1946); Meir Michael Bar-Asher, 'The Iranian Component of the Nuṣayrī Religion', *Iran*, 41 (2003), pp. 217–218.

spiritual world beyond sensory experience. The latter parallels in some ways the symbolic interpretation (*ta'wīl*) so central to Ismaili thought.

Ta'wīl (Symbolic Interpretation) and the Literature of Spring

The writings of Fatimid intellectuals, including such figures as Abū Yaʿqūb al-Sijistānī (d. after 361/971), al-Qāḍī al-Nuʿmān (d. 363/974), Ḥamīd al-Dīn al-Kirmānī (d. after 411/1020), al-Muʾayyad fi'l-Dīn al-Shīrāzī (d. 470/1078) and Ḥakīm Nāṣir-i Khusraw (d. after 462/1070), emphasise the importance of understanding the world and faith by maintaining a proper balance between their exterior, physical, literal and apparent forms (their *ẓāhir*) and their esoteric, spiritual, symbolic and intellectual realities (their *bāṭin*). The process of evincing the latter from the former is known as *ta'wīl*, or symbolic interpretation. Muslims, whether Shiʿi or Sunni, who championed the role of intellect in understanding faith, advocated the use of symbolic interpretation (*ta'wīl*). Those who defended an exclusively literal understanding of the Qur'an castigated them, often charging them with unbelief (*kufr*). They did not hesitate to respond in kind. For example, the Muʿtazilis, who referred to themselves as the People of Divine Unity and Justice (*ahl al-tawḥīd wa'l-ʿadl*), insisted that scriptural references to such things as God's hand and face must be understood allegorically, using *ta'wīl* to interpret what to them was clearly symbolic. They mocked the Ḥanbalīs for refusing to use the divine gift of intellect to understand anthropomorphic descriptions of God, contemptuously calling them *ḥashwiyya*, 'pillow stuffers' or 'dimwits'.[16]

Elucidating the connection between outward forms and inner meanings, the Ismaili savant Ḥakīm Nāṣir-i Khusraw said that by revelation or *tanzīl*, literally 'descent,' intellectual matters are expressed in a perceptible form.[17] Meanwhile, by the process of symbolic

[16] Richard M. Frank, *Al-Ghazali and the Ashʿarite School* (Durham, 1994), p. 14; Henri Laoust, *La profession de foi d'Ibn Batta, traditionniste et jurisconsulte musulman d'école hanbalite, mort en Irak à 'Ukbarā en 387/997* (Damascus, 1958), pp. 11–12; Editor, 'Ḥashwiyya', *EI2*.

[17] Ḥakīm Abū Muʿīn Nāṣir-i Khusraw, *Zād al-musāfir*, ed. Ismāʿīl ʿImādī Ḥā'irī and Muḥammad ʿImādī Ḥā'irī (Tehran, 2005), p. 368.

interpretation, or *ta'wīl*, the perceptible forms are taken back to their original intellectual state.[18] In verse, he exhorted his audience not to be content with exoteric forms, but to seek out those who can reveal the original spiritual meaning of the revelation:

> God's Word is the Ocean of Words,
> Brimful with precious, lustrous pearls.
>
> Its revelation (*tanzīl*) is like the ocean's brackish waters,
> While its symbolic interpretation (*ta'wīl*) is like pearls for the wise.
>
> As the pearls lie scattered in the ocean's depths
> Why do you scamper along its shores? Seek a diver![19]

While many Muslim exponents of *ta'wīl* employed it primarily to understand the anthropomorphic descriptions of God in the Qur'an, the Ismailis believed it was also to be applied to the canonical law (*sharīʿa*), to sacred history, and to the creation itself.[20] None of the literature surveyed in this piece falls under the genre of *ta'wīl* or designates itself by this title, but it is clear that the ethos of seeking a deeper meaning behind the exoteric phenomena of spring permeates the examples explored.

---

[18] Ḥakīm Abū Mu'īn Nāṣir-i Khusraw, *Wajh-i dīn*, ed. Ghulām Riḍā (Gholam Reza) A'wānī (Aavani) (Tehran, 1397/1977), p. 147.

[19] Ḥakīm Abū Muʿīn Nāṣir-i Khusraw, *Dīwān-i ashʿār-i Ḥakīm Nāṣir-i Khusraw Qubādiyānī*, ed. Mujtabā Mīnuwī and Mahdī (Mehdi) Muḥaqqiq (Mohaghegh) (Tehran, 1357 Sh./1978), vol. 1, p. 5; Nāṣir-i Khusraw, *Dīwān-i ashʿār-i Nāṣir-i Khusraw Qubādiyānī: Mushtamil ast bar Rawshanā'ī-nāma, Saʿādat-nāma, qasā'id wa muqaṭṭaʿāt*, ed. Naṣr Allāh Taqawī and Mujtabā Mīnūwī (Tehran, 1304–1307 Sh./1925–1928), p. 3. See also Nāṣir-i Khusraw, *Gushāyish ū rahāyish*, ed. and trans. by Faquir M. Hunzai as *Knowledge and Liberation: A Treatise on Philosophical Theology; A New Edition and English Translation of the Gushāyish wa Rahāyish* (London, 1998), p. 65.

[20] An analysis of the symbolic interpretation of creation may be found in my 'The Days of Creation in the Thought of Nasir Khusraw', in Sarfaroz Niyozov and Ramazan Nazariev (ed.), *Nasir Khusraw: Yesterday, Today, Tomorrow* (Khujand, 2005), pp. 74–83, and of sacred history in my 'Hierohistory in Qāḍī al-Nuʿmān's Foundation of Symbolic Interpretation (*Asās al-ta'wīl*): The Birth of Jesus', in Charles Fletcher and Sami G. Massoud (ed.), *Studies in Islamic Historiography* (forthcoming).

Resplendent by Your Light: An Arabic Ode

We know from numerous Egyptian accounts, including those of al-Nuwayrī (d. 733/1333), al-Qalqashandī (d. 821/1418), and al-Maqrīzī (d. 845/1442), that in Fatimid times Nawrūz, most probably observed with the annual flooding of the Nile and the beginning of the agricultural new year, was greeted with tremendous jubilation. Celebrants arrayed themselves in their finery and made merry, gifts were exchanged, charity was distributed to the poor, and poets waxed eloquent.[21] However, Prince Tamīm (d. 374/984), a talented poet and the eldest son of the Fatimid imam-caliph al-Muʿizz (d. 365/975), envisioned a spiritual meaning in the signs of nature, seeing the source of their physical blessings in the imam's generosity, bounteous munificence and spiritual light:

> In composing an ode in praise of you
> Beautiful words spring to mind
>
> But in praising someone other than you
> My tongue falters, the words lie
>
> For you are inherently gracious, exalted
> Such gifts are innate to your very nature
>
> Your right hand scatters blessed rain upon the creation
> Your forehead is dawn itself, your face a glittering star
>
> You are the illustrious one through whose light we are illuminated
> Our beloved, for whom we would give our lives
>
> Indeed, if the festival of Nawrūz is to be filled with joy
> It is only through your light that it becomes resplendent
>
> God's blessings upon you, O son of the Prophet
> For indeed you are a time-tested sword to fight life's sorrows[22]

---

[21] Narratives from the primary sources are provided in Fu'ād ʿAbd al-Muʿaṭṭī al-Ṣayyād, *al-Nawrūz wa-atharuh fi'l-adab al-ʿArabī* (Beirut, 1972), pp. 115–126. Regarding the timing of the observation, see Shoshan, *Popular Culture in Medieval Cairo*, pp. 42, 45; Paula Sanders, *Ritual, Politics, and the City in Fatimid Cairo* (Albany, NY, 1994), p. 83.

[22] Al-Amīr Tamīm b. al-Muʿizz, *Dīwān* (Riyadh, 1982), pp. 51–52. This translation benefits from Faquir M. Hunzai, *Shimmering Light: An Anthology of Ismaili Poetry* (London, 1996), p. 41.

Words of Gnosis: Spring in South Asia

The *ginān*s constitute a significant literary legacy of South Asian Ismailism.[23] The most prolific author to whom these compositions are attributed is Pīr Ṣadr al-Dīn (fl. eighth/fourteenth century), a contemporary of Imam Islām-shāh. In consonance with Ismaili literature in both Arabic and Persian, the imam, and particularly his arrival, are compared to the coming of spring, or *vasant*, one of the six seasons of the Indian calendar. This imagery is blended with that of the rich mystical traditions specific to South Asia. In a Sindhi *ginān*, for example, the imam, described as eternal spring, is depicted as the bridegroom whom every pure soul longs to wed:

> The lord is the groom for every maiden soul
> Spring eternal is the imam
> The sovereign king of all[24]

In a Gujarati *ginān*, the imam's arrival from the west is lauded, an image juxtaposed with that of the rising sun, destroying the darkness of night. The metaphor echoes the *ḥadīth* of the Prophet Muhammad, often quoted in Fatimid literature, which says that the sun's rising in the west signals the coming of the rightly guided one, the Mahdi.[25] The imam's arrival is again celebrated as the coming of spring:

---

[23] On the *ginān*s, see the following work, and the items listed in its bibliography, Shafique N. Virani, 'Symphony of Gnosis: A Self-Definition of the Ismaili Ginān Literature', in Todd Lawson (ed.), *Reason and Inspiration in Islam: Theology, Philosophy and Mysticism in Muslim Thought* (London, 2005), pp. 503–521. Please note, the transliteration of Indic scripts in this article is based on the guidelines developed jointly by the Policy and Standards Division at the Library of Congress and the Cataloging and Classification Section of the American Library Association, commonly referred to as the ALA-LC Romanization Guidelines.

[24] Pīr Sadaradīn, 'Yārā anat kiroḍīe vadhāīuṃ', *101 Ginānanī chopaḍī: Chogaḍīā sāñjanā (5) savāranā chogaḍīā (24) ghaṭapāṭanā beṭhā ginān (5) ghaṭapātanā ubhā ginān (10) venatīnā ginān (5) tathā bījā ginānavārī chopaḍī* (Mumbai, 1988 VS/1932), vol. 4, no. 29, 43, v. 12.

[25] See, for example, the poetry quoted in al-Qāḍī Abū Ḥanīfa b. Muḥammad al-Nuʿmān, *Iftitāḥ al-daʿwa wa-ibtidāʾ al-dawla*, trans. by Hamid Haji as *Founding the Fatimid State: The Rise of an Early Islamic Empire; An Annotated English translation of*

From the Western Land has arrived the lord
Vested in him are countless hopes

Shattered is the night, the sun has risen!
The imam's coming is the advent of spring

Flowers have blossomed, the season has bloomed[26]

Another Sindhi *ginān* speaks in greater depth about the imam's arrival, once again, with an emphasis on his coming from the west as the bridegroom of souls. He is described as the lord of twelve splendours, a specifically South Asian solar allusion. The imagery of spring and flowers blossoming takes an interesting turn in this composition, for the *Pīr* specifies that he is not speaking of vegetation, but of the believers bursting into bloom and becoming perfumed with the presence of the imam.

> The imam's herald travels throughout the world. In rapturous welcome, the believers shower the imam and *Pīr* with petals. The imam has appeared in the fortress of Alamūt. Brother, we are perpetually blissful, wed to the lord. By God, he has arrived; the community enjoys its fortune. Hail the advent of the Lord ʿAlī from the west. Recognise the supreme man, lord of light. Friends, know the *Pīr* to be he who has led you to the recognition of the lord of twelve splendours.[27] Serve none other than that very lord, my brother. Friend, never doubt in this. Hail the advent of the lord, as glorious as the risen sun! The imam has arrived, friends, as the spring, and flowers have burst into bloom. By God, the believers blossom, redolent with fragrance.[28]

---

al-Qāḍī al-Nuʿmān's Iftitāḥ al-Daʿwa (London, 2006), p. 68: 'The sun of God will rise from the west.'

[26] Pīr Sadaradīn, 'Pāchham desathī parabhu padhāreyā', *101 Ginānanī chopaḍī: Chogaḍīā sāñjanā (5) savāranā chogaḍīā (24) ghaṭapāṭanā beṭhā ginān (5) ghaṭapātanā ubhā ginān (10) venatīnā ginān (5) tathā bījā ginānavārī chopaḍī*, no. 41, 66–67, vv. 1–3.

[27] The twelve splendours or digits (*bār kaḷā*) refer to the sun, which represents the imam. It is contrasted with the moon of sixteen splendours or digits (*soḷ kaḷā*), which represents the *Pīr*.

[28] Pīr Sadaradīn, 'Jugame phire shāhājī munerī', *101 Ginānanī chopaḍī: Chogaḍīā sāñjanā (5) savāranā chogaḍīā (24) ghaṭapāṭanā beṭhā ginān (5) ghaṭapātanā ubhā ginān (10) venatīnā ginān (5) tathā bījā ginānavārī chopaḍī*, no. 3, 5, vv. 1–5.

A *ginān* with both Khaḍī Bolī and Gujarati features continues this symbolism. The composer begins by impressing upon the listeners matters of great import, the centrality of the Guide in the spiritual search, and the gravity of thinking of one's soul. Here, it is the word of the Guide that illuminates the soul, and the adoption of this word in the heart heralds the advent of spring. However, it is a spring in which not water, but divine light showers from the heavens:

Right now, at this very moment, comprehend this mystery
This mystery that lies within
On those who fathomed it, dawned the light of morn
Those on whom it dawned, tread upon the path
Without the Guide, how will you cross to the other shore?

A wondrous love we've found
Aches our heart, fretting about our soul
Day and night, contemplate the soul

The soul ponders the one
In whose devotion we are rapt
Those who seek in this world
The Guide they shall find
For thus is the command divine

With vigilance exult in the word of the Guide
For this is what illumines the pure soul
As when spring arrives and flowers burst into bloom
In the heart are showers of divine light[29]

The imagery of spring in the earlier *ginān*s sets the stage for a composition by Sayyid Fatḥ ʿAlī Shāh Shamsī (d. after 1206/1792) specifically about Nawrūz, which is recited annually by the South Asian Ismailis at the time of the festival. The *Pīr* describes his encounter with Imam Shāh Khalīl Allāh (d. 1232/1817) on the day of the festival. In the first verse, the imam is tellingly described as lord of the resurrection.

---

[29] Pīr Sadaradīn, 'Abhī abhī antar buj bujantar', *100 Ginānanī Chopaḍī: Sat Venatī moṭī maher karo tathā Sat vachan ne Sataguranuranā vīvānuṃ nānuṃ ginān tathā bījā ginānovālī* (Mumbai, 1990 VS/1934), vol. 1, no. 41, 77–78, vv. 1–3.

Considering the association of Nawrūz and spring with the revival of souls at the end of time, this epithet carries intriguing symbolic value, and is already a subtle indication of the sublimation of meaning that occurs throughout the composition. Saddened to learn that the imam had gone hunting in the woods, and overwhelmed by feelings of love, in search of his imam he too entered the forest, and it was there that he encountered Shāh Khalīl Allāh. While the occasion for the composition of the poem is clearly a physical encounter, it is evident that the author wishes, at the same time, to convey something of a profound spiritual experience. Symbols of transformation abound, including that of the coming of spring. The author is dyed in the eternal colour of the master, his life-breath blossoms like a flower and the empty caskets are filled with pearls, which are a symbol of supreme knowledge in the Indian poetic imagination. Most importantly, the author's ultimate desire is fulfilled when he is blessed with a vision of the lord in the form of pure light.

> On the glorious day of Nawrūz
> The most luminous imam, lord of the resurrection, had gone
>   hunting
> This humble servant's heart was filled with longing
> His very life-breath remained at the feet of the imam
>
> I was bound to my lord in rapture by love
> Being dyed in the master's eternal colour
> Such was the absorption of my thoughts in the lord of the
>   resurrection
> That the treasuries of truth overflowed with pearls
>
> I strolled merrily with the lord
> Obtaining the troves of both matter and spirit
> The souls shall be saved
> Of those who listen wholeheartedly to these words of gnosis
>
> When a soul attains the mystic way
> Its life-breath blossoms like a flower
> Love envelops it in the fragrance of aloes and sandalwood
> Pure as a swan, it lovingly glides along the lake

Shāh Khalīl Allāh was hunting near the citadel at the ring of fortresses
And graciously called for Fatḥ ʿAlī
My untold hopes were realised
The lord appeared eternally as light

Faithful brethren, venerate the lord with all your heart
Listen, O saints, such is the teaching of Sayyid Shamsī
Those who forget not the lord's bounties
Shall never be touched by sorrow[30]

The *ginān*s helped to galvanise the production of an abundance of other devotional poetry in the community. In modern times, the poet Hasanali Ramal (d. 1990) of Karachi was known for composing in an idiom inspired by nature. His penname was 'Suman,' a flower similar to a jasmine, an appropriate sobriquet for a poet so taken by gardens, birds, scents and seasons. He wrote in his native Sindhi, in Hindi, and most prolifically, in Gujarati. Widely respected as a playwright and poet both within and beyond the Ismaili community, he wrote for the Shrī Shaṅkar Vijay Sangīt Samāj and the external service of Radio Pakistan, among others.[31]

The following piece takes as its starting point not the season of *vasant*, or spring, but rather of *varṣā*, the monsoon season. Like the Persian spring, which breaks the hegemony of winter, the monsoon delivers the land from the oppressive heat of the summer (*unāḷo* or *griṣm*), when the searing dry winds known as *lū* can be fatal. The poet

---

[30] Sayyid Fateh-alī [Shāh] Shamasī (pseud.), 'Navarojanā dīn sohāmaṇā', in *101 Ginānanī chopaḍī: Chogaḍīā sāñjanā (5) savāranā chogaḍīā (24) ghaṭapāṭanā beṭhā ginān (5) ghaṭapātanā ubhā ginān (10) venatīnā ginān (5) tathā bījā ginānavārī chopaḍī* (Mumbai, 1988 VS/1932), vol. 4, no. 38, 56–57, vv. 1–2, 4–8.

[31] Many of Suman's Ismaili themed compositions are collected in his *Suman saṅgrah* (Karāchī, [1969]). The poem that follows was written in the 1980s, and so is not included in this collection. I believe I have in my possession a later, second edition of the collection, which may record the poem, but it was not available to me at the time of this writing. My access to the poem was through a copy I have of Hasanali Ramal's handwritten manuscript of his compositions, kindly provided to me by his son, Anwar Rammal of Karachi, Pakistan.

refers not to clouds (*vādaḷ*), but to 'cloudlings' (*vādaḷī*), bursting with colour, which shower the gentlest of rains. It is only in the last lines that the poet introduces spring in his prayer that it may grace the lives of the believers. In the context of allusions to spring in South Asian Ismaili literature, the intimation of the advent of the imam and his blessings is taken for granted. The word used for spring in this line, though, is not the *vasant* of the vernacular tradition, but the Persian *bahār*. So naturalised had the Persianate vocabulary become that this skilful blending of contrasting seasonal images seems quite appropriate.

There are several other noteworthy aspects of the composition, many drawn from the interactions with sister traditions of Subcontinental verse forms. The male poet writes in the voice of a female, addressing his audience as *sakhī*, translated here as sister, but literally a female friend. The feminine voice was used by several poets, both male and female, to great effect. The occasion for the poem was the celebration of the Silver Jubilee marking the twenty-fifth anniversary of Prince Karim Aga Khan as imam of the Ismaili community. The word 'Jubilee' in the poem is personified, as if Jubilee were the personal name of a sprightly girl who arrives in the courtyard joyfully dancing, with jingling little bells (*ghūṅgaru*) on her anklets. All of this is conveyed by a single onomatopoeic word, *rhūmajhūmtī*, the sound made by the little bells. The onomatopoeia, internal rhyme, and alliteration in the verses is stunning. The rains *jharamar*, the streams *khaḍakhaḍ*, the brooks *kalakal* and the birds *valaval*. Most notably, as in the other Ismaili poetry rendered here, it is abundantly clear that these verses are not simply about the coming of the rains or the longing for spring, but have deep spiritual symbolism. The poet writes, 'This is not just any rain, my sister. Swung open have the gates of blessings!'

Sister, arrived have the cloudlings
Bursting with colours
The monsoon cloudlings are here
Gently it rains, pitter-patter

Harken, sister, the thunder rumbles, rumbles
Sparkles, sparkles the lightning
Gently it rains, pitter-patter

Splashing streams, burbling brooks
Chirruping, chirruping
Birds without end
Sister, rippling ponds, moistened earth
The world has donned its finery
This is not just any rain, my sister
Swung open have the gates of blessings!
Gently it rains, pitter-patter

Sister, jingling and frolicking
Jubilee graced our courtyard
The joy in our hearts can't be contained
Scatter flowers to welcome
Beloved Karim Shah, our refuge
Sister, rejoice, rejoice
With love in your heart
Gently it rains, pitter-patter

Lush, lush in every place
The garden bursting, bursting
Bloomed, blossomed
Have succulent Suman flowers
Sister, may there be joyous colours of the rains
And the society of the sisters
May spring grace our lives
May there be sweet waves, sister
For each and every body sways
Gently it rains, pitter-patter
Gently it rains, pitter-patter

The Spiritual Resurrection: Adorning a Persian Assembly

While spring-related imagery is prevalent in literature across much of the Muslim world, it should not come as a surprise that it is particularly pronounced in Persian-influenced areas, where the pageantry of the Nawrūz festival was fertile ground for the imaginations of creative souls. The same is also true of Persian Ismaili literature, in which images of spring in general, and Nawrūz in particular, abound. The

Qurʾanic juxtaposition of spring and the coming Resurrection inspired many poets. In Ḥasan-i Maḥmūd's (d. 645/1246) *Dīwān-i qāʾimiyyāt* ('Poems of the Resurrection'), written at Alamūt after Imam Ḥasan *ʿalā dhikrih al-salām*'s (d. 561/1166) declaration of the *qiyāma* or Resurrection about a hundred years earlier, he compares the imam's advent to the arrival of Nawrūz:

> Like nature's Nawrūz, like the world of bounties, thus came Ḥasan
> Like hidden fortune, like the *qibla* of faith, thus came Ḥasan
>
> Like the source of adornment of that currency of the world
> Like grace, like gaze, like the dawn of bounties, thus came Ḥasan
>
> Like the nightingale of God's unity, sweetly singing notes of
> every tune
> Upon the rosebush in the garden, thus came Ḥasan. . . .
>
> In the pre-eternal land, kingmaker was he
> Ruler in the post-eternal realm, thus came Ḥasan. . . . .
>
> Source of the light of guidance from a lord most great, sublime
> Glory be! O glory be! O glory, thus came Ḥasan[32]

In another composition, the poet is tempted to entrust to the wind a letter to convey to his beloved. He speaks of how the beauty of her face ushers spring into the soul's garden. However, he jealously desists from entrusting the missive, lest the breeze stroke the recipient's musky tresses while delivering it. Instead, he sets out himself to meet the beloved, but try as he might, his strength fails him. He recalls that the physician administers *mufarriḥ* for weak hearts, that vivifying medicine containing rubies. Why then, he wonders, does thinking of his beloved's ruby lips sap all his heart's strength?

As the poem recounts the poet's longing, we learn that the true beloved is none other than the successor of Ḥasan *ʿalā dhikrih al-salām*, Imam Aʿlā Muḥammad (d. 607/1210), also known as Nūr al-Dīn, 'the light of faith'. The poet takes advantage of this name when he

---

[32] Ṣalāḥ al-Dīn Ḥasan-i Maḥmūd-i Kātib, *Dīwān-i qāʾimiyyāt*, ed. Seyyed Jalal Hosseini Badakhchani, *Poems of the Resurrection* (Tehran, 1395 Sh./2016), no. 50, 152–153, lns. 1523–1526, 1531, 1546. The ode is in a popular *hazaj* metre, ¯ ¯ ˘ | ˘ ¯ ¯ ˘ | ˘ ¯ ¯ ˘ | ˘ ¯ ¯.

introduces the beloved, whose light (*nūr*) ennobles his devotees while his fire (*nār*) torments his foes. In common with other Shiʿi writers, for whom the prophets and imams represent the face of God (*wajh Allāh*), i.e., those by whom God is recognised, Ḥasan-i Maḥmūd avers that the world abides by the existence of God's representative, recalling the Prophetic declaration, 'If the earth were bereft of an Imam for even a moment, it would be convulsed with its inhabitants' (*law khalat al-arḍ min imām sāʿa la-māddat bi-ahlihā*).[33] Time wonders when the imam shall take his rightful place on the throne of the world, to which Intellect responds that this will occur 'when the winds of spring's triumph convey in the mist the fragrance of victory at the end of times.'

Who shall bear to the beloved, the missive of this tearful soul?
To that portrait of loveliness, who shall bear my thousand tales?

The people of the world advised, 'Entrust your missive to the wind
That it may bear your grief to one, who liberates from woe and pain'

But bear this I could not, to entrust it to the wind
What if when conveying it, the wind caress her musky tress?

Set out I did to see that one, of rosy cheeks, stately cypress
Whose visage to soul's garden, brings splendid, glorious spring

News was heard, that lovely moon, brings to vernal charm
Violets and hyacinth, to the tulip garden

[33] This is a well-known tradition, reported in slightly different wordings in, for example, Naṣīr al-Dīn Muḥammad b. Muḥammad Ṭūsī and Ṣalāḥ al-Dīn Ḥasan-i Maḥmūd-i Kātib, *Rawḍa-yi taslīm (Taṣawwurāt)*, ed. and trans. Seyyed Jalal Hosseini Badakhchani, *Paradise of Submission: A Medieval Treatise on Ismaili Thought; A New Persian Edition and English Translation of Naṣīr al-Dīn Tūsī's Rawḍa-yi taslīm* (London, 2005), Persian p. 148, English p. 120; Abū Jaʿfar Muḥammad b. Yaʿqūb al-Kulaynī, *al-Uṣūl min al-Kāfī* (Beirut, 1428/2007), vol. 1, p. 104. For further references, see Mohammad Ali Amir-Moezzi, *Le Guide divin dans le shîʿisme originel: Aux sources de l'ésotérisme en Islam*, trans. by David Streight as *The Divine Guide in Early Shiʿism: The Sources of Esotericism in Islam* (Albany, 1994), pp. 43, 125, 229 n. 673–675. It is the most quoted tradition in Ṣalāḥ al-Dīn Ḥasan-i Maḥmūd-i Kātib's *Dīwān-i qāʾimiyyāt* (Tehran, 1390 Sh./2011). This observation, and additional Twelver sources for the tradition can be found in Muḥammad Riḍā Shafīʿī Kadkanī, '*Qāʾīmiyyāt wa jāygāh-i ān dar shʿir wa adab-i Fārsī*', ibid., p. 30.

Longingly my soul set out, pursuing perilous path
Enduring all it could, sacrificing all its strength. . . .

If doctors dispense ruby tonic, to heal a heart that's frail
Why do the beloved's ruby lips, sap all strength of my heart?

Yearning breached my heart, like a thief with lamp in hand
Gathered all chattels of self-control, and absconded in the
night. . . .

A mountain is my grief, and I an ant
Which ant can bear such a load? Such a burden mountainous?. . . .

The world abides by God's face, by his generosity
The gold of its existence, is assayed pure for all times

Sovereign of time and terre, Muhammad from whom
Their portion of light and fire, his friend and foe receive

Time asked of Intellect, 'When shall fortune of the spheres
Snatch from the adversary's head, his stolen, borrowed crown?'

Responded did Intellect, 'When the winds of spring's triumph,
Convey in the mist the fragrance, of the victory at the end of times'

'Then in glory shall he mount his throne, this ʿAlī of the time
Taking in his holy hand, the sword of Dhu'l-faqār!'[34]

The most thorough treatment of Nawrūz in extant Ismaili literature in any language probably occurs in the magnum opus of the learned Husayn b. Yaʿqūb Shāh (fl. eleventh/seventeenth century), scion of a family of Ismaili dignitaries. His hitherto unpublished *Tazyīn al-majālis* ('Adornment of Assemblies'), a blend of both prose and poetry, explores the spiritual dimension of commemorations such as Nawrūz, including

[34] Ḥasan-i Maḥmūd-i Kātib, *Dīwān-i qāʾimiyyāt*, no. 40, pp. 131–133, bayts 1212–1217, 1219–1221, 1223, 1230–1234. The composition is in the *mujtass* metre, ˘ ¯ ˘ ¯ | ˘ ˘ ¯ ¯ | ˘ ¯ ˘ ¯ | ˘ ˘ ¯, one of the favourite rhythms of Rūmī (d. 672/1273), Ḥāfiẓ (d. 792/1390) and especially Saʿdī (d. 691/1292), who composed more than half his odes in it, see Finn Thiesen, *A Manual of Classical Persian Prosody: With Chapters on Urdu, Karakhanidic and Ottoman Prosody* (Wiesbaden, 1982), pp. 146–147. It is clear in this poem that the victory of the imam is not merely symbolic, but given the political rivalries in this period, was very much conceived in material terms as well.

ʿīd al-fiṭr and ʿīd al-aḍḥā.[35] With the Safavids then in power, the formation of an Iranian nation-state further buttressed existing celebrations of the festival.[36]

The proliferation of manuscripts of the *Tazyīn al-majālis* in both Iran and Central Asia testifies to its popularity, and the fact that most copies only record sections dedicated to one or another of the festivals rather than the complete work suggests that these must have been in common use on those occasions, and were likely recited at religious gatherings for these festivals. The ode that initiates the piece on Nawrūz is written in a rather unusual form of the *hazaj* metre which, while somewhat rare, lends itself to singing, – – ⏑ | ⏑ – – – | – – ⏑ | ⏑ – – –.[37]

> Auspicious Nawrūz has arrived, O lord, may blessings abound
> Mirth pervades all around, O lord, may blessings abound. . . .
>
> Abloom is jubilation's garden, brimful is the heart's chalice
> Atwitter is the soul's nightingale, O lord, may blessings abound
>
> By the bounty of mercy divine, has passed all sorrow and suffering
> Resplendent the world has become, O lord, may blessings abound
>
> Flourish and bloom does the rose garden, filled with light and purity is the house
> Wax eloquent does the lily's tongue, O lord, may blessings abound
>
> The goblet increases good cheer, the ambergris exudes perfume
> For fragrance there is incense, O lord, may blessings abound. . . .
>
> Winter's severity has been snapped, tidings of spring reach the heart
> Every moment, say a hundred times: O lord, may blessings abound

---

[35] For this author, see Ḥusayn b. Yaʿqūb Shāh b. Ṣūfī, 'The Adornment of Assemblies by Ḥusayn b. Yaʿqūb Shāh b. Ṣūfī', chap. 4, trans. Shafique N. Virani in *An Anthology of Ismaili Literature: A Shiʿi Vision of Islam*, ed. Hermann Landolt, Samira Sheikh, and Kutub Kassam (London, 2008), pp. 296–297; Maryam Muʿizzī, 'Risāla-yi Ḥusayn bin Yaʿqūb Shāh', *Faṣlnāma-yi muṭāliʿāt-i taʾrīkhī*, 3, 3–4 (1370 Sh./1991–1992), pp. 403–425. I am currently preparing a critical edition and translation of the *Tazyīn al-majālis*, from which the translations that follow are drawn.

[36] Shapur Shahbazi, 'Nowruz ii. In the Islamic Period', *Encyclopedia Iranica*.

[37] One of only a handful of other poets to use this metre was Jalāl al-Dīn Rūmī, see Thiesen, *Classical Persian Prosody*, p. 143.

It soon becomes clear in the work, however, that Ḥusayn b. Yaʿqūb's purpose is not solely to celebrate the festival with eloquent verse. Throughout his treatise, he exhorts the believers to observe these occasions as opportunities for transformation. His treatise is addressed to 'the people of insight, whose hearts are fragrant with perfume, and the people of virtue, whose minds are the treasuries of spiritual gnosis.' Therefore, beyond simply celebrating the joyous advent of spring, in a manner typical of Ismaili luminaries, he wishes to explain subtleties of much more profound import. He informs the readers that Nawrūz is not simply when the sun enters into the constellation of Aries, signalling the moment of the equinox and the transformation of the physical world with the arrival of spring. For the believers, the true Nawrūz occurs when their actions, deeds and very existence are transformed such that their iniquities are exchanged for virtues, and their misdeeds for noble actions. While the people of exterior forms take Nawrūz to be the time when fields are to be sown, the people of interior meaning realise that this world is the sowing ground for the next world, and act accordingly. Nawrūz is hence a time for abandoning the darkness of blind following (*taqlīd*) for the light of true spiritual search and realisation (*taḥqīq*). The former pleases only the creatures, while the latter pleases the Creator. His 'Admonition for this Blessed Time [of Nawrūz]' is divided into sixteen parts, each buttressed by an Arabic quotation or two from the Qur'an, the Prophet, the imams, or wisdom literature, which is then explained in Persian, after which the author provides a line or two of sage counsel, before concluding the point with rhymed couplets (a *mathnawī*). His verse and the structure of his exordia clearly demonstrate the influence of the aforementioned *Dīwān-i qā'imiyyāt* ('Poems of the Resurrection'), written in the Alamūt era, while other portions of his writing seem to mirror the *Akhlāq-i Muḥtashamī* ('Muhtashamian Ethics') by Nāṣir al-Dīn Muḥtasham (d. 655/1257) and Naṣīr al-Dīn Ṭūsī (d. 672/1274).[38] In many senses, the tenor of this section of the *Tazyīn al-majālis* reflects an incident related from the time of Imam ʿAlī b. Abī Ṭālib (d. 40/661):

[38] Nāṣir al-Dīn ʿAbd al-Raḥīm b. Abī Manṣūr Muḥtasham and Naṣīr al-Dīn Muḥammad b. Muḥammad Ṭūsī, *Akhlāq-i Muḥtashamī* (Tehran, 1339 Sh./1960).

> ʿAlī (may God be pleased with him) saw a group dressed in finery. 'What is going on?' he asked. He was told, 'This day is one of their festivals.' He replied, 'For us, a festival is a day on which we commit no sins.'[39]

These points are illustrated in the following selected passages from this portion of the *Tazyīn al-majālis*:

> It should be as self-evident as the sun and luminous as the moon to the redolent hearts of the people of insight, the spirits of the pious laden with treasures of gnosis, and the dispositions of the supplicants before this purest companion of support, that those blessed with the good fortune of recognising the essence of our exalted lord, Ḥaḍrat-i Mawlānā (may his mercy encompass all!), must conduct themselves in a manner distinct and distinguished in every manner from the demeanour and lifestyle of negligent fools and the ignorant who have not realised the truth. Were the conduct of these two groups to be embroidered as cloth of the same weave, in no way would one be ennobled and preferred to the other. It has been said of the seekers of the world: *al-dunyā jīfa wa-ṭālibuhā kilāb*, 'The world is a corpse and those who seek it are dogs,' while of the faithful and seekers of God it has been said, *al-mu'min ḥayy fi'l-dārayn wa-ʿazīz ʿinda khāliq al-ʿālamayn*, 'The faithful are alive in both realms and are dear to the Creator of both worlds'. So how can the two bear any resemblance in their intimacy with the divine? According to sound traditions and limpid Qur'anic verses, proximity and glory are the lot of the faithful, while perfidy and depravity that of the hypocrites.
>
> Rhymed couplets:
>
> Those who seek the world are like dogs
How can such vileness be worthy of mercy?
>
> Seekers of the world are more despicable than dogs
Seekers of the faith are intimates of the Just
>
> I have penned these testaments to explain that the true Nawrūz is not the apparent one, marked by the Cusp of Aries. For

[39] Abū Ḥāmid Muḥammad al-Ghazālī, *Kīmīyā-yi saʿādat*, ed. Ḥusayn Khidīwjam, p. 566.

the faithful, the actual New Day (*rūz-i naw*) is the day they mend their ways, transforming their behaviour and their very existence. In other words, a new day will dawn upon them when they exchange their iniquities and sins for virtues and noble deeds.

First: They must transform their heedlessness into consummate struggle, for a tradition states, *al-dunyā mazraʿat al-ākhira*, 'this world is the sowing ground for the next world'. Those who don't strive, who don't sow the seeds of goodness, and instead while away their time in heedlessness, will be bereft of provisions and supplies for their journey.

Rhymed couplets:

Of faith's root, struggle is the branch
So strive that from your goal you achieve your ambition

Whiling their time away, the heedless
For the road gathered no provisions of worship

Second: They must replace worldly attachments with love for Mawlānā, for it is narrated in a tradition, *ḥubb al-dunyā ra's kull khaṭi'a*, 'attachment to the world is the root of all evil.' In another place it is said, *ṭālib al-māl fi'l-dunyā ka'l-dūdat al-qazz. Ẓannat an sutratahā taʿinahā wa'l-ladhī ẓannat ardāhā*, 'Those who seek the wealth of this world (thinking it will protect them) are like silkworms that suppose their cocoons will help them. But that very delusion is the cause of their destruction.' Thus, seekers of this world have no portion of the riches of the next.

Rhymed couplets:

Be of faith's folk, not a world-worshipper
For loving the world is the root of evil

Destroys faith does worldly wealth
Reducing acts of worship to dust. . . .

Sixth: They should supplant gossip with speaking well of others, for a tradition relates, *al-ghība ashadd min al-zinā*, 'gossip is more loathsome than adultery'. Elsewhere the Qur'an enjoins, *wa-lā yaghtab baʿḍukum baʿḍan ayuḥibbu aḥadakum an yakula laḥm akhīh maytan*, 'Nor gossip against one another. Would one of you relish eating the flesh of his dead brother?' (49:12). Hence the gossiper has no hope for divine mercy.

Rhymed couplets:

Train your tongue to speak well of others
That you may rejoice in the company of gnosis

Those who wag their tongues in gossip
Shall have no refuge from the wrath of the Wrathful. . . .

Ninth: They must exchange arrogance for submissiveness and humility, for a tradition states, *aktharu ahl al-nār al-mutakabbirūn*, 'The arrogant form the majority of hell's denizens.' In addition, Mawlānā ʿAlī (may there be prostration and glorification at his mention!) declares, *man takabbur ʿalāʾl-nās dhall*, 'Those who arrogantly consider themselves greater than others will be abased (in the next world).' Thus, the arrogant are not admitted to the sanctuary of divine splendour.

Rhymed couplets:

For the arrogant, honour is proscribed
Lost they shall be in the desert of abasement

Be humble with both great and small
That from divine wrath you may be saved

Tenth: They must trade miserliness for charity, for the Holy Prophet has said, *al-sakhī fi jiwār Allāh wa-anā rafiquh, waʾl-bakhīl fiʾl-nār wa-rafiquh Iblīs (ʿalayh al-laʿna)*, 'The charitable shall be neighbours of God and I will be their companion, while misers will be in the Fire and the devil (upon whom be curses) will be their companion.' Hence, the misers are also captive in shackles of wretchedness, with no hope of liberation.

Rhymed couplets:

Charity characterises people of the way
While upon misers is the Chosen Prophet's curse

Misers despair of blessings
While the All-Merciful showers mercy upon the charitable. . . .

Thirteenth: They must forsake despair for hope, as the divine word proclaims, 'Who are those who despair of the mercy of their Lord save those who have lost the way and the unbelievers?' (Qur'an 15:56). To despair of His threshold is naught but complete infidelity.

Rhymed couplets:

He who despairs of the favours of the Beloved
Tarries at the shore of mercy's ocean

Infidelity it is to despair of the Generous
Take hope, while also fearing God. . . .

Fifteenth: They must forsake blind imitation (*taqlīd*) for verification (*taḥqīq*) and testifying to divine unity (*tawḥīd*). Mawlānā ʿAlī (may there be prostration and glorification at his mention!) says, *al-taqlīd riḍā al-khalq wa'l-tawḥīd riḍā al-khāliq*, 'Blind imitation earns the pleasure of the creatures while (verification of) divine unity delivers one to the pleasure of the Creator.' So long as God's pleasure has yet to be sought, subservience to the pleasures of the creatures is infidelity.

Rhymed couplets:

How long will you give credence to blind imitation?
Upon your head, place the crown of divine unity

Come, join those who verify the truth, be not a blind imitator
Sprinkle not the dust of abasement on the head of honour

Sixteenth: They must exchange existence for non-existence, so that the gates of joy and forgiveness may be opened for them. This secret is the unspeakable mystery. It has been alluded to in the Qur'an and traditions in hidden narratives and silent tongues, and none can deny these words.

Rhymed couplets:

In the fire of unity, burn the ego of 'I' and 'we'
Unleashing the arrow of *lā*, of 'no (god but God),' pierce the eye of multiplicity

From the whims of your existence, no escape is there
Cease to exist, that you may light your candle with faith

In short, were we to continue to expound along these lines to one hundred thousand such points, nothing additional would be gained, for prolixity wearies the souls and dispositions of both the writer and the reader. The essence of this elaboration is that by acting contrary to the inclinations of your ephemeral nature and the desires of your carnal whims and lusts, you must transform your existence. In so doing, by divine mercy, you may discover Nawrūz, a new day. For indeed, how can all variety of dazzle and glitter, and wearing all manner of bright and colourful garments and ornaments bring about a new day (*rūz-i naw*)?

Poem:

The physical Nawrūz is brought about by a change of the year
The spiritual Nawrūz occurs but with the transformation of life itself

The Nawrūz of the people of verity lies in changing their actions
The Nawrūz of the people of falsehood lies in changing their clothes

Nawrūz is not something set to fade
Nawrūz is something safe from ever fading

These [worldly] types of Nawrūz become worn-out, to be replaced by new ones that follow in their footsteps. However, the mercy of the Sustainer is a Nawrūz that never ages and a lamp that is never extinguished by the bitter winds of renewal and degeneration. However, action and supplication are necessary to avail of His mercy (may He be exalted!). No affliction is averted without a prayer, for a tradition relates, *lā yaraddu al-balā illā al-du'ā*, 'Naught averts affliction save prayer.' So long as the supplicants seek not to change their lives in the manner related, their souls will never attain the proximity of union.

Dear friends, you have girt the belt of sincerity round the waist of belief and turned from the path of self-worship and self-seeing to undertake a journey to the destinations in the lands of affliction and God's pleasure. Despair not of His mercy (may He be exalted!). Make your day new by His eternal grace, forsake the worn instincts of your former deeds, shun wicked acts, and with the hand of hope and courage reach out to gain proximity to the Lord, until Mawlānā (may he be exalted) by his immense grace and universal generosity exalts and ennobles you.

How long can you continue gazing at the face of your hopes in this worn mirror, sullied by the rust of darkness? How long can you keep building the edifice of these foundationless walls with the mud and straw plaster of desire? Now, while you have some manner of control, burnish your hearts with the polishing rays of the righteous teacher's guidance in hand so that they shine with the light of gnosis; take up residence in the remaining stations of submission and worship, safeguarded and preserved from the misfortunes of defects and lapses; let not your feet become shackled in the fetters of pride and vanity, for divine wrath requires but the slightest cause, lest Nawrūz give way to mourning, revelry to grief, and the noble star's zenith to its nadir.

Rhymed couplets:

Penned I a few verses from the word of God
For the folk at the Beginning, as a lesson

That by this they may find the road to the Return
And rejoice in what flows from my nature

If they learn, they shall become folk of spiritual states
Into union their separation shall be transformed

If they learn not, behold, blameless am I!
Sealed I have the treatise and the book I have closed

May Mawlānā make our sustenance the felicity of Nawrūz and deliver us all from this decrepit well of darkness and misguidance. Amen, O Lord of the Worlds, and peace be upon the folk of peace!

Afterword:
The Glory of the Creation and the Glory of the Creator

In its resolution A/RES/64/253 of 2010, the United Nations General Assembly proclaimed 21 March as 'International Nowruz Day'.[40] In adopting the resolution, the UN noted that Nawrūz is celebrated as a New Year's Day by over 300 million people across the globe, and has been observed for over three millennia in the Balkans, the Black Sea Basin, the Caucasus, Central Asia, the Middle East and other regions. Its resolution cited the importance of cultural diversity, the awareness of the unity of humankind, the development of international exchanges, recognition of the importance of safeguarding intangible cultural heritage and the relevance of living in harmony with nature. It noted that 'the foundations of the traditions and rituals of Nowruz reflect features of the cultural and ancient customs of the civilisations of East and West, which influenced those civilisations through the interchange of human values.'

The study of Ismaili literature related with spring in general, and Nawrūz in particular, reveals that it was very much enriched by the diversity of cultures and customs in which it developed, drawing upon a wide-ranging panoply of languages, symbols and customs. At the same time, a common, uniting ethos also permeated much of the literature, one attuned to seeking spiritual meaning from earthly phenomena. This Ismaili sentiment was shared with others, and is well-illustrated in a story about the famous mystic, Rābiʿa al-ʿAdawiyya, related in the *Tadhkirat al-awliyāʾ* ('Memorial of Saints') by Shaykh Farīd al-Dīn ʿAṭṭār (d. 618/1221), about whom almost nothing is known, but who was later claimed by both Sufi and Ismaili authors. It is an appropriate narrative with which to conclude, as it succinctly expresses many of the sentiments in the Ismaili literature examined in this study.

---

[40] United Nations General Assembly, 'Resolution Adopted by the General Assembly on 23 February 2010: 64/253. International Day of Nowruz', New York: United Nations, May 10, 2010: http://www.un.org/en/ga/search/view_doc.asp?symbol=A/RES/64/253 (accessed 5 September 2017).

It was a glorious spring day and Rābiʿa was in her quarters. Her attendant outside was so overwhelmed by the vernal beauty that she cried out, 'Mistress, come outside, come outside! Behold the glory of creation!' To which Rābiʿa replied, 'My dear, for once, come within, come within! Behold the glory of the Creator!'[41]

---

[41] Paraphrased from Farīd al-Dīn ʿAṭṭār, *Tadhkirat al-awliyāʾ*, ed. Muḥammad Istiʿlāmī (Tehran, 2535 Shāhinshāhī/1355 Sh./1976).

19

Yemeni Ismailism in Jewish Philosophy, Sixth/Twelfth to Eleventh/Seventeenth Centuries: A General Historical Sketch*

Mauro Zonta
(Sapienza University of Rome, Italy)

Between the sixth/twelfth and eleventh/seventeenth centuries, certain Jewish philosophers employed elements of Ismaili thought for creating their own, more or less original doctrines. Among them are the scholars belonging to what has been termed 'Jewish Ismailism', a trend founded by Nathanael ben al-Fayyūmī in the sixth/twelfth century, who made use of the *Epistles of the Brethren of the Purity*, and the works of Islamic Neoplatonic authors.

In 1984, Ronald Kiener wrote a highly interesting although brief article about 'Jewish Ismailism' in sixth/twelfth-century Yemen.[1] In the last thirty years, there have been apparently no further attempts to explore this topic, although the relevant evidence can be found not only in the sixth/twelfth century, but up to the end of the tenth/sixteenth century and in spite of the fact that there are many sources which can be studied and employed with this aim, namely, to investigate the

* Editorial comments and additions in this chapter by Tzvi Langermann (TL) and the editor (OM) are framed by brackets.

[1] Ronald C. Kiener, 'Jewish Ismāʿīlism in Twelfth Century Yemen: R. Nethanel ben al-Fayyūmī', *The Jewish Quarterly Review*, n.s., 74 (1984), pp. 249–266. Kiener was the first to write on this topic. [In fact, Shlomo Pines published his 'Nathanaël al-Fayyūmī et la théologie ismaélienne', *Revue de l'histoire juive en Egypte*, 1 (1947), pp. 5–22 (reprinted in volume V of the Collected Works of Shlomo Pines). However, Pines was hesitant whether to place the author in Egypt or the Yemen, as both were under strong Shiʿi influence at the time. TL]

direct or indirect adoption of some aspects of Ismailism by Yemeni Jewish philosophers and interpreters of the Hebrew Bible.[2] Many passages from the relevant Yemeni texts, with translations and commentaries, are included in the *Yemenite Midrash: Philosophical Commentaries on the Torah*, which was published by Tzvi Langermann in 1996.[3] The first general historical outline of this question appeared in an extended article in Italian that I published in 1997, which emphasises some key lines of medieval Judeo-Arabic thought in that period and milieu.[4] The subject is also dealt with in a substantial chapter on Judeo-Arabic philosophy as a whole, which will appear in the volume edited by Ulrich Rudolph and Renate Wünsch.[5] The present paper will simply try to indicate the possible future aspects of research in this field.

Between roughly 1150 and 1550, Yemen was a central geographical area of Judeo-Arabic culture. It is probable that in this period (late Middle Ages), together with the Maghrib, Yemen was the Islamic country which witnessed a most important development of a Judeo-Arabic philosophy. As pointed out by Tzvi Langermann in 1992, this philosophy most likely entertained a close, and even symbiotic relationship with various aspects of Arab-Islamic philosophy and theology.[6] Philosophy occupied a prominent position in Yemeni Jewish communities after the death of the key figure of Jewish theology and thought in general, Moses Maimonides (1136/1138–1204). It is possible to find in the works of Jewish Yemeni authors a substantial

---

[2] [Tzvi Langermann has been trying to show that the intellectual reach of Yemenite Jewry was not at all limited to Ismaili writings – which is the impression one sometimes gets. His studies bring in Ishrāqī, Indian and other elements. See, for example 'Saving the Soul by Knowing the Soul: A Medieval Yemeni Interpretation of Song of Songs', *Journal of Jewish Thought and Philosophy*, 12 (2003), pp. 147–166. TL].

[3] Y. Tzvi Langermann, *Yemenite Midrash: Philosophical Commentaries on the Torah. An Anthology of Writings from the Golden Age of Judaism in the Yemen* (New York and San Francisco, 1996; repr., New Haven, 2010).

[4] Mauro Zonta, 'Linee del pensiero islamico nella storia della filosofia ebraica medievale', *Istituto Universitario Orientale. Annali*, 57 (1997), pp. 101–144, 450–483.

[5] Ulrich Rudolph and Renate Wünsch (ed.), *Die Philosophie in der islamischen Welt*, vol. 2 (Basel: Schwabe, forthcoming).

[6] Y. Tzvi Langermann, 'Cultural Contacts of the Jews of Yemen', in Amir Harrak, K. Kopperdryer and B. Steben (ed.), *Contacts between Cultures. Vol. 1: West Asia and North Africa* (Lewiston, 1992), pp. 218–295.

projection and extension of pre-Maimonidean and Maimonidean Judeo-Arabic philosophy.

Apart from some pages by Colette Sirat, Yemeni philosophy of the period under discussion has almost never been examined in detail in the main handbooks of the history of Jewish philosophy.[7] However, it has been the object of occasional studies. These studies have examined the philosophical and theological doctrines of some particular authors and their texts.

In chronological order, the most significant example of this literature is a work which was written in Yemeni Jewish communities, titled the *Bustān al-ʿuqūl* ('The Garden of the Intellects') by a Yemeni author, Nathanael ben al-Fayyūmī, who was possibly in contact with Maimonides. Al-Fayyūmī wrote this short philosophic-theological treatise in ten chapters around 1165. The text was discovered, in a unique manuscript, at the end of the nineteenth century and was first edited and translated into English by David Levine in 1908.[8] This work is manifestly of some interest for our topic, since it was apparently seen as an example of 'Jewish Ismailism' (see above). Moreover, it was examined and studied as a possible example of 'symbiosis' between Jews and Arabs in Yemen, to which Shlomo Dov Goitein devoted his pioneering, short but masterful study, *Jews and Arabs: Their Contacts Through the Ages*, published in 1955.[9]

After 1970, scholars began to show a greater interest in Yemeni Judeo-Arabic texts and looked at some other texts in detail. They sought to examine certain anonymous works in order to better delineate the literature of 'Jewish Ismailism'. The first example of a text similar to al-Fayyūmī's is that of two short epistles written in Arabic by an anonymous Jewish author, probably in Yemen: *On the Divine Sciences*, and *On the Unity of God, the Totality of Existence, and the Knowledge of Divine Eschatology*. Both treatises were probably written at the beginning of the ninth/fifteenth century.

---

[7] Colette Sirat, *La filosofia ebraica medievale secondo i testi editi e inediti*, ed. Bruno Chiesa (Brescia, 1990), pp. 513–517.

[8] David Levine, *The Bustan al-Ukul By Nathanael ibn al-Fayyumi* (New York, 1908).

[9] Shlomo Dov Goitein, *Jews and Arabs: Their Contacts Through the Ages* (New York, 1955; reprint with addition, 1974).

Franz Rosenthal, in a pioneering work produced in 1980, managed to identify philosophical-theological doctrines in these epistles.[10] These doctrines can be summarised as follows: according to the anonymous author, God was the first mover, without any physical attributes; the creation resulted from an emanation of separated intellects, which were organised in a numerological order. Reality is comprised of three worlds – the angelic one, that of the celestial spheres, and that of the four elements, generable and corruptible – so that it is a sort of a 'macranthropos',[11] that is, a great living creature. The human soul is a rational one, able to understand both sensible phenomena and the 'secrets of existence' – unlike any other kind of soul. These doctrines are typical of Arab Islamic Neoplatonism (in particular that of the Ikhwān al-Ṣafā'), partly mixed with some elements of al-Ghazālī's theology, which are explicitly quoted in the text.

What is more, these doctrinal positions are close to those that Joseph Qāfiḥ identified in the forty philosophical questions by Peraḥyah ben Meshullam, a medieval author whose *terminus ante quem* is 1470.[12] Since Meshullam adopted, in principle, the philosophical and theological doctrines of Moses Maimonides, he was thus another representative of Maimonidean tradition in Yemen.[13]

David Blumenthal and Yitzhaq Tzvi Langermann have carried out the most in-depth studies on specific authors and texts of Yemeni Jewish philosophy. The former dealt especially with the works of a Yemeni Jewish scholar of the first half of the eighth/fourteenth century, Ḥōṭer ben Shelōmō (lived around 1423), who wrote mostly philosophical texts. Developing a controversial hypothesis, Blumenthal tried to link Shelōmō's work with an almost mystical interpretation of Maimonides, a kind of Jewish 'illumination' similar to the

---

[10] Franz Rosenthal, 'From the Unorthodox Judaism of Medieval Yemen', in Gérard Nahon and Charles Touati (ed.), *Hommage à Georges Vajda. Études d'histoire et de pensée juives* (Louvain, 1980), pp. 279–290.

[11] [This does not necessarily imply that the cosmos has the form of a human being. My thanks to Tzvi Langermann for this comment. OM].

[12] Joseph Qāfiḥ, 'Arba'im she'elot u-teshuvot ba-filosofiah le-rav Peraḥyah ben rav Meshullam', *Sefunot*, 3, 18 (5745/1985), pp. 111–192.

[13] Ibid.

doctrine of 'illumination' (*ishrāq*) founded by Shihāb al-Dīn Yaḥyā al-Suhrawardī (d. 587/1191).

Tzvi Langermann devoted much research to the contents of philosophical Judeo-Arabic commentaries on the Hebrew Bible (especially the Pentateuch), elaborated in Yemen between the eighth/fourteenth and the tenth/sixteenth centuries. Langermann was the first to examine these commentaries employing a systematic and comparative method, thus showing that they are a proper literary genre, which reveals a sort of agreement between Neoplatonism and Jewish religious tradition.

* * * * * *

The general features of Yemeni Judeo-Arabic thought as developed between 1150 and 1550, are two at least.

On the one hand, Maimonides was regarded in Yemen as a Master of Philosophy, as was the case in European Jewish philosophy of the late Middle Ages, but in a more accommodating and moderate way.

Actually, Maimonides' philosophy was read and understood not according to Averroes (who was apparently unknown in Yemen), but according to Avicenna and even to al-Ghazālī as a philosopher, as well as according to the Neoplatonist authors who were well known to and appreciated by Ismaili scholars as well. This interpretation treads a middle course between the rationalism of Jewish Aristotelian scholars and Jewish traditionalism. It is worth noting that Maimonides was almost canonised as a semi-messianic figure. He was called the 'Moses of the age' (*Mosheh ha-zeman*), with a loan translation of the expression 'the imam of the age' (*imām al-zamān*), used to indicate the hidden imam in Twelver Shiʿism and also largely used in Ismaili Shiʿism.

The juridical and theological writings of Maimondes, including the *Commentary to Mishnah*, the *Book of Commandments*, the *Repetition of the Holy Torah* (*Mishneh Torah*), and the *Thirteen Principles of the Jewish Thought* were the most studied and commented on of all his writings. Occasional commentaries on the *Guide for the Perplexed*, such as the commentary ascribed to Zechariah ha-Rofé, who wrote around 1430, can also be found. These commentaries were produced by the authors belonging to the 'Yemeni Jewish Ismailism' tradition. However, none of the works belonging to this tradition have been published or studied in detail, except for an anonymous Judeo-Arabic Yemeni commentary to the *Guide*, partially published by Horn in 1907[14] and by Moritz Zobel in 1910.[15]

On the other hand, in the Yemeni Jewish philosophy of these centuries we notice an assimilation of the religious and philosophical trends of Islam in a simple and clear 'philosophical midrash'.

The 'Jewish Ismaili' tradition continued in the following centuries, even after the end of the Fatimid rule in Yemen in 569/1174. Indeed, almost all Yemeni Jewish works of this period seem to be imbued with doctrines spread by the Ismailis, especially in the field of cosmology. Explicit quotations from Ismaili sources, starting with the *Rasā'il Ikhwān al-Ṣafā'*, can also be found.[16]

Yemeni Jewish culture of this time also developed an undeclared connection with Zaydī thought.[17] The Yemeni Jewish authors demonstrate their knowledge of the works of a Persian Zaydī scholar, Abū Jaʿfar al-Irdibilī.[18] Furthermore, along with Jewish philosophical and

---

[14] Israel Horn, *Ein anonymer arabischer Kommentar aus dem XV. Jahrhundert zu Maimonides' Dalālat al-ḥā'irīn* (Breslau, 1907).

[15] Moritz Zobel, *Ein anonymer arabischer Kommentar zu Maimonides' Führer der Unschlüssigen* (Breslau: Fleischmann, 1910). [See now Y. Tzvi Langermann, '*Sharḥ al-Dalāla*: A Commentary to Maimonides' *Guide* from Fourteenth-Century Yemen', in Carlos Fraenkel (ed.), *Traditions of Maimonideanism* (Leiden and Boston, 2009), pp. 155–176; 'A Study of "Dalalat al-Ha'irin" and its Interpretation in the Arabophone Jewish Communities', in Sara Klein-Braslavy, Binyamin Abrahamov, and Joseph Sadan (ed.), *Tribute to Michael: Studies in Jewish and Muslim Thought Presented to Professor Michael Schwarz* (Tel Aviv, 2009), pp. 67–90 [Hebrew]; 'A Marginalium on the Phrase "Man is Political by Nature" in some Yemenite Manuscripts of Maimonides' *Guide of the Perplexed*', *Daat*, 83 (2017), pp. 95–103 [Hebrew]. TL].

[16] Y. Tzvi Langermann, 'Two Unknown Philosophical Midrashim from the Yemen \ Šeney ha-midrashim ha-filosofim ha-neʿlemim min ha-Teman', *Qiryat Sefer*, 63 (5750–5751/1990–1991), pp. 1334–1337.

[17] [An early branch of Shiʿi Islam which emerged in the 2nd/8th century, named after Zayd b. ʿAlī, the grandson of Ḥusayn b. ʿAlī. OM].

[18] On al-Irdibilī (perhaps the correct spelling should be Ardabīlī, that is, from the city of Ardabīl in Iranian Azerbaijan), see also Y. Tzvi Langermann, 'Three singular treatises from Yemeni manuscripts', *Bulletin of the School of Oriental and African Studies*, 54, 3 (1991), pp. 568–571. [The Ṭayyibī Ismailis, who probably were the main Ismaili group that influenced the Yemeni Jewish thinkers mentioned in this article,

theological works, including the works of Saʿadiya Gaon, they made use of some parts of the *Corpus Hermeticum*, texts of Indian philosophy (in Arabic translation) and probably the works of Ibn Sīnā and, as mentioned above, al-Ghazālī, which were then enjoying great acclaim in the Islamic theological schools. They apparently believed that Ibn Sīnā's philosophy was more suitable for the allegorical reading of the Bible as it had already been employed in the thought of Maimonides.

As Rosenthal wrote there were 'Jewish scholars in the medieval Yemen who had become so strongly assimilated to their Muslim, and largely Shiʿah, environment and imbued with its persuasive philosophical ideology that . . . they created an intellectual atmosphere as lively as their generally restricted circumstances would allow.'[19]

This subject deserves a deeper study, in order to better delineate the general characteristics of the Yemeni Jewish philosophy using the evidence from recently discovered texts. These texts are often known only by their titles. Such is the case with certain philosophical and scientific works discovered by Langermann in a Moscow manuscript.[20] Other philosophers could be discovered in future, who would then be added to the few authors briefly examined here.

We also have some *Commentaries on the five Books of the Pentateuch*, with *excerpta* from the Talmud and the Midrash, and from medieval authors on the Talmud, especially from Moses Maimonides. Further, there are fragments of writings of a theological or moral nature (dealing with issues such as the role of the prophecy, the nature of the divine miracle, question and answers in the nature of the Bible, religious prayers and culture, eschatology, etc.), and philosophical questions about epistemology, cosmology, psychology, ethics and natural sciences.

Out of these writings those of Ḥōṭer ben Shelōmō, mentioned above, are particularly worth noting. According to Blumenthal, the cosmological system developed by Ḥōṭer ben Shelōmō is very complex, because he attempted to insert the system of ten intellects, a result

---

regard the *Rasāʾil Ikhwān al-Ṣafāʾ* as one of their sources; they amply used and commented upon it in their works. O.M.].

19 Frank Rosenthal, 'From the Unorthodox Judaism of Medieval Yemen', p. 280.

20 Y. Tzvi Langermann, 'Yemenite Philosophical Midrash as a Source for the Intellectual History of the Jews of Yemen', in Daniel Frank (ed.), *The Jews of Medieval Islam: Community, Society, and Identity* (Leiden, 1995), pp. 335–347.

of divine emanation (a system peculiar to Ibn Sīnā), into a classic Neoplatonic scheme (intellect – soul – prime matter), apparently without being aware of the contradictions between these two constructions.[21] According to this complex cosmological system, God is certainly the first necessary Being, but not the only one. The possible beings are not the metaphysical entities, but rather individual creatures of the sublunar world.

Ḥōṭer ben Shelōmō writes in his 'Lamp of the Intellects':

> The scholars divided the existent into three parts: necessary, impossible and possible. They maintain that the necessary is what has been fully brought into existence during the six days of Creation, and will never change (. . .). The impossible is analogous to the necessary: it is that whose existence can never be possible, and whose existence is impossible. The possible is what exists if its causes predominate.[22]

God, through his will, produces the emanation of the universal intellect *ex nihilo*; from the latter emanate the ten celestial intellects; the last of the intellects is the agent intellect. While the cosmological system of Ibn Sīnā is interrupted at this point, the line of emanations continues in the works by Ḥōṭer ben Shelōmō, thus coming closer to a Neoplatonic presentation. According to Ḥōṭer ben Shelōmō, the universal soul emanates from the agent intellect, and from the universal soul emanates the so-called 'first prime matter', which serves as the basis for the formation of the celestial world.

The universal soul uses the first prime matter to model the ten celestial spheres, also giving them forms and souls, while their intellects emanate directly from the above-named ten separate intellects. The series of emanations continue from the last sphere, the sphere of the Moon, by producing the 'second prime matter', which serves as the basis for the formation of the earthly world. Here, the Neoplatonic system is grafted onto the Aristotelian one. According to Ḥōṭer ben Shelōmō, nature (as a metaphysical entity, deriving from the emanation of the universal

---

21 See e.g. David R. Blumenthal, 'An Example of Ismaili Influence in Post-Maimonidean Yemen', in Shelomo Morag et al. (ed.), *Studies in Judaism and Islam Presented to Shelomo Dov Goitein* (Jerusalem, 5741/1981), pp. 155–174.

22 Y. Tzvi Langermann, *Yemenite Midrash*, pp. 25–26.

soul) forms the second prime matter, giving rise to the four elements (fire, air, water, earth) which serve as the basis for the formation of minerals, plants and animals. Physically, man fits into this system, but his soul comes directly from the emanation of the universal soul.

The destiny of the human soul, according to Ḥōṭer ben Shelōmō's views on nature, would be the result of a compromise between the Jewish religious tradition, and the science and philosophy of his time, as taken from Ismaili scholars who were probably working in that place and time.[23] He is clearly attempting to harmonise the thought of Maimonides and Neoplatonic philosophy. From Maimonides he takes the idea of a conjunction between the human intellect and the agent intellect; from Neoplatonism, he takes the doctrine of the return of the human soul to the immaterial world from which it originally came.

The destiny of the human soul is described somewhat differently in the 'Lamp of the Intellects':

> The divine flux . . . gives life to the souls which are inside these dark and dead bodies without life. If these forms were not associated with divine Help, which rescues them from the material needs that they are plunged into, they will die and pass away.[24]

However, this does not mean that Ḥōṭer ben Shelōmō expected a physical resurrection after death and a new union between soul and body.[25] Thus, in specific details of his thought, Ḥōṭer ben Shelōmō like most, or perhaps all, Yemeni Jewish philosophers, moved away from the Jewish religious tradition. But it should be noted that he neither came under severe criticism from the exponents of religious tradition nor did he have a clear disagreement with them, as often happened in European Jewish philosophy of the eighth/fourteenth to tenth/sixteenth centuries.

---

[23] [It should also be stressed that both Maimonides and his Yemeni readers felt that they were pursuing an ancient Jewish philosophical tradition; their philosophical approach (though not the scientific content of their doctrines) was very 'traditional' in their own eyes. TL].

[24] Y. Tzvi Langermann, *Yemenite Midrash*, p. 131.

[25] David R. Blumenthal, *The Commentary of R. Ḥōṭer b. Shelōmō to the Thirteen Principles of Maimonides* (Leiden, 1974).

Index